THE BEGINNINGS OF ROME

The beginnings of Rome, once thought to be lost in the mists of legend, are now being revealed by an ever-increasing body of archaeological evidence, much of it unearthed during the past twenty-five years. This new material has made it possible to trace the development of Rome from an iron-age village to a major state which eventually outstripped its competitors and became a Mediterranean power. The study of this period raises acute questions of historical method, demanding analysis of many different kinds of archaeological evidence in conjunction with literary sources.

Professor Cornell uses the results of up-to-date archaeological techniques and takes current methodological debates into account. *The Beginnings of Rome* offers new and often controversial answers to major questions such as Rome's relations with the Etruscans, the conflict between patricians and plebeians, the causes of Roman imperialism and the growth of a slave-based economy.

Covering the period from *c.* 1000 BC to 264 BC, *The Beginnings of Rome* is the most comprehensive study of this subject. It is essential reading for all students of Roman history.

T.J. Cornell is Professor of Ancient History at the University of Manchester.

D0420585

ROUTLEDGE HISTORY OF THE ANCIENT WORLD

General Editor: Fergus Millar

THE BEGINNINGS OF ROME

Italy and Rome from the Bronze Age
to the Punic Wars (*c.* 1000–264 BC)

T.J. Cornell

London and New York

First published 1995
by Routledge
11 New Fetter Lane, London EC4P 4EE

Simultaneously published in the USA and Canada
by Routledge
29 West 35th Street, New York, NY 10001

Reprinted 1997, 2001

Routledge is an imprint of the Taylor & Francis Group

Typeset in Garamond by
Ponting–Green Publishing Services, Chesham, Bucks
Printed and bound in Great Britain by
Biddles Ltd, Guildford and King's Lynn

British Library Cataloguing in Publication Data
Cornell, Tim
Beginnings of Rome 1000–264 B.C. –
(Routledge History of the Ancient World)
I. Title II. Series
937.01

Library of Congress Cataloging in Publication Data
Cornell, Tim.
The beginnings of Rome, 1000–264 B.C./T.J. Cornell.
p. cm. — (Routledge history of the ancient world)
Includes bibliographical references and index.
1. Rome—History—Kings, 753–510 B.C.
I. Title. II. Series.
DG233.C67   1995
937´.01—dc20   94–43757

ISBN 0–415–01595–2
0–415–01596–0 (pbk)

For Mary

CONTENTS

vii

CONTENTS

FIGURES

MAPS AND TABLES

MAPS

TABLES

xiii

PREFACE

This book is about the origins of Rome. By this I mean not simply the remote beginnings of the city, but the origins of Rome as a major power in the Mediterranean world. The aim, in other words, is to trace the development of Roman society and the Roman state from their first visible beginnings down to the time, in the early third century BC, when all of peninsular Italy was firmly under Roman control. The terminal date of 264 BC has been chosen not only as a convenient stopping point, but as a symbolic moment; for in that year the Romans embarked on their first major overseas adventure, when they sent an army to Sicily to confront the Carthaginians. The start of the first Romano-Carthaginian war marked the beginning of the end for Carthage, and ultimately for all the other major powers of the Mediterranean basin. For Rome, it equally clearly signalled the end of the beginning.

As a subject for historical inquiry the question of the origins of Rome, on this broad definition, scarcely needs justification. To borrow a phrase from Polybius (1.1.5), who could be so idle or apathetic as not to want to know how Rome grew from nothing to become the dominant power in Italy? When, how and why did the city come into existence? Who were the Romans, and what were the secrets of their success? Such questions, one would have thought, would stimulate anyone endowed with even the most modest level of historical curiosity. We need not be surprised that the origins of Rome were the object of endless fascination and inquiry in antiquity, not only for the Romans themselves but also for their partners, rivals and enemies; nor that ancient accounts of early Rome have been preserved and intensively studied ever since.

What is surprising, and needs to be explained, is the fact that early Roman history has been largely ignored by scholars in the English-speaking world. This seems to be a curiously Anglo-Saxon phenomenon. Elsewhere the subject is flourishing – not only in Italy, where 'Roma arcaica' is probably more intensively researched than any other historical topic, and the volume of publications has far exceeded the limits of what a normal person could hope to take in, but also in other continental countries, including France, Belgium, Holland, Germany and the Scandinavian countries. In the English-speaking

xiv

world, however, Roman history before the Punic Wars is regarded as a marginal topic. It is hardly ever taught in school or university courses, and almost no one chooses it as a subject for research. As for publications, most important books in English have been either translated from other languages (e.g. the work of Raymond Bloch, Georges Dumézil, Jacques Heurgon, Massimo Pallottino), or written by exiles (Andreas Alföldi, Arnaldo Momigliano, Stefan Weinstock) and others who choose English in preference to their own languages (Einar Gjerstad, Par Goran Gierow, Endre Ferenczy, Jørgen Christian Meyer, Hendrik Versnel, Rudi Thomsen).

It is not easy to account for this state of affairs. It undoubtedly has something to do with the fact that in English-speaking countries ancient history is closely tied to the study of Classics, with the result that the periods chosen for historical study coincide with those that produced great works of literature; but this is surely not the whole explanation. We cannot (can we?) be so lacking in historical sense as to allow our choices to be determined by such arbitrary and irrelevant criteria. In any case English-speaking historians have not been deterred from tackling other areas that lie outside the main classical periods – Mycenaean and dark-age Greece, for example, or the Hellenistic world, or the later Roman Empire.

In my experience the most commonly advanced justification for neglecting the early centuries of Roman history is that the evidence is too uncertain. The written accounts were all produced centuries after the events they purport to describe, and there is no way of ascertaining the truth of most of what they say. In the absence of any contemporary sources, so the argument runs, the history of Rome before the Punic Wars cannot be written. There is enough truth in this formulation to make it plausible, but one of the purposes of this book is to show that the situation is not nearly as bad as that. The evidence is indeed extremely difficult, and problems of verification are acute, but it is incorrect to say that nothing can be known about how Rome began, or how it developed during the early centuries of its existence.

The problematic nature of the sources has not deterred scholars on the Continent from making the attempt. Some of these continental experts are extremely sceptical; in order to study this period one does not have to be credulous or uncritical. Moreover, the difficulties are no more acute, indeed they are probably less intractable, than those that face students of the Mycenaean age, but that has not stopped English-speaking historians from producing an apparently endless stream of publications on the Trojan War or the Greek 'dark age'. In any case, for all our many faults, I would not regard cowardice in the face of difficulty as a distinctively British or American characteristic.

The lack of any established tradition of scholarship on this subject in the English-speaking world remains a puzzle which I for one am not able to explain. But whatever the answer, the situation presents both an opportunity and a justification for a new synthesis. There is a desperate need for a new history of early Rome; this book is offered in an attempt to meet that need. I have tried to make it comprehensible to non-specialists as well as presenting new ideas that may be of interest to experts in the field. I have also tried to set out the most important problems, to acknowledge and recommend the best of previous scholarship, and to be up to date with references to current research; but in all three of these efforts I have necessarily had to be selective. Whether the finished product lives up to any of the stated aims is for the reader to decide.

This book has been many years in the making, and could not have been written without the help and inspiration of teachers, friends, colleagues and students, who over the years have enabled me to shape and clarify my thoughts on the beginnings of Rome. It would be impossible to name them all, and invidious to discriminate between them. To this general rule, however, I shall make one exception, in acknowledging the profound intellectual and personal debt I owe to my former teacher, research supervisor and friend, the late Arnaldo Momigliano. Those who were privileged to know him, and those familiar with his work, will be able to detect his influence in every part of this book. I hope that it may contain some reflection of his clarity and sureness of touch; such merits as it may possess are likely to be due, at least in some measure, to him. Alas, I was unable to show him a draft manuscript, and to have the direct benefit of his penetrating insight and criticism. If the book turns out to contain flaws in its structure, argument and interpretation, these are entirely my own responsibility.

A number of people helped in the final preparation of the text. The general editor, Fergus Millar, read the whole typescript, and suggested a number of changes and additions which I have incorporated into the final version. Fergus also deserves credit for the patience and characteristic good humour he has shown to one of the more awkward and dilatory contributors to his series, and for encouraging and commending my efforts even when they offer interpretations that are diametrically opposed to his own. I am also grateful to Michael Crawford, who read and commented on parts of the typescript and kindly allowed me to make use of a draft version of his new text and commentary on the Twelve Tables.

Special thanks are due to my mother, Margaret Cornell, who compiled the index, and at an earlier stage read through a complete draft of the book. Her critical eye, sharpened by years of editorial experience at the Royal Institute of International Affairs, corrected numerous errors of style and grammar. Richard Stoneman and his assistants at Routledge have been unfailingly courteous and helpful, and have agreed to most of my requests and suggestions on the form the book should take. The sub-editor, Margaret Deith, has worked heroically to bring consistency and order to a chaotic typescript. To all of these, and to David Saxon who drew many of the text figures, I am immensely grateful.

Much of the book was written during a period of leave granted to me by my department in the autumn of 1993. The sections on the organisation of the early Roman army, and on warfare in archaic Italy, benefited substantially from a period of research on ancient warfare which I undertook in 1994, funded by a grant from the Harry Frank Guggenheim Foundation. The last four chapters of the book cover the same ground as my contributions to the *Cambridge Ancient History* (2nd edn), vol. VII.2, 1989, and some sections represent a rewritten version, sometimes shortened, sometimes extended, of the corresponding pages of the *CAH*; a part of the final chapter is reproduced almost word for word. I am grateful to the Cambridge University Press for permission to include this material.

Finally my wife, who has no interest whatever in Roman history, has helped and sustained me during the writing of this book in ways that only she can know. I dedicate it to her, with love and gratitude.

T.J. Cornell
Department of History
University College London

ABBREVIATIONS

This list contains abbreviations of periodicals and other works referred to by initials or in severely abbreviated form. It does not include books that are frequently cited in the notes in an abbreviated form; these abbreviations will, I hope, be self-explanatory. Full details are given in the bibliography.

AC	*L'Antiquité Classique*
Acta Arch.	*Acta Archaeologica*
AION	*Annali dell' Istituto Universitario Orientale di Napoli*
AJA	*American Journal of Archaeology*
AJAH	*American Journal of Ancient History*
AJPh	*American Journal of Philology*
Annales (ESC)	*Annales (Economies, Sociétés, Civilisations)*
ANRW	*Aufstieg und Niedergang der römischen Welt* (Festschrift J. Vogt), ed. H. Temporini (Berlin, New York, 1972–)
Arch. Class.	*Archeologia Classica*
Arch. Laz.	*Archeologia Laziale*
Arch. Reports	*Archaeological Reports*
ARID	*Analecta Romana Instituti Danici*
ASNP	*Annali della Scuola Normale Superiore di Pisa*
BAGB	*Bulletin de l'Association Guillaume Budé*
BCH	*Bulletin de Correspondance Hellénique*
BCom	*Bullettino della Commissione Archeologica Comunale di Roma*
BIBR	*Bulletin de l'Institut Historique Belge de Rome*
BMCR	*Bollettino dei Musei Comunali di Roma*
Boll. Arch.	*Bollettino di Archeologia*
BPI	*Bullettino di Paletnologia Italiana*
Broughton, MRR	T.R.S. Broughton, *The Magistrates of the Roman Republic* I–II (New York 1951–2)
BSA	*Annual of the British School at Athens*
Bull. Soc. Ling.	*Bulletin de la Société de Linguistique*
CAH	*The Cambridge Ancient History*
CIL	*Corpus Inscriptionum Latinarum*
CJ	*Classical Journal*
CLP	*Civiltà del Lazio Primitivo*, Exhibition Catalogue (Rome 1976)

CPh	*Classical Philology*
CQ	*Classical Quarterly*
CR	*Classical Review*
CRAI	*Comptes Rendus de l'Académie des Inscriptions et Belles Lettres*
Crawford, *RRC*	M. Crawford, *Roman Republican Coinage* I–II (Cambridge 1974)
CSSH	*Comparative Studies in Society and History*
DdA	*Dialoghi di Archeologia*
De Sanctis, *StdR²*	G. De Sanctis, *Storia dei Romani*, 2nd edn
EAA	*Enciclopedia dell'Arte Antica Classica e Orientale*
Enea nel Lazio	*Enea nel Lazio: archeologia e mito*, Exhibition catalogue (Rome 1981)
Entretiens	*Entretiens sur l'Antiquité Classique* (Fondation Hardt, Vandœuvres-Geneva)
Eph. Ep.	*Ephemeris Epigraphica*
FGrHist	F. Jacoby, *Die Fragmente der griechischen Historiker* I–III, 11 vols (Berlin–Leiden 1923–58)
FIRA	*Fontes iuris Romani antejustiniani* 1–3, ed. S. Riccobono (Florence 1940–3)
GRT	*La grande Roma dei Tarquini*, ed. M. Cristofani, Exhibition catalogue (Rome 1990)
HSCPh	*Harvard Studies in Classical Philology*
HTR	*Harvard Theological Review*
ILLRP	*Inscriptiones Latinae Liberae Rei Publicae* (ed. E. Degrassi)
ILS	*Inscriptiones Latinae Selectae* (ed. H. Dessau)
Jacoby, *FGrHist*	See *FGrHist*
JDAI	*Jahrbuch des Deutschen Archäologischen Instituts*
JHS	*Journal of Hellenic Studies*
JRA	*Journal of Roman Archaeology*
JRS	*Journal of Roman Studies*
LCM	*Liverpool Classical Monthly*
LEC	*Les Etudes Classiques*
LIMC	*Lexicon Iconographicum Mythologiae Classicae*
MAAR	*Memoirs of the American Academy in Rome*
MEFR(A)	*Mélanges de l'Ecole Française de Rome (Antiquité)*
Mommsen, *Staatsr.*	T. Mommsen, *Römisches Staatsrecht*, 3 vols (Leipzig 1887–8)
Mommsen, *Strafr.*	T. Mommsen, *Römisches Strafrecht* (Leipzig 1899)
Mus Helv.	*Museum Helveticum*
NAC	*Numismatica e Antichità Classiche*
NSc	*Notizie degli Scavi dell'Antichità*
OCD²	*The Oxford Classical Dictionary*, 2nd edn (Oxford 1970)
Op. Rom.	*Opuscula Romana*
PAPS	*Proceedings of the American Philosophical Society*
PBA	*Proceedings of the British Academy*

PBSR	*Papers of the British School at Rome*
PCPhS	*Proceedings of the Cambridge Philological Society*
PdP	*La Parola del Passato*
Popoli e civiltà	*Popoli e civiltà dell'Italia antica*, 7 vols (Rome 1974–8)
PPS	*Proceedings of the Prehistoric Society*
Quad. Top.	*Quaderni dell'Istituto di Topografia Antica dell'Università di Roma*
RAL	*Rendiconti dell'Accademia Nazionale dei Lincei*, Classe di Scienze morali, storiche e filologiche
RBPhH	*Revue Belge de Philologie et d'Histoire*
RE	*Reallexikon der klassischen Altertumswissenschaft* (eds Pauly-Wissowa-Kroll)
REA	*Revue des Etudes Anciennes*
REG	*Revue des Etudes Grecques*
REL	*Revue des Etudes Latines*
Rev. Arch.	*Revue Archéologique*
Rev. Hist.	*Revue Historique*
RFIC	*Rivista di Filologia e di Istruzione Classica*
RHDFE	*Revue Historique de Droit Français et Etranger*
Rh. Mus.	*Rheinisches Museum für Philologie*
RIDA	*Revue Internationale des Droits de l'Antiquité*
RIL	*Rendiconti dell'Istituto Lombardo*, Classe di Lettere, scienze morali e storiche
Röm. Mitt.	*Mitteilungen des Deutschen Archäologischen Instituts (Römische Abteilung)*
RPAA	*Rendiconti della Pontificia Accademia Romana di Archeologia*
RPh	*Revue de Philologie*
RSA	*Rivista Storica dell'Antichità*
RSI	*Rivista Storica Italiana*
SDHI	*Studia et Documenta Historiae et Iuris*
SE	*Studi Etruschi*
SNR	*Schweizerische Numismatische Rundschau*
SR	*Studi Romani*
Syll.³	W. Dittenberger (ed.) *Sylloge Inscriptionum Graecarum*, 3rd edn
TAPhA	*Transactions of the American Philological Association*
TLE²	*Testimonia Linguae Etruscae*, ed. M. Pallottino (2nd edn, Florence 1968)
TLL	*Thesaurus Linguae Latinae*
TLS	*The Times Literary Supplement*
Trans. Phil. Soc.	*Transactions of the Philological Society*
Tria Corda	E. Gabba (ed.), *Tria Corda: scritti in onore di Arnaldo Momigliano* (Como 1983)
TvR	*Tijdschrift voor Rechtsgeschiedenis*
Wissowa, *Ruk²*	G. Wissowa, *Religion und Kultus der Römer* (2nd edn, Munich 1912)
ZSS	*Zeitschrift der Savigny-Stiftung für Rechtsgeschichte (Romanistische Abteilung)*

1

INTRODUCTION: THE EVIDENCE

It is customary for books on the ancient world to begin with an introductory account of the evidence. But whereas for most periods of ancient history a brief catalogue of the main sources is usually sufficient, something more is required in a book on the early history of Rome. The reliability of the written sources, and the relevance and interpretation of the archaeological material, are so controversial, and raise such complex issues, that a more extended account is called for. Discussion of particular problems will occur throughout the main part of the book, but it is important to begin with a general outline of the various types of evidence, and to define and defend the approach to them that will be taken in the following chapters.

1 HISTORICAL ACCOUNTS

The most important evidence for the early history of Rome comes from literary sources – that is, books written during the classical period and published in manuscript form. Copied and recopied, first as manuscripts and later in printed editions, these texts were preserved through the Middle Ages and down to modern times. Scholars sometimes use the blanket term 'literary tradition' to encapsulate the mass of data contained in ancient texts and representing what the Romans of the late republican and imperial periods knew, or thought they knew, about their own past. This is a convenient label, but it is important not to exaggerate the consistency and uniformity of what is in fact a variegated and often fragmentary corpus of material.

The most important texts are complete works devoted specifically to the remote past of Rome. These can be divided into two groups: those of historians, who produced chronological narratives, and those of the so-called antiquarians, who collected information about the past in all kinds of ways, both systematic and haphazard, and for all kinds of reasons – and sometimes, one suspects, for no reason at all. These eccentric individuals are difficult to characterise, but they shared a passionate and sometimes obsessive erudition, and were most definitely not historians. According to one recent study, an antiquarian can be defined as 'the type of man who is interested in historical facts without being interested in history'.[1]

The first historians whose texts we can still read lived in the first century BC. The most readable of them, and by far the most important surviving source for the history of early Rome, is **Livy**. Titus Livius (59 BC – AD 17), a well-to-do gentleman from Patavium (Padua), was almost an exact contemporary of the emperor Augustus (63 BC – AD 14). His history of Rome *From the Foundation of the City (ab urbe condita)* began to appear in the early 20s BC, and when complete at the end of his life occupied no fewer than 142 books. Only thirty-five of these are still extant, but they include the first ten books, covering the period from the origins to 293 BC. The first book dealt with the kings, the next four with the early Republic to the Gallic sack (390 BC), and the remaining five with the century from the sack to the Third Samnite War.[2]

The second major narrative source, which should be read alongside Livy, is the work of his Greek contemporary **Dionysius of Halicarnassus**, a scholar and rhetorician who lived in Rome under Augustus.[3] His *Roman Antiquities*, which began to appear in 7 BC, covered the period from the origins to 264 BC in twenty books, but we possess the complete text of only the first eleven of these, taking the story down to 443 BC, and short excerpts of the rest. Dionysius thus gave more space to the earliest period than Livy; his first book dealt with the prehistory of Italy, followed by three on the kings, and a further eight on the first sixty or so years of the Republic.

The narratives of Livy and Dionysius tell very much the same story and are often in close agreement in matters of detail. This is probably due to the use of common sources rather than the direct use of Livy by Dionysius (the reverse can be ruled out on chronological grounds). No one has ever been able to decide for certain whether the two men knew each other personally, or even if either knew the other's work. It is quite clear in any case that they differed widely in their aims, methods and approach, but they drew upon the same body of material and their accounts complement each other.

Livy and Dionysius constitute the main narrative sources down to 443 BC, after which Livy stands alone. But they can be supplemented by other accounts which cover some or all of the same ground. One of the most important, if only because of the standing of its author, is the work *On the State (de republica)* by **Cicero** (106–43 BC), the orator and statesman who was also the outstanding intellectual figure of his generation. Cicero never got around to writing the history of Rome that he sometimes contemplated, but he does offer a brief survey of the early development of its political system in the second book of the *de republica* (44 BC), a work in dialogue form on political theory. The only manuscript, which was discovered in 1820, is damaged, and there are some infuriating gaps; otherwise Cicero's outline of the early history of Rome, covering the kings and the early Republic to the middle of the fifth century BC, is the earliest continuous narrative we possess.[4]

Another important text of about the same time (probably published in the 30s BC) is the surviving portion of a universal history by the Greek writer **Diodorus Siculus**. The fully preserved text of books 11 to 20 covers the period from 486 to 302 BC, and includes the names of the Roman magistrates for each year, and notices of other Roman events in some years. One or two episodes (e.g. the Decemvirate and the Gallic sack) are treated at length. If all the references to Rome are extracted from Diodorus' text, the result is a chronicle-type account which presents significant differences from all the other sources and to which scholars have attributed great importance. This assessment is based on the assumption that Diodorus was little more than a compiler, and that his notices on Roman history were drawn exclusively from the account of an early annalist. But scholars are now less certain about this than they once were, and the idea of Diodorus as a mere cipher has been undermined in an important study by Kenneth Sacks.[5]

During the Empire the early history of the city ceased to be a major concern for serious historians; those authors who did write about the early period were mostly hacks and epitomators who relied exclusively on Livy, now firmly established as the standard account. For that reason surviving narratives of the archaic period by writers such as Florus, Eutropius and Orosius are of little value for our purpose. But at least one historian did attempt to write an independent account of the whole history of Rome. This was **Cassius Dio**, a Greek writer (also a Roman senator and consul), who was active in the early years of the third century AD. His account of the period to the Punic Wars, which occupied ten books, does not survive, but we possess substantial fragments of it as well as a fairly faithful summary by a twelfth-century Byzantine monk called **Zonaras**. Dio's work seems to have been based on republican sources and appears to be partly independent of Livy and Dionysius of Halicarnassus. It frequently provides details that are not in other sources.[6]

A continuous account that contains much relevant historical information, even if it is not strictly a narrative history, is the *Geography* of **Strabo** (*c.* 63 BC – AD 21), a work in seventeen books dealing with the whole of the known world. Book 5, on Italy, contains some extremely important sections on the early history of Rome, Latium and Etruria drawn from well-informed sources.[7]

The last important narrative source is **Plutarch** (*c.* AD 46–120), the Greek biographer whose famous *Parallel Lives* include several that fall within our period, namely Romulus, Numa, Publicola, Coriolanus, Camillus and Pyrrhus.[8] Plutarch is important because he read voraciously, and faithfully reported what he found in a wide variety of sources. He drew heavily on Livy and (especially) Dionysius of Halicarnassus, but he also provides much additional information not contained in their accounts, including recondite material taken from antiquarians and others (the Lives of Romulus and Numa are especially valuable in this respect). The Life of Pyrrhus is a key text, since it refers to the period from 293 to 264 for which we possess neither Dionysius nor Livy; indeed, it is the main source for the age of Pyrrhus.

Apart from these continuous accounts, we also possess important references to early Rome in the works of historians of other periods; two that deserve particular mention are **Polybius** and **Tacitus**. Polybius (c. 210–131 BC) was a Greek historian who wrote an account of the rise of the Roman Empire in the age of the Punic Wars. His text is a century older than any of the surviving continuous accounts of the archaic period, which makes him an especially important source in those passages where he refers back to the remote past of Rome. His account of the early treaties between Rome and Carthage (3.22–5) gives priceless information about documents of which we should otherwise be entirely ignorant, and his account of the Gauls and their wars against Rome (2.14–20) is the most reliable evidence we have on that important subject. We can only lament the loss of the so-called *archaeologia* – the digression in book 6 which gave a survey of the early history of Rome down to c. 450 BC.[9]

Cornelius Tacitus (c. AD 56 – c. 120), the historian of the Roman Principate, includes a number of well-informed digressions on archaic Rome, particularly on the origins of institutions and on topographical questions.[10]

2 THE SOURCES OF OUR SOURCES: LOST HISTORICAL ACCOUNTS

The historical sources provide us with a clear narrative framework, a well-established chronology, and a great deal of substantive information. The problem is that they were all written centuries after the events they describe, which inevitably raises the question of how historical they really are. The obvious first step is to ask where these historians obtained their information.

What were the sources of our sources? At one level this question can be easily answered. Roman historians did not, as a general rule, carry out original research; unlike the antiquarians, they did not try to discover new facts about the past, but rather to present received facts in a new way. Their aims were rhetorical, artistic, political and moral. For the most part they were content to take their information from the works of their predecessors, whom they then hoped to eclipse. Indeed, Livy's masterpiece was so successful in this respect that his predecessors (and rivals) were rapidly forgotten, and their works failed to survive. Dionysius was to some extent insulated from this process because his text was in Greek, and would not have suffered by comparison with Livy among the many Greek-speaking inhabitants of the Roman Empire who never learned Latin.

It is well recognised that Livy and Dionysius relied principally on the works of earlier historians, who had themselves done the same in their turn. There has been much debate, most of it futile, about the working methods of Livy (and to a lesser extent Dionysius), and about the identity of the sources they used at different stages of their works. This type of source analysis (or *Quellenforschung*, as the Germans call it) is of doubtful value, however, not only because it makes unverifiable assumptions about the working methods of Livy and Dionysius (for instance that they followed one source at a time), but also because it is not clear how useful it would be to know that at a certain point Livy used Valerius Antias, and at another Licinius Macer (the two first-century historians who are assumed to have been his principal sources in the early books), because we know almost nothing about these writers or their works, so naming them as sources would not advance our understanding of Livy's text or our assessment of its reliability.[11]

All we know for certain is that Livy and Dionysius came at the end of a long line of historians, each of whom had covered the history of the city from its foundation. This succession of historians is conventionally known as the 'annalistic tradition', and its practitioners as 'annalists', because they followed a year-by-year arrangement and in many cases called their works *annales* (Livy and Dionysius did not use this title, and are therefore not usually considered annalists, although they did adopt a year-by-year structure). It is not entirely certain, however, that the earliest Roman historians were annalists in this sense; some have suggested that the first proper annalist was L. Calpurnius Piso Frugi, who lived at the time of the Gracchi in the latter half of the second century BC.[12]

However that may be, the Roman tradition of historiography goes back some way before Piso. The first Roman to write the history of the city was Q. Fabius Pictor, a senator who lived in the second half of the third century BC and wrote probably a few years before 200 BC. He is an obscure figure, whose work is represented by only a handful of quotations in later authors, but we do know one fact of outstanding importance: he wrote in Greek. This indicates that Fabius was consciously applying the canons and methods of Greek historiography to the past of Rome.[13] Others quickly followed where Fabius led the way, but even less is known about them than about Fabius. Things become clearer with the development of historical writing in Latin. Here the decisive role was played by two crucially important figures: Ennius and Cato.

Quintus Ennius (239–169 BC) composed a highly original narrative poem in Latin hexameters (the Greek epic metre used by Homer), but on the theme of the history of the Roman people, from the wanderings of Aeneas after the sack of Troy down to his own lifetime. The poem, significantly entitled *Annales*, comprised perhaps as many as 30,000 lines, of which over 600 are preserved – enough to give us a flavour of the original and some idea of how it was structured. At least six books (some 10,000 lines) dealt with the period down to the Punic Wars. Ennius' work became a national epic, and was extremely influential in shaping the Romans' view of their own past.[14]

M. Porcius Cato the Censor (234–148 BC), one of the great men of his time, was the first to write history in Latin prose (during the last years of his life).

The resulting work, called *Origines* (*The Origins*), contained seven books, the first of which dealt with the origins of the Roman people (*origo populi Romani*). It covered not only the remote origins of the city, but also the age of the kings and the early Republic, probably down to *c.* 450 BC. If so, it had the same scope as Polybius' *Archaeology* and the second book of Cicero's *On the State*, which is not a coincidence.[15] The next two books dealt with the origins of all the other cities of Italy. There followed four books of historical narrative, starting with the First Punic War and describing the conquest of the Mediterranean by Rome at the head of a united Italy.[16] Around 150 fragments survive, making Cato's *Origines* the best known work of republican historiography before the time of Caesar.

We know far less about the many historians who came after Cato. These included, apart from Piso (see above), the poorly attested Cassius Hemina and Gnaeus Gellius,[17] as well as others who are little more than names to us, such as Vennonius (see below, p. 175). This brings us finally to the first century BC, and the immediate predecessors of Livy: Valerius Antias, Licinius Macer, Claudius Quadrigarius and Q. Aelius Tubero. These were the annalists *par excellence*, about whom so much has been written but so little is actually known.

The importance of these late republican annalists in the present context is that they are presumed to have been the main sources of Dionysius, and the only sources used by Livy. Consequently the assessment of the reliability of everything we read in Livy entails an assessment of the later annalists. The worry is that these late annalists are widely believed to have been less scrupulous than their second-century predecessors. They are said to have written at much greater length about the archaic period, and to have supplied the raw materials for this expansion from their own imaginations.[18] We thus arrive at the position where any statement in one of our sources, unless it can be shown to go back to an early historian such as Fabius Pictor, Cato or Piso, is suspect because it might be the capricious invention of one of the late annalists.

It has always seemed to me that this theory introduces an unnecessary complication into an already complex story. If it is true that the later annalists wrote at greater length about the early period than their second-century predecessors (which is not certain, at least not in all cases), it does not necessarily follow that they filled out their accounts with invented 'facts'. It is much more likely that the early historians had presented a bare chronicle of annual events, and that their first-century successors fleshed out this skeleton with rhetorical elaborations. This at least is what Cicero implies, when he criticises the dry-as-dust manner of the earliest historians and laments the paucity of their literary style.[19] It is also possible that the later annalists added to the stock of genuine facts by doing further research among archives that had not hitherto been exploited. We know that Licinius Macer made use of a list of magistrates recorded on linen rolls kept in the temple of Juno Moneta.[20] This was probably not an isolated example.

It would be sensible to acknowledge the extent of our ignorance in these matters. In truth we do not know precisely which sources were used by Livy and Dionysius of Halicarnassus, nor how they used them. It is arbitrary to suggest that Livy did not consult the works of early historians like Fabius Pictor and Calpurnius Piso, but only quoted them at second hand; but there is equally no reason to assume that these earlier historians were more honest and scrupulous than the later annalists, whose reliability we are not in a position to judge.[21]

All we can say is that Livy and Dionysius were dependent on an annalistic tradition that went back to about 200 BC. Given the limitations of our knowledge, we can only ask in general terms about the historical value of this tradition, as it is represented by Livy, Dionysius, and the other extant accounts. It obviously makes better sense to discuss Livy, whom we can actually read, than his lost precedessors, whom we cannot read.

In general, speculation about the competence and integrity of individual annalists is a red herring, diverting attention from the main question that needs to be addressed to the annalistic tradition as a whole. How did the Roman historians, the earliest of whom lived in the second half of the third century BC, set about constructing their accounts of the earliest history of the city? Where could they find evidence about events that had happened centuries before their time?

As far as we can tell, there were essentially four types of material that would have been available to the earliest Roman historians: relevant information in the works of Greek historians, family records, oral tradition, and ancient documents and archives. Let us examine these four types of evidence one by one.

3 THE SOURCES OF OUR SOURCES: GREEK ACCOUNTS

Greek historians were an extremely important source for Fabius Pictor and his successors. As early as the fifth century Greek historians had mentioned Rome in connection with the wanderings of Aeneas and Odysseus (see below, p. 64), but it was not until the fourth century that they began to take a serious interest in the city as a topic in its own right. This was the result of the growth of Roman power in Italy, which began to affect the political interests of the Greek cities in Italy and Sicily, and later of the Hellenistic monarchies. In these circumstances it was logical for Greek historians to focus their attention on two aspects of Roman history: the remote origins of the city, a topic which they investigated in order to discover who the Romans were and where they came from, and the most recent past, in which Rome's affairs had begun to impinge on Greek interests.

The first major Roman event to be recorded by Greek writers was the sack of the city by the Gauls in 390 BC, which was mentioned by Theopompus, Aristotle and Heraclides Ponticus (Plutarch, *Camillus* 22.2–3); later Duris of Samos described the battle of Sentinum (295 BC). Finally the sensational defeat of Pyrrhus (275 BC) created a flurry of historical research into Rome and the Romans. As far as the present subject is concerned, the most important figures were Hieronymus of Cardia and Timaeus of Tauromenium, both of whom wrote accounts of the Pyrrhic War, and introduced their readers to the Romans by describing the origins of the city.

Hieronymus (died *c.* 250 BC) was later recognised as the standard authority on the history of the successors of Alexander the Great, and was one of Plutarch's main sources for the Life of Pyrrhus; Dionysius of Halicarnassus tells us that he was also the first Greek historian to write an account of the *archaeologia* (i.e. the earliest history) of the Romans.[22] For his part Timaeus (*c.* 356–260 BC) was the leading historian of the western Greeks; his great work in thirty-eight books began with a general account, in five books, of the history and institutions of the peoples of the western Mediterranean. This was a pioneering effort, which completely superseded the casual and spasmodic curiosity of earlier Greek writers. It was Timaeus who brought Rome within the normal range of Greek knowledge, first in his general history, then again in a monograph on the Pyrrhic War.[23]

The first Roman historians would have found in the works of these Greek writers not only narrative accounts of the period of the late fourth and early third centuries, but also detailed discussion of how Rome came to be founded. As Emilio Gabba has shown, this explains the curious 'hour-glass' shape of the earliest Roman histories, which included extensive accounts of the foundation and of contemporary events, but dealt only summarily with the period in between.[24]

Unfortunately we know all too little about how the Greek historians dealt with the story of the origins of Rome, and where they found their information. But it seems certain that some of them made use of local traditions. For instance the ancient and indigenous story of Romulus and Remus had been written up in Greek sources before Fabius Pictor (Plutarch, *Romulus* 3.1); and we know that Timaeus connected local Roman customs (such as the annual festival of the October Horse) with the tradition that they were descended from Trojan refugees (Polybius 12.4b). It is uncertain to what extent Greek writers went beyond the foundation of the city and treated events of its early history. Timaeus seems to have written about Servius Tullius (Pliny, *n.h.* 33.43); and it may be that Greek historians were responsible for those stories that implied extensive Greek influence on Rome's development – for instance the legend that Numa was a pupil of Pythagoras, or that the Tarquins were descended from Demaratus of Corinth (see below, p. 124). It is unlikely, however, that Fabius Pictor would have found a systematic account of the whole regal period in any Greek writer,

8

even Timaeus; but if he did, we should still have to confront the same problem at one remove – i.e., what primary sources was it based on?

4 THE SOURCES OF OUR SOURCES: FAMILY TRADITION

Republican Rome was an aristocratic society in which status depended on a combination of birth and achievement. Roman nobles sought to justify the domination of their class, and to boost their individual claims in competition with their peers, by celebrating the achievements of their ancestors. In these circumstances it is inevitable that the great families preserved a record of their past achievements, and had ways of passing the information on to subsequent generations. That the early historians, who themselves belonged to the nobility, obtained information from this source seems likely. What we do not know is how reliable the information was or how it was transmitted. In the late Republic aristocratic houses contained ancestral portrait busts and had family trees painted on the walls, with details of the triumphs and offices held by individual ancestors; but by this date families were also sponsoring full-scale family histories in literary form. Cicero's friend Atticus, we know, wrote a history of the Junii at the request of M. Brutus, and, on behalf of other friends, histories of the Claudii Marcelli, Fabii and Aemilii.[25]

Whether the families had any documentary evidence to support their claims, and if so how far back it went, we cannot know. That they maintained a vigorous oral tradition seems certain, however, and it is probable that this was well established at least as early as the fourth century, when the Roman elite was fired by a competitive ethos. One of the ways in which family history was publicised and transmitted was the practice of delivering eulogies at funerals, a ceremony that is brilliantly described by Polybius. The funeral was attended, he tells us, by relatives of the deceased wearing the death-masks of his ancestors, and clothed in the dress suitable to the rank they achieved in their careers.

> They all ride in chariots preceded by the fasces, axes, and other insignia by which the different magistrates are wont to be accompanied according to the respective dignity of the offices of state held by each during his life; and when they arrive at the rostra they all seat themselves in a row on ivory chairs .... Besides, he who makes the oration over the man about to be buried, when he has finished speaking of him, recounts the successes and exploits of the rest whose images are present, beginning with the most ancient. By this means, by this constant renewal of the good report of brave men, the celebrity of those who performed noble deeds is rendered immortal, while at the same time the fame of those who did good service to their country becomes known to the people and a heritage for later generations.
>
> (Polyb. 6.53.8–54.2)

It is likely enough that aristocratic family traditions played a part in the formation of the surviving narrative accounts of early Rome, but it is difficult to define the precise nature of their influence. The only explicit comments are negative ones; both Cicero (*Brutus* 62) and Livy (8.40.2) tell us that funeral eulogies distorted the record by making false claims. Both seem to imply that the problem was not that people were fabricating fictitious ancestors, but rather that they were falsely claiming descent from great men of the past to whom they were not, in fact, related. If so, the amount of potential damage is considerably reduced. The context of Livy's statement also makes it seem as if the object of dispute was the identity of the individual magistrates who undertook particular tasks: which consul – Fabius or Fulvius? Or was it the dictator Cornelius? The same evidence also suggests that the false claims related to the period of the later fourth century.

One thing is certain – and rather striking. Roman aristocratic families, unlike their Greek counterparts, did not, as a general rule, concern themselves with the business of inserting their forebears into the mythical past of the city. The great patrician clans (see below, p. 245), the Claudii, Sulpicii, Cornelii and Manlii, did not try very hard to claim ancestors among the companions of Aeneas or Romulus (or, if they did, they were not successful); and their role in the traditional account of the regal period was minimal or non-existent. Some families, it is true, paraded their supposed descent from the sons of Numa, but this was a transparent fiction of relatively late date, perpetrated by *arriviste* families of no great distinction.[26]

The result of this discussion is rather inconclusive. Family tradition probably furnished some of the information collected by the early Roman historians, and may well have given rise to some minor distortions. But in general it is difficult to separate what aristocratic families provided from the contribution made by oral tradition in a wider sense; and it is to this broader category of oral tradition that we must now turn.

5 THE SOURCES OF OUR SOURCES: ORAL TRADITION

Much of what we read in the surviving sources about early Rome must be derived from oral tradition – that is to say, stories passed down by word of mouth from one generation to the next. This general point can be asserted with some confidence, simply because of the nature and form of the stories themselves. The legends of the Horatii and Curiatii, the dramatic narratives of Coriolanus, Cincinnatus and Verginia, and the whole saga of tales surrounding the rise and fall of the Tarquins, cannot possibly have been based to any great extent on documentary evidence; and while some elements may be of late literary origin, the majority certainly predate the earliest Roman literature. That the famous legends of early Rome were handed down orally is not only inherently probable, but virtually guaranteed by the absence of any serious alternative. It is also likely enough that many of them go back a long way. The most outstanding example is the foundation legend itself; that the story was already well known in the archaic period is proved by the famous bronze statue of a she-wolf, an archaic masterpiece which may be earlier than 500 BC (see below, p. 61).

At a general level there is no difficulty about this; it would be quite unreasonable to deny that much of the literary tradition is based ultimately on orally transmitted material. The trouble is that even the most time-honoured stories may be quite unhistorical, and comparative studies do not increase one's confidence in the capacity of oral traditions to preserve historical information without serious distortion.[27] The issue can only be tackled by examining each individual story on its own merits, and this will be done where appropriate in the course of the chapters that follow. In each case one must ask, first, whether there are grounds for regarding a story as ancient, or as a relatively late invention; and second whether there are reasons for thinking that it might be based on fact. Certainty can rarely be attained; it is usually a matter of probability. At all times it is important to exercise caution and to make no presumptions. The burden of proof lies as heavily on those who wish to deny as on those who wish to affirm. Where there is no evidence either way the proper course is to suspend judgement. It is quite wrong to dismiss the story of (e.g.) Verginia as fiction, simply because it cannot be shown to be based on fact. It cannot be shown to be fiction either (cf. below, p. 275).

Another major question concerns the means of transmission. Stories can be told and retold in any number of different social contexts; the question is whether we can define any formal mechanisms in early Roman society that might have facilitated the process. This is a topic that deserves more serious attention than it normally receives, even if there is relatively little firm evidence.

Two possibilities should be seriously considered. The first is drama. Dramatic performances were a feature of Roman life from the earliest times, and were associated with the annual games (*ludi*). At least two of the annual sets of games, the *ludi Romani* and *ludi plebeii*, were being celebrated as early as the fifth century, and although the earliest literary plays date only from 240 BC, it is probable that dramatic performances were instituted much earlier (Livy 7.2 suggests that drama was first introduced in 364 BC, but even that may be too late). The fact that technical words to do with the theatre, including *scaena* ('stage'), *histrio* ('actor') and *persona* ('mask', and, by extension, 'character'), were borrowed from Etruscan, points to an early date for the introduction of drama.[28] The plays regularly performed in the later Republic included the so-called *fabulae praetextae*, which dealt with Roman historical themes. For example L. Accius (*c.* 170–90 BC) presented plays on the overthrow of the kings (*Brutus*) and the battle of Sentinum (*Aeneadae vel Decius*). The earliest known example is the *Romulus sive lupus* (*Romulus or the Wolf*) by the third-century playwright Cn. Naevius; but it is perfectly conceivable that earlier drama, performed without written texts, included historical plays.[29]

The second possibility is that there was a tradition of oral poetry in Rome. A well-known theory, most famously associated with the name of Barthold Niebuhr (1776–1831), although it was first formulated in the seventeenth century, maintains that all the well-known stories of early Rome were derived from popular lays or ballads that were performed at banquets.[30] The principal evidence for this idea comes from Cicero, who had no first-hand knowledge of the banquet songs, but had read about them in Cato's *Origines*.

> Cato, that most weighty authority, stated in his *Origins* that it was the custom among our ancestors for guests at banquets to take turns to sing, to the accompaniment of the flute, the achievements and virtues of famous men.
>
> (*Tusc.* 4.3 = Cato, *Orig.* VII. 13)

In another passage (*Brutus* 75) Cicero makes it clear that the songs were no longer extant, and that Cato had spoken of the custom as something that prevailed 'many centuries before his time'. This may imply that in Cato's day the songs were no longer being performed at banquets; but it does not necessarily do so, and it certainly does not mean that Cato did not know the songs or what they contained.[31] In any case Cato's testimony, which is independently corroborated by Varro, clearly indicates that a tradition of banquet songs had once existed at Rome.

The resulting picture is unfortunately rather theoretical and difficult to substantiate in detail. It is likely enough that many of the stories preserved in the literary tradition were handed down by word of mouth in the fifth and fourth centuries, and that at least some of them were celebrated in drama and song. This is altogether much more probable than the alternative: that the stories were consciously invented after the practice of historical writing had been introduced at the end of the third century. As for the authenticity of the stories, the above arguments are sufficient to demonstrate that they should not be dismissed out of hand. There existed more than one formal means of oral transmission, and there can be no objection in principle to the suggestion that the traditional stories might be based on fact.

6 THE SOURCES OF OUR SOURCES: DOCUMENTS AND ARCHIVES

The above conclusion may seem unduly negative, or at least non-committal. If that is the best we can say, does it not follow that any attempt to write the history of early Rome will be so inconclusive as to be not worth the effort? That would indeed be the case if oral tradition had been the only major source available to the earliest Roman historians, and if the surviving narratives consisted of no more than a succession of poetic episodes like those of Horatius, Coriolanus and Verginia. But that is not what the literary tradition is really like. In fact these poetic episodes occur only infrequently in the course of a much more prosaic narrative, largely made up of routine annalistic notices.

The basic framework is present in all the main narrative accounts, and consists of the names of the chief annual magistrates, the consuls, listed at the beginning of each year, together with other items of public business that recur more or less regularly throughout the history of the Republic. Such items, which are often reported without any embellishment, include the foundation of colonies, military operations, triumphs, treaties and alliances with other cities and peoples, extensions of Roman territory, grants of citizenship and the creation of new rural tribes (see below, p. 174), temple constructions and other public works, legislation, plagues, droughts and food shortages, the deaths of prominent people (especially priests), eclipses, prodigies, and other events of religious significance.

Material of this kind must have been taken from documentary sources of an archival nature. The only possible alternative, that it is the product of fictitious invention, cannot be seriously entertained as a complete explanation for the bulk of the notices, although there may be reason to suspect the authenticity of some individual items. Most scholars accept the authenticity of the consular list (the *Fasti*) which goes back in a continuous series to the beginning of the Republic. The list can be reconstructed from the main narrative sources, which show occasional minor discrepancies but a broad measure of general agreement on the identity and order of names (see further below, p. 218). Since the consuls were eponymous – that is, they gave their names to the year and thus provided a system of dating – the practice of recording the names of the men who held the chief magistracy must go back to the very early years of the Republic, and it is certain that continuous lists were kept in written form.

The structure of the narrative sources seems to suggest that the Roman historians also had access to documents that listed not only the names of the annual magistrates, but also events that occurred during their years of office. This supposition is confirmed by Cicero, who tells us in his dialogue *On the Orator* (2.52) that the crabbed and meagre style of the earliest Roman historians was modelled on that of an official chronicle known as the *Annales maximi*. This is an extremely important reference, because it not only explains the characteristic structure that evidently underlies the surviving literary narratives, but also identifies an official document that could have provided most, if not all, of the archival material that they contain. That the *Annales maximi* were themselves a prime source for the earliest historians is implicit in Cicero's account.[32]

Not surprisingly the *Annales maximi* have prompted an enormous amount of discussion among historians of early Rome and early Roman historiography. Here it will be possible merely to outline some of the main problems, and briefly to state my own position on the question. The main sources on the chronicle are Cicero, in the passage just referred to, and a group of later texts that all derive ultimately from the antiquarian Verrius Flaccus, the most important being a passage of Servius (Auctus), *Aen.* 1.373 (on these authors see below).[33]

Cicero and Servius make it clear that the *Annales maximi* were a chronicle kept by the *pontifex maximus*, and that they recorded, year by year, all important public events. Cicero tells us that the chronicle went back to the beginning of Roman history (*ab initio rerum Romanarum*) and continued to the time of P. Mucius Scaevola, who was *pontifex maximus* in the 120s BC. Servius says that each year's entry began with the names of the consuls and the other magistrates, that the events were recorded *per singulos dies* (that is, probably, with an indication of the day on which they occurred), and that the whole compilation occupied eighty books.

Many questions arise in relation to this chronicle, particularly how it was composed and how far back it went. One firmly attested detail is that the chronicle was intimately connected with a white noticeboard (*tabula dealbata*) which the *pontifex maximus* posted outside his official residence (the Regia: see below, p. 234) in order to keep the public informed of important events. The most likely interpretation of this fact is either that the contents of the *tabula* were transferred at the end of each year to a permanent record (Mommsen called it a *liber annalis*), or that the *pontifex maximus* maintained a continuous record of events in book form, but allowed some of what he put into it to be copied on to the *tabula* for the benefit of the public. Some such explanation is far more likely than the widely held belief that the *pontifex maximus* set up a new board each year, and stored the old ones in the Regia.[34]

But the precise nature of the documents on which the record was made is a secondary issue; what matters is that the *pontifex maximus* kept some kind of chronicle, which recorded events under the heading of the annual magistrates, and that it went back to a very remote period. We can be sure of this because it recorded an eclipse of the sun on the nones (i.e. the 5th) of June in a year which Cicero dates 'around 350 years after the founding of the city'.[35] It so happens that there was an 80 per cent solar eclipse visible from Rome on 21 June 400 BC. This fact allows us to make not only the trivial observation that the Roman calendar was at that time sixteen days adrift of the Julian year, but also the decisively important inference that an authentic record of this celestial event was preserved in the *Annales maximi*.

It is certain, therefore, that the *Annales maximi* go back to the fifth century; but it is probable that the earliest entries were not very detailed. For the first century or so of the Republic the chronicle probably consisted of a list of annual magistrates with the occasional addition of events that occurred during their year of office. In some years nothing at all was recorded. During the fourth century the record became more detailed, and in the last quarter of the century it became a systematic chronicle containing a wide variety of annual events as a matter of routine. This was Mommsen's view, based on the pattern that underlies the surviving narrative accounts. In other words, the sparse and intermittent character of the fifth-century notices, and the increasing amounts of routine detail that appear in the later books of Livy's first decade, can be explained by an increase in the quantity, and an improvement in the quality, of the primary sources available to the annalists. This is an entirely legitimate inference, and in my view is almost certainly correct.[36]

This conclusion has positive as well as negative implications. The negative aspect is the fact that the documentary record of the period down to *c.* 350 BC is thin and desultory; but on the positive side the important thing is to have established that the elementary framework, skeletal though it is, does indeed rest on a solid documentary base. There is good reason to accept the authenticity of certain types of 'annalistic' information, such as reports of food shortages, temple constructions, hostile incursions by the Aequi and Volsci, foundations of colonies, the creation of new tribes, and so on. As we shall see, these various categories of information can be substantiated by independent arguments; what the foregoing discussion demonstrates is that the survival of genuine information about such matters is not wholly mysterious. The information survives because it was preserved in documents like the *Annales maximi*.

We should not forget that other documentary archives may have existed in republican Rome. The priestly colleges may have kept their own records, as indeed might other corporations such as the curiae. The plebeians had their own archive in the temple of Ceres (see below, p. 264), and we know that state documents were kept in the *aerarium* in the temple of Saturn, on the Capitol in the Treasury of the Aediles, in the Atrium Libertatis, and elsewhere.[37] Lists of consuls were undoubtedly kept from a very early period, and it is not necessary to assume that the *Annales maximi* were the only source for the first part of the *Fasti*. It is unlikely, however, that either the *Annales maximi* or any other systematic record stretched back as far as the regal period; indeed they may not even have gone back to the start of the Republic, although the consular list is probably genuine from the beginning.[38] In any case we can infer from the surviving sources that annalistic archives were available only for the Republic; the narrative of the preceding regal age is quite different in character and is manifestly based on different kinds of material, most of it oral and much of it legendary.

It does not follow, however, that the whole story of the regal period is fictitious. As we shall see, some of the legends appear to have a factual basis, and certain details, particularly the record of temple foundations, are almost certainly genuine. Moreover, the general picture of Rome as a rich and powerful city under the sixth-century kings can be confirmed, not least by archaeological evidence. It is also important to stress that even if there were no regular annalistic records dating back to the kings, the regal period nevertheless did produce documents, and at least some of these were preserved. Literacy in Rome can be dated back to the seventh century BC, and we know that the use of writing extended to the public sphere.[39] Whether any documents on papyrus or wood survived from the regal period cannot be known (but it should not on that account be ruled out); in any case certain types of document, such as treaties, laws, dedications and building inscriptions, were recorded on permanent materials such as stone or bronze. Some of these undoubtedly survived to the late Republic; indeed a few of them are still extant (see below, pp. 94, 294, etc.).

These isolated documents would not have been sufficient on their own to provide historians with a connected account of the regal period, but they made a substantial contribution to the process of historical reconstruction. Texts of laws, treaties and so on also survived from the early Republic (e.g. the Carthage treaty, the treaty of Spurius Cassius, the Twelve Tables), and quotations from them are among the most important pieces of evidence we possess. The idea, still to be found in some modern works, that these and other documents were forged in the late Republic, is absolutely unfounded. This does not mean that we should uncritically accept all the documents cited in our sources as a matter of course. Each must be treated with due caution and its pedigree judged on its merits. But what is quite inadmissible is the presumption that all quotations from, and references to, archaic documents are false unless they can be proved genuine. Given what we now know about the extent and uses of writing in archaic Rome, the burden of proof clearly lies on those who wish to deny the authenticity of a public document cited in our sources.

7 THE RELIABILITY OF THE ANNALISTIC TRADITION

We may conclude that the historical sources contain a good deal of authentic material concerning the early history of Rome before the Punic Wars. Naturally there are distinctions to be drawn between the different periods of this early history. The literary tradition on the period before the foundation of the city is entirely legendary. This was a pre-literate age, and cannot therefore have been documented in any way. It was also too remote for oral tradition to have any serious chance of surviving to historical times. It is worth saying that oral traditions about the origins of Rome can hardly have existed before the formation of a self-conscious political community – that is, before the formation of the city. It is unlikely, therefore, that the legends of the pre-Romulean period contain any vestige of historical fact.

The regal period, on the other hand, does seem to have generated both documentary evidence (admittedly meagre and sporadic) and an oral tradition that bears some relation to what actually happened. Even so, the literary tradition also contains much legendary material, and needs to be treated with extreme caution. The traditional account of the Republic, however, is different from that of the monarchy both in its formal structure and in the strength of its documentary base. But here too we should distinguish between the first century of the Republic, where the record is relatively thin, and the increasingly well-documented period of the fourth century, particularly after the changes of 367 BC. Finally, the age of the wars of conquest (from the 330s onwards) is fully historical, in the sense that it was extensively documented by written records, by accounts of Greek historians, and, perhaps most importantly, by first-hand oral tradition, since it was within the living memory of persons who could have transmitted their recollections to the first Roman historians.

Paradoxically, the period from 293 to 264 BC, which falls within this fully historical age, is the least well documented from our point of view; this is because of the loss of Livy's second decade, which means that no full-length continuous narrative survives. It should also be noted that, although the period around 300 BC is 'fully historical' in the sense indicated above, it does not follow that our sources are wholly reliable. Quite the contrary! Graeco-Roman history is different from most other fields of historical study precisely because much of the important primary evidence is literary and self-consciously historical – in other words, the work of historians. In any other field of history (other than historiography), such texts would be regarded as secondary sources by definition. It is in the nature of secondary sources that they offer interpretation and conjecture, that they tend to be biased, that they are frequently mistaken, and that they are sometimes dishonest.

Historical writing, which attempts to represent actual events by means of verbal narrative, and to construct a coherent story from a variety of more or less tractable raw data, is bound to be a distortion of reality. In this sense all history contains an element of fiction – although the view of some 'post-structuralist' literary critics, that what historians do is indistinguishable from what novelists do, is manifestly fatuous.[40] The way in which a historian bridges the gap between primary sources and finished (constructed) text depends on convention. The modern convention among professional historians is to make the relationship explicit, and as far as possible to indicate to the reader how the final product arises from the source material. It is further agreed that the historian must, if challenged, be able to support any and every statement with evidence. But in other genres (such as historical novels or biography), and in pre-modern historiography, there is much more leeway; writers are permitted to reconstruct, from their own imaginations, the feelings, aspirations and motives of persons and groups, to conjure up plausible scenes – on the battlefield, on the streets, or in the bedroom – and even to put their own words into the mouths of persons in the drama. These conventions were accepted without question in antiquity, when history was at least in part a rhetorical exercise.

For this reason historical accounts, even of the recent past, came to include a greater or lesser degree of imaginary reconstruction, set battle descriptions, freely composed speeches, and so on. In the work of any ancient historian there is always a distinction to be drawn between the structural data on which it is based and the narrative superstructure within which the data are recounted, interpreted and explained.[41] This applies as much to a historian of the Principate as to a historian of the archaic period. In the surviving accounts of early Rome the proportion of raw data is probably quite small by comparison with the amount of secondary embellishment, especially in a highly rhetorical work like that of Dionysius of Halicarnassus. Given that the primary sources were comparatively meagre and difficult to understand, and that the annalists had no clear grasp of how different the conditions of the archaic period were from those of their own age, there was bound to be a great deal of misunderstanding and unconscious distortion. Nevertheless, the fact remains that our sources do depend ultimately on a hard core of authentic data, much of which is readily identifiable.

The task of the modern historian is to extract this core and to attempt to make sense of it. Some elements, such as the consular *Fasti* and other routine annalistic notices (for example the founding of colonies or the dedication of temples) are clearly identifiable; other material, such as popular agitation for agrarian reform, is more marginal, and will require extensive discussion.

8 THE ANTIQUARIANS

Modern historians sometimes appear to assume that our knowledge of early Rome depends exclusively on what survives of the annalistic tradition, and that if this tradition is not demonstrably reliable the whole subject must lie beyond the reach of serious historical inquiry. This approach is unjustified, however, not only because the annalistic tradition rests on a fairly secure base, but because the initial premise is mistaken. The annalistic tradition is not the only source of information available to us. Not only are we becoming increasingly dependent on archaeological evidence, which incidentally lends considerable support to the traditional annalistic account; we should also remember that the literary sources contain a great deal of information about early Rome that is independent of the annalists and free from their real or supposed shortcomings. This is the evidence provided by the so-called antiquarians, men who devoted themselves to learned research into many different aspects of the Roman past.

Within the huge range of topics chosen by antiquarians as objects of research, certain areas of interest seem to have been especially important. These include legal, political and military institutions, monuments and buildings, archaic texts, chronology, the calendar, family history, religious cults, social customs, art and technology, private life, and an all-pervading interest in language. Whatever the particular subject, antiquarians almost invariably investigated the meaning and origins of technical words, personal names, place-names, archaic expressions, phrases and sayings, ritual formulae, legal terminology, and so on. Sometimes their efforts were directly aimed at language itself, as in Varro's work *On the Latin Language*, which is still partially extant. Speculation about etymology was a particular weakness of Varro, and remains to this day a curse of amateur antiquarianism, as anyone who has encountered a saloon-bar expert on 'phrase and fable' will testify.

Scholarly antiquarianism became a feature of Roman intellectual life in the second century BC, and was at least partially inspired by Hellenistic models.[42] The first great exponent was L. Aelius Stilo, who concerned himself with literary texts, grammar, and etymologies; he wrote learned commentaries on the Twelve Tables and the *carmen saliare* (the ritual hymn of the Salii, an archaic priestly college). Other noted antiquarians of the same period included C. Sempronius Tuditanus (cos. 129 BC) and M. Junius Congus 'Gracchanus' (so called because of his friendship with Gaius Gracchus), both of whom wrote about the origins and powers of the magistrates. It is worth observing that the efforts of these men marked the beginning of a split between scholarly antiquarianism and narrative historiography which was to have lasting consequences. The two activities remained separate until the eighteenth century, and to this day the breach has not been completely healed.[43]

The greatest Roman antiquarian (and perhaps the greatest antiquarian of all time) was M. Terentius Varro (116–27 BC), a pupil of Aelius Stilo, a friend of Pompey and Cicero, and a public figure in his own right. This astonishing man is said to have written 490 books by the age of 77 (another tradition gives his total output as 620 works). We know of 55 titles, but possess only one complete work: the *de re rustica*, a work in three books on agriculture, published in 37 BC. Of twenty-five books of the *de lingua Latina*, six are partially extant. The rest of Varro's life's work is represented only by fragmentary quotations. Nevertheless, his influence was all-pervasive; in the words of Nicholas Horsfall, he has perished by absorption.[44] His systematic organisation of knowledge provided the foundation for all subsequent Roman scholarship, and he was an indispensable source of factual information for later writers who occupied themselves in any way with the Roman past. The one significant exception is Livy, who along with the other late annalists paid no attention whatever to the findings of the antiquarians. Dionysius, on the other hand, made extensive use of Varro, particularly in his early books.[45]

Varro's most important work was the *Antiquitates*, divided between twenty-five books of *Res humanae* and sixteen of *Res divinae* (human and divine affairs). The latter were singled out by Christian apologists (especially St Augustine) as a major target in their attacks on pagan religion, with the consequence that we know more about them than about the books on human affairs; it is clear, however, that just as the 'divine affairs' dealt with Roman religion, so too the human affairs dealt mainly with Rome and the Romans. Cicero, in a remarkable tribute, says it made the Romans feel that they had been strangers in their own country, but were now being shown the way home.

We now know who and where we are; you have shown us the past of our country, the sequence of events, ritual and priestly laws, the traditional customs of private and public life, the position of geographical areas and of particular places, and the names, types, functions and causes of all things divine and human.

(*Acad.* 1.3.9)

Augustine tells us that the *Res humanae* were divided into four sections of six books each (following an introductory first book) on 'persons, places, times and actions' (*de civitate dei* 6.4); other than this, however, we have little precise information and few quotations.[46]

It is also not clear how the *Antiquitates* differed from the work *de vita populi Romani* (*On the Life of the Roman People*), written a few years later (the late 40s BC). This was a work in four books about the social and cultural past of Rome. Its structure was roughly chronological: the first two books dealt with the period of the kings and the early Republic, and described the institutions and private life (e.g. food, drink, domestic architecture, dress) of the early Romans, and laid stress on their simple austerity. The later books dealt with the Punic Wars and the later Republic, and illustrated the greed, corruption and moral decline that had taken place since the early days. A companion volume, the *de gente populi Romani* (*On the Ancestry of the Roman People*) dealt with the remote origins of the city.[47] It paid particular attention to chronology, a subject that Varro also treated in a work called *Annales*. It was Varro who established the system of Roman chronology that has since become conventional, with the foundation of the city in the year we call 753 BC, the first consuls in 509, and the Gallic sack in 390.[48]

Varro's activities had an immediate impact, and made antiquarian studies fashionable in intellectual circles. Cornelius Nepos, Atticus, Tarquinius Priscus, Nigidius Figulus, and many others tried their hand. Even Cicero adopted antiquarian methods in his later dialogues, as Elizabeth Rawson has shown, pointing out that what he lacked in erudition he made up for in his powers of argument.[49] In the Augustan age, whose backward-looking ideology of religious revival and moral regeneration would have been unthinkable without Varro, antiquarian studies continued to flourish. Two figures deserve particular mention. L. Cincius wrote extensively on ancient buildings, on archaic words, on constitutional and military antiquities, and on the calendar. Little survives of his output, but he is the ultimate source of some crucial pieces of evidence, notably the law about the *praetor maximus* and the account of how commanders were appointed for the forces of the Latin League (below, pp. 220, 299). The other major figure is Verrius Flaccus, who is important because of his huge influence, and because some of his work survives for us to read, even if only at second hand.

M. Verrius Flaccus was a freed slave who became tutor to Augustus' grandsons. His most important work was a dictionary entitled *de verborum significatu* (*On the Meaning of Words*), which dealt alphabetically not only with the Latin language, but with Roman antiquities in general. This great work has not survived, but we do possess part of an abridgement made in the later second century AD by Sex. Pompeius Festus, and arranged in twenty books. The only surviving manuscript of Festus' abridgement, an eleventh-century codex, was severely damaged by fire in the fifteenth century. Only the second half was preserved (from the letter M onwards) in an imperfect state; some of the entries are severely mutilated. These gaps, and the entries in the first half of the alphabet, can be partially reconstructed with the help of an epitome, made in the ninth century by Paul the Deacon, and other medieval glossaries thought to have been based on Festus.

The result, a combined Paulus-Festus with occasional additions, is a mess; but this sorry compilation provides us with hundreds of precious nuggets of information reproduced more or less faithfully from Verrius Flaccus' original text. Verrius in turn had drawn upon Varro, Cato, Aelius Stilo, Cincius, and many others, as well as on his own first-hand research, to produce an invaluable work of reference whose importance is evident even in the present wretched state of the text. Festus (Paulus) is for us one of the most important sources on the history of early Roman institutions, and will be referred to constantly throughout this book.[50]

Varro, Verrius Flaccus, and the other antiquarians of the late Republic and early Empire, provided the primary materials for later scholars whose works survive for us to read. They also had considerable influence on Roman poetry. The Greek tradition of learned verse, associated especially with the name of Callimachus, was absorbed by Latin poets, especially the 'new poets' of the late Republic; in the Augustan age they began to direct their erudition towards Roman antiquity. The best known example is Virgil's *Aeneid*, which incorporates much antiquarian information (principally from Varro) in the section about Aeneas' adventures in Italy (books 7–12). Another is the *Fasti* of Ovid, a poetic account of the Roman calendar, covering the first six months of the year (the rest was never written). It includes much historical informa-tion, as it recounts famous events that occurred on certain days (for instance the massacre of the Fabii at the Cremera on 13 February – *Fasti* 2.193–242), and it is one of the principal sources of our knowledge of early Roman religion. Ovid's account of the festivals, though presented with considerable poetic licence as the product of first-hand observation and inquiry, derives from antiquarian sources, particularly Verrius Flaccus, who wrote a prose commentary on the calendar, and Varro's *Antiquitates*, which dealt with the festivals in the eighth book of the *Res divinae*.[51]

In the imperial period the antiquarian tradition continued, but it tended increasingly to degenerate into compilation, and the summarising and excerpt-ing of earlier work, rather than new creative research. But the secondary productions of this period provide us with our most important surviving texts. Apart from Festus, the leading figures in this story are Pliny the Elder, Plutarch, Aulus Gellius, Macrobius, and the Virgil commentators.

Pliny the Elder (AD 23/4–79) was a polymath, now known through his sole surviving work, the *Natural History*. This encyclopedic study, in thirty-seven books, deals with geography, zoology, botany, mineralogy, art and technology, but touches on all manner of subjects along the way. The work is entirely derivative, and draws on hundreds of sources, which are listed in book 1; it is also lacking in judgement and often careless. Nevertheless, it frequently provides information that would otherwise be completely unknown, and some of this concerns early Roman antiquity, for which Pliny's principal sources appear to have been Varro and Verrius Flaccus.[52]

These two were also the major sources for Plutarch's charming essay, the 'Roman Questions', a literary piece which conveys, perhaps more directly than any other surviving text, the feel of Roman antiquarianism. It consists of 113 little essays on strange Roman customs, each headed by a question, such as 'Why were patricians not permitted to live on the Capitoline?' (no. 91), or 'Why do they name boys when they are nine days old, but girls when they are eight days old?' (no. 102). Varro is frequently cited; Verrius Flaccus, though not mentioned by name, was probably also used, since over forty of the questions deal with matters treated in Verrius' dictionary.[53] Another essayist whose subject matter included Roman antiquities was Aulus Gellius, whose *Attic Nights* (written in the reign of Marcus Aurelius, AD 161–180) contain numerous quotations from early Roman documents (e.g. the Twelve Tables) and literary texts. Many essays deal with early Roman law, history and institutions, and preserve crucially important information drawn from good sources.[54]

In the later empire antiquarian studies formed part of the so-called 'pagan revival'; to the intellectuals of this movement in the late fourth century the study of ancient texts, and the recollection of traditional institutions, were as important as the observation of pagan cults. The work that most clearly represents this attitude is the *Saturnalia* of Macrobius, an imaginary dialogue (modelled on Cicero's *de re publica*) set at the festival of the Saturnalia in, probably, 384, but written in the early fifth century. The discussion ranges over a wide variety of topics, but is focused on scholarly criticism of Virgil. It is rich in quotations from historical and antiquarian sources, and frequently preserves important information about the archaic age of Rome.[55]

The tradition of Virgil criticism began almost immediately after the poet's death in 19 BC. The most important surviving representative of this tradition is the fourth-century commentary attributed to Servius (a scholar whom Macrobius mentions among those present at the Saturnalia). This work is preserved in two versions: a commentary written by Servius himself, and a much longer and slightly altered version known as *Servius auctus* ('enlarged Servius'), which was put together probably in the seventh or eighth century.

The extremely erudite and well-informed additions are almost certainly taken from the otherwise lost commentary by Donatus, a fourth-century scholar whom Servius is also thought to have followed.[56] The Virgil commentaries are a rich store of information about early Rome, drawing on all kinds of sources. Varro and Verrius Flaccus are naturally prominent, but there are numerous references to earlier antiquarians and historians. Many of the fragments of Cato's *Origines*, for example, come from the Virgil comment-aries, and they are an important source of quotations from Ennius.[57]

It has seemed necessary to outline the work of the antiquarians in this way for various reasons. The first is to introduce readers to an important group of texts which are rarely considered as worthy of serious attention for their own sake. Second, they tend to be ignored in discussions of the sources for early Roman history, even in works that rely heavily on them. For many modern scholars, as was noted earlier, the literary tradition means the annalists. It is true that the annalists provide the essential narrative frame-work, but only the antiquarians give us any idea of what that framework might be based on. If it were not for the antiquarians, we should know nothing about, for example, the banquet songs or the *Annales maximi*. Our knowledge of Roman institutions, customs, monuments and so on is im-measurably enriched by antiquarian sources; without them, we should have a very different, and much dimmer, picture of archaic Rome.

The same is true even of legends. Take the foundation story itself. Livy gives us a straightforward account of the familiar saga, from Aeneas to Romulus. He occasionally notes that there were different versions of certain details. But if we examine what the antiquarians had to say, we discover an extraordinary variety of stories; thanks to antiquarian sources, we know of more than twenty-five distinct versions of the story as a whole, many of them containing no reference whatever to either Aeneas or Romulus.[58] The antiquarians, in other words, completely change the picture.

The example of the foundation legend illustrates another important point, namely that what the antiquarians tell us is not necessarily to be taken as more historical than what the annalists tell us. However learned they may have been, the antiquarians were often credulous and facile (as their feeble etymologies so amply attest), and did not possess the kind of skill and expertise that a modern scholar would be able to bring to an ancient inscription or monument. Nevertheless, the materials they were working with were genuine enough. Some modern books give the impression that in the late Republic very little survived from the city's ancient past. This absurd view is the exact opposite of the truth. The amount of evidence available to anyone in the late Republic who wished to investigate the archaic period was simply overwhelming. However poorly they understood what they found, the antiquarians are important because they can put us directly in touch with countless genuine vestiges of a forgotten past that is, almost by definition, missing from the elaborated narratives of the annalists.

9 THE SOURCES AND METHODS OF THE ANTIQUARIANS

The evidence studied by the antiquarians was far more abundant than the admittedly rather meagre documentation that would have been available, even on the most optimistic interpretation, to the historians. This was because, unlike the historians, they did not confine themselves to material relating to political and military events. Religious texts (like the *carmen saliare*, the calendars, and the procedural books of the priestly colleges), building inscriptions, dedications, private documents and legal texts – all were grist to the antiquarian mill. For instance it was the antiquarians, rather than the historians, who studied the Twelve Tables, and observed, quite rightly, that they provided evidence not only about early Roman law, but about all kinds of social and cultural realities. Cicero, for example, realised that the funerary regulations in the Tables provided evidence for early Roman burial practices.[59]

Apart from documents, there were many physical reminders of the city's ancient past in the buildings, monuments and other relics that surrounded the Romans on every side. It is sometimes assumed that little could have survived from the period before 390 BC because in that year the city was sacked by the Gauls, who destroyed everything, including all documents. Indeed the annalists used the Gallic sack as an aetiology for the shortage of documentation for the early centuries (Livy 6.1.2; Plutarch, *Numa* 1.1). This explanation, however, will not stand up to scrutiny. As we shall see (below, p. 318), the effects of the sack were nowhere near as devastating as Livy makes out. Important buildings in which documents are known to have been kept (including the Regia, the temple of Saturn and the Capitol) survived the attack unscathed, and we know that many important documents, not to speak of buildings and monuments, did, in fact, escape. In any case it is unlikely that the Roman authorities, who were careful to send the Vestal Virgins and their sacred cult objects to Caere, did not take similar precautions to protect their archives when they heard news of the impending Gallic attack.

The topography of the city was central to the studies of the antiquarians (witness Cicero's tribute to Varro, quoted above), and forms an important focus of modern research. The Romans had an immense reverence for ancient buildings, and preserved their location, form and layout more or less permanently. In this way, even if rebuilding took place, the topography of the city was preserved in fossilised form, long after its original purpose, if any, had been forgotten. The physical layout of archaic Rome can therefore be 'read' in the monumental plan of the historical city, which thus forms a kind of notional document.[60]

Many other survivals persisted in a similarly abstract form. They included institutions, customs and practices which the Romans had inherited from their ancestors, and on which they placed great value precisely because of their antiquity. Their consciously traditionalist ideology made Rome a kind of living museum, in which the past was continuously on display. This may seem surprising in a society which in the course of the Republic developed from a minor city-state into a world empire, and showed a remarkable capacity for innovation and for flexibility in adapting to change. The explanation for this paradox is not only that the Romans were experts at retaining the form of institutions while changing their substance (the best example being the restored Republic of the emperor Augustus); they also preferred to leave existing structures unchanged rather than reform them, and simply to superimpose new ones where necessary. Their approach was not unlike that of a householder who constantly buys new kitchen appliances, but cannot bear to throw the old ones away. The consequence is that the kitchen gets cluttered up with old-fashioned and redundant gadgets. Roman public life was just such a kitchen, but the Romans did not seem to mind. They found the new appliances efficient, and they quite liked the clutter, which came to seem quaint and even decorative.

A good example is the bewilderingly complex system of Roman popular assemblies. The *comitia centuriata* and *comitia tributa* (see below, pp. 179 and 265) did not replace the earlier *comitia curiata*; that archaic assembly retained a ghostly existence, and continued to meet, until the end of the Republic. Although the chief magistrates were elected by the *comitia centuriata*, they still had to submit to a second vote by the *comitia curiata*, which thereby conferred, or confirmed (scholars disagree about which of these it is), their formal powers. This *lex curiata de imperio* has been much discussed, and since the sixteenth century has been thought to contain the key to the understanding of the Roman constitution and the concept of *imperium*.[61] The idea that there is some kind of mystical essence in the notion of *imperium*, which can be unlocked by a study of these obsolete formalities, might strike the modern reader as unlikely, not to say absurd; but there can be no objection to the more hard-headed approach of the Roman antiquarians, who inferred that the *comitia curiata* and the *lex curiata de imperio* were relics of the Roman monarchy, and that they convey information about the nature of Roman kingship. In this they were undoubtedly correct.

A second area in which survivals provide invaluable evidence is religion. No sphere of Roman life illustrates so well the paradoxical combination of innovation and conservatism as religion. The Romans were notoriously conservative in the way they maintained ancient cult practices, and were punctilious in the performance of ritual acts in the manner prescribed by tradition. At the same time a remarkable feature of Roman religion was its habit of continually introducing new (usually foreign) deities and cult practices, particularly from the Greek world. This was an inherent feature, which can be traced back to the very earliest times. The old idea that the influx of foreign cults was a relatively late development, a symptom of the deterioration and contamination of the original native cult, can no longer be sustained.[62]

As in the case of political institutions, however, the old cults were not replaced by the new ones, but continued to exist as before. The result was the proliferation of a large number, and a bewildering variety, of cults, festivals and ceremonies, which continued to be observed in the classical period, even though many of them were (and perhaps always had been) obscure and mysterious. That the regular procedures of Roman religion preserved historical information was as obvious to Roman antiquarians as it is to us. The historical explanations offered in our sources may very well be arbitrary or absurd, and indeed many of them are, but that does not mean that ancient religious customs cannot be explained historically, or that we should desist from attempting to interpret the same evidence. A well-known example of how rituals can be made to yield historical information is the use of festivals like the Lupercalia, the Septimontium and the Ambarvalia to reconstruct the topography of the earliest settlements of Rome at various stages, and the extent of its territorial boundary.[63]

10 ARCHAEOLOGICAL EVIDENCE

To leave the archaeological evidence till last is to invite the sort of criticism that was made famous at the marriage feast at Cana. There is indeed a sense in which the archaeological evidence is the best available. Archaeology produces tangible relics of past societies and can put us directly in contact with the material facts of their daily existence. Archaeological finds provide the only primary data we have for the early history of Rome; there are no contemporary documents other than inscriptions, which, though important, are brief and few in number, and are themselves the product of excavations. The importance of archaeology for this period cannot be overstressed, even when account is taken of the limited range and quantity of the material currently available, and the immense problems of interpretation it presents.

Archaeology is also the only source that can reasonably be expected to provide new information. Up to now it has had a tremendous impact on the subject, which has been completely transformed, not only since the days of Niebuhr, Lewis and Schwegler, who based their accounts (written in the first half of the nineteenth century) exclusively on literary sources, but even since the time of Gjerstad, who in the 1950s and 1960s produced a comprehensive synthesis of all the archaeological evidence then available from the site of Rome.[64] Gjerstad not only dealt with recent finds, but also presented all the material from the excavations that had gone on in the city since 1870, including the crucially important campaigns in the Forum directed by Giacomo Boni between 1898 and 1905. But Gjerstad's volumes, which were intended to be definitive, marked not the end, but the beginning, of a modern revolution in early Roman archaeology.

New excavations in and around the city (often necessitated by rapid urban development), and the application of modern approaches and techniques, have radically altered our knowledge of early Rome and Latium since the 1960s. The evidence now available allows us to trace the development of iron-age communities in Latium from around 900 BC until the rise of urbanised city-states in the seventh and sixth centuries. The details of the process can be documented in a way that would have been undreamed of twenty-five years ago. Our knowledge of the archaic period (especially the late sixth and early fifth centuries) has also been transformed by sensational new discoveries, not only in Rome itself, but at other sites too, such as Lavinium (Pratica di Mare), Ardea and Satricum. Archaeological work is continuing, and further discoveries can be expected in the future.

A significant fact about the archaeological evidence from Latium is that the great bulk of it comes from funerary contexts. The most important excavations have been of cemetery sites, and most of the artefacts have been found in graves. Cemeteries are prominent not because archaeologists are morbid by nature, but because of the remarkable habit, common in ancient societies, of burying grave goods with the deceased. Most of the artefacts we study have survived because they were deliberately deposited in sealed tombs, which have remained intact until unearthed by archaeologists (or tomb-robbers). Furthermore, graves represent 'closed find deposits'; that is, the artefacts they contain were buried all together at one moment, and are therefore contemporaneous. When a number of graves are excavated in the same cemetery, the archaeologist can compare the several groups of artefacts and order them in sequence; this makes it possible to establish relative chronology and is the basis of all archaeological dating.[65] Absolute dates can be provided for the whole scheme by graves containing objects (usually foreign imports) that can be dated independently.

The cemeteries of Latium provide evidence for the period down to about 580 BC, but not thereafter. This curious hiatus presents a problem that will be discussed more fully in the relevant place (below, p. 105). Here it is sufficient to note the shift in the focus of archaeological research from cemeteries to sanctuaries, which provide most of the evidence for the subsequent archaic period. The material from sanctuaries is essentially of two kinds. In the first place there are traces of monumental sacred buildings ('temples'), consisting not only of foundations, building blocks and rooftiles, but also terracotta sculptures. Some of these were purely decorative, and include statues in the round which adorned the main roof beam (these roof statues are called *acroteria*) as well as relief sculptures on the pediment; while others were also functional, and served to protect the exposed timbers. Eaves and projecting rafters were encased in a complex array of antefixes, gargoyles and revetment plaques, while the architraves were fronted with friezes, all elaborately moulded and decorated with brightly coloured paint.[66]

These architectural terracottas constitute an important body of diagnostic material which can be analysed and classified in terms of style, iconography, provenance and date. They have been intensively studied, with valuable results. It is evident that material from the same workshops found its way to sites throughout central Italy, including southern Etruria (but it is misleading to describe it as 'Etruscan' – see below, p. 154). Finds of moulded architectural terracottas need not be associated with sanctuaries (although they often are); it is now clear that they were fitted to all kinds of public buildings, and also to the more luxurious private residences.[67] In a way this is not surprising, given the functional purpose of terracotta revetments.

Sanctuaries are also documented by material from 'votive deposits'. These are collections of artefacts, commonly found in sanctuary sites, which seem to have been deliberately buried and sealed in antiquity. For an explanation we can turn (where else?) to the Roman antiquarians. Varro (quoted by A. Gellius 2.10) tells us that it was the custom to place in underground cavities (in Latin, *favisae*) ancient bits of sculpture that had fallen off temples, together with other votive offerings that had been consecrated in the sanctuary. According to Verrius Flaccus (Paul.-Fest. s.v. 'favisae', p. 78 L), it was a way of disposing of sacred items that had outlived their usefulness. In any event these collections of votives represent another category of closed find deposit, and their contents provide us with valuable evidence. In many cases they prove that the sanctuaries in which they were found had been centres of cult activity long before the first evidence of any temple building.

The evidence shows that the golden age of archaic monumental sanctuaries lasted for about a century from *c.* 580 BC. No temple building or group of architectural terracottas can be dated much after the first quarter of the fifth century (although votive deposits indicate that cult activity continued). This is a remarkable finding because it coincides so precisely with the evidence of the literary sources. It is not simply that a long series of recorded temple dedications comes to an end in 484 BC (see below, p. 266); it is also striking that the literary sources should place so much emphasis on the events surrounding the foundation, construction and dedication of temples and sanctuaries during the period in question. On this point – the importance of monumental sanctuaries in the political, economic and cultural life of archaic Rome – the two types of evidence coincide in a remarkable way. This general observation, which will be analysed in detail in the chapters that follow, is the strongest single argument in favour of a conservative approach to the literary tradition.[68]

Tombs, sacred buildings, votive deposits – these form the traditional focus of Italian archaeology, and tend to give it an old-fashioned, artefact-based appearance. But recent decades have also seen great advances in the application of new techniques such as surface survey (pioneered in south Etruria by the British School at Rome) and the investigation of settlements. These new approaches are now beginning to yield valuable historical evidence.

It is important to remember that the function of archaeology is to provide historical evidence. This may seem a rather unfashionable point of view, and perhaps needs clarification. It is not meant to imply that archaeology should be subordinated to the study of texts, and called upon only when it contributes to a traditional narrative, still less that it should be relegated to footnotes in appendices on 'daily life' or the arts. The point is that history, if it is not to be confined to a study of kings and battles, must include those areas of life and culture that are illuminated by archaeological evidence. By the same token, it must be recognised that the issues that concern the best modern archaeologists – the organisation of settlements, demographic patterns, production, exchange and cultural processes – are historical issues. Archaeological research, if it is not to become a mindless application of mere technique, must be directed to answering historical questions.

Historians and archaeologists are therefore engaged in the same activity, but using different methods. It follows that written sources, if available, cannot and should not be ignored by archaeologists, any more than historians can avoid archaeological evidence. Attempting to write a purely 'archaeological history' is misguided.[69] The problem is that archaeological evidence and textual evidence provide the answers to very different types of question, and combining them effectively is extremely hard.

At first sight this might seem surprising. Archaeological evidence offers a body of material that is entirely independent of the data provided by written sources. It might therefore seem to be a straightforward matter to compare the two and to use the former as an independent check on the latter. Unfortunately the situation is not so simple. This is because the two bodies of data represent different kinds of reality, and have to be ordered and interpreted each according to its own rules. At the most basic level, archaeological data consist of pieces of tangible material – stones, ceramics, metals and organic matter. Even the most basic classification of this material into categories such as rooftiles, pots, coins and weapons, not to speak of such abstractions as 'cities' or 'sanctuaries', is already an act of secondary interpretation. When written sources are available, it is inevitable and perfectly proper that they should be used to assist in the business of interpretation. When an archaeologist finds a 'Greek' pot, or unearths an 'Etruscan' city, he or she is introducing categories that are derived, ultimately, from written sources.

Most archaeological 'facts' turn out to be a complex mixture of primary data and secondary interpretation. For this reason it is important to exercise extreme caution when arguing that some aspect of the literary tradition is 'confirmed' by archaeological evidence. The relationship is often the other way round. That is, the literary tradition is being used to interpret the archaeological data. A good example is the tradition about the Sabines. According to the story, the population of early Rome included a substantial element of Sabines (who had been integrated with the followers of Romulus after the rape of the Sabine women). It used to be thought (and one still finds this idea in many books) that the tradition had been confirmed by the excavation of the graves in the Roman Forum, which were found to consist of a mixture of cremations and inhumations. This was assumed to indicate the presence of two distinct ethnic groups, one of which was identified with the Sabines.[70]

The line of argument is revealing. The two burial types would probably have been taken to indicate two different ethnic groups even without the literary tradition; in the early part of this century such ethnic interpretations were fashionable. But the archaeological evidence on its own in no way justifies the identification of either set of graves as 'Sabine'. What happened, clearly, was that the archaeologists used the legend of the Sabines in early Rome to help them interpret the archaeological evidence. Almost all archaeological 'confirmations' are circular in this sense, and many are equally illusory. The recently reported discovery of a wall, perhaps dating from the eighth century BC, on the north-eastern slopes of the Palatine might conceivably form part of the fortification system of an early settlement on that hill;[71] but it does not confirm any ancient tradition, nor does it make Romulus any less legendary – any more than finds of bronze-age pottery can prove the reality of Aeneas or Evander. These examples only serve to prove the truth of the old saying, that if you ask a silly question, you get a silly answer.

Jacques Poucet, in an excellent discussion of this issue, defines the situation as follows:

Historians should be very careful when they appeal to archaeology to 'confirm the tradition' (to use the time-honoured phrase). Broadly speaking there are two situations, which need to be carefully distinguished. In a number of cases, archaeology provides only vague indications which are capable of several possible interpretations, one of them tending in the same direction as the tradition. In the name of sanity one cannot speak in such cases of confirmation of tradition. The situation is entirely different in the case of a series or organised system of archaeological data which, independently of tradition, suggest strongly, indeed affirm, a distinct state of affairs which can be taken either to strengthen, or to weaken, the traditional account. It is only in the second case that archaeology can be legitimately invoked as an argument for or against tradition. One should be under no illusions: often the archaeological picture will be neutral, and will permit no conclusion one way or the other.[72]

2

THE PRE-ROMAN
BACKGROUND

1 EARLY ITALY

Italy has always been a variegated country. The regional diversity which has characterised the peninsula since the fall of the Roman Empire, and which still persists to this day, was even more marked in pre-Roman times. Before the Roman conquest Italy was a patchwork of different peoples, languages and cultures. Unfortunately our knowledge of these pre-Roman societies is scanty, and a full reconstruction of their historical development from prehistoric times is not practicable from the evidence currently available to us. It is certainly possible to say something about their culture and way of life at the time of the Roman conquest itself (fourth–third centuries BC);[1] historical accounts of the peoples defeated by Rome can be supplemented by linguistic data from contemporary inscriptions and from place-names, and by a growing body of archaeological material. The problem is to understand the antecedents of this situation, and to determine how much can be extrapolated into the remote past, so as to provide information about Italy at the dawn of history. For the period before the emergence of Rome, the only direct evidence comes from archaeology, and this evidence must form our starting-point.

Archaeologists are agreed that a decisive stage in the cultural development of early Italy is represented by the transition from the Bronze Age (second millennium BC) to the Iron Age (early first millennium). The nature of this transition, and the matter of whether there was continuity between the two or a cultural 'break', are much-debated questions, and not easy to resolve in the present state of knowledge. The main difficulty lies in the characterisation of the intermediate phase of the Late Bronze Age (roughly 1200–900 BC). The fact remains, however, that the material culture of Italy in the Bronze Age before c. 1200 BC differed radically from the iron-age cultures that emerged in the ninth century.[2]

The most striking fact about bronze-age Italy is its cultural uniformity, which contrasts sharply with the regional diversity of later times. This uniformity is evident in the distinctive pottery of the period, a kind of highly burnished ware with incised geometric designs, which has been found the length and breadth of the peninsula in sites hundreds of miles apart, but with little or no visible variation of shapes or decorative motifs. A similar homogeneity is found in other artefacts such as bronze tools and weapons.

The sites themselves are widely distributed throughout the peninsula, but a surprisingly high proportion of them are situated in the mountainous central region; for this reason archaeologists have coined the term 'Apennine culture' to define the civilisation of the Italian Bronze Age.[3] The Apennine culture lasted from around 1800 to around 1200 BC. Although much of the evidence is the product of casual discovery rather than systematic excavation, it is nevertheless legitimate to conclude that the population was relatively sparse. Much of the land surface was covered by forest or woodland, and settlements were small; nothing larger than a small village has yet been detected. The dead were disposed of by means of inhumation.

The primary economy was based at least in part on transhumant pastoralism – that is, on a form of stock-raising that entails seasonal movement of flocks to upland pastures in the early summer and back to the lowlands again in the autumn. This custom has been traditional in Italy since time immemorial and is still practised today.[4] It used to be thought that the economy of the Apennine culture was exclusively pastoral, and that the population was nomadic; but this picture has been modified in the light of recent excavations, particularly at sites in southern Etruria, including Luni sul Mignone, Narce, and Sorgenti della Nova. These excavations have revealed permanently settled villages on defensive hilltop sites, with a mixed economy based on sedentary agriculture and animal husbandry as well as transhumance.[5] A number of similar sites have been identified in the south, especially in Apulia. In Latium bronze-age settlements have been discovered at a number of sites, including Lavinium, Ardea and Satricum. Some sherds of Apennine pottery have even been discovered at Rome itself, but so far there is no direct evidence of a permanent settlement there (see below, p. 48).[6]

In the later stages of the Bronze Age, from around 1200 BC, major changes become apparent in the archaeological record. The significance of these changes and the precise details of their chronological sequence are uncertain and much debated, but the results of the process are clear enough. These results can be considered under three headings.

First there is a marked increase in the number of sites and the range of artefacts represented in each site. These phenomena almost certainly indicate an increasing population; there are clear signs too of growth in the size of settlements. This demographic growth continues into the Iron Age. In the opinion of R. Peroni, 'if we can measure the population of an Early or Middle Bronze Age settlement in dozens, and that of a Late Bronze Age one in hundreds, it is without doubt legitimate to think of an Early Iron Age settlement as having thousands of inhabitants'.[7] Such growth implies a more intensive use of available resources. More sophisticated agricultural production is suggested by the number and variety of metal implements that have been unearthed; these are moreover among the finds that testify to advances in metalworking techniques, and to an increased level of artisan production.[8]

Second, there was a change in funerary custom, with the rite of cremation taking the place of inhumation in many parts of Italy. The new burial practice is very distinctive. The ashes were placed in an urn and buried in a shaft in the ground. Cremation graves were grouped together to form 'urnfields' very similar in character to those of bronze-age central Europe; it is a natural assumption that the practice of cremation was introduced into Italy from across the Alps.

Some confirmation of this assumption comes from the fact that although the rite of cremation had been adopted throughout Italy by the end of the Bronze Age (urnfields have been found as far south as Apulia and even Sicily), the earliest manifestation seems to have been in the Po valley. These early cremation cemeteries are associated with settlements known as *terremare*, which have been found along the southern edge of the plain between Piacenza and Bologna, especially around Parma.[9] The adoption of cremation in peninsular Italy was accompanied by new types of pottery, as the Apennine culture was gradually superseded by a new culture which, because of its close affinities with the iron-age 'Villanovan' culture (see below), has been called 'Protovillanovan'.[10]

The third crucial change that occurred at the end of the Bronze Age is the appearance of distinct cultural variations between one region of Italy and another. The emergence of clearly differentiated local cultures in Italy was well advanced by the beginning of the Iron Age, which most scholars now place at around 900 BC. It is at this point that the history of the Italian peoples can be said to begin.

2 THE ITALIAN IRON AGE

The iron-age inhabitants of Italy can be divided into two groups: those for whom cremation was the main burial rite, and those who practised inhumation (Map 1). We may note in passing that the emphasis on burial customs is a reflection of the fact that most of the excavated sites are cemeteries rather than habitations, and that most of the evidence comes from tombs. There are excellent reasons for this, as we have seen (above, p. 27), but we should always remember that the nature of the finds may be giving us a distorted view. In archaeology we frequently know more about the way of death of early societies than about their way of life. The manner in which a society disposes of its dead is a cultural fact of great importance, but it is not necessarily a crucial defining characteristic. Inhumers and cremators need not be very different in other respects, and as we now know can easily coexist in the same culture, and even in the same society. Above all, burial customs are not racial habits.[11]

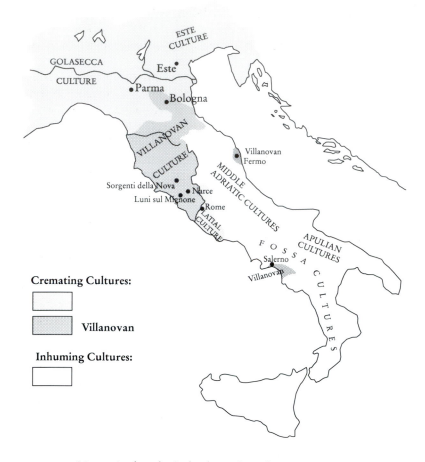

Map 1 Archaeological cultures in early iron-age Italy

With this proviso, we may proceed with our classification. The early iron-age cremation cultures are concentrated in northern Italy and in the lowland areas along the Tyrrhenian coast – that is, in Etruria, Latium and Campania. The rest of the peninsula was occupied by inhuming cultures. The only exception is a cemetery at Fermo in Picenum, where cremation graves of Villanovan type have been found. As far as we can tell, this represents an isolated pocket in an area where the normal method was inhumation.

The two main groups can be further subdivided. In northern Italy a number of distinct iron-age cultures can be defined. One of these is represented by a group of large cremation cemeteries in the lake district of Lombardy and Piedmont. This culture, which lasted without any evident break from the ninth to the fourth century BC, is generally known as the 'Golasecca culture', after the place in the Ticino valley south of Lake Maggiore where one of the

34

largest cemeteries was found. A number of 'chieftain burials', marked by the presence of rich grave goods, including weapons, armour and four-wheeled chariots, point to the existence of a warrior aristocracy similar to that of the Hallstatt culture north of the Alps, with which Golasecca has close affinities.[12]

In the north-eastern corner of the Po plain, an independent iron-age culture flourished from the ninth to the third century BC. Known as the Este (or Atestine) culture, its main sites are the cremation cemeteries at Padua, Vicenza, Oppeano Veronese and Este (ancient Ateste) itself. The most striking feature of the Este culture was the production of fine bronze artefacts decorated with embossed designs. The most impressive examples are the bronze *situlae* (buckets) that have given their name to the whole ensemble: Situla Art.[13]

The Situla people of the Este culture were in close contact with the third – and most important – iron-age culture of northern Italy. This was the so-called Villanovan culture, which was established north of the Apennines in Emilia-Romagna, and is named after the site near Bologna where it was first identified in 1853. Bologna itself was a major iron-age settlement which retained its Villanovan character from the time of its origins in *c.* 900 BC until it was taken over by the Etruscans at the end of the sixth century. The Villanovan culture is also attested throughout a wide area of peninsular Italy, where all early iron-age cremating cultures are varieties of Villanovan.[14]

Most of the evidence comes from funerary contexts, and indeed the most characteristic feature of the Villanovan culture is the burial rite itself. The ashes were placed in a biconical urn and sealed with a lid, most commonly a simple upturned bowl, but sometimes in the form of a helmet; the urn was then placed in a deep shaft (*pozzo*) and covered with a stone slab. A distinctive local variation occurs in Latium, where 'hut-urns' were used – that is, ossuaries in the form of crudely modelled dwelling-houses. This local variant, once known as 'southern Villanovan', is now generally called the 'Latial culture' (*cultura laziale*). The sites at which this Latial culture has been identified include Rome itself; we shall deal with it in more detail shortly.

In Etruria and Emilia-Romagna the Villanovan culture marks a distinct break with the preceding period. Although there are clear affinities in burial practice and grave furniture between Villanovan and Protovillanovan, the location and distribution of settlement sites are completely different. In the Iron Age large nucleated settlements developed on previously uninhabited sites, while earlier bronze-age sites (such as Luni) were abandoned. Many of the large Villanovan settlements developed in the archaic period into the city-states of Etruria, all of which can be shown to have had Villanovan antecedents.

Further south the picture is less clear. At Narce and at some sites in Latium (Satricum, Ardea, Lavinium) there appears to have been continuity of settlement from the Apennine culture down to the Iron Age, and there is no evidence of a major change in the pattern of settlement, as there is in Etruria. But the extreme scarcity of bronze-age material in Latium makes it difficult to be certain on this point; at Rome the problem is acute (and the subject of much dispute), since although there is some evidence that the site was frequented in the Bronze Age the history of the settlement cannot be traced back further than the beginning of the Latial culture.[15]

Outside the Villanovan areas of peninsular Italy the principal method of disposal was by inhumation in oblong trench graves (fosse). The inhuming cultures can be divided into three groups, which all seem to be descendants of the Apennine bronze-age tradition, but each of which developed in its own way, and was affected by different outside influences, during the course of the Iron Age. They are the fossa-cultures of Campania and Calabria, which were strongly influenced by the Greek colonies, the Apulian culture, and the Picene (or Adriatic) culture. The two latter groups were both influenced, but in different ways, by contacts with the peoples of Illyria across the Adriatic.[16]

Both of these areas (Apulia and Umbria-Picenum) are poorly documented in the early Iron Age, but later developed unusual and distinctive material cultures, and preserved independent traditions until long after the Roman conquest. The most striking feature of the Apulian culture is a type of pottery decorated with geometric designs and elaborate handles in a wide variety of forms, some of them fantastic or grotesque. Pots of this so-called 'Iapygian-Geometric' type are instantly recognisable and unique to Apulia within Italy, although similar styles are attested in the Balkans.

The cultures of Umbria and Picenum are less easily defined, but are represented by some remarkable artefacts. These include the stone grave stelae from Novilara (Pesaro), engraved with scenes of hunting and war, and the famous life-size statue of a warrior from Capestrano, a masterpiece of Italic art. Fragments of similar statues have been found in other sites in Picenum, the most notable being a helmeted head from Numana (Ancona). This was evidently a warrior society, as the weaponry found in the graves tends to confirm.[17]

3 LITERARY EVIDENCE

Literary sources have some information about the origins and early history of the Italian peoples, but the reliability and utility of this material are open to question. The relevant accounts were all produced centuries after the events they purport to describe, and there is little serious reason to suppose that they are based on sound evidence.

Greek historians and antiquarians were the first to attempt to write about the native peoples of Italy, but their earliest efforts date only from the fifth century BC. Moreover, they were primarily concerned with the Greek cities in Italy and had little direct interest in the native 'barbarians' in their own right. This situation did not change until after the Roman conquest. The first

Greek writer to make more than a token effort to uncover genuine facts about Italy and the Italians was Timaeus of Tauromenium, writing in the early third century (see above, p. 8). Timaeus' researches were prompted by his discovery of the importance of Rome as a factor in Mediterranean history. In this sense it was the Roman conquest that made Italy a fit subject for historical research, and the Romans themselves soon followed where Timaeus and others led the way.

An important figure in this story was Cato the Elder, whose *Origines* was the first systematic history of Italy ever written, based on detailed first-hand knowledge of the Italian peoples and their native traditions, archaic inscriptions and other relics. Cato's example was followed by Varro, Cornelius Nepos and other writers of the late Republic. Their findings are incorporated in works of the early imperial period which are preserved in their entirety and provide us with the earliest literary texts on Italian history that we can actually read – Strabo, Dionysius of Halicarnassus, Pliny, and Virgil's Aeneid, supplemented by Servius and the other commentators.

There are many problems, however, in using this literature as evidence for early Italian history. First, by the time of Cato (not to speak of Varro, Dionysius and the rest), genuine facts about Italy in the period before the Roman conquest would have been hard to come by. It is most improbable that the Italian peoples had any historical literature of their own (although the Etruscans are a possible exception),[18] and some were not even literate. Of the Ligurians Cato wrote: 'but they themselves have no memory of where they came from; they are illiterate and untrustworthy, and do not relate much that is true' (*Origines* II.1 Chassignet).

Another worrying factor is that the often worthless speculations of early Greek writers were taken as reliable evidence by later researchers, including Cato and Varro. Dionysius thought that very early writers such as Antiochus of Syracuse were *ipso facto* more reliable than later ones such as Timaeus; but in this he may well have been mistaken. The matter is complicated further by the fact that the native peoples of Italy themselves often accepted what the Greeks had to say about them, and hellenised their own traditions.

We can obtain a fair idea of what was known or believed about early Italian history in the Augustan age from the first book of Dionysius of Halicarnassus, which gives a comprehensive survey of what earlier Greek and Roman writers had had to say on the subject. Dionysius' aim was to prove that the Romans were Greeks, and on the basis of the evidence he presents he is able to make out an excellent case for his thesis (however preposterous it might appear to us). He traces the successive waves of Greek migrations to Italy, and the relationships that developed at each stage between the newcomers and the resident population.[19]

The first Greek immigrants were Arcadians, who arrived in southern Italy seventeen generations before the Trojan War (i.e. in the first half of the eighteenth century BC, according to the chronology adopted by Dionysius), under the leadership of two brothers, Peucetius and Oenotrus. They settled in Apulia and in Lucania and Bruttium, where they became known as Peucetians and Oenotrians (respectively). The Oenotrians were subsequently subdivided into Itali and Morgetes, named after Italus and Morges, kings who ruled in succession to Oenotrus. But according to Dionysius another group of Arcadian-Oenotrians migrated northwards into Umbria and the Sabine country, where they were known as Aborigines (here Dionysius is careful to dismiss alternative theories which made the Aborigines an indigenous people or an offshoot of the Ligurians).

The next Greeks to arrive in Italy were Pelasgians from Thessaly (although they were originally from Argos). They landed at the mouth of the Po and from there advanced into Umbria; they then made common cause with the Aborigines and helped them to drive out the Sicels, a native people of southern Etruria and Latium, regions which were then taken over by the Pelasgians and Aborigines respectively (the Sicels, of course, ended up in Sicily).

After this the Pelasgians suffered a series of calamities and disappeared virtually without trace (although Dionysius implies that the historical Faliscans were of Pelasgian descent), and their territory was occupied by the Etruscans, another native people. In a complex discussion of Etruscan origins, Dionysius rejects two other theories, one which equated the Etruscans and the Pelasgians, and another which maintained that the Etruscans came from Lydia. In Dionysius' view the Etruscans were indigenous to Italy, and consequently not Lydians; equally, they could not have been Pelasgians, since the Pelasgians had originally come from Greece.[20]

Dionysius next introduces another group of Arcadians, this time led by Evander. They arrived in Latium, where they were received hospitably by Faunus, king of the Aborigines, and founded a settlement on one of the hills of Rome, which they named 'Palatium' after Pallanteum, their home town in Arcadia. This was the earliest habitation on the site of Rome.

The next stage, which occurred during the reign of Evander, was the arrival of the god-hero Heracles. Passing through Italy after performing one of his labours, Heracles slew Cacus, a local giant, and was consequently worshipped as a divine benefactor. Such was the story; but in the historicised version preferred by Dionysius Heracles was transformed into a Hellenistic warlord, a cross between Timoleon and Alexander the Great, who earned the gratitude of the cities of the western Mediterranean by freeing them from the rule of tyrants (1.41–2). He left behind a garrison, consisting largely of Peloponnesians, on the Capitol, and then set sail for Sicily, not forgetting to found Herculaneum when his fleet put in at the bay of Naples.[21]

Last to arrive were Aeneas and the Trojans, who came to Latium during the rule of Latinus, supposedly the son of Faunus (but really, as Dionysius points out, the son of Heracles). The Aborigines were united with the Trojans, and the resulting amalgam took the name of Latins, and were ruled by Aeneas after Latinus' death. Aeneas' son Ascanius founded Alba Longa, and established a dynasty; his descendants eventually founded Rome.

Dionysius' account is a classic example of what has been called the 'hellenocentric' view of Mediterranean prehistory.[22] This characteristic approach aimed to reconstruct the events of prehistoric times by rationalising the myths and legends of the Greek heroic age. The legendary material became a coherent body of pseudo-historical tradition and was the object of intense research. Writers such as Pherecydes of Athens (mid-fifth century BC; his diligence is commended by Dionysius 1.13) and his younger contemporary Hellanicus of Lesbos were among those who attempted to impose order on the complex genealogies of the heroic sagas, and to calculate a systematic chronology using generations. By the Hellenistic period Greek historical writing about the remote past could be defined as the study of 'genealogies, foundations of cities and relationships between peoples' (Polyb. 9.1.4).

The method was hellenocentric because the Greeks connected the origins of non-Greek peoples with the activities of Greek heroes, and thus incorporated them into the general scheme. For example it was believed that India had been colonised by Dionysus and Heracles, that the Persians were descended from Perseus, and that the Celts (Galatai) were the product of a union between Polyphemus and Galatea. In many instances these Greek ideas were accepted by the 'barbarian' peoples in question and grafted on to their native traditions. This happened in part because of the cultural prestige of the Greeks, and partly because only the Greeks had devised a universal scheme for the systematic reconstruction of the prehistory of the whole inhabited world; in the Hellenistic age this Greek scheme became a common currency.

In Dionysius' account the hellenocentric structure is carefully integrated with information drawn from local tradition about customs, monuments, relics and cult practices. For example, the annual festival of the Argei, which entailed the throwing of straw effigies (called Argei) into the Tiber, was said by Dionysius to have been instituted by Heracles as one of his greatest benefactions during his sojourn in Rome, replacing the previous human sacrifices. The festival was certainly extremely ancient, and Dionysius' view (shared by most modern scholars) that the Argei were substitutes for human victims is a reasonable one; but the association with Heracles is a fanciful conjecture, perhaps suggested by the (mistaken) idea that the word Argei was somehow related to Argos.[23]

In another passage Dionysius describes the ruined cities in the Sabine territory which had once been inhabited by the Aborigines:

> . . . Mefula, about thirty stades from Suna; its ruins and traces of its walls are pointed out. Orvinium, forty stades from Mefula, a city as famous and large as any in that region; for the foundations of its walls are still to be seen and some tombs of venerable antiquity, as well as enclosures containing mass burials in lofty mounds.
>
> (1.14.3)

We need not doubt that the ruins were real enough; but the information does not in any way corroborate Dionysius' account of the Aborigines. He took his information about the ruins from Varro, and perhaps Varro too had ascribed them to the Aborigines; but the idea that the Aborigines were to be identified as Oenotrians from Arcadia was Dionysius' own deduction. We can see here the actual formation of a piece of hellenocentric pseudohistory.

It can be stated confidently that there is not the slightest chance that Dionysius' conjecture is historically correct. The same applies to all the other hellenocentric stories about early Italy. Whether or not the general run of Greek myths – about Heracles, Oedipus, Theseus, the Trojan War, etc. – have any basis in fact, the stories of their adventures in barbarian lands must be regarded as secondary elaborations of literary and antiquarian origin.

It is true that some of these stories had penetrated non-Greek traditions at a very early date. The cult of Hercules (as the Romans called him) at the Ara Maxima in Rome seems to have been established in the early archaic period, and it is therefore probable that the stories of his visit to the site of Rome and of his contest with Cacus, a figure of local legend, were also current at that time. It is less certain, but still probable, that the legend of Aeneas had been accepted in Latium as early as the sixth century BC (see further below, p. 68).

Even so there is a long way to go before one can plausibly claim that these stories represent any kind of historical reality. The same is true of the crude enumeration of tribes and peoples that passes for ethnography in literary accounts of early Italy. It is very much open to doubt whether peoples such as the Pelasgians, Oenotrians or Aborigines ever existed. Whether their alliances and conflicts (which in Dionysius are sharply defined in terms of a never-ending struggle between Greeks and barbarians) bear any relation to events that actually took place in the second millennium BC (or at any other time) is extremely unlikely.

It must be admitted that some modern historians are more optimistic, and are inclined to argue that legends of wandering Greek heroes are a traditional memory of genuine movements of peoples in the Bronze Age, or that they reflect the widespread commercial contacts of the Mycenaean civilisation.[24] Finds of Mycenaean pottery in Italy, especially in the south, are sometimes cited as archaeological confirmation of the traditional stories. Such arguments, it must be said, are quite worthless.

The Mycenaean finds in southern Italy (especially in Apulia, Sicily and the Lipari islands) are indeed impressive, and point to intensive contacts with the Aegean world in the Bronze Age – but it should be noted that precious little Mycenaean material has been found in central Italy;[25] but this does not justify the conclusion that the heroic legends are based on fact. One might just as well argue that the presence of Mycenaean sherds in southern Britain confirms the medieval legend of Brutus the Trojan, a descendant of Aeneas who founded London and became the ancestor of the British.

It is not simply the logical point that sherds of broken pottery cannot prove or disprove a specific story, or the immense interval of time that has to be presupposed between the events themselves and the first appearance of the stories in written sources. Rather, scepticism must be based on the fact that the universal scheme of prehistory that is presupposed in all hellenocentric stories was the product of erudite conjecture by scholars. The great E.J. Bickerman showed how this process occurred: the legends were manufactured by literary men, and form a body of pseudohistorical tradition which originated not in popular memory but in the lamplit studies and libraries of Athens and Alexandria.[26]

A few generations ago it might have seemed reasonable to match these literary accounts to the available archaeological evidence. Until recently scholars were indeed in the habit of using labels such as 'Oenotrian' or 'Pelasgian' to describe classes of artefacts, and of asking themselves whether or not the 'Villanovans' were Etruscan, or Pelasgian, or indeed both. In this they were following the lead of their Hellenistic predecessors, with whom they had much in common. In the Hellenistic period (sometimes called the second great age of Greek colonisation) it was natural for Greeks to assume that all historical and cultural changes were the result of migration and invasion; and it was equally natural for western scholars during the colonial era to think in the same way, and to interpret archaeological changes in terms of invasionist theories.

Today it is easy to see that these versions of prehistory are based not on evidence but on cultural prejudice. Nothing in the archaeological record of the Italian Bronze and Iron Ages proves, or even suggests, that any major invasions took place between c. 1800 and c. 800 BC. But even if migrations did in fact cause some of the changes in material culture that have been observed, there is no chance whatever that the supposed movements have anything to do with the heroic legends recounted in the literary sources.

4 THE LANGUAGES OF ITALY

The distance between the literary sources and the archaeological data is enormous and unbridgeable. But it is no greater than the gap that separates both from the third body of material, namely linguistic evidence.

From the meagre evidence that survives scholars have been able to identify about forty separate languages or dialects that were spoken in Italy before Roman rule made Latin the universal language (Map 2). Some of these are documented by a reasonably large body of textual material, while others are known only from one or two fragmentary inscriptions. Some are not directly attested at all, and their existence has to be inferred from circumstantial evidence and from such indications as place-names. The classification of the languages of pre-Roman Italy has long been established as an important goal of linguistic research, and we can do no more here than summarise some of the main findings of experts in this difficult field.[27]

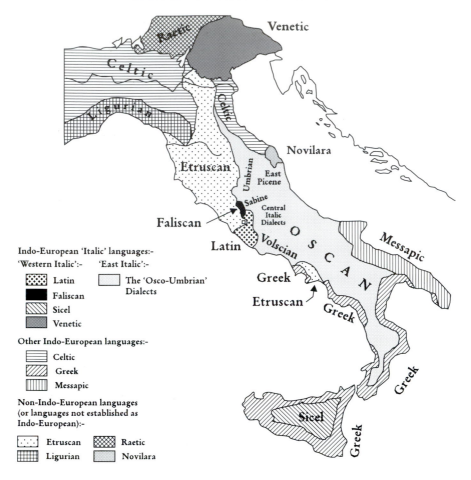

Map 2 The languages of pre-Roman Italy, *c.* 450–400 BC

It is conventional to differentiate between the languages which belong to the so-called Indo-European family of languages, and those which do not. Indo-European (henceforth 'IE') is the term commonly used to describe the languages spoken throughout Europe and parts of western and southern Asia which show marked similarities in vocabulary, grammar and morphology, and which have since the nineteenth century been supposed to derive from a common stock (although whether a single IE language ever existed at a precisely identifiable time and place is perhaps doubtful). The IE family can itself be subdivided into groups of languages which are closely related to one another in distinction to other groups, for instance the Germanic, Slavic or Iranian groups. Scholars frequently invoke the image of an IE family tree, with the various groups or sub-families sprouting like branches from the main trunk. One of these branches is formed by languages spoken in Italy, which constitute a distinct group of so-called 'Italic' languages.

The Italic languages include Latin, originally spoken only in the tiny region of Latium, to the south and east of the lower Tiber valley. There is some evidence of dialectal variations between the Latin spoken in Rome and that of other Latin communities; one such dialect is perhaps represented by the language of the Faliscans, who lived on the right bank of the Tiber to the north of Veii (see Map 2). It was once generally thought that 'Faliscan' was a separate language, but a recently discovered inscription has shown that some of the morphological peculiarities of Faliscan were also characteristic of the language spoken at Satricum, a Latin community some 80 kilometres to the south. This would suggest that 'Faliscan' is in fact no more than a dialect of Latin.[28]

Some other Italian languages seem to be especially closely related to Latin (and to Faliscan, if that is a separate language); they include Venetic, the language spoken in north-eastern Italy, and possibly also the language of the Sicels, a native people of eastern Sicily (but this 'Sicel' language is extremely badly documented). These languages form a subgroup which some scholars have labelled 'West Italic'. The other Italic languages form a single closely related group which in historical times was spread throughout central, eastern and southern Italy. Its two principal elements were Umbrian, represented by inscriptions from several of the cities of Umbria and especially by the long religious text inscribed on the bronze tablets of Iguvium (Gubbio), and Oscan, the language spoken by the peoples of the southern Apennines, the Samnites, Lucanians and Bruttians, as well as by most of the inhabitants of Campania. Oscan or Oscan-type dialects are also assumed to have been spoken by the inhabitants of the central Apennine region (the Abruzzi district), such as the Sabines, Marsi, Paeligni, Marrucini, Vestini and Picenes, as well as by the Aequi and Volsci, although in these cases the documentary evidence is thin or even non-existent.

We now come to the languages of Italy that are IE but which have no particular affinities either with each other or with the Italic languages proper. The most important of these are Greek, spoken in the Greek colonies that were established around the coasts of southern Italy from the eighth century BC onwards, Celtic, spoken in most of the Po valley and along the Adriatic coast from Ravenna to Rimini, and Messapic, spoken in the 'heel' of Italy.

Finally we turn to the non-IE languages. Of these Etruscan is by far the most important, and the one that presents the gravest historical problems (see below, p. 46). Others include Raetic, spoken in the region of the upper Adige, a language of which we know little, but which is of especial interest because it seems to show affinities with Etruscan. A language about which almost nothing is known is Ligurian, which is, however, generally presumed not to be IE; other languages that are attested only in isolated examples, such as the language of the mysterious Novilara inscriptions, also come into this category.

What is the historical significance of these linguistic data? The most obvious explanation would seem to be that many of the historic languages of Italy, including those of IE origin, were introduced from outside by migrating peoples, and that the resulting patchwork was the product of successive movements of population in prehistoric times. This is, after all, demonstrably true of the most recent arrivals, such as Greek and Celtic. The Greek-speaking settlements of southern Italy were first established as colonial foundations by Greek immigrants in the eighth and seventh centuries BC, and migrating Celts from beyond the Alps brought their language with them into the northern plain in the sixth and fifth centuries. Another historically documented change was the spread of Oscan into Campania, Lucania and Bruttium by invaders from the central Apennines who occupied these regions in the fifth century.

By adopting a simple invasion model (or 'migration hypothesis') one could reconstruct the linguistic history of Italy as follows: the various IE languages entered Italy in successive waves; the first brought in the Western Italic group (Latin, Faliscan, Sicel), and a second was represented by speakers of the Central Italic languages (the Osco-Umbrian dialects). These languages are closely related and occupy a unified geographical area, which would seem to indicate that they represent a more recent stratum. The earlier 'Western Italic' languages were thereby squeezed into small pockets around the margins of the Italic world. Finally Messapic, the IE language of eastern Apulia, was introduced by migrating peoples from across the Adriatic. Greek and Celtic were relatively late intrusions, as we have seen.

As for the non-IE languages, the majority opinion among scholars seems to be that they are pre-IE survivals forming part of a 'Mediterranean' substratum. They are all to be found in the western part of Italy, a fact which lends some support to the idea that the IE languages of Italy were introduced across the Adriatic from the Balkans rather than from central Europe across the Alps. But other explanations are possible, most obviously the theory that at least some of the non-IE languages were themselves brought to Italy from outside. Etruscan, the language spoken in a fertile region that was neither remote nor backward, is more easily explained as an intruder than as a survival. The difficulty, however, is that mass migration is only one means by which languages can spread from place to place; scholars have suggested many alternative models, and it is no longer possible to infer prehistoric migrations from linguistic data alone.[29] Thus Etruscan may be intrusive and a relatively late arrival (by comparison with the IE Italic languages), but it does not necessarily follow that 'the Etruscans' migrated to Italy from elsewhere, still less that this hypothetical migration can be identified with any event recorded in historical sources. In terms of linguistic history, the 'late arrival' of Etruscan could still mean a date before 2000 BC.

5 WHO WERE THE ETRUSCANS?

The question of Etruscan origins is a good illustration of the problems we have been discussing, in particular of the difficulty of combining literary, linguistic and archaeological evidence. Historically, the Etruscans were the people who inhabited the roughly triangular region on the west coast of Italy bounded by the rivers Tiber and Arno. Although they apparently called themselves 'Rasenna' (Dion. Hal. 1.30.3), they were known to the Romans as Etrusci or Tusci, and to the Greeks as Tyrrhenians or Tyrsenians, names that survive in the language of modern geography (Tuscany, the Tyrrhenian Sea). Etruscan civilisation reached its cultural zenith in the period from the eighth to the fifth century BC, when powerful city-states emerged. These are conventionally divided into a southern group, including Veii, Caere, Tarquinii and Vulci; a northern group, comprising Volaterrae, Populonia, Vetulonia and Rusellae; and an inland group, including Arretium, Cortona, Perusia, Clusium and Volsinii.

In many ways early Rome was very like its Etruscan neighbours, and had close (though not always friendly) links with them; according to tradition the first war between Rome and Veii occurred under Romulus. In the fourth and third centuries the Etruscan cities gradually fell victim to the growing power of Rome. The defeat and capture of Veii in 396 BC was the first stage in the Roman conquest of Etruria, which was finally completed when Volsinii was destroyed in 264 (see below, pp. 362–3). Even so, the remaining Etruscan cities preserved much of their ancient culture and unique social organisation well into the Roman period; their language continued to be spoken at least until the first century BC, when it finally gave way to the universal spread of Latin.

Archaeologically the Etruscans are known to us through the evidence of their cities, some of which have been partially excavated, and of their rich cemeteries, which were laid out like like cities of the dead outside the walls (the modern term 'necropolis' precisely describes this situation). The beginning of Etruscan civilisation is usually placed in the eighth and seventh centuries BC, when the great necropolises began to be developed with elaborate chamber tombs containing aristocratic burials (this development coincides with a change, in most centres, from cremation to inhumation). Their rich decorations and exotic grave goods provide evidence of a remarkable 'orientalising' culture (see further below, p. 85), and the emergence of dominant aristocratic groups. This important social change was accompanied by the growth and development of the larger settlements (and the absorption of some smaller ones), and, in the later seventh century, of the monumental organisation of their sacred and public areas. At this point they can properly begin to be called cities.[30]

As far as the archaeological evidence goes, this social, economic and political transformation was internally generated, though undoubtedly stimulated by contacts and exchange with the outside world (particularly the

Greek colonies). There is no sign of any decisive break in continuity of settlement, or in the composition of the population, from the preceding Villanovan phase. In other words, it looks as if the Etruscan civilisation emerged directly from the Villanovan, and consequently that the people who professed the Villanovan culture in iron-age Etruria were in fact Etruscans. 'It is now generally agreed,' writes David Ridgway, 'that the peninsular Iron Age culture conventionally termed "Villanovan" represents the outward and visible sign of the Etruscans in their Iron Age stage.'[31]

Linguistically the Etruscans remain something of a mystery. The Etruscan language is attested in thousands of inscriptions dating back to around 700 BC. They are written in a version of the Greek alphabet, and can be read without difficulty (so it is not a question of 'decipherment', which strictly entails the explication of an unknown script or code). The problem is that Etruscan is a completely unknown language; it has no known cognates, and is certainly not Indo-European. This remains true even though many Etruscan words, and the majority of the surviving texts, can be broadly understood. The explanation of this paradox is that most Etruscan texts are short and formulaic, and their function is obvious from the context. The majority are either dedications or epitaphs. For example, a bronze votive statuette in the British Museum bears the following dedication to the god Selvans:

ecn turce larthi lethanei alpnu selvansl canzate

('this gave Larthi Lethanei a gift(?) to Selvans Canzate(?)'). Scholars disagree about the meaning of *alpnu*, some preferring an adverb ('gladly') to a direct object ('gift'), while the meaning of the final word is completely unknown. That it is a divine epithet is a pure guess.[32]

A small number of Latin–Etruscan bilinguals, a few glosses (i.e. explanations of individual Etruscan words by Greek or Latin writers), and educated conjecture (sometimes dignified by the phrase 'the combinatory method') have allowed scholars to compile a vocabulary of upwards of 200 words whose meaning can be approximately established. But the grammar and morphology are very imperfectly understood, and the precise meaning of many Etruscan texts remains unclear.[33] As noted earlier, the isolated presence of this mysterious language in a region like Etruria is problematic, however much some modern experts try to play down the issue.

The outlandish nature of their language was one of the main reasons why the Etruscans aroused the curiosity of Greek and Roman observers, who regarded their presence in Italy as a historical problem. The question was couched in terms of provenance. Who were they, and where did they come from? A variety of solutions was put forward, the most famous being those of Herodotus (1.94), who said they migrated from Lydia in Asia Minor under the leadership of a prince named Tyrrhenus, and of Dionysius of Halicarnassus, who maintained that they were not intruders at all, but were indigenous to Italy (1.30.2).

Modern scholars have inherited this ancient controversy, and have attempted to resolve it with the help of archaeological and linguistic evidence. At the risk of oversimplifying, it can be said that by the middle of this century the great majority of scholars accepted the theory of the 'eastern' provenance of the Etruscans.[34] Following Herodotus, they argued that a migration from Asia Minor brought the Etruscans and their language to Italy, and they dated this event, on archaeological grounds, to the eighth century BC. On this view, the invading Etruscans took over the existing Villanovan settlements and turned them into cities; the orientalising culture of the succeeding centuries was explained, not as the result of contact with the Greeks and other peoples of the eastern Mediterranean, but as an expression of the culture that the 'oriental' Etruscans had brought with them.

Unfortunately, this tidy construction is built on unsound foundations. The archaeological evidence now available shows no sign of any invasion, migration, or colonisation in the eighth century, and the artistic trend we call 'orientalising', which affected all of western peninsular Italy, including the Greek cities, is more satisfactorily explained by trade and exchange. Its sources appear to be located in Egypt, Cyprus, the Levant, Syria and Urartu (Armenia), rather than Asia Minor; it is worth saying also that no one has ever succeeded in establishing any connection between the Etruscan language and Asia Minor, or anywhere else in the Near East for that matter.[35] Finally Herodotus, on whom everything depends, does not place the migration of the Tyrrhenians in the eighth century, but in the remote past – long before Heracles, and consequently many generations before the Trojan War. In other words, the alleged coincidence of literary, linguistic and archaeological evidence is illusory.

As things stand at present, the development of Etruscan civilisation in the eighth century can be explained without reference to any supposed oriental invasion. As for Herodotus, there remains a theoretical possibility that some kind of prehistoric migration took place (although how Herodotus' Lydian informants could have known about it is a puzzle), and that it was responsible for bringing the Etruscan language to Italy. As we have seen, a date before 2000 BC would be perfectly possible in terms of linguistic history. The trouble is that such a prehistoric migration would cease to have any serious significance in a discussion of the development of Etruscan civilisation. Today the controversy over Etruscan origins has resolved itself in favour of the solution first proposed by Massimo Pallottino in 1947: that is, the formation of Etruscan civilisation occurred in Italy by a gradual process, the final stages of which can be documented in the archaeological record from the ninth to the seventh centuries BC.[36] Whether or not any prehistoric migration took place is of marginal relevance to this historical process of development. For this reason the problem of Etruscan origins is nowadays (rightly) relegated to a footnote in scholarly accounts.

3

THE ORIGINS OF ROME

1 ARCHAEOLOGY IN ROME AND OLD LATIUM: THE NATURE OF THE EVIDENCE[1]

The earliest settlements of Old Latium arose on the low hills or spurs that extend from the central Apennines into the coastal plain. Rome itself, which occupies a group of hills overlooking the Tiber, possesses many natural advantages as a place of settlement (Map 3). In a defensible position with a good supply of fresh water and easy access to the sea, it controlled the main natural lines of communication in central Italy. These were the Via Salaria (the 'Salt Road'), as it was known in Roman times, which ran along the Tiber valley and connected the interior with the salt beds at the mouth of the river, and the coastal route from Etruria to Campania, which crossed the Tiber at the lowest available point; this was a natural ford, slightly downstream from the Tiber island, at a bend in the river beneath the Capitoline, Palatine and Aventine hills. Tradition maintained that this area, where there was a cattle market (the Forum Boarium) and a river harbour (the Portus Tiberinus), was frequented from the very earliest times.

Whether by coincidence or not, the Forum Boarium has yielded some fragments of Apennine pottery, dating from the middle Bronze Age, which are among the earliest traces of human activity in the area.[2] Similar finds have been recorded elsewhere in Latium, for example at Ardea, Pratica di Mare, Ficana, Satricum and Castiglione.[3] It is important to note, however, that the material is sporadic and consists of tiny handfuls of sherds. At present it is impossible to know whether they represent permanent settlements, or if so whether they were continuously occupied down to the Iron Age.[4]

The first traces of permanent habitation on the site of Rome date back to around 1000 BC, and consist of a handful of cremation graves in the Forum. Similar tombs have been found at sites in the Alban Hills, at Pratica di Mare (Lavinium), and possibly at Ficana,[5] as well as in the Sabine country at Palombara Sabina and Campo Reatino.[6] This material marks the emergence, for the first time, of a distinctive archaeological facies in Old Latium, which archaeologists have labelled the 'Latial culture' (*cultura laziale*). The first

48

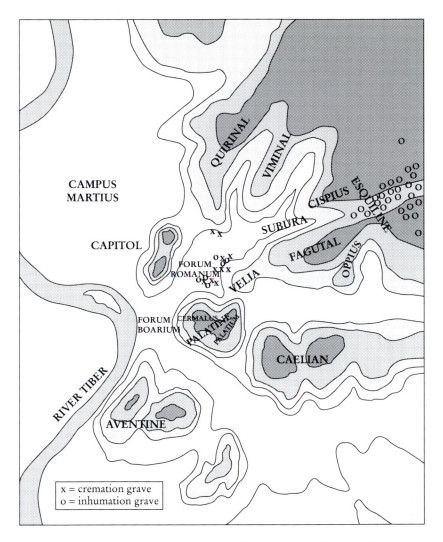

Map 3 The site of Rome, showing principal features and early burial find-spots

phase, lasting from *c.* 1000 to *c.* 900 BC according to the generally accepted chronology (see Table 1),[7] belongs to the final period of the Italian Bronze Age, in which the Latial material forms a localised variant of the Proto-villanovan culture.

In its earliest phases the Latial culture is documented solely by tombs, and its most characteristic feature is the burial rite itself. An urn containing the ashes of the deceased was placed together with some miniaturised pottery and bronze objects in a large circular jar (*dolium*) and buried in a pit (Figure 1). Although the rite of cremation was widespread in Italy in the late Bronze

Table 1 The Latial culture. Principal chronological definitions

Phase	Dates BC	Cultural definition	Historical definition
I	*c.* 1000 – *c.* 900	Final Bronze Age (Protovillanovan)	Pre-urban
IIA	*c.* 900 – *c.* 830	Early Iron Age (Villanovan)	"
IIB	*c.* 830 – *c.* 770	"	Proto-urban
III	*c.* 770–730/20	"	"
IVA	730/20–640/30	Early and middle orientalising	"
IVB	640/30–580	Late orientalising	Urban (archaic period)

Figure 1 Latial culture: cremation burial.

Age, and is a characteristic feature of the Protovillanovan culture in general, it is only in Latium that we find such precise and coherent symbolism in funerary practice, with the utensils of daily life accompanying the ashes. In some cases a crudely modelled human figurine was also included. The most striking feature of all is the hut-urn – that is, a container for the ashes shaped like a miniature dwelling-house. Hut-urns are present in some of the Latial tombs of the first period, and in phase II become standard equipment in cremation burials.

Very little is known about the communities to which these earliest cremations belonged. No settlements of the first Latial phase have yet been identified, although occasional finds of 'Protovillanovan' material have been recorded in habitation contexts in Latium, for example at Ficana, and in votive deposits, e.g. at Campoverde.[8] The funerary evidence itself is too limited to allow wide-ranging inferences about the character of the settlements.

Much better evidence is available, however, for the second phase, which marks the beginning of the Iron Age in Latium. There is no break in continuity from the preceding period, but the volume of material increases substantially, and a number of sites make their first appearance at this time. These sites include Satricum, Antium, Osteria dell'Osa (near the ancient city of Gabii), Decima, La Rustica and Laurentina (see Map 5, p. 296).

Most of these sites were unknown twenty years ago, and came to light only in the 1970s, when there was intensive archaeological activity in Old Latium. The results of this work have been spectacular, and have completely transformed our knowledge of the Iron Age in Latium, which is now better documented than any other part of Italy. As far as the early Iron Age is concerned, the most important site is at the so-called Osteria dell'Osa, a cemetery on the shores of Lake Castiglione, where hundreds of tombs have been systematically excavated using the most modern techniques.[9] Classification and analysis of the finds have provided much fascinating information about the communities of Old Latium at this remote period.

Let us begin by summarising the funerary evidence provided by the cemetery at Osteria dell'Osa. During the first part of the second Latial phase (IIA, *c.* 900–830 BC) cremation and inhumation were practised simultaneously. To put it another way, the rite of cremation was used selectively. It was reserved exclusively for males, but evidently for only a privileged group, since the inhumation graves contain members of both sexes. The process must have involved considerable effort and expense; burning a corpse is far from easy, and the miniature artefacts deposited with the ashes would have had to be specially made for the purpose. It seems therefore that those who were cremated were persons of some standing in the community.

The grave furniture (*corredo*), consisting of miniaturised pottery and bronzes, is virtually the same in all the cremation graves, and forms a clearly defined symbolic whole. This standard *corredo* comprises three or four storage containers for food and drink, together with cups, bowls and plates.

The bronzes consist of a brooch, a razor and miniaturised weapons, usually a spear and sometimes a sword as well. The symbolic function of this complex of objects is evident enough; it signifies the passage of the dead person from one life to another, and provides him with the equipment he needs for day-to-day existence and for the performance of his social roles in the community. It emphasises his status as a warrior (the weapons) and as head of a household (the hut-urn). The variety of pots perhaps signifies a banquet, or at any rate something more elaborate than a simple meal.[10]

There is also evidence of more specialised functions. For example one tomb (no. 126) contained a statuette of a person making an offering (Figure 2), a miniature bronze sacrificial knife, a ritually broken vase and some tiny pots of a type otherwise found only in votive deposits in sanctuaries. That the tomb contains the mortal remains of some kind of priest or holy man seems evident. Another tomb (no. 128) is unique in having the entire *corredo* in a large rectangular hut-urn in place of the normal *dolium*. The urn is over six times the size of the normal hut-urns, and represents an altogether more substantial type of dwelling-house; for example it has two doors, implying

Figure 2 Osteria dell'Osa, terracotta figurine.

that it was subdivided into rooms. It is not unreasonable to see this unique tomb as belonging to the chief or leader of the community.[11]

The inhumations are simpler, the dead being placed full length in rectangular trench graves. The males are usually accompanied by two or three pots (of normal size) and a brooch, but no weapons. Women likewise were inhumed with a few vases, some personal ornaments such as brooches, rings, and glass and amber beads, and usually a spindle whorl. A small number of the female graves have more carefully worked pottery and particularly abundant personal ornaments; these examples also contain several spindle whorls instead of just one, together with bobbins, loom weights and other items to do with weaving. It would seem that special prestige attached to those women who were involved in the weaving of cloth as well as the spinning of wool.

In the Osteria dell'Osa cemetery two distinct groups of burials can be discerned, both belonging to phase IIA. The two groups each comprise a small cluster of cremation tombs surrounded by a larger number of inhumations. The groups are characterised by subtle differences in the form and decoration of the vases, types of brooch, and the structure of the tombs themselves. The two groups are certainly contemporary, and are best explained as representing distinct family units, each consisting of several households.[12]

In the later part of this period the practice of cremation appears to cease altogether, and phase IIB (c. 830–770 BC) is represented only by inhumations. It is sometimes asserted that inhumation 'replaced' cremation at this stage, but a curious feature of the Osteria dell'Osa cemetery (which seems also to be true of other sites) shows that this is at best misleading. In phase IIB the great majority of adult burials seem to be female. The ratio of adult male to female burials in phase IIB is similar to that of adult male to female *inhumations* in phase IIA. The typical male *corredo* remains undistinguished, and in particular contains no arms.

In other words, cremation tombs disappear from the archaeological record at the end of IIA, but are not replaced by a corresponding number of inhumations in IIB. These facts strongly suggest that a special funerary rite continued to be reserved for men of standing in the community, but one which has left no trace in the archaeological evidence.[13] The most obvious possibility is that they were cremated and that the ashes, instead of being buried, were deposited somewhere above ground.

In every important respect the finds at Osteria dell'Osa are reproduced in all the early iron-age cemeteries of Old Latium,[14] and the site can therefore serve as a model for the historical reconstruction of the daily life of the early Latin communities in general.

2 THE CHARACTER OF THE SETTLEMENTS

The funerary evidence implies a very simple form of social structure, in which distinctions between groups were based on kinship, and the status of individuals depended on age, sex and functional roles within the family and the community. There is no evidence of economically differentiated classes or any other kind of permanent social stratification.

There are few signs of wealth, and it is unlikely that these small village communities were able to produce anything in the way of a surplus. Rather, the evidence suggests a subsistence economy based on the cultivation of primitive cereals and legumes, supplemented by stock-raising. An analysis of the botanical remains found in the cemetery in the Roman Forum produced the following distribution of grain types: einkorn wheat (*Triticum monococcum*) 10 per cent, emmer wheat and/or spelt (*Triticum dicoccum et/sive spelta*) 58 per cent, barley (*Hordeum vulgare*) 32 per cent. Legumes included vetch (*Vicia faba*) and peas (*Pisum*).[15] Animal bones from tombs in Rome and elsewhere show a predominance of pigs over cattle and 'caprovines' (i.e. sheep and goats; the similarity of the two species is such that their bones are not easily distinguished).[16] This is not surprising in that the Latin countryside is well suited to the keeping of pigs; but we must remember that in a funerary context we can only expect to find remains of animals used to provide meat, not of those raised for wool or for dairy or draught purposes. The production of wool is, however, presupposed by the presence in many tombs of spindle whorls, loom weights, and so on.

At present it is still not possible to present a fully detailed account of the subsistence economy of these early Latin communities. What is required is a controlled scientific analysis of plant and animal remains from domestic contexts in habitation sites. The necessary samples must be available after the recent excavations at Ficana, Satricum and Lavinium, but so far no results of any tests have been published.[17]

As far as we can see there is very little evidence for a specialised division of labour. Pottery was simple hand-made 'impasto', and seems to have been produced by each household for its own domestic use. The slight but perceptible differences in pottery styles between the two family tomb groups at Osteria dell'Osa (see above, p. 53) make this virtually certain. The presence of spindle whorls in almost all female tombs also clearly points to domestic production of textiles. The only specialised craft was metal-working. Here it is probable that the needs of the small village communities of the region were met by locally based craftsmen who themselves handled the necessary trade with the metal-producing regions (principally Etruria and Calabria).

During the earliest phases the communities were small villages; the population of the settlement at Osteria dell'Osa has been estimated at around 100 persons.[18] There is some evidence, however, that the villages were concentrated in groups. For instance, the village at Osteria dell'Osa appears to have been one of several small settlements around the shores of Lake Castiglione. At Rome there may have been habitations on several of the hills surrounding the Forum – certainly the Palatine (which at one stage was perhaps the site of more than one village)[19] and possibly also the Capitol and

Quirinal. Surface surveys have indicated that there were similar groups of small village settlements at Ardea and Lavinium, and it is the obvious explanation of the scattered groups of burials in the Alban Hills.

In the course of phase IIB, however, the pattern of settlement changed, as groups of villages began to coalesce and to form larger nucleated units. For example, at Lake Castiglione a large unified settlement began to form on the site of the later city of Gabii, and at Rome the habitation area was extended from the Palatine to include the Capitol and Forum; the Esquiline became the chief cemetery. A similar 'proto-urban' phenomenon had occurred around 100 years earlier in Etruria, where the introduction of the Villanovan culture was accompanied by the formation of large nucleated settlements on the sites of the later Etruscan cities. By the beginning of the eighth century Latium had 'caught up', and from then on Etruria and Latium developed in parallel.[20]

The change signifies an increase in the size of the population of Old Latium. The older sites grew in size, and in the course of phase IIB several new sites were established, apparently for the first time. Moreover, we know from surface surveys and casual finds that several as yet unexcavated sites in the north and east of the region were also inhabited by the end of the ninth century. They include Antemnae, Fidenae, Crustumerium, Corniculum and Tibur.[21]

On the other hand, there is no evidence of any comparable demographic growth in the Alban Hills region. The situation is not very clear because much of the material from this region comes from casual discoveries, mostly made in the last century, and no systematic modern excavations have taken place. The fact remains, however, that the area seems to have experienced an eclipse in phase IIB, and if it did not become depopulated (as some scholars suppose), the most that can be said is that the pattern of tiny scattered settlements continued. There was certainly no proto-urban development.[22]

The relative decline of the Alban Hills region and the growing importance of other centres in the plain is one of the conclusions to emerge from a recent brief study of trade routes and communications in Old Latium (Map 4).[23] This sets up two contrasting models for the late Bronze Age and the late ninth and eighth centuries. The former shows the Alban Hills at the centre of a network of communications connecting southern Etruria, coastal Latium and both inland and coastal routes to Campania (see Map 4a). In the second Rome has become the nodal point of routes from Etruria to the south; the rise of new centres such as La Rustica, Laurentina and Decima, as well as the eclipse of the Alban Hills, can be explained by this model, a crucial feature of which is the rise of Veii at the expense of Caere as the main centre in south Etruria (see Map 4b).

As far as we can see the new settlement patterns did not bring about any immediate changes in the social structure of the communities, which are therefore properly termed 'proto-urban' rather than urban. This is a matter

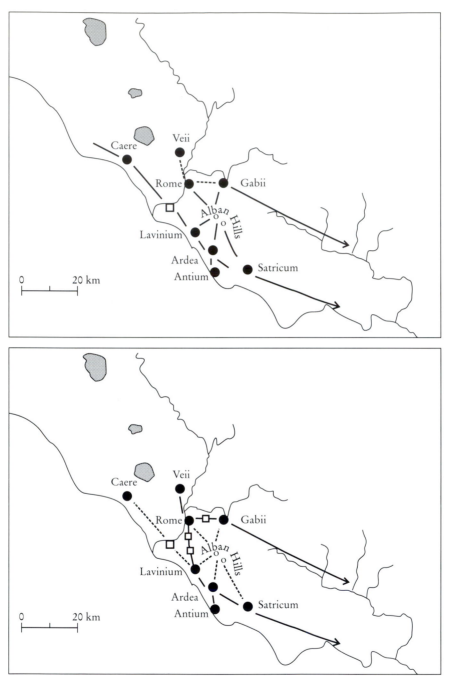

Map 4 Trade routes and communications in Old Latium
(from Sestieri, 1992, pp. 74–5)

to which we shall return in Chapter 4. Equally there was no perceptible change in the form of the settlements, which continued to consist of primitive wattle-and-daub huts with thatched roofs supported by timber posts. Their basic design can be reconstructed from hut-urns and from the foundations that have been unearthed at many settlement sites in Old Latium, dating from the ninth century BC onwards. These huts have a timeless quality. They are not essentially different from the huts used in the Apennine Bronze Age, or indeed from those used even today by shepherds and charcoal burners in central Italy. An important point is that such huts can be built in a matter of hours from easily available materials and require no specialised skills.[24]

Huts continued to be the main form of dwelling in periods III and IVA. In Rome hut foundations dating to the mid-eighth century BC were unearthed on the Palatine in the 1930s, and more recently traces of eighth-century fortifications have been reported on the north-east slopes of the hill. Since Romulus is said to have founded his city on the Palatine at this very time, these discoveries have given rise to much enthusiastic comment; to some observers they seem to provide archaeological confirmation of the traditional account of the origins of Rome. This traditional account, and the historical questions it raises, form the subject of the following sections.

3 THE ANCIENT TRADITION[25]

The majority of the ancient sources are agreed that the city of Rome was founded by Romulus, a member of the royal house of Alba Longa, a mythical city in the Alban Hills. He and his twin brother Remus were the sons of Rhea Silvia, daughter of King Numitor. Numitor was deposed by his brother Amulius, who made Rhea a Vestal Virgin in an effort to prevent the emergence of any rival claimants to his throne. When she nevertheless became pregnant and gave birth to twin boys, Amulius ordered them to be drowned in the Tiber. But the twins were washed ashore at the foot of the Palatine, where they were suckled by a she-wolf and subsequently rescued by shepherds.

When they grew up they became leaders of a band of shepherd warriors and for a time lived the life of brigands. But after they had discovered their true identity they attacked Alba, overthrew the wicked Amulius and restored their grandfather to his throne. They then resolved to lead a colony from Alba and to found a city at the place where they had been rescued. In this way Rome was established, taking its name from Romulus, who became its founder and first ruler after killing his brother in a petty quarrel.

These elements form the bare bones of a story that is richly embellished in the surviving accounts. There is a fair degree of unanimity about the main structure, but the sources record endless disputes on matters of detail.[26] We happen to possess the text of a work wholly given over to curious and obscure variants of the traditional story. Known as the *Origo gentis Romanae* (*The*

Origin of the Roman Race) and attributed to the late-imperial historian Aurelius Victor, it probably drew upon an antiquarian work of the Augustan age, which itself had collected together the more or less bizarre deductions and speculations of scholars of the second and first centuries BC.[27]

Controversy centred upon such matters as the parentage of the twins. In most accounts their father was the god Mars; but other versions also circulated, the most interesting of which asserted that their mother had been impregnated by a spark from the hearth – a motif which has many parallels in Italic myth.[28] Another point at issue was the story of the she-wolf, which some historians rationalised by suggesting that the foster-mother of the twins was a local prostitute, since the Latin word *lupa* (= 'she-wolf') was also a slang word meaning 'tart'. There was dispute about the date of the foundation (see below), and about the circumstances of the death of Remus. In some versions the killer was Romulus himself, in others one of his companions; and a certain Egnatius, a writer cited in the *Origo gentis Romanae*, even went so far as to suggest that Remus was not killed at all.[29]

The episode of Romulus and Remus was itself part of a wider story. It is a famous paradox that Roman history began long before Romulus. The twins were descended on their mother's side from a long line of kings of Alba, and ultimately from Aeneas the Trojan, who had married the daughter of Latinus, the king of the Aborigines, and whose son Ascanius (or Iulus), founded Alba Longa and gave his name to the Julian clan. In the developed version the Aeneas legend was integrated with the story of the settlement on the site of Rome established by Evander, an Arcadian who had migrated to Italy before the Trojan War and was firmly established on the Palatine when Aeneas arrived. Nor is this the end of the matter; other mythical persons, such as Faunus, Saturnus and Hercules, also play a part in the story of pre-Romulean Rome, and in some versions are said to have established settlements there.

Just as the rescue of the twins was not the beginning of the story, so the death of Remus was not the end. The act of foundation was a complex process and had a long sequel. Whatever the fate of Evander's settlement (which is not made clear in the sources), the site was deserted by the time of Romulus, who was obliged to seek far and wide for colonists for the new city. He opened an asylum on the Capitol, and fugitives of all kinds – paupers, debtors, criminals and runaway slaves – were welcomed. As most of them were unattached males, he organised the rape of the Sabine women in order to provide them with wives. A war then ensued against the Sabines, but ended in an agreement between the two peoples, who merged as a single community under the joint rule of their respective leaders, Romulus and Titus Tatius. After Tatius' death (in obscure circumstances; his partner did not escape suspicion), Romulus ruled alone for many years, successful in peace and war.

His reign ended mysteriously. The sources give two accounts of what happened: the pious version, in which he was assumed into heaven and made a god (and worshipped under the name Quirinus), and the cynical version, in which he was murdered at a meeting of the Senate, each senator taking away some part of his dismembered body.[30] As one might imagine, in the time of Caesar and Augustus this discrepancy was discussed with enthusiasm, and was of more than academic interest.

A striking feature of the tradition is that the foundation of the city is presented not as a single act but as a slow and gradual process. In this sense there is a contrast between the foundation legends of the Greeks and the Roman conception of the origin of the city. Rome was not created all at once by Romulus; on the contrary, he merely initiated a long process of formation. The Romans believed that the state (res publica) was the result of this gradual process, to which each of the kings contributed (Cicero, Rep. 2.37; Polyb. 6.10.14). The elder Cato argued in his Origins that the Roman constitution was superior to those of the Greek states precisely because it was the product of the collective wisdom of past generations and not the work of a single individual (Cic., Rep. 2.3). In the same way, the physical growth of the city, from Romulus' modest Palatine settlement, was also a gradual process, each king extending the urban area and contributing to its monumental development. According to Livy (2.1.2), each of the early kings was in his turn a founder of part of the city: omnes deinceps conditores partium certe urbis.

On the other hand, the historiographical tradition, which from the beginning was influenced by Greek ideas, assimilated the story to a Greek foundation legend (ktisis), and presented Romulus in the guise of a founder hero who established the city all at once and out of nothing. The most extreme example of this tendency occurs in Dionysius of Halicarnassus, who in the second book of the Roman Antiquities credits Romulus with the creation of a fully fledged 'constitution' and of a monumental urban settlement.[31]

This contradiction cannot be easily resolved. It is not simply a matter of individual sources presenting different points of view (although Dionysius of Halicarnassus is out on a limb). In almost all of the surviving narratives we can detect the presence of two contrasting tendencies. On the one hand we find a modernising tendency, which assumed that there was little difference in kind between the social world of primitive Rome and that of the late Republic. On this view, Aeneas, Evander, Romulus and Numa inhabited a world of urbanised city-states with fully developed political, military and religious institutions. In physical appearance the cities of Latium, even at the time of the Trojan War, were just like those of the Hellenistic age, with walls, streets, market-places, temples and monumental public buildings.

This modernising view is balanced, however, by a contrasting tendency to imagine the city of Romulus as a settlement of rustic shepherds, living a simple and virtuous life in primitive thatched huts. This romantic notion is found especially in the Augustan poets, but it did not originate with them. As early as the second century BC Roman writers were stressing the contrast between the simplicity of primitive Rome and the elegant and luxurious decadence of their own time.[32] The Romans of the classical period were able to visit and to wonder at a crude shepherd's hut on the Palatine, which was preserved as a relic of the earliest settlement and was called 'the house of Romulus' (*casa Romuli*: see Map 10, p. 386).[33]

The Roman foundation legend provides evidence, first and foremost, of how the Romans of later times chose to see themselves, and how they wished to be seen by others. The story carries a strong ideological message. The most revealing sign of this is the way it defines the identity of the Roman people as a mixture of different ethnic groups, and of Roman culture as the product of various foreign influences. There could hardly be a greater contrast with the foundation myths of the Greek cities, which insisted on the purity and continuity of their origins (in some cases, as at Athens, maintaining that the population was 'autochthonous' – that is, sprung from the soil). In attempting to prove that the Romans were of the purest Greek stock, Dionysius of Halicarnassus faced a virtually impossible task.

The Roman saga was characteristic of a people who had built up their power by extending their citizenship and continuously admitting new elements into their midst. From this point of view we can appreciate the powerful appeal of the *Aeneid*, an epic poem which to this day retains a special significance for migrants and refugees.[34] Rome was also unique among ancient societies in its practice of assimilating freed slaves, who automatically became Roman citizens on manumission. By the end of the Republic many of even the most aristocratic Romans had servile blood in their veins, and a large proportion of the population of the city consisted of slaves or freedmen.[35] In these circumstances we can well understand why the Romans were not ashamed to admit that Romulus' followers included runaways and exiles from every land – although this was an aspect of the story that greatly embarrassed poor Dionysius of Halicarnassus (whose strictures on the practice of large-scale manumission in the Rome of his day (4.24.4–6) are highly instructive).

4 THE ORIGIN OF THE LEGENDS: ROMULUS AND REMUS

The motley and disreputable origin of some of the first inhabitants is only one of many 'shameful' elements in the story of Romulus and Remus. The predatory (or meretricious!) foster-mother of the twins, the murder of Remus, and the rape of the Sabine women are the most noteworthy of these discreditable features, and all of them were at various times exploited by Rome's enemies and by Christian critics of her pagan traditions. These facts led H. Strasburger to conclude that the story of Romulus was not an ancient indigenous legend, but was rather a product of anti-Roman propaganda, fabricated probably in Magna Graecia in the late fourth century BC by some resentful victim of Roman imperialism.[36]

This theory, although influential and argued with subtlety and skill by its supporters, is clearly mistaken. There are good reasons for believing that the story was current in Rome in the archaic age. The best evidence is the magnificent bronze statue of a she-wolf, now in the Palazzo dei Conservatori, which is undoubtedly archaic and probably dates from the sixth century BC (Figure 3).[37] We know, moreover, that by around 300 BC at the latest the story of the twins had become the standard version in Rome, and that it was officially proclaimed to the world in 269 BC when a representation of the she-wolf and twins appeared on one of the first issues of Roman silver coins (see below, Figure 32c, p. 395).[38] This could not possibly have happened if the story had been fabricated only a few years earlier by a hostile propagandist.

Figure 3 The 'Capitoline Wolf' (Musei Capitolini, Palazzo dei Conservatori).

The evidence adduced by Strasburger in favour of his theory in fact points to the opposite conclusion, namely that the story was accepted in Rome precisely because it was an old and indigenous legend, and because its main features, uncongenial though they may have appeared to later apologists, were too well established in the tradition to be ignored or suppressed.[39] It is also clear that the story contains folk-tale elements which are echoed in myths and legends from many societies throughout the world. These legends concern the birth and upbringing of persons who grow up to become kings, founders, religious leaders, heroes or conquerors. Well-known examples include Cyrus of Persia, Semiramis the founder of Babylon, Sargon the founder of the Akkadian dynasty, Ion the ancestor of the Ionians, the Trojan princes Paris and Aeneas, the Greek heroes Perseus and Oedipus, the usurper Aegisthus (the murderer of Agamemnon), Cypselus the tyrant of Corinth, the Sassanian king Shapur, and Pope Gregory the Great. It will be evident, moreover, that the Christian nativity story contains many of the same mythical elements.[40]

An ideal type can be constructed, roughly as follows. The child is conceived in a union that is in some way irregular, miraculous or shameful: a princess and an unknown stranger or lower-class person (e.g. Sargon, Cypselus), an incestuous relationship (Moses, Gregory), or, very commonly, a mortal and a god (Semiramis, Ion, Aeneas). In many cases the father is a god, the mother a virgin (Perseus, Jesus, Romulus and Remus). In the next stage the child is ordered to be killed by a wicked king (often the child's father, grandfather or uncle), who has been warned by a dream or oracle that the child will one day kill or overthrow him (Cyrus, Oedipus, Perseus, Romulus, Jesus, Shapur, and the rest – the list is endless). The method chosen is usually to abandon the child in a forest or on a mountainside (Oedipus, Paris, Aegisthus, Semiramis, etc.), although in many stories the child is placed in a box, boat or basket and cast adrift, at sea or in a river (Perseus, Sargon, Cypselus, Romulus, Moses, Gregory).

The child is then rescued by a shepherd, gardener or fisherman, who either rears the child himself (Sargon, Romulus, etc.) or hands the baby over to his employer – either a local king (Oedipus, Perseus), princess (Moses) or abbot (Gregory). In many of these tales the foundling child is substituted for the recently stillborn baby of the foster-parents. The most striking feature of many of the stories, however, is the intervention of an animal, which carries out the immediate rescue and sometimes itself suckles the child. This event in the life of Romulus and Remus (wolf) was also experienced by Cyrus (bitch), Semiramis (doves), Paris (bear), Aegisthus (goat), and many others.

As they grow up, these children of destiny tend to exhibit signs of their future greatness by their precocious behaviour and natural charisma. They become leaders of their own age group (in some stories, for example that of Cyrus, they play the king in a royal game); eventually their true identity is revealed by tests, tokens, scars or simply by the fulfilment of the original prophecy, which sometimes happens by accident, as when Oedipus unwittingly kills his father. In many stories there is an element of rivalry, violence and even murder: Cyrus beats the boy who disobeys him in the royal game, Moses kills the Egyptian, and Romulus kills Remus.

It will be seen from this brief selection that the same popular motifs recur in stories from all parts of the Mediterranean and the Middle East, and from all periods of ancient history. A diffusionist explanation (e.g. that the same story or stories were borrowed by the Greeks from near-eastern sources, and by the Romans from the Greeks) is highly unlikely. This is confirmed by the fact that characteristic elements of these stories are also attested in the folk mythology of Scandinavia, India, Central Asia, and even from southern Africa, Polynesia and South America. To give just two examples: Birta-Chino, the founder of the Turkish race, was reared by a wolf, and Tiri, the founder-hero of the Yuracarés tribe of Brazil, was fed by a leopard.[41]

The recurrence of the same motifs in so many different contexts cannot be explained by literary or oral diffusion, or by common inheritance within a particular ethnic or linguistic family. The stories are not characteristically Indo-European or Semitic; they are manifestly both, and more besides. Rather, they must be seen as popular expressions of some universal human need or experience, occurring independently in times and places that are worlds apart. Everything suggests, therefore, that the legend of Romulus and Remus was both ancient and indigenous.

By way of confirmation we may note in passing that similar stories, involving miraculous conception, exposure in the wild, rescue by animals and upbringing by shepherds, are recorded of Italian kings and founders, like Silvius of Alba Longa and Caeculus of Praeneste.[42] If we possessed a full text of Cato's *Origines*, or the works of Varro or Verrius Flaccus, we should be able to say more about these local legends. As it is, we are given tantalising hints by fragmentary texts and by figured monuments like the fourth-century Etruscan stele from Bologna showing a child being suckled by an animal (probably a lioness), and similar scenes on a bronze mirror from Bolsena (Figure 4), and on the foot of a cista from Praeneste.[43]

5 THE ORIGIN OF THE LEGENDS: AENEAS AND THE TROJANS[44]

In the received tradition the Romulus story was combined with that of Aeneas. No one doubts that this represents an artificial synthesis of two originally separate legends, but there is dispute about when and how the synthesis occurred. If Romulus was already acknowledged as the founder of Rome in the archaic period, it might seem to follow that Aeneas was a relatively late addition. But matters are more complicated than that, and there are good grounds for thinking that Aeneas too was recognised in Rome and Latium at an early date.

The Aeneas legend was of Greek origin, with its roots in the epic. In the *Iliad* Aeneas is a prominent though uninspiring figure belonging to a minor branch of the royal house of Troy. His importance derives from the fact that he alone of the major Trojan heroes survives the sack. A famous passage in the *Iliad* prophesies that he and his descendants will one day rule the Trojans.[45] But since there was no trace of any plausible dynasty of Aeneadae ruling in the Troad in historical times, the Greeks began to speculate that Aeneas had moved away from Troy and established his ruling dynasty somewhere else.[46]

Suggestive place-names, local pride and the fertile imagination of poets and antiquarians did the rest. As early as the sixth century BC, a place called Aeneia in Macedonia was issuing coins showing Aeneas carrying his father Anchises from the ruins of Troy.[47] It is possible too that at that time the new Troy was already being sought in the far west. This idea was perhaps made popular by

Figure 4 Etruscan mirror from Bolsena, with animal suckling children.

the Sicilian poet Stesichorus in about 550 BC, although the evidence for this is far from secure;[48] but the story of the westward migration of refugees from Troy was certainly well established in the fifth century, and was referred to by Thucydides (among others).[49]

As far as we know, the earliest reference to Rome as a foundation of Aeneas occurred in the works of Hellanicus of Lesbos and Damastes of Sigeum,[50] two Greek historians writing at the end of the fifth century. We have no idea what Rome meant to these early writers, but it was probably little more than a name to them. Their interest, after all, was not in Rome but in Aeneas. It was only later, probably around the end of the fourth century and when the

Romans first began to have political dealings with the Greeks, that Greek writers began to take serious notice of Rome for its own sake. By that time the connection between Rome and Aeneas was well established.

As we have seen, the Aeneas story was one of those hellenocentric legends of literary origin that was adopted as part of the native tradition by the people on whom the Greeks had foisted it. This fact is not in itself difficult to explain. In general it is not surprising that the Romans were willing to embrace a story that flattered their pride by associating them with the legendary traditions of the Greeks, whose cultural superiority they were forced to acknowledge – albeit sometimes grudgingly. More specifically, in Greek myth Aeneas possessed qualities which the Romans liked to see in themselves, such as reverence for the gods and love of his fatherland.[51]

The Trojan legend was also useful to the Romans in that it gave them a respectable identity in the eyes of a wider world, and one that could be used to advantage in their dealings with the Greeks. And not only with the Greeks: the political utility of the legend first manifested itself in 263 BC during the war against Carthage, when the people of the Sicilian town of Segesta allied themselves to the Romans because of their common Trojan descent.[52] 'Trojan' propaganda became especially important in the early second century BC when Rome began to intervene in the affairs of Asia Minor.[53] Perhaps it was at this time, and for clear political reasons, that the Romans' claims to a Trojan origin were first seriously contested.[54]

Finally, we should note that by claiming to be Trojans the Romans were saying that they were not Greeks, and in a sense defining themselves in opposition to the Greeks. But one of the most interesting features of the Aeneas legend is that although it was at first used to stress the enmity between Greeks and Romans, in the hands of Virgil and other writers of the first century BC it became a means to reconcile them, and to make Roman rule acceptable in the Greek world.[55]

The Aeneas legend is therefore an important part of the complex history of political and cultural relations between Rome and the Greeks, and, as we have seen, what made it important was its acceptance by the Romans themselves. When this happened is a matter of controversy. One school maintains that the Romans first laid claim to the Trojan legend when it became politically useful to them – that is, in the late fourth or early third century BC. J. Perret suggested that the connection between Rome and Troy was fabricated out of nothing by King Pyrrhus of Epirus when he invaded Italy in 280 BC. Pyrrhus claimed descent from Achilles, and wished to present his attack on the Romans as a new Trojan War. Now Pyrrhus certainly did not invent the connection between Rome and Troy; it can be stated with confidence that Perret was unsuccessful in his efforts to set aside the evidence of early texts such as the fragment of Hellanicus. But it remains a distinct possibility that it was Pyrrhus who first made the Romans think of themselves as Trojans.[56]

But this late dating is not widely favoured today, and most scholars prefer to think that the Aeneas legend was already established in central Italy long before – perhaps in the sixth century BC or even earlier. On this view early Greek writers such as Hellanicus were influenced, however indirectly, by local tradition, rather than the other way round. The theory has become attractive because recent archaeological finds have increasingly demonstrated that the natives of central Italy were deeply influenced by Greek culture in the archaic period – a subject to which we shall return repeatedly in the course of this book.

The story of Aeneas and the Trojans was well known in Etruria in the sixth century. Representations of Aeneas have been found in Etruscan sites, not only on imported Greek vases but also on objects of local manufacture, in particular on a red-figure amphora now in Munich and a scarab belonging to the de Luynes collection in Paris, both showing Aeneas carrying Anchises.[57] Some small terracotta statuettes of Aeneas and Anchises from a sanctuary at Veii imply a hero-cult, but the date of these objects is far from certain; experts are now inclined to place them in the fourth century BC or later – that is, after the Roman conquest of Veii in 396 BC.[58] If this evidence is discounted, there is no reason to suppose that Aeneas was the object of a hero-cult in archaic Etruria, still less that he was regarded as an ancestor or founder. We can say only that he was a known and evidently well-liked mythical figure.

As far as Rome and Latium are concerned, it is sometimes suggested that the Aeneas legend was established there through Etruscan mediation, and first took root during a period of Etruscan rule in the sixth century (see below). But this theory is not compelling, if only because it is far from certain that Rome was ruled by the Etruscans in the sixth century; it is also unnecessary, because the latest archaeological research has furnished much evidence of direct contact between Latium and the Greek world in the archaic age.

The most important site in this connection is Lavinium (modern Pratica di Mare), which in historical times claimed Aeneas as its founder. Lavinium was famous as a religious centre and a place of pilgrimage for the Latin peoples, including the Romans. The cult of the ancestral gods of the Roman people, the Penates, was located there, and even in the time of the emperors the Roman chief priests and magistrates were obliged to attend in person at the annual celebrations of the cult. The Penates were at one stage identified with the mysterious sacred objects which Aeneas had rescued from Troy, and which play such an important part in the developed legend (see e.g. Virgil, *Aeneid* 2.293,717; 3.12,148–9). The idea that Lavinium held the Trojan Penates was already current by around 300 BC,[59] and may well be much older. The shrine of the Penates is perhaps to be identified with the 'sanctuary of the thirteen altars' (Figure 5) which was uncovered in a brilliant campaign of excavations by the University of Rome in the 1950s and 1960s (see further below, p. 109). The sanctuary goes back to the archaic period and shows heavy Greek influence in architectural design and in religious ideology.[60]

Figure 5 Lavinium: The thirteen altars.

One of the most startling discoveries was a sixth-century dedication to Castor and Pollux (*ILLRP* 1271a), a Greek cult which according to tradition was adopted in Rome in the early fifth century and honoured with a temple in 484 BC. The Lavinium inscription gives powerful support to this tradition, which was further strengthened in 1982 when excavations in the Forum revealed massive archaic foundations beneath the Temple of Castor.[61] On the other hand the suggestion that the Dioscuri should be identified in some way with the Trojan Penates remains controversial.[62]

Aeneas himself was also worshipped at Lavinium with the strange cult-name of 'Pater Indiges' or 'Indiges'. This must imply a secondary elaboration of a pre-existing cult – that is to say, Aeneas was at some stage equated with a local god called Indiges. The shrine of Aeneas or Indiges took the form of a tumulus on the bank of the river Numicus; it was visited by Dionysius of Halicarnassus in the first century BC and described by him in detail (1.64). Recent excavations at Pratica di Mare have revealed a monument which has been identified as the hero shrine described by Dionysius. It is a rich tomb of the seventh century BC surmounted by a sacred building of fourth-century date. But even if the identification is correct (which seems doubtful, if only because the monument is not on the bank of a river), we would not be able to say for certain when the original, and certainly ancient, cult of Indiges came to be associated with Aeneas.[63] Other evidence concerning Aeneas at Lavinium is equally inconclusive, and as things stand at present we cannot be certain that the Trojan legend was established there before the fourth century BC.[64]

It nevertheless remains probable that Lavinium was among the first of the Latin cities to lay claim to a Trojan origin. The fact that the cults of Aeneas and the Penates continued to be celebrated at Lavinium even in Roman times suggests that Aeneas was connected with Lavinium before he was connected with Rome, and that this connection was already established when Lavinium was subjected to Roman rule after the Latin War of 340–338 BC. At present the evidence does not allow us to be more precise than this; but in view of what is now known about the hellenisation of Latin culture in the archaic period, it would not be at all surprising if archaeologists were to come across definite proof of a cult of Aeneas at Lavinium in the sixth century.

6 THE ORIGIN OF THE LEGENDS: EVANDER AND HERCULES

It is reasonable to argue, then, that Aeneas probably, and Romulus certainly, were known in Rome before the end of the sixth century BC, and that a composite foundation legend involving both had already begun to circulate. The credentials of other parts of the story, for example that concerning Evander, are much less certain. We have no idea when or by whom the Evander story was invented, although it was present in all the earliest Roman histories.[65] Modern scholars believe that Evander, an obscure Arcadian hero who appears fleetingly in Hesiod, was introduced into the Roman story in the late fourth or third century BC.[66] By that time Rome was established as a military power noted for the quality and size of its manpower resources. The Greek word for such a condition was *euandria* (εὐανδρία), and this may have influenced the choice of a hero with the name Εὔανδρος (i.e. Evander). This is not as silly as it sounds; some Greek writers made great play of the fact that the name of Rome in Greek ('Ρώμη) meant 'strength'. According to an anonymous author cited by Plutarch, the city was founded by Pelasgians who called it Rhome because of their military strength.[67]

The starting-point for all this was the idea that there was something Arcadian about Rome, which is probably a much older conception. In a pioneering study J. Bayet argued that the Arcadian legend in Rome arose from the similarity between the Lupercalia and the Arcadian cult of Zeus Lykaios, and the identification of Faunus with Pan.[68] This assimilation could have been brought about through the influence of Greek traders landing at the Forum Boarium, the river harbour at the foot of the Palatine. Bayet's suggestion that this area might have been frequented by traders at a very remote period, and before the city of Rome had come into being, seems now to be supported by archaeological evidence. Excavations near the church of Sant'Omobono in the Forum Boarium, which have been intermittently carried out since the 1930s, have unearthed a deposit containing sherds of Euboean, Pithecusan, Corinthian and Cycladic pottery of the eighth century BC. The quantity of this material has led some archaeologists to suspect not only that Greek merchants visited the site, but that some of them had actually taken up residence there.[69]

The same reasoning can provide an explanation for the Roman cult of Hercules, which was also studied by Bayet.[70] According to the legend Hercules visited Rome on his way back to Greece with the cattle of Geryon. The cattle were stolen by Cacus, a local giant, who lived in a cave near the Palatine. When Hercules slew Cacus, cults were set up in his honour by the local people at the instigation of Evander. Two major sanctuaries were established, the Great Altar (Ara Maxima) and the shrine of Hercules Victor, both situated in the Forum Boarium. The cult of Hercules in Rome was closely connected with commerce, and this fact, together with the location of the shrines, suggests that it was introduced by Greek traders. This was the view of Bayet, who also drew attention to versions of the Hercules–Cacus story in the Greek cities of southern Italy.

An alternative theory, not ruled out by Bayet, is based on the close affinities between Hercules and the Phoenician Melqart, and maintains that the Roman Hercules was of Phoenician origin. It has been suggested that the cult was introduced by Tyrian merchants who took up residence in the Forum Boarium; but this interesting suggestion has not yet been substantiated by archaeology.[71]

7 THE HISTORICAL VALUE OF THE LEGENDS

The foregoing discussion has shown that the traditional stories of the origins of Rome can be explained historically, and if taken seriously can be made to yield valuable information about the development of early Rome. But in spite of the extreme antiquity of many of the stories, it would not be correct to say that they are historical in the normal sense of the word.

With a few fringe exceptions,[72] everyone agrees that the Roman foundation story, from Aeneas to Romulus, is legendary and has no right to be considered a historical narrative. The name 'Romulus' is an eponym formed from the name of the city, and perhaps means simply 'the Roman' (cf. Siculus = Sicilian); we may take it as certain that no such person as 'Romulus' ever existed. As a character in the Greek epic Aeneas is perhaps more substantial; although he must stand or fall along with the rest of the Homeric heroes and with the saga of the Trojan War itself. But the reality of Aeneas, even if it could be established, would not provide a warrant for the story of a Trojan migration to Italy, which is a very different matter. And it goes without saying that the credentials of Evander, Hercules and their like are virtually non-existent.

Nevertheless, many modern historians, perhaps a majority, are inclined to believe that at least some of the legends 'reflect' or 'echo' actual historical events. The principal argument is that there can be no smoke without fire, and that the legends must be in some way 'based on fact'. It hardly needs saying that this is a naive assumption, and that the practice of rationalising the stories, by eliminating miraculous elements and obvious exaggerations, in order to reveal the factual core,[73] is poor historical method. So too is the distasteful habit of denouncing anyone who expresses doubts as 'hyper-critical' or as a reincarnation of Ettore Pais.[74]

These elementary points have been forcefully stated in a recent book by J. Poucet. Poucet relentlessly attacks the orthodox 'historicising' approach, and argues instead that the whole edifice is constructed out of unhistorical materials ('matière non-historique')[75]. In particular he challenges the widely held belief that archaeological discoveries and linguistic studies have provided independent confirmation of parts of the tradition.

For example, sherds of Apennine pottery from a secondary deposit in the Forum Boarium cannot reasonably be called confirmation of the legend of Evander, or of any other part of the story of pre-Romulean Rome. Nor can alleged 'Mycenaean' borrowings in the Latin language, even assuming that such borrowings exist (which seems doubtful).[76] A more serious suggestion is that archaeology has to some extent confirmed the prominent role played by Alba and Lavinium in the Roman foundation story. It is true that the most important sites to yield material from the earliest phases of the Latial culture include Pratica di Mare (Lavinium) and places in the Alban Hills; on the other hand, they also include Rome, which on present evidence cannot be shown to be a later settlement. The tradition, however, maintains that the cities of

Latium were all colonies of Alba Longa, and that Rome was the latest of them; but on this point tradition is disproved by the facts.[77]

The rather strange idea that Lavinium and Alba were much older than Rome probably arose from a chronological difficulty. Since they were founded by Aeneas and Ascanius, they had to be dated shortly after the Trojan War, which according to the calculations of Greek scholars took place around 1200 BC.[78] But the Romans had reasons of their own for assigning Romulus to the eighth century. The consequence was that Romulus could not be the son or grandson of Aeneas, as some early versions had maintained.[79] Historians who recognised the difficulty therefore had no alternative but to assume a long interval between Aeneas and Romulus, an interval that was filled by the dynasty of Alban kings.

The tradition that the cities of Latium were colonies of Alba contains a modernising fallacy and cannot be historically true in a literal sense. The same applies to the idea that Alba exercised a political hegemony in Latium before its destruction by Tullus Hostilius.[80] The archaeological evidence, as we have seen, indicates the presence in the Alban Hills of small groups of village settlements in the earliest phases of the Latial culture (periods I and IIA – the 'pre-urban' phase). In subsequent phases these settlements failed to develop in the same way as others, and were eclipsed in importance by the proto-urban communities in the plain (see above, p. 55).

It is possible that the tradition represents a dim memory of this shift, which it has distorted and modernised with its talk of colonisation and political hegemony, and its assumption that 'Alba Longa' was an urbanised city-state. It is possible, but not very likely. We should note that in putting the matter thus we are not using the archaeological evidence to confirm the tradition, but using the tradition in order to interpret some very enigmatic archaeological evidence. Equally we cannot accept the suggestion of some scholars that archaeological evidence confirms the story of the destruction of Alba Longa by Tullus Hostilius. The 'eclipse' (but not necessarily the disappearance) of the Alban villages at the beginning of the eighth century BC may be 'reflected' in the story of the sack of a city in the middle of the seventh, but it seems unlikely to me. In any event there can be no question of archaeological confirmation, as Poucet has rightly observed.[81]

It is altogether more probable that the prominence of Alba and Lavinium in the tradition arises from their historic importance as religious centres. The national festival of the Latin peoples took place each year on Monte Cavo (Mons Albanus), the highest point of the Alban Hills. The festival, known as the Latiar or Feriae Latinae, was held in honour of Jupiter Latiaris, who was identified in legend with Latinus, the eponymous ancestor of the Latins (Festus p. 212 L). Similarly, Lavinium played host to representatives of the Latin peoples at the annual celebrations of the cult of Aeneas and the Penates, and for this reason claimed to be the first city of Latium and the metropolis of Rome.

As one might expect, there was rivalry between the two shrines. This competition is manifested in the story that the statues of the Penates were removed from Lavinium to Alba Longa but twice returned miraculously to their place of origin (Varro, *LL* V.144). There was also dispute about the miraculous story of a sow that had given birth to thirty piglets, symbolising the thirty peoples of the ancient Latins. According to one version the sow led Aeneas to Lavinium, where a bronze statue of her and her young could still be seen in the time of Varro.[82] But according to Fabius Pictor the sow led the founder to Alba Longa, which took its name from the colour of the sow (*alba* = 'white').

In historical times the Alban Hills, including the shrine of the Latiar on Monte Cavo, were part of the territory of Rome. The conquest of this region undoubtedly took place under the monarchy, and there is no reason in principle to deny that the king who organised it was called Tullus Hostilius. Where the tradition went wrong was in assuming that the religious predominance of the Latiar arose from a political hegemony exercised by Alba over its colonies, and that after the victory of Tullus Hostilius this hegemony passed automatically to Rome. The three central elements of the legend – colonisation, political hegemony, and the city of Alba Longa itself – are modernising anachronisms and cannot be considered historical.

One point on which there is said to be substantial agreement between the tradition and the archaeological evidence is the foundation of Romulus' settlement on the Palatine, dated by the Romans themselves to the mid-eighth century BC. The discovery on the Germalus (one of the summits of the Palatine) of iron-age huts dating from phase III of the *cultura laziale* was once thought to have vindicated tradition in this instance. But we now know that permanent occupation of the site began long before, and that the hut foundations are not the earliest evidence of settlement, even on the Palatine itself, where material from phase I has been found in a deposit beneath the huts, and an isolated phase I cremation burial was unearthed under the House of Livia, between the Germalus and the Palatium.[83] This evidence, together with the phase I burials in the Forum, indicates that the site was inhabited from around 1000 BC.[84]

The recent discovery of an eighth-century wall on the north-eastern slopes of the Palatine has received much publicity in the press, but the detailed evidence so far remains unpublished.[85] It is therefore too early to comment on the significance of the finds, except to say that any suggestion of a connection with the foundation story must face the objections raised in the foregoing paragraph. In any case we do not know why the Romans chose to date the foundation to the mid-eighth century, and there is a strong suspicion that their reasoning may have been arbitrary.

It seems clear that the various dates given by historians for the foundation (Fabius placed it in 748 BC, Cincius in 728, Cato in 751 and Varro in 754) were linked to estimates of the length of the regal period as a whole, and to calculations of the date of the beginning of the Republic, which could be established (within reasonable limits) with the help of the *Fasti*. Most probably the date was fixed simply by counting back seven generations of thirty-five years: thus, 509 + (7 × 35) gives the Varronian date of 754. Other explanations are possible, but whatever the precise method it seems likely that the foundation date was fixed by some kind of mechanical calculation.[86]

Archaeology has also been invoked in support of the tradition that the Palatine was the original nucleus of the city. But matters are not quite so straightforward. Early material has been discovered on the Palatine, as we have seen, but also in other parts of the city. The horizontal stratigraphy of the Forum cemetery (which moves away from the Palatine towards the Esquiline)[87] is interesting but hardly decisive. And we must always bear in mind that other areas of the city, such as the Caelian or the Aventine, have not been explored by archaeologists in the way the Palatine has. The archaeological evidence on its own, then, does not tell a very clear story.

Nevertheless, there are good grounds for thinking that in this instance the tradition is perfectly sound. Apart from general probability – the Palatine is, after all, a prime site for a settlement – we can use the evidence of the Lupercalia. This ancient festival, in which naked youths called *luperci* ran around the Palatine, is best interpreted as a ceremony of purification which originally encircled the whole of the community.[88] The archaeological evidence is therefore consistent with tradition, but not adequate on its own to confirm it. Once again it is tradition that helps us to interpret the archaeological evidence, rather than the other way round.

8 ARCHAIC FORMULAE AND INSTITUTIONAL 'FOSSILS'

All things considered, it seems unlikely that any of the narrative accounts of the beginnings of Rome are historical in the normally understood sense. Nevertheless, there is a chance that antiquarian texts describing archaic institutions may preserve genuine information about the pre-urban period.

One such text is the Elder Pliny's list of thirty 'Albensian peoples (*populi Albenses*) who used to take meat on the Alban Mount' – that is, peoples who used to take part in the Latin festival. He quotes the list in the course of a discussion of how many of the ancient peoples of Latium had 'disappeared without trace' in his time. The list is as follows: Albani, Aesolani, Accienses, Abolani, Bubetani, Bolani, Cusuetani, Coriolani, Fidenates, Foreti, Hortenses, Latinienses, Longani, Manates, Macnales, Munienses, Numinienses, Olliculani, Octulani, Pedani, Polluscini, Querquetulani, Sicani, Sisolenses, Tolerienses, Tutienses, Vimitellari, Velienses, Venetulani, Vitellenses.[89]

The most interesting thing about this document is not what it contains, but what it does not contain. Some of the names clearly belong to recognisable historic places, such as Bola, Corioli, Fidenae and Pedum, but none of these were in the first division of Latin towns. The major centres of the historical period, such as Tibur, Praeneste, Tusculum, Aricia, Lavinium, etc. are missing. The most conspicuous absence of all is naturally Rome itself. Some of the peoples are otherwise quite unknown. Others are defined in relation to geographical districts, such as the Tolerienses and Tutienses, who presumably belong to the valleys of the rivers Tolerus and Tutia.[90]

These and other indications have led scholars to conclude that the list refers to the pre-urban period in Latium, and specifically to the system of scattered villages that existed at the beginning of the Iron Age.[91] The names that have attracted most attention are those that seem to refer to villages on the site of Rome itself; if so, the text bears witness to a period before the consolidation of Rome as a single nucleated centre. These pre-Roman peoples include the Velienses, the people of the Velia (the ridge extending north east from the Palatine to the Esquiline), and the Querquetulani, the inhabitants of the Caelian (which according to Tacitus (*Ann.* IV.65.1) was originally called the *mons Querquetulanus*).

How could such a list have been preserved? An explanation can be found in the religious context, in the fact that it is a list of participants in a cult. It would not be at all surprising if the names of the original members of such a group were remembered long after they had been superseded in political importance by the city-states of the historical period. The list could then have acquired a formulaic character and have been preserved in a fossilised form for ceremonial purposes – not unlike the Cinque Ports or the Chiltern Hundreds in England. If so, it is more than likely that the list was permanently inscribed at an early date (the early sixth century is perfectly possible), and that the inscription was copied either by Pliny or, more probably, by an earlier historian or antiquarian whom Pliny consulted.[92]

Another echo of the pre-urban stage was preserved in the annual Roman festival of the Septimontium. This ancient ceremony took place on 11 December and involved the inhabitants of the 'seven mounts', which according to Festus comprised the two summits of the Palatine (Germalus, Palatium), the Velia, the Caelian, and the three spurs of the Esquiline (Oppius, Cispius, Fagutal).[93] It is reasonable to suppose that this festival too dates from a very early period (note that two of the mounts, the Velia and the Caelian, also appear in Pliny's list of Albenses); most scholars are agreed that it represents a stage of development at which the various summits were occupied by separate villages. The separation of the Germalus and the Palatium suggests moreover that it antedates the unification of the Palatine.[94]

A point of some interest is that the Septimontium group excludes the Quirinal, which archaeological and other evidence suggests was inhabited very early. This fact implies a separation, which is hinted at in other texts, between the people of the mounts (*montes*) and the people of the hills (*colles*), that is, the Quirinal and the Viminal.[95] This distinction appears to be reproduced, at least in part, in other institutions and cult ceremonies which

74

imply an opposition between the Palatine and the Quirinal. The clearest example is the division of the Salii, the dancing warrior-priests, into two corporations: the Salii Palatini who were associated with the Palatine and served Mars, and the Salii Collini who were linked with the Quirinal and served Quirinus.[96] The *luperci*, the naked youths who took part in the Lupercalia, were also divided into two groups, the Luperci Quinctiales and the Luperci Fabiani. This fact is of special interest because the Roman clan of the Fabii was closely connected with the Quirinal (Livy 5.46.2). These facts are best understood as the result of a fusion of two originally separate communities, one on the Palatine, the other on the Quirinal.[97]

There are many other indications of an ancient bipartite division in the organisation of early Rome. Apart from the priesthoods, we may note that the Romans had two names: Romani and Quirites – an extremely puzzling fact which has never been satisfactorily explained. Again, the Lares Praestites, the guardian gods of the state, were represented as twins – *di gemelli*.[98] Since Lares were probably deified ancestors, a *lar familiaris* being the founder of a family, it would seem to follow that there is some connection between the Lares Praestites and the twin founders of the city, another puzzling phenomenon which might be explained if the Roman state was the product of a union between two communities.[99]

9 THE SABINES AND EARLY ROME

But the clearest evidence is undoubtedly the tradition that the original population of Rome was a mixture of Roman and Sabine elements, a story that begins with the rape of the Sabine women and ends with the fusion of the two peoples under Romulus and Titus Tatius. The idea that a significant part of the population was of Sabine origin pervades the tradition at every level. Of the first four kings, two were Latin (Romulus and Tullus Hostilius), and two were Sabine (Numa Pompilius and Ancus Marcius) – or three if one counts Titus Tatius. Even more significant, given the evidence we have just been discussing, is the fact that tradition connected the Sabines and Titus Tatius with the Quirinal (Varro, *LL* V.51).

Is there any truth in this tradition? For over a century the question has been one of the most hotly debated in the whole field of early Roman history. The majority opinion would seem to be that in this instance the legends echo a genuine fact about the ethnic composition of early Rome; but eminent scholars such as Mommsen, Pais, Dumézil and Poucet have all sought to deny this, and to argue instead that the tradition is based on later events which have been arbitrarily projected back to the time of Romulus.[100]

It is true that supporters of the tradition have been guilty of misusing certain kinds of linguistic and archaeological data, and have invoked theories, some with racist overtones, that are now discredited. Nobody now believes that the use in the Forum cemetery of two distinct burial customs – cremation and inhumation – signifies the presence of different racial groups, although this belief was once widespread (see above, p. 33). J. Poucet is undoubtedly right to point out that archaeology has not succeeded in verifying the tradition. On the other hand, it has not succeeded in disproving it either.

On reflection this is not surprising. Archaeology in the Sabine district is only in its infancy, although significant progress has been made in recent years.[101] What the latest research shows, if anything, is that the Sabines were culturally very close to the neighbouring Latins and Faliscans. This means that it would be difficult to differentiate between Romans and Sabines from material finds alone. As A. Momigliano put it, 'I do not know what, archaeologically, makes a Sabine in Rome.'[102]

As far as linguistic evidence is concerned, certain basic Latin words, such as *bos* ('ox'), *scrofa* ('sow'), *popina* ('kitchen'), and perhaps even *lupus* ('wolf'), are thought to be Sabine borrowings. This is likely enough, although it should be stressed that there can be no certainty in the matter. These words and others like them show dialectal peculiarities not typical of Latin, and they are best interpreted as loan words from some other Italic language. In the circumstances (i.e. in the light of tradition among other things), it seems reasonable to identify that language as Sabine, which was certainly Italic, although we do not know enough about it to be positive. Let us be clear. The linguistic evidence does not support or confirm the tradition; rather, the tradition suggests a possible interpretation of the linguistic evidence.[103]

It must be admitted that at present there is no strong external support for the traditional stories about Sabines in early Rome. On the other hand there is no good reason to deny the possibility of a significant Sabine component in the population of monarchic Rome, which we know to have been an open and cosmopolitan society (see further below, p. 157). The infiltration of Sabines is documented at the end of the sixth century by the arrival of the Claudii, which need not have been the first episode of its kind. Other aristocratic families claimed a Sabine origin; they include the patrician Valerii, who are said to have been established in Rome long before the Claudii. This makes it difficult to accept that Sabine incursions began to occur only under the Republic.

Finally, it is difficult to understand why, if Sabine incursions first occurred in the fifth century, the Romans of later times should have wanted to project them back to the time of the origins. In particular it is more than surprising that in doing so they should have created the disreputable story of the rape of the Sabine women. If this story was a late invention, it becomes open to rationalising criticism; and it would be difficult to improve upon the observation of de Beaufort, in 1738, that if Romulus was really as handsome and gifted as the story suggests, one would expect women to have chased after him, rather than the other way round.[104]

It should be said, however, that Dumézil and Poucet are fully aware of this objection (indeed I found the reference to de Beaufort in Dumézil).[105] They meet it by saying that the story of the rape of the Sabine women is a version of an ancient myth that forms part of the Indo-European heritage of the Roman people. In its original form this myth described the formation of a complete society of gods from the fusion of two opposing but incomplete groups, one of which possessed magical strength and bravery, the other wealth and fecundity. According to Dumézil the basic elements of this myth can be reconstructed from the Icelandic saga of two warring groups of gods, the Aesir and the Vanir, who correspond in the Roman story to the followers of Romulus and Titus Tatius respectively.[106]

In the fourth and third centuries BC the Romans 'historicised' this ancient myth – that is to say, they transformed it into a pseudo-historical narrative and passed it off as a record of what had transpired in the time of Romulus. It was only at this secondary stage that the Sabines were introduced; the idea was suggested by the influx of Sabines into Rome in the fifth century, and the final treaty between Romulus and Titus Tatius was framed in the same terms as the incorporation of the Sabines into the Roman state in 290 BC (in this way Dumézil and Poucet revert once again to the view of Mommsen). The validity of this interpretation must be assessed in the broader context of the general theory of Dumézil, and the whole question of Indo-European survivals in Rome. These matters will be considered in the next section.

10 ROME'S INDO-EUROPEAN HERITAGE

The mythical interpretation of the tradition about the Sabines is only a small part of a wide-ranging theory about the Indo-European ancestry of the Roman people, a subject to which G. Dumézil devoted a lifetime of scholarly inquiry. The comparative study of the social structures, religious beliefs and mythical tales of India, Iran, Scandinavia, Ireland and above all Rome led him to the conclusion that their peoples organised their societies, and structured their mental outlook, in accordance with a well-defined Indo-European pattern. The key to this pattern is a tripartite division of human activity in terms of function. Dumézil's three functions are derived from the supposed division of the original Indo-European society into priests and rulers (first function), warriors (second function), and producers (third function).

In Rome the 'ideology of the three functions' (as Dumézil called it) is most evident in religion. The three functions are represented by the gods Jupiter, Mars and Quirinus, who according to Dumézil were at the centre of Roman religion in the earliest period of the city's development. Whether the three functions were also represented in the social structure of early Rome is more problematic. In his early works Dumézil argued that the three 'Romulean' tribes, the Ramnes, Luceres and Tities, were functionally defined castes of priests, warriors and producers (respectively); but later he abandoned this theory (for which there is no supporting evidence in our texts), and argued instead that the framework of the three functions 'remained only ideological and formed a means of analyzing and understanding the world'.[107]

As far as the story of the origins is concerned, Dumézil believed that the narrative of the early kings was constructed out of Indo-European myths, and that it expresses the ideology of the three functions. According to Dumézil Romulus and Numa represent two contrasting aspects of sovereignty, and thus in combination exemplify the first function (as do Indra and Mitra in Indian mythology);[108] Tullus Hostilius naturally embodies the second (warrior) function, while Ancus Marcius can, with rather less ease, be made to fit the requirements of the third, economic, function.

These ideas, which are presented with immense learning and clarity of expression in a long series of books, have had great influence, particularly on French-speaking historians and students of religion. Elsewhere, especially among Italian historians and archaeologists, they have met with resistance. Although traces of Indo-European myth and functional ideology are undoubtedly present in the stories of early Rome, and in particular in early Roman religion, the problem is to determine the extent and meaning of these traces. Do they really pervade everything, and does comparative analysis of Indo-European myths and social structures really provide the key to understanding all of the Roman legendary tradition?

Dumézil's theories can be criticised on four distinct levels. First there is the simple objection that Indo-European mythical patterns, and especially the ideology of the three functions, are not always as clear to the ordinary observer as they are to Dumézil and his followers. For instance, it is not self-evident that the traditional account of the first four kings expresses the operation of the three functions. True, Numa and Tullus can be convincingly interpreted as contrasting functional stereotypes, but Ancus makes a poor representative of the third function. The evidence adduced by Dumézil to link Ancus with wealth and production is marginal and the argument is patently unconvincing.[109] As we have seen, the idea that early Rome was once divided into three castes of priests, warriors and producers was abandoned even by Dumézil himself; Rome had its three tribes, but nothing links them with a division of functions. In short, there is evidence of functional differentiation in the early Roman tradition, and evidence of tripartite organisation in Roman society. Unfortunately, the functionalism is not tripartite, and the tripartition is not functional.

Second, attention should be given to the views of A. Momigliano, who until his death in 1987 was the leading critic of Dumézil.[110] The main thrust of Momigliano's criticism is that by attempting to isolate a static and unvarying Indo-European pattern underlying Roman institutions and beliefs, Dumézil and his followers cannot explain the important historical facts about early Rome, which was a constantly changing and developing society.

My objection to Dumézil's views ... is not only that his evidence is weak, but that his theories are unnecessary. Nothing is explained in Roman history if we believe that in a prehistoric past Roman society was governed by a rigorous separation of priests, warriors and producers. The fundamental fact of Roman society remains that warriors, producers and priests were *not* separate elements of the citizenship.[111]

Third, there is a problem about the sources and the mechanism by which the Indo-European heritage was transmitted. According to Dumézil the stories about the origins of Rome were put together in the fourth century BC, when the creators of the tradition (Dumézil is not very clear about precisely who they were) fashioned a pseudo-history out of the old Indo-European myths. From this it follows that the ideological framework continued to exercise its hold over the minds of the Romans even at a time when their society had been totally transformed and bore no relation whatever to the supposed Indo-European ideal. Indeed Dumézil pays no attention to problems of transmission, and assumes that the same Indo-European mentality lies behind all Latin texts, irrespective of date or authorship. Few historians are likely to be convinced by a method that assumes an unconscious attachment to a traditional Indo-European ideology in writers such as Livy, Virgil or Propertius.[112]

Fourth, even if we allow that the stories of the origins of Rome are expressions of a functional mythology, does it necessarily follow that they are unhistorical? The alternative is to suppose that instead of historicising myths, the Romans imposed a mythical framework on to a historical tradition. After all, Dumézil himself argues that when the Romans created the story about the Sabine War they took the myth of the war between the magician gods and the rich gods and 'simply modernised its details, adapting them to their own 'geography', 'history', and customs and introducing the names of countries, peoples and heroes suggested by actuality'.[113] Would it not be possible to eliminate the quotation marks, and to argue that the materials 'suggested by actuality' were drawn from an ancient tradition, possibly based on fact, that the original population of the city resulted from a fusion of Latin and Sabine elements?

We could equally suppose that the stereotyped figures of Numa and Tullus were created by imposing functional specialisation upon two kings who were respectively celebrated in tradition for religious reforms and a successful war – achievements which in themselves make perfectly credible history. Finally, if the mysterious fourth-century pseudo-historians had really manufactured the story in order to give expression to the operation of the three functions, surely they would have come up with a more convincing representative of the third function than the enigmatic Ancus Marcius, most of whose actions have nothing whatever to do with wealth or production? The basic question is: was it the Romans who turned Indo-European mythology into history, or was it Dumézil who turned Roman history into Indo-European mythology?

11 CONCLUSIONS

To sum up, we may say that the archaeological evidence now available gives a picture of the development of early Latin communities, from small villages to larger nucleated settlements, during the course of the early Iron Age. It is possible that certain religious customs and ceremonies date back to this primordial phase, and retain a memory of a time when the site of Rome was itself occupied by separate villages. Archaeology and literary tradition combine to suggest that the Palatine was the site of a very early settlement. Some institutions and formulae point to a distinction between the Palatine and the Quirinal, which is perhaps to be linked to the tradition that in the beginning the city was a joint community of Romans and Sabines. This tradition is consistent with linguistic evidence, but cannot be said to be directly confirmed by it; the archaeological evidence is equivocal on this point, and neither strengthens nor weakens the traditional story.

In general the narrative accounts of the origins of Rome, from Aeneas to Romulus, cannot be considered historical. They represent a complex mixture of popular legend, folk-tale, and learned conjecture, and are important for the study of Roman historiography and the development of Roman self-consciousness. Whether this process was informed by an unconscious attachment to a tripartite functional ideology inherited from a prehistoric Indo-European past is arguable. The three functions are certainly present in some early Roman religious institutions, most notably the three *flamines maiores*, priests who were specifically attached to the cults of Jupiter, Mars and Quirinus, representing sovereignty, war and production (respectively);[114] but the interpretation of other Roman institutions and legends in terms of the three functions is much more questionable.

Finally, the 'traditional' date for the foundation of the city, which historians and antiquarians of the late Republic placed in the middle of the eighth century BC, should not be taken too seriously. Everything suggests that it was fixed by means of an artificial process of mechanical calculation. Archaeological evidence clearly indicates that the site was permanently occupied centuries before 754 BC; on the other hand it was not until considerably later that any major change occurred in the organisation and structure of the community, of a kind that can be linked to the crucial processes of urbanisation and state-formation. These developments, which can legitimately be defined as the foundation of a city-state, cannot on present evidence be pushed back beyond the middle of the seventh century – that is, more than a hundred years after the so-called 'traditional' date. The nature of these structural changes will form the subject of the next chapter.

4

THE RISE OF THE CITY-STATE

1 ARISTOCRATS, CLANS, AND THE 'ORIENTALISING' PHASE

During the eighth century BC the communities of Old Latium underwent a gradual transformation. For most of Latial phase III (*c.* 770–730/20 BC) there was no radical break in the pattern of everyday life (or death). There was continued growth in the size of the population, and a consolidation of the nucleated settlements that had developed at the major sites at the end of the preceding phase. A rise in both the quality and quantity of material found in the cemeteries of Latium points to an increase in the general level of wealth and prosperity. There must have been a rise in productivity, caused at least in part by improved agricultural techniques. For this period we have the first traces of polyculture – the cultivation, that is, of vines and olives – and there is evidence of increasing specialisation of labour. Wheel-made pottery makes its first appearance at the start of phase III, and while examples are relatively rare at first, by the end of the eighth century it had become standard and largely displaced home-made impasto. By that stage pottery was an independent specialised craft.[1]

The last decades of the eighth century witnessed radical changes in the social structure, which became more pronounced in the orientalising period (Latial phase IV). The appearance at this time of exceptional wealth in some of the tombs points to the beginnings of permanent social stratification and the emergence of a dominant aristocracy. The changes are documented, as before, by the evidence of cemeteries, the most important being those at Osteria dell'Osa, La Rustica, Laurentina, the Esquiline necropolis at Rome, and above all that at Castel di Decima, a site which was first discovered in 1953, but was not systematically explored until the 1970s when hundreds of tombs of the orientalising period (*c.* 730–580 BC) were excavated. The material from Decima is not yet published, but interim reports and the publication of some of the most important tombs have given a glimpse of the fabulous wealth of its ruling elite.[2]

The most ostentatious burials contain rich jewellery and treasure in the form of bronze tripods, cauldrons, armour and chariots. Fragments of gold and silver vessels have also been found. Imported ceramics include proto-Corinthian ware, Etruscan bucchero and Phoenician amphorae. The richest tombs have been compared to the 'princely tombs' (*tombe principesche*) of Praeneste, which were excavated in the nineteenth century and are now on display in the Villa Giulia museum in Rome (Figure 6).[3]

A brief description can be given of some of the more notable Decima tombs that have been published in full or in part. Tomb XV is a warrior grave dating from the last years of the eighth century. The corpse, a relatively young man, was buried with many personal ornaments of silver and bronze, iron weapons and a chariot. His accompanying treasure consisted of two tripods, numerous bronze vessels and a large collection of imported ceramics including a Phoenician wine amphora and five Greek vases. Tomb CLIII, the grave of a woman, is one of the richest so far discovered. The bronzes and fine ceramics run to around ninety individual items, and include several sets of *bucchero sottile*, the fine black-glaze ware that was an Etruscan speciality. The exceptional feature of this tomb is the extreme richness of the personal ornaments on the body, which was covered from head to foot with gold, silver and amber jewellery.[4]

The young woman buried in tomb CI was similarly accoutred, if anything even more richly, and interred with a chariot. This is one of a number of examples from Latium of female tombs containing chariots. The phenomenon is of interest because it implies that chariots were marks of status rather than instruments of war. In Etruscan art chariots are shown in processions and evidently had a ceremonial function. So too in Rome chariots were used on the occasion of a triumph. There are also indications that the chariot was a mark of royalty. In his account of the monarchy Livy reports that women of the royal family drove around the city in carriages (Livy 1.48). In later times the use of carriages in the city was a privilege reserved exclusively for Vestal Virgins, whom Mommsen regarded as republican surrogates for the king's daughters.[5] If so, the royal character of their privileges would seem to be confirmed. With these thoughts in mind, archaeologists have labelled tomb CI at Decima the 'Tomb of the Princess'. However that may be, the important point is that women seem to have enjoyed relatively high status in the aristocratic society of this period, a fact which left traces in later Roman tradition and custom.

In general the evidence implies the formation of a wealthy aristocracy that had succeeded in concentrating the surplus of the community into its own hands and in perpetuating its domination through inheritance. An interesting feature of the Decima necropolis is that some of the tombs are grouped together in what seems to be a deliberate manner. Seven such groups have been discerned, each containing an average of three tombs. It is striking that tombs within a given group are sometimes separated chronologically from one another by as much as twenty-five years; this seems to indicate that the

Figure 6 Items from 'princely tombs' at Praeneste: (a) gold fibula; (b) gilded silver bowl; (c) ivory plaque with Egyptianising motifs (Museo Nazionale di Villa Guilia).

memory of the dead was being perpetuated over a considerable period at the tomb. A comparable state of affairs can be observed at Laurentina, where tombs are arranged in distinct groups, each forming a rough circle, with one or two rich burials at the centre, surrounded by more modest ones.[6]

These instances can be seen as forerunners of the chamber tomb, a kind of family vault, in which successive depositions were made. Chamber tombs become common in Etruria in the second half of the seventh century, and several examples are now known in Latium, for example at Osteria dell'Osa and at Torrino near Laurentina; in both places tombs containing up to a dozen burials have been found.[7] At least one chamber tomb has been identified at Rome itself (tomb 125 of the Esquiline cemetery), and others have been found at Satricum, among which tomb II (late seventh century) is especially worthy of note. It contained at least four burials and was richly equipped with weapons, bronzes and imported ceramics, and can be added to the list of princely tombs in Latium.[8]

The purpose of chamber tombs was to emphasise and perpetuate family solidarity, and their appearance has been taken as evidence of the importance at this period of extended patriarchal families or clans. In historical times the clan (*gens*) was a patrilineal descent group whose members (*gentiles*) claimed descent from a common ancestor. This common descent, whether real or fictitious, was reflected in the system of nomenclature. Each individual member of a *gens* had two names: a personal name or *praenomen* (e.g. Marcus, Titus, Sextus) and a clan name or *nomen gentilicium*, sometimes in the form of a patronymic (hence Marcius, Titius, Sextius). We may compare the names of the Scottish clans: MacDonald, MacGregor, etc.[9]

The importance of clans in the social organisation of early Italy is a matter of vigorous and longstanding dispute. It is one of those areas in which the volume of scholarly literature is out of all proportion to the tiny amount of factual evidence we happen to have. It is neither possible nor worth while to discuss modern theories in detail here; it will be sufficient to outline briefly the points that seem to be reasonably well founded.

First, the institution of the clan was not unique to Rome, or even to Latium. Many of the Italic peoples had clans, including the Etruscans, as is proved by inscriptions which show that the two-name system was widespread throughout the peninsula. Second, the clan system extended to all social classes. All free Romans, of whatever rank, possessed clan names, and this appears to have been true from the archaic period onwards. Admittedly, some scholars maintain that there was once a time when only patricians had clans, or when plebeians did not have clans; but there is no evidence for either of these propositions (which are not quite the same). In modern accounts one frequently comes across phrases such as *plebeii gentes non habent* ('plebeians do not have clans'), but these expressions, though in Latin, are modern coinages and have no ancient authority.[10]

Third, we know that the *gens* became an established feature of the social structure of Etruria during the early seventh century BC, when the earliest surviving two-name inscriptions were produced; in Latium the direct evidence is somewhat later, but we can be reasonably certain that the *gens* was established there before about 600. What needs to be emphasised is that the onomastic system characteristic of the *gens* seems to have spread in conjunction with the process of urbanisation. This feature of the evidence runs counter to a well-entrenched nineteenth-century theory that the *gens* originated as a 'pre-political' organisation, which was weakened and ultimately eclipsed by the rise of the state. In fact, the evidence implies the contrary.[11]

It is also worth noting that in the literary accounts of the period down to Romulus all the leading figures possess only one name (Numitor, Amulius, Faustulus etc.), whereas after the foundation of the city the two-name system is consistently found: Numa Pompilius, Hostus Hostilius, Mettius Curtius – to name only a few of the earliest examples. This feature of the tradition seems clearly to reflect a genuine historical process, a fact that it would be difficult to attribute to chance; it can only mean, as Jan Bremmer has argued, that the main elements of the foundation story were already current in the archaic age – perhaps as early as the first half of the sixth century BC.[12]

The appearance of chamber tombs in the later eighth century, the development of clan structures, and the concentration of wealth in the hands of a dominant class form the background to an important cultural movement which archaeologists have labelled 'orientalising'. The evidence is most noticeable in the luxury artefacts that have been found in the princely tombs (*tombe principesche*) at Praeneste, Decima and elsewhere in Latium. These famous tombs have their counterparts in other areas of Tyrrhenian Italy, for example at Vetulonia, Tarquinii and Caere. In particular, the fabulous Regolini-Galassi tomb at Caere contained orientalising objects very similar to those found in the Bernardini tomb at Praeneste. Princely tombs are also attested in Campania, and as far south as Pontecagnano. The contents of these tombs are remarkably similar, and they must be viewed as a single series.[13] How are we to account for their appearance over such a wide area?

Archaeologists were at one time convinced that such tombs were characteristically Etruscan, and that the examples in Latium and Campania revealed the presence of conquering Etruscan warlords in those areas; even at Cumae, a Greek city, the discovery of a princely tomb of the standard type was thought to indicate the presence of Etruscan interlopers.[14] But this theory, which is ultimately based on the idea that the Etruscans came from the east, is not only dubious in itself (cf. above, pp. 46–7); it is also unnecessary. The discoveries at Decima and elsewhere have shown that the Praeneste tombs are not unique in Latium, and there is no need to postulate the presence of Etruscan warlords in order to explain them.[15] Finally, and most decisively, we now know that the orientalising phenomenon in Italy was the result of Greek influence. The objects found in the princely tombs of Etruria, Latium and Campania are no different from those found in contemporary Greek sites. The orientalising phenomenon, after all, affected Greece no less than Italy.

Greek art and culture were profoundly influenced from the later eighth century by contacts with the ancient Near East. The Greeks imported luxury objects from Egypt, Palestine, Syria and Mesopotamia. It has been established that this trade was largely channelled through the Levant, where Euboean Greeks had set up a trading post at Al Mina on the Orontes shortly before 800. This trade had a significant influence on Greek art, which began to imitate oriental motifs and styles. The decoration of Greek painted pottery began to incorporate free-flowing naturalistic designs, especially exotic plants and animals, in place of the former geometric patterns. The most important of the new pottery styles was proto-Corinthian, which first appeared around 725.[16]

In Italy the matter is complicated because the native peoples were exposed to oriental culture and to orientalising Greek culture simultaneously. Italian orientalising was therefore a mixture of direct and indirect influences, which stimulated local imitations of both eastern and Greek orientalising styles (for example in the development of 'Etrusco-Corinthian' and 'Italo-Corinthian' pottery).[17] In any event there is no need to look further than the Greeks for an explanation of the change; such trade as there was between Italy and the Near East was probably carried by Greek merchants, at least in the first instance. The question of whether there was any direct contact between native Italians and Phoenicians in the orientalising period remains uncertain (see above, p. 69). However that may be, it is evident that the arrival of the Greeks in Italy was decisive, and provoked a cultural revolution.

2 GREEK COLONISATION AND ITS EFFECTS

The earliest Greek settlement in Italy was on Ischia, the island that lies just off the northern tip of the Bay of Naples. The ancients called it Pithecusae or Aenaria. It was here that some Euboean adventurers established a permanent settlement in the years around 770 BC. Within a generation a flourishing community had grown up, engaging in trade with the native peoples of the mainland. Archaeologists have unearthed thousands of graves belonging to the settlement, and have built up a vivid picture of its daily life.[18] There can be little doubt that the chief motive for the settlement was the search for metals, for which there was a heavy demand in the Greek world. Etruria was a major producer of copper and tin, which are found at Mount Amiata, the Tolfa mountains, and above all the area called the *colline metallifere* – the 'metal-bearing hills'; and iron ore occurs in plenty on the island of Elba. Excavations on Pithecusae have revealed iron-smelting works and buildings used for metal-working.[19]

Historians are undecided whether the Euboean settlement on Pithecusae should be regarded as a colony (*apoikia*) or merely as a trading post (*emporion*); but David Ridgway has recently argued that it displays features of both, and advises his readers not to agonise too much about a distinction that was probably not important to the settlers themselves.[20] In any event, Pithecusae prepared the way for further Greek colonisation in the western Mediterranean, a process that implied more than commercial adventure. The Greeks who took part in the colonising movement were seeking to make a better life for themselves. Like nineteenth-century homesteaders they aimed to create an improved version of the society they had left behind, in an environment where land would be available in plenty and where they could achieve a standard of living undreamed of in their overcrowded and impoverished homeland.[21]

A generation or so after the arrival of the first settlers at Pithecusae, a full-scale colony was established at Cumae on the mainland opposite. The new foundation flourished and soon outstripped its predecessor; and it was rapidly followed by a host of further colonies around the shores of southern Italy and Sicily. By the fifth century southern Italy was known as 'Great Greece' (Megale Hellas, or, in the more familiar Latin form, Magna Graecia). The Greek colonies enjoyed great prosperity, and one of them, Sybaris, became a byword for luxury.

The arrival of the Greeks in Italy had a profound impact on the social, economic and cultural life of the native peoples. The hellenisation of Etruria, Latium and Campania began in the eighth century and had a major influence on the structural changes that occurred in the orientalising period, and especially on the formation of the aristocratic order. We cannot be sure whether contact with the Greek settlements was the *cause* of social stratification and the emergence of an aristocracy in Italy, or whether it merely impinged on a process that would otherwise have taken place independently.[22] We should note for instance that the *gentile* structure of the Italian aristocracies is a feature which they do not share with the Greeks. But there is no doubt that Greek influence was important in shaping the aristocratic society of Italy, and in providing a cultural model by which it could define itself.

The aristocracy of early Greece, as Oswyn Murray in particular has shown, was characterised by its cultural outlook and its way of life. Membership of the aristocratic class was a matter of status and honour, and was associated with well-defined activities and values. Greek aristocrats achieved their position of esteem by inheritance and by leadership, especially in war. The mere fact of wealth (a *sine qua non*, it need hardly be said) was less important than the means by which it was acquired and spent. The aristocratic ethos demanded conspicuous consumption and an extravagant style of life. Honour and prestige were reinforced by mutual recognition and interaction. The most important of these reinforcing mechanisms were feasting, guest-friendship, and gift-giving.[23]

The main source of information about early Greek aristocracies is Homer.

The *Iliad* and the *Odyssey*, which were composed in the late eighth century BC, give a vivid picture of the daily life of the heroes, a picture that was at least partly based on the contemporary world. The social environment of the heroes is portrayed with great clarity, and has provided modern historians with an opportunity for extensive sociological analysis.[24] We may briefly note here some of the findings of modern research which are important for our present purposes.

Homer's heroes lived in a competitive world in which personal esteem (*time*) was the principal goal. Such esteem required continual displays of generosity in the entertainment of one's peers. Feasting with male companions is an important activity in the epic, and consumes much of the heroes' time and most of their surplus resources. But through their generosity they obtained support for warfare and raiding, and were thus able to replenish their stocks of wealth and enhance their personal standing. The heroes also maintained a widespread network of contacts and obligations. There is considerable mobility in the world of Homer; Odysseus was not the only one who travelled. Mobility was made possible by the institution of guest-friendship, which imposed on the hero a sacred obligation to offer hospitality to any man of his class who might come visiting. The network was reinforced by the exchange of gifts, which conferred honour on both parties and gave physical expression to personal relationships and obligations.[25]

Movable wealth, which could be acquired by warfare and by gift exchange, consisted largely of luxuries and prestige items, especially metal. Gold and silver, iron and bronze – these metals filled the storerooms of the Homeric heroes, and were drawn upon whenever gifts were needed. Usually they were worked in the form of tripods, bowls, cauldrons, armour or weapons. These apparently functional objects were not for use, but for display. Their symbolic or prestige value was further enhanced if they were exotic or had an interesting pedigree.

> It is my earnest hope, Telemachus, [says Menelaus in book XV of the *Odyssey*] that Zeus the Thunderer and Lord of Hera will grant you a safe journey and make your home-coming all that you desire. By way of presents you shall have the loveliest and most precious of the treasures that my palace holds. I am giving you a mixing bowl of wrought metal. It is solid silver, with a rim of gold around the top, and was made by Hephaestus himself. I had it from my royal friend, the king of Sidon, when I put up under his roof on my way home. And now I wish it to be yours.
>
> (lines 111–19)

The relevance of Homer to the matter in hand hardly needs to be spelt out. If we are searching for a social context to explain the princely tombs of central Italy, we need look no further than the world of Odysseus. It is not simply an apt comparison; it is the model which the Italian aristocracies consciously adopted.

The evidence is unequivocal. The princely tombs of Etruria, Latium and Campania contain treasures that would not have disgraced even the most ebullient Homeric hero. The objects are strikingly uniform in type, even though the tombs are dispersed over a wide area that crosses several linguistic and ethnic frontiers. The ultimate provenance of the treasures varies enormously, but the same 'international eclecticism' is common to all the princely tombs.[26] They can therefore be seen as the material expression of a shared culture (or *koinē*, to use the specialist jargon), brought about by frequent interaction between aristocratic individuals and groups.

We know that in central Italy at this date there was extensive mobility at the highest social level (see below, p. 158). The evidence implies that social standing was recognised internationally, and that aristocrats could move freely from one community to another without regard to ethnic and linguistic barriers. In the same way Homer's heroes expected to be given hospitality and gifts wherever they went, regardless of whether their hosts were Greeks, Trojans, Lycians, Sidonians or Phaeacians. The rules of guest-friendship applied universally. True, they were broken by the Cyclops, but he was beyond the pale of ordinary humanity and obviously did not know how to behave. He is the exception that proves the rule.[27]

There can be little doubt that networks of obligation and guest-friendship linked the *aristoi* of the Greek colonies to their native counterparts, and that the circulation of prestige goods in Italy occurred by means of gift exchange. This conclusion appears to be corroborated by the 'gift inscriptions' that are found on objects in sixth-century Etruscan tombs.[28] Although the value of this evidence has been questioned, the fact of gift exchange in the aristocratic society of Tyrrhenian Italy can be taken as certain.

It is equally clear that feasts and drinking parties were an important feature of daily life in upper-class circles. The ceramic ware that fills so many rich Italian tombs is not just any old crockery, but belongs to a specific type of 'banquet service', and includes a range of vessels used in communal eating and drinking parties. These feasts occurred not only at funerals, as the context of the finds might lead one to infer. Fragments of a complete banquet service have recently been discovered in the debris of an aristocratic house at Ficana (Figure 7) – clear proof that feasting was part of the daily life of Latin aristocrats.[29] Concerning the origin of the custom it has been pointed out that the many Greek loan words in Etruscan include technical terms for vases and drinking vessels (e.g. *askos*, *kylix*, *olpe*, *lekythos*, etc.), which tends to confirm that the banquet, an important feature of Etruscan culture in the archaic period, was inspired by Greek models.[30]

Finally, it can now be affirmed that the *tombe principesche* themselves were modelled on Greek prototypes, and that the paradoxical habit of displaying one's wealth through funerary luxury was inspired by the example of the

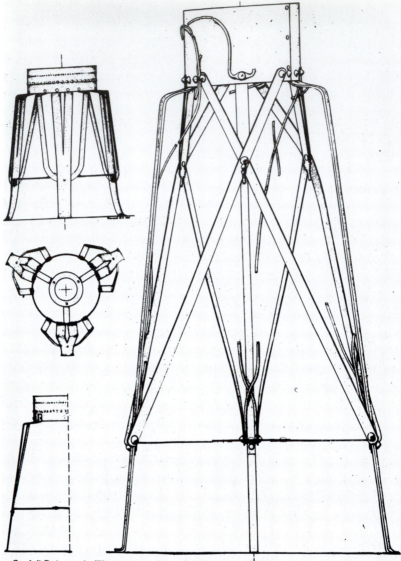

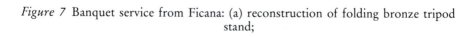

Castel di Decima, tomba XV: ricostruzione dei tripodi di bronzo (cat. 82/30-31).

Figure 7 Banquet service from Ficana: (a) reconstruction of folding bronze tripod stand;

(b) group of vases.

Greek *aristoi*. The wealthy Fondo Artiaco tomb at Cumae, excavated at the beginning of this century, is now dated to *c.* 720 BC and can be confidently described as the earliest in the series of Italian princely tombs. Recent excavations at Eretria in Euboea have now unearthed six tombs in a closely similar style, and have proved that its origins are to be sought in Greece.[31]

The arrival of the Greeks, then, prompted far-reaching changes in the social habits of Tyrrhenian Italy at the end of the eighth century BC. But this was only the beginning. From now on Hellenism was to be a pervasive influence, the single most important factor of change and development in Roman (and Italian) history. So far we have noted its effects on the lifestyle and ethos of the aristocracy. But in the course of the archaic period Greek ideas affected every aspect of life at all levels of society. Art, architecture and religion were already being transformed in the orientalising period. But the most far-reaching change occurred in the political sphere in the second half of the seventh century. This change was the formation of the city-state.

3 URBANISATION

One of the most important signs of the development of city-states in central Italy is the change that can be observed in the physical character of the settlements. This was a long and gradual process, beginning in the early Iron Age (ninth to eighth centuries BC), when systems of small hilltop villages began to coalesce into larger nucleated settlements. This so-called 'proto-urban' phenomenon is particularly well documented in southern Etruria. At Tarquinii, for instance, a number of small hut settlements, separated from one another at a distance of a few kilometres, each with one or more attendant cemeteries, gave way in the course of the eighth century to a single nucleated centre on the so-called Civita plateau; meanwhile the separate village cemeteries were relaced by a general necropolis on the neighbouring hill of Monterozzi. A similar development can be traced at Caere and Veii.[32]

In Latium the situation is less clear, but it seems likely that here too a similar process occurred, with the development of concentrated settlements on sites previously occupied by separate villages. This seems to have happened at Rome at the end of phase IIB (early eighth century BC), somewhat later at Gabii (probably after *c.* 750), and perhaps also at centres such as Lavinium, Ardea and Antium, although at these sites the process itself, and the date, remain conjectural.[33] The structure of these larger nucleated settlements is difficult to visualise; all that can be said is that as far as present evidence goes they consisted of large concentrations of huts, with no evident signs of planning or formal organisation of space.

It was not until the middle of the seventh century BC that any change becomes evident. At that point the emerging aristocratic elite began to display its wealth and prestige in the construction of monumental chamber tombs, surmounted by gigantic tumuli, and placed in isolated splendour away from the main necropolis, often along the main road leading into the settlement.[34] An even more remarkable development is the appearance of monumental palaces or 'stately homes' in the Etruscan countryside. Two examples are now known, at Murlo near Siena and at Acquarossa south of Lake Bolsena.[35] The discovery of these sites some thirty years ago was a complete surprise, and their full significance is still hard to assess. Both palace complexes were rebuilt in the sixth century, and decorated with fine architectural terracottas; but their seventh-century predecessors, though poorly attested, represent the earliest examples of monumental architecture in permanent materials that have so far come to light in Etruria. Both centres, it should be said, were violently destroyed in the last decades of the sixth century, victims of the political upheavals that overtook central Italy at that period (cf. below, p. 293).

In the main centres of population the development of permanent monumental architecture and urban planning occurred somewhat later – during the second half of the seventh century BC. It was also at that period that the great planned necropolises began to appear. The most famous is at Caere, where the Banditaccia cemetery, which comes closer than any other to the description of a 'city of the dead', began to be laid out in the years before 600 (Figure 8). The other famous example of an 'urbanised' necropolis, the Crocefisso del Tufo cemetery at Volsinii (modern Orvieto), dates from the sixth century.

But it is at Rome that we have the clearest and earliest evidence of urban development within the area of habitation itself. The archaeological evidence is still patchy, but enough is now known to give a skeletal picture of the

Figure 8 Cerveteri, Banditaccia necropolis.

remarkable transformation that occurred in the late orientalising period. The first definite sign of change occurred around the middle of the seventh century when the huts by the so-called Sacra Via and the Equus Domitiani were demolished and a rough beaten floor was laid.[36] This was the first Forum. Some years later, perhaps around 625 BC, the pavement was renewed and this time extended in a north-westerly direction to take in the Comitium.[37] From about the same time we have the first evidence of permanent houses, built of stone and with tiled roofs; this material was found on the Velia. Similar buildings on the Palatine date from the early sixth century.

The earliest public building so far identified was the Regia, a mysterious edifice at the eastern end of the Forum which in republican times was a shrine of Mars and Ops Consiva, but under the monarchy was probably part of a larger complex in which the king resided. This interpretation, which agrees with the literary tradition (e.g. Paulus-Festus' dictionary entry, 'Regia: a royal residence'), gains support from the comparison with the palaces at Murlo and Acquarossa, to which the Regia shows certain similarities (see below, p. 240).

At the opposite end of the Forum, a building was erected on the northern edge of the Comitium, dating from about 600 BC; it has been plausibly identified with the Curia Hostilia, the first Senate House, which tradition ascribes to Tullus Hostilius (whence its name).[38] Around 580 BC the Comitium was redeveloped, and a monumental sanctuary constructed on its southern side. In 1899 Giacomo Boni uncovered the remains of the sanctuary beneath a black marble paving, which was clearly the 'Black Stone in the Comitium' mentioned in ancient sources (Festus p. 184 L: *niger lapis in Comitio*). The sanctuary contained an altar, the lower part of a column (which in its original state perhaps supported a statue), and the truncated remnant of a block of stone bearing an inscription in archaic Latin (Figure 9). At the time of its discovery the inscription caused a sensation because it contained the word *recei* (= *regi* in classical Latin, from *rex*, 'king'), and therefore appeared to confound the then fashionable view that the Roman monarchy was a myth.[39]

Whatever the severely mutilated text might be saying – the surviving portion is extremely difficult to interpret, and the rest must be supplemented by guesswork – recent studies have clarified the significance of the monumental context.[40] It is the sanctuary which the Romans called the Volcanal (i.e. the shrine of Vulcan), and connected in various ways with Romulus. Some sources (apparently including Varro) thought that it was the tomb of Romulus. That is strange because there was no tomb at the site; moreover all the various accounts imply that Romulus' body disappeared, and consequently that he could not have had a tomb.[41] Perhaps what Varro really meant was that it was a cenotaph or 'heroon'. Other sources describe it not as a tomb but as the place where Romulus met his death.[42] As for the famous inscription, it is probably the one mentioned by Dionysius of Halicarnassus (II.45.2), who records that Romulus dedicated a statue of himself to Hephaestus (sc. Vulcan) and set up an inscription 'in Greek characters' (i.e. in archaic script) describing his achievements.

A votive deposit beneath the Niger Lapis contains material going back to the first half of the sixth century, and provides evidence of the foundation of the cult. This appears in the form of a fragment of an Attic black-figure *krater* (large mixing-bowl) showing the Greek god Hephaestus returning to Olympus, and dating from *c.* 570–550 BC (see further below, p. 163).[43]

Figure 9 Sanctuary of the Niger Lapis: archaic inscription.

Votive deposits are an important source of information for this period. They provide evidence, for example, of cult activity at the site of the temple of Vesta. Objects found in a well can be connected with the cult activities of the Vestals. The first building on the site dates from *c.* 560.[44] Votive deposits on the Capitol and Quirinal from this period testify to cult activity at these places also.[45] In the Forum Boarium, huts dating back to the eighth century were demolished at the end of the seventh and a sanctuary established there before 600. Sacrificial remains and a great amount of imported pottery, both Greek and Etruscan, belong to this period. These items include two Etruscan inscriptions.[46] A temple was constructed on the site in the second quarter of the sixth century, destroyed a generation or so later and then rebuilt, this time decorated with terracotta friezes and the acroterial statues of Heracles and Athena of which large fragments are preserved (see below, p. 149).[47] It is natural to connect this building with the temple of Fortuna attributed to the sixth-century king Servius Tullius.

The foundations of a huge archaic temple are still visible on the Capitol. This was the great temple of Jupiter, Juno and Minerva which was built under the Tarquins and dedicated in the first year of the Republic. Archaeological evidence, in the form of fragmentary architectural terracottas, confirms the date of the temple, and the remaining traces of the foundations and sub-structure confirm what the tradition tells us about the immense scale of the building. It measured some 61 metres long by 55 metres wide, making it one of the largest temples in the Mediterranean world by contemporary stand-ards.[48]

Taken as a whole, the evidence gives a clear picture of the physical development of Rome in the later seventh and sixth centuries BC, from a primitive hut settlement to a truly urban community. This archaeological picture is consistent with that of the literary sources, which make frequent reference to the public works undertaken by the kings. The tradition relating to the foundation of temples is generally agreed to be reliable.[49] This does not mean that all trace of the earlier hut settlement had vanished; on the contrary, scattered groups of huts would have continued to occupy much of the site down to the end of the sixth century and probably beyond.[50] But from the mid-seventh century onwards the huts had progressively given way to more sophisticated types of building and to a better organised and planned use of urban space. Public squares and communal sanctuaries occupied the central areas of the city, which as time progressed were graced with increasingly large and elegant public buildings. Many of these buildings went through several stages of construction in the course of the sixth century. By around 500 BC Rome must have been one of the showplaces of the western Mediterranean, a city with a physical setting to match its position as the most powerful state in central Italy (see below, pp. 198–214).

This general picture has recently been confirmed by excavations that have been going on since the mid-1980s on the northern slopes of the Palatine. The finds are as yet unpublished, and the brief reports that have so far been released give only a general indication of what has been discovered.[51] It seems certain, however, that in the late sixth century BC this area of the city was reorganised and a row of large private residences was constructed, with their entrances along the Sacra Via. At least four of these stone-built archaic houses have been identified, and an outline description of one of them has been published. The plans indicate that it was a large *atrium*-type house, of the kind that was later standard at Pompeii. The house consisted of rooms surrounding a large cruciform central space, lit by an opening at the centre (*compluvium*), with a basin underneath to catch the rain (*impluvium*).

The house was immense, and occupied most of an irregular quadrilateral plot measuring 22 x 25 x 31 x 38 metres, the eastern edge of which was a garden (see Figure 10). The narrow entrance gave on to a large hall (*atrium*), flanked by two wings on either side of the *impluvium*. Beyond the *impluvium*, at the south end, was the main reception area (*tablinum*), which measured some 7 x 9 metres, a huge room by any standards. It was considerably bigger than the early (fourth century BC?) 'House of the Surgeon' at Pompeii, which it otherwise resembles in layout.[52]

The director of the excavations, Andrea Carandini, has pointed out that in the late Republic this was the most fashionable residential area of the city, and that leading Roman aristocrats, including Cicero and Clodius, had their town houses there. The house described above was probably the precursor of the house of L. Licinius Crassus, consul in 95 BC. The excavations seem to show that the archaic houses, dated by Carandini around 530–520 BC, were subsequently preserved in their original form until the end of the third century, when they were destroyed by fire (probably the one recorded in 210 BC) and rebuilt. This suggests that the houses were the ancestral homes of leading families from the archaic period onwards, and that in the fourth and third centuries the prestige of these families was enhanced by the fact that they were living in houses that were hundreds of years old.

The process of urbanisation is better documented at Rome than anywhere else in Old Latium. Relatively little attention has been paid to the habitation areas of sites outside Rome, and much of what has been done remains unpublished. Among the better known sites, Lavinium, Satricum and Ficana have produced evidence of urban development similar to what we have witnessed in Rome. The principal feature of the change is the replacement of huts by permanent stone buildings in the sixth century, and the appearance at a number of sites of monumental sanctuaries. These sanctuary sites are discussed more fully below (section 7).

4 THE CITY-STATE: THEORETICAL PROBLEMS

We have seen in the previous section that the physical character of the settlement was transformed in the later part of the seventh century BC, when it began to take on the appearance of an urban centre. This change has been interpreted as an 'urban revolution', a decisive historical turning-point which marks the beginning of the history of Rome. An influential version of this theory was advanced by the Swedish archaeologist E. Gjerstad shortly after the Second World War.[53] Gjerstad insisted on a sharp division in the historical development of the site between the 'pre-urban' and 'urban' epochs. The

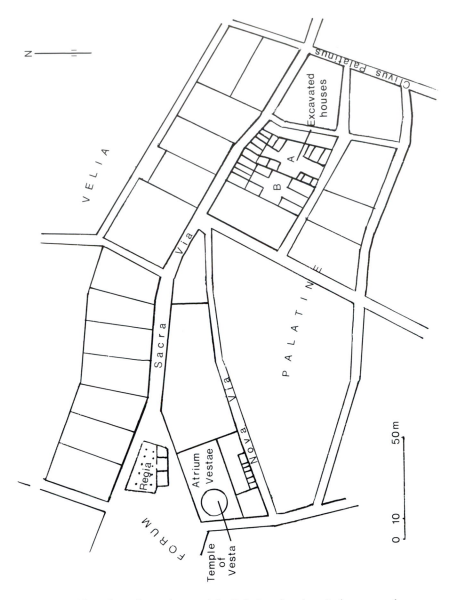

Figure 10 (a) Plan of northern slopes of the Palatine showing sixth-century houses.

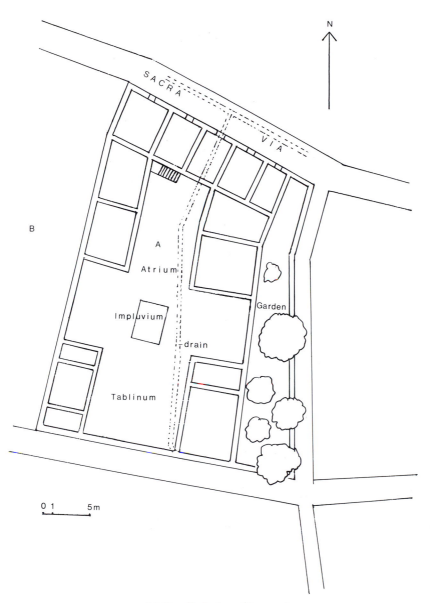

(b) Detailed plan of house A.

beginning of the latter was marked, he thought, by the first paving of the Roman Forum, a development which he dated to *c.* 575 BC. According to the revised chronology adopted in this book, the date of the first Forum must be raised to *c.* 625 BC, but this need not affect Gjerstad's basic pre-urban/urban division.

Gjerstad maintained that the whole history of the Roman kings belongs to the urban epoch; dismissing Romulus as a mythical eponym, he argued that the first king of Rome was Numa Pompilius, whose reign therefore began in *c.* 575 BC. More controversially, he further suggested that the regal period lasted until the middle of the fifth century, and that the beginning of the Republic coincided with the publication of the Twelve Tables in 450 BC. This chronological scheme entailed a radical revision of the historical record concerning the early Republic, which few scholars have been able to accept. After more than twenty years of fierce debate, the balance of scholarly opinion is now heavily in favour of the traditional chronology of the beginning of the Republic (see below, p. 222).

This is part of a more general feeling of dissatisfaction with the methods and results of the Swedish school. As for the paving of the first Forum, critics have not only revised the date (from *c.* 575 to *c.* 625), but have also questioned the interpretation that Gjerstad put upon it. The idea that the city came into being at a single decisive moment has been dismissed as a romantic illusion deserving no more credence than the ancient foundation legends. The theory of an 'urban revolution' has been replaced by that of a gradual process of spontaneous evolution, which is held to be closer to the archaeological record and more in keeping with the secular ideas of the twentieth century.[54] The most powerful voice to have spoken in favour of this approach belongs to the archaeologist H. Müller-Karpe, who contrasted the ancient legends of *Stadtgründung* (city foundation) with the modern concept of *Stadtwerdung* (city development); Rome, he suggested, evolved gradually from an original inhabited nucleus on the Palatine, which expanded to take in the other hills during the course of the Iron Age.[55] Gjerstad, on the other hand, had imagined a number of independent village settlements on the various hills, which were brought together in a deliberate act of unification in *c.* 575 BC.[56]

The paving of the Forum and the development of monumental architecture in Rome towards the end of the seventh century are recognised by the adherents of the 'Stadtwerdung' school as important developments, but as forming only one of many stages in the long process of urbanisation, the beginnings of which should be placed in the eighth century. To choose any one stage as marking a decisive transition from a pre-urban to an urban community is on this view a rather arbitrary procedure – a matter of verbal definition; what counts is to reconstruct the main stages of the process, rather than to identify any particular stage as 'urban'.

This objection could be raised against a recent study by R. Drews, which reacts against the prevailing evolutionism and seeks to replace it with a more 'creationist' view.[57] Arguing that a city can be defined as 'a compact settlement of streets and houses', Drews suggests that cities arose in central Italy when huts were replaced by permanent houses with stone foundations and tiled roofs – a transition that occurred in the seventh century BC. This raises questions of fact: in suggesting that the change happened all at once and produced an 'urban revolution', Drews goes way beyond the evidence.[58] Rather, the little we know suggests that the replacement of huts by houses was a gradual process, conforming if anything to the theory of gradual evolution. Moreover, although Drews regards it as simply 'common sense', it is hard to see why a development in building technique should be singled out as the decisive feature of city life.

Similar problems arise with any attempt to apply a universal or 'autonomous' definition of urbanism to the archaeological evidence. According to Müller-Karpe the site of Rome already possessed the features of an urban settlement in the eighth century: a large inhabited nucleus, an 'extra-urban' cemetery (on the Esquiline), specialised craft production, and a stratified social structure (these developments are all attested in phase III of the Latial culture).[59] The classic example of this kind of approach is V. Gordon Childe's famous study of 'the Urban Revolution', which specified no fewer than ten indices whose concurrent appearance in the archaeological record could be held to mark the advent of urbanism.[60] In a recent article A. Guidi has tried to apply Childe's ten criteria to the material from Rome and Latium.[61] His conclusion is that a 'proto-urban' settlement existed at Rome already at the end of the ninth century BC, and that it developed into an urban community in the course of the eighth.

The difficulty here is not so much the interpretation of the factual evidence (although there is little doubt that eighth-century Rome does not satisfy the ten criteria),[62] but rather the theoretical validity of the method. What Childe outlined was a set of features that characterised a certain type of urban community. Some of them are not specific to cities as such but are merely necessary conditions of urbanism (such as a concentrated settlement or craft specialisation); others are not even that, and need not always be present (for example naturalistic art). This would suggest that Childe was not setting out a universal definition of urbanism, but rather delineating the features of a predetermined model or ideal type.[63]

It is clear from the general context of Childe's paper, and from the nature of the criteria he set out, that the model he had in mind was the type of city that developed in Mesopotamia in the third millennium BC.[64] The most characteristic feature of cities in the ancient Near East was the presence of a centralised redistributive economy based on a temple or palace, and regulated by a scribal bureaucracy – a type of urban community that never existed in Greece or Italy in the classical period. But if we adopt Childe's general method rather than his specific findings, we ought rather to search for indices of a culturally appropriate model – in this case, obviously, the typical Graeco-

Roman city-state (*polis* or *civitas*). Instead of asking when Rome became a city, we should attempt to discover when the characteristic features of the city-state became evident at Rome.[65]

This is the question Gjerstad tried to answer. The paving of the Forum and the Comitium are crucial stages in the development of Rome not (or not *only*) because it changed the physical layout of the settlement, but because it symbolised the formation of a political community. As Gjerstad repeatedly emphasised, the Forum was a central meeting-place which served as both a market and a civic centre.[66] The appearance of house architecture in place of huts is an important technical development, but greater political significance attaches to the construction of monumental public buildings designed for communal or civic use. Religious buildings are especially important. There is evidence of cult activity in parts of Rome from very early times, but as far as the rise of the city-state is concerned what matters is the first evidence of *communal* religious activity and the establishment of *public* cults.

In Rome the most important civic cults were those of Vesta and of Capitoline Jupiter.[67] The cult of Vesta, and the construction of a temple in the Forum connected with the Regia, are securely documented in the archaeological record from the second half of the seventh century. The evidence from the Capitol is more difficult to intrepret. A votive deposit from the Capitol contains material that can be assigned to a long time-span down to the end of the Latial culture; the latest objects date from period IVB (630–580 BC), and give an approximate date for the moment when the votives were ceremonially placed in a sealed deposit. Some kind of monumental structure was then built on top of it – presumably a sanctuary or even a temple. The site is some distance from that of the great temple of Jupiter Optimus Maximus that was constructed at the end of the sixth century (see above, p. 96), but it may nevertheless be its precursor.[68]

The archaeological evidence thus bears witness to a dramatic reorganisation of Rome in the last decades of the seventh century BC. It was described by Gjerstad as a *synoikismos*, which we may translate as 'unification'. This notion has been criticised on the grounds that the evidence for separate villages on the tops of the various hills of Rome is poor, and that in any case a large nucleated settlement, including the valley of the Forum, existed long before the Forum was formally laid out as a paved open space (see above, p. 101). Such criticisms are misplaced, however, because they do not fully address the point that Gjerstad was making, and they also misrepresent the Greek idea of *synoikismos*. Gjerstad was thinking principally of a political unification of the community and the subordination of local autonomy to a single centralised authority.[69]

This too is the true meaning of *synoikismos*, namely the creation of a unified political community. As far as the Greek *polis* was concerned, physical or topographical unification was entirely secondary and was not even necessary. Sparta for instance was a unified *polis* from a very early date, but even in the classical period was topographically diffuse, consisting as it did of five unwalled villages. Equally striking is the tradition about the *synoikismos* of Athens, described for us by no less an authority than Thucydides (2.15.2). According to this account, Theseus abolished the magistracies and councils of the various townships of Attica and compelled their inhabitants to use Athens, *although they continued to live in the same places as before*.[70]

At Rome the formation of a city-state coincided with major developments in the organisation of urban space and in architectural technique. These changes can all be placed within a relatively brief space of time (the decades on either side of 625 BC), and must have been deliberately put into effect. We are entitled, in my opinion, to refer to this process as the foundation of Rome, even if we cannot name the person or persons who founded it. At this point the true history of Rome begins.

5 LITERACY AND ITS USES: THE CALENDAR OF NUMA

The formation of the city-state was accompanied by other social and cultural changes which were causally related to it. One of these was the development of literacy. The western alphabet was invented, probably around 800 BC, by an unknown genius who adapted Phoenician signs to represent linguistic sounds in Greek.[71] Around 700 BC, if not before, the alphabetic script was being used in Italy to represent Etruscan; and the earliest Latin inscriptions can be dated not much later.[72] Since the alphabet is itself a Greek modification of the Phoenician script the Italian peoples must have taken the idea from the Greeks; no one these days thinks that the Etruscans or Latins independently created their own alphabet from Phoenician. This can be confirmed by the fact that the Italian alphabet is closest to the one used by the Euboeans, who were the first Greeks to settle permanently in Italy.

As it happens, one of the earliest known pieces of Greek alphabetic writing occurs on a gold drinking-cup found in a tomb at Pithecusae, the first Greek settlement in Italy.[73] One of the oldest – but it is not absolutely the oldest. That record is held, at present, by a recently discovered inscription from Latium – to be precise, from the cemetery of Osteria dell'Osa. It consists of four or five letters scratched on a small globular vase found in a tomb (no. 482) dating from the end of phase IIB (i.e. before *c.*770 BC).[74] What it signifies, and where it comes from, are unanswered questions, but it certainly suggests contact with the Greek world. It is widely believed that the Etruscans passed on the art of writing to the Latins, but there are good reasons, reinforced by the new find, for thinking that the process of transmission was more complex, and that both Etruscans and Latins learned directly from the Greeks, but also influenced each other.[75]

A surprisingly large number of inscriptions on stone, bronze or ceramic surfaces survives from archaic Italy. Around 120 Etruscan texts survive from the seventh century BC, and a further 800 or so can be dated to the sixth and fifth centuries. Latium is less well represented (at present around seventy Latin inscriptions can be assigned to the same time-span), but there are special reasons for this, and it would be wrong to assume that literacy was less well established or less widely used in Latium than Etruria. In fact there are good reasons for thinking that writing played an important part in the public and private life of archaic Rome, and was widely used for social, administrative and commercial purposes.[76]

At the beginning of this section it was stated that the rise of the city-state and the advent of literacy were causally connected. This was not meant to imply that literacy is a necessary condition for urbanism, or indeed for the formation of a state; indeed, examples of both processes can be found in non-literate societies, for example among the Incas. Nevertheless, there is a case for saying that literacy made possible the particular form of city-state that developed in the Graeco-Roman world. In particular, the formal and artificial institutions of the Graeco-Roman model, requiring the complex organisation of time and space, seem to presuppose a literate mentality. This is the conclusion of a famous series of studies by the Cambridge anthropologist Jack Goody, and in spite of criticisms it remains compelling.[77]

Literacy not only allows one to record masses of complex data; it also makes it possible to reorganise and reclassify the same data, to retrieve some or all of them at will, and to use them for an infinite variety of different purposes. This revolution in information technology was a basic requirement for the Graeco-Roman city-state, which was characterised by complex artificial institutions in which citizens were divided and subdivided into different kinds of functional groups. The operation of these institutions further depended on the formal division and public organisation of space and time. The census and the reforms of Servius Tullius (on which see below, p. 173) would be unthinkable in a non-literate community.

Another example of the product of a literate mentality in archaic Rome is the calendar, which tradition ascribes to King Numa Pompilius. Our knowledge of the Roman calendar before the reforms of Julius Caesar is based on literary sources and an inscribed calendar of the early first century BC, partially preserved on the wall of a house at Antium. This document, the so-called *Fasti antiates maiores*, enables us to distinguish the republican elements in the many other preserved calendars of early imperial date. It is widely accepted that the basic structure of the pre-Julian calendar goes back to the archaic period, probably to the time of the monarchy. This dating is based on Mommsen's observation that the earliest elements are written in large capital letters, and that entries in small capitals represent later additions. Since the festival days in large letters include no reference to the cult of Jupiter Optimus Maximus, which was instituted as the principal state cult under the Tarquins, Mommsen argued that the original (large-letter) calendar must be earlier. Although it is not universally accepted, everything suggests that Mommsen's view is right.[78]

The calendar itself is complex, and lists different kinds of information simultaneously. It is set out in thirteen columns, representing the regular twelve months and the additional ('intercalary') month that was inserted every other year. In the columns the days are listed, each bearing a letter from A to H to show its position in the nundinal cycle (a 'week' of eight days), together with another letter or set of letters to indicate its status. The letter F (*fastus*) marked an ordinary working day, C (*comitialis*) one on which assemblies could be held. On days marked N (*nefastus*) certain types of business were forbidden. The letters EN (*endotercisus*) indicated that the day was divided between the afternoon, which was F, and the morning and evening, which were N. Two days (24 March, 24 May) were marked QRCF (*quando rex comitiavit fas*), meaning that the day became F once the king had dismissed the *comitia curiata*. This designation manifestly goes back to the regal period.

The calendar also lists the three fixed points within each month, the Kalends, Nones and Ides, which originally corresponded with the phases of the moon. Finally, the letters NP (probably *nefastus publicus*) were attached to the days of the great public festivals, the names of which were also given in abbreviated form – e.g. LUPER[calia], FORDI[cidia], SATUR[nalia], etc. The calendar is a fundamentally important document for the study of Roman religion, since the list of festivals (*feriale*) which it contains goes back to the regal period. But it is also important for two other reasons. First, it represents more clearly than anything else the operation of a centralised political authority. It is an elementary point, but one that deserves to be forcibly emphasised, that the calendar, which can be dated to the sixth century with certainty, and perhaps even earlier, is the product of an organised city-state. Second, the form of the calendar, with its different kinds of information listed in a single document, is clearly linked to the development of literacy; indeed it presupposes it.[79]

6 CHANGES IN FUNERARY PRACTICE

The state of the archaeological evidence for sixth-century Latium represents a strange reversal of what had obtained previously. The finds from the orientalising cemeteries in Latium (Decima, Laurentina, Lavinium, etc.) are far more impressive, both in quantity and quality, than anything so far found in Rome. But after *c.* 600 the city of Rome becomes the most important archaeological site, and the Latin centres fade from view. This is because the major iron-age sites in Old Latium are cemeteries, and no cemetery has produced any material later than *c.* 580 BC. The gap in the funerary record extends to most of the sixth and fifth centuries. How are we to account for this curious phenomenon?

One possible explanation would be that the Latins had found some way of disposing of their dead other than by interment. Another theoretical possibility is that cemeteries of the sixth and fifth centuries exist in Latium but have not yet been discovered. But such explanations are extremely unlikely, especially as in some cemeteries, such as Praeneste, La Rustica and the Esquiline in Rome, fourth-century tombs have been found alongside those of the late orientalising period, but with no trace of the intervening archaic period.[80]

The only alternative, and this must be the true explanation, is that we do in fact possess graves of the sixth and fifth centuries, but do not know how to recognise them as belonging to that period. The reason we cannot date them is because they contain no datable material. Burials without grave furnishings have been recorded in recent excavations of Latial cemeteries and have been mentioned in passing in published reports; but one suspects that in earlier excavations, such as those of the late nineteenth century on the Esquiline, they were passed over as unworthy of serious attention.[81]

The unavoidable conclusion is that the Romans and Latins of the sixth and fifth centuries BC buried their dead in simple graves without accompanying goods or artefacts. But why? Such a question seems natural, although on reflection it is the practice of burying goods with the dead, rather than the failure to do so, that ought to strike us as odd. It is a sign of how familiar we have become with archaeology and its findings that we expect ancient tombs to contain artefacts, and are surprised when they do not.

At all events the evidence points to a radical change in funerary custom in Latium at the beginning of the sixth century. The explanation is almost certainly cultural and ideological rather than strictly economic. The disappearance of grave furnishings is unlikely to be the result of worsening economic conditions or a decline in the prosperity of the society; there is no suggestion of any such decline in the rest of the evidence, but rather the contrary. In any case economic constraints might deter people from burying treasure with the dead, but would not stop them from including cheap artefacts such as pottery.

In an important study G. Colonna suggested that the change might be connected with some form of legal restriction.[82] He drew attention to the regulation in the Twelve Tables limiting the expense of funerals (Table X, 2–6, from Cicero, de legibus 2.58–62). These rules were similar to provisions in the laws of Solon and other archaic Greek law codes, as the Romans themselves noted (Cicero, ad loc.). The view of the sources, that the Romans sent an embassy to Athens in 454 BC to study Solon's laws before producing a code of their own, is open to the objection that Solon's laws were out of date by 454 BC (see below, p. 275). But Colonna argues that restrictions on funerary extravagance can be seen to date back to the early sixth century (which is when Solon was active), and that the Twelve Tables were therefore a codification of existing laws and practices, some of which went back more than a century.

The theory is attractive, and acceptable up to a point. It is likely enough that the tenth Table codified norms of behaviour that were established long before the mid-fifth century, and that there is a link with the change in funerary practice that occurred at the beginning of the archaic period. But it would be wrong to put too much emphasis on prohibition as the cause of the change.[83] There are a number of problems in such an approach. In the first place, the new funerary practice was adopted throughout the whole of Latium Vetus and also in the southern Etruscan city of Veii (although the rest of Etruria was not affected). This area was not under the control of a single political authority until the Roman conquest of Veii in 396 BC, so it is hard to see how any kind of general restriction could have been imposed in the sixth century. Second, the theory is too positive in its assumptions about the efficacy of legislation. Experience suggests that legislation rarely succeeds in bringing about the results its promoters intend. This is particularly true of social legislation – that is, of laws designed to change attitudes, behaviour, or patterns of consumption ('sumptuary' laws). Such laws, which are invariably full of loopholes, are easy to evade and usually impossible to enforce. One is tempted to formulate a rule of thumb for historians: the least likely explanation for changes in social behaviour is that they are wished for by governments.

There *is* a connection between the law codified in the tenth Table and the change in funerary practice in the early sixth century, but it is less straightforward than one might imagine. Let us note, first, that the change was less sudden and dramatic than is implied in the simplified account given above. The height of extravagance in aristocratic burials in Latium was reached in the middle orientalising period (*c.* 675–640). Later graves are more modest in terms of the treasures they contain, and there is a perceptible decrease in the number of objects deposited. In other words the change in attitudes and beliefs was gradual. There is a strong possibility, therefore, that the change in funerary practice gave rise to the legislative norms, rather than the other way around.

An important point about the provisions of the tenth Table is that they affect the conduct of funerals, rather than the contents of graves. Nothing in the tenth Table would have prevented a person from burying treasure in a tomb, had he or she so wished. It is no good objecting that we do not have the full text of the Table; if there had been such a regulation, Cicero would certainly have mentioned it in his discussion in the *de legibus*. Most of the known laws on funerary restriction, both Greek and Roman, are concerned with the conduct of funerals: the number of mourners, the clothes that they could wear, the amounts of food and drink they could consume, and the way they were to behave. Grave goods as such are rarely mentioned.[84]

Social historians make a distinction between 'prospective' and 'retrospective' funerary practices – that is, between practices for the benefit of the living, and those intended for the dead.[85] The change that took place in the late seventh century can perhaps be seen as a shift from the latter to the former. The burials of the late orientalising period, particularly those associated with chamber tombs, seem to reflect a change of emphasis from the essentially private commemoration of the deceased to the public celebration of the standing and prestige of a family. We have to imagine aristocratic funerals as elaborate public events, involving banquets, entertainments and large crowds. Expenditure came to be concentrated on them rather than on treasure to be buried with the deceased; and it was these aspects that attracted the attention of later legislators and moralists. Grave goods were not included in sumptuary legislation because they were no longer part of regular funerary practice.[86]

This hypothetical shift coincides with a major change in the organisation of society. Stated simply, what happened was that the emerging aristocratic families and clans became competing elements in a wider community. The result was that the activities of the elite had a communal focus, and their surplus resources were diverted from private consumption of prestige luxuries to expenditure in a public context, particularly on gifts to communal sanctuaries. This hypothetical model implies a close connection between the change in burial practice in the years on either side of 600 BC and the emergence of an urbanised community in the same period. This was certainly not a coincidence. The public orientation of funerary practice (and, more generally, of patterns of elite expenditure), the appearance of sacred and secular public buildings, the organisation of urban space, and (possibly) the imposition by a central authority of norms of behaviour – these developments can be seen as further symptoms of the pathological condition we have diagnosed as the rise of the state.

7 SANCTUARIES

One of the most striking indications of the formation of the city-state at this period is the development of public communal sanctuaries. Although many of these holy places had been the centres of cult activity from a very early period, it was the sixth century that witnessed a widespread process of monumental development, in some cases leading to the construction of temples. The earliest known example of a temple in central Italy is the one uncovered before the Second World War in the Forum Boarium at Rome, at a site near the church of Sant'Omobono. This temple dates from before 550 BC, and is no doubt to be identified with one of the two temples in that area attributed by tradition to King Servius Tullius (see below, p. 147).

Other early examples from Rome include the Capitoline temple (late sixth century) and the temple of Castor (early fifth century). Many other archaic temples are recorded in the literary sources, for example those of Diana on the Aventine, and of Saturn in the Forum. In most cases these temples were built on the sites of existing sanctuaries, consisting of open-air altars.

Sometimes these archaic monuments continued to be preserved alongside the temple buildings. For instance, an archaic altar at the west end of the Forum, beneath the Clivus Capitolinus, has been plausibly identified as the Altar of Saturn (Ara Saturni).[87] Other sanctuaries, such as the Volcanal in the Comitium and the Great Altar of Hercules, continued as open-air shrines until the late Republic.

Archaeological research has revealed a similar pattern in southern Etruria and at other Latin centres. The remains of archaic temples (late sixth to early fifth centuries) have been found at Veii, Orvieto, Lanuvium, Ardea and Satricum, often in association with evidence of earlier cult activity. Some important shrines were situated outside the main inhabited areas of the cities. These so-called 'extra-mural' sanctuaries form an important group. One of the most impressive sites is at Pratica di Mare (ancient Lavinium), where several such sanctuaries have been found. One, on the eastern side of the city walls, has yielded large numbers of terracotta offerings in a votive deposit extending from the sixth to the fourth century BC, including over sixty large-scale statues, at least four of them representing Minerva (Figure 11). The excavators therefore identified the site, no doubt rightly, with a sanctuary of Minerva mentioned in literary sources. Architectural terracottas point to the existence of temple buildings.[88]

Another major site at Lavinium is the open-air sanctuary to the south of the city, made famous by the discovery, in the early 1960s, of a row of thirteen stone altars.[89] This complex is probably to be associated with the cult of the Penates (see above, p. 66), which was common to all the peoples of Latium. The best explanation of the altars, which differ from each other in style and date, is that the several Latin communities each maintained its own altar, just as the Greek cities had their individual treasuries at Delphi.

This interpretation can help to explain the function of extra-urban sanctuaries in general. Although all religious shrines in archaic Italy seem to have been 'international' in the sense that they were offered, and were prepared to accept, dedications from all comers (no doubt on condition that they had money and/or high status), it appears that the extra-urban sanctuaries were established for the specific purpose of attracting outsiders, and inviting other communities to participate in joint celebrations. This would explain why Servius Tullius founded his 'federal' cult of Diana on the Aventine, which was outside the sacred boundary of the city (below, p. 298).

Another function served by some of the extra-urban sanctuaries was the encouragement and supervision of international trade. This aspect has recently been illuminated by the discoveries at Gravisca and Pyrgi, two coastal sites in south Etruria. At Gravisca, the port of Tarquinii, a sanctuary was established in the early sixth century to Aphrodite, Hera and Demeter, Greek divinities close to the hearts of the numerous Greek traders who frequented the place. The names of these traders, which are documented by the many

Figure 11 Lavinium: statue of Minerva.

dedications they offered at the shrine, show that they came mostly from the eastern Aegean – from Samos, Ephesus and Miletus. But the most famous visitor was Sostratos of Aegina, who dedicated a stone anchor to Apollo (Figure 12); Sostratos is otherwise known from Herodotus (4.152), who described him as the most successful merchant of all time. Further evidence of his activities is provided by the many sixth-century Greek vases found in Etruscan sites bearing the trademark SO, in Aeginetan letters. That SO stands for Sostratos, and that the vases (and their contents?) were among the merchandise traded by him, seems extremely probable.[90]

Another international trading port (in Greek: *emporion*) of the same kind

Figure 12 Gravisca: the 'Sostratos anchor'.

was located at Pyrgi, one of the harbours of Caere. Here excavations have revealed a sanctuary comprising two large temples, the smaller of which (temple B) is a peripteral (Greek-style) building, measuring about 20 by 30 metres, and dating from the late sixth century. The second, and slightly larger, temple A (c. 24 x 35 m), dating from around 460 BC, is a typical Etrusco-Italic temple with three cellae, but the fragmentary sculptures from its rear pediment portray a scene from the Greek myth of the Seven against Thebes (Figure 13). However, the famous bilingual inscription from the same sanctuary (see below, p. 212) is written in Etruscan and Phoenician, and indicates that Phoenician traders, as well as Greeks, were resident in the port, and occupied a position of some influence in the affairs of Caere. The temples form part of a great monumental complex, only parts of which have been excavated. One building has been identified as a brothel; according to this plausible fantasy the *emporion* offered lucrative market opportunities, the chance to trade in protected and privileged surroundings, and exotic sexual diversions – everything, in other words, that the international businessman could possibly want.[91]

This 'emporic' model can be extended to other major sanctuaries along the Tyrrhenian coast, most of which were situated in harbour sites, were at least partly dedicated to the cult of erotic deities (Aphrodite/Venus, Fortuna, Mater Matuta), and were frequented by foreign traders. They include a site at the mouth of the Liris (later Minturnae), Antium and Ardea; but the most important examples in Latium were undoubtedly Lavinium and Rome itself, where the Forum Boarium, with its hellenising cults, its location outside the sacred boundary of the city, and its association with the river harbour (Portus), was evidently the haunt of foreign merchants, many of them resident.[92]

By way of conclusion, two brief points can be made about the archaic sanctuaries of Tyrrhenian Italy. First, the extra-urban sanctuaries, especially those situated on or near the coast, explain the route and the mechanism by which Greek and Phoenician goods, ideas and persons were able to penetrate the societies of central Italy so effectively, and with such far-reaching results, during the seventh and sixth centuries BC. It is precisely these coastal *emporion*-sanctuaries that have produced all the most exciting and important Greek and Phoenician finds during the past thirty years or so. These discoveries have revolutionised the study of early Roman and Latin culture. Second, it is worth repeating that sanctuaries not only dominate the archaeological evidence for the period of the sixth and early fifth centuries; they are also a topic of overriding importance for the literary tradition. The amount of space our sources devote to the construction of the Capitoline temple, the 'federal' cults of Diana, the shrines of Lavinium, and the cult of Jupiter Latiaris (among others) is, in the circumstances, truly remarkable. This cannot be a coincidence, and it must reinforce the argument that the literary tradition is based on fact.

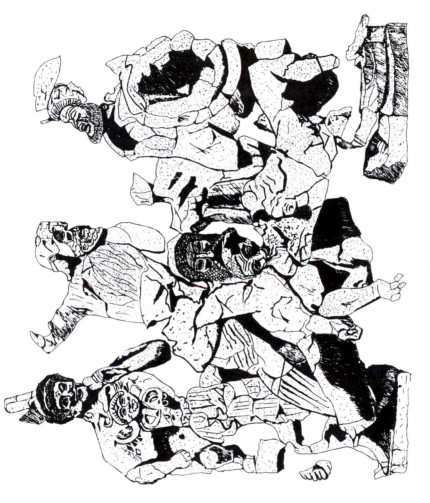

Figure 13 Pyrgi: sculptures from the pediment of temple A.

8 INSTITUTIONS

So far our discussion of the city-state has concentrated on archaeological and epigraphic evidence, and has therefore been largely concerned with monumental aspects of urbanism and with cultural developments. In the nature of things archaeology cannot tell us much about the details of social structure or institutions; and the earliest epigraphic documents are more important as evidence of literacy and its uses than for any substantive information they might contain. If we want to know about the earliest institutions of the Roman state, it is to the literary sources that we must turn.

The sources tell us that the population of early Rome was divided into three tribes, called Tities, Ramnes and Luceres, which were themselves subdivided into thirty smaller units called curiae, ten to each tribe. The tribes were the basis of the earliest military organisation of the state: the army consisted of 300 cavalry and 3,000 infantry, each tribe supplying 100 and 1,000 men respectively.[93]

According to tradition the Ramnes took their name from Romulus, and the Tities from Titus Tatius. There is less certainty about the Luceres, but the majority of the sources state that they were named after Lucumo, an Etruscan warrior who helped Romulus.[94] This tradition provides the warrant for the modern theory that the tribes represent three different ethnic groups, Romans, Sabines and Etruscans, who together made up the population of early Rome.[95]

According to Varro the tribes were local divisions (*LL* 5.55). This can be reconciled with the ethnic theory by connecting the Ramnes with the Palatine (where Romulus founded his settlement), the Tities with the Quirinal (the 'Sabine' hill), and the Luceres with the Caelian, which had Etruscan associations (cf. below, p. 134).[96] But these particular locations are arbitrary, and on any balanced view the local character of the tribes would seem to tell against an ethnic interpretation. As a matter of fact no source explicitly states that the tribes were ethnic units, or even that the Ramnes were the followers of Romulus, the Tities of Titus Tatius, and the Luceres of Lucumo (which is not necessarily the same thing). The only partial exception is Florus (2.6.1), but he has no independent authority and is merely offering us an inference of his own. It is, admittedly, an easy inference, but when we remember that the basis for it is no more than the supposed derivation of the names of the tribes from mythical heroes, it becomes clear how flimsy the whole construction is.

Modern research is rightly sceptical of attempts to interpret archaic social divisions in terms of 'natural' or pre-existing kinship groups, and has established that they tend to be artificial creations characteristic of organised states.[97] To this extent the traditional account of the founding of the tribes by Romulus is closer to the truth than nineteenth-century ethnic theories. If there is any reality in the traditional scheme which makes the tribes the basis of the curiae and of the army, we have no alternative but to accept that all

114

these institutions were interrelated and artificially instituted for political and administrative purposes. The idea that three different ethnic groups each formed ten curiae, and that the army consisted of equal units of Romans, Sabines and Etruscans, is absurd. The same objection can be raised against Dumézil's theory that the three tribes represent functional groups of priests, warriors and producers (see above, p. 77).

In later times the names of the three Romulean tribes survived because six of the cavalry centuries in the *comitia centuriata* were known as the 'earlier and later Ramnes, Tities, and Luceres' (*Ramnes priores, Ramnes posteriores, Tities priores*, etc.). This curious duplication was said to be the work of King Tarquinius Priscus, who increased the size of the cavalry, but was prevented from giving new names to the additional centuries by Attus Navius (on this extraordinary story see below, p. 252 and n. 40). Apart from the six cavalry centuries, we know of no other institution in the Republic that retained the names of the three Romulean tribes. We do not know whether later Romans were able to name the tribe to which they belonged, even if they knew their curia, since it is equally uncertain whether they knew which curiae belonged to which tribe. This is just one of many puzzling questions about the curiae, to which we may now turn.

As has been pointed out, the thirty curiae were subdivisions of the three tribes, ten to each tribe. But unlike the tribes, the curiae retained certain residual functions in the public life of the Roman Republic. They formed the constituent units of an assembly, the *comitia curiata*, which met to pass the law conferring *imperium* (the right of command) on the senior magistrates (the *lex curiata de imperio*), and for other formal purposes, such as witnessing adoptions and wills (although this archaic method of making a will had become obsolete by the late Republic). These assemblies had a purely formal function, and by the late Republic the curiae were each represented by a single lictor (attendant).[98]

The curiae also played a part in the religious life of the state. Certain annual festivals, in particular the Fornacalia in February and the Fordicidia (15 April), were celebrated by the curiae. The last day of the Fornacalia, the 17 February, was called the Quirinalia, but was popularly known as the 'feast of fools', because all the curiae met together on that day, and those who did not know which curia they belonged to were able to take part (Ovid, *Fasti* 2.531–2). This tradition indicates that in classical times membership of a curia had little significance for most citizens; but it also implies that in theory the curiae comprised the entire citizen body, and that every Roman citizen was deemed to belong to a curia, even if he did not know which it was.

This inference helps to answer the first question we need to ask about the curiae: whether they included the whole community, or only a part of it. The evidence we have is admittedly sparse, but it offers little serious support for the view that the curiae were confined to patricians. This patrician theory is another way of saying that the patricians were the original citizens; if the military and political organization of early Rome depended on the tribes and curiae, it follows that civic rights and obligations, the functions of citizenship, were restricted to members of the curiae. This theory, it must be conceded, is backed by the authority of both Niebuhr and Mommsen;[99] nevertheless, there is precious little support for it in the sources.

Membership of the curiae depended on *gentile* affiliation. That is to say, one belonged to a given curia by virtue of having been born into a given *gens*. But this does not mean that one had to be a patrician. Admittedly, some scholars maintain that the *gentes* were exclusively patrician and that only patricians had *gentes*, but this theory is probably mistaken (see above, p. 84); in any case it still would not follow that the curiae were exclusively patrician, because there is no evidence that Romans who did not belong to *gentes*, if indeed such people existed, could not belong to curiae.

Each curia had a leader with the title *curio*, who had to be over 50 years of age and held office for life. One of these leaders was chosen as head of all the curiae, the *curio maximus*. In the early Republic this post was always held by a patrician, which is not surprising; but in 209 BC a plebeian *curio maximus* was elected, which means that the curiae included plebeians in the third century, and probably always had.

What kind of groups were the curiae? It seems virtually certain, as we have seen, that the division of the people into curiae was based on birth: one entered a curia by being born into it. This conclusion emerges from the fact that specified *gentes* belonged to specified curiae, and from the definition given by the antiquarian Laelius Felix (*ap.* Gellius, *N.A.* 15.27), who described the curiae as *genera hominum* ('kinds of men'). There has been much discussion of the meaning of this phrase, but since *genus* means a natural category, and since Laelius Felix contrasted the *comitia curiata*, based on 'kinds of men', with the *comitia centuriata*, based on wealth and status, and the *comitia tributa*, based on residence, there is no realistic alternative to interpreting the phrase as meaning that the curiae were groups whose membership was determined by birth.

It does not follow from this, however, that the curiate organisation was based on kinship. Although the members of a clan were united by real or supposed kinship, there is no evidence that the several clans grouped within a given curia, still less those grouped within the curiae of a given tribe, believed themselves to be kinsmen. It is still possible that they did, but the nearest thing to evidence is the fact that the word curia is translated in Greek sources (e.g. Dion. Hal. 2.7.3) as φρατρία (= 'brotherhood'), an archaic Greek social group, but this is hardly conclusive, especially as it is not even certain that the brotherhoods were based on kinship.[100]

The word curia is also used to signify a building where meetings took place. The Curia Hostilia, for instance, was the earliest senate house, later replaced under Caesar by the Curia Julia. The use of the same word for a division of the people and a meeting place perhaps supports the traditional etymology from *co-viria* (i.e. a gathering of men).[101] There is some evidence, moreover, that each of the thirty curiae had its own meeting hall, and was associated with a particular locality in the city. A reference in Pliny the Elder (*n.h.* 18.8) to purification of boundaries at the Fornacalia may indicate that the curiae were local divisions with defined territories (cf. Dion. Hal. 2.7.4). This need not conflict with our earlier conclusion that the curiae were divisions of the people with hereditary membership; it simply suggests that when the curiae were created the families resident in various localities were grouped together to form curiae (and the curiae themselves grouped to form local tribes).

We might well imagine that in the course of time the growth and mobility of the population would tend to dissolve the connection between residence and membership of a curia. The names of the curiae, of which eight are known, offer little assistance: some appear to be associated with particular places (Veliensis, Foriensis), others to be clan names (cf. Dion. Hal. 2.47.4; Plutarch, *Rom.* 20.3), though if so the clans in question are very obscure ones (Titia, Faucia, Velitia, Acculeia), while others are frankly mysterious (Tifata, Rapta). The fact that one of the curiae was called Rapta perhaps gave rise to the naive tradition that the curiae were named after thirty of the Sabine women raped by Romulus and his men.[102]

The important points to emerge from this survey are as follows:

(1) The three tribes and thirty curiae were once a vital element of Rome's political and military organisation. In the historical period residual traces of this original system survived in religious practice, in the formalities of the *comitia curiata* and in fossilised relics such as the six cavalry centuries. We have here a good illustration of the characteristic Roman habit of combining innovation and conservatism, by which new institutions, instead of replacing old ones, were simply grafted on to the existing structure. The old forms were not abolished, but continued to exist alongside the new ones in a fossilised and redundant form (cf. above, pp. 24 f.).

(2) The three tribes and thirty curiae were artificial units deliberately instituted for administrative and political purposes. Tradition implicitly recognises this fact when it attributes the tribes and curiae to Romulus. They cannot have come into being before the foundation of the city-state; indeed, the formation of the city-state coincides with the introduction of the tribes and curiae. If this is correct, we can date them to around the middle of the seventh century BC.

An important point is that the complex and regular structure of tribes and curiae appears to be unique to Rome. Although we know of curiae in other Latin communities, and of something similar at Iguvium in Umbria,[103] there is no known parallel in ancient Italy for the threefold tribal division, and its curial subdivisions, which we find in Rome. In particular it seems that there was no equivalent to the Roman tribes in the Etruscan cities, while in Umbria, where the Iguvine Tables offer us an obscure but important glimpse of the religious organisation of the city of Iguvium, the term *trifu* (= Latin *tribus*) refers to the whole community not to a part of it. The *trifu*, it seems, is a single community envisaged as a division of the wider (Umbrian) ethnic group.[104]

In Rome, by contrast, the city itself was artificially divided into tribes. This distinction is exactly parallel to that found in the Greek world between polis (city-state) communities and *ethne* ('ethnic states'). Recent studies have shown that tribal divisions are characteristic of *poleis* but not of *ethne*, and are a product of the 'archaic rationality' that polis organisation represents.[105] The conclusion is inescapable: in the seventh century BC Rome, perhaps alone among the native communities of central Italy, began to take on some of the features of the Greek *polis*.

5

TRADITIONAL HISTORY: KINGS, QUEENS, EVENTS AND DATES

1 THE SEVEN KINGS

Early Rome was ruled by kings. Of that there can be no doubt.[1] But when it comes to reconstructing the history of the regal period, all we can be certain of is that much of our information is legendary. Traditionally there were seven kings, some of whom are probably historical, at least in the sense that men named Numa Pompilius, Tullus Hostilius, and so on, may indeed have ruled at Rome. But that does not take us very far (and is not certain in any case).[2] Paradoxically, some of the actions for which they were supposedly responsible are more easily authenticated than the kings themselves. For example, although Romulus is legendary, institutions attributed to him can be shown to be historical and to date back to the early regal period. This is simply another way of saying that information about institutions and structures is more reliable than that dealing with individual persons and events. This was the principle behind Mommsen's account of early Rome, which dealt at length with the 'regal constitution', but made no reference to the individual kings. Mommsen's principle remains valid to this day, and is too readily forgotten by those scholars who are determined, at almost any cost, to show that the kings were historical figures.

It is clear enough that the earliest kings of Rome are mythical or semi-mythical persons. The first king, Romulus (traditionally 753–717 BC), probably never existed. His name appears to be a crude eponym formed from the name of the city; it has the form of an adjective, and means simply 'Roman'. His biography is a complex mixture of legend and folk-tale, interspersed with antiquarian speculation and political propaganda. The principal elements of the story, after the founding of the city, are the affair of the Sabines, leading to the joint rule of Romulus and Titus Tatius, victorious wars against Caenina, Fidenae and Veii, and the creation of the earliest institutions of the Roman state.

The successors of Romulus, Numa Pompilius (716–674 BC) and Tullus Hostilius (673–642 BC), are little more than contrasting stereotypes, the one pacific and devout, the other warlike and ferocious. These two may conceivably be historical,[3] although the surviving accounts of their reigns are a mixture of legend and conscious antiquarian reconstruction. Tradition credited Numa with all the major religious institutions of the state, including the calendar and the priesthoods. The central episode in the saga of Tullus Hostilius was the war against Alba Longa. This war provided the setting for the legend of Horatius, one of the most famous of all Roman stories. Horatius was the victorious survivor of the battle between the Horatii and the Curiatii, two sets of triplets who fought as champions on behalf of Rome and Alba Longa (respectively – although Livy says that there was some uncertainty about this). On his triumphant return to the city, Horatius was met at the gate by his sister, who had been betrothed to one of the Curiatii. When she shed tears on learning of their fate, Horatius killed her in a fit of rage.[4] The war itself, which led to the conquest of Alba Longa and its territory, is historical in the sense that the region of the Alban Hills became part of Roman territory at some point in the regal period. For all we know, this could have been accomplished by a king named Tullus Hostilius.

The fourth and fifth kings, Ancus Marcius (641–617 BC) and L. Tarquinius Priscus (616–578 BC), are more rounded, and perhaps more historical, figures than their predecessors. Ancus was of Sabine origin, and a grandson (on his mother's side) of Numa. He was celebrated by tradition for building the first bridge across the Tiber (the Pons Sublicius), for extending Roman territory as far as the coast and for the foundation of Ostia at the mouth of the river. The Romans of later times remembered him as a popular and beneficent ruler; Ennius and Lucretius called him 'Ancus the Good'.[5] His successor, L. Tarquinius Priscus, was of part-Etruscan origin, and enjoyed a successful reign as a warrior, constitutional innovator and civic benefactor. He increased the size of the Senate and the cavalry, and instituted games and public entertainments. His military victories were won over the Sabines, the 'Ancient Latins', and, if we believe Dionysius of Halicarnassus, the Etruscans.

The sixth king, Servius Tullius (578–534 BC), is the most complex and enigmatic of them all. The widely differing accounts of his origins and background – in short, of who he was – form only one part of the puzzle. The manner in which he obtained the throne, and the nature of the far-reaching reforms he then instituted, are equally problematic. There is no doubt, however, that the achievements attributed to him – the reorganisation of the citizen body, the construction of temples, public buildings and fortifications, and important initiatives in international affairs – have a firm historical basis and can in some cases be directly confirmed by independent evidence. Another point is that the nature of the kingship changed under Servius Tullius, who did not (unlike his predecessors) obtain the throne in a regular manner, but relied on popular support and became not so much a king as a kind of proto-republican magistrate (see further below, p. 235).

The last king, L. Tarquinius Superbus (Tarquin the Proud, 534–509 BC), was a tyrant pure and simple. The son of the elder Tarquin, he seized the throne by force after murdering his father-in-law Servius. He was cruel and capricious, but also flamboyant and successful. Under his rule, Rome became the dominant power in central Italy, and its prosperity was reflected in the monumental development of the city. The crowning achievement of Tarquin's reign was the construction of the great temple of Capitoline Jupiter, one of the largest and most impressive structures in the Mediterranean world at that time. Just as the temple was completed, but before he had a chance to dedicate it, Tarquin was expelled from the city by a group of aristocrats who set up a republic in his place.

2 THE CHRONOLOGY OF THE REGAL PERIOD: GENERAL

The first step in any attempt to check the historical credentials of this traditional narrative must be to compare it with the archaeological record. In doing so one is immediately struck by an apparent discrepancy in the chronology. Tradition makes the regal period last for nearly two and a half centuries, stretching back from the fall of Tarquin to the foundation of the city in 754/3 BC. But, as we have seen, the archaeological evidence suggests that the formation of the city-state occurred in the later part of the seventh century. There are two ways of resolving this difficulty. The first is to shorten the reigns of the kings, and to suppose that they ruled for around 120 years altogether instead of 240. The alternative is to retain the traditional chronology and to split the regal period in half: on this view the earlier kings would belong to the pre-urban phase, and the dramatic transformation of the community in the later seventh century would coincide with the arrival of the Tarquins.

Perhaps surprisingly, the majority of modern experts opt for the second of these alternatives. Almost all recent accounts of early Rome either state or imply (or take it for granted) that the accession of Tarquinius Priscus coincided with a major break in the historical development of regal Rome. I say surprisingly because no such break is recorded in the sources (although scholars frequently assert the contrary), and because if one thing is certain about the regal period, it is that the traditional chronology is historically impossible. It seems hardly necessary to state that an aggregate of 244 years for seven kings is without historical parallel and cannot be taken seriously.[6]

On any rational view the Roman king-list must be adjusted in one of two ways. Either we must suppose that there were more than seven kings, or we must shorten the chronology. Indeed there are good reasons for doing both; as we shall see, the canonical list of seven kings is almost certainly incomplete, and the simplest way to resolve the conflict between the tradition and the archaeological record is to date all the historical developments of the regal period, including the kings themselves (if they are authentic), in the period between c. 625 and c. 500 BC.

But this revision goes against the prevailing current of modern scholarly opinion, which inclines to accept the traditional chronology, and to assume that the accession of Tarquinius Priscus marked an important turning-point in the history of the regal period. This notion needs further discussion, and the contrary view being presented here requires a detailed defence. In modern studies the rise of the Tarquin dynasty is presented in a number of different ways. Some experts regard it as the beginning of the historical age of Rome, and consign the earlier period to legend.[7] Others stress the primitive character of the preceding phase, and contrast it with the prosperous and sophisticated urban culture introduced by the Tarquins: this view is summed up in the now rather hackneyed description of sixth-century Rome as 'la grande Roma dei Tarquini'.[8] A third strand in contemporary scholarship places heavy emphasis on ethnicity: on this view the accession of Tarquinius Priscus represents the end of a 'Latino-Sabine' period, and the start of an Etruscan phase.[9]

These three ways of defining the issue are not mutually exclusive; on the contrary, they are frequently combined, and most modern accounts contain aspects of all three. It is widely believed that the Tarquins ushered in a period of Etruscan rule, and that for a time Rome became an 'Etruscan city'. On this view it was the Etruscans who were responsible for all the political, economic and cultural changes that Rome underwent during the last century of the monarchy; it was the Etruscans, in short, who made Rome into a city. This Etruscan hypothesis can be found, in one form or another, in virtually every recent book or article on the archaic age of Rome.[10] In the opinion of the present writer, however, it has no warrant either in the written sources or in the archaeological record, and is one of the most pernicious errors currently obscuring the study of archaic Rome.

3 THE CHRONOLOGY OF THE REGAL PERIOD: THE TARQUIN DYNASTY

We may begin by observing that the main support for this imposing construction is the fact that the transformation of the city which archaeology reveals in the later years of the seventh century BC coincides with the traditional date for the accession of Tarquinius Priscus. Remove this chronological prop, and the whole edifice collapses. Yet we have already seen that the conventional dates of the kings are unacceptable as they stand. Moreover, there are particular reasons for questioning the traditional chronology of the Tarquin dynasty, especially the fact that the last king, Tarquinius Superbus, is presented as the son of Tarquinius Priscus. This is simply impossible on the traditional chronology, as a brief examination of the story will show.

Priscus was a mature adult when he obtained the throne in 616 BC. We are therefore asked to believe that he was born some 150 years before the death of his son in 495. Since Priscus died in 578 BC, his son Superbus must have been at least 80 years old when he fought in the battle of Lake Regillus

(499 or 496 BC). That is improbable enough; what makes the whole saga impossible is that Superbus' mother, Tanaquil, had accompanied the elder Tarquin to Rome, and was therefore a grown woman before 616 BC. These difficulties were known to our sources, particularly to Dionysius of Halicarnassus, who devotes two chapters to exposing the absurdities of the traditional story (4.6–7).

Naturally there was no lack of ingenious attempts to get around the problem. Some historians (quoted by Dionysius 4.7.4) suggested that Tarquinius Superbus (and his brother Arruns) were the sons of a second wife whom Priscus had married late in life (in spite of the well-established tradition that Tanaquil was still alive at the time of her husband's death, and played a crucial role in subsequent events). Dionysius himself preferred to follow the second-century annalist, L. Calpurnius Piso, who suggested that Tarquinius Superbus was in fact the grandson, not the son, of Tarquinius Priscus, and many modern scholars have accepted this modified version.[11] But Piso's solution is a transparent rationalisation which goes against the authority of the oldest tradition (including Fabius Pictor, fr. 7b Jac.) and creates all kinds of further difficulties.[12]

The original account of the Tarquin dynasty (as presented by Fabius Pictor) can be represented by a family tree:

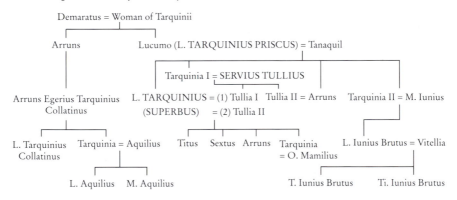

Figure 14 The Tarquin dynasty.

There is nothing impossible about the relationships indicated in this family tree. Admittedly the marriages of the sons of the elder Tarquin are incestuous, but the marriage of close kin is so common in royal families (often in breach of the rules applying in the societies over which they rule) that it scarcely constitutes a problem.[13] In any event our main concern here is chronology. The family tree makes good sense in terms of its own internal chronology, but becomes nonsensical if the reigns of its three kings are extended to cover a period of 107 years – i.e. 38 (Priscus) + 44 (Ser. Tullius) + 25 (Superbus) – figures which are fairly implausible in any case.

An obvious answer to the puzzle would be that their reigns were shorter, and that the dynasty came to power, not in the later seventh century BC, but at some time in the sixth – let us say between 570 and 550. This is a simple solution, and I think it is probably right. The matter is complicated, however, by the tradition that Tarquinius Priscus was the son of Demaratus, a Corinthian aristocrat who had migrated to Tarquinii in order to escape the tyranny of Cypselus. The generally accepted date for Cypselus' *coup d'état* at Corinth is 657 BC, which fits the traditional Roman chronology precisely, but would not be compatible with the revised dating proposed above.

It must be said, however, that the date of the Cypselid tyranny is far from secure. Scholars such as Julius Beloch and Edouard Will have made a strong case for lowering the date of Cypselus' seizure of power to *c.* 620 (Will) or 610 BC (Beloch).[14] A simple solution might therefore seem to present itself: by adopting the low chronology for Cypselus we should be able to bring the accession of Tarquinius Priscus down to the sixth century.

But this is probably not the answer. The tradition that Tarquin was the son of Demaratus was certainly established early. It is referred to by Polybius (6.11a.7), and was probably in Fabius Pictor. Whether it is historically true, however, is another matter. The migration of Demaratus may well be authentic, at least in a symbolic sense. Our sources use the story to explain the spread of Greek culture in Etruria. Demaratus is said to have brought with him a large body of dependants, who included skilled craftsmen: hence the strong Greek (and especially Corinthian) influence on Etruscan art. Tacitus (almost certainly drawing upon the researches of the emperor Claudius) says that Demaratus taught the Etruscans the art of writing (*Annals* 11.14); and Cicero believed that Greek culture was brought to Rome by Tarquin, who had been given a Greek education by his father (*Rep.* 2.34).

The general picture is borne out by archaeological evidence which confirms the decisive importance of Corinthian influence on Etruscan civilisation during the second half of the seventh century. The story may indeed be literally true, in the sense that Corinthian craftsmen did live and work in the centres of southern Etruria at this time;[15] and in the conditions of the archaic period it is entirely credible that an aristocratic émigré and his retinue could take up residence in a foreign community without loss of social position.[16]

Demaratus himself may well be historical; but the idea that he fathered a king of Rome is quite another matter. To all appearances this is a secondary extension of the tradition. The story of Demaratus, if true, will have been preserved in Greek sources (or Etruscan ones, but that is far less probable) which are unlikely to have been interested in Rome. How it came to be connected with Rome is a matter for conjecture; but the most probable answer is that the connection arose in the late fourth century BC, when Roman contacts with the Greeks of Magna Graecia created a new interest in the origins and early history of the city. As Gabba has shown, this was the crucial period for the formation of the Roman historical tradition, which was promoted by the growing interest in Rome among the Greeks.[17] In particular, there is evidence that Greek intellectuals sought to explain the development of Roman culture and institutions as the result of early contacts with the Greeks. The most striking example is the story that Numa, the founder of Roman cult, was a pupil of Pythagoras. As it happens, we can trace the roots of this tradition back to the late fourth-century thinker Aristoxenus of Tarentum, who is said to have written that Pythagoras' pupils included Romans (fr. 17 Wehrli).

It was probably also at this time that someone first thought of making Romulus the son or grandson of Aeneas; and the story that the Twelve Tables were modelled directly on the laws of Solon may have arisen in the same milieu. These stories are all artificial and secondary attempts to reify, or indeed to personify, complex cultural interactions that in some cases can be shown to be based on genuine fact. The undoubtedly historical influence of Greek, especially Corinthian, ideas on the material culture of southern Etruria and Latium during the orientalising period was thus connected directly with the migration of Demaratus and his followers to Tarquinii. What better way of bringing Rome into the picture than making the king who had come from that very city the son of Demaratus?

Problems arose, however, when Roman historians and antiquarians in the second century BC began to examine the chronological implications of these pleasing anecdotes. The work of Hellenistic chronographers had made this possible, and the discrepancies that emerged were problematic, not to say embarrassing. The discovery that several centuries separated Romulus from Aeneas made it necessary to fabricate the dynasty of Alban kings. On the other hand, the realisation that Numa lived two centuries before his alleged teacher Pythagoras could not be resolved so easily. This tradition, which was still officially accepted in Rome in 181 BC (Livy 40.29.9–14), was eventually abandoned.[18]

As for Demaratus and Tarquin, it is probable that Greek chronographers had canonised the 'long' chronology for the Cypselids, and had firmly placed the start of the Corinthian tyranny in O1.30.4 (= 657 BC).[19] No doubt this was what caused the Roman historians to assign more than 100 years to the Tarquin dynasty, and to give such inordinately long reigns to the last three kings. Unfortunately, the stretching of the absolute chronology played havoc with the relative dating of episodes within the saga; and it was in response to this problem that Piso proposed the solution that won the approval of Dionysius of Halicarnassus and his modern followers – that Tarquinius Superbus was the grandson, not the son, of Tarquinius Priscus. In fact this revision of the traditional story deserves no more credence than the dynasty of the Alban kings, and should be consigned to the same dustbin.

We may sum up by observing that the chronology of the surviving accounts is the product of artificial and secondary manipulation. The tradition itself presupposes a shorter chronology: the rule of the Tarquins, which ended in 509, lasted for no more than two generations and therefore began around 570 BC at the earliest. It is possible, indeed probable, that the tradition itself is unreliable, and that the history of the later regal period was more complex and disturbed than our sources allow; but that is another matter, to be discussed shortly. What is important for the present purpose is that the supposedly 'traditional' date of 616 BC for the accession of the elder Tarquin deserves no credence whatsoever; and that the much vaunted coincidence with developments in the archaeological record is a mare's nest.

The chief advantage of placing the start of the Tarquin dynasty between 570 and 550 BC is that it leaves room for the earlier kings and their achievements within the general framework of the development of the city. The events and innovations associated with these earlier kings are real enough, but good sense requires that they be dated to the period after c. 625 BC. In the first place they presuppose an ordered system of social and political institutions based on artificial divisions of the people into tribes and curiae (see further above, p. 114). This was, traditionally, the work of Romulus. Second, a carefully articulated programme of religious cults, supervised by differentiated priestly authorities and centred on an organised public calendar, is attributed to Numa. Third, the military conquests of Tullus Hostilius and Ancus Marcius presuppose the existence of a defined territory and the formation of an effective communal army. These institutional, religious and military developments had undoubtedly taken place before the end of the regal period. On the other hand they cannot be earlier than the formation of Rome as an organised city-state; indeed they themselves were an integral part of that formative process.

Insofar as they are authentic, then, the accomplishments of the earliest kings belong to the historical period of the city-state, not to the pre-urban epoch. The same applies to the kings themselves, if they are historical persons. Since we have established that Rome first emerged as a city-state in the last decades of the seventh century BC, it follows that the early kings, if historical, must be placed in the period between c. 625 and c. 570 BC.[20]

A small point, but one that is perhaps worth mentioning, is that the revised dating appears to find some support in the archaeological evidence. The first building on the site of the Regia, ascribed by tradition to Numa, dates from the last decades of the seventh century;[21] while traces of an archaic building on the north side of the Comitium, dating from the beginning of the sixth century, have been identified as belonging to the Curia Hostilia, which was traditionally built by Tullus Hostilius.[22] These instances may appear to confirm that Numa and Tullus were ruling in the late seventh and early sixth centuries BC respectively; but they should not be pressed too hard. As a religious building the Regia was inevitably connected with Numa; the case of the Curia Hostilia deserves serious attention, however, and is no worse than other arguments of this nature (e.g. the use of the Sant'Omobono temple to 'confirm' the date of Servius Tullius).

4 THE TARQUINS: A NEW PHASE OF ROMAN HISTORY?

We have already commented on the conventional view that the regal period falls into two distinct parts, the break coming with the accession of Tarquinius Priscus. The aim of the present section is to demonstrate that this convention is entirely modern, and that in spite of frequent assertions to the contrary it has no support from the ancient sources.

It should be noted, first, that Tarquinius Priscus succeeded to the throne in a legal and regular manner. The assertion of some historians that he was an usurper[23] is simply wrong. Ancus Marcius died in his bed (the only king other than Numa to do so), and Tarquin was appointed in his place after the performance of all due formalities – *interregnum*, popular vote, *lex curiata*, inauguration.[24] Whether any of this is historical does not matter; the question at issue is how tradition presents it. The constitutional nature of Tarquin's position is highlighted by the contrast with his successors, who *were* usurpers. Servius Tullius was the best loved of all the kings, so it is rather remarkable that the sources unanimously affirm (albeit not without embarrassment) that he seized the throne illegally. Cicero and Livy say, in virtually identical words, that he was *the first* to rule without a vote from the people,[25] thus reinforcing the point that his predecessor had been properly elected. This was used against Servius by the younger Tarquin, in Livy's account:

> Tarquinius . . . abused the king . . . who, after the shameful death of his own father, Tarquinius Priscus, had seized the power; there had been no observation of the interregnum, *as on former occasions*; there had been no election held; not by the votes of the people had sovereignty come to him, not with the confirmation of the Fathers, but by a woman's gift.[26]

Tarquin's harangue is hypocritical, to be sure, but that does not detract from the force of the point he has to make. We may conclude that the sources do not support the idea that the first Tarquin seized power and introduced a new type of monarchy. Rather, they make it quite clear that the break with tradition came, not with Tarquin, but with Servius Tullius.

The traditional narratives are equally unaware that the elder Tarquin made a decisive contribution to the urban development of Rome, although modern scholars are apt to assert that this alleged aspect of his activity is 'confirmed' by archaeological evidence. In describing the growth and development of the city the sources do not single out any one king. Quite the reverse: the Roman tradition insisted that it developed gradually, and that all the kings contributed to it. All of them were, one after another, founders of parts of the city, as Livy pointed out (above, p. 59).

As for the Tarquins, it is important to note that the same building and engineering operations are ascribed to both of them. Both Priscus and Superbus are said to have constructed sewers, viewing stands for the circus, and the temple of Jupiter Optimus Maximus on the Capitol. The most likely explanation for such duplications is that the original tradition attributed these works simply to a king Tarquinius. Since there were two kings of that name, historians assigned the works to one or the other, with the result that in the synthetic annalistic vulgate they came to be associated with both of them. Where the duplication was obvious, historians proposed a compromise: the elder Tarquin drew up the plans, or laid the foundations (or both), and his younger namesake completed the task.

This compromise solution has its supporters even today, but is clearly unsatisfactory. That the duplications (or 'doublets', as they are called) are artificial can be simply demonstrated by the example of the sewers. It is sufficient merely to quote the following passages:

> Tarquinius Priscus was carrying out the project (sc. the sewers) using the common people as labourers, and the only question was whether more hardship would be caused by the intensity of the work or by its duration. Since large numbers of citizens were seeking to escape from their exhaustion by committing suicide, the king devised a strange remedy, unheard of either before or since: he crucified the bodies of the dead, so that they might be looked upon by their fellow citizens and torn to pieces by birds and wild beasts.
>
> (Pliny, *n.h.* 36.107)

> Tarquinius Superbus forced the people to construct sewers; and when this hardship caused many to hang themselves, he ordered their bodies to be crucified.
>
> (Cassius Hemina fr. 15 P)

The conclusion is obvious: the same story has been attached to two different Tarquins (QED).

A similar result emerges from examination of the traditions surrounding the Capitoline temple. The main sources resort to the usual compromise: Tarquinius Priscus vowed the temple and began its construction, and his son continued it, although he was deposed before it was fully complete. It was dedicated at the start of the Republic by one of the first consuls, M. Horatius. Archaeological evidence confirms a date at the end of the sixth century, and the association of the temple with M. Horatius, otherwise a wholly obscure figure, seems genuine; Horatius' name was probably inscribed above the portico.[27] These details prove that Tarquinius Superbus was involved in the building of the temple; but it is doubtful if his father had anything to do with it.

In the first place there is unquestionably a doublet in the accounts of how the building was financed. Valerius Antias wrote that it was paid for out of the spoils of Apiolae, a town captured by Tarquinius Priscus, whereas other texts say that the booty came from Pometia, taken by Tarquinius Superbus.[28] Apiolae is simply a Greek translation of Pometia, and given the context (and the fact that Apiolae is otherwise unknown) it is virtually certain that the two places are one and the same. One of the two versions must be rejected, and in view of the evidence set out in the preceding paragraph it is clearly Priscus who must give way.

There are many other reasons for dismissing the alleged connection of the temple with Priscus, not least the enormous interval that elapsed between his death and the beginning of the Republic, when the building was finished. Even on the revised chronology suggested earlier in this chapter, a period of more than thirty years is implied, which seems excessive for the construction of a temple made largely of wood, bricks and terracotta. The temple was large, but it was no Gothic cathedral. The argument that the project was temporarily abandoned during the reign of Servius Tullius is a desperate one, requiring as it does the rejection of Tacitus' clear statement in favour of the silence of other sources.[29] It may be that Tacitus (or his source) simply assumed, without any explicit evidence, that work continued under Servius Tullius; even so, we are not entitled to deduce from the silence of other sources that there was a definite tradition that work did *not* continue under Servius.

The matter is clinched by a story about the terracotta statues and decorations that went with the temple. This story has sometimes been used as evidence that Tarquinius Priscus was the real builder of the temple,[30] but in fact it proves the opposite. According to Varro (cited by Pliny, *n.h.* 35.157) the cult statue of Jupiter and a terracotta quadriga that adorned the roof of the temple were made by a Veientine master-craftsman named Vulca. Curiously enough, the text specifies that Vulca was commissioned by Tarquinius Priscus, but this must be a mistake. It is unthinkable that decades should elapse between the original order and the final delivery of the sculptures, and on the traditional chronology the sequence of events becomes absurd. In fact this is another doublet, since Plutarch's detailed account (*Publicola* 13) tells us that the Veientine sculptors (presumably including Vulca, though he is not named) were commissioned by Tarquinius Superbus, and that they delivered the terracottas at the beginning of the Republic. It goes without saying that Plutarch's version is the only one that makes sense, and must be preferred to Varro's.[31]

Once it is admitted that Tarquinius Priscus had little or (more probably) nothing to do with the Capitoline temple, the argument that he was traditionally seen as the great monumental builder of the city collapses. As they stand, the sources do not give prominence to this aspect of his activities. Cicero, our oldest surviving source for the reign of Priscus (his account in *de republica* 2.35–6 is preserved in its entirety), makes no reference whatever to buildings, apart from the vow of the Capitoline temple (which, however, was built by the younger Tarquin, using the spoils of Pometia, in Cicero's version – *Rep.* 2.44). It is no good objecting that in the *de republica* Cicero is only interested in the constitution and not in the physical development of the city; this is controverted by e.g. 2.33, the addition of the Caelian and Aventine by Ancus Marcius, and by the reference just cited to the building of the Capitol. It is to be noted that in the tradition generally Tarquin the Elder is the only king apart from Numa who is not credited with an enlargement of the city boundary.[32]

In Livy and Dionysius the most important facts about Tarquinius were his victorious campaigns against the Latins, Sabines and Etruscans, and his reform of the Senate and the cavalry, both of which were doubled in size. His public works are mentioned only in passing. One detail, however, has received much attention from modern historians. This is the brief notice that he made land around the Forum available for private dwellings, and constructed shops and porticoes.[33] This is sometimes taken to mean that Tarquin virtually replanned the city, but it quite evidently means nothing of the kind. In particular, the texts do not say that Tarquin laid out the Forum; rather, they presuppose the existence of the Forum, to which he made additions and improvements. If Livy and Dionysius had wanted to say that he created the first Forum, they would have done so. Once again it is necessary to stress that the point here is to establish what the tradition has to say, not to reconstruct what really happened.

The literary tradition, then, does not give any grounds for believing that the accession of Tarquinius Priscus marked the beginning of a new phase in the history of Rome, or that major urban developments took place under his reign. Both ideas are modern interpretations based on an artificial and probably misguided combination of literary and archaeological data, reinforced by a third element to which modern historians attach great importance – namely, the fact that Tarquinius Priscus was an Etruscan. Underlying most modern accounts is the assumption that, while Latin and Sabine kings were acceptable, an Etruscan would have been beyond the pale; on this view Tarquin's accession can only have taken place as a result of some kind of upheaval, probably involving the use of armed force. Second, since it is universally supposed that Rome became urban as a consequence of becoming Etruscan, it is naturally tempting to identify this supposed 'etruscanisation' with the arrival of the Tarquins. It cannot be too strongly emphasised, however, that the prominence given to this racial factor in most recent accounts has no basis in the sources and reflects a distinctively modern type of prejudice. This issue will be addressed more fully in the next chapter.

5 WHO WAS SERVIUS TULLIUS?

As we have seen, the break, when it came, came with the sixth king, Servius Tullius. He more than any other transformed the city, both in its physical aspect and in its political organisation, and is sometimes regarded as a second founder. It is also clear, as we have seen, that he obtained the throne by means of an illegal seizure of power, something that our sources are unable to conceal, however much they tried to mitigate its implications.

But who was this man? The origins of Servius Tullius – his ancestry, birth and upbringing – form a major historiographical crux, not simply because the annalistic tradition contains a bewildering variety of discrepant versions, but because of the existence of a radical alternative, deriving from Etruscan sources, which presents a wholly different account of who he was and how he came to power. No study of early Rome can avoid a detailed analysis of this fascinating tangle.[34]

According to the native Roman tradition Servius Tullius was born a slave, and was brought up in the royal palace. That he was no ordinary boy, however, was soon revealed by a miraculous event. One day while he was sleeping, his head burst into flames, without any evident cause and without doing him any harm. From this time on he enjoyed the special protection and favour of King Tarquin and, more particularly, of Queen Tanaquil, who interpreted the miracle as a portent of his future greatness. When he grew up, Servius became Tarquin's most faithful lieutenant, holding military commands and other positions of responsibility (esp. Dion. Hal. 4.3), and eventually received the hand of his daughter in marriage. On Tarquin's death, Tanaquil arranged for Servius to win the throne.

Tarquin was assassinated, in a bizarre episode, by two hired killers acting on behalf of the sons of Ancus Marcius, who saw Servius Tullius as a threat to their own ambitions. All they managed to achieve, however, was the very result they had feared. Tanaquil ordered the wounded Tarquin to be taken into the palace, and although he soon died, she concealed the fact and announced to the crowd from an upstairs window that the king was recovering, and had appointed Servius Tullius to act in his place in the meantime. Servius then had the Marcii condemned to permanent exile and secured his own position; after a few days, during which the people became used to seeing Servius bearing all the marks of royalty, Tarquin's death was announced and Servius' first act as king was to supervise his funeral.

Our sources are agreed on the main points of this interesting narrative. The main problem concerns Servius' parentage. His mother was a slave named Ocresia (or Ocrisia) from Corniculum, who had been taken prisoner when her home town was defeated by Tarquin. The servile origin of Servius is acknowledged in all the sources and is the most important single fact about him. Some modern scholars argue that this story arose as a naive aetiological deduction from his first name (since Latin *servus* = 'slave').[35] But this is highly unlikely, for several reasons. In the first place, it would not have been necessary to invent an explanation for what was, in fact, an ordinary Roman *praenomen*. Servius was one of the fifteen or so *praenomina* regularly used by the upper classes; it was not one of the most common, but it is certainly attested, and was especially favoured by the patrician Sulpicii.[36] The emperor who succeeded Nero, for instance, was Servius Sulpicius Galba. No slave he.

On the other hand the name *is* connected etymologically with *servus*, and it is perfectly possible that it was once used of children of servile origin – for instance the sons of slave concubines. Other appellative names were probably used in the same way – e.g. Spurius for bastards, Quintus for the fifth child, Sextus for the sixth, and so on, even though in later times they lost their literal meaning and became simple proper names. It is more probable, therefore, that Servius Tullius was so called because he was (or was believed to be) of slave origin, rather than the other way round.

Second, the tradition that he was born in slavery was to the Romans both shameful and embarrassing. It offended their sense of propriety that one of their kings, indeed the most revered of them, should have carried this stigma – a point that was not lost on his rival Tarquinius Superbus (in Livy's account), or on later detractors of Rome. Mithridates, for instance, sneeringly observed that the kings of Rome had included *servos vernasque Tuscorum*, a clear reference to Servius Tullius.[37] It is therefore inconceivable that the Roman tradition would have invented a servile origin for a king whose name needed no special explanation in any case.

In fact the Romans were clearly embarrassed by the story, and tried to compensate for it – the most notable of their efforts being Livy's claim (1.39.5) that Ocresia was really an aristocratic lady who was saved from slavery by Tanaquil and instead permitted to live in the palace as her companion. An integral part of this version, which is also alluded to in other sources, is that Ocresia was the widow of a leading citizen of Corniculum who was killed in the war against Rome. Servius was the posthumous son of this nobleman, his mother having been pregnant at the time of her capture. It scarcely needs saying that this is a face-saving variant, which gives Servius a respectable pedigree and relieves him of the shame of having no father,[38] or of being the son of a slave woman and a client of the king, as in Cicero's account (*Rep.* 2.37; Plut., *Fort. Rom.* 10). Incidentally, Cicero adds the interesting information that Tarquin's fondness for Servius Tullius caused the inevitable rumours to circulate among the people.

Alongside these stories, which presuppose that Servius had a natural father (known or unknown), there was another version which maintained that his father was a god. According to this remarkable account, he was conceived when his slave mother was impregnated by a phallus which had appeared in the hearth of the palace. It was interpreted as a manifestation of either the household god (*lar familiaris*), or of the fire god, Vulcan. The motif of the phallus in the hearth, and more generally the sexual and procreative symbolism of fire, are characteristic features of ancient Italic myth, and recur in connection with Romulus, in an obscure variant recorded by Plutarch, and other legendary figures. For example Caeculus, the founder of Praeneste, was conceived when his mother was struck by a spark as she squatted by the fire.[39]

This is not the place to pursue the fascinating problems of Italian myth and religion that are raised by these stories. In the present context it is enough to notice that they belong to a well-known type of legend, widespread in time and space throughout the ancient Mediterranean and the Near East, that attributes supernatural origins not only to city-founders like Romulus, but also to founders of dynasties, such as Sargon, Cyrus and Ptolemy Soter, and to tyrants and usurpers, for example Cypselus, Agathocles and Hiero II.[40] These stories have complex psychological roots; but at a simple level it is evident that they serve to confer legitimacy on charismatic figures of obscure background who come 'from nowhere' to achieve positions of leadership. In a society where vertical mobility is discouraged and seen as a threat to traditional values, such myths have an important role in reinforcing existing hierarchies. In the case of Servius Tullius, the two strands in the native tradition have the same function. For a slave to become king is an outrage; but it becomes acceptable if it turns out (as in the rationalised version) that he was 'really' a prince all the time, or if he was the son of a god and enjoyed divine favour (as in the supernatural version).

We may now turn to the alternative Etruscan tradition. This is recorded by only one source, but one that deserves a great deal of respect, namely the scholar-emperor Claudius. It is not uncommon for politicians and statesmen to turn to the writing of history in their spare time or in retirement; indeed, one might say it happens all too often. But it is truly remarkable when a historian, who has devoted his life to the pursuit of scholarly research, finds himself thrust into a position of political power, as happened to Claudius on 24 January AD 41. This unexpected elevation gave Claudius unheard-of opportunities for the publication of his research. In AD 48 he urged the Senate to open its doors to men from Gaul; and in the course of his speech, he treated the senators to a learned digression on the history of archaic Rome:

> Once kings ruled this city; however, they did not pass it on to successors within their own families. Members of other families and even foreigners came to the throne, as Numa, coming from the Sabines, succeeded Romulus; he was a neighbour certainly, but at the same time he was a foreigner, as was Tarquinius Priscus who succeeded Ancus Marcius. Tarquinius, prevented from holding office in his own land because he was of impure blood – for he was the son of Demaratus of Corinth and his mother was from Tarquinii, a lady noble but poor, as she must have been if she needed to give her hand to such a husband – subsequently migrated to Rome and gained the throne. Between Tarquin and his son or grandson (for even this is disputed between writers) Servius Tullius intervened. If we follow our Roman sources, he was the son of Ocresia, a prisoner of war; if we follow Etruscan sources, he was once the most faithful companion of Caelius Vivenna and took part in all his adventures. Subsequently, driven out by a change of

fortune, he left Etruria with all the remnants of Caelius' army and occupied the Caelian hill, naming it thus after his former leader. Servius changed his name (for in Etruscan his name was Mastarna), and was called by the name I have used, and he obtained the throne to the greatest advantage of the state.

(The 'Table of Lyons', *ILS* 212.I.8–27)

The alternative tradition which Claudius refers to in the second half of this passage is otherwise completely unknown to us. His words imply, moreover, that he expected it to be unfamiliar to his audience of senators, even to those whose knowledge of early Roman history went beyond Livy. In short, Claudius was announcing a discovery. Like the true scholar he was, he could not resist putting forward a new idea, even when it was not required by his argument, still less by the occasion on which he was speaking.[41]

The prima-facie implication of Claudius' words is that he had found new evidence about Servius Tullius in Etruscan sources. Can we be more precise about these sources, and about the nature of the evidence they contained? First, we can be sure that Claudius was referring to written Etruscan sources. This is evident from the wording of the text. When 'our' sources are contrasted with 'Etruscan' sources (*si nostros sequimur, . . . si Tuscos*), the adjectives *nostros* and *Tuscos* evidently agree with *auctores* (= 'writers'), carried over from the earlier parenthesis.[42] It follows that the sources in question were literary works, either histories or antiquarian studies.

There is no way of knowing for certain whether these works were written in Etruscan, or whether they were by romanised Etruscans writing in Latin. The former possibility should certainly not be ruled out. Claudius himself may have been able to read Etruscan, but even if he could not, he was well acquainted with people who could.[43] It is possible, but far less likely, that his knowledge of the Etruscan tradition was second-hand, and based on references to Etruscan sources in the works of Roman historians or antiquarians. The main reason for excluding this possibility is that the Etruscan version was unknown to the mainstream annalistic tradition. It is not simply that Livy, Dionysius of Halicarnassus, and the other extant narratives contain no trace of it; it is also obvious that Claudius could not have written *si Tuscos (auctores sequimur)* if the Mastarna story had been in Fabius Pictor, say, or Valerius Antias.[44]

The Etruscan tradition reported by Claudius does contain some elements that were already known to Roman antiquarians, and his discourse seems to take account of this. In particular, he refers to Caelius Vivenna as someone who needed no introduction, and whose adventures would have been generally familiar. Claudius may have made the characteristic scholarly error of overestimating the erudition of his audience; but we know that antiquarians such as Varro and Verrius Flaccus had written about Caeles Vibenna (as he is more usually called) in connection with the Caelian hill and the Vicus

Tuscus (the 'Etruscan quarter' of Rome); Caeles is also mentioned by Dionysius of Halicarnassus.[45] Verrius Flaccus seems to have been the best informed of these scholars. He knew that Caeles Vibenna was one of two brothers, that they were from Vulci, and that they came to Rome in the time of the Tarquins (Varro and Dionysius had made Caeles Vibenna an ally of Romulus). Verrius may also have mentioned Mastarna, but this is based on an uncertain restoration of the fragmentary text.[46]

If Verrius Flaccus knew more than his predecessors, it was because he had access to Etruscan traditions. Verrius was a specialist on Etruscan matters, on which he had written a monograph;[47] and the information he gave about the Vibenna brothers, in so far as we can reconstruct it from the fragmentary entry in Festus, can be directly confirmed by Etruscan evidence.

The brothers Caeles and Aulus Vibenna were widely celebrated in Etruscan tradition.[48] They feature in legendary scenes depicted on funerary urns from Chiusi and on a bronze mirror from Bolsena (Figure 15). The name *Aules V(i)pinas* appears on a fifth-century red-figure cup by an Etruscan artist who imitated an Attic cup of the school of Duris; this may be evidence of some kind of hero-cult.[49] Even more remarkable is the bucchero vase from the Portonaccio sanctuary at Veii, inscribed *Avile Vipiiennas*. This object, now dated to the first half of the sixth century BC, was perhaps offered by Aulus Vibenna in person.[50]

But by far the most important Etruscan evidence comes from the François Tomb at Vulci. The wall paintings of this unique tomb, which are generally agreed to date from the second half of the fourth century BC, illustrate episodes from Greek mythology and Etruscan history, the one balancing the other (Figure 16).[51] The historical scene shows men armed with swords killing defenceless and unarmed opponents. The corresponding picture, on the opposite side of the chamber, presents a scene from the *Iliad*: the sacrifice of Trojan prisoners at the funeral of Patroclus. Some kind of symbolic parallel is evidently intended. The figures in both paintings are identified by having their names written beside them; and it is this fact that gives the historical painting its startling relevance to the present subject. The victorious warriors include Mastarna (written *Macstrna*) and the Vibenna brothers (*Avle* and *Caile Vipinas*), and one of the victims is named *Cneve Tarchunies Rumach* – that is, Gnaeus Tarquinius of Rome.

Certain features of the painting allow us to reconstruct the episode in a more precise way. Most of the figures are naked, though the victims have mantles loosely draped over them. One of them, however, named *Venthical* [. . .]*plsachs*, wears a breastplate; he is shown reaching vainly for a shield, as *Avle Vipinas* pulls his head back by the hair and plunges his sword into the side of his chest. The likely interpretation of these details is that the victims have been surprised while sleeping, and that *Venthical*, who wears a corslet and has arms to hand, had been keeping watch but had fatally nodded off.

As for the victors, all but one are naked. The exception is *Larth Ulthes*,

Figure 15 Etruscan mirror from Bolsena, showing the Vibenna brothers.

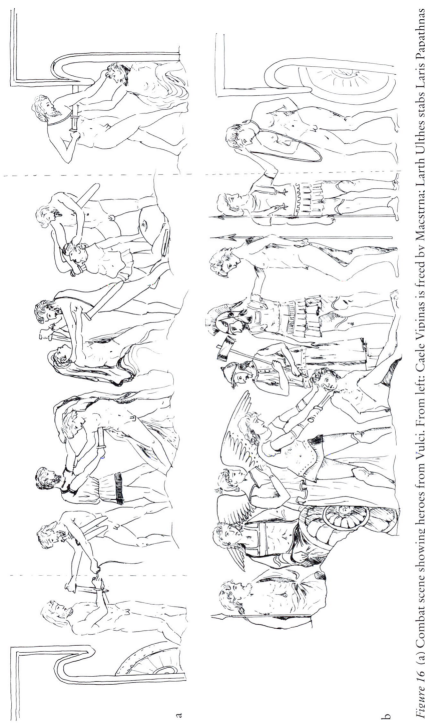
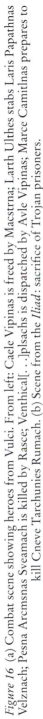

Figure 16 (a) Combat scene showing heroes from Vulci. From left: Caele Vipinas is freed by Macstrna; Larth Ulthes stabs Laris Papathnas Velznach; Pesna Arcmsnas Sveamach is killed by Rasce; Venthical[. . .]plsachs is dispatched by Avle Vipinas; Marce Camitlnas prepares to kill Cneve Tarchunies Rumach. (b) Scene from the *Iliad*: sacrifice of Trojan prisoners.

who wears a bordered tunic (and is shown in the act of stabbing *Laris Papathnas Velznach*). The fact that some of the figures are clothed is sufficient to undermine Coarelli's theory that the nakedness is a form of 'heroic nudity';[52] rather, Alföldi was right to argue that it is due to the special circumstances of the episode. The nature of these circumstances is revealed by the scene to the far left of the frieze, which shows *Macstrna* freeing *Caile Vipinas*. Alföldi's interpretation is that not only *Caile Vipinas*, but also his naked companions, *Macstrna*, *Avle Vipinas*, *Rasce*, and *Marce Camitlnas*, had all been taken prisoner, disarmed, stripped and bound; but *Larth Ulthes* has crept in to set them free, bringing with him an armful of swords, with which they are now killing their erstwhile captors.[53] Two details confirm this interpretation. First, *Macstrna* has two swords: one he uses to cut the rope binding *Caile Vipinas*' wrists; the other, which hangs around his neck, is clearly for his friend to use once he is free. The second relevant detail is that, in the corresponding scene on the opposite side of the chamber, the Trojan prisoners are shown naked, and their Greek captors are clothed and fully armed. This surely puts the issue beyond doubt.[54]

It seems evident that what is represented here is one of those adventures mentioned by Claudius, involving Caeles Vibenna and his faithful companion Mastarna. The fact that Mastarna is shown releasing Caeles Vibenna seems to emphasise the special friendship between them, and is a most remarkable confirmation of Claudius' words. This detail, in conjunction with all the other evidence, proves beyond doubt that Claudius was drawing, directly or indirectly, on a genuine Etruscan tradition.

Let us now move on from the specific episode to consider its general historical context. First, who or what do these groups of warriors represent? A conspicuous feature of the painting is that the defeated warriors are all identified with a word ending in -*ach* (or -*achs*) indicating their local or ethnic provenance. Thus *Cneve Tarchunies Rumach* is from Rome; *Laris Papathnas Velznach* probably from Volsinii, *Pesna Arcmsnas Sveamach* perhaps from Sovana. In the case of *Venthical* [. . .]*plsachs* the relevant part of the text is missing and his place of origin cannot be identified.[55] On the other hand, their victorious opponents are designated by personal names only, which probably means that they were well-known local heroes.[56] From the Vulcentane point of view, then, the picture shows 'our boys' getting the better of a group of foreign enemies.

One of the latter is a Tarquinius from Rome, which suggests strongly that the episode has some bearing on Roman history during the age of the Tarquins. Can we be more precise? Some historians maintain that the picture represents a victory of Vulci in a war against Rome and its allies; and others have even suggested that it illustrates the defeat and death of King Tarquin and his replacement by Mastarna. But these interpretations go way beyond the evidence and simply beg the question. Nothing in the picture indicates that *Cneve Tarchunies* was a king, and his first name, Gnaeus, suggests prima facie that he is not to be identified with either Tarquinius Priscus or Tarquinius Superbus, both of whom were called Lucius. On the other hand, we cannot exclude the possibility that other members of the Tarquin family ruled at Rome. Moreover, there is something of a question mark over the *praenomen* of the first Tarquin. According to Livy his name Lucius was a Latin version of his Etruscan name Lucumo. But we happen to know that *lucumo* (Etr. *lauchme*) was the Etruscan word for 'king', and there must be a suspicion that name and title have been confused. If his name was not in fact Lucius (or Lucumo), it must have been something else. In other words, it is theoretically possible that *Cneve Tarchunies* is none other than Tarquinius Priscus; but although some scholars seem to regard this identification as certain,[57] it should be noted that there is no positive evidence in its favour.

On the other hand, *Cneve Tarchunies* is the only one of the defeated group to have a beard; the others are beardless youths.[58] If, as many experts believe, the wearing of a beard is a sign of age and status, there is a case for seeing *Cneve Tarchunies* as the leader of the group. It does not follow, however, that he is the ruler of Rome or that he in any way represents the Roman state, still less that his companions are kings or leaders of states allied to Rome. *Tarchunies* could be a private adventurer or *condottiere*, operating with a personal following of armed dependants. The same goes for the victorious group, which other evidence suggests may well have been a private band of precisely this type. As far as the evidence of the painting goes, however, we can only make the point negatively: it does not necessarily show an episode from a war between Vulci and Rome, or between Vulci and a Roman-led coalition.

Finally, let us consider Mastarna-*Macstrna*. The biggest problem is his name. It is most unusual, indeed virtually unheard of, for anyone involved in the history of archaic Rome not to have the standard two names (*praenomen* and *nomen gentilicium*). In the tomb painting also *Macstrna* is unusual in this respect, although the victorious group includes another example, namely *Rasce*, the killer of *Pesna Arcmsnas*. This is an unsolved puzzle.[59] The most likely answer is that these are not 'real' names, but nicknames which for some reason became the standard way of referring to well-known local heroes. A widely canvassed explanation of *Macstrna* is that it is an etruscanised version of the Latin word *magister*.[60] This word, from which the term 'magistrate' is derived, occurs in official titles at Rome, particularly for positions of military leadership. An alternative title for the dictator was *magister populi*, and his assistant was known as *magister equitum* ('Master of the Horse'). According to one theory the nature of Roman kingship changed in the sixth century, and the old *rex* was replaced as chief executive by a lifelong *magister populi*. When Rome became a republic, this office was retained for use in emergencies: hence the institution of the dictatorship.[61]

If *Macstrna* is connected with *magister*, we can resolve the issue in the following way. A companion of Caeles Vibenna became (at some point) the ruler of Rome with the title *magister* (*populi*). From then on, and in later Etruscan tradition, he was known as *Macstrna*, which was either a nickname meaning something like 'the Leader',[62] or a misunderstanding of the Latin title, which was wrongly assumed to be a personal name, and became *Macstrna* in Etruscan – i.e. *magister* with the onomastic suffix *-na*.[63] The process is exactly parallel to that whereby the Etruscan title *lucumo* was taken by the Romans to be a personal name and rendered Lucius.

If *Macstrna* is a nickname or title, the person called *Macstrna* in the painting must have had another 'real' name; and in the circumstances it would be tempting to suggest that this real name was Servius Tullius. Indeed, the temptation is almost overwhelming in view of Claudius' statement that Mastarna and Servius Tullius were alternative names for the same king. The tendency of recent scholarship has been to accept this attractive reconstruction, which may be essentially correct. But there are certain difficulties which cannot be ignored. In the first place the argument from nomenclature (outlined in the preceding paragraph) is rather convoluted, and depends entirely on the connection between *Macstrna* and *magister*. This connection is plausible but far from certain.[64] Second, acceptance of Claudius' Etruscan version entails the complete rejection of the native Roman tradition concerning Servius Tullius, which seems a rather drastic step.

Let us first be clear that the two versions are incompatible. The faithful servant of Tarquinius Priscus can hardly be the same man as the adventurer who accompanied Caeles Vibenna on all his escapades. The two are so different that it makes sense to keep them apart. Nevertheless, their careers seem to run on curiously parallel lines. Both were dependants who served their masters faithfully, and took over from them when they were killed. But it is difficult to see how they can be combined into a single person unless some way can be found of identifying Caeles Vibenna with Tarquinius Priscus; and that, one suspects, would be beyond the ingenuity of even the most resourceful scholar.[65] On the other hand, the similarities can perhaps be explained once it is understood that this was an age of adventurers, in which private armed bands struggled for supremacy and their leaders attempted to seize political power. As we shall see, there is considerable evidence for this phenomenon in the sixth century, and it may have been a fairly frequent occurrence for a chief to be replaced by a rival, or to be supplanted by a deputy.

In other words, there is room for more than one Mastarna, and for that matter more than one Servius Tullius. We have to reckon with the possibility that there were more kings in sixth-century Rome than are dreamed of in the simplified narratives of the annalists. On balance, it is probably sensible to keep Servius Tullius and Mastarna distinct from one another, while recognising that they have something in common and that they may be examples of the same general phenomenon. On this view Claudius' Etruscan sources did not say explicitly that Mastarna was the Etruscan name for Servius

Tullius; rather, what they said about Mastarna convinced Claudius that he must be identical with Servius Tullius. For example, the Etruscan sources may have indicated that Mastarna became king of Rome in succession to a king Tarquinius. In that case, if it did not occur to Claudius to question the canonical list of seven kings, he would have had no alternative but to identify Mastarna with Servius Tullius.[66]

6 THE NATURE OF KINGSHIP AT ROME

We may conclude this chapter with a few remarks on the nature of Roman kingship, as it is represented in the sources, and on the changes that occurred in the last decades of the monarchic period. The most obvious peculiarity about the Roman kingship is that it was not hereditary. In the developed legend of the origins of Rome, the son of Aeneas founded a hereditary dynasty at Alba Longa. But this Alban dynasty was an antiquarian fiction devised for chronographic reasons; the reality of Roman kingship (and perhaps of kingship in other Italian city-states) was different. No king of Rome inherited the throne from his father; the only partial exception is the last king, Tarquin the Proud, who was the son of the elder Tarquin. But Tarquin's reign did not follow on directly from that of his father; and since he was by all accounts a usurper who seized the throne illegally, it is an exception that proves the rule, and indeed confirms that in normal circumstances hereditary succession was excluded.

According to the received tradition, the rule was observed even in the case of kings who were survived by legitimate sons. The clearest instance of this is the accession of Tarquin the Elder, who was chosen as king even though his predecessor, Ancus Marcius, had left two grown-up sons.[67] The story is complicated, however, by the fact that Tarquin is said to have arranged for the sons of Ancus Marcius to be sent away from Rome a few days before the election of a new king. The Marcii were also supposedly responsible for the murder of Tarquin himself; but, as we have seen, this mysterious tale is rather nonsensical, since the assassination produced the very result the Marcii had set out to prevent, namely the accession of Servius Tullius as Tarquin's successor. The point is, however, that there is an underlying expectation in this narrative that a king's sons would have some kind of claim; we find the same expectation in an account of the death of Tullus Hostilius preserved in Dionysius of Halicarnassus (III.35.3–4). According to this version (from which Dionysius is careful to distance himself), the death of Tullus Hostilius and all his family in a fire was the work of Ancus Marcius, who wanted the throne for himself but feared that it would pass to one of the king's sons.

How these elements of the traditional account are to be explained is open to debate. The most probable interpretation would seem to be that the Roman monarchy was an elective system, but one in which connections, sometimes blood relationships, existed between some of the kings and their successors.

We are given to understand, for instance, that kings were able to designate their chosen successors by giving them positions of responsibility; thus Tarquinius Priscus was the 'right-hand man' of his predecessor Ancus Marcius, and was succeeded in his turn by his own favourite, Servius Tullius.

A further sign of this connection between kings and their successors is that they were frequently related by marriage. Servius Tullius was the son-in-law of Tarquinius Priscus, and Tarquinius Superbus was the son-in-law of Servius Tullius.[68] There is a folk-tale element in such stories: an outsider marries the king's daughter and thereby obtains the kingdom. A classic instance of this motif is the story of Aeneas, who married Lavinia, daughter of King Latinus, and on his death became the ruler of the Latins. In general the process means no more than that the most evident way a king can show favour to a would-be successor is to offer him his daughter's hand. This is more probable than the suggestion that in Rome the succession 'passed through the female line'.[69] Nevertheless, it is undeniable that in the story of the Roman monarchy women are sometimes instrumental in the process of succession, and play an important king-making role. This is especially evident in the story of Tanaquil.

An important feature of Roman monarchy is that many kings were outsiders – literally so in the cases of Numa and Tarquinius Priscus, the former a Sabine, the latter of mixed Greek and Etruscan ancestry. Another point of special interest is that the kings were not of patrician blood. This is manifestly true of Numa and Tarquinius Priscus, who were immigrants, and of Servius Tullius, about whom one of the few things on which our sources agree is that he was not of patrician birth.[70] This conclusion is confirmed by, but does not depend on, the fact that in historical times the Pompilii and Tullii were plebeian *gentes*. The later plebeian status of the Hostilii and the Marcii would further indicate that the third and fourth kings of Rome were not patricians. By contrast, it is most noteworthy that none of the great patrician clans (Fabii, Cornelii, Valerii, Aemilii, etc.) produced a king.

This is unlikely to be an accident, and it prompts the suggestion that the king of Rome had to be an outsider, and that members of the native (patrician) aristocracy were not eligible. It is true that Dionysius of Halicarnassus, in a series of dubious notices, reports that some of the kings were admitted to the patriciate on their accession. This seems improbable for various reasons, but in any event it merely serves to confirm the general point being made here, that the kings were not chosen from among the patricians.

The procedures for choosing a king were complex. The key institution was the *interregnum*. When a king died, the patrician heads of families (*patres*) took turns to hold office as *interrex* ('between-king'), each serving for five days. According to Livy the *interregnum* lasted for a year, after which an election was held. The process thus involved both the patricians and the people's assembly. It is not clear from the sources whether the people were merely asked to give assent to a single candidate who had been selected in advance by the *patres*, or whether they were given a genuine choice between candidates. It is also uncertain how this 'election' relates to the so-called *lex curiata de imperio*, the decree of the curiate assembly that conferred *imperium* on the king (and, in later times, on the consuls). In any event, the *patres* themselves had subsequently to ratify the people's decision. This was the so-called *auctoritas patrum*, which until 339 BC was necessary before any popular decree could become legally binding. The appointment of a king, therefore, was made 'with the authorisation of the Fathers, by command of the People' (*auctoribus patribus, iussu populi*).

In this process, which was repeated in republican times in the event of the death of both consuls, or if a year ended with no new consuls elected, it is evident that the decisive role was played by the patricians through their control of the *interregnum* and the *auctoritas patrum*. It was the patricians, in short, who chose the king, although it seems clear that they were not themselves eligible for the kingship. This means that the patricians were kingmakers. It also seems that they were what anthropologists call 'stake-holders',[71] since they were the traditional guardians of the auspices (*auspicia*). They conferred the auspices on the king, who held them for life; on his death, 'the auspices returned to the Fathers' (*auspicia ad patres redierunt*). This interesting phrase, which has been the object of much scholarly attention,[72] seems to imply that the patriciate was the ultimate repository of the auspices, and that the king held them in trust. If this interpretation is correct, it would confirm that the king was not himself a patrician or a representative of the *patres*. The king's tenure of the auspices was conferred by a special religious ceremony in which the gods were asked to signify their approval of the new king with favourable omens (a full account in Livy 1.18.6–10). In this way the king was 'inaugurated', a word that has passed into our language.

From the sources, then, we can gather that the king was an outsider, sometimes a foreigner, but in any case chosen from outside the patrician aristocracy, and that his election was a complex process involving the previous king, the patricians, the people, and the gods. But as we have seen, during the later period of the monarchy these formalities were subverted, and power fell into the hands of usurpers and tyrants. This is clear even from the traditional annalistic narrative, which divides the second phase of the regal period between two stereotyped figures, the beneficent reformer Servius Tullius, and the cruel tyrant Tarquinius Superbus. But enough evidence has slipped through the interstices of this simplified account to allow a rather more complex picture to be drawn.

7 ADVENTURERS AND TYRANTS

One of the most important features of the society of central Italy in the archaic period is the presence of *condottieri*[73] – aristocratic warlords whose power rested on the support of armed personal dependants, who are variously styled 'clients' (*clientes*) or 'companions' (*sodales*). These armed bands formed what were essentially private armies, operating independently of state governments, moving freely across state frontiers, and frequently changing their allegiances. Well-known examples include the Sabine leader Attus Clausus (Appius Claudius), who in 504 BC migrated to Rome with a private retinue of 5,000 armed clients; and Cn. Marcius Coriolanus, noted for his 'large following of companions, and many clients banded together for warlike gain', who joined the Volscians and became their leader in a war against Rome. A similar phenomenon is implied in the story of the Fabii, the patrician clan who in 479 BC fought a private war against Veii with the support of their own clients and companions.[74]

This situation has been further illuminated by an inscription recently uncovered at Satricum (Figure 17). The so-called Lapis Satricanus, which can be dated with some confidence around 500 BC, records a dedication to Mars by the companions (*sodales*) of a certain Poplios Valesios (i.e. Publius Valerius).[75] The Publius Valerius in question may be none other than the famous P. Valerius Publicola, who dominated the Roman state in the early years of the Republic. However that may be, the interest of the inscription in the present context is that it provides contemporary evidence of a group who define themselves not as citizens of a state or members of an ethnic group, but as companions of an individual leader. The otherwise rather unusual word *sodales* seems to have a particular social significance in this context and to refer to the armed followers of an independent warlord. The most obvious comparison is with the Homeric *hetairoi*, and it is no accident that this is exactly how Dionysius of Halicarnassus translates it (9.15.3).

These facts recall two important details of Claudius' account of Mastarna. First, Claudius describes Mastarna as 'the most faithful *companion* of Caelius Vivenna' (*Caeli . . . Vivennae sodalis fidelissimus*); and secondly he says that after Caelius' misfortune Mastarna left Etruria with the remnants of Caelius' army (*cum omnibus reliquis Caeliani exercitus*). In other words, this was not the army of a state (e.g. Vulci), but a private band defined in terms of its leader. Such groups appear to have been a significant feature of the aristocratic society of central Italy from at least the middle of the sixth century BC down to the early years of the fifth. The history of the later regal period can be seen as a struggle between competing warlords, some of whom succeeded in asserting their rule, either by persuasion or by force. When Claudius says that Mastarna and the remnants of Caelius' band occupied the Caelian, something more hostile than mere settlement may be implied; the Latin word *occupare* often has the sense of 'seize by force'. Somewhat later, Lars Porsenna of Clusium 'occupied' the Janiculum, and then, if we follow a variant tradition (on which see below, p. 217), took the city itself. The mysterious figure of Porsenna is perhaps best understood as an independent warlord.

There were probably others who were able to dominate Rome, at least for a time. For instance, there is a possibility that Aulus Vibenna ruled at Rome.

Figure 17 The Lapis Satricanus. This famous inscription was discovered at Satricum in 1977 on a block that had been reused in the construction of the second phase of the Temple of Mater Matuta (early fifth century BC). The inscription must therefore have been engraved at an earlier date – i.e. around 500 BC at the latest.

A tradition that is at least as old as Fabius Pictor connected Aulus Vibenna with the Capitoline hill. The hill was supposed to have received its name when a human head was dug up during the construction of the temple of Jupiter. The head belonged to 'Olus' – hence the childish etymology: *caput Oli*. The story is interesting because historians and antiquarians identified Olus with Aulus Vibenna of Vulci, about whom they knew some interesting facts. For example, he came to Rome after being banished from his own country; he was killed by a slave of his twin brother; and according to one late source he had ruled as king (*rex*) in Rome.[76] If so, like Mastarna and Lars Porsenna he failed to establish himself either decisively or for long enough to be remembered as a king in the later vulgate tradition. Others such as Valerius Publicola and Appius Claudius were remembered as republican leaders rather than kings, though the difference may not be as clear-cut as the annalists liked to think; yet others may have tried their hand but failed in the attempt. A dim memory of an unsuccessful coup of this kind is perhaps retained in the story of Appius Herdonius, who for a few days in 460 BC seized the Capitol with a band of 4,000 armed clients.[77]

A second and closely related aspect of the Roman monarchy in the later sixth century BC is its tyrannical character. This emerges clearly from the sources, which portray Tarquinius Superbus in all the lurid colours of a typical Greek *tyrannos*. The standard modern interpretation sees this as a purely literary phenomenon, the annalists having modelled their accounts of Tarquin's reign on Greek accounts of Pisistratus, Periander, Gelon, and the like. There is undoubtedly some truth in this, but it does not tell the whole story. There are strong grounds for supposing that the rulers of Rome in the sixth century really did resemble their tyrannical counterparts in the contemporary Greek world. This was partly for what we may call structural reasons – they were the product of similar historical circumstances, and reacted to them in the same way – but it was also because Rome (and other city-states in central Italy) had close and direct contacts with the Greek world at this time. It would be reasonable to suppose, and reliable evidence confirms, that the later Roman kings were well aware of what contemporary Greek tyrants were doing, and consciously set out to imitate them.

Like the Greek tyrants, the later Roman kings pursued an ambitious foreign policy, patronised the arts and undertook grandiose building projects. Success in these ventures boosted their prestige and helped compensate for the inescapable fact that they were unconstitutional rulers who had gained power illegally, sometimes by force. Their most pressing need was to legitimise their position, and their greatest efforts, and some of their most permanent achievements, were designed to meet this need. Since they lacked traditional legitimacy, they tended instead to appeal to charismatic authority, and tried in particular to suggest that they owed their supremacy to the protection and favour of the gods.

In this connection Servius Tullius is a crucial figure. Mention of divine protection and favour recalls the legends of Servius' birth and upbringing. To argue that these stories were current already during his lifetime might seem a bold step; but it is remarkable that one of the most important sixth-century monuments, located in the Comitium, the civic centre of Rome, was a shrine of Vulcan (Hephaestus), the god who supposedly fathered the king and protected him as a boy.[78] It is not fanciful to suggest that the ruling monarch publicly encouraged the notion of a personal connection between himself and the god worshipped in the shrine in the Comitium.

According to tradition, Servius also claimed a special relationship with Fortuna, the goddess of good luck, to whom he dedicated numerous shrines throughout the city. One of these was a temple in the Forum Boarium, the very place where an archaic temple, dating from the sixth century BC, has been discovered, near the church of Sant'Omobono. Servius' good fortune was evident in the fact that he rose to power from obscure beginnings. According to the story he owed this divine favour to a love affair with the goddess, who is said to have visited him secretly at night, entering his room through a window later known as the Porta Fenestella.[79] This legend has been interpreted by scholars as evidence of the ritual known as 'sacred marriage'.

The ancient rite whereby a ruler consorts with a divinity and thereby achieves both legitimation and the fertility and well-being of his kingdom is widely attested in the ancient world, particularly in the Near East.[80] The union was deemed to take place when the king spent a night in the temple of the goddess. In some cases there was actual copulation, the role of the goddess being assumed by a female slave, priestess or temple prostitute. When a sacred marriage was first consummated at the start of a new reign, the 'goddess' would announce the fact from the temple, and thus confirm her approval of the new king. In some figured monuments from Cyprus and other parts of the Near East, she is represented making her pronouncement from an upstairs window. This well-known motif of 'the goddess at the window' (Figure 18) cannot but recall the story of how Tanaquil ensured the throne for her favourite, Servius Tullius, by addressing the people from a window in the palace. The window is also an important detail in the story of the love affair between Servius and Fortuna. Interestingly, Plutarch connects the two stories

Figure 18 The 'goddess at the window'.

(of Fortuna visiting Servius, and of Tanaquil addressing the people) in his discussion of the Porta Fenestella in the *Roman Questions*.[81]

The similarities between elements of the Roman legend and the near-eastern sacred-marriage rituals are remarkable and cannot be due to co-incidence. Equally they cannot be dismissed as the result of late, Hellenistic, contamination. That the sixth-century Roman kings claimed to enjoy the personal favour of divine powers, and that they adopted Greek and near-eastern models of kingship in their search for legitimacy and charismatic authority, may seem far-fetched; but the evidence that is now available indicates that that is precisely what they did. Two pieces of evidence, in particular, combine to make this interpretation virtually certain.

The first is the bilingual inscription from Pyrgi, the port of Caere, some 50 km north west of Rome. The text, which is partly in Etruscan and partly in Phoenician, records the dedication of a sanctuary to the Phoenician goddess Astarte (Etruscan Uni) by the ruler of Caere, Thefarie Velianas, shortly after 500 BC (see below, p. 232). The purpose of his dedication was to acknowledge that he owed his position of power to the help and favour of the goddess. The text does not make it clear whether Thefarie Velianas saw himself as the consort of the goddess; nevertheless, it is worth noting that in the ancient Near East it was Astarte or Ishtar (Sumerian Inanna) who conferred power on the king and fertility on his people in ceremonies of sacred marriage.

The second piece of evidence is a terracotta statue group from the archaic temple in the Forum Boarium in Rome. This fragmentary group, which belongs to the second phase of the temple and dates from about 530 BC, consists of two standing figures, representing Hercules and Minerva (Figure 19). The most persuasive interpretation is that it represents the apotheosis of Heracles, a scene from Greek mythology in which the goddess Athene (= Minerva) introduced the hero to the company of gods on Mount Olympus.[82]

The interest of the sculpture in the present context is its possible ideological significance. In a series of studies J. Boardman has demonstrated that Pisistratus, the sixth-century Athenian tyrant, sought to strengthen his position by identifying himself with Heracles and claiming the assistance and support of Athene.[83] An echo of this use of myth occurs in Herodotus' anecdote about Pisistratus driving into Athens with a six-foot girl clad in armour and masquerading as Athene (Herodt. 1.60). As Ampolo has observed, this Athenian evidence can serve to explain contemporary developments in Rome, where the kings sought to define their position in terms of Greek and near-eastern models of kingship. The same is true of rulers in other Italian cities, among whom we may include Thefarie Velianas of Caere.[84]

We may conclude, therefore, that tradition preserves a genuine memory of the archaic age when it presents the last kings of Rome in the guise of Greek tyrants. This important finding also serves to authenticate another alleged aspect of their rule, namely its populist character. The Greek tyrants were essentially anti-aristocratic figures, who ruled in the interests of the lower classes, particularly the class of independent small farmers. They expropriated the wealth of their aristocratic opponents and redistributed it among their friends and supporters; at the same time they attacked their political privileges and extended civil rights to wider groups.[85]

This is precisely what is said to have happened under the later kings of Rome. Ancus Marcius was a patron of the *plebs* and was too easily swayed by the voice of the people, according to Virgil's famous characterisation (*Aeneid* 6.815–6); Tarquinius Priscus canvassed for popular support and carried out reforms that angered the aristocracy. But the last two kings went much further. As we shall see (below, p. 190), Servius' thorough reform of the state is best understood as an attempt to undermine the traditional bases of aristocratic power; and Tarquinius Superbus openly persecuted the aristocracy. In the end it was they, rather than the proletariat, who organised the plot to overthrow him.

The popular and anti-aristocratic regime of the last kings is confirmed by the Romans' later attitude to the institution of kingship. In the republican period the very idea of a king was viewed with an almost pathological dislike. It is hard to believe that this was due solely to the popular memory of the last Tarquin's misdeeds; it is much more likely to be an element of the powerful aristocratic ideology of the ruling class of the Republic. This class was dominated by a narrow oligarchy of 'nobles' who claimed the exclusive

Figure 19 Statue group from the Sant'Omobono sanctuary (Musei Capitolini).

149

right to compete for positions of power and influence, and dignified this state of affairs with the name of 'liberty' (*libertas*). The Romans were always conscious of the basic incompatibility of monarchy and *libertas*, and by taking precautions against the incidence of the former they hoped to defend and preserve the latter. The tradition is very likely correct when it says that the first acts of the founders of the Republic were to make the people swear never to allow any man to be king in Rome and to legislate against anyone aspiring to monarchy in the future. What was truly repugnant to the nobles was the thought of one of their number elevating himself above his peers by attending to the needs of the lower classes and winning their political support.

This explains why all the serious charges of monarchism (*regnum*) in the Republic were levelled against mavericks from the ruling elite whose only offence, it seems, was to direct their personal efforts and resources to the relief of the poor. This was the case, as we shall see, with Sp. Cassius, Sp. Maelius, and M. Manlius Capitolinus. Later the murders of the Gracchi were justified also on the grounds that the brothers had aimed at kingship. However absurd this charge may have been, it was not made simply for rhetorical effect. At the time it was no doubt genuinely believed by those whose openly expressed hatred of kingship concealed a profound subconscious fear of the lower classes.

6

THE MYTH OF
'ETRUSCAN ROME'

1 'ETRUSCHERIA'

Everyone who studies the archaic period takes it for granted that Rome went
through an 'Etruscan phase' during the monarchy. But what exactly does this
mean? Some speak bluntly of an Etruscan conquest; others, more vaguely, of
an Etruscan ascendancy; and others, more neutrally, of an Etruscan presence.
These formulations cover a wide spectrum of opinion, and it will be best to
keep them distinct in the discussion that follows. But all are agreed that, in
some sense, archaic Rome was an 'Etruscan city'.

Before we proceed, it is worth reminding ourselves that it was not always
like this. In the eighteenth century the discovery of the monuments and
cemeteries of Etruria stimulated a new interest in the Etruscans, particularly
among Italian scholars, who found in the civilisations of pre-Roman Italy a
focus for their feelings of local and national patriotism. This movement
continued into the early nineteenth century and played its part in the
Risorgimento. The Etruscans exercised a particular fascination as a people
who were civilised and literate long before Rome became important, and who
had for a time succeeded in uniting most of Italy (or so it was supposed).
There was a strong anti-Roman strain in the work of these scholars, who saw
ancient Rome as a conquering oppressor, and its modern counterpart as a
centre of clerical reaction and an obstacle to nationalist aspirations.[1]

Eighteenth-century writing on the Etruscans combined antiquarian learning with far-fetched theories (for instance about their origins) and enthusiastic
fantasies about their influence. The Etruscans became the originators of all
art, literature, philosophy and science – in short, the founders of civilisation
(it is necessary to remember that at this period Greek vases were thought to
be Etruscan). The more extravagant manifestations of this erudite speculation
were rather contemptuously labelled '*etruscheria*'. Nevertheless, the antiquarians achieved a great deal, and their results prepared the ground for the
pioneering study of Karl Otfried Müller, whose two volumes on *Die Etrusker*
appeared in 1828. Müller identified and organised what was best in *etruscheria*
and created the modern study of the Etruscans as we know it today. The

updated second edition of his book by W. Deecke is still required reading,[2] and all subsequent books of any seriousness on 'the Etruscans' are basically new versions of Müller. The most important feature of his work, however, was its strong emphasis on the deep influence of the Etruscans on the political and religious life of Rome. The notion of Etruscan Rome, so prevalent in modern work on archaic Italy, goes back essentially to Müller.

Paradoxically, however, Müller's work had little immediate effect on Roman historians. Partly this was because of the Romantic movement, and its exaltation of the Greeks. The Etruscans suffered a serious blow in 1806, when Luigi Lanza proved that the allegedly Etruscan painted vases were in fact Greek,[3] and with the rediscovery of Greek architecture and sculpture the Etruscans were bound to lose prestige in comparison. A second reason was the fact that Niebuhr, who disliked Müller personally, reacted against his work and in the second edition of his *Römische Geschichte* (1827) minimised the role of the Etruscans, retracting as he did so the theory he had put forward in the first edition (1811), that Rome originated as an Etruscan colony.[4] Niebuhr even went so far as to deny the Etruscan origin of the Tarquins. The principal Roman historians of the mid-nineteenth century, such as Schwegler, Ihne and Lewis, followed suit. For his part Mommsen accepted the Etruscan provenance of the Tarquins, but described it as an 'unimportant fact', which had no effect on Rome's development.

> The history of the Tarquins, [he writes,] has its theatre in Latium, not in Etruria; and Etruria, so far as we can see, during the whole regal period exercised no influence of any essential moment on either the language or customs of Rome, and did not at all interrupt the development of the Roman state or of the Latin league.[5]

The reinstatement of the Etruscans as the decisive factor in the development of early Rome belongs to the twentieth century, particularly to the years after the First World War. In part this was the result of systematic archaeological research, not only in the Etruscan cities but also in Rome, which made it clear beyond doubt that archaic Rome and Etruria shared the same material culture; but it was also connected with the revaluation of Etruscan art which began with the discovery of the Apollo of Veii in 1916. The ideological background to this story is too complicated to go into here; suffice it to say that anti-German hostility and Fascism have a great deal to do with it. The debate about the originality of Etruscan art went together with attempts to prove that the Etruscans were indigenous to Italy and that their civilisation was an expression of native Italian genius (the same, indeed, as that which later produced the Renaissance). This formed the background to the growth of Rome; the native vitality of Etruscan civilisation could be set beside the creative originality of Latin literature as an essential ingredient of *romanità*.[6]

In the changed atmosphere of the period after the Second World War, the Etruscans continued to attract attention, but now, as part of the reaction against the Fascist cult of *romanità*, there was a revival of anti-Roman *etruscheria*. This reached its height in the 1950s and 1960s, particularly in the wake of the sensational Paris exhibition of 1955, which spawned a mass of popular books on 'those mysterious Etruscans'.[7] An important symptom of the anti-Roman backlash was the renewed insistence that archaic Rome was conquered by the Etruscans, an event deliberately concealed by nationalistic Roman historians, and that any sign of artistic creativity or cultural sophist-ication in Rome must be the result of Etruscan influence. At the beginning of the century the best Roman historians were still minimising the role of the Etruscans;[8] but soon all were swept along by the tide. The notion of archaic Rome as an Etruscan city has become embedded in modern scholarship, and any attempt to challenge it requires an extended discussion.

2 ETRUSCAN RULE IN LATIUM AND CAMPANIA

We may begin with the theory of an Etruscan conquest of Rome in the late seventh century and its occupation until the end of the sixth. The conquest is normally seen as part of a wider pattern of expansion which led to the formation of an Etruscan 'empire' extending from the Po valley to the gulf of Salerno. The literary sources assign an Etruscan origin to the cities of Capua, Nola, Herculaneum and Pompeii (among others), and the Etruscan occupation of Campania is confirmed by the discovery, at a number of sites, of Etruscan inscriptions dating from the sixth and fifth centuries.[9] It is widely believed that this must have been preceded by the conquest of Latium, and in particular that it presupposes Etruscan control of the crossing of the Tiber at Rome.

The argument is superficially plausible. The Etruscans must have got to Campania somehow, and the most direct way would be to march overland through Latium. It is obvious enough, however, that this kind of reasoning is insufficient on its own to support the idea that Rome was under foreign occupation for over a century. Quite apart from the fact that there were other routes to Campania, the whole formulation is too vague and circumstantial to be compelling. Serious questions need to be asked. Who exactly were these Etruscans? Etruria and its people did not form a single political entity, but on the contrary consisted of independent and often warring city-states. What kind of Etruscan communities existed in Campania, and how and when were they established? Above all, is there any specific evidence for an Etruscan conquest of Rome (or any other place in Latium)?

The origins of the Etruscan presence in Campania are problematic, largely because of the uncertain implications of the archaeological evidence. Some important excavated sites, such as Capua in northern Campania, and Ponte-cagnano on the gulf of Salerno, have an archaeological history similar to that of the great iron-age centres in Etruria, with Villanovan and Protovillanovan phases going back to the ninth century BC. In the orientalising period they imported Etruscan bucchero pottery in large quantities, and then produced their own in imitation. Etrusco-Corinthian material typical of the late orientalising phase has also been found. In the sixth century the Campanian cities continued to import material from Etruria, but also developed their own distinctive tradition of architectural terracottas. These have affinities with those of Etruria and Latium but are not derived from them; Frederiksen suggests that the two styles have common origins going back to the late seventh and early sixth centuries BC, and that they may be independently derived from mainland-Greek and Ionian models.[10]

The non-Greek centres in Campania seem therefore to have developed along lines parallel to those of their counterparts in archaic Etruria, and to have particular affinities with Clusium and Vulci; but they also retained their own burial practices and distinctive artistic styles, which Frederiksen took to be 'signs that the Etruscanization of Campania did not go excessively deep'.[11] Nevertheless, we are still entitled to call these places Etruscan, for two reasons: first because of the clear and abundant testimony of literary sources, and secondly because of the many Etruscan inscriptions, mostly of the fifth century (although the earliest texts, from the Salerno region, date from c. 600 BC) that have been found at sites in Campania, including Capua, Nola, Suessula, Pompeii and Pontecagnano. The alphabet used in these inscriptions is of a type found in southern Etruscan cities, especially Veii and Caere, but retaining archaic features which these places had dropped by around 500 BC.[12]

The evidence suggests that a substantial Etruscan-speaking population was resident in the Campanian cities from before 500 BC. How had this situation come about? One possibility is that the Etruscans had been there from the beginning, and that Capua, Nola, and the rest had always been Etruscan settlements. This is quite possible archaeologically, and it would be consistent with the statement of Velleius Paterculus (1.7), himself a native of Campania, that these cities were founded some 830 years before his time (i.e., c. 800 BC). Most scholars, however, reject this notion, and argue instead that Campania was colonised by the Etruscans at a later stage. If so, the Etruscan colonists would have taken over existing settlements and imposed their rule on the indigenous inhabitants. This is precisely what is alleged also to have happened at Rome.

The date of the Etruscan invasion of Campania, which on this view would be crucial also for the development of Rome and Latium, is much disputed. The Elder Cato is reported as saying that Capua was founded by the Etruscans 260 years before its capture by the Romans, which gives a date of 471 BC (the Romans having taken the city in 211).[13] This seems very late, and in view of the epigraphic evidence in particular most scholars either reject Cato's date out of hand, or argue that he has been misquoted. According to Beloch, Cato dated the Etruscan 'foundation' to c. 600 BC, by counting back from the time when Capua was given Roman citizenship (338 BC).[14] Others believe that Cato had referred not to the capture of Capua by the Romans, but to its capture by the Samnites in 423 BC (Livy 4.37.1); the foundation date would then work out at 683 BC.[15] A third group of experts reject Cato altogether in favour of Dionysius of Halicarnassus, who reports an attack on Cumae by a force of Etruscans and others in 524 BC; although Cumae was saved, it was this invasion that first established Etruscan power in Campania.[16]

There is no need to enter into a detailed discussion of the merits of these various suggestions. The important thing to note is that the debate revolves around the possible interpretation of ancient texts; the archaeological evidence, so far from being decisive, can be made to fit any one of a wide range of possible dates. The Campanian sites show 'Etruscanising' traits from a very remote period, but the presence of actual Etruscans is much harder to detect from material evidence (except when it is inscribed). And it is quite another matter to decide when, or even whether, an Etruscan 'conquest' might have taken place. It is notoriously difficult, not to say impossible, to deduce political facts from material finds. In other words, we are dealing with the sort of question that archaeology is not equipped to answer – a point we shall do well to remember when we consider the case of Rome.

The foregoing discussion has both direct and indirect relevance to Rome. Directly, the Etruscan penetration into Campania is said to presuppose Etruscan control of Rome and Latium. But there is no need for such an assumption, especially in view of the nature of Etruscan 'rule' in Campania. This should not be seen as the result of an imperial conquest of unoccupied territory by a unified Etruscan state (as far as we know there never was such a thing); rather, the evidence we have reviewed suggests a process of emigration by small groups from individual Etruscan cities, who established themselves, by force or persuasion, as a significant element of the ruling class in settlements that already existed as going concerns. In this way they gained control of autonomous communities and pursued their own interests, rather than acting as dependencies of a centralised Etruscan metropolis. That being the case, there was no need for a direct overland link to be maintained and, consequently, no need for 'the Etruscans' (we can see how meaningless this term is in a geopolitical context) to control Rome. On the other hand, commercial contacts between Etruria and Campania flourished during the archaic period. In so far as this trade was conducted by land, it is obvious that strategically placed centres on the main routes, such as Praeneste and Rome, would benefit from the traffic and try to encourage it as much as possible. But there is no need to suppose that their political independence would be thereby threatened.

What happened in Campania also has an indirect bearing on the possibility of an Etruscan conquest of Latium. A comparison of the two cases can show how flimsy the evidence is for a period of Etruscan dominance in Latium. Etruscan rule in Campania is clearly documented, both by literary texts which state that the area was colonised by the Etruscans, and by epigraphic evidence which reveals a dominant Etruscan element in the population of the non-Greek cities. Such documentation is lacking in the case of Rome and Latium. The literary sources do not say that Rome was under Etruscan control (but rather the opposite), and there is not much of a case to be made for Etruscan rule in Latium either. The elder Cato believed that parts of southern Latium were once Etruscan, and may even have written that 'almost all of Italy was once in the power of the Etruscans' (*Origines* I.13 = fr. 62 P). But the context of the fragment makes it clear that it referred to the time of the legendary Metabus, an Etruscan who ruled as tyrant at Privernum before the arrival of Aeneas (Virg., *Aeneid* 11.540). Cato was dealing with events long before Rome was even founded, and his comments have no relevance to the situation in the archaic period.[17]

3 THE TARQUINS AND THE NATURE OF ETRUSCAN RULE IN ROME

As for Rome, it is sometimes suggested that the rule of the Tarquins is in itself a sign of Etruscan domination, and that it can only have come about as a result of a forcible seizure of power. There is no hint of this in the sources, however, which tend rather to stress the fact that Tarquinius Priscus was not actually Etruscan at all, since he was the son of a Corinthian refugee; in the traditional story he left Tarquinii because he found that his foreign (i.e. non-Etruscan!) parentage was a hindrance to his political ambitions. So far from taking Rome by armed force, he migrated there with his wife and his dependants for personal reasons – principally because he knew that Rome was a place where he would be accepted, and where he would be able to make his fortune.

This simple story is often rejected as a romantic myth, created by Roman historians who wished to conceal the fact that Rome was actually subjected to Etruscan rule. Alföldi, for example, argued that Rome was conquered and ruled by a succession of rival Etruscan cities in the sixth century, but that this unpalatable truth was suppressed by Fabius Pictor, who perpetrated a cynical cover-up.[18] The idea that a 'patriotic tradition' deliberately papered over the fact of Etruscan rule has become a kind of received wisdom, and is widely repeated in general handbooks.[19]

It hardly needs saying that these theories go against the evidence of the sources; their purpose, after all, is to subvert the traditional account and to replace it with a different and supposedly more convincing alternative. The justification for such a position seems to be a general feeling that the tradition is not convincing as it stands; that in fact the cultural supremacy and profound influence of the Etruscans must also have entailed political domination,[20] and that the story of the peaceful integration of Tarquin and his family is too good to be true. In the harsh world of political reality, our knowing experts seem to say, things don't happen like that; rather, experience dictates that *realpolitik* should take precedence over romance. This kind of reasoning seems to underlie the revisionist version of events that is found in so many modern books, although, truth to tell, in most cases their authors do not trouble to justify their stance and explain why they reject the traditional account.

In fact, the traditional story of the migration of Tarquin is not at all unbelievable. Tradition portrays Rome in the archaic period as an independent city which maintained its own identity in spite of the absorption of outside elements and foreign ideas. The Romans of later times were well aware of their mixed origins, and made a positive virtue of their ancestors' willingness to admit foreigners into their midst. The Tarquins were not the only outsiders to rule at Rome. Other examples included the Sabines Titus Tatius and Numa, the Etruscan adventurer Mastarna, and Attus Clausus, the ancestor of the Claudian house, who migrated to Rome at the beginning of the Republic. He was admitted to Roman citizenship, given land for himself and his followers, and allowed to enter the Senate as a patrician. Within a decade he had become consul (495 BC).[21] The episode of Attus Clausus (Appius Claudius) exemplifies the way in which groups and individuals of foreign origin could be incorporated into the social structure of the city. Studies of the consular *Fasti* have shown that in the early Republic the supreme office was frequently held by representatives of immigrant families, some of them Etruscan.[22]

This picture is confirmed by epigraphic evidence. A small number of Etruscan inscriptions (probably four at most) have been found at Rome, dating from the regal period.[23] Three of them are on votive offerings, and testify to the high social standing of those who dedicated them; but for the same reason they cannot necessarily be taken to prove that these persons had taken up residence in Rome. We know that it was not unusual for out-of-town visitors to make dedications in sanctuaries.[24] Nevertheless, two of the texts show dialectal peculiarities that have been plausibly interpreted as a distinctly Roman form of Etruscan.[25] If so, we have evidence that Etruscan speakers were a well-established group within the Roman upper class, and that their presence goes back a long way. This is confirmed by the fourth Etruscan text, which comes from a grave on the Esquiline dating from the first half of the seventh century BC.[26]

On the other hand, the Etruscan texts form only a small minority of the archaic inscriptions from Rome. This situation is in sharp contrast to that in the non-Greek cities in Campania, where Etruscan is completely dominant, thus confirming the view of the sources that these cities had been subjected to Etruscan rule. In Rome the majority of archaic inscriptions are in Latin, including public documents such as the Forum Cippus at the shrine of the Niger Lapis. This epigraphic material confirms the picture given by the rest of the evidence – of a predominantly Latin-speaking population but one that was willing to admit outsiders, including Etruscans.

An open-door policy was one of the most important features of Roman society throughout its long history; the image of Rome as an 'open city', so memorably popularised by Roberto Rossellini, is not modern, but, on the contrary, older than Romulus.[27] Historically it makes Rome unique, but in the archaic period it was by no means peculiar to Rome. Recent research has revealed the ethnic diversity of the aristocratic societies of southern Etruria in the seventh and sixth centuries BC, where inscriptions have revealed the presence of high-ranking individuals of Greek, Latin and Italic origin. The most notable are the Greek *rutile hipukrate* (Rutilus Hippocrates) at Tarquinii, the Italic *ate peticina* (Attus Peticius) at Caere, the Latin, possibly Roman, *kalatur phapena* (Kalator Fabius), also at Caere, and the well-heeled *tite latine* (Titus Latinius), buried in a rich seventh-century tomb at Veii, whose name (like that of Lucius Tarquinius at Rome!) speaks for itself.[28] As Carmine Ampolo has shown, this evidence implies that the cultural uniformity of Tyrrhenian central Italy was accompanied by a high degree of horizontal social mobility, characterised not only by intermarriage but also by the free movement of individuals and groups between communities.[29]

The evidence bears witness to the existence in Tyrrhenian Italy of a phenomenon that actually extended throughout the Mediterranean world at this time. In archaic Greece too, the horizontal mobility of aristocratic families and individuals between city-states was a well-established feature, reinforced by gift-giving networks, inter-communal festivals, athletic contests, and intermarriage (the *locus classicus* being the story of the marriage of Agariste – Herodotus VI.126–31). The implication is that in archaic society personal standing, wealth and family background were more important than residence, ethnic origin or anything resembling nationality or citizenship. Indeed, one of the conclusions to be drawn from this discussion is precisely that such concepts as nationality and citizenship are anachronistic in the context of the seventh and sixth centuries BC.

To sum up, the idea that the rise of the Tarquins entailed the subjection of Rome to Etruscan rule is based on a crude and anachronistic misreading of the evidence. In fact the simple story of how the elder Tarquin made a purely personal decision to leave Tarquinii and seek his fortune in Rome is another case in which the ancient tradition turns out to be more credible than the modern theories that aim to replace it.

This conclusion involves an important consequence, namely that our sources were right to present the Tarquins as independent kings of Rome who happened to be Etruscan. It is sometimes said that the Roman tradition tried to play down the fact of their Etruscan origin; but it is altogether more probable that this ethnic factor has been exaggerated in modern accounts. The ethnic diversity of archaic Rome, together with the fact that all the Roman kings were in some sense outsiders (see above, pp. 142–3), suggests that the Etruscan origin of the Tarquins was incidental, at least in the sense that it did not necessarily have any far-reaching political or cultural implications.

Once that is admitted, it is no longer necessary to assume that the accession of the elder Tarquin should have coincided with an increase in the level of Etruscan influence in Rome, still less that it should represent a *terminus post quem* for all cultural contacts between Rome and Etruria. The archaeological evidence is said to indicate an intensification of such contacts in the last decades of the seventh century BC. In fact it does nothing of the kind, but even supposing it did, there would be no grounds for identifying the change with the arrival of the Tarquins, or for claiming the archaeological evidence as 'confirmation' of the traditional date. Such arguments, though frequently encountered in modern scholarship, are a travesty of historical method.

In fact, evidence of all kinds – literary, epigraphic, linguistic and archaeological – indicates clearly that contacts between Rome and Etruria go back long before the arrival of the Tarquins, even on the traditional chronology.[30] As far as the tradition is concerned, the story of Tarquin's move to Rome would seem to imply that the city was already open to penetration from Etruria. The presence of Etruscans in Rome was not a consequence of Tarquin's rise to power, but rather a precondition for it.

4 ETRUSCAN CULTURAL DOMINATION

If Rome was not conquered and ruled by the Etruscans during the archaic period, it nevertheless remains possible that its culture was transformed as a result of contacts with Etruria. The majority of modern scholars consider this cultural influence to have been extensive and profound. The Etruscans are held to have been responsible for the development of Rome as a city, and for major changes in Roman institutions, arts and religion. Archaic Rome was therefore an Etruscan city, not because it was subjected to Etruscan rule by military conquest, but because it was transformed by contact with a more advanced civilisation. In this formulation, Etruscan influence on Rome is being defined as a form of cultural imperialism; that is to say, scholars who reject the idea of direct conquest are inclined to adopt a neo-colonialist model of Etruscan domination in its place.

In the way it is usually applied, this model assumes a priori that all changes, developments and advances in the 'native' culture were brought about by the influence of the superior 'penetrating' culture;[31] a further implication is that Roman society was inherently stagnant and inert, and that in its relationship with Etruscan culture it was wholly passive. A great deal of modern writing on this subject takes it for granted that the Romans were simple, artless and unimaginative, and hence that anything involving art, imagination, technical skill, philosophical awareness or spirituality had to be borrowed from the Etruscans.[32] Greek influence is not excluded, but can be accommodated to the pan-Etruscan hypothesis, which maintains that Rome came into contact with Greek culture only through Etruscan mediation. Notice, for instance, how scholars use imports of Attic pottery as evidence for Etruscan influence on Rome.[33]

As an argument the hypothesis all too easily becomes circular and self-validating. Once it is assumed that the Etruscans were responsible for all major changes, any evidence of a major change can be put down to the

Etruscans. Although it is not often recognised as such, this is a version of what archaeologists call diffusionism, or an 'invasion hypothesis' – the theory, that is, that all cultural change is the result of outside influence, and in particular of migrations of people. In the present case crude invasionism is sometimes invoked. For instance Ogilvie, in a chapter entitled 'The arrival of the Etruscans', writes as follows:

> The Etruscans came to Rome and settled in force – as craftsmen, merchants, builders, religious experts, doctors and rulers. It was not a case of an alien usurpation of the throne for a temporary period; it was a deep interpenetration of society at every level.[34]

This remarkable statement is not prefaced by any background, and Ogilvie offers no explanation of how, when or why the supposed mass of Etruscans 'arrived'. He does not seem to believe in an Etruscan conquest (which would at least have answered these questions); the Etruscan migration is simply assumed as given. One thing is for sure: there is no evidence for it whatsoever. The arrival of the Etruscans, in the manner described by Ogilvie, is an entirely hypothetical event based on invasionist assumptions. Notice that this is not at all the same as the horizontal mobility we spoke about earlier. Ogilvie is not simply saying that the population of Rome included Etruscans (among other immigrants); he is saying that the society was transformed by the arrival ('in force') of Etruscans, whose specialised skills (enumerated in the quoted passage) made possible a range of cultural advances.

The application of this invasionist model to the study of 'Etruscan Rome' has produced thoroughly misleading results. All kinds of innovations which have no obvious connection with the Etruscans are arbitrarily credited to them. For example it is frequently asserted that it was the Etruscans who introduced a luni-solar calendar to Rome,[35] an assertion that appears to be wholly unfounded. It is not possible to set out the evidence because there isn't any. We know nothing whatever about religious calendars or time-measurement in Etruria, and the only reason for connecting the Roman calendar with the Etruscans is the general (and entirely circular) argument that they were responsible for all cultural developments in archaic Rome. On the negative side it must be said that the pre-Julian calendar shows few signs of direct Etruscan influence. The suggestion that the name April (*Aprilis*) is derived from Etruscan is no more than a guess,[36] and the only festival with any plausible Etruscan connections is the Volturnalia (27 August). The name of the god Volturnus, who seems to have been a god of rivers (in Rome naturally associated with the Tiber), may be Etruscan, although even this is not certain.[37] In general, however, it has to be said that Etruscan elements in the Roman calendar are conspicuous by their absence.[38]

Many aspects of Roman religion are considered to be of Etruscan origin. A striking example is the theory that the Etruscans brought to Rome a completely new concept of divinity: whereas formerly the Romans had believed in vague impersonal forces, the Etruscans taught them to personalise their gods, to represent them with human attributes, and to house them in temples.[39] The simple way to respond to this suggestion is to point out, once again, that it is not founded on any serious evidence. But it is worth asking how it came to be made in the first place. More particularly, is there any evidence for an early stage when the Romans did not envisage their gods in human form?

It is certainly true that the Roman gods, as we know them from later times, were conspicuously devoid of personality; the iconography and mythology of later Roman religion are entirely Greek. Some deities, such as Vesta, were never represented in human form, while others, particularly those belonging to collective groups such as the Lares and Penates, were little more than functional abstractions. The traditional explanation for this state of affairs is that the impersonal abstractions represent the original character of Roman belief, and that personalised gods and goddesses were the product of later development (and, of course, foreign influence). This interpretation appealed to scholars at the turn of the century because it conformed so closely to the evolutionist ideas that were fashionable at that time, and in particular to the theory that primitive religions are focused on impersonal spirits residing in natural phenomena ('animism'). Anthropomorphic deities, on this view, represent a more advanced stage of religious belief.[40] It also has the support of an ancient witness, Varro, who wrote that for the first 170 years of their history (i.e. down to 583 BC) the Romans worshipped their gods without any images.[41]

It is difficult to know what evidence Varro might have had for this assertion. But even if he was right, which now seems doubtful, it does not follow that the change to human images of the gods was the result of Etruscan influence. Before we decide on that issue, it would be useful to discover how the early Etruscans visualised their gods. But that is not easy, for the obvious reason that we do not possess any relevant information. It is interesting, however, that experts on Etruscan religion tend towards the view that the Etruscans also had only a vague and amorphous concept of divinity. Pallottino's account has a familiar ring to it: 'their conception of supernatural beings was permeated by a certain vagueness as to number, attributes, sex and appearance.' He goes on to say, predictably enough, 'thus one is naturally led to the conclusion that the great individual deities were solely due to foreign, or, to be more specific, Greek, influences, playing upon this vague and amorphous religiosity.'[42]

Whether this is right or wrong (I suspect it is wrong), the key element is the mention of Greek influences. What is absolutely clear is that both Etruscan and Roman ideas of deity were profoundly affected by Greek influences from a very early period. Both Etruscans and Romans adopted Greek gods such as Heracles and Apollo; and they both sought to equate their own gods and goddesses with appropriate figures from the Greek pantheon (thus, Greek Hermes = Etruscan *Turms* = Roman *Mercurius*; Greek Aphro-dite = Etruscan *Turan* = Roman *Venus*; Greek Hephaestus = Etruscan *Sethlans* = Roman *Vulcanus*, etc.). This is well known.[43] I would merely emphasise three points: first, Etruscan and Roman representations of these deities invariably drew upon Greek iconography and mythology; second, evidence of this syncretistic process (sometimes called *interpretatio graeca*) goes back to the very beginning of the archaic period; and third, Greek influence on Roman views of the gods was the result of direct contacts between Rome and the Greek world. The last point is decisive since it rules out even an attenuated version of the proposition under discussion, namely that anthropomorphic gods were a Greek idea, but one which the Etruscans brought to Rome.

Modern research has produced abundant evidence for direct Greek influence on early Roman religion. Some of the more important items can be briefly reviewed. The terracotta acroterial sculptures from the second phase of construction of the Sant'Omobono temple, which date from *c.* 530 BC, include near-lifesize statues of Minerva and Hercules. In an important study Anna Sommella Mura demonstrated that the two statues fit together to form a group representing a scene from Greek mythology, to wit Pallas Athene introducing Heracles to the gods on Mount Olympus (see p. 148, above).[44] The style and iconography are pure Greek, probably Ionian; the sculpture was therefore the work of a Greek craftsman who must have been at least temporarily resident in Rome.

It is probably not an accident that this representation of the apotheosis of Hercules was set up on the roof of a temple overlooking the Forum Boarium. Nearby was the site of an ancient cult of Hercules which according to legend was much older than Rome itself; the sanctuary had associations with foreign trade, befitting its location near the ancient river harbour. Finds of early Greek pottery have led some scholars to speculate that a community of Greek merchants and artisans was established in this area of the city as early as the eighth century BC.[45] If so, there is every chance that the cult of Hercules was indeed set up centuries before the age of the Etruscan kings, and that if the Romans had to be taught to imagine their gods as personal beings, they had learned to do so long before the sixth century.

Actually the whole idea of an aniconic stage in the earliest Roman religion is highly questionable. This is not simply because evolutionism has now gone out of fashion,[46] but because the direct evidence seems to show that personal, hellenised gods were worshipped in Rome from the very earliest times. One of the most remarkable examples comes from the sanctuary of the Niger Lapis in the Comitium, which Filippo Coarelli has convincingly identified as the shrine of Vulcan (Volcanal) referred to in written sources. A votive deposit associated with the earliest phases of the sanctuary was found to contain a fragment of an Attic black-figure cup showing Hephaestus returning to Mount Olympus on a donkey, a well-known Greek myth (Figure 20). The presence of this scene in this context cannot be a coincidence. It confirms the identification of the shrine with the Volcanal, and proves that by this date (580–570 BC) the Romans had already equated Vulcan with Hephaestus.[47]

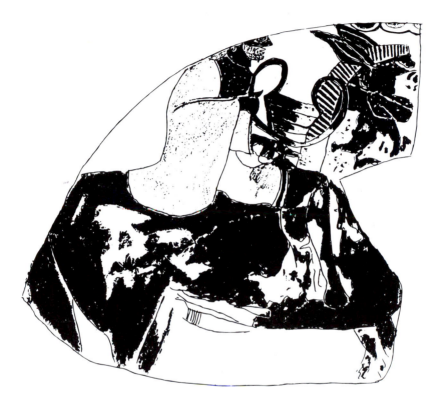

Figure 20 Fragment of an Attic cup from the Volcanal.

5 ROME AND ETRUSCAN CULTURE: ALTERNATIVE MODELS

The archaeological evidence now available offers a picture of archaic Rome far removed from that of a primitive settlement on the periphery of the Etruscan world, passively awaiting enlightenment from a superior civilisation. What we see instead is a vigorous independent community developing its own hellenising culture, and taking a full and direct part in the circulation of goods, people and ideas that transformed the western Mediterranean at this time. Scholars today speak of a cultural *koinē*, a linguistic metaphor implying the spread of a common cultural idiom throughout Tyrrhenian Italy.[48] The interchange of goods, ideas and persons between Etruria, Latium and Campania, and between these areas and the outside world, produced a

163

common material culture shared by peoples with distinct ethnic and linguistic identities.

In defining the relations between these groups scholars have begun to abandon the old 'imperialist' models of cultural superiority and diffusion, and instead to concentrate on the idea of interaction. Particularly fruitful in this context is the concept of 'peer polity interaction', which seeks to explain cultural change through contacts, exchange and competition between auto-nomous political units within the same geographical region.[49] This is precisely the situation we find in Tyrrhenian Italy during the archaic period. According to leading advocates of the model, interactions in such a context lead not only to uniformity of material culture and its symbolic functions (for example the association of certain objects or assemblages of objects with high social status), but also to parallel developments in political and religious institutions. It is also suggested that high levels of interaction are likely to promote intensification of production and increasingly complex and hierarchical systems of organisation.[50]

This is a much better way of explaining not only artistic developments such as the orientalising movement, but also societal processes such as urbanisation and state-formation. As we have seen when considering the adoption of Greek mythology and divine iconography, Rome was in the mainstream of cultural development in Tyrrhenian Italy during the seventh and sixth centuries. It is neither necessary nor sufficient to look to Etruscan influence to explain the major transformations we see occurring at this time. It will be remembered that the same point was made about the development of literacy; the adoption of the alphabet in central Italy should not be seen as a simple linear transmission from Etruscan to Latin or vice versa, but as a more complex interactive process involving speakers of both languages (see above, p. 104).

Naturally this is not to deny the importance of contacts between the Etruscans and Rome in the archaic period – quite the contrary. Rather, the point is to emphasise how difficult it is to identify a specifically Etruscan contribution to the development of a culture that was common to all the non-Greek cities of Tyrrhenian Italy. Even to try to distinguish what is exclusively Etruscan is probably misguided, at least in the analysis of archaeological evidence for processes such as monumental urbanisation. For example in domestic architecture, the replacement of huts by houses with stone founda-tions and tiled roofs is at present better documented at Rome and other Latin centres than in Etruria, and there is no evidence of Etruscan priority.[51]

The same is true of infrastructural elements such as drainage works. In Rome the urban development of the low-lying valleys between the hills, and particularly of the Forum valley, required the reclamation of marshy areas by means of drainage. The achievement of this task is usually attributed to the Etruscans, who are thought to have been especially skilled in hydrology. The evidence is that the countryside of southern Etruria is riddled with drainage tunnels (*cuniculi*) designed to divert streams and to channel surface moisture away from waterlogged areas. Some of them are remarkable feats of hydraulic engineering.[52] The trouble is that *cuniculi* of the same type can be found in Latium as well as south Etruria, and since they are impossible to date there is no way of telling whether the Etruscan ones are earlier or later than the Latin ones. Of course on the standard (invasionist) view the phenomenon is easily explained. Thus Tim Potter writes:

> These remarkable structures vividly demonstrate how accomplished the Etruscan engineers became in the control of water. They were undoubtedly responsible for the Cloaca Maxima, which drained Rome's Forum area, and may well have designed the forty-five kilometres of *cuniculi* that are known from the Alban Hills.[53]

This statement begs the question because nothing compels us to assume that the engineers in question were Etruscans. There is nothing inherently Etruscan about a drainage tunnel. The mention of the Cloaca Maxima, however, is a reference to the story that the great Roman sewer was constructed by one of the Tarquins. Here it is important to stress the point that has been well made by Christian Meyer, namely that there is no necessary connection between the actions of a king of Rome and the fact that he was of foreign extraction.[54] One might as well connect the foundation of the Bank of England (1696) with the fact that William III was a Dutchman. Certainly the sources do not suggest that the Cloaca Maxima had anything to do with Tarquin's ethnic background. Rather, they link it with the tyrannical nature of his rule, since the people had to be dragooned into working on the project.[55]

6 THE EVIDENCE OF THE SOURCES

The purpose of the discussion so far has been to challenge a modern approach which makes the Etruscans responsible for all kinds of innovations, ideas, customs and institutions. This approach is founded not on the evidence but on mistaken a-priori assumptions. That is not to say, however, that the matter of Etruscan influence on early Rome is ignored in the sources. On the contrary, it appears that historians and antiquarians in the late Republic developed an interest in this question, which resulted in a more or less agreed list of Etruscan borrowings. The main items in this list can be found in Livy and Dionysius of Halicarnassus, in derivative authorities like Florus and Silius Italicus, and particularly in the composite ethnographic accounts of Diodorus and Strabo.[56]

All the sources agree that the dress and insignia of the kings were borrowed from the Etruscans. Some of these ceremonial trappings were inherited by the curule magistrates – the purple-bordered robe (*toga praetexta*), the folding chair made of ivory (*sella curulis*), and the *fasces*, the bundles of rods and axes, carried by attendants called lictors, and symbolising the magistrate's power to inflict physical punishment. Other elements of the regal insignia were preserved in the costume and accessories of the *triumphator* – the embroidered purple robes (*toga purpurea, tunica palmata*), the chariot, the gold crown and the ivory sceptre surmounted by an eagle. Further Etruscan borrowings included musical instruments, and their use in war and on formal public occasions; certain ritual procedures, especially those used in the ceremonial foundation of a city, and divination by examining the innards of sacrificial animals; and a particular style of architecture that influenced the design of both sacred and secular buildings.

Two observations may be made about this list. First, the sources do not agree about when or how the various items were introduced to Rome. Strabo is the only writer to imply that they were all brought by the Tarquins (and even he is not explicit on the point). Livy tells us, for example, that the royal insignia were adopted by Romulus. Dionysius is aware of this version, but himself prefers to believe that they were conferred on Tarquinius Priscus after his victory over the Etruscans (an event not registered by Livy). Another tradition dates them to the reign of Tullus Hostilius.[57] Similar discrepancies surround the introduction of Etruscan methods of divination, foundation rituals, and so on. It follows that the sources offer no support for the modern view of an 'Etruscan period' during the later monarchy; rather, they assume that the city was open to Etruscan influences from the time of its foundation, although it was at no time overwhelmed by them. This seems to me to be a balanced view, and one that fits the evidence better than the more extreme modern theories.

Second, it is evident that the traditional list of Etruscan borrowings is limited to external adjuncts of Roman public institutions and ceremonies, and does not extend to the institutions and ceremonies themselves. Of the triumph, for instance, it has been well said that, in spite of its many Etruscan trappings, 'the ancients never claimed, as modern scholars have done, that the institution itself was borrowed from the Etruscans'.[58] Again, if the symbols of Roman political authority were Etruscan, it does not follow that Roman political institutions or juridical concepts of power were also of Etruscan origin. There is, admittedly, an impressive body of scholarly opinion that ascribes an Etruscan origin to the concept of *imperium*, but this view is based on a-priori theories about an 'Etruscan monarchy' in the sixth century which we have seen to be unfounded.[59]

An essential ingredient of *imperium* was the right of the holder to take the auspices, which was conferred by the ceremony of *inauguratio*. Our sources insist, however, that *auspicium* and the whole science of augury were not of Etruscan origin.[60] The only form of divination specifically attributed to the Etruscans was extispicy (i.e. examination of entrails), which throughout Roman history remained the preserve of special Etruscan priests called *haruspices*. This was always a distinct and marginal area of Roman religious life, which may not even go back to an early date. The practice of summoning *haruspices* from Etruria to interpret signs is not recorded as a regular event until the Second Punic War.[61]

A similar problem surrounds the dating of Etruscan foundation rituals. We are relatively well informed about these ceremonies (for details see below, p. 203), which were regularly performed when the Romans founded colonies during the middle Republic; but it is quite another question whether they go back to the archaic period. We need not accept the pious Roman legend that Romulus founded Rome in accordance with sacred protocols dictated by Etruscan priests,[62] although the tracing of the *pomerium* ('sacred boundary') by Servius Tullius may have more serious credentials. However that may be, the important point is that the Etruscan rituals associated with the foundation of a city are precisely that – rituals. They do not mean that the Etruscans invented town planning or city life, as some historians seem to think.[63] Similarly in architecture, the existence of a distinctive 'Tuscanic' style (as Vitruvius calls it) does not justify the inference that it was the Etruscans who first began to build permanent houses in place of huts, or that they introduced the idea of providing the gods with temples. In fact city life, town planning, houses and temples were all originally Greek; the spread of these features in central Italy was part of the formation of a hellenising *koinē* in which the specific Etruscan contribution, where visible at all, was limited to technical or marginal aspects.

As far as the 'Tuscanic' temple is concerned, there is good reason to think that it was first developed in Rome, where the earliest examples have been found.[64] 'Tuscanic' probably means Etruscan, but Vitruvius may have fallen victim to a tendency, prevalent in his time, to regard as Etruscan anything venerable or archaic (see below); alternatively, he could have been misled by his Greek sources, given that down to the third century Greek writers referred to all the native inhabitants of peninsular Italy indiscriminately as Tyrrhenians (i.e. Etruscans), as Dionysius of Halicarnassus perceptively observed (1.29.2). A Greek writer would not think twice about calling an Italic temple Tyrrhenian.

We know, certainly, that the great temple of Capitoline Jupiter at Rome was built by Etruscan craftsmen, and its terracotta sculptures were made by artists from Veii (see above, p. 129). But this means only that the Romans were able to call upon the services of the best available craftsmen, and in the late sixth century, as the statues from the Portonaccio temple amply attest, the finest school of terracotta sculpture was situated at Veii (Figure 21).[65] The facts testify to the cosmopolitan character of Rome, rather than to its dependence on Etruria. In any case, what this evidence most emphatically does not prove is that the Capitoline cult, of Jupiter, Juno and Minerva, was itself of Etruscan origin. The Etruscan character of the Capitoline triad has, however, become a piece of received wisdom, endlessly repeated in secondary works, even though it was decisively refuted by Luisa Banti as long ago as 1943.[66]

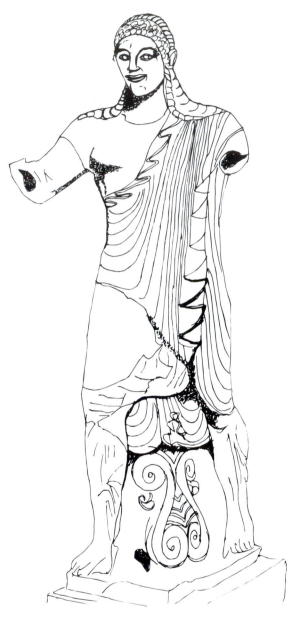

Figure 21 The 'Apollo of Veii': acroterial statue from the Portonaccio Sanctuary, Veii (Villa Giulia).

7 CONCLUSION

The evidence of the sources suggests that the encounter with the Etruscans had only superficial effects on Roman life and culture. Formal dress, magisterial symbols, ceremonial trappings, ritual technicalities and architectural forms – these amount to little more than outward tokens. This conclusion is precisely matched by the evidence for Etruscan influence on the Latin language. The number of Etruscan words in Latin is comparatively small, and most of those are technical, as Alfred Ernout pointed out more than sixty years ago.[67] The only word of socio-political importance that might conceivably be Etruscan is *populus*, but the evidence is far from certain.[68] In any case it is an exception that proves the rule.

A second feature of the traditional list of Etruscan borrowings is that it is largely confined to archaic aspects of Roman political and religious life which survived in fossilised form down to the late Republic. This can be related to a perceptible Roman tendency, often remarked upon by scholars, to treat the word 'Etruscan' as equivalent to 'ancient' or 'outmoded'. This habit may be due in part to an etruscanising fashion at Rome in the late Republic and early Empire;[69] but a more important reason was that the Etruscan civilisation which the Romans of that time were able to observe (as represented in monuments, works of art, such texts as may have been accessible, and whatever survived of an authentic Etruscan way of life in the first century) seemed to be, and probably in fact was, archaic and backward by comparison with their own.

What I am suggesting is that in the archaic period Rome, although different in language, and probably also in self-conscious ethnic identity, from the Etruscan cities, was nevertheless comparable to them in material culture, social structure and institutions. But during the course of the first three centuries of the Republic their paths diverged; Roman society and culture were transformed, first by the internal political changes that gave power to the plebs, secondly by conquests which revolutionised Rome's economy and brought it into direct contact with other civilisations, and third by a continuing open-door policy which changed the composition of the citizen body. The Etruscan cities experienced none of this; on the contrary, they remained largely static and comparatively isolated, so that in the age of the Punic Wars, perhaps even down to the time of the Social War (91 BC), they retained an archaic culture and a fossilised social system similar to that which had obtained at Rome before the emancipation of the *plebs*.[70]

In the late Republic Etruscan civilisation seemed to the Romans alien, mysterious, even barbaric;[71] that there had once been a time when they and the Etruscans had shared the same culture was something of which they were not remotely aware. But noting that their archaic temples (for example) were similar in design and decoration to those in Etruria, they assumed that they were 'Etruscan', and explained their presence in Rome as the result of borrowing. The Romans were by no means ashamed of such borrowing; on the contrary, they made a positive virtue of the fact that they owed most of their institutions and customs to other peoples. What made this not only tolerable but even a source of pride was the fact that they had achieved mastery over their erstwhile superiors; and it was ideologically potent because it helped them to come to terms with their complete dependence on Greek culture during the last centuries of the Republic. That they had beaten their teachers at their own game became something of a Roman conceit. This is well illustrated by a famous rhetorical passage from a fragment of an anonymous Roman historian. The setting is a debate between a Carthaginian envoy and a Roman spokesman named Kaiso:

> When the Carthaginian had spoken thus, Kaiso replied: 'This is what we Romans are like (I shall tell you things that are beyond dispute, so that you may report them back to your city): with those who make war on us we agree to fight on their terms, and when it comes to foreign practices we surpass those who have long been used to them. For the Tyrrhenians used to make war on us with bronze shields and fighting in phalanx formation, not in maniples; and we, changing our armament and replacing it with theirs, organised our forces against them, and contending thus against men who had long been accustomed to phalanx battles we were victorious. Similarly the Samnite [oblong] shield was not part of our national equipment, nor did we have javelins, but fought with round shields and spears; nor were we strong in cavalry, but all or nearly all of Rome's strength lay in infantry. But when we found ourselves at war with the Samnites we armed ourselves with their oblong shields and javelins, and fought against them on horseback, and by copying foreign arms we became masters of those who thought so highly of themselves. Nor were we familiar, Carthaginians, with the art of siege warfare; but we learned from the Greeks, who were highly experienced in this field, and proved superior in siegecraft to that accomplished race, and indeed to all mankind. Do not force the Romans to engage in affairs of the sea; for if we have need of naval forces we shall, in a short time, equip more and better ships than you, and we shall prove more effective in naval battles than people who have long practised seafaring.'[72]

I have reproduced this passage in full not only because of its intrinsic interest (and the fact that it is not easily accessible; to my knowledge no English translation of it has been published), but because of the reference to the Etruscans, who are said to have taught the Romans to adopt hoplite armour and tactics. This statement is taken seriously by modern historians, who are apt to repeat it as reliable evidence.[73] No doubt the fact that it fits their preconceived ideas about 'Etruscan Rome' has led them to overlook the rhetorical and unreliable nature of the source from which it comes. The truth of the matter is that the hoplitic style of fighting was of Greek origin, and it was adopted in Tyrrhenian Italy some time before 600 BC. In view of Rome's cultural status at this time, it is highly unlikely that she would have lagged behind the Etruscan cities in adopting a Greek innovation in warfare, or that the Etruscans would have had to act as intermediaries in its transmission.[74]

Just as in the case of the alphabet, or the borrowing of Greek mythology and religious iconography, so too in this instance the spread of Greek ideas in the communities of Tyrrhenian Italy was based on a complex mixture of direct and indirect influences brought about by peer polity interaction. We see here a clear example of 'the strength of the urge to conform to the practices of one's peers, even when it was only to fight them'.[75]

The paradoxical conclusion is that, so far from attempting to minimise or conceal Etruscan influence on early Rome, our sources are actually guilty of the opposite tendency, and have if anything exaggerated the extent of this influence. Even such supposedly obvious Etruscan features as the regal insignia may be a more general product of the orientalising koinē. Crowns, sceptres and purple robes are fairly universal symbols of monarchy, and their use in Etruria and Rome was no doubt affected, at least in part, by near-eastern and Greek influences. As we have seen, the tyrannical monarchies that are attested in Rome and some Etruscan cities during the sixth and fifth centuries owed much to Greek and near-eastern models.

The clearest example of all is dress. Larissa Bonfante writes: 'Just as the Church today retains certain ordinary fashions of the Middle Ages, the religious and ritual costume of Rome preserved much of what had been everyday Etruscan dress in the late sixth and early fifth centuries BC.'[76] This statement would be unexceptionable, in my view, if it simply omitted the word 'Etruscan'. What we have here, and what is so well analysed in Bonfante's excellent study, is the typical costume of the aristocrats who dominated the communities of central Italy during the archaic period. Its main elements were ultimately of Greek origin, but a distinctive regional style developed as a result of mutual imitation and interaction between the communities of the region itself. Call it Italic, Etrusco-Italic, or what you will; the point is that this costume was not specifically characteristic of any one ethnic or linguistic group.

Let us now sum up the results of this discussion. Rome was never an Etruscan city. It was an independent Latin settlement, with a cosmopolitan population and a sophisticated culture. Its material life was similar to (indeed often indistinguishable from) that of neighbouring Etruscan cities, but that does not make it Etruscan, nor does it imply any cultural supremacy or priority on the Etruscan side.

It is important to be clear about the purpose of this discussion. The aim is not to prove that Etruscan influence on early Rome has been exaggerated in modern studies (although in some of them it undoubtedly has), but rather that the idea of 'Etruscan Rome' completely misconceives the nature of the relationship between Rome and the Etruscans. On the model of a cultural *koinē*, 'Etruscan Rome' is as misleading a description of Rome as 'Roman Etruria' would be of archaic Etruria. Rather, the Etruscan cities, Rome, and other communities in Tyrrhenian central Italy shared the same common culture, formed from an amalgam of Greek, orientalising, and native Italic elements. In attributing an Etruscan origin to various features of archaic Rome modern historians are committing the same error as their late-republican predecessors, who assumed that archaic Romans and Etruscans were profoundly different from one another in their institutions, customs and mental outlook. Nothing could be further from the truth. The supposed opposition is both false and anachronistic, and any attempt to separate authentic and original elements of Roman culture from alien Etruscan intrusions is doomed from the start.

This is not to deny that there were differences between Rome and the Etruscans, just as there were differences between the Etruscan cities themselves; but these differences are not always visible in the archaeological record (which provides the only primary evidence we have), and when they are they do not necessarily coincide neatly with ethnic and linguistic divisions. A good example is funerary custom. This is a subject on which we have abundant archaeological evidence, and for once it enables us to detect important differences between different Etruscan cities, and between the Etruscan cities and Rome. We have already referred in an earlier chapter to the change in burial practice that occurred in Latium in the late orientalising period, when the number and quality of grave goods declined sharply; after about 580 BC the Latins (including the Romans) buried their dead in simple graves without any accompanying goods or artefacts. This situation contrasts with that in the Etruscan cities, where elaborate burials with expensive tomb furnishings continued throughout the sixth and fifth centuries (see above, pp. 105 ff.).

Stated thus, the data seem to point to a straightforward division between Latins and Etruscans; different burial practices, we know, do not necessarily coincide with distinctions of race or language, but in this case it might seem that they do. But there is a complication, namely that the change in funerary custom that occurred in Rome also affected the Etruscan city of Veii, which in this instance went along with its Latin neighbours rather than with the other Etruscan cities. This is only one of a number of resemblances between Rome and Veii at this period,[77] and it goes together with the evidence that the two cities were at the forefront of developments in architecture and sculpture in the late sixth century. Rome and Veii formed a cultural axis which cut across linguistic and ethnic boundaries. This merely confirms the time-honoured archaeological principle that can serve as a motto for this chapter: race, language and culture do not necessarily coincide.

7

THE REFORMS OF
SERVIUS TULLIUS

1 THE LOCAL TRIBES

At the end of Chapter 4 we noted that the 'curiate constitution' left only vestigial traces in the later republican system. The reason for this is that it was superseded by new forms of organisation that were introduced in the course of Roman history. The first and most famous of these reforms was traditionally ascribed to King Servius Tullius. Servius divided the people into new tribes to replace the old tripartite division, and carried out the first *census*, a characteristic Roman institution by which the citizen population was not only enumerated but carefully distributed into ranks and status groups according to wealth and property. Indeed it is possible to argue, on the evidence of the sources, that Servius Tullius invented the idea of Roman citizenship.

Servius' measures are described in elaborate detail by the sources, but it is widely recognised that these accounts cannot be accepted at face value. What we find in Cicero, Livy and Dionysius (to name the three principal sources) are versions of the system that existed in the middle Republic; and this mid-republican system was the result of a long process of change and development. In studying the evidence we need to consider three questions: (i) is it possible to reconstruct the earliest stage of the 'Servian' system? (ii) does this earliest stage go back to the time of Servius Tullius? If not, what is its date? and (iii) what was the purpose of the reform?

We may begin by considering the reform of the tribes. In later times the tribes were local divisions of the Roman people, and membership of a given tribe depended on residence. According to a unanimous tradition this system of local tribes was first instituted by Servius Tullius, in place of the three original 'Romulean' tribes. The developed system of local tribes, which existed in the late Republic and persisted through the Principate, was based on the division of Roman territory in Italy into thirty-five tribes, four of which were in the city of Rome itself, the remaining thirty-one incorporating the rest of the *ager Romanus*.[1]

One certain fact about this system is that it did not come into being all at once, but was the product of gradual development. As Roman territory expanded in the fourth and third centuries BC, new tribes were created to incorporate newly won territory. We know that fourteen new tribes were instituted in a series of stages between 387 and 241 BC, after which it was decided not to add any more to the total, but to include new territory in the existing tribes. Since the final total was thirty-five, it follows that before 387 BC there were twenty-one tribes. This much is securely documented and historically certain. Difficulties arise when we come to examine the origins and history of the twenty-one earliest tribes.

It is probable that the twenty-one oldest tribes go back at least to the beginning of the fifth century. This can be asserted with some confidence, for two reasons. First, before the conquest of Veii in 396 BC (which was the occasion for the addition of four new tribes in 387) no significant increases in Roman territory are recorded for around a hundred years. For most of the fifth century Rome was defending itself against attack, rather than expanding at the expense of its neighbours. Second, an important notice of Livy (2.21.7) records that twenty-one tribes came into being (*tribus una et viginti factae*) in 495 BC. A passage of Dionysius also presupposes the existence of twenty-one tribes at the time of Coriolanus (*c.* 490 BC: 7.64.6).

Livy's phrase *tribus una et viginti factae*[2] is unfortunately ambiguous: it could mean 'the twenty-one tribes were formed', which would imply that the system of local tribes was first instituted at that time, and not under Servius Tullius, as Livy elsewhere maintains. Alternatively, the phrase could equally well mean 'the tribes became twenty-one' – that is to say, one or more new tribes were added to the pre-existing ones, so as to bring the total to twenty-one. This second interpretation is the more likely on general grounds, and is the one most widely adopted by modern scholars.[3]

The twenty-one oldest tribes include the four urban regions, the *tribus Palatina, Collina, Esquilina, Suburana*, and seventeen country tribes, the Aemilia, Camilia, Claudia, Clustumina, Cornelia, Fabia, Galeria, Horatia, Lemonia, Menenia, Papiria, Pollia, Pupinia, Romilia, Sergia, Voltinia, and Voturia. Of these seventeen rural tribes (which I have listed in alphabetical order) one immediately strikes the observer as an 'odd one out', namely the Clustumina. All the others have clan-type names, ending in *-ia*, and the majority of them (the Aemilia, Cornelia, Fabia, etc.) are in fact the names of known patrician clans. The Clustumina, however, has a geographical name, like those of the later rural tribes. Moreover, it comprised the former territory of Crustumerium, which was overrun by the Romans in 499 BC, according to Livy (2.19). This evidence suggests that the Clustumina was the most recent of the twenty-one oldest tribes, and that its creation was the event recorded by Livy under 495 BC when the tribes 'became twenty-one'.[4]

At least one other tribe appears to be of republican origin: this is the Claudia, which can hardly be earlier than 504 BC, when the Claudii migrated to Rome. Both Livy (2.16.5) and Dionysius (5.40.5) state that the formation of the *tribus Claudia* was a consequence of the migration of the Claudii. It is possible that the Claudia was formed at the same time as the Clustumina, and that both were added to the list of tribes in 495 BC. It may not be a coincidence that Appius Claudius, the leader of the immigrant clan, was consul in that year.

Apart from the Claudia and the Clustumina there is no reason in principle why some or all of the remaining nineteen tribes should not have been formed under the kings. But this is very uncertain, and it must be firmly stated that we have reached the limit of what can be achieved by the method of working from the known to the unknown. Anything that is said about the history of the local tribes before 495 BC must be largely conjecture.[5] The situation is aggravated by the fact that the traditional accounts, which agree in tracing the institution of local tribes back to Servius Tullius, contain puzzling discrepancies about the details of the Servian reform.

While some accounts say that Servius created the four 'urban' tribes, others maintain that he instituted the rustic tribes as well; an additional problem about the second group is that the number of rustic tribes attributed to Servius is impossibly high. Among the sources quoted by Dionysius,[6] a certain Vennonius is credited with the opinion that Servius created thirty-one rural tribes, to make thirty-five in all.[7] Since that was the classic figure arrived at only in 241 BC, we must deduce either that Vennonius was ignorant of the historical development of the tribes, or that Dionysius somehow misunderstood or misquoted him.

More problematic is Dionysius' reference to Fabius Pictor, who is quoted as saying that Servius divided the country into twenty-six tribes, to make thirty in all. This too appears impossible, since the tribes numbered only twenty-one in 495 BC. Dionysius himself seems to be aware of the difficulty, because he describes Vennonius and Fabius Pictor as 'less trustworthy' than a third source, Cato the Censor, who did not name a figure (but Dionysius implies that Cato nevertheless credited Servius with the formation of at least *some* rural tribes).

There are serious difficulties here, particularly as regards Fabius Pictor, whose testimony cannot be lightly discarded, especially as it appears to be confirmed by a fragment of Varro:

> He [sc. Servius Tullius] divided the fields outside the city into 26 regions, giving individual allotments to free citizens.[8]

One explanation of the difficulty, which was first suggested by Niebuhr and was later refined by F. Cornelius,[9] is that Rome's territory was more extensive under Servius Tullius than in the early fifth century, and that military reverses had caused it to contract, so that by 495 the original thirty tribes had been reduced to twenty-one. The ingenious arguments used to support this unlikely hypothesis have been shown to be fallacious, however, and it is now generally rejected.[10]

A more acceptable theory maintains that Servius' twenty-six rural divisions were not in fact tribes, but smaller units called *pagi*, which Fabius Pictor mistakenly identified with tribes. Dionysius deals at length with the *pagi* established by Servius, and with the rural festival of the Paganalia, in a way that implies that he too equated tribes and *pagi*;[11] the fragment of Varro, on the other hand, speaks only of 'regions', not of tribes, which may mean that Varro reproduced the same data as Fabius Pictor but offered a different interpretation of them. But what Varro really thought cannot be known, given that we have only an isolated fragment. It is also uncertain whether his statement has independent value as evidence; he may or may not have relied solely on Pictor as his source.[12]

The majority of modern historians would probably accept that Servius Tullius divided the whole Roman territory into just four tribes.[13] These comprised the four regions of the city, each of which also included a section of the surrounding country.[14] The country areas were themselves subdivided into regions (*regiones* or *pagi*), of which there were twenty-six in all. Some time later a second reform took place, which confined the original four tribes to the city, and replaced the Servian *regiones* with a new division of the country into rustic tribes, which may or may not have been formed by grouping together the earlier *regiones*. At any rate the new rustic tribes were fewer in number than the *regiones* – at most seventeen in all.

When did this second reform take place? Can we be more precise about when and how the rustic tribes were instituted? The range of possible answers extends from the view that the seventeen earliest rustic tribes were created all at once in 495 BC,[15] to the idea that Servius Tullius himself, having originally created the four tribes, subsequently changed his mind and at a later census brought in the rustic tribes[16] – at most fifteen of them, because on any interpretation the Claudia and the Clustumina date from after 504 BC. Of course, once it is admitted that the seventeen earliest rural tribes need not have been established all at once, it becomes possible to postulate any number of intermediate stages; and in the present state of our knowledge, further speculation along these lines soon becomes unprofitable.

Nevertheless, it is reasonable to ask whether any of the rustic tribes date back to the time of the kings, or whether they are all of republican origin. Here it is worth pausing to examine the names of the tribes, which may have a bearing on the question of their origins. Ten of the seventeen earliest rustic tribes are named after leading patrician clans, whose members are represented in the consular *Fasti* of the early Republic. This might appear to suggest that the rustic tribes were established only at that time. Furthermore, it could be argued that tribes named after patrician clans are unlikely to have originated under the monarchy, especially if the later kings were popular leaders ('tyrants'), who attempted to curtail the power of the aristocracy.

But there are serious difficulties in the view that the names of the tribes point to a date at the beginning of the Republic. First we may note that six of the tribes bear the names of clans which are not represented in the *Fasti* at all. Second, some of the 'tribal' clans, such as the Aemilii, Fabii and Cornelii, appear from the *Fasti* to have become dominant only in the 480s and later, while others, like the Sergii, Romilii and Papirii, do not appear in the *Fasti* until the middle of the fifth century. On the other hand, some of the clans which dominate the earliest years of the Republic, including the Postumii, the Sulpicii, and above all the Valerii, did not give their names to tribes.[17]

The argument thus lacks its basic requirement, namely a strong positive correlation between the 'tribal' clans and the groups that were politically important in the first two or three decades of the Republic. Indeed, the evidence of the *Fasti* has encouraged sceptical historians such as Beloch and Alföldi to argue that some of the tribes were created later in the course of the fifth century – the Romilia in the 450s, the Papiria in the 440s, and so on.[18] This sort of reconstruction is absolutely unacceptable, however, since it entails abandoning firm evidence in favour of scholarly conjecture. The starting-point for any theory must be the fact that there were twenty-one tribes in 495 BC. It is of course possible that this datum is unsound (although this seems unlikely, since it fits so well with everything we know about the development of the Roman state in the sixth and fifth centuries, and is entirely consistent with the latest archaeological evidence), but if it is unsound we are left with nothing whatever on which to build any reconstruction.

There remains the point that tribes bearing the names of aristocratic clans are *ipso facto* unlikely to have originated under the kings; but this is not an argument that can be pressed, given our ignorance of political conditions under the monarchy. Naming the tribes after aristocratic clans may indicate that the king who created them was minded – or compelled – to make concessions to the nobility; it may have been a meaningless gesture, offered in exchange for greater concessions wrested from the nobility. Even if the clans which gave their names to the tribes were the dominant landowners in the districts in question, which is quite probable, that fact need not in itself be politically significant. It has been well said that 'the patrician *gentile* name does not imply patrician domination any more than the eupatrid name of an Attic deme implies eupatrid domination of that deme'.[19]

The names themselves do not, therefore, point to a republican origin for the rustic tribes; if anything, the same evidence might rather suggest that they were formed under the monarchy. We have seen that the patricians were members of clans that had acquired special privileges under the kings; and the best explanation for the tribes named after 'unknown' clans (Camilia, Pollia, Voltinia, etc.) is that these had once been important patrician clans, but that they had died out, or had fallen into obscurity, before the end of the monarchy – they may even have been casualties of the revolution that brought it down.[20]

This explanation is certainly more likely than an alternative theory which maintains that the tribal names such as Galeria, Lemonia, Pollia, etc. are not those of clans at all, but are geographical names. It is poor method to assume that a tribal name must be geographical simply because no clan of that name is recorded in our meagre evidence. The weakness of the argument can be illustrated by the case of the Romilia tribe, which we know was named after a clan. But we know this only because one of its members, T. Romilius Rocus Vaticanus, appears in the *Fasti* as consul in 455 BC and as one of the Decemvirs in 451. He is the only patrician Romilius known to history. But if it had not been for his successful career – if he had died in infancy or had fallen in battle against the Volscians – the Romilii would have vanished without trace, the *tribus Romilia* would be ranked along with the Camilia, Lemonia, and the rest, and the name would no doubt be interpreted as geographical.

It should be noted, moreover, that two other '*gentile*' tribes, the Horatia and the Menenia, are named after patrician clans that are not represented in the *Fasti* after 378 and 376 BC (respectively) and were defunct in the late Republic. In the light of these examples, there can be no objection in principle to the hypothesis that the tribes Camilia, Galeria, Lemonia, Pollia, Pupinia and Voltinia took their names from long defunct clans that had failed, for whatever reason, to make the *Fasti*. They all represent perfectly plausible clan names, and some are indeed attested as personal names in later times – for example Galerius, the name of a consul in AD 68, and of an emperor in 305. Persons called Camilius, Voltinius, etc. are also known from imperial times.[21]

Evidence that any of the earliest rustic tribes (other than the Clustumina) bore geographical names is virtually non-existent. Medieval and modern place-names such as Rio Galera and Santa Maria in Galeria in an area to the east of Rome have been used by scholars to identify the location of the Galeria tribe;[22] but to argue from this evidence that the Galeria tribe has a geographical name[23] is literally preposterous. The toponyms clearly derive from the name of the tribe, not the other way round. The same objection can be raised against statements in antiquarian sources that the Lemonia tribe took its name from a *pagus Lemonius* (Paul.- Fest. p. 102 L) and the Pupinia from an *ager Pupinius* (Festus p. 264 L). These notices have been taken far too seriously by modern historians: their true worth can be assessed by comparing the entry in Festus (Paulus) p. 331 L, which states that the Romilia tribe was so called because it included land that had been captured by Romulus!

Thus far the origin of the local tribes has been discussed as it were *in vacuo*, without reference either to their function in relation to other institutions or to their place in an overall scheme of reform. What were the local tribes for? The question is easy to ask but extremely difficult to answer. It seems certain that they were connected with the census, which in later times, and probably from the very beginning, was based on the tribes; they must in that case have been part of the same package of reform that brought about the centuriate organisation, as tradition indeed affirms. But the precise nature of the relationship between the tribes and the centuries is problematic and elusive. This question will be tackled shortly.

For the present it will suffice to take note of the general point made most forcefully by H. Last, that the tribal reform changed the basis of Roman citizenship and redefined the links by which individual Romans were bound to the community.[24] In particular the reform replaced the old Romulean tribes and curiae, which were dominated by aristocratic clans, and which had an exclusive membership based on birth. From now on membership of a tribe, and consequently entitlement to Roman citizenship, depended on residence and on registration at the census, which was organised locally through the tribes. These aspects will be considered further below.

2 THE CENTURIATE ORGANISATION

Servius Tullius is said to have divided the people into classes according to their wealth, and subdivided each class into smaller groups called centuries. The citizens were also divided into age groups, so that each class consisted of equal numbers of centuries of *iuniores* (men aged between 17 and 45) and *seniores* (men aged 46–60). This is said to have had an explicit military purpose. The *iuniores* were to serve as front-line soldiers, the *seniores* as a 'home guard' to defend the city. The men in each class were equipped (evidently at their own expense)[25] with different kinds of armour and weapons, reflecting their place in the hierarchy. The details are best set out in tabular form.

Table 2 The centuriate organisation

Class	Property rating (asses)	Defensive armour	Offensive weapons	Number of centuries: iuniores	seniores	Total
I	100,000	Helmet, round shield, greaves, breastplate	Spear, sword	40	40	80
II	75,000	Helmet, oblong shield, greaves	Spear, sword	10	10	20
III	50,000	Helmet, oblong shield	Spear, sword	10	10	20
IV	25,000	[Oblong shield]	Spear, javelin [sword]	10	10	20
V	11,000 [12,500]	—	Sling, stones [javelin]	15	15	30
Infantry total						170
Supernumerary centuries:						
Equites (cavalry): 18; Engineers: 2; Musicians: 2; Proletarians: 1						23
Total number of centuries						193

Sources: Livy 1.43; Dionysius of Halicarnassus IV, 16–18. The two sources offer virtually identical information. Differences are indicated by square brackets [], which contain variants and additions found in Dionysius but not in Livy.

It is generally agreed that this system as it stands cannot go back to the time of Servius Tullius. What Livy and Dionysius have given us is a description of the system that existed at a much later period, probably in the fourth and third centuries, when it no longer performed a military function, but was a division of the people for political purposes in the *comitia centuriata*. The principal reason for this conclusion is that the centuries in the scheme as described are clearly units of very different size; they cannot have functioned as military units, and they certainly cannot be units of 100 men, although that is of course the literal meaning of the term, and it is reasonable to assume that when it was first introduced the *centuria* did indeed consist of 100 men.

But in the 'Servian' hierarchy it is obvious that the centuries of the richer classes would have been much smaller than those of the relatively more populous poorer classes. Cicero (*Rep.* 2.39) and Dionysius (4.18.2) make this point explicitly, but it is in any case unimaginable that the numerical ratios of the centuries in the various classes could possibly reflect the social structure of a real community. In fact we may reasonably assume that the numbers of centuries in the various classes are in inverse proportion to the actual numbers of citizens. Another obvious anomaly is that there were equal numbers of centuries of *seniores* and *iuniores*, although in fact the latter must have heavily outnumbered the former; the ratio was probably around 3:1. The unavoidable conclusion is that the senior centuries were invariably much smaller than their junior counterparts.

Before we proceed any further it will be well to glance briefly at the sources. The accounts of Livy and Dionysius agree precisely in all respects except on details of the armour and weapons borne by the two lowest classes, the census rating of the fifth class, and the location in the class system of the centuries of engineers and musicians.[26] These discrepancies are of small importance in themselves, but they are significant in that they show that Livy and Dionysius were following different annalists; on the other hand, the basic agreement on all major points demonstrates that the annalistic accounts go back to the same ultimate source, which, as Mommsen first recognised, was almost certainly an official document called the *descriptio classium*, mentioned by Festus (p. 290 L).[27]

The fact that Livy and Dionysius disagree on the nature of the armour and weapons carried by the various classes almost certainly means that the official document made no mention of weapons, and that they represent the result of learned research and conjecture by antiquarians and annalists. If so, the account of the armament of the different classes, which certainly appears to be artificial and contrived, should be treated with the gravest suspicion. The most that can be accepted without reserve is the distinction between the heavily armed infantry of the first three classes, and the light-armed troops of classes IV and V. These conclusions are important, as we shall see.

A brief note is needed on the method of assessment. Membership of the classes depended on an assessment of the value of a family's estate; the paterfamilias and all free-born males within his *potestas* were then assigned to the appropriate class. The assessment of the value of an estate was measured in bronze *asses*, the *as* being a pound of bronze. There is no need to infer from the fact that the ratings are given in *asses* that the organisation described by Livy and Dionysius dates from a time after the Romans had begun to use coinage; weights of metal could be (and in Rome almost certainly were) used as a measure of value and even as a means of exchange long before the Romans decided to issue specially designated pieces of metal in the form of coins.

Even so, some scholars have argued that the rating in *asses* points to a relatively late date for the 'Servian' class system described by Livy and Dionysius. The argument rests on the assumption that the valuations have been calculated in so-called 'sextantal' *asses*, that is, *asses* weighing two ounces, or one-sixth of a Roman pound. This devalued sextantal *as* was introduced in the Second Punic War, around 211 BC, at the same time as the *denarius*, a silver coin rated as equivalent to ten sextantal *asses* (the word *denarius* means literally 'a tenner'). From this it has been inferred that the class system described by Livy and Dionysius belongs to the period after *c.* 211 BC.[28]

But this conclusion is far from secure. In the first place the only reason for thinking that the census ratings are defined in sextantal *asses* is that Dionysius, who was writing in Greek for a Greek readership, has converted the sums into drachmae at a rate of ten *asses* to the drachma; since the Attic drachma was equivalent to a *denarius*, it follows that Dionysius (or his source) was using the sextantal standard. But this may simply have been a mistake by Dionysius or his source. All one can legitimately infer from this evidence is that the sums were converted into Greek drachmae some time after *c.* 211 BC.[29] But even if we suppose for the sake of argument that the values *are* expressed in sextantal *asses*,[30] that need not mean anything more than that the figures were updated and converted to the new monetary system introduced in 211 BC. This could mean either that the *descriptio classium* was itself updated by the censors, or that the historians who transcribed the document converted old-fashioned sums into monetary terms that would be understood by their readers. However that may be, the census ratings reported by Livy and Dionysius have no bearing on the question of the date of the 'Servian' organisation itself.

3 THE ORIGINS OF THE CENTURIATE ORGANISATION: FRACCARO'S THEORY

In an important and influential paper published in 1930 Plinio Fraccaro observed that the centuriate organisation as described by Livy and Dionysius is based on a structure that corresponds precisely to that of the Roman legion.[31] Throughout its long history the legion consisted of sixty centuries of heavy infantry, backed up by a smaller number of light-armed troops (*velites*). In the middle Republic the *velites* amounted to 40 per cent of the number of heavily armed legionaries – equivalent therefore to twenty-four centuries, although the *velites* were not in fact brigaded in centuries.

In the 'Servian' scheme a similar division can be observed in the distinction between the first three classes, which were heavily armed, and classes IV and V, which comprised light-armed troops with no defensive armour and only light offensive weapons and missiles.[32] Fraccaro noticed that if this distinction is applied to the units of the 'Servian' field army – that is, the centuries of *iuniores* – the result is precisely sixty centuries of heavy infantry in the first three classes (40 + 10 + 10), backed up by twenty-five centuries of light-armed troops from classes IV and V (10 + 15).

At the same time he drew attention to two curious facts about the Roman army of the republican period. First, although a *centuria* strictly signifies a unit of 100 men, the standard republican legion with its sixty centuries comprised not 6,000, but 3,000 men, supplemented by 1,200 supporting *velites* (rather than 2,400), to make a total of 4,200, the normal complement of a legion according to Polybius (6.20.8). Second, the Roman army during the Republic always consisted of more than one legion. From 311 BC onwards the standard number was four legions,[33] but before that Roman armies normally comprised two legions. If the facts are set out in this way, an explanation for both peculiarities automatically suggests itself. An army consisting of two legions of 3,000 heavy infantry (plus 1,200 *velites*) must be the result of a division of a single legion of 6,000 heavy infantry (plus 2,400 *velites*) into two halves, each of which artificially retained the original number of centuries at reduced strength.

The assumption that originally there was only one legion of 6,000 heavy infantry is founded not only on the literal meaning of the term *centuria*, but also on the fact that the term *legio*, literally meaning 'levy', ought strictly to refer to the whole army. Moreover, in the Republic each legion had six military tribunes, and a tribune was originally the commander of a tribal contingent of 1,000 men (see above); this original meaning is reflected in the fact that in Greek sources the word tribune is translated χιλίαρχος (= commander of 1,000).

Why should the original legion have been split into two legions at half strength? Fraccaro found the answer in a suggestion that had already been made by military historians such as H. Delbrück and G. Veith.[34] They had argued that such a change in the structure of the army, resulting in two identical armies in place of one, would most probably have occurred at the beginning of the Republic, when two equal magistrates (the consuls) began to share the command that had formerly been held by the king. Fraccaro accepted this argument, and concluded that since the core of the Servian organisation was a division of men of military age into units that are reproduced in the structure of a Roman legion, it must have come into being at a time when there was only one legion, based on a corps of 6,000 heavy infantry divided into sixty centuries. It follows that the Servian organisation was earlier than the consulship; in other words, it must have been introduced under the monarchy.

This brilliant insight of Fraccaro's has rightly been seen as a breakthrough in the study of the subject, and its central arguments remain persuasive to this day. Following Fraccaro, we can reconstruct the early history of the Roman army as follows. Originally it consisted of 3,000 infantry, 1,000 from each of the three Romulean tribes, 100 from each of the thirty curiae. In the course of the regal period the growth of Roman power led to a corresponding increase in manpower. There are various indications in the tradition that at a certain point the original number of soldiers was doubled. Dionysius suggests that this happened after Romulus' defeat of Caenina (2.35.6); Livy perhaps implies something similar at the time of the destruction of Alba Longa (1.30.1); and Festus (p. 468 L) hints that under Tarquinius Priscus the whole citizen body, not just the cavalry, was doubled in size and divided among the *Ramnes, Tities, Luceres priores et posteriores*.

What these rather dubious reports imply is that Servius Tullius took over from the earlier military organisation not only the century as the basic unit (each curia supplied 100 men), but also the number of sixty centuries – i.e. ten each from the Ramnes, Tities and Luceres *priores et posteriores*. His reform was therefore a new way of forming the sixty centuries. But this reconstruction, although endorsed by Fraccaro, seems far less likely than the alternative possibility that it was Servius' extension of citizenship to immigrants and other previously disfranchised groups that led to an increase in the number of available fighting men. On this view it was because approximately 6,000 heavily armed infantrymen were counted at the first census that the number of centuries was fixed at sixty.

4 THE HOPLITE PHALANX

There can be little doubt that the original reform had a strongly military character. For that reason alone it is likely that the first census made no distinction between *seniores* and *iuniores*, but simply counted all men of military age. There are also good reasons for thinking that at first the centuriate organisation was much simpler than the complex arrangement of five graded property classes as described by Livy and Dionysius. The meagre evidence confirms what one might reasonably expect concerning the military requirements of Rome in the archaic age, namely that the fundamental purpose of the census was to register all those who were both physically fit and economically capable of equipping themselves for military service. Within this group it was necessary to make only one basic distinction – between those who were able to serve as heavy infantry, and those who would only be able to fight as *velites*. Evidence for a basic division of this kind can be found in antiquarian sources, which refer to a distinction between a single class, the *classis*, and the rest, who were 'below the class' (*infra classem*). The most important of these texts is Gellius VI.13:

> The so-called *classici* were not all the men in the five classes, but only those of the first class, who were assessed at 125,000 *asses* or more. The term *infra classem*, on the other hand, was applied to those of the second class and the rest of the classes, who were assessed at less than the amount stated.[35]

This distinction goes back to a time when the *classis* was the effective part of the army. The word, which was derived from *calare* (= 'to call' or 'summon') is sometimes found in contexts where it can only mean 'the army'.[36] The most convincing interpretation of the evidence is that of G.W. Botsford, who argued that the *classis* comprised those citizens who could afford to equip themselves with heavy armour and were required to fight in massed ranks in the manner of Greek 'hoplites'.[37] The Greek 'hoplite' was a heavily armed soldier, wearing bronze body armour, helmet and greaves, and carrying the characteristic circular bronze shield (*hoplon*). But the protection which the heavy armour provided was offset by a corresponding loss of speed and manoeuvrability, so that the hoplite was only truly effective when fighting in a line alongside other hoplites. A massed body of hoplites, technically known as a phalanx, was virtually irresistible as long as the men who formed it were disciplined enough to keep their place in the line.[38]

When this type of armament, and the tactics associated with it, made their appearance in the Greek world, probably in the years around 700 BC, they rapidly superseded all other modes of combat. By around 675 BC the hoplite phalanx had become the standard form of military organisation among the Greek states. What is important for us is the fact that this type of warfare spread to Italy in the seventh century BC. Archaeological evidence, particularly from warrior graves, shows that the hoplite panoply had been widely adopted in the communities of the Tyrrhenian lowlands by *c.* 625, and representations of the phalanx are known from before 600 BC.[39] In view of the precocious development of Rome at this period it is reasonable to assume that hoplite weaponry and the tactical use of the phalanx were well established there in the sixth century.

It has long been recognised that the Servian reforms presuppose the adoption of hoplite tactics at Rome. The latest studies of the archaeological evidence show that this development had occurred by the sixth century, and therefore provide strong support for the traditional date of the original reform. There can no longer be any justification for the once fashionable view that the introduction of hoplite tactics at Rome, and consequently the centuriate reform, took place after the middle of the fifth century.[40]

The armour and weapons supposedly borne by the first three classes are entirely consistent with a body of heavy infantry fighting in phalanx formation. Strictly speaking, however, only the soldiers of the first class have the full hoplite panoply, including the characteristic round shield – the *clipeus*. In Dionysius of Halicarnassus this is described precisely as an 'Argive' shield – that is, a hoplite shield *par excellence*. On the other hand, the men of classes II and III not only have less in the way of defensive armour; they also carry an oblong shield (*scutum*), which is far less suitable for hoplite warfare of the classic type.[41]

The evidence we have permits two possible reconstructions of the original Servian *classis* and its subsequent development. First it has been suggested that the original Servian legion, the *classis*, should be identified with what later became the first class, and consisted of just forty centuries. The rest of the citizens were *infra classem*.[42] This view is supported by texts such as the passage of Gellius quoted above, which explicitly state that the *classis* comprised just the first class; another important passage is the notice of Festus which informs us that the first class was also called the *classis clipeata* – that is to say, it was distinguished by its use of the *clipeus*.

A Servian *classis* of forty centuries also accords well with the theory that Servius created just four tribes; it would mean that the three old tribes, providing thirty centuries of infantry, were now replaced by four new tribes, providing forty centuries of infantry. Admittedly, this rather neat hypothesis implies that a further change would have been necessary when the rural tribes were introduced; but some sort of change must in any case be presupposed in order to account for a later legion of sixty centuries with no visible relationship to the number of tribes. The increase in the number of centuries from forty to sixty could be explained in the following way: at some stage the *infra classem* were subdivided into four groups (classes II-V), and then or later it was decided to add the top two of these, each containing ten centuries, to the original *classis*, to form a legion of sixty centuries.[43]

The second possible reconstruction of the origin and development of the *classis* would retain Fraccaro's theory of a Servian legion composed of sixty centuries, and identify it with the *classis*. Some time later the twofold division *classis–infra classem* was replaced by the more complex system of graded property classes. This entailed splitting the *classis* into three classes (I–III), and the *infra classem* into two classes (IV–V) plus the proletarii. Since the term *classis* was from now on applied only to the first class, and *infra classem* to the four lower classes, this change effectively meant that the *classis* was reduced in size, and that the groups now enrolled in classes II and III were relegated to the *infra classem*.[44]

It is important to realise, however, that this change did not have any bearing on the organisational structure of the army. The legion continued to be made up of sixty centuries of heavy infantry with light-armed support. But the distinction between heavy and light infantry no longer coincided with that between *classis* and *infra classem*. The latter opposition ceased to have any military application, and was confined to socio-legal contexts. This point is highly contentious; for that reason it is necessary to digress briefly from the main theme of the sixth-century reform, and to examine the subsequent history of the centuriate order in a brief excursus. It will become apparent that this later history has an important bearing on the nature of the original reform.

5 SUBSEQUENT DEVELOPMENTS

It is extremely unlikely that the division of the people into graded property classes had a military purpose. It is true that Livy and Dionysius give the various classes distinct types of armour and weapons, but this looks highly artificial; the idea, for example, that classes II and III were formed in order to differentiate between men who could afford greaves and those who could not, is patently absurd. This is not to say that the heavy infantry were all armed exactly alike; it is inevitable that there would be individual differences between soldiers who provided their own equipment. It is less likely, however, that in the context of hoplite warfare there would be separate infantry units bearing different kinds of equipment. In particular, it may be doubted whether there was ever a time when part of the Roman army used round shields (*clipei*), while another section used oblong *scuta*.[45] Rather, the *scutum* should be seen as a later development replacing the *clipeus*, a change that took place when hoplite tactics gave way to the looser manipular style which was practised in the fourth century. Both Livy and Diodorus explicitly connect the new mode of fighting with a change from round to oblong shields (Livy 8.8.3; Diodorus 23.2.1).

All things considered, it seems extremely improbable that the five-class system was introduced in order to create a set of separate military units. The citizens were distributed among the classes in such a way that the first class of wealthy citizens, who were relatively few in number and formed only a small minority of the population, contained almost as many centuries as the rest of the classes put together. At the same time the classes were split into two age sets, the *seniores* and *iuniores*, comprising an equal number of centuries within each class. The numerical distribution of centuries among the classes therefore ran counter both to the social structure and to the demographic profile of the community, and cannot possibly have served a military purpose. On the contrary; the introduction of the new system in place of the simple distinction between *classis* and *infra classem* marks a decision to end the military role of the original Servian system and to adapt it instead for specific political and fiscal purposes.[46]

Politically speaking, the aim was clearly to create an assembly heavily weighted in the interests of well-to-do and conservative elements. The centuries, which functioned as voting units in the *comitia centuriata*, were so distributed as to ensure that the old could outvote the young, and the rich could outvote the poor.

On the other hand, the reformed system also had a fiscal dimension, since the property tax, known as *tributum*, which was introduced at the end of the fifth century, was imposed on the citizens in varying proportions according to class.[47] We are not well informed about how this was done, but the most likely reconstruction is that the centuries were used as the basis of a rating system. That is to say, the government could decide in advance how much it needed to raise, divide the sum by the number of centuries, and thus determine how much the citizens of each class should pay. Thus, the citizens of the first class would pay $\frac{80x}{193}$, x being the total sum to be raised. The second class would be required to pay $\frac{20x}{193}$, and so on. This is not idle speculation; it is precisely how the system is described in a little-noticed passage of Dionysius of Halicarnassus (4.19). But Dionysius also commits two major errors: first, he assumes that the system of five classes was used as the basis of recruitment for the army, so that the burden of military service, no less than the burden of taxation, fell most heavily on the wealthiest class; secondly, he attributes the five-class system to Servius Tullius.

The truth of the matter, however, is that the five classes resulted from a reform of Servius' original system. Is it possible to date this reform? The most probable answer is that it occurred at the end of the fifth century, and that it is connected with an innovation recorded by Livy under the year 406 BC. That was when the Roman state first began to pay wages to its soldiers, to compensate them for loss of income during prolonged campaigns (Livy 4.59.11–60.8; cf. Diod. 14.16.5), and it was then that the *tributum* was first imposed. Military pay (*stipendium*) and tribute are closely linked in the traditional narratives, which continually refer to them in the period after 406; this is unlikely to be either invention or coincidence, and we may legitimately infer that military pay, and the imposition of taxes to pay for it, were indeed instituted at that time.[48] This would be an appropriate context for the introduction of the five classes, which distributed the burden of taxation in accordance with people's wealth, and compensated them with corresponding political privileges.

On the other hand, it is probable that the reformed centuriate system no longer had any integral connection with the recruitment and organisation of the field army. For instance, it is hardly likely that two-thirds of the strength of the heavy infantry were drawn from the first class, and only one-sixth each from the larger second and third classes. This argument also tells strongly against Fraccaro's view that the system of five classes was an original feature of Servius Tullius' scheme.

I would venture to suggest that the moment when the citizen body was divided into five property classes, and split between juniors and seniors, was also the time when the centuriate organisation was detached from the field army. From now on the legions were recruited indiscriminately from all five classes (*ex classibus*, as Sallust put it – *Bell. iug.* 85) – that is, from all Roman citizens who possessed the minimum property qualification for membership of the fifth class. Within this group distinctions in equipment and tactical function were henceforth based on age, not on economic status (with the exception that the light-armed, the *velites*, were drawn from the youngest *and* the poorest, according to Polybius 6.21.7). This change coincides with the introduction of a new form of tactics, the so-called manipular system, in place of the old hoplite phalanx.

At the end of the fifth century, then, there was a major reorganisation of the political structure of the community, which coincided with a thorough reform of the army. This reform introduced pay for the soldiers, new types of armour and weapons, and new tactics. Livy confirms that these innovations occurred simultaneously: 'The Romans had formerly used round shields; then, after they began to serve for pay, they changed from round to oblong shields; and their previous formation in phalanxes, like the Macedonian army, became a battle line formed in maniples . . .', etc. (Livy 8.8.3).

If this general reconstruction is correct, it follows that the centuries of the *comitia centuriata* no longer bore any relation to the centuries of the legion, which continued to have a formal existence even though under the manipular system they had no tactical function. The field army was no longer an armed version of the *comitia centuriata*. The process of recruitment was organised not by classes and centuries, but by tribes. Men of military age who possessed the minimum property qualification were summoned to Rome and assembled in tribes; the tribunes of each legion then took turns to choose recruits from groups selected from each tribe in succession, in an order determined by lot. This system, described by Polybius, was in operation before the Second Punic War, and it was probably instituted, together with the other reforms, around 406 BC.[49]

The introduction of pay for soldiers was a logical and necessary innovation once the Romans had decided to raise heavily armed troops indiscriminately from all five classes, rather than from those (now confined to classes I to III) who could afford to equip themselves as hoplites. A point which deserves attention in this context is the fact that this same period provides the earliest recorded instances of indemnities imposed by the Romans on defeated enemies. The first case was that of the Faliscans in 394 BC. Indemnities became a regular feature of Roman military policy in the fourth century,[50] and frequently entailed the requisitioning of military supplies, such as clothing and equipment, for the Roman army. This indicates that Roman soldiers were no longer serving at their own expense, but were receiving food and equipment, in addition to wages, as a regular condition of service. If this practice was already established in the 390s, as seems likely, it would be reasonable to connect it with the reforms of 406 BC. This conclusion is consistent with the hypothesis that from that time service in the legions was no longer the preserve of a wealthy group who could afford their own armour and weapons, but had been extended to all citizens who could meet a relatively modest property qualification. They probably included the great majority of free adult males; the only group to be excluded was the proletariat, which probably did not become numerically significant until the later fourth century.

We may sum up this discussion by saying that the earliest form of the centuriate organisation was based on a simple division of the citizens into two groups, the *classis*, consisting of those who could afford to equip themselves as hoplites, and the *infra classem*, who served as light-armed. This arrangement lasted down to 406 BC, when it was adapted for political and fiscal purposes and transformed into a system of five classes of seniors and juniors. A notice in Livy (4.34.6) referring to the *classis* in operation against Fidenae in 426 BC suggests that the earlier organisation was still functioning at that date. As for its origins, Fraccaro's reasons for dating it to the regal period remain valid; we may also take note of another of his observations, namely that if the centuriate organisation had come into being under the Republic, the Roman tradition would not have insisted on attributing it to a king.[51]

The original Servian system was probably centred on a *classis* of sixty centuries. This cannot be certain, but it is on balance more likely than the alternative reconstruction which postulates a *classis* of forty centuries. This means that in the sixth century Rome was capable of fielding an army of 6,000 hoplites. By the standards of the archaic age this was a formidable total; any state with a military capability of that order was a force to be reckoned with in the Mediterranean world. But the notion that in the sixth century Rome was the major power in central Italy is consistent with a range of other evidence, including archaeology. Taken together, these considerations combine to suggest that tradition was right to attribute the *classis* to Servius Tullius.

Our reconstruction of the development of the centuriate organisation implies that it was first introduced as a military system, and only later adapted for political purposes. This statement needs some qualification, however, if only because it is questionable whether military organisation can ever be entirely separated from politics. This is especially true in the context of an ancient city, in which military service was not the specialised preserve of a professional group, but on the contrary was an integral function of citizenship; in such circumstances any change in the basis of military organisation is bound to be *ipso facto* political.

Scholars have frequently argued that the principal purpose of Servius' reform, or indeed its sole purpose, was to create a hoplite army using the tactics of the phalanx. The earlier army, on this view, fought in disorganised fashion with primitive weapons; warfare, at this early period, is said to have consisted largely of single combats between aristocratic champions.[52] This may be so; but there is no compelling reason to believe that organised hoplite warfare was first introduced by the Servian reform. Archaeological evidence suggests that the use of hoplite equipment in central Italy goes back at least to 600 BC, and it is possible, indeed likely, that the Romans had adopted the technique of fighting with massed hoplites in a phalanx some time before

Servius Tullius. Indeed, some such conclusion is essential if we are to accept that major conquests like those attributed to Tullus Hostilius and Ancus Marcius were carried out by the pre-Servian or 'Romulean' army.

What Servius introduced was a new way of organising the army, which goes together with a new definition of citizenship. Previously the army had been based on the three Romulean tribes, and amounted to a federation of armed groups dependent on the aristocratic clans which dominated the curiae. Servius changed all that, by introducing local tribes as the basis of citizenship – which had the effect of incorporating immigrants and others who had formerly been excluded from the curiae – and organising the *classis* by means of centuries. This brings us to the heart of the matter: the relation of the tribes to the centuries. This is the most vexed question of all, and it is the key to understanding the purpose of the Servian reform.

6 CENTURIES AND TRIBES: THE PROBLEM

It may be stated as a fact that there was a relationship between the centuries and the tribes. The difficulty is that we do not know what it was. The confusing state of the evidence concerning the origin of the local tribes, especially the rural tribes, aggravates the problem.

Of one thing we can be reasonably certain: the centuries were not subdivisions of the tribes, and there was no direct numerical relationship between them. Admittedly, the view that Servius instituted only four tribes, coupled with the hypothesis that the *classis* comprised forty centuries, would permit the convenient assumption that each tribe contained ten centuries (perhaps an especially attractive notion in view of the fact that each of the three Romulean tribes had also contained ten centuries). But this solution only serves to postpone the main problem, because it has to be conceded that such a system would need to be restructured when the rural tribes were introduced.

Some scholars have suggested that the later system was based on twenty local tribes, and have offered elaborate reconstructions of the relationship between the supposed twenty tribes and the centuries.[53] But such theories face insurmountable objections.

First, and most obviously, such theories presuppose a period when the number of tribes remained fixed at twenty, which can only be done by rejecting Livy's notice about the twenty-one tribes in 495 BC, and assuming that the twenty-first tribe, the Clustumina, was not added until the end of the fifth century. Such a procedure is arbitrary, as we have seen, and cannot be accepted as sound method. In fact it is probable that there never was a time when the tribes numbered twenty; it is more likely that the total went from nineteen to twenty-one with the addition of two new tribes (the Claudia and the Clustumina) in 495.

Second, a system based on a fixed numerical relationship between the tribes and centuries makes no allowance for changes in the size or the structure of the citizen body. In order for it to work effectively, all tribes would have to have approximately the same number of citizens and the same social structure; in particular, the number of well-to-do persons eligible for service in the *classis* would need to be roughly the same within each tribe. This approximate equality would be upset by internal mobility, whether horizontal or vertical, and completely undermined by any large-scale addition of new citizens as a result of immigration or conquest. New citizens would have to be incorporated in one or more of the existing tribes, which would create a general imbalance, or one or more new tribes would have to be created, which would necessitate a complete overhaul of the system. As L.R. Taylor rightly observed, 'the coordination of tribes and centuries would have required a complete reorganisation of the centuriate assembly on each of the five occasions from 387 to 299 when new tribes were added'.[54]

Rome was a dynamic society with a growing population and a constantly changing social structure, and it is unlikely that Servius Tullius or any other reformer would have introduced a system that required a static population in order to function properly. Indeed, this consideration may provide the clue we are looking for. That is to say, we might perhaps suspect that the institutions created by the Servian reform were flexible in character, and that their purpose was precisely to cope with changes in the composition of the citizen body. The clearest example of this is the census. The most remarkable feature of the Roman census, which differentiates it from comparable institutions in other ancient societies, is that it was repeated at frequent and fairly regular intervals. In the classical Republic a census was held roughly every five years.

The census was a complete review of the citizen body. It redefined its membership and composition by compiling a list of all adult male citizens and assigning them to their appropriate tribe, class and century. By constantly repeating this task the state was able to adapt to changes in the size and structure of the population. In short, at each census the city-state was reconstituted. At the end of the proceedings the officials conducting the census (special officials called censors were not instituted until 443 BC) performed a purificatory ritual called the *lustrum*, which entailed a sacrifice and a solemn procession around the assembled citizens in the Campus Martius. Whoever did this was said to 'found' the *lustrum* (*lustrum condere*), a curious phrase which is perhaps best understood as elliptical, and as signifying that the ceremony was regarded as a symbolic refounding of the city.[55] It is no coincidence that our sources present Servius Tullius, the creator of the census, as a new founder of Rome.

The centuries are the key to the flexibility of the system. Membership of the centuries was determined afresh at every census, and the assignment of citizens to centuries was the principal task of the censors (or equivalent) in the archaic period. The centuries can best be understood as a means of combining a vertical division of the people based on locality (the tribes) with a horizontal division based on property (*classis/infra classem*).

The starting-point for the conduct of the census was undoubtedly the tribes. As L.R. Taylor pointed out, 'the only practicable basis for a census is local'.[56] This means that the people were counted tribe by tribe, and within each tribe assigned on the basis of their property to the *classis* or the *infra classem*. The simplest form of military organisation would then have been to form the *classis* from tribal contingents. Those who agree with Beloch, that the forty centuries of the first class were made up of two centuries from each of twenty tribes, evidently believe that that is precisely what happened. But this kind of reconstruction is unacceptable for a number of reasons, as we have seen. So, if the centuries were not co-ordinated with the tribes, how were they formed? How did the censors (or equivalent) assign the citizens to their appropriate centuries, if not by their tribes?

7 CENTURIES AND TRIBES: A POSSIBLE SOLUTION

The available evidence does not permit us to answer this question with any certainty, and what follows is admittedly only a hypothesis; but it is one that makes sense because it resolves the difficulties we have been discussing and because it offers a clear political motive for the entire Servian reform. The suggestion is simply that the citizens within each tribe were divided equally among all the centuries. Thus, if (as seems likely) the *classis* consisted of sixty centuries, all those within a given tribe who possessed the necessary property qualification for service in the *classis* were divided into sixty groups of equal size. The sixty groups from all the tribes were then added together to form the sixty centuries. In this way the sixty centuries would always be of equal size, even if the total available manpower fluctuated through demographic shifts, and regardless of any change in the number of tribes or in the relative strengths of particular tribes. Internal mobility between the tribes, or between the *classis* and *infra classem*, could be dealt with by adjustments at the census, and the system could equally accommodate the addition of new citizens to any of the existing tribes, as well as increases in the number of tribes themselves.

The same basic principle would have been applied to the *infra classem*, if that group was also divided into centuries (which is not certain); and it was also doubtless extended to the five classes, and the groups of juniors and seniors, when they were introduced at the end of the fifth century. At that point, as we have seen, the centuriate system lost its direct connection with the army, which from then on was recruited directly from the tribes in the manner described by Polybius, although the basic structure of the legion based on sixty centuries continued to exist, at least formally.

Before this reform, however, recruitment was based on the centuries. Although at the time of Servius Rome was capable of fielding a maximum of

6,000 hoplites, it is probable that this total rapidly expanded, and that the centuries within the *classis* came to number more than 100 men. But it is unlikely that the Romans regularly fielded all their available hoplites; rather, the armies that were actually mobilised were of varying sizes, according to perceived military needs. The legion of 6,000 (or, later, two legions of 3,000) heavy infantry represented only the theoretical strength of the army. What remained constant was the division of the legion into sixty centuries, reflecting the division of the property-owning citizens into sixty centuries, which functioned as levy-units or cadres from which the field army could be drawn.

We have hypothesised that the division into sixty centuries was reproduced in each of the local tribes. This made it possible for the Romans to make use of the tribal organisation when raising an army, but also to base the levy on the centuries. In fact, this reconstruction is the only one that can make sense of all the evidence.

That the size of a Roman field army varied according to perceived strategic requirements is suggested by common sense, and is confirmed by the practice of the later Republic. Polybius (6.20.8) describes the enrolment of soldiers 'up to the number fixed in advance' (τὸ προκείμενον πλῆθος); the legion could vary between a standard complement of 4,200 and an exceptional 5,000, but in Polybius' time the total size of Rome's forces could also be adjusted by varying the number of legions and the strength of the supporting allied contingents. In the archaic period, however, when the army consisted of one legion (or, in the early Republic, of two legions), there must have been some mechanism for adjusting the number of men under arms at any given time – that is, for varying the size of the legion(s).

The centuriate system as we have reconstructed it provided the necessary mechanism, since the state needed only to divide the total number of troops required by sixty, and then to raise the resulting number from each century. This is the method described by Dionysius of Halicarnassus (4.19), and there is every reason to suppose that it reflects what actually happened in early Rome.[57] But Dionysius' account appears to be in direct conflict with an earlier statement (4.16) that Servius Tullius carried out the levy on the basis of the new local tribes. Gabba explains this discrepancy by supposing that Dionysius has reported two different versions: one of these was from an annalist who mistakenly attributed to Servius Tullius the method of recruitment by tribes that was practised in the middle Republic, and is described for us by Polybius; the other version, according to Gabba, was based on 'an excellent antiquarian source', and describes the levy based on the centuries which preceded the tribal mode of recruitment, and which probably goes back to the sixth century.[58] Other scholars have assumed that the levy was always based on the tribes, and have either overlooked or dismissed Dionysius 4.19. But all are agreed that, unless the tribes and centuries were numerically co-ordinated (which we have seen to be untenable), the two versions of Dionysius are irreconcilable.

Reconciliation *is* possible, however, on the theory that is being presented here. If the centuriate division was reduplicated in each of the tribes, then it would be possible for recruitment to be both organised by tribes and based on the centuries as levy-units. This could work in one of two ways: either the state could require all the tribes to supply a certain number of men for each century, adjusting the figure in accordance with the total force required; or it could select a certain number of tribes and order them to mobilise their available manpower. With this system the state could raise a specific number of troops by means of the formula $F = \frac{M}{t} \times s$, where F is the number of the forces required for a given campaign, M the total available manpower of the state, as calculated at the census, t the total number of tribes, and s the number of tribes selected.

Although it might seem unlikely at first sight, this latter method turns out to be one that was actually employed in archaic Rome, at least on some occasions. One such occasion was in 418 BC, when, according to Livy, 'it was decided to raise troops not from the whole population at large, but from ten tribes only, selected by lot; from these ten the *iuniores* were enrolled' (Livy 4.46.1). This passage has frequently puzzled scholars, who have either attempted to explain it away,[59] or to use it as evidence that the tribal levy, as described by Polybius, was already functioning in the fifth century.[60] But it presents no problem if the tribes and centuries were integrated in the way I have described, and I take this reference to be an important piece of supporting evidence for my thesis.

8 POLITICAL IMPLICATIONS OF THE CENTURIATE REFORM

If the reconstruction outlined above is accepted, the true political purpose of the Servian reform becomes clear. On this assumption a major consequence of the reform was that the centuries, as levy-units from which the main tactical units of the army were drawn, each amounted to a cross-section of the whole community, and comprised men from all the tribes. This would have meant that the army could not be split by regional divisions or clan loyalties. The effect of such a reform would be to minimise the power of locally dominant aristocratic clans, and to maximise the central power of the state. We may note in passing that a measure designed to check the growth of aristocratic power could hardly have been introduced under the Republic, when the patricians controlled the government.[61]

The Servian reform was comparable to, and may well have been inspired by, contemporary developments in the Greek world. The closest parallel, among the cases we know about, is the reorganisation of the Attic tribes by Cleisthenes. An important part of his revised constitution was a new method of recruitment for the army, which was made up of contingents supplied by the tribes.[62] Each of the ten new tribes was composed of three sections (*trittyes*), one from the city, one from the hinterland and one from the coast, so as to form a cross-section of the whole community. The aim, Aristotle tells us, was to break up the old centres of local power by 'mixing up' the citizens (*Ath. pol.* 21.2).

If the centuries were units of equal size and similar composition, they would have formed suitable constituencies in a political assembly. This raises the question of whether the centuriate system was designed to function as a political assembly from the moment of its inception. Our sources take it for granted that it was,[63] but many modern historians reject this assumption, partly on the grounds that the purpose of the reform was military, and that the political function of the centuries must therefore have been a later development, and partly because a political assembly would have no place under a monarchy.[64]

These are footling objections. It is obvious that a reform introducing new divisions of the people could have both military and political purposes, as the example of Cleisthenes shows; indeed, as we have seen, in the context of an archaic city military organisation cannot in fact be separated from politics. And if it is true that the Roman army had used hoplite weapons and hoplite tactics before Servius Tullius, as was suggested above, then the new organisation must be understood as having primarily political aims. As for the second objection, that under a monarchy there would be no need for a political assembly, one need only point to the *comitia curiata*, which undoubtedly existed in the regal period.

It is perfectly reasonable to suggest that Servius, an illegal usurper whose power rested on the support of the hoplite army, should have created a political assembly based on a new military organisation, in place of the existing assembly based on the curiae. Throughout its history the centuriate assembly always retained traces of the fact that it was essentially an assembly of the people in arms. It met outside the *pomerium* in the Campus Martius (Laelius Felix *ap.* Gellius 15.27.5); it was known as the 'army of the city', and was summoned by trumpets; during its meetings red flags flew on the Capitol and the Janiculum to signify that guards were posted to watch for a possible enemy attack. 'This practice was observed,' writes Cassius Dio, 'only in the case of centuriate assemblies, for these were held outside the wall and all who bore arms were obliged to attend them' (Dio 37.28.3). Strangely enough, scholars such as H. Last have inferred from this evidence that the purpose of the Servian reform was exclusively military, and that the political functions of the centuries were a later development.[65] This is not only a *non sequitur*; one could equally argue that the assembly had a military character precisely because it went back to the time of the original reform, and was specifically designed to represent the 'people in arms'.[66]

As for the possible functions of the centuriate assembly under the monarchy, there is plenty of scope for plausible conjecture. Some of its later functions, such as approving decisions concerning peace and war, could perfectly well have originated during the monarchy. It is also possible that the king asked the army to approve his choice of senior officers. This would fit very well with the theory that the consuls were originally army commanders (*praetores*) who took over the state after the expulsion of the king. In that case we could assume that in electing the consuls the army (i.e. the *comitia centuriata*) was simply exercising a privilege that it already possessed.

This reconstruction helps to resolve what would otherwise be a rather perplexing difficulty: why should the founding fathers of the Republic have created the *comitia centuriata*? One might have thought that the interests of the patrician aristocracy would have been better served by the old *comitia curiata*, which on the standard view was the only assembly to have existed under the kings. If the purpose of the centuriate reform was to check the locally entrenched power of the aristocracy, is it likely that the aristocrats who overthrew the kings would have introduced an assembly based on the centuries? The question becomes even more difficult to answer when we remember a peculiar feature of the procedure of the *comitia centuriata*, namely the fact that the six cavalry centuries, which consisted mainly, if not exclusively, of patricians, voted after the first class. This means that, in the original centuriate organisation, the cavalry was subordinated to the infantry.[67]

These problems disappear, however, if we accept that the centuriate assembly was created by Servius Tullius precisely in order to reduce the influence of the patricians, and that it already existed as a functioning institution at the end of the monarchy. However much they might have disliked the Servian organisation, the founding fathers of the Republic would not have been able to turn the clock back, and to abolish the *comitia centuriata* or even to reduce its power. We can well imagine that an assembly composed of the people in arms would have been unwilling to accept any diminution of its role, and would have had the power to enforce its wishes.

These considerations may also have a bearing on the judicial role of the *comitia centuriata*. Tradition records that in the first year of the Republic the *comitia centuriata* became a court of appeal in capital cases, as a result of a law proposed by P. Valerius Publicola, one of the first consuls. According to Cicero the Lex Valeria was the first legislative enactment of the *comitia centuriata* (*Rep.* 2.53).

The historicity of the Lex Valeria has been questioned on various grounds, some of them hypercritical;[68] the most serious objection is that similar Valerian laws granting a right of appeal (*provocatio*) to the people are also recorded under 449 and 300 BC. Only one of these, that of 300 BC, is reckoned to be authentic, the two earlier ones being 'duplications' or 'anticipations'. But this argument will not stand up to scrutiny, as will be explained in due course (below, p. 277).

On the positive side, it should be noted that the existence of a people's court (*iudicium populi*) to try capital cases on appeal is presupposed in the

Twelve Tables, which affirmed that such cases must not be decided except by the greatest assembly (*nisi maximo comitiatu*).[69] Here as elsewhere the Twelve Tables were probably not introducing a new principle but merely confirming an existing law. As it happens, there are good reasons for thinking that the citizens' right of appeal was first established at the beginning of the Republic. A recent discussion of this subject asserts that 'having established the new republican magistracy with implicitly extensive coercive powers the aristocracy is not likely to have imposed a major restriction on their exercise forthwith'.[70] But in view of what was said above about the origins of the *comitia centuriata*, one might rather be inclined to assert the contrary. That is to say, the aristocracy not only conceded to the centuriate assembly the right to elect the consuls, but was also obliged to give it the final say in capital cases.

The centuriate army was the creation of the kings, and we might reasonably doubt whether the aristocrats who staged the coup in 509 could automatically count on its support. They had every reason to be wary of the army, and to try to win its loyalty by not only confirming but also extending the rights and privileges of the *comitia centuriata*.

The idea that a popular assembly could act as a court of appeal may not have arisen *ex novo* as a result of the law of 509 BC. As it happens, our sources suggest that the kings had sometimes referred appeals to the people,[71] a tradition that should not be dismissed out of hand. The Macedonian monarchy, under which the army passed judgement in cases of treason, serves as a parallel.[72] We might conjecture that a king was not obliged to allow an appeal,[73] but at the beginning of the Republic the appellate function of the people in arms was for the first time conceded as a right.

However that may be, the foregoing discussion has established that the centuriate organisation could have functioned as an assembly from the time of its creation by Servius Tullius; and the importance of the *comitia centuriata* in the constitution of the Republic indicates that it almost certainly did.

8

THE POWER OF ROME IN
THE SIXTH CENTURY

The implication of the foregoing chapters, particularly those dealing with institutions and with archaeological evidence, is that Rome during the later monarchy was a large city with a strong army and a sophisticated culture. The aim of the following sections is to examine these aspects in more detail, and in particular to attempt an assessment of the physical dimensions of the city at various stages, the extent of its territory and the size of its population. We shall then proceed to consider Rome's relations with her Latin neighbours, and the city's position in a wider Mediterranean setting.

1 THE WALLS OF ROME

The extent of the city cannot yet be determined with any precision. Although the sources are reasonably forthcoming about the enlargement of the settlement under the kings, their statements are far from unanimous and often contradictory. For instance, the addition of the Caelian is firmly attributed to Tullus by Dionysius (3.1.5), to Ancus by Cicero (*Rep.* 2.33; cf. Strabo 5.3.7), and rather less clearly to Romulus, Tarquinius Priscus and Servius Tullius by other writers.[1] This is not an issue that can be settled at present by archaeological evidence.

Equally problematic is the matter of Rome's earliest fortifications, the object of much confusion and dispute in the scholarly literature. Substantial traces still remain of the republican city wall – the most impressive portion being that which stands in the Piazza dei Cinquecento outside the entrance to the main railway station. The course of this massive enceinte can be followed for almost the whole of its length, which amounts in total to more than 11 kilometres; it embraces an area of some 427 hectares, and includes all of the traditional seven hills of Rome.[2]

The ancients believed that this wall had been built by King Servius Tullius, but in this they were mistaken. Modern research has established that the republican walls, which protected the city from Pyrrhus and Hannibal, and played their part in the civil wars of the first century BC, were constructed in

198

the fourth century, after the destruction of the city by the Gauls.[3] A precise date is given by Livy, who places it in 378 BC (6.32.1).

Various attempts have been made to reconcile these discrepant pieces of information. It has been suggested for instance that the fourth-century walls follow the line of an earlier defensive circuit, which is revealed at certain points by traces of grey 'cappellaccio' masonry, and that these are the remains of a wall built by Servius Tullius. The trouble with this theory is that the best-preserved section of the earlier fortification in cappellaccio occurs on the Aventine, to the north of the church of Santa Sabina (overlooking the Lungotevere Aventino).[4] But we know that the Aventine was outside the sacred boundary of the city (the pomerium – see below) in the time of Servius. Admittedly this is not a decisive objection: one could argue that even at the time of Servius the pomerium and the course of the city wall did not coincide, surprising though that may seem.

Another relevant fact is that at the weakest point of the circuit, the section between the Quirinal and the Esquiline where there is no natural line of defence, the republican wall was supplemented by a massive earthwork (agger) and ditch (fossa). Excavations of the agger appear to have shown that it was considerably earlier than the wall, but it is impossible to date more precisely. The find of a small sherd of Attic red-figure pottery, dating from c. 480 BC, does not necessarily prove that the agger belongs to the fifth century.[5] The agger probably had to be repaired from time to time, and was certainly tampered with when the wall was built in 378 BC. One tiny sherd could easily have found its way into the earth fill long after the original construction of the agger, and cannot in any case be made to bear the weight that some scholars have tried to place upon it.[6]

In these circumstances we are left with arguments of a more general order. In the first place we may note that earth ramparts were used to defend the vulnerable parts of hilltop sites elsewhere in Latium. Some of these earthworks have been dated as early as the eighth century BC (Ficana, Decima, Laurentina), others to the seventh (Satricum, Lavinium, Ardea). At Ardea there was a complex system of three separate earth banks, defending the three contiguous plateaus that form the site. The largest of the three aggeres was 600 m long, 40 m wide and 15 m high, fronted by a ditch 20 m deep. This was clearly a first line of defence, since the plateau it enclosed, now called Casalazzara, was not part of the inhabited area.[7]

The case of Ardea suggests a possible parallel with Rome, where the agger is a long way from the nucleus of the city; the area immediately to the west of it is unlikely to have been inhabited in the archaic period. Whether there was an inner line of defence is uncertain. In an interesting passage (LL 5.48), Varro speaks of an earth wall (murus terreus) at the Carinae, the valley between the Velia and the Esquiline. At one time the Carinae must have marked the eastern boundary of the settlement; this is confirmed by the tradition about the tigillum sororium, a timber beam stretched across a roadway at precisely this point. According to legend the *tigillum* was the beam beneath which Horatius had to pass in order to purge himself of blood-guilt after the murder of his sister (hence the popular etymology: 'sister's beam').

The most persuasive interpretation of this myth is that the *tigillum* marked an ancient gateway into the city, through which warriors had to pass in a ceremony of purification at the end of a campaign in order to be readmitted to the civic community.[8] It is not easy to relate this to a precise stage in the city's development, but it seems certain that the inhabited area extended beyond the Carinae in the sixth century. Varro's *murus terreus*, then, probably belongs to the pre-urban period, and was a distant precursor of the *agger* (unless the *agger* itself is much older than the sixth century).

The evidence suggests one of two possible conclusions. The first is that in the sixth century Rome was partially defended against attack from the north east by a rampart and ditch running from the Esquiline to the Quirinal; but that elsewhere it relied on the natural defences of individual hills. There was no complete circuit of artificial fortifications. In support of this conclusion it can be argued that if Rome did have effective all-round defences, the Gauls would never have been able to capture it in 390 BC.[9] As we shall see, the behaviour of the Romans before and during the Gallic raid can be explained only on the assumption that the city was virtually defenceless (below, p. 320).

The second possibility is that even in the sixth century the *agger* was part of a more comprehensive system forming a complete circuit around the city. The principal argument in favour of this view is the unanimous verdict of the literary sources – something that deserves to be taken seriously. But we must be careful to examine what the sources actually say, rather than what we should like them to say. First it should be noted that Servius Tullius is not the only king to be credited with the construction of city walls. On the contrary: some sort of fortification is ascribed to all of them – with the exception of Numa, who was presumably too busy with religion to have time for walls. But the sources which attribute city walls to Romulus, Tullus, Ancus, and the rest are not in conflict; indeed, such notices often occur in the same source.[10]

The point is that as each king made additions to the city, he adjusted the defensive circuit accordingly. Thus, in Dionysius of Halicarnassus, Romulus fortified the Palatine, Aventine and Capitoline hills (2.37), Tullus enclosed the Caelian within the city's defences (3.1.5), Ancus fortified the Aventine (3.43), Tarquinius Priscus replaced the existing rough-and-ready fortifications with walls of squared stone (3.67.4), and Servius Tullius added the Esquiline and Viminal, enclosing them in a new walled circuit which was still visible in Dionysius' own day (i.e. the 'Servian' Wall of 378 BC) (4.13.3–14.1). A similar development is presupposed in Strabo, whose account deserves to be quoted in full:

The first inhabitants [of Rome] walled the Capitolium and the Palatium and the Quirinal, which last had been so easy for outsiders to ascend that Titus Tatius took it at the first onset .... Again Ancus Marcius took in the Caelian and the Aventine together with the plain between them, which were separated both from one another and from the parts that were already walled, but he did so only from necessity; for, in the first place, it was not a good thing to leave hills that were so well fortified by nature outside the walls to be used as strongholds against the city by any who wished, and, secondly, he was unable to fill out the whole circuit of hills as far as the Quirinal. Servius, however, detected the gap, for he filled it out by adding both the Esquiline and the Viminal. But these too are easy for outsiders to attack; and for this reason the Romans dug a deep trench and took the earth to the inner side of the trench, and extended a mound about six stadia on the inner brow of the trench, and built thereon a wall with towers from the Colline Gate to the Esquiline .... Such then are the defences of the city, although they [now] need further fortifications.

(Strabo, *Geography* 5.3.7, p. 234 C)

The main point of interest in this extremely intelligent and observant account is the unmistakable reference to the *agger*. Although their accounts differ in a number of ways, Strabo and Dionysius are agreed on one vital point: that the achievement of Servius Tullius lay in the fortification of the vulnerable stretch connecting the Viminal and the Esquiline. The two authors partly state and partly imply that the rest of the circuit was already complete before Servius' time. Now this seems illogical; one would have expected the most vulnerable section to have been fortified first, not last. After all, a chain is only as strong as its weakest link.

The best interpretation of these sources is that they each combine two elements: first, a tradition, which I take to be well founded, connecting the *agger* with the name of Servius Tullius; and secondly an assumption, which I take to be unfounded, that *at every stage of its development* the city was surrounded by artificial defences. For Strabo and Dionysius it was simply unthinkable that Rome should ever have been without walls.

A similar prejudice can be found in some modern writers. Recent excavations at Lavinium have revealed traces of a fortified enceinte dating from the seventh century BC; in the sixth century city walls of squared blocks of *cappellaccio* were erected, apparently surrounding the entire habitation area. If Lavinium had walls in the sixth century, so it is argued, the same must be true of Rome.[11] But this argument is scarcely compelling, because like is not being compared with like. Lavinium was a tiny place, its urban centre measuring no more than 30 hectares in area with a perimeter of around 2 kilometres. 'Servian' Rome was of a different order of magnitude, and belongs in the same category as the larger city-states of Greece and Etruria (cf. below, Table 3).

Few if any of the major Etruscan cities had complete walled circuits in the sixth century. The walls at Tarquinii and Caere, for example, belong to the fourth century and do not in either case surround the whole of the site.[12]

These cities relied for the most part on natural defences, as did Veii, which did not equip itself with walls until the late fifth century, shortly before its epic struggle with Rome.[13] On the Greek mainland cities with complete walled circuits were rare in the sixth century. Athens did not surround itself with walls until after the Persian wars, and Sparta and some others never did so. On the other hand, the Ionian cities were surrounded by walls at a very early date (in some cases before 700 BC), no doubt prompted by the threat of attack from the organised kingdoms of Anatolia.[14] The situation in Sicily and Magna Graecia is more uncertain: some cities (Naxos, Leontini, Posidonia) had walled circuits in the sixth century, while others, including Cumae, seem to have been unfortified towns surrounding a defensible acropolis.[15]

In conclusion, then, we may say that the argument from analogy proves little; if anything, the situation in the Etruscan cities tips the scales against the idea that Rome was completely surrounded by walls in the sixth century. On the other hand, there are good grounds for accepting the link between Servius Tullius and the so-called *agger*.

2 THE SACRED BOUNDARY AND THE 'CITY OF THE FOUR REGIONS'

The strongest reason for thinking that it was Servius Tullius who organised the defences of the city is the fact that he is celebrated in tradition as the man who fixed its boundaries. The definition of a formal boundary represents an important stage in the process of urbanisation, and is something we should expect to have occurred at Rome in the sixth century. It is also something we should expect to be associated with Servius Tullius, who more than anyone else is presented as the person who gave the city-state formal definition as a properly constituted and self-conscious community. This king and his activities deserve further discussion here. Servius is said to have divided the city into four administrative regions, which became part of a reformed system of tribes; he also organised the countryside into districts (see above, p. 176). This division of the urban and rural space is parallel to Servius' formal redistribution and classification of the people in the first census (see further above, Chapter 7).

As noted above (p. 191), in historical times the census was completed by a ritual purification of the newly reconstituted citizen body, a procedure known as the *lustrum*.[16] This is one of several indications in the Roman tradition that Servius Tullius was regarded as a second founder of the city. Another is the story of his miraculous birth and the idea that he was the son of the god Vulcan (above, pp. 132 ff.). These legends irresistibly recall the association of Romulus and Vulcan at the sixth-century shrine in the

Comitium – the Volcanal/heroon of Romulus (above, p. 94). Coarelli has put forward the attractive theory that the Volcanal was established by Servius Tullius, and that it was he who first propagated the myth of the founder as an ideological symbol of the newly emerging city-state.[17]

But the clearest expression of the idea that Servius was the second founder is the tradition that he defined the *pomerium* or sacred boundary of the city. The *pomerium* was a religious boundary traced by the founder of a city in accordance with an Etruscan ritual.[18] The procedure was adopted in historical times by the founders of Roman colonies; the details are described for us by historians and antiquarians. Here is Cato the Elder:

> Founders of a city used to yoke a bull on the right, and a cow on the inside [i.e. on the left and proceeding in an anticlockwise direction]; then, clad in the Gabine manner – that is, with part of the toga covering the head and the rest tucked up – they would hold the plough-handle bent in so that all the clods fell inwards, and ploughing a furrow in this manner they would describe the course of the walls, lifting the plough over the gateways.

> (Cato, *Origines* I.18a = fr. 18 P)

Some of our sources assume that this procedure was adopted by Romulus, and that Servius Tullius enlarged the *pomerium*. But their statements about the Romulean *pomerium* are extremely confused, and are regarded by some scholars as relatively late and artificial constructs based on the assumption that the city of Romulus would be inconceivable without a *pomerium*.[19] Livy significantly makes no mention of the *pomerium* in his account of Romulus, and introduces the subject for the first time when dealing with Servius (Livy 1.44.4). Many scholars have followed Livy in assuming that Servius Tullius was the first to lay out the sacred boundary in the Etruscan manner.

The *pomerium* of Servius Tullius was marked by stone *cippi* (Varro, *LL* 5.143) and remained as the sacred boundary of the city until the time of Sulla, who once again enlarged it – a symbolic and ideologically significant gesture.[20] The Servian *pomerium* enclosed the 'city of the four regions', and its course can be reconstructed from the sources with a fair degree of precision. The four regions were called Suburana, Esquilina, Collina and Palatina (and numbered I–IV in that order – Varro, *LL* 5.45). The city of the four regions embraced an area of *c.* 285 hectares. Of all the indications we have, this is the most likely to represent the actual extent of the city of Rome in the sixth century BC.[21]

Of one thing we can be fairly certain: Rome was by far the biggest city in Latium at this date. The simple measurement of surface area is a crude indication that takes no account of local topography or the possibility of large open spaces within the city. Nevertheless, such information as we possess indicates that the other Latin cities were on a much smaller scale, and that for anything comparable we have to turn to the larger cities of Etruria and Magna Graecia. The evidence is most easily set out in the form of a table.

Table 3 The urban areas of cities[22]
(in hectares: all figures approximate. NB 100 ha = 1 km²)

Latium:			
	Laurentina		5
	La Rustica		5
	Decima		10
	Antium		25
	Lavinium		30
	Satricum		40
	Ardea		40
Rome:			
	Palatine/Velia	(early 8th century BC)	50
	Septimontium	(late 8th century)	80
	Four regions	(mid-6th century)	285
	'Servian' Walls	(4th century)	427
Etruria:			
	Volsinii		80
	Caere		148
	Tarquinii		121
	Vulci		90–140
	Veii		194
Magna Graecia/Sicily:			
	Cumae		72.5
	Metapontum		141
	Locri		232
	Agrigentum		450
	Tarentum		510
Greece/Aegean/Asia Minor:			
	Thasos		52
	Mytilene		155
	Rhodes		200
	Halicarnassus		350
	Athens and Piraeus		585

3 TERRITORY AND POPULATION

The earliest indications of the extent of Rome's territory come from certain ancient festivals concerned with boundaries. Such ceremonies as the Terminalia, the Robigalia, and particularly the Ambarvalia, in which a procession of priests traced a boundary around the city (Strabo 5.3.2 p. 230 C), appear to date from a time when Rome's territory extended for about 5 Roman miles (a little over 7 km) in each direction, and thus embraced an area of between 150 and 200 square kilometres.[23] Physical traces of this ancient boundary also survived in the late Republic, for example the Fossae Cluiliae, a primitive earthwork which lay five Roman miles to the south of the city and supposedly marked the boundary between Roman territory and that of Alba Longa.

These territorial limits were soon extended. Tradition records that after the destruction of Alba Longa by Tullus Hostilius the Romans absorbed its population and annexed its territory. Tullus' successor, Ancus Marcius, made further gains when he led a series of successful campaigns down the Tiber valley. As a result the towns of Tellenae, Politorium and Ficana were destroyed, and their territories annexed. The *ager Romanus* now extended as far as the coast, where Ancus is said to have founded Ostia at the river mouth. By campaigns such as these Roman territory had been considerably enlarged by the end of the sixth century.

We can obtain a more precise idea of its limits from a reconstruction of the area that was incorporated within the earliest rural tribes; as we saw (above, pp. 174 ff.), the seventeen earliest rural tribes had been established by 495 BC, and the majority (probably all except the Clustumina and the Claudia) went back to the regal period. The territory under direct Roman control by the end of the regal period measures around 822 km^2 according to Julius Beloch's estimate. Further conquests at the beginning of the Republic would have pushed this figure up to around 900 km^2 by 495 BC.[24]

This means that by the end of the monarchy more than one-third of the total land area of Latium Vetus was in Roman hands. A comparison with the territories of the other Latin communities is revealing, and exactly bears out the impression given by the table illustrating the relative sizes of urban sites (Table 3). Following Beloch's reconstruction of the territorial boundaries of the Latin cities (see Figure 22), we can calculate that Rome's biggest rivals, Tibur and Praeneste, had territories of 351 and 262.5 km^2 respectively, but of the rest only Ardea and Lavinium had more than 100 km^2 each (see Figure 22). These figures are conjectural, but are of the correct order of magnitude. Adjusting the boundaries would produce marginally different figures and alter the relative proportions, but the general picture would stay the same.

Beloch, the founder of modern historical demography, realised that population levels are a function of the area and productivity of available cultivated land.[25] If we know the size of Rome's territory in the sixth century, and can estimate the likely yield of the cultivated parts of it, we can arrive at a figure for the maximum population that it could sustain. Naturally the result will be imprecise, and will depend on such variables as the amount of land under cultivation in any one year, the likely annual yield in conditions of ancient agricultural practice, and an assessment of how much food a person needs to keep alive and reasonably healthy (an issue on which experts cannot agree, even today). Nevertheless, it is possible to establish the range within which a correct answer will fall – in other words, a correct approximation.

Scholarly estimates based on such methods range from Beloch's own figure of 20,000–25,000, which is probably too low, to De Martino's 40,000–50,000, which may be too high.[26] In a careful reassessment of all the evidence, Ampolo

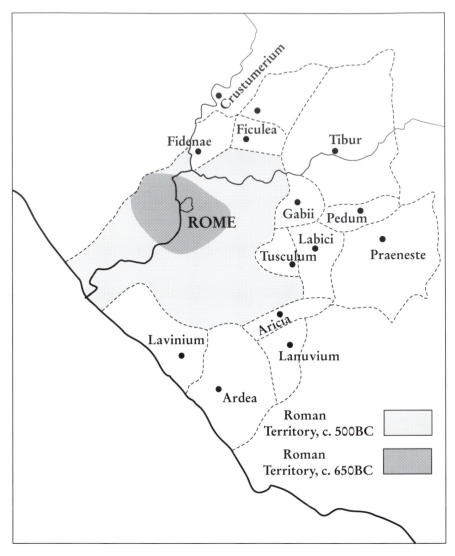

Figure 22 Territories of the Latin city-states, *c.* 500 BC.

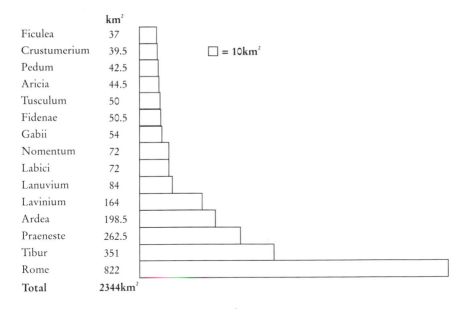

	km²
Ficulea	37
Crustumerium	39.5
Pedum	42.5
Aricia	44.5
Tusculum	50
Fidenae	50.5
Gabii	54
Nomentum	72
Labici	72
Lanuvium	84
Lavinium	164
Ardea	198.5
Praeneste	262.5
Tibur	351
Rome	822
Total	**2344km²**

□ = 10km²

Figure 22 continued

has argued for a maximum population of 35,000 in the late sixth century.[27] These figures are all within the same general range, and we may consider a reasonable approximation to lie between the extremes of 20,000 and 50,000, most probably between 25,000 and 40,000. Such estimates are consistent with the results achieved by Jacques Heurgon, in an important discussion of the population of Etruscan Caere, based on the number of graves in the Banditaccia cemetery; he calculated that the average size of the population during the six and a half centuries from 700 to 50 BC was around 25,000, but that it was probably greater in the archaic age than in the late republican period.[28] Once again we are directed to the conclusion that Rome was on the same scale as the major Etruscan cities, if anything slightly larger.

These findings tend to confirm, and are themselves confirmed by, the size of the centuriate army as reconstructed by Fraccaro (above, p. 181 ff.). This reconstruction presupposes a body of over 9,000 free men of military age (a *classis* of 6,000, with upwards of 2,400 *infra classem* and 600 cavalrymen). This figure would represent no more than 30 per cent of the total population – somewhat less if we allow for old men, proletarians and slaves, who would not be counted in the army total. In other words, the centuriate system presupposes a minimum total population of 30,000 – the same result by an independent method.

It is important to note, however, that these estimates differ radically from direct statements in the sources concerning the size of the population. A tradition going back to Fabius Pictor (*ap.* Livy 1.44.2) maintains that the number of men 'capable of bearing arms' (*qui arma ferre possent*) amounted to 80,000, an absurd total which must be some kind of mistake.[29] A more difficult problem is presented by the series of census figures given in our sources for the early Republic, which can be tabulated as follows:

Table 4 Recorded census figures, 508–392 BC

508	130,000	Dion. Hal. 5.20; Plut., *Publ.* 12
503	120,000	Hieronym. *Ol.* 69.1
498	150,700	Dion. Hal. 5.75.4
493	110,000	Dion. Hal. 6.96.4
474	103,000	Dion. Hal. 9.36.3
465	104,714	Livy 3.3.9
459	117,319	Livy 3.24.10; Eutrop. 1.16
392	152,573	Pliny, *n.h.* 33.16

These figures are extremely puzzling. They can on no account be genuine totals of adult male citizens, which is what the census figures of the late Republic represent.[30] Even if we suppose that they include all men, women and children, as Pliny seems to imply in his statement about the 392 census, they still seem far too high. Nevertheless, it is worth saying that they fluctuate roughly in accordance with the fortunes of Rome and its allies during the period in question. For instance, the decline after 498 could be explained by the loss of southern Latium to the Volscians (see below, p. 304). Coarelli has recently used this as evidence in their favour, but his argument still does not answer the basic objection, that the figures imply too high a population density for the known size of the *ager Romanus* in the fifth century.[31] Niebuhr's theory that they include the population of Rome's Latin allies is not wholly far-fetched, but is nevertheless rather speculative.[32] On the other hand, one cannot simply dismiss them as fabrications, as Brunt for example does, because they register fluctuations which no Roman annalist or antiquarian would have been aware of; their view of Roman history in the fifth century BC was one of uniform linear progress.[33]

However the figures are to be explained, they cannot be regarded as evidence for population size in the fifth century; they must be rejected in favour of the more soundly based calculations set out earlier, which give an approximate figure of 35,000 for the total population of Rome at the end of the sixth century. This would make Rome a large and powerful city-state by the standards of the archaic period, and lends support to the traditional picture of what has come to be known as 'la grande Roma dei Tarquinii'.

4 'LA GRANDE ROMA DEI TARQUINII'

The phrase 'la grande Roma dei Tarquinii' was first coined by Giorgio Pasquali in a famous article published in 1936.[34] Earlier work, particularly by the American scholar Tenney Frank and his pupil Inez G. Scott, had already suggested that the archaeological evidence (especially the architectural terra-position of Rome in the sixth century;[35] but Pasquali's paper was the first systematic attempt to combine archaeological data with Beloch's calculations of the size of the city and its territory, Fraccaro's reconstruction of the centuriate reform, and literary accounts of Roman power under the Tarquins. In the post-war period this well-articulated thesis was largely forgotten in the noisy debate about the dating of archaeological finds, and in the exaggerated emphasis placed upon the role of the Etruscans in the development of early Rome. What Pasquali took to be evidence of cultural sophistication and contact with the Greek world was dismissed as a mere symptom of a passing phase of Etruscan rule.

This tendency culminated in the important and influential work of Andras Alföldi, whose *Early Rome and the Latins*, published in the mid-1960s, argued that Rome in the sixth century was an insignificant place and that the literary tradition was a deliberate fabrication; so far from being the leading city in Latium, Rome was itself an Etruscan vassal. The climax of Alföldi's vigorous account was an eighteen-page chapter of sustained polemic against the myth, as he saw it, of 'la grande Roma dei Tarquinii'.[36]

Thirty years later, we can safely say that the debate aroused by this publication has been decisively resolved – against Alföldi and in favour of Pasquali. In spite of its learning and rhetorical power, Alföldi's book contains inherent weaknesses that have been fatally exposed;[37] but what has finally tipped the scales against him is the accumulation of new archaeological evidence. This material was recently assembled and put before the public in a grand exhibition entitled, naturally, 'la grande Roma dei Tarquinii', and staged in Rome to coincide with the World Cup finals in 1990. By all accounts the exhibition, like the performance of the Italian national team in the semi-final, was not a success, but the magnificent catalogue remains as testimony to an incontrovertible fact: Rome was a great city in the later sixth century BC.[38]

In these circumstances there is no longer any good reason to doubt what the sources tell us about the ambitious and successful foreign policy of the later kings. In particular we can accept that under Tarquinius Superbus the Romans had managed to establish an extensive hegemony in Latium. Natur-ally we cannot properly define the nature of this hegemony; it will suffice merely to summarise what the sources tell us. Tarquin is said to have organised the Latins into a military alliance under Roman leadership (Livy 1.52). He also captured Pometia by storm, gained control of Gabii by means of a ruse, colonised Signia and Circeii, and won over Tusculum by marrying his daughter to its leading citizen Octavus Mamilius. At the time of the coup that led to his expulsion, he was engaged in besieging Ardea.

There is nothing incredible in these reports. The story that the spoils of Pometia paid for the construction of the Capitoline temple may well be an authentic tradition connected with the building (cf. Tac., *Hist.* 3.72). If Pometia is correctly identified with Satricum, which seems extremely likely, recent excavations there have confirmed the richness of the site at this period. It is also worth noting that architectural terracottas from Circeii, one of Tarquin's colonies, appear to have been produced in Roman workshops.[39] The treaty which Rome made with Gabii was preserved in the temple of Semo Sancus in Rome, and was still there in the time of Augustus (Dion. Hal. 4.58.4).

Two further pieces of evidence confirm the fact of Rome's ascendancy at this time. First, the anonymous author of the appendix to Hesiod's *Theogony* wrote that Agrios and Latinus, the sons of Odysseus and Circe, 'ruled over the famous Tyrsenians, very far off in a recess of the holy islands' (lines 1011–16). If the appendix to the *Theogony* is correctly dated to the sixth century, these lines represent a contemporary allusion to the power of the Latins under Roman leadership during the later monarchy. It is worth mentioning that the appearance of Circe in this passage was almost certainly suggested by the place-name Circeii.[40]

The second and most crucial piece of evidence is the treaty between Rome and Carthage transcribed by Polybius (3.22), and dated by him to the first year of the Republic. This is probably the most important single text from the entire literary tradition about early Rome, and it deserves close attention.

5 THE TREATY BETWEEN ROME AND CARTHAGE

Polybius quotes the treaty as the first of a series of Romano-Carthaginian treaties preserved on bronze tablets in the Treasury of the Aediles on the Capitol; and he dates it to the consulship of L. Junius Brutus and M. Horatius – that is, to 507 BC on his chronology (see below, p. 218). In the treaty the Romans and Carthaginians agree to be friends, and undertake not to act contrary to one another's interests. In particular, the Romans agree not to sail 'beyond the Fair Promontory', and to abide by certain conditions when trading in Libya and Sardinia; as for the Carthaginians, they pledge themselves

> not to injure the people of Ardea, Antium, Lavinium(?), Circeii, Terracina, or any other city of the Latins who are subjects of Rome. As for the Latins who are not subjects, they shall keep their hands off their cities, and if they take any such city they shall hand it over to the Romans unharmed. They shall build no fort in Latin territory. If they enter the territory in arms, they shall not spend a night there.[41]

The treaty evidently treats Rome as the ruling power in Latium, and as controlling the coast as far south as Terracina, 100 kilometres south of Rome. If it is a genuine document of the late sixth century, we need go no further;

the annalistic accounts of Tarquin's miniature empire in Latium are directly confirmed.

That the document is genuine is accepted by all serious scholars. Not even Alföldi was prepared to suggest that it was a forgery, and we need not spend time on establishing the authenticity of a text that was accepted without question by Polybius, one of the most hard-headed and reliable historians of antiquity. But it is a serious question whether Polybius (or his informant) was right to date the treaty to the first year of the Republic. This has been a major scholarly crux ever since the date was first called into question by Mommsen in 1858.[42]

One of Mommsen's main arguments was the fact that Diodorus, sup-posedly drawing upon Fabius Pictor, clearly states that the first treaty between Rome and Carthage was concluded in 348 BC (Diod. 16.69.1). Livy too refers to a treaty in 348 (7.27.2), his first mention of any contact between the two cities. But the issue is complicated because in his next reference to a treaty, under 306 BC, Livy speaks of it being renewed 'for the third time' (9.43.13; cf. 9.19.13; *Epit.* 13). It is not therefore a case of Polybius against the rest – though even if it were, many experts would back the judgement of Polybius against all comers. The identity of Diodorus' source is much less certain than Mommsen thought, but in any case it would not be surprising if Fabius and other early historians had no knowledge of the earliest treaty, because Polybius himself makes it clear that the bronze inscriptions had only just come to light – probably around 152 BC.[43]

The principal argument in favour of Polybius' date for the first treaty is the fact that its contents accord with the historical circumstances of the sixth century BC. A later date is ruled out by the fact that the Pomptine district and much of southern Latium was overrun by the Volscians at the beginning of the fifth century and not regained by Rome until the middle of the fourth century. The only alternative is to date Polybius' first treaty to the mid-fourth century, and that is indeed what Mommsen proposed, identifying it with the treaty of 348 referred to by Livy and Diodorus. On this view Polybius' second treaty, which he does not date precisely, was concluded a few years later, perhaps in 343 (cf. Livy 7.38.2).

Scholars who reject Polybius' date have made much of the fact that a similar political and military situation is presupposed in both treaties.[44] But that is actually the point at which their argument is most vulnerable; what emerges clearly from a comparison of the first two treaties is not the similarities but the differences. Polybius himself noted that the oaths sworn by the Romans differed markedly between the two treaties: in the first they swore the archaic oath 'by the stone' (in which the person taking the oath throws a stone, on the understanding that he himself will be cast out like the stone if he breaks his word), whereas in the later treaties they swore by Mars and Quirinus.[45] This important distinction clearly suggests that the two treaties belong to different epochs.

There are also significant differences in the terms of the two treaties. In the second treaty the Carthaginians are careful to prevent the Romans from founding cities in Sardinia or Libya – a clear reference to their overseas colonising activities in the fourth century (see below, p. 321); the draftsmen of the first treaty, however, do not seem to have considered this a possibility worth guarding against. Finally, and most decisively, Polybius refers to the archaic language of the first treaty, which he says could be understood only with difficulty, even by the most learned Romans; but he mentions no such difficulty in connection with the later treaties, which must imply that the first was much earlier.[46]

The most probable date for Polybius' second treaty is 348 BC, since Rome's sphere of influence is still confined to Latium. A later treaty, even one of 343 BC, would have had to include Campania as well as Latium among the coastal territories under Rome's control.[47] If the second treaty was signed in 348, and if it was separated from the first by a substantial interval, the first treaty must go back to the period before the Volscian invasions of the 490s. A clear reason, therefore, for accepting Polybius' date for the first treaty is that there is no realistic alternative.

But there are also strong positive grounds for dating the first treaty to the late sixth century. Carthaginian interest in the area of the Tyrrhenian Sea is well attested at this period, and it is probable that the treaty with Rome was one of a number of such agreements which the Carthaginians made with friendly states in the area. Aristotle refers to treaties between Carthage and the Etruscans as classic examples of a particular type of trading agreement (*symbolon*) which provided for a mutual exchange of rights and privileges; according to Aristotle, the contracting parties became 'like citizens of one city' (*Politics* 1280a36). The purpose of these *symbola* seems to have been to ensure rights of access to foreign trading ports and to protect the interests of merchants resident in them. The presence of communities of Phoenician traders in Etruscan ports is indicated by the existence of a coastal settlement called Punicum (S. Marinella) in the territory of Caere, and by the bilingual Etruscan-Phoenician inscriptions from Pyrgi (Figure 23), another Caeretan port (see above, pp. 112, 148; below, p. 232).

When the Pyrgi inscriptions were discovered in the early 1960s, historians immediately realised that they injected a decisive new element into the debate about the Polybian treaty. Aristotle was already on hand to show that the Carthaginians were interested in making agreements to protect their traders operating in Tyrrhenian waters; the Pyrgi finds now made it clear that this trade was being carried on around 500 BC – at the very time when, according to Polybius, they made a similar treaty with Rome. The discovery also gave substance to a story in Herodotus, who records that around 535 BC the Carthaginians and Etruscans joined forces to defeat the Phocaean Greeks in a naval battle in the Sardinian Sea (1.166–7).

In the circumstances it is natural that the Carthaginians should have wanted

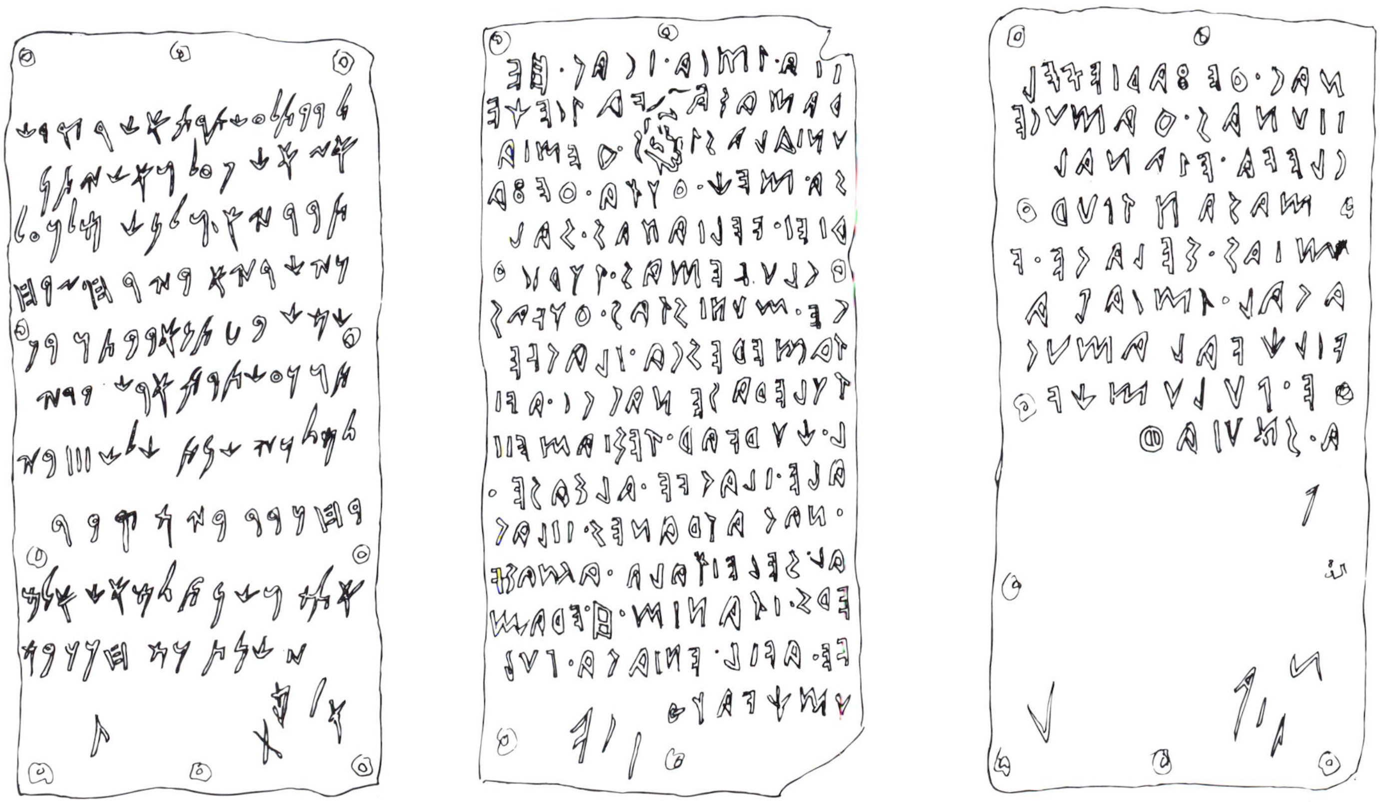

Figure 23 The Pyrgi inscriptions.

to establish good relations with the city on the Tiber that controlled a long stretch of the central Italian coastline, and it would obviously have made sense for them to keep on good terms with the new republican regime that seized power in Rome after the expulsion of Tarquin, when all previous agreements would have been automatically terminated. For their part the new Republic's leaders might have hoped to gain recognition for themselves by a formal agreement with Carthage, and at the same time would have wanted to assert their claim to the position of hegemony in Latium which the kings had formerly possessed. The first year of the Republic is therefore a plausible context for a treaty between Rome and Carthage.

9

THE BEGINNINGS OF
THE ROMAN REPUBLIC

1 THE EXPULSION OF THE KINGS

The end of the Roman monarchy is presented in our sources as an episode in the dramatic saga of the family of the Tarquins. It may be useful to summarise the main outlines of this famous story, which, though immortalised in Livy's prose narrative and the verses of Shakespeare and Lord Macaulay, may not be as familiar to modern readers as it once was.[1]

According to the story Tarquinius Superbus was overthrown in 509 BC by a group of aristocrats who set up a republican government under two elected annual magistrates, the consuls. The incident that prompted the coup was the rape of Lucretia by Sextus Tarquinius, the tyrant's second son. The virtuous Lucretia killed herself, and the outrage provoked by this tragedy led to an uprising against the ruling family. Curiously enough the leaders of the revolt were themselves close relatives of the tyrant (cf. above, p. 123). They included L. Junius Brutus, the king's nephew, and L. Tarquinius Collatinus, his cousin once removed and husband of the unfortunate Lucretia. Her father, Sp. Lucretius, was also in the plot, along with an influential friend, P. Valerius Publicola.

The king, who was conducting a war against Ardea, hastened back to Rome on hearing news of the coup, but found the gates barred against him; meanwhile the leaders of the revolt went to Ardea and won over the army, which expelled the king's sons.[2] Brutus and Tarquinius Collatinus became the first consuls, and Brutus made the people swear never again to tolerate a king and to punish with death anyone who tried to restore the monarchy. He then proposed that all members of the Tarquin clan should be banished. He himself escaped the effects of this measure because he was related to Tarquin through his mother; but his colleague, Tarquinius Collatinus, was a member of the *gens* and consequently had to resign his office and leave the city. His place as consul was taken by Valerius Publicola.

The domestic drama continued when Brutus' two sons became involved in a conspiracy to restore the Tarquins, along with the Vitellii, the brothers of Brutus' wife, and the Aquilii, the nephews of the exiled Collatinus. The plot was revealed by a slave, and Brutus himself was obliged to carry out the execution of his sons and their associates in a scene of typical Roman severity.

Meanwhile, Tarquin had fled to Etruria, first to Caere and then to Veii and Tarquinii, and persuaded these cities to attack Rome on his behalf. But their efforts were thwarted at the battle of Silva Arsia, at which the Romans were victorious in spite of the loss of their consul Brutus.[3] Tarquin then turned to Lars Porsenna, the king of Clusium, who marched on Rome and besieged it from the Janiculum (508 BC); but he was prevented from capturing the city by Horatius Cocles, who held the Sublician Bridge against the enemy until it could be demolished. This and other acts of Roman heroism[4] persuaded Porsenna to relent, and instead to send his forces, under the command of his son Arruns, against the Latin town of Aricia. The expedition ended in failure, however, when Arruns was defeated and killed by the Latins and their allies from Cumae.

Porsenna withdrew, but Tarquin went on to enlist the aid of his son-in-law, Octavus Mamilius of Tusculum,[5] who mobilised the Latin League in his support and led a general revolt against Rome. This initiative ended with the defeat of Mamilius and the Latins at the battle of Lake Regillus (499 or 496 BC), whereupon Tarquin took refuge with Aristodemus the Effeminate, the tyrant of the Greek city of Cumae and the leader of the Cumaean army that had helped the Latins at the battle of Aricia. The hated king spent his last days as an exile at the court of Aristodemus, and his death in 495 BC brought the whole saga to a conclusion.

It is perhaps not surprising that this action-packed drama has failed to carry much conviction among modern scholars, who have attacked its historical credentials in all kinds of ways. Some of the leading dramatis personae – Lucretia, Brutus, Valerius Publicola, even Lars Porsenna – have been dismissed as figments of pure legend.[6] The chronology has been challenged, with many scholars rejecting the traditional sixth-century date in favour of a later one – around 470 BC, or even after 450. Others have suggested that the transition from monarchy to republic was not a sudden revolution, but rather a gradual process lasting many years, perhaps even centuries, and consisting in the slow decay of the old kingship and the introduction of a series of successive forms of republican magistracy, before the consular system of the classical Republic was at last established. Finally, it is widely supposed in modern books that the end of the Roman monarchy marked the end of a period of Etruscan rule in Rome, and the liberation of the city from a period of foreign occupation. In its strongest form this theory maintains that the fall of Tarquin was only a minor symptom of a much wider phenomenon, namely the decline of Etruscan power and the fall of an Etruscan empire in central Italy.

These theories, which will be discussed in detail presently, can be reconciled with one another in various ways, but they all entail the rejection of most or all of the traditional story. The question we have to ask is whether the evidence really justifies such radical scepticism, and the replacement of the traditional account with a story of our own making. Admittedly, it is impossible to check the credentials of the tradition in a direct manner, since we have no way of knowing how it was transmitted to the Roman historians, or what sources they were able to draw upon. All that can be said is that it has the appearance of a historical romance, and forms a self-contained saga of connected stories – stories, it must be said, of extraordinary power and beauty. This feature clearly points to an oral tradition. These were stories that deserved to be told and retold, and were doubtless known and passed on through generations of Romans. That they formed the subject of epic poems or ballads is likely enough; Lord Macaulay was not alone in sensing the poetic character of the tales.[7] Another interesting suggestion is that of Jacques Heurgon, who has emphasised the dramatic character of the events, and has argued that they might have been re-enacted as tragic performances.[8]

In the present state of our knowledge such theories are no more than speculation, and cannot help to decide the issue one way or the other. But there is no reason in principle why the tradition should not be a romanticised version of events that really happened. It is arbitrary to dismiss the rape of Lucretia (for instance) as fiction, when we have no way of knowing whether it is fiction or not. The history of many ruling families has been characterised by ruthless brutality and personal tragedy, and as a dynastic history the bare catalogue of events within the Tarquin family is, in itself, perfectly credible.

It needs to be emphasised, however, that the traditional account makes sense principally as a dynastic saga. The revolt against Tarquin was a plot hatched within the family by men who might have hoped to succeed to the kingship themselves. This picture of a palace revolution sits rather uncomfortably with the notion of a political uprising inspired by republican ideals. The conflict between Brutus and Collatinus is also puzzling as it stands. If the name Tarquinius was so odious, why was Collatinus elected consul in the first place? And if family connections with the Tarquins were so unacceptable, how did Brutus escape suspicion?

The role of Lars Porsenna is also difficult to fathom. The main annalistic tradition suggests that he was prevented from taking the city, but was so impressed by the bravery of the Romans that he came to terms with them, and used Rome as a base for his expedition against the Latins. But in that case what happened to Tarquin? The story makes no sense because it presupposes that Porsenna's aim was to reinstate the deposed tyrant. The difficulty becomes even more acute if we consider a variant tradition, according to which Porsenna succeeded in capturing the city and imposed humiliating terms on the Romans (Tac., *Hist.* 3.72; Pliny, *n.h.* 34.139). This unpalatable version is arguably more credible than the alternative (patriotic) one, but in that case the whole episode has to be reinterpreted. One plausible suggestion is that, so far from attempting to restore the Roman monarchy, Porsenna actually abolished it.[9]

On this view we might be tempted to argue that the overthrow of Tarquin was followed by a confused period of turmoil in which various members of his family and other leading figures struggled for power,[10] replacing one another in rapid succession, until the intervention of Lars Porsenna put an end to their aspirations; with his withdrawal the Republic was finally and firmly established.

One can argue about details, and speculate endlessly about what might really have happened during these years; but the important question is whether the broad outline of events is correct. Is it true to say that at the end of the sixth century BC Rome ceased to be ruled by a monarch, and became a republic governed by annual consuls? The historicity of Lucretia, Brutus, Horatius and the rest is a secondary issue in comparison with this basic question. Equally it is of little consequence whether the change took place in a matter of days, as tradition maintains, or over a period of a few years, during which the city may have been occupied by the forces of Lars Porsenna. The same point can be made about the chronology. Whether the Roman Republic began in 509 BC, or 507 or 504 or 502, is not of great importance at this distance. What matters is that an approximate date should be established; and tradition clearly points to a date shortly before 500 BC. It is this general proposition that has been challenged by the more radical modern critics, and that needs to be tested against the available evidence.

2 THE PROBLEM OF CHRONOLOGY

We may begin with the problem of dating, which will lead on to other related issues. The Romans calculated the date of the beginning of the Republic by means of the consular *Fasti*, the list of annual consuls, which went back to around 500 BC. Our sources provide us with slightly differing versions of the list for the period before 300 BC. But the discrepancies are only minor, and the striking thing about the surviving versions is that they show a substantial measure of agreement despite being based on a variety of different sources.[11] All of them go back to a point shortly before 500 BC, with only a few years separating the longest version, the so-called *Fasti Capitolini*, which go back to 509 BC, from the shortest, Livy, whose starting-point is equivalent to 502 or 501 BC.[12]

The Romans made the eminently reasonable assumption that the beginning of the list marked the year when the first consuls took office, and therefore served to date the start of the Republic. It was then a relatively simple matter to synchronise the republican era with other systems of dating. Dionysius of Halicarnassus was able to inform his Greek readers that the Republic began in the first year of the 68th Olympiad, the year in which Isagoras was archon at Athens – that is, in 508/7 BC (Dion. Hal. V.1.1). Dionysius was saying nothing new. Some 150 years earlier Polybius, one of our oldest sources, had written that L. Junius Brutus and M. Horatius were 'the first consuls after the expulsion of the kings, and the founders of the temple of Jupiter Capitolinus. This was 28 years before the crossing of Xerxes to Greece.'[13]

It is likely enough that the Romans, who were not stupid, had always been aware that the list of consuls could serve to indicate how many years had elapsed since the start of the Republic. The idea that this elementary deduction was first made by some Roman equivalent of Sherlock Holmes in the fourth or third century BC is absurd (but seems to be widely believed by scholars). As far as we know, the consuls had always given their names to the year in which they held office, and such a system of eponymous dating (as it is called) requires that lists of past consuls be kept. This simple prima-facie argument suggests that at any time in the history of the Republic a well-informed Roman would have had no difficulty in stating when it had begun.

A number of texts seem to confirm this hypothesis. Dionysius of Halicarnassus quotes a document recording a census 'in the consulship of L. Valerius Potitus and T. Manlius Capitolinus, in the one hundred and nineteenth year after the expulsion of the kings' (I.74.5). The consulship in question is that of Varronian 392 BC – that is, probably, 389 or 388 BC in reality (cf. below, p. 399) – which once again gives a date of 508 or 507 BC for the Republic. The document cited by Dionysius is usually dismissed as a late fabrication, but on completely inadequate grounds.[14] In fact it may well be authentic.[15] The pedantic and humourless Dionysius was no doubt speaking the truth when he said that he had seen it with his own eyes, and in view of what was stated earlier there is no reason in principle why the censors of 392 (389/8) BC should not have known how many years had passed since the expulsion of the kings.

The same point can be made about a more famous text concerning Cn. Flavius, the radical reformer of the late fourth century BC (on whom see below, p. 374). At the end of his turbulent aedileship Flavius dedicated a shrine to Concordia (always a sign, in Rome, that one had been fomenting discord), with a bronze inscription dating it '204 years after the dedication of the Capitol' (Pliny, *n.h.* 33.19). Since the Capitoline temple was dedicated in the first year of the Republic, and since Flavius was aedile in 303 BC (Varronian 304), we can be certain that the Republic began in 507 BC and that this fact was well established in the late fourth century. Or can we?

Some modern writers are deeply sceptical of the tradition that the Capitoline temple was dedicated in the first year of the Republic; the coincidence seems too good to be true or, in the words of one recent critic, 'too obviously symbolic to be accepted'.[16] Cn. Flavius clearly believed that the temple was dedicated 204 years before his aedileship, but we cannot be sure that he based his calculation on the consular *Fasti*, or even whether he believed that the dedication occurred in the first year of the Republic. It is possible that Flavius dated the temple by some other means, and that the date of the first consuls was artificially fixed, perhaps long after Cn. Flavius, so as to make it coincide with the dedication.

This at least is what Robert Werner has argued, in a long monograph dedicated entirely to the question of the beginning of the Republic.[17] Werner suggests that there was a distinct 'Capitoline era', independent of the *Fasti*. The argument is superficially attractive because of a well-known passage of Livy, which quotes an ancient law, 'written in archaic words and letters', stating that 'he who is the chief magistrate (*praetor maximus*) on the Ides of September shall hammer a nail [into the wall of the temple]' (Livy 7.3.5). The Ides of September was the anniversary of the dedication of the temple, and it follows that the nails fixed in the wall would, like notches in a stick, mark the number of years that had elapsed since the original dedication.[18]

Werner believes that the consular list was artificially lengthened in the third century BC, in order to make the beginning of the Republic coincide with the dedication of the Capitol; this was done by the insertion of spurious names into the first part of the list. Werner's efforts are directed to identifying the impostors and expunging them; the result is to lower the date of the first consuls to around 472 BC. The revised dating can be made to fit with other evidence and with general historical arguments. In 474 BC an Etruscan fleet was defeated off Cumae by Hieron of Syracuse. This event is widely regarded as marking the final collapse of Etruscan power in central Italy, and, for Werner, its aftermath provides a suitable context for the expulsion of the Etruscan kings from Rome. His conclusion is that 'the Roman republic owed its existence to a Greek victory over the Etruscans'.[19]

In this reconstruction everything depends on the supposition that the *Fasti* of the early Republic are a fraudulent imposture. But before one attempts to identify the perpetrators, and to show that they had both motive and opportunity, one should first try to establish that a fraud has, in fact, been committed. This Werner is quite unable to do. Most of his arguments against the authenticity of specific names in the traditional list are too feeble to merit discussion;[20] in general his method amounts to assuming in advance what sort of names ought to be in the *Fasti*, and rejecting those that do not fit the assumed criteria. In particular he dismisses the so-called 'plebeian' names (on which see further below, pp. 252ff.), on the grounds that plebeians could not hold the consulship in the early Republic (even though we are told of this restriction by the very same sources that provide us with the names of the consuls). The procedure is a classic case of the logical fallacy known as *petitio principii* (in English, 'begging the question'); and as Momigliano pointed out,

> the *petitio principii* is particularly flagrant in the case of the so-called plebeian names because on the one hand it is not certain that they were plebeian and on the other hand it is not certain that plebeian names deserve to be rejected from the *Fasti*.[21]

There are also serious difficulties in Werner's theory of a distinct 'Capitoline era' based on the annual nails. For one thing, the relevant passage of Livy seems to imply that the annual ceremony of fixing the nail had lapsed by the early fourth century BC.[22] Cn. Flavius' affirmation that 204 years had passed since the dedication of the Capitol does not necessarily indicate a distinct Capitoline era, independent of the *Fasti*. In fact it is much more probable that Flavius simply took it for granted that the temple was dedicated by one of the first consuls, and based his calculation on the *Fasti*.

The majority of modern historians accept that the *Fasti* are broadly reliable, and that the beginning of the list coincides with the dedication of the temple. It might seem that for these historians the question of the date of the Republic is thereby resolved; but matters are not quite so simple. It should be noted that although the *Fasti* may go back to the same year as the temple, they do not necessarily go back to the beginning of the Republic.

There are two other possibilities. First, we might suppose that the Republic began earlier, but that the practice of naming the year after the consuls, and of recording their names (which is practically the same thing), began only when the temple was dedicated. It is conceivable, for instance, that there was some kind of archive associated with the temple, which recorded the names of the magistrates in office on each anniversary of the dedication; in this way, the consular *Fasti* and the annual nail-fixing ceremony would be different aspects of the same thing.[23] The possibility that the annual consulship might be older than the consular *Fasti* is only a theoretical one, however, and has never to my knowledge been seriously advocated, although it was implicitly recognised by Mommsen as long ago as 1858;[24] on the other hand there is some scholarly support for the rather paradoxical alternative, namely that the consular *Fasti* are older than the Republic.

This theory has been advanced with great ingenuity and subtlety by the Swedish scholar Krister Hanell, in one of the most important and stimulating books ever written about early Rome.[25] Hanell suggested that the primary task of the consuls was to act as eponymous officials – that is, to give their names to the year – and that there is no reason in principle why they should not have existed under the monarchy. The situation would not be unparalleled: there were eponymous yearly magistrates in ancient Assyria (the *limmu*) and in Sparta (the ephors), both of which were ruled by kings. We should also remember that in Greek cities eponymous officials continued to hold office even under tyrannies, for example at Athens under the Pisistratids.

Hanell's view is that the introduction of eponymous dating at Rome was only part of a major change in the official method of measuring time, and was accompanied by a reform of the calendar. Links between the pre-Julian calendar and the Capitoline cult allow him to conclude that the reform was introduced at the time when the temple was dedicated.[26] It follows that the coincidence between the beginning of the *Fasti* and the dedication of the temple is not the result of chance, but rather of a functional relationship between them. On the other hand the *Fasti* have nothing to do with the institution of a republic, which on Hanell's view emerged only gradually in the course of the fifth century, when the power of the kings slowly withered away, and was taken over by the eponymous annual officials who served under them.

Hanell's theory was very influential because it opened up the possibility of revising the traditional date for the fall of the monarchy without having to reject the evidence of the *Fasti*. This challenge was taken up most famously by Hanell's compatriot Einar Gjerstad, who invoked archaeological evidence to support his view that the kings of Rome continued to rule until after the middle of the fifth century BC.[27] Many of Gjerstad's arguments are notoriously weak or unsound. For instance he contends that monuments traditionally attributed to Servius Tullius can be dated archaeologically to the early fifth century, and consequently that the reign of Servius Tullius belongs to the early fifth century. It is now generally agreed that Gjerstad's archaeological dates are wrong; but even if they were correct, they would not justify the inferences he bases on them. If buildings attributed to Servius turn out to belong to the fifth century, the natural assumption would be that they have been wrongly attributed to him, not that his reign has been wrongly dated.[28]

The main prop for Gjerstad's theory, however, is his observation that there is no break in the continuity of the archaeological record of Rome until the middle of the fifth century, when the volume of imported artefacts suddenly declines and the city becomes isolated and impoverished. Gjerstad equates this cultural break in the mid-fifth century with the end of Etruscan influence, and suggests that it can be accounted for by the expulsion of the Etruscan kings. It follows that the monarchy must have come to an end around 450 BC.

Further support for this reconstruction is sought in the *Fasti*, of all places. Gjerstad noted that some of the consuls of the early Republic have Etruscan names; he concluded that they must have held office under the rule of Etruscan kings. Indeed he went further: the Etruscan names are not scattered indiscriminately through the early part of the *Fasti*, but are concentrated in two distinct groups, the first in the years from 509 to 490 BC, the second in the period from 461 to 448. These two groups correspond, in Gjerstad's opinion, with the reigns of the two Tarquins, and the intervening period of the 480s and 470s with that of the Latin Servius Tullius.

This argument from the *Fasti* serves to illustrate an important point about the methods employed by Gjerstad and other like-minded revisionists. It is not the case that they are presenting a new version based on archaeology in contrast to the traditional story based on literary sources. In fact Gjerstad's reconstruction depends on a complex mixture of archaeological and literary data. Once again it must be emphasised that the archaeological evidence cannot tell an independent story of its own; only by interpreting it in the light of written sources can it be made to speak at all.[29]

In general Gjerstad's theory about the end of the monarchy is pretty improbable. It strains belief that the Romans preserved historical information about the age of the Tarquins and about the first half of the fifth century, but failed to realise that the two periods overlapped, and that events that are separated in the traditional story by more than 100 years were in fact happening simultaneously. Why did the Romans get their own history so wrong, and, if they did, can we seriously believe anything they tell us?

Not surprisingly Gjerstad has convinced no one, and his theories are now little more than a curiosity;[30] but it is nevertheless worth discussing them because they raise questions of method in the handling of archaeological data, and because many of their underlying assumptions are still alive and well, and continue to inform the theories of present-day scholars.

With this in mind we should note that all the revisionist theories we have been considering are concerned not only with the date of the fall of the monarchy but also with the nature of the change itself. Gjerstad and Werner both assume that the end of the monarchy marks the end of a period of Etruscan rule in Rome; their arguments are designed to show that the departure of the Etruscans from Rome is more likely to have happened in the fifth century than at the end of the sixth. Hanell's theory, on the other hand, presupposes that the change from monarchy to republic was not a sudden revolution, but rather a gradual process that was not completed until the middle of the fifth century. On this view the fall of the Roman monarchy was, like the fall of the Roman Empire, a non-event.[31]

Looked at in this light, the question of dating becomes secondary. The idea that in ridding themselves of kings the Romans were also ridding themselves of Etruscan domination is extremely widespread in the scholarly literature; Gjerstad and Werner are eccentric only in attempting to revise the chronology. Similarly, Hanell's view that the Republic emerged gradually from the embers of a dying monarchy is shared by many other historians who differ from him only in that they are less concerned with the chronological issue; in a way this is hardly surprising, given that a non-event is, by definition, rather difficult to date.

The remainder of this chapter will be concerned with these two important questions: (1) Are we justified in speaking of the 'departure of the Etruscans' from Rome, and what exactly does this phrase mean? (2) Did the monarchy come to a sudden end, or did it merely fade out of sight? Only when we have answered these questions can we resolve the matter of dating, to which we shall return at the end of the chapter.

3 THE 'DEPARTURE OF THE ETRUSCANS'

The standard view, which can be found in the majority of modern works, is that the expulsion of the kings marked the end of a period of Etruscan domination in Rome. Precisely what is meant by this depends on how one understands the notion of 'Etruscan rule'. Those who believe that Rome was subordinated to Etruscan political control in the sixth century, and that in the age of the Tarquins the city was under foreign occupation, naturally regard their overthrow as an act of liberation and an assertion by the Romans of their national independence. But this view must be rejected because, as we have seen, the whole idea of an Etruscan conquest of Rome is unfounded (above, Chapter 6).

On the other hand there is no denying that Rome in this period had extensive contacts with Etruria, and that its population contained a significant Etruscan element. If we discount the idea of liberation from Etruscan rule, it nevertheless remains possible that the overthrow of the Tarquins entailed an anti-Etruscan backlash of some kind. This can be envisaged in a variety of different forms: the expulsion from the city of persons of Etruscan origin, a conscious rejection of Etruscan cultural influence, a reduction in trade with Etruria, or indeed a combination of some or all of these.

There is no need to outline the different versions of this general theory, since the entire construction is founded upon quicksand. There is absolutely no evidence – not a single scintilla of evidence – for any of it. The literary sources give no indication that the hatred incurred by Tarquinius Superbus had anything to do with his being an Etruscan (I leave aside the fact that in the sources the Tarquins are presented as being of Greek, not Etruscan, descent); and the archaeological evidence is equally silent, which is hardly surprising, since material evidence is not capable of expressing opinions of any kind, least of all ethnic prejudices.

Such evidence as we do have points in an entirely different direction; but this evidence, if noticed at all, tends to be either arbitrarily dismissed or grossly distorted. Consider for example the Etruscan names in the consular *Fasti*. These are either rejected as unhistorical on the grounds that Etruscans would not have been able to hold high positions after the expulsion of the kings, or (as we have seen) taken as evidence that the kings had not yet been expelled. In fact they prove something quite different. What they prove is that the overthrow of the Tarquins did not entail the wholesale expulsion of Etruscans from the city.[32]

In fact the traditional accounts make it quite clear that only the *gens Tarquinia*, the agnatic clan of the Tarquinii, was driven out of Rome. There are precise parallels for this kind of act (e.g. the case of the Alcmaeonid clan at Athens – Herodt. 5.71; Thuc. 1.126; Plut., *Solon* 12.3), which would be characteristic of the aristocratic society of the archaic age. The departure of the Tarquinian clan is also in a sense a mirror image of its arrival, many years earlier. We have already seen (above, p. 157) that the story of the migration of Tarquinius Priscus, with his family and retainers, fits the conditions of archaic society much better that the modern notion of an Etruscan conquest of Rome; so too Livy's account of the departure of the Tarquin clan is historically more credible than any supposed anti-Etruscan movement in the city.[33]

The whole idea that the events surrounding the fall of the Roman monarchy were part of a wider ethnic conflict between Etruscans and Latins is a modern fabrication. The story that after his expulsion Tarquin received help from

Octavus Mamilius and the Latins (a more credible version than that which makes him a protégé of Lars Porsenna) confirms this observation. The evidence suggests a more complex set of alignments, with Rome and Lars Porsenna on the one side, Octavus Mamilius, the Latins, and Aristodemus of Cumae on the other. Tarquin's position in all this remains mysterious, but it is probable that he was an element of secondary importance. However that may be, the message of the sources is absolutely clear: the Romans got rid of Tarquin, not because he was an Etruscan, but because he was a tyrant.[34]

There is equally no evidence of any deliberate rejection of Etruscan culture in the aftermath of the coup, or of a disruption of commercial links between Rome and the Etruscan cities. Indeed, it was precisely the fact that no such break can be detected at the end of the sixth century that led scholars such as Bloch and Gjerstad to postpone the 'departure of the Etruscans' until a generation or two later.

It is true enough that in the middle years of the fifth century there are clear signs of a decline in cultural activity and a downturn in foreign trade. But however we choose to understand the nature of this apparent recession (see further below, p. 266), in the present context it is sufficient to point out that it need not have any connection with the fall of the monarchy or indeed with any supposed 'departure of the Etruscans'.

As far as the monarchy is concerned, it goes without saying that a change in the nature of the political regime need have no effect whatever on cultural trends and economic developments. But does the evidence point to the end of 'Etruscan Rome'? Those who believe that it was the Etruscans who brought prosperity and urban civilisation to Rome might be tempted to argue that their departure from the scene would lead to cultural impoverishment. This is a *non sequitur*, but in any case its premise is false. It is only a modern prejudice that cultural activity in archaic Rome was monopolised by Etruscans. The same is true of trade and commercial activity. The volume of imported Attic pottery found in Rome declines rapidly after the middle of the fifth century, but there is no reason why this fact should have any bearing on Rome's relations with Etruria. If anything, it reflects a change in commercial relations with the Greek world. The idea that only Etruscans were attracted to Greek culture, and that they alone traded with Greeks, is based purely on prejudice and on any reasonable view should be dismissed as absurd.

Finally, it should be noted that the so-called 'fifth-century crisis' affected not only Rome, but the whole of Tyrrhenian Italy and indeed other places in the western Mediterranean, including Carthage. The archaeological record of sites in Magna Graecia, Campania, Latium and coastal Etruria during the second half of the fifth century is extremely meagre; imports of Attic pottery virtually cease, artisan production stagnates, public building comes to an end, and the quality of artistic endeavour declines.[35] It is obvious, therefore, that the particular version of this general phenomenon that we find in Rome cannot be accounted for by local political upheavals, however violent; and it is absurd to postulate the end of Etruscan influence as a cause of a condition that also affected the Etruscan cities themselves.[36]

4 THE NEW REPUBLIC

Once they had got rid of Tarquin the founders of the Republic replaced the kingship with the curious institution of a collegiate magistracy, in which two men shared the supreme power. It seems that their original title was praetors, a term of uncertain meaning, and only later that they came to be known as consuls (but the more familiar term will be used here to avoid confusion).[37] The consuls were elected by the *comitia centuriata* and held office for a year. They held *imperium* (they were still obliged to submit to the formality of a vote of the *comitia curiata*) and they inherited many of the insignia of power from the kings; but in order to avoid the appearance of having merely substituted two kings for one, the Republic's founders arranged that the consuls should take it in turns to hold the *fasces* (Livy 2.1.8).

But the power of the consuls was limited in other, more substantial, ways. One of the first consuls, P. Valerius Publicola, is said to have passed a law giving citizens a right of appeal (*provocatio*) against a sentence pronounced by a consul (cf. above, p. 196); as a symbol of this right of appeal the axe was removed from the consular *fasces* within the city boundary. Naturally the historicity of the Lex Valeria is uncertain, but there are good grounds for supposing that some sort of right of appeal existed in the early Republic, and it is hypercritical to dismiss the Lex Valeria out of hand.[38]

The consuls' freedom of action was also restricted by the annual and collegiate nature of their office. The rule that political offices should be both collegiate and of fixed duration became a basic principle of Roman constitutional practice, and was applied to all subsequent magistracies, the only partial exception being the non-collegiate dictatorship (see below). The effect of having two consuls of equal power was that the activity of one could be frustrated by the other, since it was agreed that in any dispute the negative view should always prevail. The limitation of a consul's term to one year also restricted his freedom of independent political action. To be sure, it was possible to be consul more than once, but apparently not for successive terms.[39]

The exception to these rules was the dictatorship. In cases of emergency a dictator was appointed (by one of the consuls, in a mysterious ceremony which had to happen at night) to act as supreme commander and head of state. The dictator himself appointed an assistant, the Master of the Horse (*magister equitum*). This, together with the fact that an alternative name for the dictator was *magister populi* (probably, commander of the army), indicates that his primary function was to act as a military commander.[40] The consuls remained in office, but were subject to the dictator's authority, against which there was no appeal. On the other hand, his term of office lasted for only six months (or for the duration of the emergency, whichever was the shorter).

This very remarkable set of institutions had no parallel, as far as we know, either in Italy or anywhere else in the Mediterranean. For this reason some modern historians have been moved to doubt whether it could have been simply invented all at once and out of nothing at the start of the Republic. Rather, they have suggested that it may have developed gradually over a period of years or by a series of intermediate stages, and that the transition from monarchy to republic was a more complex and extended process than the surviving sources would have us believe. Their evidence can be summarised under three headings.

First, the existence under the Republic of a ceremonial official with the title *rex sacrorum* (or *rex sacrificolus*) perhaps indicates that the Roman kingship did not die, but, like an old soldier, only faded away. Livy tells us (2.2.1) that the post of *rex sacrorum* was created at the start of the Republic in order to carry out the ritual functions of the former king; however, it is easy to speculate that in fact the *rex sacrorum* was not a surrogate, but the real king stripped of his political powers and reduced to a ceremonial figurehead. The parallels for this process, sometimes called 'reductio ad sacra', are legion, and include not only the so-called 'constitutional monarchies' that survive in some modern countries (most obviously the United Kingdom), but also instances from the ancient Greek world, most notably that of the 'king archon' at Athens.

Second, the ancient law quoted by Livy concerning the hammering of a nail (above, p. 220) most interestingly required that the ceremony be performed on the Ides of September by the *praetor maximus* ('chief magistrate'). This could be (and often has been) taken to imply that there was a time when the Republic was headed, not by two equal consuls (more strictly, 'praetors'), but by a single *praetor maximus*.

Third, the dictatorship, the mysterious office which in Rome came into operation only in emergencies, is attested as a regular annual magistracy in other Latin towns. Aricia and Lanuvium were each ruled by a dictator; and a curious tradition held that at Alba Longa, before its destruction by the Romans, the kings had been replaced by annual dictators (Livy 1.23.4; Dion. Hal. V.74.4 [= Licinius Macer, fr. 10 P]). This has given rise to the hypothesis that at Rome too there may have been an intermediate stage, between the end of the monarchy and the introduction of the dual consulship, when power was exercised by a regular annual dictator. After the consular regime was established, the dictatorship was retained for use only in emergencies.

Let us examine some of the more important theories that have been proposed. First, the most straightforward interpretation of the law concerning the annual nail ceremony is that there was once a single supreme official called the *praetor maximus*. One could argue either that the king was replaced in a revolution by an annually elected *praetor maximus*, or, with

Hanell, that the *praetor maximus* was an annual official who was appointed by the king, but who in the course of time took over most of the king's powers and in the end replaced him altogether. The principal objection to both forms of this theory is that the *Fasti* record two names for each year; and it is a very unsatisfactory recourse to argue that the *Fasti* have been interpolated, and that one of the two names recorded for each year is false.[41]

A more acceptable solution would be that there were two *praetores* each year, but with unequal powers: one, the *praetor maximus*, outranked the other. This suggestion is very close to another well-known theory, advanced by historians such as Beloch, and more recently by De Martino, that at the start of the Republic Rome was governed by an annual dictator; on this view the two names recorded for each year in the *Fasti* would be those of the dictator and his assistant, the *magister equitum*.[42]

It is largely a matter of taste whether one wants to regard *praetor maximus* as an alternative title for the dictator. Alföldi, for example, regards the two offices as identical. De Martino takes a different view. His theory is that the series of annual dictatorships ended in 451 BC with the decemvirate. When the experiment of an annual board of ten proved a failure, two unequal praetors were instituted, one of whom was the *praetor maximus* (on this view the law quoted by Livy dates from after 450 BC). After 444 the two unequal praetors were sometimes replaced by three or more military tribunes with consular power (see further below, pp. 334 ff.); the 'consular tribunate' became the regular regime during the early fourth century, until 367, when the dual consulship was introduced for the first time.[43]

De Martino is not alone in dating the consulship to 367 BC.[44] The suggestion is attractive because it provides an explanation for the otherwise puzzling and apparently unique institution of two equal magistrates; its purpose in the context of the reforms of 367 BC would have been to allow the two orders to share power, by giving one consulship to the patricians, the other to the plebs. Unfortunately there is a decisive objection to this theory. As we shall see (below, p. 337), although the dual consulship was introduced (or restored) in 367 BC, it was not until 342 that regular power-sharing was established. It follows that the idea of two equal magistrates was not devised in order to give equal rights to the two orders. Nothing is gained, therefore, by postponing the introduction of the consulship to 367 BC, and the theory is not an improvement on the traditional account, which maintains that in 367 the Romans simply restored the dual magistracy that had originally been introduced at the beginning of the Republic.

Another problem arises from the phrase *praetor maximus*. Strictly speaking *maximus* is a superlative and ought to mean the greatest of three or more; the grammatically correct term for the more important of two praetors would be *praetor maior*, not *praetor maximus*. This difficulty can be resolved by supposing that there were in fact three or more elected annual magistrates, of whom one was supreme. That would account for the *praetor maximus*, but it more or less rules out the identification of the *praetor maximus* with the dictator, and it once again runs up against the fact that the *Fasti* record two names for each year in the early Republic.[45]

Proponents of this theory are therefore forced either to reject the evidence of the *Fasti* (at least in part), or to argue, with J. Heurgon, that the regime of the *praetor maximus* was very short-lived, and was replaced, after only a few years, by two equal magistrates.[46] The trouble with this solution is that it takes us back to where we started. That is to say, if the Romans were able to institute a dual magistracy in *c.* 503 BC, why could they not have done so a few years earlier, immediately after the expulsion of the kings? Heurgon's reconstruction goes some way towards reconciling the evidence with a revisionist theory, but it effectively makes any such theory unnecessary.

This point raises an important general issue. The case for revising the traditional account is largely circumstantial, and is based on the assumption that the developed republican system is unparalleled and too extraordinary to have been created all at once and out of nothing. How compelling is this argument? Before attempting an answer let us first be clear about the facts. In the present state of our knowledge, there is virtually no direct evidence to support a revisionist interpretation. I say 'virtually' because the law concerning the *praetor maximus* constitutes an exception. But this text is unique: it is the only item of direct evidence to suggest that the early Republic was regularly governed by anyone other than two equal magistrates.

But the precise significance of the term *praetor maximus* is far from certain. Although *maximus* is a superlative, the inference that there must have been more than two *praetores* should not be pressed. There are examples in early Latin of *maximus* being used of the greater of two (e.g. Terence, *Adelph.* 881, where one of the two brothers declares himself the elder 'qui sum natu maxsumus'), and it would be rash to rule out such a usage in the text under discussion. But if the *praetor maximus* was one of two *praetores*, it would not necessarily follow that they formed an 'unequal college'. It is equally possible that the *praetor maximus* was the senior of two *praetores* with equal power, his seniority consisting in the fact that he was the elder (*natu maximus*, as in Terence!), that he had been elected first, or that he was the one holding the *fasces* at the time in question.[47] In other words, the term *praetor maximus* is compatible with the traditional narrative of the origins of the Republic, and does not necessarily justify a radical revision.

This brings us back to the question of general probability. Is it really unthinkable that the king was replaced immediately by a college of two equal magistrates? That there are no known parallels or precedents is not as strong an argument as some historians seem to think. Our knowledge of sixth-century constitutions (particularly in Italy) is so woefully thin that we cannot know whether the Roman consulship was a unique institution or not. In a famous book on this subject S. Mazzarino argued that pairs of collegiate magistrates are represented on a sixth-century terracotta frieze from Velitrae.[48] Whether this interpretation is right or wrong – and given the nature of the evidence it can be no more than a hypothesis[49] – it draws attention to the real possibility that collegiate magistracies might have existed elsewhere in Italy before 500 BC.

5 OTHER ITALIAN REPUBLICS

How the communities of non-Roman Italy governed themselves is a difficult question documented only by brief, enigmatic and mostly late inscriptions. The evidence from the Etruscan cities is particularly important, because it is fairly plentiful and some of it is early; moreover we can be certain that some aspects of the consulship (for example the *fasces* and other trappings) were also borne by Etruscan magistrates. On the other hand, the Etruscan material is also the most difficult to interpret, since our knowledge of the language is so poor. Words such as *maru*, *purθne*, and above all *zilaθ*, which occur quite frequently in Etruscan inscriptions, have been plausibly interpreted as official titles, but whether they were collegiate magistrates, and if so whether their powers were equal or unequal, is a matter of dispute.[50]

Much of the evidence is inscrutable; we should remember, moreover, that the Etruscan cities were independent states which are unlikely to have had uniform institutions. Nevertheless, there is a good case for saying that in some Etruscan cities at least there was a hierarchy of different magistrates with specialised functions, and that one of them, who had the title *zilaθ purθne*, was superior to the rest.[51] This was a relatively sophisticated system; elsewhere in Italy things seem to have been simpler. The standard term for a magistrate in Oscan-speaking communities was *meddíss* (Latin *meddix*), but each autonomous group was headed by a supreme official called the *meddíss toutviks* (*meddix tuticus*), who seems to have served alongside other, inferior, *meddices*.[52]

This evidence has been used to support the theory of a single *praetor maximus* at Rome, just as the dictators at Aricia, Lanuvium and Nomentum have given encouragement to those who argue for a regular annual dictatorship. But that is not the end of the matter, since there is also evidence that other cities had collegiate magistrates who may have had equal powers. A number of Latin cities, the most important of which was Praeneste, were ruled by two *praetores*,[53] and similar systems may have existed outside Latium. For example, the Umbrian cities of Fulginium and Asisium had two eponymous magistrates called *marones*, who appear to be comparable to the Roman consuls, although we know nothing about them beyond their title.[54] The number of examples could be extended.[55]

We should not therefore rule out the possibility that in introducing the consulship the Romans were imitating other republics. But we cannot be certain because the evidence for all the parallel cases is late (third century BC at the earliest), and there is no guarantee that any of them goes back as early as the sixth century. They may all be later than Rome, and were perhaps imitations of the Roman model, rather than the other way round.[56]

In any event it is clearly a mistake to study Rome in isolation. What happened at Rome at the end of the sixth century, even if occasioned by particular local circumstances, undoubtedly formed part of a wider movement of change affecting not just the Italian peninsula but the Mediterranean world as a whole. In the Greek cities tyrannies were overthrown and replaced by constitutional systems combining aristocratic rule with the participation of property-owning citizens; to my mind the traditional accounts imply a change of precisely this kind at Rome. It is less clear, however, that a similar transition occurred in other communities of Tyrrhenian Italy at this time, although it is sometimes blandly assumed that in the years on either side of 500 BC all the city-states in Etruria, Latium and Campania changed from monarchies to republics, perhaps with an intervening period of 'tyrannical' rule.[57]

While it is certain that republican governments were eventually set up in all the cities of central Italy about which we know anything, and that there is no trace of monarchy anywhere after the early years of the fourth century BC, nevertheless the details of the process are unclear. As far as Latium is concerned, there is little trace of kingship in the surviving tradition, which makes no reference to kings after the destruction of Alba Longa, and if anything implies that the Latin cities were governed by aristocratic regimes in the archaic period. Rome, with its tyrannical monarchy, may have been unique among the Latin cities in the sixth century. None of the Latin leaders whom we hear about, such as Octavus Mamilius of Tusculum or Turnus Herdonius of Aricia, is described as a king. We are told that Tarquin installed his son Sextus as king of Gabii, but this was a puppet regime imposed by trickery; and when the people of Gabii heard about the revolution in Rome, they lost no time in putting Sextus to death.

In Etruria, on the other hand, monarchy seems to have been more firmly rooted. Clusium was still under royal control at the end of the sixth century, if Lars Porsenna is correctly described as king ('rex') in our sources,[58] and we know that other Etruscan cities retained their monarchies well into the fifth century. A king of Veii is attested in the 430s, and the city was still a monarchy at the time of its capture by Rome in 396 BC. Admittedly Livy, who gives us this information, also implies that a period of republican government intervened between these two dates, and that by the end of the fifth century Veii was unique among the Etruscan cities in having a king; but Livy is not necessarily to be trusted on this point.[59]

An inscription commemorating the career of Aulus Spurinna, a republican magistrate at Tarquinii, refers to a king of Caere named Orgolnius. The events recorded in the inscription are difficult to date, but it seems to me most probable that Orgolnius reigned at some point in the fifth century; others, including M. Torelli, the most recent editor of the text, would place him as late as the 350s BC.[60] The inscription in any case proves that Caere had kings after Tarquinii had become a republic.

Further information about the situation in Caere in the fifth century comes from the Pyrgi inscriptions, which record a dedication by the ruler of Caere, Thefarie Velianas. In the Etruscan text his title is *zilaθ*, which is normally understood to be equivalent to the Latin *praetor*,[61] but it seems he was no annual magistrate, because he is said to be in the third year of his rule. It is theoretically possible that he was in his third consecutive annual term, but in that event one would have expected a different form of words (the equivalent of '*zilaθ* for the third time'). His tenure was conceivably for a limited number of years, like a modern presidency, but was most probably for life. This is borne out by the Phoenician version of the text, which calls him *melek* (= 'king'); someone must have thought this was an appropriate translation of the Etruscan *zilaθ*. The most striking feature of the inscription, however, is its suggestion that Thefarie Velianas owed his position to the protection and favour of the goddess Uni-Astarte; this recalls the charismatic autocracy of the Greek tyrants and the later Roman kings, and prompts the inference that Thefarie Velianas was some kind of tyrant.[62] The same can perhaps be said about Orgolnius, who is described as *rex* in the Latin *elogium* of Aulus Spurinna; indeed Orgolnius must have been one of the successors (if not *the* successor) of Thefarie Velianas.

All this suggests that monarchy remained the standard form of government in the Etruscan cities in the fifth century, whereas in Latium republican institutions had become the norm already in the sixth. If so, we could argue that in this sense at least Rome was reacting against Etruscan influence by rejecting its kings. But it is important to stress that this conclusion is based on an impressionistic reading of inadequate evidence, and cannot be regarded as certain.

The same point can be made about the observation of A. Rosenberg, who distinguished the simple form of collegiate magistracy that existed among the Latins, Oscans and Umbrians from the complex and hierarchical systems of the Etruscans, whose supreme officials ruled alone with dictatorial or indeed monarchical power. Rome was unique because it combined elements of both systems in a dual magistracy where both holders possessed the full *imperium*.[63] This theory has its attractions, although the evidence is not sufficient to prove it conclusively, and it is probably overschematic as it stands.[64]

6 THE SEPARATION OF POLITICAL AND RELIGIOUS FUNCTIONS

Rosenberg's theory makes it easier to accept that the Romans might indeed have replaced their kings, at a stroke, by a wholly novel form of republican magistracy. The important point is that they did not create it out of nothing; on the contrary, the end product was a hybrid form of government ('Zwitterstaat') based on principles drawn from a variety of sources and put together to make an original synthesis. This kind of creativity would be typical of Roman cultural eclecticism, and consistent with the innovative spirit shown by the Roman governing class in later times.[65] There is nothing surprising or improbable in the idea that the founding fathers of the Roman Republic were intelligent and resourceful men; the events recorded by tradition reveal the actions of an 'alert and ruthless aristocracy'.[66] These observations bring us back, finally, to the traditional account, and to the interpretation of it that seemed more than adequate to Mommsen, namely that the unusual features of the republican constitution testify to the political genius of the Roman people.[67]

The element of the new regime that seems most clearly to reveal the political skills of its creators is the institution of the *rex sacrorum* (or *rex sacrificolus*), a priest whose task it was to perform the religious functions of the erstwhile king. In the later Republic this 'priest-king' was an obscure figure, whose ritual duties had become an obsolete formality. These duties were connected with the operation of the calendar. He performed sacrifices on the first day (the Kalends) of each month, and announced the dates of the month's festivals on the Nones (i.e. the ninth day before the full moon, known as the Ides). He also sacrificed in the Comitium on certain days of the year. At a strange ceremony on 24 February he had to run away after completing the sacrifice. This 'king's flight' (*regifugium*) was interpreted by Roman antiquarians as a re-enactment of the expulsion of Tarquin, an explanation that modern authorities have generally rejected.[68]

On the other hand, modern scholarship has accepted the ancients' view that the *rex sacrorum* was a religious surrogate for the real king. The institution is normally explained as the product of religious conservatism – the belief that the gods would not tolerate change in cult practice or organisation, and that, in this instance, they would not permit rituals traditionally conducted by the king to be conducted by anyone other than a king. A special priestly 'king' therefore had to be created.

Our sources make it clear that the *rex sacrorum* was prohibited from holding political office and from membership of the Senate (Livy 40.42.8) – a unique restriction which did not apply to other Roman priests. Indeed it was normal practice for members of the political elite to hold priestly offices, and to combine their priesthoods with membership of the Senate, magistracies and military commands. Even the *flamen dialis*, who was surrounded by taboos that were incompatible with political and military office, was an *ex officio* member of the Senate. The unique disqualification of the *rex sacrorum* must have arisen from a deliberate decision by the founders of the Republic to separate the title of 'king' from the exercise of political power.

Livy tells us that the *rex sacrorum* was subordinated to the authority of the *pontifex maximus*. In the later Republic the *rex sacrorum* was chosen by the *pontifex maximus* and, along with the three major *flamines*, was a member of the pontifical college. The *pontifex maximus* not only presided over the college; he supervised all aspects of state cult, as well as exercising disciplinary authority over the *flamines* and the Vestal Virgins. An interesting entry in Festus (p. 198 L), however, tells us that in former times the order of precedence was different: that the king came first, followed by the three major *flamines*, with the *pontifex maximus* in fifth place. The 'king' in question may have been the *rex sacrorum*, but the text does not say so, and in any case it is probable that the information reflects the state of things that existed in pre-republican times, when the chief religious authority in Rome was the real king.

The later hierarchy has been interpreted as the result of a 'pontifical revolution', in which the *pontifex maximus* usurped the religious position of the king (or *rex sacrorum*). In particular it should be noted that the pontifices were in charge of the calendar, the area in which most of the duties of the *rex sacrorum* lay. Another sign of the replacement of the king by the *pontifex maximus* is the fact that in the Republic the latter's official duties were carried out in an ancient building in the Forum called the Regia. But there is good reason to suppose that in former times the Regia was the house of the king. This is indicated not only by its name (*regia: domus ubi rex habitat*, Festus p. 347 L), but also by the discovery, during excavations of the building, of a sixth-century bucchero fragment inscribed with the word *rex*.[69] Finally, we should note that some of the cult activities of the *rex sacrorum* took place in the Regia, although in the late Republic he resided elsewhere (Festus p. 372 L).

Livy tells us that the *rex sacrorum* was subordinated to the *pontifex maximus* at the beginning of the Republic, and that this was a deliberate political act (2.2.1). The difficulty with this interpretation is that it fails to explain why the founders of the Republic thought it necessary to institute a *rex sacrorum* at all. If it was possible for the *pontifex maximus* to take over the king's role as overseer of the calendar, to usurp his pre-eminent place among the Roman priests, and even to occupy his house, it hardly makes sense to explain the institution of the *rex sacrorum* by the supposed reluctance of the gods to tolerate change. The evident fact of a pontifical revolution represents a formidable obstacle to the standard view of the *rex sacrorum* as the product of religious conservatism.[70]

One way of resolving this difficulty is to argue that the *rex sacrorum* was indeed created by the founders of the Republic as a replacement for the king, but that his subordination to the *pontifex maximus* was a subsequent development. On this view the pontifical revolution, which is envisaged as either a gradual process or a sudden change, is variously dated to the fourth or third century BC.[71] But this theory, in whatever form, faces difficulties in its turn. One is that it is not supported by any evidence (a major obstacle given that a change of such importance at that date is unlikely to have gone unrecorded), but its main weakness is that it does not meet all of the original objections.

234

At this point we need to restate the problem. It is not true to say that all the king's sacred tasks were transferred to the *rex sacrorum* (or to the *rex sacrorum* and the *pontifex maximus*); on the contrary, some were taken over by the consuls. The religious functions of the consuls included sacrificing on behalf of the community, taking the auspices, making public vows and dedicating temples. It will be remembered that the Capitoline temple was dedicated in the first year of the Republic by one of the consuls, M. Horatius, not by the *rex sacrorum* or the *pontifex maximus*; and this became the regular procedure in the years that followed. It is reasonable to assume that, if the coup had not taken place, the Capitol would have been dedicated by Tarquinius Superbus in person.[72] More broadly, we can be certain that all the religious duties of the consuls were inherited from the kings.

If some of the king's sacred duties could be passed on to the consuls, and others be taken over by the *pontifex maximus* (assuming this was not a later development), the question becomes more acute: why was it necessary to create a *rex sacrorum*? The argument from religious conservatism is clearly unsustainable, and it becomes altogether difficult, if not impossible, to accept that the *rex sacrorum* was created at the start of the Republic. If we rule out a later date (which would be frankly inconceivable), we are left with only one alternative, paradoxical though it may seem: that the *rex sacrorum* came into being before the foundation of the Republic.

This suggestion becomes tolerable if it is set beside the evidence for changes in the character of the Roman monarchy in the sixth century. As we have seen, the later kings, particularly the last two, were usurpers who ruled in the manner of tyrants. At first sight this might seem to imply that a new, charismatic, form of authority simply replaced the traditional kingship. But it is equally possible that the old king was not abolished so much as kicked upstairs – that is, reduced *ad sacra* – while the new-style leader seized the reins of political and military power.

We are very close here to the theory that the Republic proper was preceded by a transitional stage in which power was wielded by lifelong magistrates. The figure who fits most easily into this 'proto-republican' framework is Servius Tullius, the most 'democratic' of the seven kings.[73] According to S. Mazzarino, Servius Tullius was not a king but a life-magistrate; his title was not *rex* but *magister populi*.[74] This theory, though attractive, can be little more than speculation, since it rests on the rather flimsy idea that Mastarna (or *Macstrna* – see above, pp. 139f.) is an etruscanised form of the word *magister*. Nevertheless, the theoretical possibility remains that Rome was once ruled by a magistrate or *magister populi* who held office for life. This would certainly provide a good explanation for the later institution of the dictatorship, which on this view was a temporary reversion, in an emergency, to the type of monarchic rule that had preceded the dual consulship.

Once again the Pyrgi inscriptions provide an illuminating parallel. Thefarie Velianas, it will be remembered, was the charismatic, tyrannical ruler of

Caere, holding lifelong power but bearing the title of a republican magistrate. Nothing prevents us from supposing that the usurpers who ruled Rome in the later sixth century were 'proto-republican' tyrants of the same type; indeed everything suggests that that is precisely what they were.

What was said earlier about the *rex sacrorum* is consistent with this hypothesis, and indeed tends to confirm it. The *rex sacrorum* would be the old king reduced to a minor ceremonial role involving sacrificial duties and supervision of the calendar. Meanwhile the tyrant (or *magister populi*) took over politically important religious functions such as the conduct of the auspices and the dedication of sanctuaries (it was Thefarie Velianas, let us not forget, who made the dedication at Pyrgi, just as Servius Tullius dedicated the temple of Diana on the Aventine). When the tyranny was overthrown at the end of the sixth century, the *rex sacrorum* was permitted to continue in office; but the Founding Fathers took steps to ensure that he was subordinated to the *pontifex maximus* and that he should be excluded from political office.

The hypothesis being advanced here is that Rome in the sixth century was under the rule of a double monarchy. This might seem improbable, but in fact double monarchies of this kind are quite common. One of the clearest examples is the case of medieval and early modern Japan, where sovereignty was shared between the *shōgun*, a figure comparable to the *magister populi*, and the emperor (*tenshi* or *mikado*), who was a *rex sacrorum*.[75] Moving to ancient Italy, we find a curious example of double kingship in the legend of the kings of Alba Longa. Our sources tell us that rivalry between the descendants of Aeneas was resolved by an agreement that power should be shared, between the Silvii, who would rule the kingdom, and the Julii, who would possess sacred authority.[76] Diodorus, whose account is preserved only in the Armenian version of Eusebius' *Chronicle*, adds that his position made him 'like a second king'.[77] This story is probably to be connected with the fact that at the time of its destruction Alba Longa supposedly had a dictator and a *rex sacrorum*.[78] The same thing is attested later at Lanuvium, where a dictator and a *rex sacrorum* coexisted[79] – the very situation we have hypothesised for Rome.

These parallel instances make it possible (though they do not necessarily make it probable) that in the later sixth century Rome went through a 'proto-republican' stage, under a life magistrate (*magister populi*) who ruled alongside the king reduced *ad sacra*. This suggestion is no more than a hypothesis, and cannot be verified in the present state of our knowledge, but it provides the best explanation of that lonely and mysterious figure, the *rex sacrorum*.

7 CONCLUSION

In conclusion let us sum up the foregoing discussion and attempt a tentative reconstruction. In saying that a revolution around 500 BC created the Roman

Republic, our sources are probably right. A domestic crisis may have provided the spark, but Rome was soon engulfed in a greater conflagration that affected all of Tyrrhenian Italy. The central figure in this was Lars Porsenna of Clusium. His role in the downfall of the Tarquins is mysterious, if we reject as naive the story that his invasion was prompted by an appeal from the affronted tyrant. It is probable that Porsenna occupied Rome for a time, and there can be no doubt about the broad pattern of what happened next: his forces launched an assault against the Latins, but were decisively defeated at the battle of Aricia.

These facts are endorsed by an important passage of Dionysius of Halicarnassus (7.3–11), which recounts the life and deeds of Aristodemus, the tyrant of Cumae. Since this narrative presents the story from an exclusively Cumaean point of view, we can be sure that it is based, not on Roman annalistic sources, but on an independent Greek account. Dionysius probably took it from Timaeus, who would have drawn upon local Cumaean sources.[80] This evidence provides independent confirmation of the events involving Lars Porsenna and, crucially, gives a date of 504 BC for the battle of Aricia. If this date was given by Dionysius' Greek source, as seems likely, and if the Roman tradition was right to situate Porsenna's attack in the aftermath of the fall of Tarquin, then the standard chronology for the beginning of the Roman Republic is decisively confirmed.[81]

The overthrow of the monarchy had nothing to do with Tarquin being an Etruscan. There is no evidence that his expulsion was accompanied by any kind of anti-Etruscan reaction. Cultural and commercial links between Rome and Etruria continued much as before, and Etruscan immigrants went on living in the city unmolested. The outward insignia of royal power, which may have been of Etruscan origin, were not done away with but were transferred, wholesale, to the consuls. The Capitoline temple, which was built and decorated by Etruscan craftsmen, was dedicated by one of the consuls and became the cult centre of the new Republic. There was no question of the temple being abandoned or its terracotta sculptures smashed, still less of it being razed to the ground.[82] It is probable that these symbolic items – the insignia, the form of the temple, and the style of its architectonic decorations – were so much a part of a common cultural language that they were not seen as distinctively Etruscan (see above, p. 171); but that would merely reinforce the point that political events at this period should not be understood in terms of a clash between distinct cultures or ethnic groups.

This does not mean that the transition from monarchy to republic was necessarily smooth. In fact, there are signs in the archaeological record of widespread destruction in the city at this time. In particular, the Regia, the Comitium, and the sanctuary at Sant'Omobono were all burnt down around 500 BC.[83] This may not be a coincidence, and it perhaps suggests that the fall of the monarchy was more violent and disruptive than our sources are prepared to admit. The most striking fact is that the Sant'Omobono temple was not rebuilt after its destruction, and the site was abandoned for over 100 years.[84] This is significant because the Sant'Omobono sanctuary was so closely associated with the person of the monarch; the cult was a symbol of the charismatic personal rule of the tyrant (see above, p. 148). The destruction and subsequent abandonment of the site can therefore be interpreted as a symbolic and anti-monarchical gesture. And we may note in passing that the archaeological date of *c.* 500 BC for the destruction is consistent with the traditional chronology, and provides further evidence in its support.

What happened at Sant'Omobono contributes to the general impression that the revolution took the form of an oligarchic coup against a populist tyranny. We have suggested that in the later sixth century the traditional authority of the old kingship had been relegated to a purely ceremonial role in the person of the marginalised *rex sacrorum*; political and military power were now in the hands of charismatic personal rulers whose position depended on mass support, and above all on the support of the army. That they were 'proto-republican' figures who held life magistracies by virtue of a popular vote is a reasonable conjecture. It was Servius Tullius who reformed the basis of citizenship and organised the citizens who could bear arms into a political body; such changes were bound to undermine the traditional foundations of aristocratic power. Accounts of the rule of Servius' successor, Tarquin, leave us in no doubt about the anti-aristocratic nature of the Roman monarchy at this time.

If these kings had enjoyed popular support, the leaders of the aristocratic coup might not have had everything their own way. It is possible, not to say probable, that they were forced to make concessions, in particular to the army. The need to compromise would explain the importance of the *comitia centuriata* in the new constitution; as we saw earlier (above, p. 197), the electoral, legislative and judicial powers of this assembly of the 'people in arms' can be explained if the founders of the Republic were obliged to confirm, and indeed to extend, the functions it had already exercised under the kings. One attractive hypothesis is that the king had been in the habit of asking the army to approve his choice of senior officers. If there were two senior army commanders under the king (as Dionysius of Halicarnassus suggests at 4.85.3), we could speculate that it was they who overthrew their master and took over the state. This would provide a simple explanation for the institution of the dual consulship.[85]

However that may be, it is not justifiable to reject the traditional account of the origin of the consulship simply on the grounds that a college of two equal magistrates seems strange and unusual. The consulship might have been the product of circumstances, as has just been noted, and it was perhaps not as unusual as some modern historians appear to think. Similar collegiate magistracies may already have existed elsewhere to provide a model for the founders of the Republic. Our knowledge of constitutional developments in Italian city-states at this time is extremely poor, and we cannot simply dismiss the tradition that the dual consulship went back to the beginning of the Republic.

APPENDIX: A NOTE ON THE REGIA

Much attention has recently been focused on the Regia, the building in the Forum that was first excavated in the late nineteenth century.[86] Its earliest levels were subsequently explored in a brief campaign by the American Academy in Rome in the mid-1960s. The results of these soundings have never been fully published, but the main findings have been outlined in two important papers by the leader of the American team, the late Frank E. Brown.[87] These reports have strongly influenced recent discussions of the origins of the Republic,[88] and for that reason some account of them is necessary, although I have consigned it to an appendix because in my opinion the evidence currently available does not prove anything either way.

The American excavations revealed that the republican Regia was preceded by a series of earlier buildings on the same site, going back to the late seventh century BC. In his first published account (1967) Brown suggested that the earlier phases formed a temple complex, which went through several phases of rebuilding. But at the end of the sixth century this complex was destroyed by fire, and replaced by a wholly new type of building, the Regia. These data, in Brown's opinion, confirmed the traditional account, because they seemed to show that the republican Regia originated around 500 BC as a purpose-built structure for a newly created official, the *rex sacrorum*.

In 1974, however, Brown changed his mind. According to his revised version, the republican Regia was only the latest (in fact the fifth) of a series of similar buildings on the same site; the first Regia was now dated to *c.* 625 BC. It is true that the earlier structures differed from one another in their ground plans, and that the fifth Regia (of *c.* 500 BC) was a new design which then remained unchanged until the Principate, in spite of successive reconstructions. This architectural sclerosis (as it has been called) may indicate that there was something especially significant about the rebuilding at the end of the sixth century, and that the new plan in some way symbolised the introduction of a new, republican, *rex sacrorum*;[89] but this is a very weak argument, with none of the force of Brown's original reasoning.

Brown himself (in his second article) regarded the earlier buildings as precursors of the republican Regia, since all of them had the same basic elements – two small rooms connected by a vestibule and facing on to a colonnaded courtyard of irregular shape. He deduced from this that the building must have had the same function from the beginning, and that it cannot have been a residence at any stage of its history. The republican Regia was not a house but a sacred building containing shrines of Mars and Ops Consiva (probably to be identified with the two rooms in the excavated building). In the late Republic the *pontifex maximus* was the occupant of the

Regia, but did not live there: his official residence was the nearby *domus publica*. The *rex sacrorum*, meanwhile, had his own residence on the Velia, the *domus regis sacrorum* (if this was not the same as the *domus publica*).[90] Brown noted, moreover, that none of the kings is said to have lived in the Regia, with the partial exception of Numa. The others lived in different parts of the city. Numa is a particularly interesting case because although some of the sources make the Regia his residence, others say, rather more precisely, that he performed his official duties there but had his dwelling on the Quirinal.[91]

It would seem to follow, therefore, that the Regia was the building in which the king, and later the *pontifex maximus*, performed certain sacred tasks; but whether the king in question was the real *rex*, or only the *rex sacrorum*, is anybody's guess. Even Brown was moved to speculate, following a bold conjecture of De Francisci's, that the first Regia was built in the late seventh century for a *rex sacrorum*, a priest whom the kings had created and to whom they hived off the more tedious of their religious obligations.[92]

More recently Filippo Coarelli has offered a new interpretation of these confusing data.[93] His starting-point is the fact that the Regia, the house of the Vestals (with the temple of Vesta), and the *domus publica* are next door to one another, and are closely linked by their religious functions. By combining archaeological and literary evidence Coarelli has been able to argue that the three elements once formed a single unified complex of buildings dating back to the regal period. This complex was a palace containing the king's residence and its associated household cults, in particular the hearth (Vesta), the gods of the store-room (Lares and Penates), and cults which symbolised the king's role as warrior (Mars) and provider of wealth (Ops Consiva). Coarelli based his reconstruction partly on the evidence of sixth-century palace complexes that have recently been discovered in Etruria, complete with internal sanctuaries and architectural features similar to the Regia.[94]

As for the houses of the kings, Coarelli believes that they are all to be located in the general area of the Regia complex, and were indeed extensions of it. Tullus Hostilius lived on the Velia, on the site of the later temple of the Penates, Ancus Marcius at the top of the Sacra Via, where the later temple of the Lares stood, and Tarquinius Priscus at the top of the Nova Via, near the Porta Mugonia and the temple of Jupiter Stator. According to Coarelli's reconstruction of the topography of the upper Sacra Via these sites are all roughly contiguous, and could indeed have been parts of a single palace complex covering the east end of the Forum and the western slope of the Velia.[95]

When the monarchy was overthrown at the end of the sixth century the complex was split up into separate units, and its various sacred areas became the centres of public cults: the temples of Vesta, the Lares and the Penates, and the shrines of Mars and Ops Consiva in the new 'Regia' (formerly the name of the whole complex). A small residential section of the palace became a residence for the *rex sacrorum* (later the *domus publica*, the house of the *pontifex maximus*). The *rex sacrorum*, on this view, was a public functionary created by the founders of the Republic to take over the formerly 'private' cults of the palace, just as the Vestal Virgins took over from the unmarried women of the king's household the task of tending the 'public' hearth in the temple of Vesta.[96]

This brilliant theory remains compelling even if one wants to dispute the topographical details of the course of the upper Sacra Via and the location of the houses of the kings.[97] The key element is the recognition that the Regia was originally a palace complex including the *atrium Vestae*, the *domus publica* and the small sacred building later known as the 'Regia'. I would only disagree with the order of events as reconstructed by Coarelli, and would be inclined to interpret the same data in a slightly different way.

The principal difficulty is that the last two kings are said to have lived at different sites on the Esquiline, a tradition which cannot easily be fitted into the theory unless we assume that the scale of the Regia complex exceeded that of the Golden House of Nero. A better solution would be to revert to the hypothesis outlined earlier (above, p. 236), namely that the later monarchs were tyrants (or life-magistrates) who seized the reins of power and reduced the king to a purely ceremonial role, leaving him to languish in the Regia as a *rex sacrorum*. When the Republic was formed at the end of the sixth century, the palace was split up and brought into the public domain. The *rex sacrorum* was evicted, and his place taken by the *pontifex maximus*, who was housed in a part of the old palace significantly named the *domus publica* (just as the former household gods were renamed *lares publici* and *penates publici*).[98]

10

PATRICIANS AND PLEBEIANS

1 THE NATURE OF THE PROBLEM

The domestic history of Rome during the first two centuries of the Republic is dominated by the conflict between the patricians and the plebeians. Although the surviving sources have a great deal to tell us about this epic struggle, conventionally known as the 'Conflict of the Orders', their accounts conspicuously fail to explain its true character, and do not allow us to reconstruct it with any confidence. The reason for this paradoxical situation is that the main issues of the conflict were resolved long before the first historians of Rome were born, so they themselves had only a hazy idea of the events they were attempting to describe. The problem is aggravated by the fact that the late republican annalists interpreted the events of the struggle in terms of the political divisions of their own day. This procedure is perfectly understandable, and should not be dismissed as frivolous or dishonest; nevertheless, the annalists unwittingly contrived to distort the facts, and the results, which are incorporated in the surviving accounts of Livy, Dionysius, and the rest, are often anachronistic and misleading.[1]

One undoubtedly misleading aspect of the ancient narratives is their assumption that the division of the Roman people into two distinct groups was a permanent and original feature dating back to Romulus. According to Cicero, Dionysius and Plutarch, Romulus divided the people into patricians and plebeians, and made the latter serve the former as clients. It was therefore an institutionalised system of subjection that went back to the beginnings of Roman history. This primordial 'dualism' was universally accepted until recent times. Historians of the nineteenth century added further refinements in line with theories that were then current. It was suggested, for instance, that the patricians were the original citizens of Rome, organised in clans and distributed among the curiae (which on this view were composed exclusively of patricians). The plebeians were a disfranchised underclass who had no political or legal rights; either they were clients, attached to the patrician clans (this was Mommsen's opinion), or they were outside the original community altogether, as Niebuhr believed. According to Fustel de Coulanges they had no proper family structure and no domestic religion (which he thought was characteristic of the patrician clans); they were an amorphous rabble, and lived like wild beasts.[2]

Another influential nineteenth-century theory maintained that patricians and plebeians were descended from different ethnic groups. This notion enjoyed a tremendous vogue in the period from the 1870s to the First World War. Essentially there were two competing models. One traced the patricians back to the original Latin inhabitants, and identified the plebeians with later immigrants, captives, and foreign clients, who were admitted to the community on sufferance and with an inferior status. On the alternative model the plebeians were the indigenous Latin population, who were subjected to the rule of conquering invaders, identified as Sabines or Etruscans according to taste.[3] In another version of this invasionist model the indigenous 'Mediterranean' population of Latium was overrun by Aryan invaders.[4]

Every kind of evidence was deployed in the debate, and scholars utilised the latest discoveries in linguistics, archaeology and physical anthropology. For instance, Giacomo Boni, the excavator of the Forum cemetery, maintained that the plebeians were an autochthonous Mediterranean race with flattened skulls, who practised the rite of inhumation; the patricians, on the other hand, were Aryans, and consequently 'dolichocephalous' (i.e. they had long skulls). They disposed of their dead by cremation, which one might have thought would make their skulls difficult to measure.[5] Economic and social anthropology was also invoked, as historians identified the patricians as pastoralists, and the plebeians as agriculturalists (or vice versa);[6] others did not hesitate to define the plebeians as an indigenous race with a matriarchal organisation, supposedly a characteristic of aboriginal Mediterranean societies (of which the Etruscans, well known for their uppity women, could be seen as a survival). The Aryan invaders naturally put a stop to all that; not for nothing were they called patricians.[7]

It is easy at this distance to point out the absurdities as well as the dangers inherent in these theories, which together make up such a dismal chapter in the history of scholarship. It is worth dwelling on them briefly, not only because their racist legacy is still with us and appears all too frequently in modern books,[8] but also because the same methods are still being employed, *mutatis mutandis*, in the discussion of other problems. The most obvious error is the notion that archaeological or linguistic evidence can be used to confirm or validate historical theories. Such evidence may be consistent or inconsistent with a given theory, but only in unusual circumstances can it properly be held to confirm or refute it. Normally the relationship is the other way round: that is to say, a historical theory or hypothesis serves to interpret archaeological or linguistic evidence. Arguments based on archaeological or linguistic 'confirmation' are almost always circular. This does not mean they are wrong, but simply that they do not constitute proof. On the other hand, as the above example makes clear, it is not difficult to find archaeological or

linguistic confirmation for the most absurd hypotheses. The fact that archaeological evidence makes no sense until it is subjected to interpretation merely
goes to show that archaeologists can usually find what they are looking for.

The idea that the distinction between patricians and plebeians was of racial
origin manifestly subordinates the evidence to a-priori theories; and what is
striking is how remote this idea is from historical reality. The main objection
to it, and for that matter to all theories of a primordial dualism, is that it
presupposes a permanent and static division that conflicts with everything we
know about archaic Rome. As we have seen, Rome was a dynamic and
constantly changing society, with a diverse and ever growing population
whose most striking characteristic was its capacity to absorb and integrate
new elements. That anyone could ever have thought that the Conflict of the
Orders arose from a primordial division of the community into two ethnic
groups is almost beyond belief.

The important breakthrough in the modern study of this subject came with
the realisation that the Conflict of the Orders was the product of historical
development. The pioneer in this (as in so much else) was the great De Sanctis,
who suggested that the patriciate did not come into existence, fully fledged,
at the beginning of Roman history, but that it gradually developed into an
exclusive group with well-defined privileges during the course of the archaic
period.[9] This idea was subsequently taken up and pursued, in different
directions, by scholars such as Last, Magdelain, Ranouil and Palmer.[10] A
rather different approach has been adopted by Momigliano and Richard, who
focus their attention on the *plebs*, and argue that the history of social conflict
in the early Republic is best understood in terms of the development and the
changing fortunes of the plebeian organisation.[11] Kurt Raaflaub has emphasised that not only the groups involved, but also the issues at stake in the
struggle, must have been transformed in the course of the fifth and fourth
centuries.[12]

It seems to me that these new approaches are entirely justified, but that if
anything they do not go far enough. In the discussion that follows it will be
argued that there was no 'Conflict of the Orders' (properly so called) until
the fourth century, when the battle over the Licinio-Sextian Rogations began
(see below, p. 333). Only at this period are we justified in speaking of a
struggle between patricians *qua* patricians and 'plebeians' in the sense of other
Roman citizens who were not patricians. This polarised situation, in which
all Romans belonged to one or other of the two orders, was the result, not
the cause, of the Licinio-Sextian Laws. In the fifth century matters were rather
different. In particular, the *plebs* were involved in a struggle against oppression by rich landowners, who naturally included the patricians; but this
class conflict originally had nothing to do with attempts to break the patrician
monopoly of office by persons who were outside the charmed circle of the
patriciate. Only by analysing the component elements of these essentially

different conflicts can we begin to make sense of the evidence. Such an analysis will be attempted in the following sections.

2 THE PATRICIANS, THE SENATE, AND THE CAVALRY

During the relatively well-documented period of the middle Republic the patricians formed a clearly identified group within the Roman nobility. Patrician status was hereditary. That is to say, it appertained only to the legitimate (natural and adopted) children of a patrician father. It was not necessary for both parents to be patricians, at least after 445 BC; in that year the Lex Canuleia overturned a provision of the Twelve Tables that had ruled mixed marriages illegitimate. What the situation had been before the Twelve Tables is uncertain (see further below). The main attributes of the patricians were prestige, derived from the acknowledged fact that they were descended from the most ancient aristocracy of the city, and the possession of certain privileges in public life. These included the right to wear a special kind of shoe (the *calceus patricius*), and exclusive access to certain offices. In the later Republic these were confined to archaic priesthoods and positions of ceremonial significance (for instance the post of *interrex*), but it is certain that they had once been more extensive; indeed, tradition maintained that the patricians had once exercised a virtual monopoly of political and religious office.

We know that patrician status was the exclusive preserve of certain clans; this is evident from the frequent use of the term *patriciae gentes* ('patrician clans') to describe the patrician order as a whole. For instance the jurist C. Ateius Capito distinguished the *populus* from the *plebs* on the grounds that only the former included the patrician clans.[13] The fact that the patricians belonged to particular clans is reflected in the tradition that the patriciate developed gradually during the regal period, with the addition of aristocratic clans from outside Rome. They include the 'Trojan families' (for example the Julii) who were brought to Rome after the destruction of Alba Longa, and the Claudii, the Sabine clan that migrated to Rome in 504 BC. Other patrician clans, notably the Valerii, also claimed a Sabine origin; they would have been among the new families who, according to some sources, were added to the patriciate after the war between Romulus and Titus Tatius (Dion. Hal. 2.47.1). Finally, we may notice the mysterious distinction within the patriciate between the 'greater and lesser clans' (*maiores gentes, minores gentes*). The significance of this distinction is problematic, but it confirms that the patriciate consisted of particular clans.

The word 'patrician' (*patricius*) is an adjective formed from *pater* ('father'); and the patrician clans were so called because they produced *patres*. But what does *patres* mean in this context? Many historians have argued that it means senators. *Patres* was indeed a regular way of referring to the Senate in the

Republic, and the traditional story of Romulus' senate lends support to the idea that the patriciate was a senatorial aristocracy. According to this theory the *patres* (senators) were drawn from patrician clans, which were called patrician precisely because they supplied *patres* to the Senate. This could mean one of two things: either that the king was obliged to select his senators from a restricted circle of patrician clans, or that a clan became patrician once its head had been chosen as a *pater* by the king.[14]

The latter interpretation presupposes that the *patres* were heads of clans, a notion that has been widely canvassed in the scholarly literature. Niebuhr indeed went so far as to suggest that each curia was divided into ten clans, and that the Senate comprised the 300 clan leaders.[15] Niebuhr arrived at this seemingly bizarre conclusion not because he was soft in the head but because, in his opinion, the clans were artificial entities, like the tribes and curiae, rather than 'natural' kinship groups. This is by no means impossible, although it would be difficult to prove. But the main objection, which is decisive not only against Niebuhr but against all those who believe that the *patres* were clan heads, is that historically the clans were acephalous groups. It is only a confusion, which afflicts the sources no less than their modern successors, between clans and families that has given rise to the notion (in this case exclusively modern) that the *patres* were heads of clans. In fact a clan comprised several families, each with its own independent *paterfamilias*. Since there was no system of primogeniture in Rome there was no natural way in which any one *paterfamilias* could become head of the clan, and we know nothing whatever about any artificial method such as election. In short, the idea that each clan had a single head is absolutely unwarranted; and the phrase *pater gentis*, which is bandied about in books on Roman law, is a modern invention.[16]

This objection, however, does not affect the more general assumption that *patres* (senators) were drawn from patrician clans, or the theory that the essence of patrician privilege lay in the fact that the patriciate was the class from which senators were drawn. The theory has the virtue of simplicity, and coincides with the assumptions that underlie the annalistic narratives, which tend to describe the Conflict of the Orders as a struggle between the *plebs* and the Senate. This coincidence might appear to strengthen the case, but in fact it is merely a symptom of the anachronistic approach of our sources, whose view of events was conditioned by the conflicts between the tribunes and the Senate in the last century of the Republic. The truth of the matter is that the annalists have grossly exaggerated the importance of the Senate in early Rome, and that modern scholars, almost all of whom define the patriciate as essentially a senatorial order, have been misled by this tendency of the tradition. The theory that *patres* means 'senators', and that the patriciate was the class to which the *patres* belonged, is simple and economical, and enjoys the support of the great majority of scholars. Nevertheless, there are serious difficulties in the theory, and I doubt if it can be right. The reasons can be set out as follows.

(1) There is no evidence that the Senate was ever an exclusively patrician body. We know that, from very early times, it consisted of two groups, the *patres* and the *conscripti*. The formal designation of senators was *patres conscripti*, or *patres et conscripti*. Admittedly, some experts take *conscripti* as an adjective qualifying *patres*, and the phrase *patres et conscripti* as a hendiadys,[17] but this interpretation can be ruled out, not only because tradition treats the *conscripti* as separate from the *patres*, but because the formula used to summon the Senate called upon 'those who are Fathers and those who are enrolled' (*qui patres quique conscripti*), which puts the matter beyond doubt.[18] It is also worth observing that although we are told a great deal about the effort to break the patrician monopoly of the consulship and the major priesthoods, we hear of no comparable move to have non-patricians admitted to the Senate. The reason must be that the Senate was not an exclusively patrician body.[19]

If it was not necessary to be a patrician to be a senator, the patriciate can hardly be defined as a 'senatorial order'. Nevertheless, we might still argue that the *patres*, by virtue of their patrician status, had special privileges in relation to the Senate. Thus Momigliano and Richard have suggested that the *patres* had a hereditary right to a place in the Senate, whereas the *conscripti* were chosen *ad hominem*, so that the two groups resembled the hereditary peers and life peers in the British House of Lords.[20] On this view the patriciate consisted of those clans whose family heads (*patres familiarum*) automatically became senators (*patres*). The trouble is that this suggestion is not supported by any evidence, and appears to be born of necessity. Indeed it goes against the only firm evidence we do have, namely the statement of Festus that the kings (and later the consuls) had a free choice when enrolling senators (see below).

(2) The second reason for not defining patrician privilege as eligibility for membership of the Senate (or, on Momigliano's view, the automatic right to enter the Senate) is that the Senate as such did not have any effective functions. In the middle Republic the Senate was the governing body of the state and had immense authority and prestige; but this situation was the result of fundamental changes that took place in the later fourth century BC, as we shall see (below, p. 370). Before that period it was an elusive and ill-defined body of limited importance. Even in the mid-republican period the most striking thing about the Senate was that strictly speaking it had no constitutional powers whatever and virtually no autonomy of action. Its resolutions had no legal force, and it could not even meet unless summoned by a magistrate. These facts reinforce the traditional interpretation of the Senate as a body of advisers for the magistrates, and, before them, the kings.[21] This traditional view is based on the analogy between the Senate and the private institution of the *consilium*. It was the custom for a Roman *paterfamilias*, before taking

any important decision concerning his family or property, to consult the advice of an *ad hoc* council of senior relatives and friends. He was under no obligation to follow their advice, however, and his power over the family remained absolute.

The idea that the Senate originated as a *consilium* for the king is an attractive one that makes good sense of the evidence. But the analogy entails two further consequences: first that the king was free to choose whomever he wished to advise him from among his closest associates, and second that the *consilium* had no permanent existence, but lasted only for the duration of the matter in hand.[22] As it happens this is precisely how Festus defines the Senate in the archaic period. His words are worth quoting:

> There was once a time when it was not considered disgraceful for senators to be passed over, because, just as the kings by themselves used to choose (or to choose as replacements) men who would serve them as public advisers (*in publico consilio*), so under the Republic the consuls (or military tribunes with consular power) used to choose for themselves their closest friends from among the patricians and then from among the plebeians. This practice continued until the law of the tribune Ovinius put an end to it. Ovinius' law bound the censors by oath to enrol in the Senate the best men from all ranks. The enforcement of this law had the consequence that senators who were passed over, and thus lost their place, were held in dishonour.[23]

This seems to mean that before the Lex Ovinia (*c.* 339 BC) membership of the Senate depended solely on the personal favour of the current holder(s) of the *imperium*, and that there was no guarantee that a senator under one regime would necessarily be a senator under succeeding regimes. This point is confirmed by Festus, who specifically states that before the Lex Ovinia senators who were passed over (*praeteriti*) were not held in disrespect, whereas it was later a mark of the greatest disgrace to be excluded from the Senate. The clear implication of the passage is that in early times the Senate was little more than an *ad hoc* body of advisers with a constantly changing membership, not a permanent corporation of lifelong members. In short, before the Lex Ovinia, the Senate as such did not exist.

This radical view, which, be it noted, comes from the pen of a Roman antiquarian and not from a modern historian, deserves to be taken seriously. Admittedly it has no support from the rest of the sources, which presuppose the existence of a permanent Senate from the earliest times; but this may be based on no more than the unthinking assumption, which came naturally to the annalists and to conservative political thinkers such as Cicero, that the Senate had always been an important part of the Roman political system. It may be one of those cases where an antiquarian could have blown the received tradition sky high, if he had chosen to do so.[24]

(3) The third difficulty in taking the *patres* as senators arises directly from

the foregoing discussion. If the Senate was not a permanent body with a well-defined membership, how are we to account for those functions which are attributed to the *patres* as such, and which in the late Republic were carried out by patrician senators? These included holding the office of *interrex* and giving formal approval (*auctoritas patrum*) to decisions of the people's assembly. Under the monarchy the only decision we know the people were called upon to make was to elect a new king (or to approve a candidate put forward by the *patres*). The *auctoritas patrum* is further proof that the patricians controlled the appointment of the king. These powers, and the fact that, in an *interregnum*, the auspices were said to 'revert to the fathers', would not make any sense if the *patres* were those patricians whom the king from time to time felt moved to consult. The logic of such a position is that when there was no king there were no *patres*, which is absurd.

The inescapable conclusion is that the *patres* who controlled the *inter-regnum* procedure, gave their approval to decisions of the *comitia*, and had reversionary possession of the auspices, cannot be adequately defined as senators, or even patrician senators. It is not in the least surprising that in the late Republic the patricians who held the post of *interrex* were leading senators who had held senior magistracies. Equally it is understandable that, after the *auctoritas patrum* had been reduced to a meaningless formality by the Lex Publilia and the Lex Maenia (see below, p. 341), the task of delivering this formal approval was taken over by the patrician senators.[25] But in the earlier Republic and under the monarchy the *patres* who performed these roles cannot have been 'senators'. This leads me to the fourth, and to my mind decisive, argument against the identification of *patres* and senators.

(4) The clearest sign that *patres* should not be equated with (patrician) senators is the fact that the term *patres* is often used to mean patricians in a more general sense. Indeed, in Latin sources (especially our main source, Livy) the standard designation of the people we call patricians is none other than *patres*. Although the adjective *patricii* is sometimes used as a substantive (e.g. Livy 3.13.4), *patres* is far more common. The result is deeply confusing, and it is hardly surprising that translators render *patres* either as 'patricians' or as 'senators' according to context (Greek writers such as Dionysius did the same, referring either to οἱ πατρίκιοι or to ἡ βουλή). The unfortunate consequence of this practice has been that scholars tend to make an unreal distinction between patricians and *patres*, and have lost sight of the fact that the two are synonymous.[26]

The point is made abundantly clear by the use of *patres* in contexts where the reference cannot be to senators as such. An example is Livy's interesting account of the episode of Kaeso Quinctius, the hot-headed son of Cincinnatus, who in 463 BC organised a gang of young patrician louts in a campaign of street violence against the *plebs* and their tribunes.[27] In the course of his narrative Livy makes an interesting distinction between Kaeso's young patricians, the *iuniores patrum*, and their more responsible elders, the *seniores patrum*. The latter may conceivably be a reference to senators, but Livy certainly did not mean to say that the young *patres* in Kaeso's street gang were senators![28]

In using *patres* for patricians in general Livy was following established usage. The most striking example of this usage occurs in references to the prohibition on intermarriage in the Twelve Tables. Both Cicero and Livy report the rule in similar fashion – that there should be no right of legitimate marriage between *plebs* and *patres* – which almost certainly reflects the wording of the original law.[29] Here *patres* obviously means not senators, but the whole patrician order, including both sexes. The texts therefore imply, confusingly, that patrician mothers were also Fathers.[30]

The evidence compels the conclusion that *patres* was not the exclusive title of patrician senators. Of course patrician senators were *patres*, but that is because all patricians were *patres*. We have seen that in archaic Rome the Senate was not a permanent body of lifelong members, and that if anything it functioned as an *ad hoc* body of advisers to the king (and subsequently the consuls). Even if at one time the Senate consisted exclusively of patricians, the right to be considered for membership was probably only an incidental feature of patrician status, not the defining criterion.

The same comment can be made about the theory that the patriciate was an equestrian order – the idea, that is, that the patricians were the class from which cavalrymen were drawn. It is likely enough in general that when Rome went to war the patricians served in the cavalry. Aristocracies have a natural affinity with horses (often extending to personal appearance, as we know); this applies not just to our western Middle Ages, but to social elites in all times and places.[31]

Mommsen and many other historians have argued that the six cavalry centuries, which survived the Servian reform as a unique relic of the old Romulean system, were reserved for patricians.[32] There was certainly something special about these centuries, which, even after the cavalry was increased by the addition of a further twelve centuries, kept their old names (Ramnes, Tities, and Luceres, *priores* and *posteriores* – see above, p. 115), and retained a separate identity as the *sex suffragia* (the 'six votes'). There is no firm evidence, however, that the *sex suffragia* were centuries of patricians, although an obscure passage of Festus could be taken to imply the existence in the *comitia centuriata* of units called *centuriae procum patricium* ('centuries of patrician notables').[33] If that is the correct interpretation of the Festus passage, it is difficult to imagine which units these could be other than the *sex suffragia*. The argument is clearly tenuous; but even if it be sound, it does not follow that the definitive characteristic of patrician status was service in the cavalry. Being good with horses does not make one an aristocrat; rather, being an aristocrat makes one (among other things) good with horses. In other words, we may draw the same conclusion about cavalry service as about membership

250

of the Senate: even if restricted to patricians, which is far from certain, it was only an incidental feature of patrician status.

3 THE ORIGIN AND NATURE OF PATRICIAN PRIVILEGE

As we have seen, tradition maintains that the patriciate originated during the regal period. Some modern historians, however, believe that it emerged only under the Republic, when the men who expelled the king and held office during the early years of the new regime attempted to form themselves into a closed aristocracy, and to arrogate to themselves and their descendants exclusive rights of access to positions of political and sacred power.[34] This process was described by De Sanctis as 'the closing of the patriciate',[35] a concept that has been widely accepted by subsequent scholarship, in my opinion rightly. But De Sanctis was also right, I believe, to argue that the aristocracy which staged this takeover of the government had already come into existence as a social elite during the regal period. Naturally, as with all aristocracies, its power was based ultimately on wealth, as De Martino has rightly stressed; and its emergence can be documented archaeologically by the chamber tombs of the orientalising period.[36] In other words, it is unrealistic to imagine the patriciate being formed out of nothing at the beginning of the Republic; it must already have existed, in embryonic form, under the kings.

The main argument of those who see the patriciate as a post-monarchical development is that the kings themselves do not appear to have been patricians.[37] But we have already seen that a different interpretation is possible, namely that the patricians were 'stakeholders' who controlled the appointment of the king, although they were not eligible for the kingship themselves (above, p. 143). Their choice tended to fall on outsiders, which was a way of avoiding internal rivalries and tensions among themselves. This hypothesis is supported by ethnographic parallels and makes sense of the evidence we have. At any rate it is certain that the *interregnum*, as its name suggests, was an institution of the monarchic period, and it would seem to follow that the patricians' control of the *interregnum* also dates back to the time of the kings.[38]

The exclusive privileges connected with the *interregnum* and the *auctoritas patrum* suggest that the patriciate was already a well-defined group with distinct political privileges before the beginning of the Republic. The religious character of patrician privileges is also important. This religious dimension is particularly evident in the notion that the auspices in some sense 'belonged' to the patricians, and reverted to them on the death of the king to whom they had been entrusted for the time being. The religious nature of patrician privilege also emerges from the fact that all the major priestly offices were reserved for them.[39] These patrician priesthoods included not only membership of the chief religious corporations (of the Pontiffs, Augurs, *duumviri sacris faciundis*, Fetiales and Salii), but also the posts of *rex sacrorum* and the major *flamines* (of Jupiter, Mars and Quirinus). The fact that all the main state priesthoods were reserved for patricians shows that, whatever else it may have been, the patriciate was essentially a class defined by religious prerogatives.

This patrician monopoly of religious office must go back to the regal period. Some of the priesthoods in question (especially the major flaminates) were extremely archaic and, if the interpretation offered in an earlier chapter is accepted (above, p. 234), had already become anachronistic relics by the start of the Republic. It is also striking that almost all Roman priesthoods were traditionally established under the kings (the only known exception is the college of *septemviri epulones*, formed in 196 BC), and indeed are recorded as going back to the beginning of the regal period (only the *duumviri sacris faciundis* are attributed to the age of the Tarquins). This tradition is probably historical, in the sense that the king, however powerful he may have been in military and judicial contexts, did not enjoy a monopoly of religious authority. Even if the tradition about the *rex sacrorum* is interpreted to mean that the king was once the most important figure in the priestly hierarchy, the same evidence indicates that he coexisted with a wide range of other religious authorities. Clashes between the king and priestly power are indeed recorded in the tradition, the most notable instance being the conflict between Tarquinius Priscus and the augur Attus Navius. One of the many interesting features of this episode is that the king came off second best.[40]

We may therefore conclude that under the monarchy certain clans had acquired the exclusive right to fill the principal sacred offices, and thus to control the religious life of the state. This gave the patricians a unique relationship with the gods, and no doubt underpinned the belief that the auspices reverted to them when the kingship fell vacant. They claimed the sole right to hold the position of *interrex*, and they alone were able to confer the auspices on the king whom they had effectively chosen. If it is true that the later kings were usurpers, the patricians must have lost ground; indeed the most probable interpretation of the actions of the last kings is that they were designed to restrict the growth of patrician power. The revolution, when it came, was an aristocratic coup against a populist and tyrannical monarchy; and there can be no doubt that the patricians were in the forefront of the group that seized power at the start of the Republic.

4 THE 'CLOSING OF THE PATRICIATE'

The most controversial question concerning patrician privilege under the Republic is whether it was necessary to be a patrician in order to hold the consulship. Our sources assume that it was, but the *Fasti* suggest that in the earliest decades of the Republic not all consuls were patricians. The most striking example is the very first consul, L. Junius Brutus. The Junii were an important plebeian clan, whose members were tribunes of the plebs in the fifth and fourth centuries, and reached the consulship as plebeians in the later fourth century. The famous Brutus who murdered Caesar was a plebeian, and yet claimed descent from the founder of the Republic.[41] This is not therefore a case where 'tradition' is in conflict with a modern interpretation of the *Fasti*; rather, the tradition is itself confused and self-contradictory. The apparently 'plebeian' consuls of this period can be listed as follows:

Table 5 Consuls of uncertain status in the fifth century

Name	Year(s) in office
L. Junius Brutus	509
Sp. Cassius Vicellinus	502, 493, 486
Post. Cominius Auruncus	501, 493
M' Tullius Longus	500
M. Minucius Augurinus	497, 491
P. Minucius Augurinus	492
T. Siccius Sabinus	487
C. Aquillius Tuscus	487
T. Numicius Priscus	469
P. Volumnius Amintinus Gallus	461
L. Minucius Esquilinus Augurinus	458
Q. Minucius Esquilinus	457
Sp. Tarpeius Montanus Capitolinus	454
A. Aternius Varus Fontinalis	454
T. Genucius	451 (designate)
M. Genucius Augurinus	445

Source: Drummond, *CAH* VII² 2, 175.

There are three possible solutions to the difficulty. One is to reject all the 'plebeian' names as fictitious interpolations, on the grounds that the consulship was reserved for patricians. But this solution manifestly begs the question (cf. above, p. 220), and there is no need to waste time on it.[42] A second and more serious suggestion is that the consuls in question were really patrician, even if later bearers of the same names were plebeian. It was indeed possible for individual patricians to become plebeian, by a mysterious process known as 'transition to the plebs' (*transitio ad plebem*); their descendants would also be plebeian, with the result that patrician and plebeian lineages coexisted within the same clan.[43] Another way of explaining how the same name could be borne by both patricians and plebeians is to suppose that the latter were descended from freed slaves, since it was the custom for a freedman to take the gentilicial name of his former master and to pass it on to his descendants.[44]

However we choose to explain it, the fact is that the later Roman nobility included plebeians who bore patrician names (most notably the Claudii Marcelli); it is therefore possible to argue that the 'plebeian' names in the early

Fasti are actually those of patricians whose clans died out or faded into obscurity, but were survived by plebeian namesakes who became prominent in the later Republic.[45] This ingenious theory might explain some of the problematic names in the early lists, and is borne out by one instance (the case of the Sempronii) where the presumed development is known to have taken place.[46] But it is unlikely to be true in all cases, and as a general explanation it must be rejected. It was certainly common in the later Republic for plebeians to bear patrician names, but within the ranks of the nobility it was an extremely rare phenomenon. Of the hundreds of *gentile* names in the republican *Fasti* (over thirty of them patrician), only four are shared by patricians and plebeians – viz. Claudius, Servilius, Veturius and Sempronius.[47] It is therefore highly improbable – indeed, it strains belief – that as many as seven (a clear majority) of the problem cases should involve clans that produced patrician consuls in the fifth century, and then went on to produce plebeian consuls in succeeding centuries.[48]

There is a second objection to this theory which only needs to be stated to reveal what must be the correct answer to the problem. If it were true that the supposedly plebeian consuls of the early Republic actually belonged to patrician clans that subsequently died out, one would expect them to be spread at random through the fifth-century *Fasti*. In fact they are concentrated at the beginning of the list, as shown in Table 6.

Table 6 Status of office-holders to the end of the fifth century

Period (BC)	Total no. of offices	Offices held by patricians	Offices held by 'plebeians'
1 509–483	57	45 (79%)	12 (21%)
2 482–456	56	52 (93%)	4 (7%)
3 455–428	61	56 (92%)	5 (8%)
4 427–401	99	98 (99%)	1 (1%)

Note: The period from 509 to 401 has been divided into four equal sections; the Decemvirates have been excluded. The offices include those of consul, suffect consul and military tribune with consular power. The one non-patrician office-holder in period 4 is Q. Antonius Merenda (*trib. mil. c.p.* 422 BC), a problematic case.[49]
Source: Broughton, *MRR*.

The table shows that the proportion of office-holding patricians in the fifth century increased to the point where they gained a virtual monopoly; this is particularly striking for the second half of the century, because at that period the number of available posts almost doubled with the introduction of the consular tribunate (see below, p. 334). The evidence points unmistakably to the conclusion that the patricians, although always in a strong majority, did not achieve a complete monopoly of political power until the second half of the fifth century. The few non-patricians who achieved high office in the early Republic were an isolated minority, and were unable to pass on their distinction to their descendants. It is extremely significant that the most successful of them, the three-times-consul Sp. Cassius, is portrayed as a popular leader who was tried and executed in 486 BC after allegedly trying to revive the monarchy.[50] Whether we should call such people plebeians is questionable; but it is virtually certain that they were not patricians.

The process by which the patricians turned a majority share into a monopoly can reasonably be called the 'closing of the patriciate', although it should be noted that that is not precisely what De Sanctis meant by 'la serrata'. What he had in mind was the tendency of the patricians to form themselves into an exclusive hereditary caste, in particular by discouraging intermarriage between the orders. It seems likely, however, that both processes went together, and culminated in the middle of the fifth century. That, after all, was when the Decemvirs enacted (in the eleventh Table) the notorious rule that there should be no *conubium* between patricians and plebeians.

It is sometimes suggested that this enactment did no more than confirm long-standing practice;[51] but there are good reasons for thinking that it was indeed an innovation. After all, this is the unanimous view of our sources, which should not be lightly dismissed; second, the outcry that led to its repeal within a few years implies that it was seen as an outrageous novelty; and third, the evidence we have seems to show that mixed marriages had formerly been perfectly acceptable. For instance the wife of Cincinnatus was named Racilia (Livy 3.26.9). It is possible that the Racilii were an otherwise unknown patrician *gens* (as Mommsen thought), but it seems unlikely. Similarly, Coriolanus' wife Volumnia was a plebeian, although his mother Veturia was a patrician. It follows that, whatever the status of Coriolanus himself, he was either the product of a mixed marriage or himself party to one.[52] The Tarquin family was also involved in mixed marriages, since Lucretia was a patrician, while the Junii, Aquilii and Vitellii were plebeian (see above, p. 123).

On the other hand, it is widely believed that the patricians used a distinctive form of marriage ceremony known as *confarreatio*, so called because the ritual involved cakes of spelt (*far*). If this ceremony was confined to patricians, and was essential for a valid patrician marriage, as many scholars suppose, then it would follow that mixed marriages were not regarded as legally valid, and that resulting children would not inherit patrician status.[53] However, there is absolutely no evidence that *confarreatio* was ever restricted to patricians. Strictly speaking, the purpose of *confarreatio* was to bring about not the marriage as such, but rather the acquisition of what the Romans called *manus* (see below, p. 285); since the whole issue of *manus* was concerned with property transfer and succession, it is unlikely that *confarreatio* was much used outside the ranks of the propertied classes. But that is not the same thing as saying that it was confined to patricians, nor does it have any bearing on the issue of mixed marriages, which are likely to have involved only better-off 'plebeians'.

That such people existed is beyond question, as we shall see in the discussion that follows. And it was no doubt from their ranks that the non-patrician consuls of the early Republic were drawn. The process we have called the 'closing' of the patriciate had the effect of excluding them from the consulship and from permanent social integration with the patricians by means of intermarriage. The process was complete by around 450, and had a polarising effect; and it transformed the face of Roman politics by driving wealthy non-patricians towards the plebeian organisation.

5 THE RISE OF THE *PLEBS*

The formation of the patriciate did not coincide with the rise of the *plebs*. This statement is paradoxical only in the sense that on a broad definition the *plebs* comprised the totality of non-patrician Roman citizens. Of course on this negative definition the *plebs* came into being as soon as the patriciate began to emerge as a distinct social group. But it is doubtful if at that period (the monarchy and early Republic) the rest of the population outside the patriciate was envisaged as a definite element in society, still less that the term 'plebeians' was applied to all of them. Rather, the evidence seems to suggest that the *plebs* originated as a distinct group with a positive and self-conscious identity during the early Republic. It was not the primordial entity that is assumed in dualistic theories, but the product of a secondary development, later than the patriciate and independent of it. Like the patriciate, the *plebs* was not formed in opposition to any particular group, but rather had its own identity and its own agenda that distinguished it from the rest of the population. In any event it is most improbable that the original aim of the plebeians was to challenge the position of the patricians as such, but rather to fight for their own interests; in Raaflaub's words, the initial aims of the *plebs* were 'protection and defence' rather than any immediate attempt to break down patrician exclusiveness.[54]

In origin the *plebs* was an organised group, consciously formed at a time of crisis. Tradition places this event in 494 BC, when a large number of the poor, oppressed by debt and arbitrary treatment, withdrew from the city *en masse* and occupied the Sacred Mount, a hill overlooking the Tiber a few miles upstream from Rome (an alternative version, mentioned by Livy (2.32.3), specified the Aventine, a hill with strong plebeian associations, which was also outside the city boundary). Here they created their own organisation, which was like an alternative state. They formed their own assembly, known as the *concilium plebis*, and elected their own officials, the tribunes. At first the tribunes were probably two in number, which suggests that they were set up in opposition to the consuls, as Cicero confirms.[55] At the same time a temple to Ceres, Liber and Libera was dedicated on the Aventine, and became a cult centre for the *plebs*.

The first question we need to ask about the plebeian organisation is: who were the *plebs*? The word *plebs* means 'the masses' (it is related to the Greek *plēthos* – 'multitude'), and is used in classical Latin as a general term for the lower classes. In phrases such as *plebs urbana* ('urban mob') and *plebs sordida* ('the great unwashed') it was plainly a derogatory term. It may always have been so, in which case the adoption of it by the plebeians themselves (even in formal language, as in the phrases *tribunus plebis, concilium plebis* and *plebiscitum*) is an example of the way in which such terms can be taken up and used with pride by those against whom they were originally directed.[56]

However that may be, the implication of the term *plebs*, and the clear message of the traditional accounts, is that the plebeians who staged the First Secession (as the withdrawal in 494 became known) were drawn from the poorest and most disadvantaged people in the community. It is not necessary to identify them with any particular group – for example urban artisans as opposed to farmers, or, for that matter, peasants as opposed to urban workers.[57] The likelihood is that they included both, and that the organised plebeian movement embraced an undifferentiated mass of poor people who shared a common sense of distress and were united by a their commitment to the cause. In this sense it was the plebeian movement that created the *plebs*, not the other way round.[58]

Even if the *plebs* included a substantial proportion of small farmers and agricultural workers, which seems likely enough given the nature of the ancient economy, it is still improbable that in its early stages the plebeian movement included many (or even any) of the hoplites – that is, of the relatively well-off peasant proprietors who could afford to equip themselves for service in the heavy infantry. To this extent Momigliano was justified in arguing that the *plebs* were largely drawn from the *infra classem*. Raaflaub, on the other hand, suggests that 'the plebeians must have dominated the phalanx'.[59] This cannot be right. If the First Secession had been an uprising by the hoplite infantry, the conflict of the orders would not have lasted two days, let alone two centuries.

Whether the *plebs* can be formally identified with the *infra classem* is more doubtful. Momigliano laid stress on an archaic formula that appears to contrast *populus* and *plebs*; this can be explained if *populus*, which seems originally to have meant 'the army', is interpreted as a reference to the *classis*.[60] Even so, it would not follow that the *plebs* were excluded from military service, but only that they did not serve in the hoplite phalanx. The role of the *infra classem* was to support the phalanx by fighting as light armed soldiers; they were the citizens who, in the later reorganisation of the *comitia centuriata*, were assigned to the fourth and fifth classes (cf. above, p. 185).

This interpretation would make some sense of the traditional accounts of the plebeian secessions, which are represented in part as a refusal by the *plebs* to perform military service. On the other hand, the sources do not assume that the army consisted entirely or even predominantly of plebeians. For instance, Appius Claudius is said to have dismissed the danger of a secession in 493 BC on the grounds that the *plebs* made only a minimal contribution to Rome's fighting strength, and that the patricians could easily provide an army from among their own clients.[61] If the plebeians were mostly *infra classem*, and served as light armed troops, the nature of the secession becomes clear; the withdrawal of the *plebs* was a serious matter for Rome, but it was hardly decisive, and would not have been able to bring the state to its knees.[62]

This discussion raises an issue that has lately received much attention, namely the fact that the social structure of early Rome was based on a complex set of status categories expressed in terms of binary oppositions: patrons and clients, *patres* and *conscripti*, *classis* and *infra classem*, *equites* and *pedites*, *seniores* and *iuniores*, *adsidui* and *proletarii*, and, if the above interpretation is correct, *populus* and *plebs*. Most of these pairings occur in official formulae or archaic documents such as the Twelve Tables, and can therefore be taken as good evidence for the nature of status categories in the early Republic. The important point is that in most cases these distinctions do not coincide, but represent contrasts between different kinds of groups. We are dealing with a pattern of overlapping and intersecting status categories, characteristic of a society that was sufficiently complex for the same person to belong to several different groups at the same time, and in which there was a very large range of possible combinations.[63]

This observation puts the final nail in the coffin of the old patrician–plebeian dualism. In the archaic formulae, *patres* were contrasted with *conscripti*, the *plebs* with the *populus*. It does not follow that the *populus* was exclusively patrician, nor that the *conscripti* were plebeians. Rather, *patres* and *plebs* were at opposite ends of a complex social hierarchy, and were separated by intermediate groups who could themselves be variously classified and differentiated. The *plebs* were opposed not just by the patricians, but by those who had a vested interest in maintaining the status quo, including the farmers who formed the hoplite phalanx, and those well-to-do persons who, although not of patrician status, nevertheless managed to reach the consulship in the early Republic. To call these men plebeians, in the circumstances of the years before and after 500 BC, would be quite mistaken.

6 THE 'STATE WITHIN THE STATE'[64]

To what extent the First Secession is an authentic historical event is difficult to say. The traditional accounts are a mixture of legend and romance, most famously represented by the story of Agrippa Menenius, who persuaded the *plebs* to return to the city by telling them the parable of the limbs and the belly (i.e. that a healthy body requires the co-operation of all its parts).[65] Other episodes in the struggle, for instance the agitation of 471 BC associated with the plebeian leader Volero Publilius, are equally uncertain. At this period it is probably not worth trying to analyse individual episodes in detail since the sources are confused and there is no way of verifying any one account against another. It would be more profitable to summarise the main results of these conflicts, by saying that by the middle of the fifth century BC a fully developed plebeian organisation had come into being, with its own assembly and magistrates and with its own distinctive modes of political action. The principal features of this plebeian organisation can be briefly enumerated.

The tribunes of the *plebs*

According to the second-century historian Piso there were originally two tribunes, but their number was increased to five in 471 BC; Livy and Dionysius, on the other hand, say that the first two tribunes of 494 immediately co-opted three additional colleagues. Diodorus, however, states that in 471 'for the first time in Rome four tribunes of the *plebs* were elected'.[66] The significance of these different versions is difficult to assess, and attempts to relate the number of tribunes to the number of tribes, or the number of classes, are probably misplaced. In any event, by the middle of the fifth century the number of tribunes had been increased to ten, an event dated by Livy to 457 BC.[67]

The tribunes' authority was based on what the Romans called a *lex sacrata*. This was a collective resolution reinforced by a solemn oath. Having elected their tribunes, the plebeians swore to obey them and to defend them to the death; anyone who should harm them became *sacer*, a term for which the English word 'accursed' is an inadequate translation. The formula *sacer esto* ('let him be accursed') was pronounced on persons who by their actions harmed the gods.[68] Such a person became forfeit to the god in question, and on death was surrendered into his power; anyone who killed the offender was therefore carrying out a sacred duty, and did so without incurring any penalty or blood-guilt.[69] In this way the tribunes of the plebs became 'sacrosanct' (i.e. inviolable).

The *lex sacrata* is otherwise attested as a military institution among Italic peoples such as the Volsci or the Samnites. In times of crisis these peoples would raise armies by means of a compulsory levy, and the soldiers so enrolled would be sworn to follow their leaders to the death.[70] In a Roman context the *lex sacrata* has affinities with the military oath; the fact that the plebeian leaders were called tribunes perhaps encourages the analogy (since the senior officers of the Roman armies were known as *tribuni militum*).

The *lex sacrata* gave the plebeian tribunes extensive powers which derived ultimately from their inviolability. They were able to enforce their will by coercion (*coercitio*). They could impose fines, imprisonment, or even the death penalty, against anyone who challenged their authority or who made a physical or verbal assault on their persons.[71] Because of their sacrosanctity the tribunes were able to protect individual plebeians from ill treatment by the rich and powerful, and from arbitrary punishment by the magistrates, by giving them 'assistance' (*auxilium*). At first this was an extra-legal procedure in which the tribune intervened personally, and rescued plebeians by threatening opponents with the dire consequences of the *lex sacrata* if they should try to use force against him. In other words it was a form of organised self-help by the *plebs*, who backed their actions by lynch-law disguised as divine justice. Although Livy suggests that in 494 and 471 the patricians accepted the plebeian institutions by 'agreement' (*pactio*), and for all Dionysius' talk, in the same context, of 'treaties', the surviving accounts leave little room for doubt that in the first half of the fifth century the plebeian organisation was an extra-legal body which the hard-line patricians refused to recognise. The battle for recognition and legal acceptance was clearly an important part of the struggle in the early days, and was effectively decided in 449 BC, when the Valerio-Horatian Laws re-established the plebeian organisation after the Decemvirate.

It was probably after the *plebs* had gained recognition that the tribunes acquired the right to 'intercede' in the general legislative, deliberative and executive procedures of the government, and thus in effect to bring its business to a standstill. This was the famous tribunician 'veto' (in Latin *intercessio*). If any such interventions occurred in the early period of the Republic, they would have been examples of the use of *de facto* power based on the sanction of the *lex sacrata*, rather than the exercise of a legal right; but at some stage (perhaps once again the settlement of 449 BC), the tribunician veto became a recognised right and a formal part of the constitution of the state. In the later Republic, the veto could be used to put a stop to virtually anything, and became an extremely powerful weapon in the armoury of the tribunes. But it is unlikely that the veto could have functioned in this indiscriminate way as early as the fifth century; it must have been restricted, perhaps to contexts where the persons of individual plebeians were seen to be directly threatened by the actions of the magistrates. When Sulla restricted the use of the tribunician veto in 81 BC, perhaps in exactly this way, he was undoubtedly attempting to restore what he saw as its original function.[72]

The *concilium plebis*

One of the tribunes' most important functions was to hold meetings of the plebeian assembly (*agere cum plebe*). The assembly was called the *concilium plebis*, and was in principle open to all citizens other than patricians, although at first, as we have seen, probably only a minority took part as active members of the organisation. In 471, as a result of a reform by the tribune Volero Publilius, the *concilium plebis* was reorganised on the basis of the local tribes; from now on, it decided on proposals by means of the group-vote system (that is, a majority of votes within a tribe would determine the vote of that tribe, and a majority of the tribes would then determine the outcome).

This reform raises some interesting questions. First, how had the *concilium* been organised before Publilius' reform? The sources offer the surprising answer that in its early days the plebeian assembly had been based on the old curiae.[73] That is of course possible; but it is worth considering another possibility, namely that Roman antiquarians were so used to the group-vote principle in all political assemblies that they overlooked the obvious alternative (obvious to an outsider, that is). It is surely conceivable that the earliest meetings of the *plebs* were not divided into groups at all, but, like Greek assemblies, were open meetings whose decisions were arrived at by simple majority of all those present and voting. That the plebeian movement was directly influenced by Greek political ideas and practice is very likely.[74]

However that may be, it is certain that the *plebs* did not at any stage make use of the centuriate system. This might seem surprising at first sight, especially if one of the purposes of the centuriate reform was to curtail the locally based power of the aristocracy (see above, p. 196). This suggests two important conclusions. The first is that the original purpose of the plebeian organisation was not to challenge the power of the aristocracy; secondly, the plebeian movement was not broadly equivalent to the infantry army (which was the essence of the centuriate system), but, on the contrary, consisted largely of people who were outside the ranks of the *classis*.

On the other hand, the use of the tribes suggests that the purpose of the Lex Publilia (if we may call it that for convenience) was to make the plebeian assembly more democratic by ensuring that the rural plebs were properly represented in assemblies which took place within the city, and which would otherwise have been dominated by the urban population, who for practical reasons found it easier to attend in person. If so, and it is hard to see any other reason for the reform, it follows that the *plebs* cannot have been restricted to artisans, traders, and other 'urban' groups.

Plebiscites

Resolutions of the *plebs*, which in historical times were decided by a majority vote (using the tribal system) on proposals put forward by the tribunes, were known as plebiscites (*plebiscita*). These were binding on the *plebs*, and in so far as they concerned the plebeian organisation itself (its 'constitution' as we might say), they are unproblematic. An example is the Lex Publilia (strictly, the *plebiscitum Publilium*), which concerned voting procedure in the plebeian assembly.[75] The matter is more complicated in the case of plebiscites dealing with substantive issues, particularly those concerning the whole community. The question of the validity of plebiscites was tackled by one of the Valerio-Horatian Laws of 449 BC, and will be discussed in due course (below, p. 277). But we know of at least one plebiscite that seems to have passed into law before 449 BC. This is the so-called *lex Icilia de Aventino publicando* of 456 BC.[76] The result of this measure, according to Dionysius, was that public land on the Aventine, including areas that had been occupied illegally, was reclaimed and distributed in lots to the plebeians for building houses.

The problem, naturally, is to explain how the *plebs* were able to make any kind of binding decision in respect of public land (*ager publicus*), which as its name suggests belonged to the Roman people as a whole; one would have thought that only a formal public law of the Roman people (*lex publica populi Romani*) could dispose of public land.[77] Dionysius was acutely conscious of the difficulty, and his account offers an elaborate way round it. According to this version, the measure was not a plebiscite at all; the tribune who first thought of it, L. Icilius, did not propose it to the *plebs*, but submitted it to the consuls and the Senate. After some discussion the law was approved by the Senate and then enacted by the centuriate assembly summoned by the consuls. The problem here is that the law evidently bore the name of Icilius (as in Livy), whereas a centuriate law of the kind described by Dionysius would have been named after the consuls. In any case it is clear enough that Dionysius' account deserves no credence; he (or his source) has sacrificed all historical plausibility on the altar of constitutional propriety.[78] It is character- istic of his picture of early Rome that everything should be accomplished by due legal process, and in particular that tribunes should behave properly by acknowledging the superiority of the Senate and submitting all proposals for prior approval. The account reflects the ideology of the late republican 'optimates'.

Nevertheless, the fact that the annalists were so troubled by the Lex Icilia, and were prepared to go to such absurd lengths to overcome the problem, must count strongly in favour of its general authenticity. That it was a genuine law is further supported by the fact that it was recorded on a bronze pillar in the temple of Aventine Diana, and was still extant in the time of Dionysius.[79]

Livy, whose many charms include a complete lack of interest in con- stitutional problems, says nothing about all this; indeed he has little to say about the law at all, beyond its name and the fact that it was passed in this year, but he does add a crucial detail which provides the key to the puzzle. He tells us that in 452 the plebeians agreed to the appointment of patrician *decemviri* 'on condition that the Icilian Law concerning the Aventine and the other *leges sacratae* should not be abrogated'.[80] The implication is that the Lex Icilia was itself a *lex sacrata* – that is to say, its authority was based on nothing more than a collective oath of the *plebs*. De Sanctis rightly deduced that the law was a unilateral decision by the *plebs* to occupy public land on the Aventine, and to protect individual settlers against eviction, if necessary by force.[81]

We may reasonably conclude that all the plebiscites of the early fifth century were unilateral resolutions of the *plebs*, backed by oaths and dependent for their effectiveness on plebeian solidarity. Livy confirms this when he suggests that the *plebs* demanded legal recognition of the *leges sacratae* as the price of accepting the first Decemvirate.

The aediles and the temple of Ceres

At the First Secession the plebeians are also said to have created two aediles, to serve as annual officials alongside the tribunes. In later times the duties of the aediles included the upkeep of the streets and public buildings in the city, maintaining public order, supervising markets, organising games and over-seeing the food supply. Some of these functions can only have developed after 367 BC, when the aediles became regular state magistrates, but there is no reason to doubt that most if not all of them have their roots in the early period when the aediles were officers of the *plebs*. For instance, the Plebeian Games (*ludi plebeii*), which are first attested in the third century BC, may go back to the beginnings of the plebeian organisation in the fifth century. It would be entirely characteristic of the *plebs* to institute their own games in imitation of the official state celebrations, the Roman Games (*ludi Romani*), which were probably first held under the kings.[82] It is also possible that market supervision was one of the earliest functions of the plebeian aediles, if markets developed in connection with meetings of the plebeian assembly.[83]

These are matters for speculation. We are on much firmer ground with the title *aedilis*, which is certainly to be connected with the temple (*aedes*) of Ceres, Liber and Libera, the plebeian cult centre on the Aventine. It is unfortunately not clear how the temple and the cult first came to be associated with the *plebs*. According to the traditional account (Dion. Hal. 6.17.2–4) the temple was vowed after the battle of Lake Regillus by the patrician dictator A. Postumius, and was funded by spoils of the campaign; in this respect it was no different from the aristocratic cult of Castor, whose temple originated at the same time. On the other hand, the vow to Ceres (the goddess of grain crops) was the consequence of a food shortage, which would have afflicted the *plebs*; and the temple was dedicated in the year after the First Secession by the consul Sp. Cassius, a popular leader, and this may not be a coincidence. We should also note that under the *lex sacrata* a transgressor was pronounced *sacer* to Jupiter, and his belongings became the property of Ceres. This suggests that the plebeian connection with Ceres goes back to the beginning.

If so, it is worth noting that the cult had strong Greek associations. Even if the triad of Ceres, Liber and Libera is not demonstrably of Greek origin,[84] it is beyond question that the identity of the three deities with their Greek counterparts (Demeter, Dionysus and Persephone) was recognised from the start; the most probable theory is that the cult was adopted from southern Italy, where cults of Demeter were common.[85] The Greek associations of the cult of Ceres are confirmed by two further details. First, we happen to know that the painted terracotta sculptures that decorated the temple were the work of two Greek artists, Damophilos and Gorgasos (Varro *ap.* Pliny, *n.h.* 35.154). Second, Cicero tells us explicitly (*pro Balbo* 55) that the rituals used in the cult were of Greek origin and were called by Greek names; moreover, they were performed by priestesses who came from the Greek world, usually from

Magna Graecia. We cannot be sure that these Greek features of the cult go back to the 490s BC, but the rest of the evidence makes it probable that they do; and the arguments that have been used to support a later date are extremely weak.[86]

Momigliano has argued that the plebeian movement made use of Greek models in the course of its development; given the evidence we now have for the importance of Greek influence on all aspects of Roman life in the archaic period, this conjecture seems well founded. One sign of this Greek influence is the fact that Ceres was the patron goddess of written laws – *legifera Ceres* as Virgil calls her (*Aeneid* 4.58). This was a direct translation of the Greek epithet *thesmophoros*, which when applied to Demeter originally had a different cultic significance, but was later taken to mean that Demeter had invented laws and given them to men.[87] This notion probably originated at Athens and spread to other cities, including some in Italy, such as Thurii and Cumae, in the fifth century. From here it would have reached Rome, where it became customary at this period to keep copies of public enactments in the temple of Ceres.

From 449 BC, according to Livy, decrees of the Senate were consigned to the care of the plebeian aediles, to be kept in the temple of Ceres (3.55.13). This measure has been misunderstood by modern authorities, who find it incredible that at this period the state should charge plebeian leaders with the official task of keeping public documents.[88] But that is not the point. Rather the measure should be understood as a concession to the *plebs*, who demanded, and were hereby granted, the right to know what the Senate had resolved, and to keep a written record of it. Livy confirms this when he adds (ibid.) that previously the consuls had been in the habit of suppressing or altering senatorial decrees. It is true that decrees of the Senate (*senatus consulta*) did not have the force of law, and at this date were not the important instruments of policy that they later became; but they are significant in this context because meetings of the Senate, unlike those of the *comitia*, were held behind closed doors, and their proceedings were not made public. There was no need for a comparable law concerning enactments of the *comitia*, since there was nothing to stop the *plebs* from keeping a record of them, and the evidence we have suggests that that is exactly what they did.

The notice confirms the plebeians' commitment to the idea of written law. This was a Greek invention, and the *plebs* had already adopted it for their own plebiscites, which the aediles recorded and kept in the temple of Ceres. Indeed, one tradition maintains that the original function of the aediles was to act as archivists. Zonaras writes:

> In addition to the tribunes, two aediles were chosen, who were to assist them in the matter of documents. They took charge of all the records of the *plebs*, of the people, and of the Senate, and kept them, so that nothing that was transacted should escape their notice.[89]

The plebeian movement was a remarkable phenomenon, as far as we know without parallel in the history of the ancient city-state. Two general observations may be made here. First, it was a revolutionary organisation, at least potentially. In a society which at no time in its history recognised the right of free association, the *plebs* had no alternative but to create a union which would have to defend itself, if necessary by violence, against the forces of the state. The clearest sign of this is the *lex sacrata*, which allowed the *plebs* and its officers to intervene in the political arena and to enforce their will by a system of lynch-justice. The outline is vague and the detailed events recorded in our sources for the fifth century cannot be relied on; but the formation of an extra-legal plebeian movement in the early fifth century should not be doubted. The later vestiges of the movement, which were so important in the political history of the later Republic, were gradually recognised and integrated with the institutions of the state, a process which began in 449 BC. Before that, the *plebs* had to rely on self-help and unilateral action.

Second, Mommsen was absolutely right to define the plebeian movement as 'a state within the state'. Objections to this on the grounds that the *plebs* lacked certain aspects of state apparatus, e.g. that they had no council and raised no armies, are mere quibbles.[90] It is true that the *plebs* did not aspire to complete autonomy (except during a secession, when they threatened to detach themselves permanently from the rest of the community), but that is not really the point. What is remarkable is not only the way in which plebeian institutions matched those of the state, but the fact that their organisation was in many ways more advanced and sophisticated. In the period down to 367 BC the plebeian institutions were either integrated into the constitution, or were themselves imitated by the 'patrician state'. The fact that the *plebs* had two sets of elected magistrates perhaps inspired the innovation of 447 BC, when two quaestors were elected to assist the consuls.[91] The quaestors were elected in an assembly organised by tribes (the *comitia tributa*), clearly modelled on the *concilium plebis*. The *comitia tributa* was also used for the election of 'curule' aediles, state magistrates who were created in 367 BC in direct imitation of the plebeian aediles. Finally, if the suggestion made above is accepted, it was the plebeians who first established an archive, probably in imitation of Greek practice, and pioneered the notion that official decisions should be systematically recorded and preserved. We should not be surprised, therefore, that the demand for a codification of the laws should have been among the stated aims of the plebeian movement.

7 PLEBEIAN GRIEVANCES: DEBT AND FOOD SHORTAGES

The formation of the *plebs* took place against the background of an economic recession which, as we have seen (above, pp. 225–6), affected not just Rome but the whole of Tyrrhenian Italy. The nature and causes of this crisis are hard to assess on the meagre evidence available to us. The symptoms include a marked decline in public building, documented by the record of temple constructions. Our sources report the dedication of several major temples in the first years of the Republic. Apart from the great temple of Capitoline Jupiter (509 BC), they include those of Saturn (497), Mercury (495), Ceres (493), Fortuna Muliebris (486) and Castor (484). But after 484 the tradition, which is meticulous in recording details of this kind, has no further record of any temple dedications until that of Apollo in 433, itself an isolated case, apparently prompted by a plague (Livy 4.25.3). The explanation for this pattern is to be found in the disastrous series of military reverses that Rome suffered from the late 490s onwards. Temples in the Roman Republic were normally financed by war booty, and were therefore constructed as a consequence of successful campaigns.[92] The record of temple foundations is therefore entirely consistent with what our sources tell us about the incursions of the Volsci and Aequi, and the military difficulties of Rome and her allies during the early fifth century (cf. above, p. 306).

The archaeological evidence bears out this picture. Not only is there a dramatic reduction in the volume of fifth-century material from Rome and other Latin sites (especially imported fine pottery); the artistic quality of locally produced pottery also declines. As far as buildings are concerned, there is virtually nothing from Rome that can be dated to the period from c. 474 to c. 400 BC (see above, p. 28). This accords with the record of temple dedications in the literary tradition. The evidence is extremely poor and can only be used to support a vague and generalised picture of 'crisis' at this time. Nevertheless, it is consistent (this point must be repeatedly stressed), and offers a plausible context for the plebeian struggle. The literary sources connect plebeian agitations with economic distress, and refer specifically to indebtedness, food shortages and land hunger. That these problems constituted the principal grievances of the *plebs* is likely enough; the difficulty is to document them in detail and to discover how the plebeians set about attempting to obtain redress.

By all accounts the principal cause of the First Secession was a debt crisis. Our main sources concentrate on a single episode which serves to highlight the nature of the crisis. This is the story of an ex-soldier who had been imprisoned and tortured by his creditor, after a series of misfortunes had forced him into debt. His farm had been destroyed by enemy action, and a tax demand had forced him to borrow; usury had deprived him of his ancestral property, then of his other belongings, and finally of his freedom. The appearance of this pathetic figure in the Forum caused an outcry, and the emergence on to the streets of other debt slaves (*nexi*), some of them in chains.[93]

The conditions that are presupposed in this story sound plausible enough. Debt-bondage was (and in many parts of the world still is) a widespread form of exploitation, characteristic of the Greek city-states in the archaic period, and of Rome in the fourth century BC. The harsh regulations concerning defaulting debtors in the Twelve Tables (III.1–6) testify to the importance of indebtedness in the fifth century. But there are difficulties in seeing it as the main grievance of the *plebs* at the beginning of the Republic. First, the issue of debt and debt-bondage curiously disappears from the traditional narrative after the First Secession, and does not recur until the fourth century, when it is repeatedly mentioned as one of the main causes of plebeian discontent. Second, the anecdote of the 'distinguished veteran' is a commonplace, including a number of probable anachronisms, most notably the reference to property tax (*tributum*), which did not exist at this date.[94] The circumstances of the story most easily fit the conditions of the fourth century, when the *tributum* was a regular imposition. It may well be that the story is modelled on a fourth-century prototype.[95]

Why do the narrative sources make no reference to the problem of debt after the First Secession? Two answers are possible. Either the issue of debt-bondage is anachronistic in this context, and has been artificially introduced as a plausible cause of the Secession, or the record for the rest of the fifth century is defective. On this latter view the debt crisis of 495 BC was authentic enough (although the anecdote of the veteran may be a secondary elaboration) and was remembered because of its connection with the Secession, but for the rest of the fifth century no information about debt-bondage was recorded or remembered. At present I see no way of deciding between these alternatives, although on balance I would favour the second, partly because debt was given such prominence in the Twelve Tables, and partly because the conditions for debt-bondage existed in the fifth century, and it is difficult to believe that it was not already widespread.

One difficulty in the story of the First Secession is the apparent discrepancy between its cause and its outcome, at least in the accounts of Cicero and Livy.[96] The *plebs* rebelled because of debt, and ended up with tribunes. They do not seem to have campaigned, in 494 or later, for cancellation of debts or for abolition of the system of debt-bondage. Why not? The probable answer is that their initial target was not the system of debt-bondage as such, but particular cases of outrageous treatment, against which the assistance of tribunes was an effective remedy. The nature and function of debt-bondage will be discussed in detail later (below, p. 330); but for the present it should be noted that bondage (*nexum*) offered certain advantages to the debtor if the alternative was death or slavery abroad. In other words, total abolition of *nexum* might have seemed contrary to the plebeians' interest, and was in any case unlikely to be practicable. If the *plebs* did not agitate in the fifth century for any reform of the system, or pass resolutions calling for cancellations of debts, their grievances in this area, however serious, would not have left any trace in the historical record.

An issue that *is* given prominence in the sources is the occurrence of food shortages. Periodic food crises were endemic in the Graeco-Roman world, although famines – that is, catastrophic shortages leading to large-scale starvation – were relatively rare, as Peter Garnsey has recently demonstrated.[97] The Roman annalistic sources refer to shortages on fourteen separate occasions between 508 and 384 BC, and make it clear that they were a matter of serious concern;[98] frequently the government intervened directly, and sent embassies to Etruria, Campania and Sicily to procure additional supplies.

These notices are almost certainly authentic. We know that grain shortages were among the items regularly noted in the *Annales maximi*, and sometimes Livy gives unembellished references that probably reflect the character of this primary source.[99] Moreover, the fact that no further shortages are recorded after 384 BC can be taken as a sign that the fifth-century notices are genuine, for two reasons. First, in the fourth century one of the principal causes of food crisis – enemy action – was largely eliminated; as we shall see, the Romans of that period took care to fight their wars on other people's territories, rather than their own. Second the growth of the city made it necessary to import grain on a regular basis, and not just in times of exceptional shortage; and in any case their military power was such that they could no doubt always procure whatever they needed, by force if necessary, in order to pre-empt the effects of a food crisis.

What is entirely uncertain, however, is whether these food crises, and the steps that were taken to deal with them, had anything to do with the plebeian organisation. The cult of Ceres, itself vowed in response to a grain shortage, implies some connection, especially when we remember that the Greek cities of southern Italy and Sicily, from which the cult and its rituals were derived, were also the places to which the Romans went in search of emergency supplies. It is possible that the plebeian organisation, and particularly the aediles, who in later times were responsible for the city's food supply, were more closely involved in the procurement, storage and distribution of grain than our sources are prepared to admit.[100] This is possible, perhaps even probable, but cannot be proved. Equally uncertain is the connection, if any, between the plebeian struggle and the episode of Sp. Maelius, who was put to death in 439 for trying to make himself king. A man of non-aristocratic origin, Maelius had obtained private supplies of grain from Etruria, and sold it at a rock-bottom price to the poor at a time of shortage. The popularity he gained was seen as a dangerous threat to the Republic, and he was killed by the patrician C. Servilius Ahala. Maelius may have been a leader of the *plebs*, but the story is fraught with difficulties; as Garnsey rightly notes, 'the authentic core of this multi-layered fabrication defies identification'.[101]

8 PLEBEIAN GRIEVANCES: AGRARIAN PROBLEMS

Another major source of discontent, and one that allegedly provoked much agitation by the *plebs*, was the issue of land distribution. The background to this is not easy to understand, because of our ignorance of the nature of land-holding in early Rome.[102] However, two facts of prime importance can be extracted from the meagre documentation. The first is that the freehold properties of the peasants were extremely small. Romulus is said to have given each of his followers a plot of land measuring 2 *iugera* (1 *iugerum* = 0.25 hectares = 0.625 acres). This legend may not be entirely fanciful, since we know that 2-*iugera* plots were distributed to settlers in early Roman colonies.[103] Other evidence suggests that smallholdings of 7 *iugera* or less were common in early Rome. This is surprising because even a plot of 7 *iugera* is less than half the minimum that would be required, using the methods of Roman agriculture, to support a family. The difficulty can be resolved, however, by taking account of the second of the two facts referred to earlier. Land in private ownership accounted for only a part of the total extent of Roman territory. The rest was public land (*ager publicus*), an extremely important category that is fundamental to the understanding of Roman agrarian history.

It is likely that public land comprised a substantial portion of Roman territory from the earliest times. Mommsen, indeed, explained the 2-*iugera* tradition by suggesting that these small plots were the gardens surrounding the houses of individual families, and that in the earliest period (before the reforms of Servius Tullius) they alone were held in private ownership, whereas the agricultural land outside the city was held in common owner-ship.[104] No one today believes that all Roman agricultural land was once communally owned, still less that it was worked collectively; nevertheless, public land was always important, and the peasants depended on it for survival. Most, if not all, public land was the result of conquest, and the extent of such land grew in parallel with Roman expansion. It then became available for grazing or cultivation by individual families, who were thus able to supplement their incomes.

The trouble was that access to public land came to be controlled by the rich and powerful, who occupied large portions of it and treated them as part of their ancestral estates, while the poor were driven off and reduced to poverty and dependence.[105] The process can only be described in general terms, but it appears that the power of the large landowners arose partly from the fact that they were able to give rights of access to their own clients and dependants, or (what amounts to the same thing) to demand support and loyalty, and perhaps payment in kind and labour services, from those to whom they granted rights of occupation. This may well explain statements in the sources suggesting that plebeians as such were excluded from the *ager publicus*.[106]

At all events the issue of public land was at the centre of political controversy throughout the history of the Republic, and according to the sources was one of the principal targets of plebeian agitation. What the plebeians appear to have demanded, at least in the earliest period, is that

Roman public land, especially newly conquered areas, should be distributed in allotments that would become the private property of their recipients (a form of distribution known technically as *assignatio viritana*), rather than remaining the property of the state and thus open to encroachment by rich landlords. In the period from 486 to 367 BC the sources record around twenty-five separate attempts by the plebeian leaders to have public land redistributed in this way. Some of these reports may be unhistorical, but it is arbitrary to reject the entire tradition as an invention, as some modern scholars have done.[107]

The arguments that have been used to support this extreme stance are manifestly inadequate. The fact that in the surviving narratives some of the episodes have been assimilated to the events of the Gracchan age does not mean that the episodes themselves have been invented out of nothing. All it means is that in their accounts of agrarian conflicts in the early Republic the annalists made use of obvious Gracchan analogies. It would be quite unreasonable to expect them to have done anything else. The resulting narratives are full of anachronistic and unreliable detail; but that is not the point at issue. The question is whether we can accept reports, some of them extensively elaborated but others completely unembellished, that in a given year the tribunes agitated for agrarian reform.[108]

It is also argued that because most of the agrarian proposals were abortive they cannot have been recorded. In the present context this argument is less compelling than it may seem. De Martino rightly points out that plebeian demands for land distribution were not simply idle proposals but the stuff of serious politics; whether successful or not, these agitations were important events.[109] Second, we may ask why the *plebs* were unsuccessful. The sources occasionally suggest that the senators persuaded some of the tribunes to veto the proposals of their own colleagues (e.g. Livy 2.44; 4.48; 4.49.6). This probably *is* a Gracchan anachronism, especially if Badian is right to argue that Octavius was doing something unheard of when he persisted in using his veto against Tiberius Gracchus.[110] In fact the idea of tribunes interceding against their colleagues to block agrarian proposals is nonsensical at this date. It is much more probable that the *plebs* consistently passed these bills, but were unable to get the plebiscites passed into law. Livy's report, under 441 BC, that the tribune Poetelius tried unsuccessfully to get the consuls to lay an agrarian proposal before the Senate, sounds much more plausible. The important point for this discussion, however, is that if the various proposals were passed as plebiscites, then a memory of them might well have survived.

The idea that the notices are all invented 'anticipations' of the Gracchan proposals is also open to the serious objection that none of them contains any hint of what was the central feature of the Gracchan land laws, namely the limitation on the size of holdings of *ager publicus*. As far as the sources are concerned, the first such *lex de modo agrorum* was the Licinian Law of 367 BC (see below, p. 329). Another argument in favour of these agrarian notices (or, at least, against the view that they were invented) is that they are concentrated in two distinct groups, the first in the period from 486 to 474 BC, the second in the years after 424. The location of the second group is highly significant, because it coincides with a period of Roman military success and the acquisition of new areas of *ager publicus* (below, p. 313). This cannot be an accident, and is to my mind the strongest argument in favour of the annalistic record.[111]

The earlier group of instances is more problematic. These were all the result of the activities of Sp. Cassius, who as consul in 486 proposed the first ever agrarian law (Livy 2.41.3). The surviving narratives present Cassius very obviously as a forerunner of the Gracchi. The most interesting sign of this is his alleged proposal to distribute allotments not just to Roman citizens, but to the Latins and other allies as well.[112] Livy and Dionysius present significantly different accounts of the proposal. Livy writes that the Hernici, who had recently been defeated and forced to become allies, were deprived of two-thirds of their territory, which Cassius proposed to share between Romans and Latins (2.41.1). Dionysius, on the other hand, says that the Hernici were not deprived of any territory (8.77.2), but were made allies and were included by Sp. Cassius in his scheme to distribute some existing *ager publicus*, currently under illegal occupation by the rich. The allotments were to be shared between Romans, Latins and Hernici (8.69.3–4).

The best interpretation of these discrepant versions is that of De Sanctis, who rightly observed that the supposed agrarian law has been combined with the Hernican treaty in an artificial and arbitrary manner.[113] One of the provisions of the treaty was that the profits of any victory won jointly by the Romans, Latins and Hernici were to be divided between them, and that all three would have a share in the settlement of any conquered territory (see below, p. 301). The similarity to the alleged terms of the agrarian law is obvious, and it hardly needs saying that some confusion has evidently taken place. De Sanctis was right to insist that in 486 the Hernici did not in fact lose an inch of territory (*pace* Livy), and that Dionysius' notion of Latins and Hernici sharing in a redistribution of part of Rome's territory is impossible. But it does not necessarily follow that the proposed agrarian law was a fiction, as De Sanctis believed; it is equally possible that Cassius did propose a *lex agraria*, and that either by confusion or wilful manipulation its terms were reconstructed on the basis of the provisions of the Hernican treaty. The genuine core of the tradition might be no more than that Sp. Cassius was put to death for aiming at tyranny; but one cannot rule out the possibility that the would-be tyrant was also remembered as the author of an agrarian law.[114] The difficulty, as always, is to decide where to place the boundary between genuine tradition and secondary elaboration; and in this case it is hard to see where the balance of probability might lie.

11

THE TWELVE TABLES

1 THE DECEMVIRATE

The Greek historian Polybius, writing in the middle of the second century BC, described the Roman constitution as a balanced mixture of monarchy, aristocracy and democracy. This excellent system, he believed, was the product of a historical process of trial and error which culminated in the Valerio-Horatian Laws of 449 BC. From that moment, he tells us, the Roman political system continued to progress, until it reached perfection at the time of the Hannibalic War (6.11.1). This idea, that the events of 449 BC marked the end of the formative stage of Rome's political development, was not dreamed up by Polybius, but was already well rooted in the Roman historiographical tradition. It was certainly in Cato's *Origines*, from where it was borrowed by Cicero.[1] As far as the Romans were concerned, the revolution that created the Republic as they knew it was not the overthrow of the monarchy at the end of the sixth century BC, but the upheaval that occurred in the middle of the fifth.

The dramatic events of 451–449 BC arose from the plebeian demand for the laws of Rome to be codified and published. Agitation for this measure supposedly began in 462 BC in the tribunate of C. Terentilius Harsa, and continued for more than ten years. In 454 an embassy is said to have been sent to Athens and other Greek cities to study their laws, particularly those of Solon (Livy 3.31.8). Finally in 451 the two sides agreed to suspend the constitution and to appoint a body of ten men to govern the state with consular powers and to draft a code of laws (*decemviri legibus scribundis*). According to Cicero (*Rep.* 2.61) the tribunes of the *plebs* abdicated together with the consuls in favour of the Decemvirs, who were not subject to appeal. To judge from Livy's account, all ten were patricians; but one of them, T. Genucius, has an apparently plebeian name and belongs to that problematic category we examined earlier (see above, p. 253).

In their year of office these Decemvirs produced ten 'tables' of laws. In the following year (450) two more were added by a second college of Decemvirs, this time including several plebeians.[2] The second Decemvirate then began to behave tyrannically, and at the end of their term refused to stand down. This provoked a crisis, which was aggravated by a military disaster and a series of scandals, most notably the attempted rape of Verginia by Appius Claudius, the leader of the junta and the only one who held office in both Decemvirates. When Appius ordered one of his minions to seize the girl, her father killed her to save her from the tyrant's lust. This event, which forms the subject of some of the finest pages in the whole of Livy (3.44–8), prompted a secession of the *plebs* to the Aventine, and brought the crisis to a head. The 'ten Tarquins' were overthrown, Appius Claudius killed himself, and the old constitution was eventually restored. The settlement that followed was framed in a series of enactments proposed by the consuls of 449, L. Valerius Potitus and M. Horatius Barbatus.

The above outline is a brief and inadequate summary of what our sources have to say about a complex series of events. As one might expect, modern scholars have attacked the traditional narrative from every point of view. This raises issues of principle which it is necessary to touch upon; but it would be beyond the scope of this book to examine all the detailed problems that arise in reconstructing the events themselves. It will suffice merely to indicate some of the main areas of debate, and to give a general idea of where the main problems lie.

A matter about which the sources themselves seem to be uncertain is the purpose of the Decemvirate as an institution. On the one hand, it is presented as a new kind of magistracy, designed to reintegrate the *plebs* into the state by doing away with the tribunes and aediles, but at the same time replacing the consulship with a body of ten men (the obvious comparison therefore is with the tribunate) who would take over all magisterial functions. This interpretation would make sense if the new office were to be open to all citizens, including plebeians. As we have seen, Livy seems to have thought that the Decemvirate was confined exclusively to patricians, but he may be wrong about the all-patrician membership of the first Decemvirate, and he is certainly wrong about the second.

This discrepancy has led some scholars to reject the name of T. Genucius from the list of Decemvirs in 451, and to dismiss the second Decemvirate as complete fiction.[3] It scarcely needs saying, however, that such a gross example of question-begging cannot possibly be justified. There is no doubt that the whole episode of the Decemvirate has attracted a great deal of secondary elaboration, extending at times to pure romance, and that parts of the surviving narrative are almost certainly fictitious. But identifying the fictitious parts is no easier than deciding which parts might be based on genuine fact. The second Decemvirate may or may not be factual; for it to be damned as fictitious something more convincing is needed than the observation that it contains plebeian names.

If the Decemvirate was to be a new annual magistracy to replace both patrician consuls and plebeian tribunes, then we should not be surprised to read that after one year a new college of Decemvirs was elected, nor that one or both colleges included plebeians. On this interpretation, then, the second Decemvirate makes excellent historical sense. The problem is that the sources also imply that the purpose of the Decemvirate was to act as a commission to draft a code of written laws, and that it was to remain in being only for as long as it took to complete its task. This interpretation is implicit in Livy's statement that the second Decemvirate was elected because of a general belief that the ten tables issued in the first year were inadequate, and that two more were needed; and in the story that the second set of Decemvirs tried to perpetuate their term of office by not publishing the final two tables, and thus pretending that they still had work to do.[4]

There is a real contradiction here: if the Decemvirate was designed as a permanent replacement for the consuls and tribunes, the drafting of laws was only an incidental and temporary function; on the other hand, if it was set up for the duration as a temporary body of lawgivers, why suspend the consuls and tribunes? This difficulty applies equally to the modern theory that the first Decemvirate differed from the second in that the former was a special commission of lawgivers, the latter a permanent governing body.[5] This is an unsatisfactory compromise because in that case we should expect the consuls and tribunes to have been suspended at the start of the second Decemvirate.

A second problem arises from the character of the regime of the Decemvirs. The developed tradition draws a sharp contrast between the first (good) college, and the second (bad) one. Some modern historians argue that the distinction is an aetiological legend which served to explain the presence in the Twelve Tables, generally acknowledged as 'a good thing', of the notorious ban on intermarriage between the two orders. This 'most inhuman law', as Cicero called it, was put down to a second body of wicked Decemvirs; since it occurred in the eleventh Table, there was nothing for it but to attribute the twelfth Table to the wicked Decemvirs as well, although it dealt with the relatively innocuous business of intercalation.[6] Unfortunately, this theory creates more problems than it solves. If the second Decemvirate was invented to explain the eleventh Table, why do all the sources say that the last two tables were ratified and published by Valerius and Horatius, the consuls of 449?[7] And if the aim was to explain a law that prohibited mixed marriages, why invent a mixed college of Decemvirs, containing both patricians and plebeians? The fact that the developed story is so full of internal contradictions must surely indicate that it cannot have been the product of wholesale conscious invention.

The traditional narrative is more probably the result of a complex process of piecemeal elaboration. It is certain that the two Decemvirates, and the division of the Twelve Tables into groups of ten and two, were already part of the historical tradition in the middle of the second century BC (Cassius Hemina fr. 18 P); and the idea that the Decemvirate became a self-serving oligarchy that brought about its own overthrow was almost certainly in

Polybius.[8] The later annalists may have elaborated certain episodes in the story, but there is no evidence that they invented any of them. Scholars have noted similarities to events of the late Republic such as the dictatorship of Sulla, the Catilinarian conspiracy, and the two triumvirates; but none of these parallels is especially close, and in spite of the enormous effort of generations of sceptics, there is no serious evidence that any part of the story was invented in the first century BC.[9]

The story of Appius Claudius and Verginia was evidently the target of much secondary elaboration, but the main elements may derive from a very old story; Niebuhr, Lord Macaulay and more recently De Sanctis thought that Verginia was the subject of a traditional popular ballad. The figure of Appius Claudius may have been the victim of a late republican historical tradition hostile to the Claudii,[10] and some have thought that Verginia is altogether too good a name for a chaste young maiden. There are also obvious typological analogies between the stories of Lucretia and Verginia. But these objections do not in themselves prove that the story is a late invention;[11] indeed it is perfectly conceivable that it has some basis in fact.

The story of the embassy to Athens has also been the object of much discussion and debate. It is unlikely to be true in a literal sense. It has been well said that, if Roman envoys had really visited Athens in 454 BC, Pericles would have given them something more up to date than the laws of Solon.[12] But the story represents a different kind of truth, in the sense that the surviving fragments of the Twelve Tables show many signs of Greek influence, and even include a Greek loan-word: *poena*.[13] The source of this influence is most likely to have been the Greek cities of the south, and it is reasonable to assume that the Decemvirs made efforts to acquaint themselves with other written laws. An alternative tradition maintained that they were advised by a Greek philosopher-in-exile, Hermodorus of Ephesus, whose statue was later set up in the *comitium*.[14]

These variant traditions should be seen as rival attempts to personalise what was in fact a more complex and long-standing tradition of contacts between Rome and the Greek world. The whole question neatly illustrates how scholarly attitudes have changed during the course of the present century. The evidence of Greek influence on the Twelve Tables was once taken as a sign that they must be later than the fifth century, but is now seen as consistent with the traditional date. In view of the evidence now available (much of it archaeological), showing that the cultural life of archaic Rome was profoundly hellenised, it would indeed be astonishing if the Twelve Tables did *not* show traces of Greek borrowings.[15]

The reconstruction of detailed events is not in itself a matter of great significance in the present context, except in so far as it bears on the general question of the reliability of the sources. As far as events are concerned, the important thing is not so much what happened, or how or why, but rather the results of what happened. Here the answer is straightforward: whatever the precise nature of the upheaval that undoubtedly took place in the middle of the fifth century, it produced the document known as the Twelve Tables. This fundamentally important historical document will be described in section 3; but first we may glance briefly at the other main result of the rule of the Decemvirs, namely the settlement that followed their overthrow, and the restoration of the old regime. According to tradition, this was the product of the so-called Valerio-Horatian Laws.

2 THE VALERIO-HORATIAN LAWS

The Valerio-Horatian Laws cemented the alliance of convenience that the *plebs* and the patriciate had formed in order to get rid of the Decemvirs. Here again there has been controversy over the authenticity of the legislation, with some scholars denouncing it as fiction, others taking a more conservative line. As so often, there is no conclusive evidence either way, so dogmatism is out of place. It is also a mistake to adopt a blanket approach, either by taking it for granted that all early laws are fictitious, or by naively assuming that because some elements of the tradition have been vindicated (e.g. by archaeological discoveries), all of it must be historical. Modern commentators will inevitably be guided in the first instance by their general approach to the tradition as a whole; but that does not absolve them from the necessary duty of assessing each case on its merits.

First we should consider the law which recognised the sacrosanctity of the plebeian officers – not only the tribunes, but also the aediles and a third body of whom we otherwise know nothing, the board of ten judges (*iudices decemviri*).[16] According to Livy the interpretation of this law was disputed by Roman legal experts, although the precise technical distinctions they argued about are not clear to us (or at least not to me).[17] The important point is that these experts did not question the authenticity of the law, but only the nature of its provisions. Its effect was to give statutory recognition to the plebeian organisation, and as such it was a great victory for the *plebs*. We cannot know for certain whether the law is authentic; the best we can say is that there is no reason in principle why it should not be.

If the downfall of the Decemvirs and the Second Secession are regarded as broadly historical events, the restoration must have been accompanied by some kind of settlement. There is no reason to doubt that the settlement effectively recognised the tribunate and the plebeian organisation, which became thereafter an established part of the political system. Whether this was achieved by a formal statute proposed by the consuls, or by a more informal agreement, as Diodorus suggests (12.24.2), is not of great consequence.

A second law concerned the citizens' right of appeal (*provocatio*). This law has been impugned on the grounds that the sources record three identical laws granting the right of appeal, in 509, 449 and 300 BC, and that all three are associated with a Valerius – the first with P. Valerius Publicola, the second with the consul of 449, and the third with M. Valerius Corvus (cos. 300). It is alleged that only the third and most recent of these Leges Valeriae can be authentic.[18] The charge cannot be made to stick, however, because there is no way of proving that the three laws were, in fact, identical. As far as the 449 law is concerned, the sources themselves indicate that its specific purpose was not to grant the right of appeal *per se*, but to prohibit the creation of magistracies not subject to appeal. Such a law itself presupposes the prior existence of a right of appeal (which is confirmed by the Twelve Tables – IX.1–2), and, as we have seen (above, p. 196), there are good reasons for supposing that it goes back to the time when the magistrates were first created – i.e. the beginning of the Republic. It may be that the first law was artificially associated with Valerius Publicola, but that cannot be certain.

In any event there are absolutely no grounds for thinking that the law of 300 was the first to establish the right of appeal. We know nothing about its contents, and there can therefore be no objection in principle to the hypothesis that its purpose was to modify an existing law. Livy (10.9.3–6: our only source for this law) himself tells us that it was *diligentius sanctam* – 'more carefully set down' (sc. than the previous laws). It was the habit of Roman legislators to deal repeatedly with the same subjects, sometimes over periods of several centuries; and it was a feature of Roman statutes that they tended explicitly to incorporate continuing provisions of existing laws as well as the particular modifications that were the primary intention of the legislator. Thus it came about that Roman reformers frequently re-enacted earlier statutes, even when these were still in force. A classic example is the agrarian law of Tiberius Gracchus, which laid down a limit of 500 *iugera* for the amount of public land any one citizen could occupy, even though this limit was already in existence, and had been for many years.

The same argument can be applied to the third of the Valerio-Horatian Laws, which is perhaps the most controversial of all, although to my mind it is the one that can be most easily authenticated. The law is said to have given legal validity to plebiscites, by enacting 'that what the tribally assembled *plebs* might order should be binding on the people' (Livy 3.55.3). Once again the problem is that apparently identical measures were passed in 339 BC (the Lex Publilia) and in 287 (the Lex Hortensia), and once again there is no lack of experts prepared to argue that only the third and latest of these laws is historical.[19] But this sceptical interpretation cannot possibly be correct, because a number of plebiscites are recorded in the period before 287 BC which obviously did have the force of law. And it is not a matter of a few isolated examples; on a rough calculation it can be said that more than thirty-five plebiscites are recorded in the period from 449 to 287 BC.[20] Some of these may be doubtful; but it would be hypercritical to deny the historicity of such fundamental measures as the Leges Liciniae-Sextiae (367 BC), or the Lex Ogulnia (300 BC).

The probable answer to the puzzle is that the law of 449 conceded the general principle that the plebeian assembly could enact legislation, but in some way restricted its freedom to do so unilaterally, for instance by making plebiscites subject to the *auctoritas patrum* or to a subsequent vote of the *comitia populi*, or indeed to both. This would explain the difficulties the plebeian leaders are said to have had in getting popular proposals passed into law – for instance the many abortive attempts to introduce agrarian laws in the period after 424 (see above, p. 270), which can hardly have failed because of opposition among the *plebs*, as Livy rather unconvincingly suggests. On this view the supposed restrictions on plebeian legislation would have been partly removed by the law of 339, and completely abolished by that of 287.[21]

This explanation, that the laws of 339 and 287 did not replicate that of 449, but re-enacted it while introducing specific modifications, is the only one that fits the facts as we know them. It is no good objecting that there is no clear evidence for any restriction in the Lex Valeria-Horatia, or for its removal by the Lex Publilia or the Lex Hortensia;[22] since our sources do not set out the detailed provisions of these laws, it is hardly surprising that we have no evidence for their provisions. The explanation we have offered is therefore admittedly hypothetical, but given the nature of the sources it can hardly be anything else.

A number of other measures are recorded for 449, including some plebiscites which reinforced the plebeian organisation, and another which backed up the Lex Valeria-Horatia on appeal;[23] as we have seen, it was also decided (by another Valerio-Horatian Law?) that the aediles should be allowed to keep records of senatorial decrees in the temple of Ceres. Finally, the consuls ordered the Twelve Tables to be inscribed in bronze and displayed in the Forum.[24] Their subsequent history is unclear, but it seems that the tables themselves were no longer extant in the time of Cicero. If they were, we should know about it. Livy seems to imply that they were destroyed in the Gallic attack of 390 BC, but he is not very clear on this (6.1.10). The important point is that the text of the laws survived independently of the official bronze tables. Portable copies on perishable material could be, and no doubt were, made; and Cicero tells us that in his time school-children learned the text by heart. We can therefore be reasonably confident that when our sources quote from the Twelve Tables, they are giving us extracts from a document of the middle of the fifth century BC. Normally such confidence is lacking, and this circumstance gives the Twelve Tables a unique status as a historical source.

3 THE NATURE OF THE CODE

We do not possess a full text of the Twelve Tables; our knowledge of their contents is based on quotations and indirect references of various kinds in the works of later authors. Assembling these scattered fragments and ordering them under different headings have been the work of modern scholarship. Only rarely do we know the number of the table to which a given law belongs, but most scholars follow the conventional arrangement first established in the early nineteenth century by H. Dirksen.[25] Although some modernisation of the language took place in the course of the Republic, most of the direct quotations can be shown to go back to an early version of the text, and give a clear idea of the archaic style of the original.

The laws are in the form of terse injunctions and prohibitions in simple but often obscure language. A few examples will illustrate the point. 'Whoever shall have been lacking witness, he is to go every other day to clamour(?) at the door' (II.3). 'They are to make a road. Unless they laid it with stones, he is to drive carts where he shall wish' (VII.7). 'If he has maimed a limb, unless he agrees with him, there is to be retaliation' (VIII.2). They are characterised by grammatical ambiguity – most notably in the use of undefined pronouns and changes of subject. The results are sometimes bewildering: 'If he [i.e. a plaintiff] summons to law, he [the defendant] is to go. If he does not go, he [the plaintiff] is to call [someone else] to witness. Then he is to seize him' (I.1), or even comical: 'if the weapon flew from [his] hand rather than [he] threw it' (VIII.24). This latter example represents an attempt to distinguish deliberate from accidental homicide, but reveals a marked inability to generalise or express abstractions.

The wording is often obscure, and not only to us; some words and phrases were already puzzling Roman experts at the start of the second century BC, when the first learned commentaries began to be produced.[26] But enough can be made out from the surviving fragments to give us a remarkable documentary record of Roman society in the archaic period, as well as a fascinating glimpse of the early development of Roman law and legal practice. But it is difficult to say what was the original purpose of the codification, or how it fits into the story of the struggle of the orders.

It should be noted that the Twelve Tables do not amount to a code in the modern sense. The Decemvirs made no systematic attempt to set out the whole of the law, and the areas they did cover were not dealt with comprehensively. The main areas of concern are: the family, marriage and divorce; inheritance, ownership and transfer of property; assaults and injuries against persons and property; debt, slavery and *nexum*. Other topics include procedures, such as the summoning of defendants to court, and regulations of a religious character, for example the rules governing the conduct of funerals. As far as we can judge, the whole subject of public and constitutional law was omitted, which is perhaps surprising in view of Livy's report that the plebeians had demanded that the powers of the consuls should be defined in writing (3.9.5).

Exactly why the Decemvirs chose to set out the law on some matters, but not on others, is a puzzle. But it seems most likely that their choice was determined by the need to specify the law in doubtful or disputed areas, but to leave unstated rules which were settled or taken for granted. Good examples of this are the provisions concerning slavery and debt.

4 THE LAWS: SLAVERY, DEBT AND *NEXUM*

The existence of slaves is implied by a number of provisions in the Twelve Tables, such as those dealing with the liability of slave owners if their slaves caused damage to the persons or property of other citizens (XII.2); but there was no attempt in the Twelve Tables to set out the law of slavery, to define what a slave was, or how a person became a slave. The probable reason is that the institution of slavery was taken for granted and that the rules governing enslavement and the rights of masters over slaves were settled and neither questioned nor disputed by anyone.[27]

That slavery existed as a well-established institution in early Rome is one of the important social facts that can be deduced from the Twelve Tables. It is not clear, however, whether slaves formed a significant proportion of the total population, although the probability is that they did not. It is also unlikely at this date that slave labour was used in agricultural production; the anecdotal evidence implies that slaves were mostly employed in domestic service – a type of work for which there would have been considerable demand among the wealthier classes, if the recently discovered archaic houses are anything to go by (see above, p. 97).

Most slaves would have been either captives or home-bred. Booty in war normally included human beings, especially women and children, who were then enslaved. Although the Romans were not involved in wars of conquest during the fifth century, the regular pattern of annual raiding against the Aequi and Volsci undoubtedly entailed, whenever possible, the seizure of captives. House-born slaves (*vernae*) were the offspring of slave women. Such children were invariably of slave status, regardless of who their father was (often, no doubt, the master of the house). The fact that many slaves were the natural children of Roman citizens is perhaps one of the reasons for the frequency of manumission at Rome, and for the very remarkable fact that the freed slaves of Roman citizens themselves received the Roman citizenship.

Manumission is not dealt with directly in the surviving portions of the Twelve Tables, but Table VII.13 refers to it incidentally in laying down that a slave who was freed by will on condition of a payment to the heir can obtain freedom, even if the heir has sold him to a third party, by paying the same sum to the purchaser. The clause illustrates the complexity of Rome's social and legal development by this date. We learn not only that slaves could be freed through fulfilment of a condition in a will, but also that slaves controlled funds (the so-called *peculium*) from which they could make payments, and that they could be bought and sold.

If masters could free their slaves in this indirect way, it is certain that they could also do so directly, not only by will, but during their lifetimes by one or both of the methods that were used later, namely by enrolling them as citizens at the *census* – a method that tradition dates to the time of Servius Tullius (Dion. Hal. 4.22.4) – or by the so-called *manumissio vindicta*, a legal action before a magistrate. This too was believed to have been instituted before the Twelve Tables.[28]

It seems that at the time of the Twelve Tables the rule was already established that Roman citizens could not be enslaved at Rome.[29] This is clear from the harsh law of debt in Table III, which sets out in detail the procedures to be followed in a case of default. If the debt was not settled within a fixed period after judgement had been pronounced in court against the debtor, the creditor was empowered to sell him into slavery *trans Tiberim peregre* ('abroad, across the Tiber'). This phrase implies not only that enslavement of a Roman citizen had to take place outside Roman territory (that is the sense of *peregre*), but also that it was forbidden within the territory of the Latin allies (because it had to be not only *peregre*, but also *trans Tiberim* – i.e. in Etruscan territory); the law therefore throws interesting light on the scope of the Latin treaty (see below, p. 299). Some commentators have inferred that at the time of the Twelve Tables the Tiber marked the limit of Rome's territory;[30] but in that case *trans Tiberim* alone would have been sufficient. The law evidently laid down two distinct conditions (*trans Tiberim* and *peregre*), both of which had to be fulfilled in the event of a sale. So far from suggesting that Rome possessed no territory on the right bank in 451 BC, this provision of Table III proves the opposite.[31]

This is one of many historical problems that arise in the study of this section of the Tables. Another is the fact that sale into slavery was laid down as an alternative to the death penalty in cases of default; and that where there were multiple creditors, the body of the debtor was to be cut into pieces. That at least is how Gellius, our main source, understood the phrase *partis secanto*.[32] There has been much debate about this clause. For instance, even Gellius was surprised by the fact that there was no record of this cruel provision ever having been put into effect. The answer may be that Gellius has misunderstood the words of the Table, which may have meant something quite different;[33] alternatively, the frightful sanction may have functioned – indeed may have been intended – purely as a deterrent in order to compel the parties to adopt an alternative. Sale abroad would have had obvious advantages to both parties, but even that may have had the purpose of forcing them to arrange a prior settlement, most obviously a bondage contract.[34]

Nexum ('debt-bondage') was clearly distinct from sale into slavery, first because the *nexi* ('bondsmen') retained their status as Roman citizens, and second because they continued to live at Rome (and consequently had not been sold abroad across the Tiber). The law was careful to specify that prior settlement was possible before the execution of the judgement, and it may be that this was the intended result. If so, we may be able to answer the question of how the law was supposed to benefit the *plebs*. In one sense it is obvious that the law in Table III merely confirmed the *de facto* power of the creditor; and indeed it has been argued that the whole purpose of written law codes in archaic societies was to strengthen the position of the rich and powerful, and to reinforce their dominance in society.[35] But this seems too extreme. It would be unreasonable to expect the law of debt to do anything other than provide redress for the creditor (and naive to think of law in general as an instrument for neutralising social inequality). That was not what the *plebs* expected, and it was not what the Twelve Tables gave them. But the Tables did regulate the ways in which debtors could be punished, and defined clear procedures for the execution of judgement by creditors. For the *plebs* this was no doubt preferable to arbitrary action.

First, seizure (*manus iniectio*) could only take place after a judgement in court and a thirty-day period of grace; then after a second court appearance the creditor could bind the debtor in chains. For the next sixty days the debtor could either look after himself at home, or allow himself to be kept a prisoner by the creditor, who was obliged to feed him. During the sixty-day interval that had to elapse before the debtor could be killed or sold abroad, there was the possibility of settlement – the most obvious method being an agreement whereby the debtor gave his labour services to the creditor as a virtual slave. Whether a person in such a condition was properly called a *nexus* is arguable. Alternatively the debtor could enter a *nexum* contract with a third party, to whom he surrendered himself as a bondsman in exchange for money with which he paid off his existing debts. That there were different categories of *nexum* is implied in Livy's description (2.23.8) of *nexi* as *vincti solutique* ('those who were in chains and those who were not'), which may reflect a distinction between those who were in bondage as a result of default and those who voluntarily 'entered into *nexum*'.

We should note that *nexum* is presented by our sources as the result of an agreement voluntarily entered into by the debtor.[36] Table VI.1 indicates that it was a verbal contract similar to *mancipium*:

> *cum nexum faciet mancipiumque, uti lingua nuncupassit, ita ius esto*
> ('When he shall perform *nexum* and *mancipium*, as his tongue has
> pronounced, so is the law to be').

Mancipium, later *mancipatio*, was a form of conveyance for the types of property known as *res mancipi* – that is, real estate, slaves, and working animals. The procedure involved the weighing out of bronze (i.e. money) in front of witnesses. A similar act *per aes et libram* ('with bronze and scales') was therefore required for a *nexum* contract.[37]

It is important to be clear about the nature of debt in archaic agrarian societies. It may strike the observer as puzzling that moneylenders should have been prepared to advance loans to impoverished peasants who had no serious prospect of repaying them, and no security other than their own persons. The knowledge that one would be entitled to cut a defaulter into pieces is unlikely to have given much satisfaction. The explanation is that we are not dealing with moneylending, 'credit', and interest payments; rather it is a matter of 'loans' made by wealthy landowners, often no doubt paid in kind, in the form of seed-corn or the bare means of subsistence. The purpose of the 'loan', which was secured on the person of the debtor, was precisely to create a state of bondage. In reality it was a payment for the labour services of a bondsman, who effectively sold himself (or one of his children) to the 'creditor'. The very nature of the contract, *per aes et libram*, was similar to a sale. From the lender's point of view the object of the exercise was to obtain the labour services of the debtor rather than profit through interest.

Debt-bondage is an institutionalised form of exploitation in agrarian societies where alternative forms of bonded labour such as chattel slavery are either prohibited by law (as in the Third World today) or insufficiently developed (as in the 'archaic' societies of the ancient world). In such societies poverty, social inequality, and the primitive structure of economic activity do not permit the development of a free labour market. The result is that production comes to be based on dependent labour that is constrained by institutionalised legal mechanisms such as the fiction of 'loans' and 'debts'. It is virtually certain that the function of *nexum* in early Rome was to provide dependent labour for exploitation by large landowners. Economic and social inequality forced many poor Romans to sell themselves or their children as bonded labourers on the large estates of the rich. Slavery, properly so called, was restricted to the domestic work of the larger urban households.

These considerations suggest a possible solution to another puzzle. In Table IV.2 we read:

> *si pater ter filium venum duit, a patre filius liber esto*
> ('If a father thrice sells a son, the son is to be free from the father').

Later Roman legal writers such as Gaius and Ulpian took this clause to refer to cases where the father sold the son into slavery, and regained his power over him in the event of his being manumitted. The Decemvirs, on this view, considered it unreasonable for a father to keep on doing this, and limited him to a maximum of three such sales. But one might well question whether a Roman citizen could become the slave of another Roman by an act of sale by his father. Moreover it seems unlikely that in reality repeated manumissions would give a father the opportunity to sell his son three times.[38] It has been argued that what really happened was the 'hiring out', rather than the sale, of the son.[39] But this view entails the rejection of Gaius' assumption that the transaction took the form of *mancipatio* (whence the process of freeing a son after three goes was called 'emancipation'). The best way to resolve the problem is to suppose that the father was not selling the son into slavery, which could not happen at Rome, but 'hiring' him out as a *nexus*. This brings us back to the point that *nexum* was a form of *mancipium*, or *mancipatio*.[40]

283

5 THE LAWS: FAMILY AND PROPERTY

The power of a father over his son brings us to the central institution of Roman society, and the one that forms the focus of the Twelve Tables – the family. The Roman *familia* comprised the whole household, including property as well as persons, and was under the control of the head of the household, the *paterfamilias*. According to the technical definition a *paterfamilias* was the oldest surviving direct male ascendant. He exercised a virtually unrestrained authority over all persons and property within the household, who were said to be in his power (*in potestate*). His sons, even though they might be mature adults with children of their own, had no independent legal status or rights of property, and were not released from their father's authority until his death, whereupon they became *patresfamiliarum* in their own right.

This was a unique, in many ways a bizarre, state of affairs. A Roman male of mature years, even though he might be a person of great consequence – a senator, or even consul – could not be a party to any legal transaction, make a gift, manumit a slave or make a will, so long as his father remained alive. He owned nothing. Ways were found of releasing sons from *patria potestas* (see n. 38), but instances of this were not common. For practical purposes most fathers gave their sons money to live on and allowed them independence in a day-to-day sense, but this was not recognised by law and could be revoked by the father at any time. The son's personal fund was known as *peculium*, which points to an important truth: the legal status of persons *in potestate* was formally equivalent to that of slaves.[41]

Everything within the *familia* – inanimate property and all living creatures, animals and humans – was alike treated as items of property at the arbitrary disposal of the *paterfamilias*. His legitimate children were distinguished from the rest in that they were free: hence the standard Latin word for children – *liberi* (i.e. 'the free ones'); but this freedom, in a family context, was potential not actual, and only became a reality on the death of the last surviving direct male ascendant. We see here an element of the unresolved conflict that always existed in Roman society between the status of an individual within the family and his position in the community at large. A free adult male was a Roman citizen with full rights, who could vote, serve in the army and hold political office, regardless of his position at home.

The father's power (*patria potestas*) included the right to kill members of his family or to sell them (the nature of the sale of a *filiusfamilias* is discussed above). Naturally the right of life and death (*ius vitae necisque*) was rarely exercised, except at birth, when it was not uncommon for fathers to dispose of unwanted children, especially girls.[42] In the case of badly deformed infants, the Twelve Tables enjoined that they should be quickly killed (IV.1). Dionysius of Halicarnassus tells us (2.15) that Romulus ordered citizens to raise all their male children and the firstborn girl, unless the child were deformed, in which case it could be killed provided five neighbours approved. But this cannot ever have been a real law, and it comes from the highly suspect 'constitution of Romulus' in Dionysius, which derives from a political pamphlet of the first century BC.[43] This document attributes to the founder a set of laws that enshrine what the author of the pamphlet regarded as desirable social behaviour.

The alleged law of Romulus conflicts with the father's freedom of action embodied in *patria potestas*; but it does conform to reality in the sense that the *paterfamilias* was in practice subject to moral constraints and the limits of what was regarded as acceptable. On all important matters he was traditionally expected to consult the advice of senior relatives and friends, who formed a 'domestic council' (*consilium domesticum*); and although he was not obliged to accept their advice, custom dictated that he normally should.

The authority exercised by a husband over his wife was known as *manus*. *Manus* could be acquired by one of three methods: *confarreatio*, a religious ceremony (see above, p. 255), *coemptio*, a transaction using bronze and scales, by which the husband symbolically 'bought' the bride, and *usus*, whereby *manus* was automatically acquired after a year of cohabitation. Since purchase and 'use' were means of acquiring ownership, it appears that a wife was treated, like other members of a household, as an item of property 'owned' by her husband (or her husband's *paterfamilias*); it is worth noting, however, that *manus* was less extensive than *potestas*, and did not for instance include the *ius vitae necisque*.[44] The three ways of acquiring *manus* were probably all known before the Twelve Tables, and it is likely that all three were specified in the code.[45] However, it is also clear that the Twelve Tables recognised the desire, and made available the means, to avoid *manus*; this was achieved by the wife spending three nights in the year away from home, which was considered sufficient to break the period of 'use' (Gaius 1.111: Table VI.5).

A marriage without *manus* was clearly recognised as legitimate; its consequence was that the wife, instead of leaving her father's family and entering that of her husband, remained within the *potestas* of her father. Such marriages were probably in a minority at this period, although by the end of the Republic they had become the norm. Both types of marriage had advantages and disadvantages for the woman, though this would not have been the primary consideration of the men who framed the law. An unmarried woman or a woman married without *manus* became *sui iuris* (i.e. legally independent) on the death of her last direct male ascendant; if married with *manus*, she achieved independence on the death of her husband.[46] A woman in this condition could own property and stood to inherit equally with her brothers and sisters (or with her children, if married with *manus*) under the rules of intestate succession.

However, the law insisted that a woman who had neither father nor husband should be supervised by a guardian (*tutor*), whose consent was necessary before she could carry out any transaction; guardianship was also prescribed for minors, lunatics and spendthrifts. A range of rules on these matters was laid down in Table V. This Table deals generally with rights of property and succession, matters which are central to the code as a whole.

The most striking features of the society presupposed in the Twelve Tables are the family unit, private ownership of property, and the absolute control over both that was exercised by the *paterfamilias*. It is important to note that the society of the Twelve Tables identified property rights with individual ownership; in spite of a-priori modern theories, the Romans clearly did not think of the family as the owner of property, or make any distinction between the family estate and what the *paterfamilias* owned as an individual.[47] The clearest indication of this is the recognition of the right of the *paterfamilias* to make a will:

> *uti legassit super familia pecuniave tutelave sua, ita ius esto*
> ('As he has disposed by will concerning his family, or goods, or guardianship, so is the law to be') (Table V.3).

As we have seen, a will could include conditions, which the law evidently regarded as valid. This indicates a high level of legal sophistication, and should warn us that the simplicity of the language does not necessarily imply a naive or 'primitive' legal system.

Finally, we should note that the surviving fragments of the Twelve Tables give no support whatever to theories about the *gens* as a primordial social unit. The *gens* has no place in the regulations concerning property or succession (despite frequent assertions to the contrary by scholars). It is true that members of the *gens* (*gentiles*) had a claim in cases of intestate succession. Here the rule was that in a case of intestacy the property went to automatic heirs (*sui heredes*), that is, persons in the *potestas* of the deceased. In the absence of automatic heirs, the inheritance went to the nearest agnates (Table V.4), most commonly brothers and sisters. But in the absence of agnates (Table V.5) the property was to go to the *gentiles*. So too Table V.7 gives power over a lunatic and his property to his agnates and (sc. in the absence of agnates) *gentiles*.

But these clauses do no more than give expression to the Roman belief that members of a *gens* were related by descent from a common ancestor, even though no agnatic ties could be demonstrated. It is important to stress that it is the *gentiles* as individuals who are specified as heirs by default, not the *gens* as a group. It is incorrect to say that in the absence of agnates the property 'should go back to the *gens*'.[48] The *gentiles* are no more thought of as members of a corporate group than the agnates. It is possible that these clauses in the Twelve Tables are a ghostly reflection of an earlier stage in the development of Rome when property was held in common by the *gens*; but they certainly do not prove it or even make it probable. It may also be noted that neither here nor anywhere else in the Twelve Tables is it suggested that *gentiles* refers exclusively to patricians.

6 THE LAWS: ECONOMIC IMPLICATIONS

To judge from the Twelve Tables the economic life of Rome in the middle of the fifth century BC was predominantly agricultural. The regulations governing the respective rights of neighbours, damage to property, and ownership of land are entirely concerned with farmland, cereal crops, vines, fruit trees and livestock. In a sense this is an unsurprising fact. At all times and places in antiquity most people were engaged in the business of subsistence, and consumed the bulk of what they produced. Trade consisted largely of exchange of local produce, and manufacture of localised craft production. The wealth of the upper classes was derived from extensive landholdings, and was expended on culturally defined modes of conspicuous consumption. This general view of the ancient economy, based loosely on Finley, is certainly applicable to archaic Rome.

The conspicuous consumption of the elite stimulated trade in exotic luxuries from abroad, but the total value of this trade was probably relatively insignificant (and was in any case in decline by the middle of the fifth century). Traders were evidently persons of little standing. At any rate there is nothing in the Twelve Tables dealing with commercial transactions, credit, industrial production or investment; all the clauses that deal with purchase are concerned with *res mancipi* – that is, real estate, draught animals and what are called 'rustic praedial servitudes' (rights to walk, to drive animals or carts, or to take water, through someone else's property). The bias is surely significant.

It is equally noticeable that arable farming, viticulture and arboriculture are far more prominent than stock-raising; the livestock that is mentioned consists for the most part of draught animals (*iumenta*, rather than flocks and herds, which are barely referred to). This pattern is reproduced in the rest of the evidence, particularly the religious calendar and the faunal and botanical remains from archaeological sites.[49] Out of nearly fifty fixed festivals in the old calendar only two are concerned with pastoralism. They are the Parilia and the Lupercalia, both extremely ancient and believed by tradition to have been celebrated by the shepherd society in which Romulus and Remus grew up. The common festival of the Latins, the Feriae Latinae, also had a pastoral character. But the majority of the rural festivals in the calendar deal with arable farming and viticulture (the cultivation of olives is noticeably absent).[50]

What the various data suggest is that pastoralism was a relatively insignificant part of the rural economy. This needs saying because of a well-entrenched scholarly tradition that early Rome was a pastoral society, a situation that continued, according to some, down to republican times.[51] Another widespread theory, which goes back in essentials to A. Piganiol, interprets early Roman history in terms of a conflict of two opposing tendencies, mentalities and ways of life – the agrarian and the pastoral.[52] On this view the power and standing of the patrician clans depended on the possession of extensive flocks and herds, and wealth in general consisted of cattle and sheep.

The Twelve Tables and the calendar do not bear out this picture. It is true that the word for money, *pecunia*, which occurs frequently in the Tables, derives from *pecus* ('herd'), and ancient sources speak of fines being assessed in cattle and sheep.[53] But cattle and sheep were if anything used only as notional measures of value, and it does not follow that they were a major form of capital accumulation, still less a means of exchange. The idea that payments were actually made (and fines levied) in cattle and sheep is an unnecessary and perhaps absurd assumption.[54]

It is clear in any case that by the time of the Twelve Tables a proper monetary system was in operation, and that transactions were made in bronze measured by weight. The 'bronze and scales' method of transfer is itself a proof of this, and payments in bronze are specified as penalties for certain types of injury in Table VIII.3–4. Roman money was not yet being issued in the form of coins; that was a development of the years around 300 BC (see below, pp. 394–7). But as Crawford points out, the most important stage in the early history of money is the designation by the state of a fixed metallic unit, and in Rome that stage can be dated early; indeed it is an attractive suggestion that it was Servius Tullius who designated the *as* (a pound of bronze) as the Roman monetary unit.

This is probably the most satisfactory explanation of a fragment of Timaeus, allegedly attributing coinage to Servius.[55] It is worth adding, however, that bronze ingots or 'currency bars' bearing primitive designs in the form of a twig or 'dry branch' (usually referred to in Italian as 'ramo secco') have been found in hoards throughout northern and central Italy, including Latium. These coin-like objects, which clearly represent a form of mobile wealth if not of currency, are now known to have been produced as early as the sixth century BC. It is possible, therefore, that Servius Tullius, in addition to fixing a basic unit of bronze, also issued marked ingots weighing the amount in question.[56]

7 THE LAWS: SOCIAL DISTINCTIONS

One of the reasons why Servius Tullius established a system of monetary evaluation was to classify Roman citizens according to wealth at the census. One of the basic distinctions was between landowners, who were known as *adsidui* and were liable to military service, and the *proletarii*, who were the landless poor and generally excluded from the army except in dire emergencies. This is one of the few social distinctions between Roman citizens to affect their legal position in the Twelve Tables. In Table I.4 we read:

> *adsiduo vindex adsiduus esto. proletario civi quis volet vindex esto*
> ('For an assiduus an assiduus is to be guarantor. For a proletarian citizen whoever wishes is to be guarantor').

The clause evidently refers to some aspect of litigation procedure, but its precise import is a matter for conjecture. This is unfortunate as we cannot tell whether it benefited proletarians or disadvantaged them (although the natural interpretation would be the former). One important historical inference is that the Servian reforms, which created the distinction between *adsidui* and *proletarii*, must be dated before 450 BC.[57]

There is dispute about whether the distinction is equivalent to that between *classis* and *infra classem*; the probable answer is negative. The *classis/infra classem* distinction is most likely to represent two different levels of *adsidui*, the *proletarii* being excluded altogether from the Servian system (and from regular military service). At this period they were probably few in number, and were virtually disfranchised in that they had no say in the earliest form of the centuriate assembly, and had only a restricted voice in the assembly of the *plebs*, in which the tribal voting system guaranteed a majority to those who had properties in the rural tribes. This reinforces the view that the *plebs* were concentrated in the ranks of the *infra classem* rather than the proletariat.

A second important status distinction mentioned in the Twelve Tables is that between patron and client. A problematic clause, normally placed in Table VIII, reads:

> *patronus si clienti fraudem fecerit, sacer esto*
> ('If a patron shall have wronged a client, he is to be accursed') (VIII.21).

This is a surprising inclusion, given that on the standard view patron–client relations in Roman society were based on informal trust (*fides*) rather than legal obligation (although the source of Dionysius 2.10 naturally includes the rights and duties of patrons and clients among the laws of Romulus). Indeed some historians have challenged its authenticity on that account.[58] But the vague form of the injunction, and the nature of the penalty (the only example of the *sacer esto* formula in the Twelve Tables), perhaps suggest that the non-legal character of the relationship between patron and client is being recognised and reinforced, with a divine curse being invoked on a person guilty of breach of trust.

The idea was perhaps to remind patrons of their moral obligation to protect their clients, but without introducing any legal sanctions. Whether it had any practical effect may be doubted. It is noteworthy that the clause is one-sided, and does not impose any corresponding obligation on the client to abstain from *fraus* (whatever that might precisely be). The reason is obvious enough: a patron, who was in the position of power, had all kinds of sanctions against an erring client, most obviously to withdraw the protection on which the client depended. He had no need for pious assistance from the Decemvirs. As for the wronged client – heaven help him! That, indeed, is exactly what this clause is saying.

The phenomenon of patronage exists to some degree in all societies, and arises from inequalities of wealth and status. The relationship between patrons and clients is an instrumental one based on the reciprocal exchange of favours, benefits and services. It is of the essence that the exchanges are unequal, and consist of different kinds of personal service. Patrons are powerful people who give protection and benefits to those whom they choose to favour; the latter, the clients, respond with deference, respect, loyalty and support. The precise nature of the goods and services exchanged will differ from one society to another, but the essential nature of the relationship, a system of vertical links tying the rich and powerful to poorer and weaker persons, remains the same.[59]

In Rome patron–client relations were a central feature of social intercourse at all periods, which is hardly surprising, since the basic terms are derived from Latin (*patronus*, *cliens*, etc.). It is not enough, however, merely to demonstrate the existence of patron–client relationships in early Rome; rather we need to understand how they functioned and how important they were in the life of the community. All the indications are that in the archaic period patronage was the dominant form of social relationship, and that it was clearly and openly acknowledged as such.

The sources are no doubt wrong to suggest that the citizen body was neatly divided into two groups, of patrons and clients, and that the latter were subdivided into separate clienteles each attached to an individual patron. But modern theorists are equally mistaken when they imagine that clients were wholly dependent on the great houses and were not part of the citizen body at all; or that the lower class of citizens were all clients of the great houses, and that the *plebs* were excluded both from patronage and from Roman citizenship.[60] These tidy constructions are undoubtedly too rigid. In fact archaic Rome, like its later republican counterpart, is likely to have consisted of interlocking networks of patronage in which people of moderate standing, who were dependent on the favour and goodwill of their more powerful neighbours, were at the same time able to extend their patronage to dependants of their own. To see the distinction as a simple one between rich and poor is too simplistic; clients were not impoverished down-and-outs. Indeed our sources make clear what we should otherwise have been able to conjecture: that the most desirable and favoured clients were well-off.

In the competition for status, patrons would have found that they had clients in common, and the more desirable clients would have received the patronage of more than one grandee. Nevertheless, in the archaic period there were more instances than later of fixed clienteles – that is, of families that were completely bound by ties of dependence to rich and powerful patrons. This is evident from stories like the episode of Appius Claudius, who emigrated to Rome with a retinue of 5,000 clients.

The traditional role of the Roman client was to greet his patron at his house for the morning 'salutation', and then to attend him on his way to the Forum. In the early period this personal attendance sometimes took the form of armed service, as bands of clients became private armies in the service of the great leaders. The best example of this feudal organisation is the story of the

Fabii, who fought a private war against the Etruscans of Veii in 479 BC supported only by their companions (*sodales*) and dependants (*clientes*) (cf. above, p. 144). Supposedly 306 adult male Fabii took part in this campaign, and their armed retinue numbered several thousand. The numbers are certainly exaggerated (as also in the case of Appius Claudius); but the number 306, which seems to be traditional, would be a plausible total for the whole army, including companions and clients. The companions (*sodales*) are likely to have been the most favoured and privileged clients (cf. above, p. 144), but the nature of their status has been hidden by the use of terms indicating affection and friendship; here as elsewhere patronage merges into other categories of relationship.

At the other end of the spectrum patronage can be directly exploitative, and protection can become a protection racket – that is, the obtaining of obedience and support by threats, and if necessary by force. The goods and services exchanged can be materialist in the crudest sense, when the patron provides the barest means of subsistence, and the client is obliged to provide labour services. At this point the relationship shades into servitude, and it is probably not incorrect to see *nexum* as an extreme form of patronage.

Patron–client relations are central to an understanding of the 'Conflict of the Orders', and of the solitary reference in the Twelve Tables to the distinction between patricians and plebeians – the notorious ban on inter-marriage in Table XI. This is normally taken to be an attempt to make the patriciate a closed order by prohibiting exogamy. If all non-patrician citizens were plebeians, that would indeed be the necessary inference. But we have seen that a dualistic interpretation of Roman society as comprising two mutually exclusive groups is probably incorrect. Patrician dominance, which became stronger in the course of the early decades of the Republic, depended on the support of well-to-do non-patricians who found it to their advantage to back the existing system. The social mechanism that made this possible was patronage. The wealthy non-patrician clients were certainly not plebeians. On the contrary, their loyalties brought them into direct conflict with the organisation of the *plebs*. The plebeian movement, for its part, was a self-help group that provided an alternative refuge to those who were excluded from the benefits of patronage.

We can envisage two processes taking place in the course of the fifth century. First, the growth of the plebeian movement and the development of its organisation began to attract ambitious individuals from among the well-to-do, who found the prospect of wielding independent power as leaders of the *plebs* preferable to a subservient role as clients of the patricians. The emergence of wealthy and aspiring plebeians changed the face of the plebeian struggle, and brought about a direct confrontation with the patriciate as such. In particular, the plebeian leaders began to demand the right to hold the consulship. We cannot be sure when this phase of the struggle began, but it may well have been before 450 BC.

The second, parallel, process was the patricians' response to these develop-ments; in essence this amounted to an attempt to ostracise the plebeian movement and to impose disabilities on its leaders. On this view the notorious clause of the eleventh Table was designed to prohibit marriages between patricians and leading plebeians (that is, leaders of the plebeian movement); its aim would have been to discourage wealthy non-patricians (the group who would normally have expected to intermarry with the patriciate) from going over to the *plebs*.[61]

One advantage of this admittedly hypothetical reconstruction is that it can explain both the imposition of the ban in the eleventh Table and its repeal by the Lex Canuleia of 445 BC. Since the process of intermarriage, if permitted, would have served to integrate patricians and the leading plebeians, we can imagine that radical elements among the *plebs* might have been opposed to it. This is the only possible explanation of how the second Decemvirate, consisting of both patricians and plebeians, could have introduced the measure set out in the eleventh Table. On the other hand, moderate elements within the patriciate, together with many of the socially aspiring plebeian leaders, might have opposed the law from the start. We have seen that a political alliance of precisely this sort was responsible for the compromises of 449 after the downfall of the Decemvirs; and it was perhaps the same group that gave impetus to the movement for the repeal of the marriage ban in 445 BC. Only if it had substantial patrician support could Canuleius' measure have become law; it was, after all, a plebiscite, and would have been subject to the restrictions imposed by the Lex Valeria Horatia (above, p. 278).

12

WARS AND EXTERNAL RELATIONS, 509–345 BC

1 ROME AND THE LATIN LEAGUE

The half century from *c.* 525 to 475 BC was a period of turmoil and unrest in central Italy. The evidence hints darkly at political upheavals, violent changes of regime, tyrannies and the anarchic conflicts of warlords supported by private armies. The impression given by the written sources is borne out by archaeology. In Etruria a number of settlements, mostly smaller urban centres, disappeared at this time, either abandoned or destroyed.[1] The most notable victims were the 'seigneurial' centres at Acquarossa and Murlo, which were sacked at the end of the sixth century (cf. above, p. 93).

As we have seen (above, p. 237), the fall of the monarchy at Rome was part of this wider picture. Although tradition presents the overthrow of the last king as a bloodless coup occasioned by a domestic incident, archaeological evidence hints at something more violent; and there are good reasons for rewriting the story of Lars Porsenna of Clusium, who probably captured the city and may therefore have been responsible for driving out the Tarquins. But when Porsenna's army was defeated at Aricia in 504, the stage was set for a conflict between Rome and the other Latin peoples, with the Romans attempting to regain the ascendancy they had had at the time of the Carthage treaty a few years earlier, and the Latins determined to resist.

This hypothetical reconstruction is probably the best way to make sense of the event that dominates the early years of the Republic, namely the war between Rome and the Latins which reached its climax in the epic battle of Lake Regillus in 499 BC (or 496: see Livy 2.21.3–4). Victory went to the Romans, led by the dictator A. Postumius Albus, whose descendants celebrated his achievement for centuries thereafter. The war ended in 493 BC with a treaty, known to posterity as the Treaty of Spurius Cassius (*foedus Cassianum*) from the consul who negotiated it on Rome's behalf. These events are real enough, even if the detailed episodes associated with them are legendary.

A good example of how fact and legend are interwoven in the episode of Lake Regillus is the story of the Dioscuri, the divine twins Castor and Pollux, who are said to have intervened on the Roman side in the battle, and afterwards were seen watering their horses at the Fountain of Juturna in the Forum, where they announced the Roman victory to the anxiously waiting populace. As a result, a temple was built on the spot where they were seen, and dedicated in 484 BC (see above, p. 68).[2]

Since Castor and Pollux belong to Greek mythology, it would be easy to dismiss this whole story as a late invention modelled on similar Greek legends, of which there are many; but recent archaeological research has vindicated the tradition in the most remarkable way. Near the shrine of the thirteen altars at Lavinium a bronze plaque was unearthed in 1959 inscribed with a dedication to Castor and Pollux. It can be dated to the late sixth century, which proves that the cult was established in Latium before the time of the battle of Lake Regillus;[3] and recent Danish excavations of the substructure of the temple of Castor in the Forum have shown that the earliest building does indeed go back to the early fifth century.[4] Since most Roman temples were financed from booty, tradition is probably correct in saying that this one was founded in honour of deities who were believed to have helped the Romans in a battle. It is by no means inconceivable that the story of their miraculous appearance was already current at the time. Reported sightings of divine beings at great battles – gods, angels, the Virgin Mary, etc. – are copiously documented, from remote antiquity to the First World War and beyond.[5]

The most problematic question to arise from this war and its aftermath, however, is the nature of the coalition of Latin states that fought against Rome and afterwards concluded the Cassian treaty. Modern scholars have coined the term 'Latin League' to describe this coalition; although there is no precise equivalent in Latin, it is worth noting that Dionysius of Halicarnassus referred to a *koinon*, the standard Greek term for a 'league'. But this word is notoriously vague and ill-defined,[6] and the difficulty is aggravated in the case of the Latins by the fact that most accounts fail to distinguish carefully enough between a political alliance of city-states and other forms of association and communal activity which we know united the Latin peoples from very early times.

Reference has been made in an earlier chapter to the religious festivals, celebrated at different sites in Latium, in which some or all of the Latin communities took part (above, pp. 66–8). The most important of these common festivals was the Feriae Latinae, celebrated each year on the Mons Albanus. The ceremony involved the sacrifice of a bull and the distribution of portions of meat to representatives of the participating communities. There can be no doubt about the importance of this annual celebration in the ethnic consciousness of the Latins. In the historical period it was the Latin cult *par excellence*; the presiding deity was Jupiter Latiaris, who was identified in legend with Latinus, the eponymous ancestor of the tribe (Festus p. 212 L).

The ceremony was evidently an expression of tribal solidarity, and constituted an annual renewal of the ties of kinship that united the Latin peoples.

Participation in the cult was a badge of membership; the Latin name (*nomen Latinum*, the standard expression in the sources for the Latin nation) could be said to consist exclusively of those peoples who received meat at the annual banquet on the Alban Mount. If one of the Latin peoples failed to obtain its proper share of the meat, the whole ceremony had to be repeated (see e.g. Livy 32.1.9; 37.3.4).[7]

The Feriae Latinae was not the only cult that the Latin peoples shared in common. Festivals of the same kind were also celebrated at Lavinium, an important religious centre, as we have seen. There was a major common shrine in the grove of Diana at Aricia, and from casual references in the literary sources we hear of others near Tusculum and at Ardea (Pliny, *n.h.* 16.242; Strabo 5.3.5, p. 242 C) (Map 5). It is in this context that we can best understand the tradition that Servius Tullius founded a temple of Diana on the Aventine as a common shrine for all the Latins. Since the Aventine was outside the *pomerium*, the sacred boundary of the city, the Dianium was clearly an extra-urban sanctuary of the kind that already existed at other places in Latium.

There is no reason to doubt that the cult of Diana was, in fact, founded by Servius Tullius, although the original sixth-century shrine was probably not a temple, but an open-air sanctuary with an altar. The inscription which recorded the founding of the cult still survived in the time of Augustus.[8] The Aventine cult of Diana, like many of the cults founded at this time, was influenced by Greek ideas; the cult image of the goddess was modelled on that of Ephesian Artemis – or, rather, on the copy of the Ephesian Artemis that had been set up shortly before in the Ephesion at the Greek colony of Massilia (Marseilles), with which Rome had been friendly since the early sixth century (Strabo 5.1.4, p. 180 C; Justin 43.5). Representations of the Roman cult statue on coins of the late Republic confirm the sixth-century date.[9]

These shared cults go back to the pre-urban period and are the clearest sign of the fact that, throughout their history, the Latins were conscious of belonging to an integrated community that transcended the boundaries of individual groupings. They shared a common name (the *nomen Latinum*), a common sentiment, and a common language. They worshipped the same gods and had similar political and social institutions. A shared sense of kinship was expressed in a common myth of origin. Finally, the archaeological record shows that a distinctive form of material culture was diffused throughout the region of Latium Vetus from the period of the Final Bronze Age onwards (see above, p. 48).

Another aspect of this sense of unity is the body of social and legal privileges that were shared in common by the Latins and were in historical times defined as specific rights (*iura*). These included *conubium*, the right to contract a legal marriage with a partner from another Latin community; *commercium*, the right to deal with persons from other Latin communities and to make legally binding contracts (especially important was the right to own real estate within the territory of another Latin community); and the

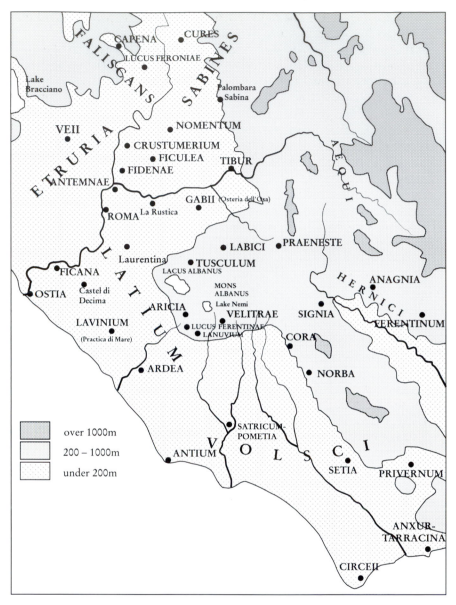

Map 5 Early Latium

so-called *ius migrationis*, the right to acquire the citizenship of another Latin state simply by taking up permanent residence there.

This community based on shared religious sentiment and reciprocal private rights is to be firmly distinguished from the political and military league of Latin states which we know existed at the end of the sixth century. The principal reason for keeping them separate is the consistent and unequivocal view of our sources that Rome was never a member of a general Latin alliance. In fact, the traditional account maintains that the League was a political coalition of Latin states formed in opposition to Rome. Its meetings took place outside Roman territory at the grove of Ferentina near Aricia, and its purpose was to organise resistance to the growth of Roman power.

Our sources refer to this league as a going concern early in the regal period. For example, Dionysius of Halicarnassus describes a war between the Rome of Tullus Hostilius and an organised coalition of Latin states meeting at Ferentinum (*sic*: Dion. Hal. 3.34.3). Dionysius' report is probably unhistorical, but it may be an anachronistic reflection of a situation that actually existed in the later part of the sixth century. In the time of Tarquinius Superbus we hear of another meeting at Ferentina, at which a certain Turnus Herdonius of Aricia attempted to stir up the Latins against Rome (Livy 1.50; Dion. Hal. 4.45). Turnus was, however, outwitted by Tarquin, who had him killed and then persuaded the Latins to accept an agreement in which they formally acknowledged the supremacy of Rome. The treaty entailed joint military co-operation, with Rome and the Latin League each contributing an equal number of troops to the allied army, but with the Romans taking command (Livy 1.52.6). The terms of this treaty, whether historical or not, clearly anticipate those of the *foedus Cassianum*, as we shall see.

When the Latins broke away from Rome after the fall of the Tarquins and the occupation of the city by Porsenna, their resistance was once again organised from Ferentina, this time under the leadership of Tusculum and Aricia. This phase of Latin history is documented by an important fragment of Cato's *Origines*, which records a joint dedication of a grove of Diana at Aricia by a group of Latin peoples. The text, which was probably transcribed by Cato from the original dedicatory inscription, reads as follows:

> Egerius Baebius of Tusculum, the Latin dictator, dedicated the grove of Diana in the wood at Aricia. The following peoples took part jointly: Tusculum, Aricia, Lanuvium, Laurentum (i.e. Lavinium), Cora, Tibur, Pometia, Rutulian Ardea. . . .
>
> (Cato, *Origines* II.28 C = fr. 58 P)

The quotation as we have it tells us nothing about the date or significance of the event in question, nor is it clear how the passage fitted into Cato's narrative. But the majority of scholars are agreed that the most suitable context for it would be the period around 500 BC, when the Latins were co-ordinating their efforts against Rome.[10]

The grove of Diana mentioned by Cato is probably not the same as the Lucus Ferentinae, although both were situated in the territory of Aricia. The Dianium has been located below the north-eastern edge of the crater of Lake Nemi; parts of the historic sanctuary were excavated in 1888 and in the 1920s.[11] The grove of Ferentina, on the other hand, was situated near the course of the later Via Appia, and is probably to be identified with the Laghetto di Turno (Lacus Turni) near Castel Savelli, about 2 km west of Albano.[12] It follows that the fragment of Cato does not itself record the formation of the anti-Roman alliance, but rather a parallel religious event.

The cult foundation recorded by Cato probably represents an attempt by the Latins to isolate Rome and to set up a new 'federal' cult of Diana which would rival – and perhaps supplant – the shrine on the Aventine at Rome. It is not really a serious objection to this view that some sources seem to regard the Arician cult of Diana as older than the 'Servian' cult at Rome (e.g. Statius, *Silvae* 3.1.59ff.). The Diana cult at Aricia was indeed very ancient, and displays a number of primitive features, most notably its priesthood, an unenviable post for which only runaway slaves were eligible. It offered a precarious form of immunity to the fugitive, who obtained it by killing the incumbent in single combat. In order to qualify as a challenger, he had first to pluck a branch from a sacred tree (Virgil, *Aeneid* 6.137); this was the famous 'golden bough', immortalised by Sir James Frazer.[13] The winner of the contest then reigned as 'king of the wood' (*rex nemorensis*) for as long as he could defend himself against aspiring successors.

Such features are not likely to have been instituted at the meeting recorded by Cato, and must go back a long way before the sixth century. But the difficulty can easily be overcome by assuming that the document quoted by Cato did not record the intial foundation of the cult of Diana at Nemi, but rather an attempt to give it a new role as a religious centre for the Latin League. The list of peoples given in the fragment is probably not complete, and cannot be taken as a full list of members of the Latin League at the end of the sixth century.[14] An alternative list given by Dionysius of Halicarnassus (5.61.3) is suspect for a number of reasons – it is probably based on erudite conjecture rather than on genuine records – and cannot safely be used to supplement Cato.

Cato's evidence does, however, confirm the leading part taken by Tusculum, the city which heads the list and whose representative, Egerius Baebius, performed the dedication as *dictator Latinus*. This apparently official title is another important element of the text. It can be argued that the Latin dictator was the chief official of the Latin League, and that it was as dictator that Octavus Mamilius commanded the confederate Latin forces at Lake Regillus. The alternative is to assume that the 'Latin dictator' was a purely religious functionary, but on the whole this seems less likely.[15]

2 THE *FOEDUS CASSIANUM* AND ITS CONSEQUENCES

This was the coalition which the Romans defeated at Lake Regillus and with which they concluded the Cassian treaty in 493 BC. There is no reason to question these basic elements of the tradition. Spurius Cassius, whose name was mentioned in the text, was a historical figure who appears in the *Fasti*. The treaty itself was inscribed on a bronze pillar which was set up in the Forum and was still there in the time of Cicero (*pro Balbo* 53; cf. Livy 2.33.9), and Dionysius of Halicarnassus gives an account of its contents (6.95). Dionysius' version has every appearance of a genuine document of the fifth century BC, and the most reasonable view is that it is based, directly or indirectly, on the inscribed text in the Forum.[16]

The treaty summarised by Dionysius was a bilateral agreement between the Romans on the one side and the Latins on the other. It lays down perpetual peace between the two parties, and a defensive military alliance by which each will go to the aid of the other if it is attacked. Each agrees not to assist or give free passage to enemies of the other. The spoils of any successful campaign are to be shared equally. Finally, provision is made for the settlement of commercial disputes between the citizens of different states.[17]

An important issue which is not dealt with in Dionysius' version of the treaty is the question of the organisation and command of the allied army. However, we are given some valuable information on this point in a fragment of the antiquarian L. Cincius, quoted by Festus (s.v. 'praetor', p. 276 L). Cincius tells us that, down to the consulship of P. Decius Mus (340 BC), the Latins used to meet at the spring of Ferentina to discuss arrangements concerning the command. He goes on to describe the procedures that were followed 'in a year when it was the responsibility of the Romans to supply a commander for the army by order of the Latin name'.

The meaning of this passage is unfortunately ambiguous. The phrase *quo anno* ('in a year when') might seem to imply that there were years when the allied supreme commander was not summoned from Rome, and consequently that the command was exercised in turn by the Romans and the Latins in alternate years.[18] But this does not seem ever to have happened. The most probable interpretation of the passage is that there was a regular annual meeting of the Latins at Ferentina, but not necessarily a regular annual campaign; so that it was only in years when military action was contemplated that a commander would be needed – a commander who was invariably summoned from Rome.[19]

The alliance enabled the Romans and the Latins to campaign effectively against the enemies who threatened them in the years following the Cassian treaty. These incursions will be discussed in the next section; here we need only note that the alliance made organised resistance possible and saved Latium from being overrun. Indeed, it may have been the pressure of hostile forces on the borders of Latium that brought Rome and the Latin League together in the first place, and gave rise to the treaty.[20]

In 486 BC, so we are told, the Hernici were brought into the alliance. The Hernici were an Italic people, apparently related to the Sabines,[21] who inhabited the strategically vital region of the Trerus (Sacco) valley. In the absence of any archaeological or epigraphic material the Hernici are now little more than a name to us. The only relics are some impressive remains of polygonal walls, dating from the pre-Roman period, which can still be seen at the chief Hernican centres: Anagnia, Verulae, Ferentinum and (especially) Aletrium (Figure 24). But we do not know whether these places were fully developed urban settlements in the fifth century. More probably they were fortified places of refuge. An isolated reference in Livy (9.42) suggests that the Hernici were organised in a league centred at Anagnia.

Figure 24 Aletrium: remains of polygonal walls.

This alliance was also said to be the work of Spurius Cassius, who was consul for a third time in 486 BC. The Hernici are said to have been admitted on terms identical to those of the earlier Cassian treaty (Dion. Hal. 8.69.2). It was probably a separate pact between the Romans and the Hernici rather than a tripartite agreement involving the Latin League as well. In any event it seems likely that the addition of the Hernici enhanced the position of Rome as the pivotal element of the alliance; by co-ordinating the efforts of two disparate sets of allies she inevitably came to control them both. The inclusion of the Hernici therefore had the paradoxical effect of weakening the position of the allies and strengthening that of Rome.

As for the question of how the military alliance worked in practice, all we can say is that the Latins and Hernici fought in separate contingents under a unified (Roman) command. We cannot know what proportion of the total allied force was contributed by each of the three partners. The same uncertainty naturally surrounds the question of the division of the spoils. An equitable division of the spoils would presumably have entailed a distribution to the various contingents in proportion to their size. In any event the division of the spoils was a matter of great importance, and one that is frequently referred to in the course of the traditional narrative of the warfare of this period. Clauses about the division of booty are a common feature of ancient treaties, and offer a revealing glimpse into the function of warfare in the ancient world.[22]

Booty consisted of movable goods, livestock, slaves and land. In the nature of things, the distribution of land acquired by conquest presented a special problem, particularly where the Latins were concerned, since the Latin League did not constitute a unitary state, but rather a coalition of states. Probably the same was true of the Hernici. To divide a single tract of land into separate allotments belonging to different sovereign states would have been unthinkable. The problem was overcome by the institution of the colony. By this simple device conquered land was allotted to colonists who were organised into a new political community. The new community became an independent sovereign state with its own citizenship and its own territory.

3 EARLY LATIN COLONIES

The sources record the foundation of many such colonies during the fifth and fourth centuries (see Table 7 below, p. 303). Most were on the borders of Latium, or indeed at formerly Latin sites that had been reconquered from invading enemies. In most cases the territories of the colonies did not border on that of Rome. It was therefore logical for the new settlements to become members of the Latin League. As such they were obliged to send contingents to the allied army along with the other Latins, and they also possessed full Latin rights. Consequently they were known as 'Latin colonies' (coloniae Latinae). An exception to this pattern was Ferentinum (not to be confused with the grove of Ferentina, above, pp. 297f.), which was conquered (or reconquered) from the Volsci in 413 BC (Livy 4.51.7–8). Since Ferentinum was in Hernican territory, it was attached to the Hernican federation, rather than to the Latin League. The same principle probably applies to Veii and other places such as Labici which were directly incorporated into the Roman state (see below, p. 303).

It is important to stress that the appellation 'Latin colony' refers solely to the legal status of the newly founded community, and has nothing to do with either the ethnic origin of the settlers or the manner in which it was founded. In any Roman colonial enterprise the largest single group of settlers would normally have been drawn from Rome. Beloch cannot have been far wrong in asserting that normally at least 50 per cent of the colonists would be Romans.[23] The rest would be either Latins, or Hernicans, or both.

Although the Roman colonists would invariably be the largest single group of settlers, they might still constitute a minority of the total population, since many of the early colonies were established at existing towns, whose surviving inhabitants were then enrolled in the colony. This is actually recorded as happening at Antium in 467 BC, where native Volscians were included together with Romans, Latins and Hernici (Livy 3.1.7; Dion. Hal. 9.59.2). It is noteworthy that the sources misunderstand this story, and attempt to explain the presence of allies and native Antiates by suggesting that an insufficient number of Romans volunteered to join the colony (incidentally this misunderstanding is a strong argument in favour of the authenticity of the event).

As for the question of how a colony came to be founded, the sources tell us that the Roman state was responsible for the entire exercise. It has recently become fashionable, however, for scholars to reject this tradition and to argue instead that the colonies were founded by the Latin League.[24] This line of argument is based on the untenable view that the Latin League was a federal state that included Rome among its members. The strict constitutional position must have been that all matters regarding the distribution of conquered land had to be decided jointly by Rome and the allies in consultation. But to say that a colony was founded by Rome is probably only a technical error. It is most likely that in practice the decisions were taken by the Romans, and that the consultation of the allies was a formality. Roman officials were probably always responsible for the practical tasks of founding the colonies and distributing land. This conclusion proceeds both from the analogy of the military command and from the fact that in every case the largest single group of colonists were Romans. In any event the idea that the Romans took little or no part in decisions regarding the early colonies is clearly mistaken. As it happens, on more than one occasion Livy gives us the names of the commissioners who supervised colonial enterprises – and they are always Romans. For example, the 'Triumvirs' who led the colony to Ardea in 442 BC were Agrippa Menenius Lanatus, T. Cloelius Siculus and M. Aebutius Helva, all prominent members of the Senate (Livy 4.11.5–7).

The record of colonisation during the fifth and early fourth centuries can be tabulated as follows:

Table 7 Early Roman/Latin colonies with attributed or probable dates

Fidenae	Romulus
Signia	Tarquinius Superbus
Circeii	Tarquinius Superbus
Cora	Tarquinius Superbus
Pometia	Tarquinius Superbus
Fidenae*	498 BC
Signia*	495 BC
Velitrae	494 BC (reinforced 492)
Norba	492 BC
Antium	467 BC
Ardea	442 BC
Labici	418 BC
Velitrae*	401 BC
Vitellia	395 BC
Circeii*	393 BC
Satricum	385 BC
Setia	383 BC
Sutrium	382 BC
Nepet	382 BC

* = second recorded foundation

One point arising from this list calls for brief comment. Under the year 209 BC Livy gives a list of all the colonies that had been founded by the Romans until that date (Livy 27.9). The problem is that his list, which contains thirty colonies in all, includes only seven of the early colonies enumerated above in Table 7, viz. Signia, Norba, Setia, Circeii, Ardea, Sutrium and Nepet. The rest are ignored.

Livy's omission of colonies whose foundation he himself had recorded in his earlier narrative is indeed a difficulty, and has led some scholars to argue that many of the earlier notices are false. But the omissions can be more satisfactorily explained on the assumption that the communities in question no longer had the status of colonies in 209 BC. Some had perhaps ceased to exist altogether (e.g. Fidenae, destroyed in 426 BC), while others were incorporated in the Roman state as communities of Roman citizens after the Latin War of 340–338 BC (e.g. Velitrae and Antium).[25]

It is possible, however, that some of the earlier colonial settlements never became Latin colonies. For example, if the conquered land bordered on the *ager Romanus*, it may have been simply annexed and assigned *viritim* (i.e. in individual allotments) to Roman citizens who were not formed into a new community but remained citizens and were directly administered from Rome. This procedure was adopted when Veii was conquered in 396 BC, and may have happened earlier, for example at Labici in 418 (Livy 4.47.6–7). It is likely that in these cases some of the land was assigned to allies in accordance with the treaties. If so, they would automatically have become Roman citizens on taking up residence within Roman territory. In the same way it is probable that Romans and Latins were able to take part in the settlement of Ferentinum when it was recaptured in 413 and handed over to the Hernici. It seems that the treaties gave the Latins and Hernici the right to take part in any programme of colonisation that the Romans might undertake, and that this right continued to be exercised. Strangely enough, we know about this because of an incident involving Ferentinum; Livy records that some Ferentinates had enrolled as settlers in a Roman citizen colony in 195 BC, and had thereby obtained Roman citizenship (Livy 34.42.5).

4 THE INCURSIONS OF THE SABINES, AEQUI AND VOLSCI

It was suggested above (p. 299) that the formation of the military alliance between Rome and the Latin League was a response to an external military threat. The colonies at Velitrae, Signia and Norba probably represent an attempt by the alliance to strengthen the borders of Latium against the threat of hostile invasions.[26] But in spite of these precautions the security of Latium was seriously threatened at the end of the 490s by incursions of the Volsci and Aequi, who first begin to feature prominently in the traditional narrative at this time.

For most of the fifth century the Volsci were in control of the Monti Lepini (the hill country to the west of the Sacco valley), most of the Pomptine plain, and the whole of the coastal district from Antium to Terracina which in the sixth century had been part of the 'empire' of Tarquinius Superbus (cf. above, pp. 209–10). The Volscian occupation of southern Latium cannot be documented in any detail; but the literary sources indicate that it took place at the beginning of the fifth century. A brief remark in Livy shows that the strongholds of Cora and Pometia were in their hands by 495 BC (2.22.2); Antium was overtaken before 493 (Livy 2.23.4), and was shortly followed by Velitrae, on the southern edge of the Alban massif.[27]

Our knowledge of Volscian culture and society is meagre in the extreme. Onomastic evidence and general probability suggest that they were an Italic people who had moved down from the central Apennines before the end of the sixth century. This is supported by the fact that another branch of the Volscians was established at an early date in the region of the middle Liris valley, around Sora, Arpinum and Atina (see e.g. Livy 10.1). Linguistic evidence is furnished by the so-called *tabula Veliterna*, a four-line bronze inscription from Velitrae, dating from the third century BC and written in a language that is usually taken to be Volscian.[28] The language of the inscription has close affinities with Umbrian, and for this reason scholars generally postulate a 'northern' origin for the Volscians, and suppose that they migrated down the Liris valley from beyond the Fucine Lake during the course of the sixth century.[29]

In any event it is most probable that the appearance of the Volscians in the southern part of Latium was the result of a migration from the interior, and that it was part of a wider movement of peoples which affected most of the Italian peninsula in the fifth century BC. The sources report a succession of tribal migrations at this time which resulted in the spread of the Sabellian peoples and the diffusion of the Osco-Umbrian dialects throughout the central and southern regions of the peninsula.

These migrations were supposedly the result of a series of 'sacred springs'. According to legend the sacred spring (*ver sacrum*) was a ritual response to a famine or similar crisis. In such circumstances all the produce of a given year would be sacrificed to Mars. The animals were slaughtered, but the children were spared and designated *sacrati*. When they reached maturity they would be sent out into the wild to fend for themselves, following the lead of a wild animal; they would then settle wherever the animal stopped to rest, and form a new tribe.[30] This myth accounted for the origin of the Picentes, for example, who had followed a woodpecker (*picus*) in their migration down the Tronto valley to Asculum (Ascoli Piceno) and the Adriatic coast; similarly the Samnite tribe of the Hirpini had followed a wolf (*hirpus*) in their southward trek from the Sabine hills. The Roman foundation legend itself contains similar elements, since Romulus and Remus were envisaged as leaders of a band of young shepherd warriors living in the wild. The myth is based on an assumption that is real enough, namely that the pressure of overpopulation in a region of poor natural resources was the primary cause of emigration.

The migrations set off a chain reaction, and the shock waves were felt the length and breadth of the peninsula. In Magna Graecia, the effects were catastrophic, as Iapygians, Lucanians and Bruttians pressed down upon the Greek cities on the coast. The disastrous defeat of Tarentum by the Iapygians in 473 BC was 'the worst the Greeks have ever suffered' according to Herodotus (7.170). In the south west city after city was overwhelmed by the Lucanians, until by about 400 Velia and Naples were the only remaining centres of Hellenic culture along the entire length of the Tyrrhenian coast.[31]

Inland from Naples, Oscan-speaking Samnites occupied Campania and formed themselves into a new Italic nation (the 'Campani') after taking over the principal cities. This movement probably began as a gradual infiltration of Samnite immigrants rather than as an organised invasion. At Capua the Etruscan inhabitants admitted the newcomers into the citizen community after an initial period of resistance; but this gesture did not prevent the Samnites from overthrowing the Etruscan ruling class in a violent coup one night in 423 BC.[32]

Returning to Latium, we can see that the incursions of the Sabines, Aequi and Volsci were local manifestations of this wider phenomenon, and that they had similar effects on the settlements in the coastal plain. As we have seen, the Volscians occupied the cities of southern Latium during the 490s; in the north east, in the area between the Tiber and the Anio, Roman territory was repeatedly attacked by the Sabines; and in the east the cities of Tibur, Pedum and Praeneste were threatened by the Aequi, a mountain people who inhabited the upper Anio valley and the surrounding hills.

We know nothing about the language and culture of the Aequi, although it is a fair presumption that they too were an Italic people speaking an Oscan-type dialect. Once again the archaeological evidence consists solely of remains of polygonal fortifications that can be seen at a number of hilltop sites in the mountains above Praeneste. These hill-forts should presumably be equated with the 'strongholds' (*oppida*) which are referred to in the literary sources (e.g. Livy 2.48.4; 10.45; Diod. 20.101). It was from these mountain fastnesses that the Aequi made their frequent raids into the Latin plain.[33]

There are good grounds for thinking that Tibur, Pedum and Praeneste were overrun by the Aequi at the start of the fifth century. Tibur had taken part in the foundation of the grove of Diana at Aricia (see above, p. 297), but then vanishes from the record until the fourth century. Praeneste is said to have defected from the Latin League to Rome in 499 BC (Livy 2.19) – not an impossible occurrence, given that one of the consuls of 499, C. Veturius, belonged to a clan that had long-standing connections with Praeneste[34] – but that is the last we hear of Praeneste for the rest of the century. Pedum is likewise missing from the traditional account of the fifth century, apart from a brief appearance in the saga of Coriolanus. The best explanation of these silences is that the three cities had been taken over by the Aequi. This possibility becomes a virtual certainty when we take account of the fact that in the wars against the Aequi the principal scene of action was the Algidus pass and the region around Tusculum,which is presented as the most vulnerable of the Latin cities. This state of affairs would not make sense if the Latins still controlled Praeneste.

The chief victims of the Volscian and Aequian attacks were therefore the outlying Latin cities, which protected Roman territory from the worst effects of enemy action. But in the case of the Sabine incursions it was Rome itself that was directly affected. If tradition is to be believed, wars between the Romans and the Sabines had been going on since the time of Romulus. There is also considerable evidence for peaceful infiltration as well as by armed hostility. Many of the noblest Roman families, including the Valerii, claimed a Sabine origin, and the story of the migration of the Claudii in 504 BC is evidence that the process of integration was still going on in the republican period. Sporadic warfare between the Romans and the Sabines also continued down to the middle of the fifth century.

The wars against the mountain tribes in the early part of the fifth century had a disastrous effect on the economic and cultural life of Rome and the Latins. This point is not simply an a-priori inference from the fact that half of Latium fell into enemy hands; it is also confirmed, as we have seen (above, pp. 225–6; 265–6), by clear evidence of an economic recession in Rome in the fifth century, which is most easily explained by the military reverses Rome suffered at the hands of the invading highlanders. The most serious of these setbacks occurred in the years 490–488 BC, when the Volscians, led by the Roman renegade Cn. Marcius Coriolanus, invaded Latin territory in two devastating annual campaigns. Capturing one city after another, Coriolanus' forces advanced as far as the Fossae Cluiliae on the outskirts of Rome (see above, p. 205). In the traditional story the city was saved only by the entreaties of Coriolanus' wife and mother, who persuaded him to turn back.[35]

Leaving aside the romantic details, we can reasonably accept that the story reflects a genuine popular memory of a time when the Volscians overran most of Latium and threatened the very existence of Rome. The chronology is insecure, however, since none of the leading persons in the story appears in the consular *Fasti*; but the Romans' belief that the events took place in the early years of the fifth century is probably correct in general terms.

The Volscian wars continued intermittently throughout the fifth century. Their raids into Latin territory either alternated, or coincided, with those of the Aequi. During the period from *c.* 494 to *c.* 455 a Roman campaign against one or other, or both, of these peoples is recorded virtually every year; after the middle of the fifth century, the record becomes more sporadic (see below, p. 309). The spectacular successes of the Volscians under Coriolanus were never repeated, as far as we know, although occasionally we hear of armies of Aequi and Volsci advancing right up to the gates of Rome (e.g. Livy 3.66.5 – 446 BC).

The most memorable episode of the Aequian wars is the story of L. Quinctius Cincinnatus, who, during an emergency in 458 BC, was summoned from the plough to assume the dictatorship. Within fifteen days Cincinnatus had assembled an army, marched against the Aequi (who were besieging a consular army encamped at Algidus), defeated them, triumphed, laid down his office, and returned to his ploughing. It must be admitted, however, that this exemplary story tells us more about the moralising ideology of the later Roman elite than it does about the military history of the fifth century BC. Even if Cincinnatus was a historical character (as he probably was), the supposedly crushing victory of 458 BC is more than a little suspect, especially as the Aequi came back the following year, and again in 455.

On the other hand, the story of a major Roman victory over the Aequi and Volsci at the Algidus in 431 BC (Livy 4.28–9) is more likely to be a genuine event. The episode shares certain features in common with the sagas of Coriolanus and the battle of Lake Regillus. These narratives are exceptional in that they are embroidered with a wealth of incidental detail that is qualitatively different from the transparent rhetoric that we find elsewhere. A particular feature of the story of the battle of the Algidus (and of that of Lake Regillus) is the record of names and exploits of individual combatants on both sides.[36] This feature, which gives the battle descriptions an 'epic' character, is not due in the first instance to Livy (although he exploits it to the full), but is rather a sign that the events had been celebrated in popular memory, and had perhaps formed the subjects of historical ballads (see above, p. 12).

But such episodes are exceptional. For the most part the literary tradition consists of a vacuous and insipid narrative of annual campaigns of which the most we can say is that they probably took place. The accompanying details that we find in Livy and Dionysius of Halicarnassus are transparently rhetorical exercises and are not taken seriously by anyone. But it is obviously an important question whether the basic structure – the bare record of events, stripped of all rhetorical embellishment – is soundly based and derived from an authentic tradition.

Of one thing we can be certain. The Roman annalists did not simply fabricate a never-ending series of Roman victories. Although some Roman successes are no doubt exaggerated (e.g. the alleged victory of Cincinnatus), it is noteworthy that as a general rule major Roman victories are comparatively rare in the tradition as we have it. This point can be illustrated by the record of Roman triumphs between the overthrow of the kings and the Gallic sack.[37] The record reveals the comparative infrequency of triumphs during this period. In the middle Republic triumphs were held, on average, in two out of every three years,[38] and they were especially common at the time when the first Roman histories were being written – that is, in the late third and early second centuries BC. By contrast, only twenty-two triumphs (and ovations) are registered for the whole of the fifth century; this must suggest that the tradition is not simply a fraudulent projection into the remote past of the conditions of the middle Republic.

Whatever later generations of Romans might have wanted to believe about the heroic achievements of their ancestors, the fact is that they did not succeed in effacing the dismal memory of the fifth century as a period of hardship and adversity. Indeed the sources frequently record Roman defeats.[39] But the most striking feature of the surviving narratives is that most of the annual campaigns are presented neither as victories nor as defeats, but as indecisive and often uneventful raiding expeditions. This seems an unlikely pattern for an annalist to invent; it is much more probable that it represents the true character of actual events.

We should note that the warfare of the fifth century was a very different kind of phenomenon from the organised military activity of the Roman state in the later Republic. What the sources reveal is an indistinct pattern of annual razzias. Warfare is recorded regularly, but there is no continuity from year to year. One year the Volsci might attack, the next year the Aequi, the next both together – in a seemingly random pattern. On the Roman side, each year's campaign was treated as an entirely self-contained affair. New consuls would take office, and a new army would be enrolled. Every spring and autumn special rituals were performed to mark the beginning and end of the campaigning season. This rhythmic pattern of annual warmongering was certainly not confined to Rome, but was characteristic of Italic society in general during the archaic age.

In central Italy during the fifth century there was little difference in practice between warfare and brigandage – a fact acknowledged by Livy, who frequently speaks of periods in which there were was 'neither peace nor war' (e.g. Livy 2.21.1; 2.26.1; etc.). At all events the rationale behind these wars was always the same. They were predatory raids by highland peoples upon the relatively prosperous and advanced settlements on the plain. The principal objective was always the acquisition of booty. The capture of large quantities of spoil is referred to again and again in the traditional accounts of the campaigns, and the importance of this feature is confirmed by the explicit provisions in the *foedus Cassianum*.

The annual pattern of raiding and counter-raiding seems to have diminished considerably after the middle of the fifth century. The Sabines disappear from the record after 449 BC, and attacks by the Aequi and Volsci are reported far less frequently. In the period of thirty-two years between 442 and 411 BC campaigns against the Volsci are recorded in only three years (431, 423 and 413), and against the Aequi in only four (431, 421, 418 and 414). The most likely explanation is that the Aequi and Volsci gradually developed a more settled mode of existence, rather than that the record is defective in some way. This deduction is based on the fact that the sources continue to report other 'routine' events, such as plagues and grain shortages, during the period in question. They also give full accounts of wars against the Etruscan city of Veii, and it is to these wars that we must now turn.

5 THE CONFLICT BETWEEN ROME AND VEII

Situated on a rocky plateau some 15 kilometres to the north of Rome, Veii was the nearest of the Etruscan cities to the borders of Latium. Rome and Veii shared a common border along the right bank of the Tiber, and it is hardly surprising that the sources should trace their rivalry back to the very beginning of Roman history. Intermittent wars between Rome and Veii must have occurred under the monarchy, even though we cannot reconstruct them in detail from the unreliable narratives of the literary sources. The evidence for the three major conflicts that occurred during the Republic, however, is much more secure. The three encounters were well-defined events which we may legitimately call the First, Second and Third Veientine Wars. This feature clearly differentiates the struggle between Rome and Veii from the more primitive pattern of organised brigandage that characterised the Aequian and Volscian wars. The difference arises simply from the fact that Veii, like Rome but in contrast to the Aequi and Volsci, was a centralised city-state.

During the past half century our knowledge of Veii and its territory has been greatly increased by archaeological finds, which have resulted partly from the extensive field survey of south Etruria (including much of the *ager*

Veientanus) that was carried out by the British School at Rome between 1950 and 1974.[40] The main results of this work can be briefly outlined.

During the sixth century Veii was a flourishing urban centre. Not much is known about the actual layout of the town, although the evidence of surface finds suggests a fairly open pattern of loosely scattered buildings running the whole length of the plateau from the north-west gate to the sanctuary at Piazza d'Armi. There was probably some concentration around the point where the major roads converged, which formed the centre of the later Roman town, but this has yet to be confirmed by excavation. The sanctuary sites at Portonaccio, Campetti and Piazza d'Armi have been more systematically explored, and it is clear that at each of them substantial buildings were erected during the sixth century. The famous acroterial statues from the Portonaccio temple (see above, p. 168) are an indication of the wealth of the city and of its high level of artistic achievement.[41]

Veii controlled an extensive and fertile territory, measuring some 562 km².[42] Field surveys have revealed an even and relatively dense pattern of rural settlement in the sixth and fifth centuries, indicating that most of the land was under cultivation or grazing. Its productive capacity was greatly improved by the elaborate system of drainage tunnels (*cuniculi*) which are common in the *ager Veientanus*, the majority of them probably dating from the fifth century. The territory of Veii was also served by a network of carefully engineered roads which were probably constructed during the seventh and sixth centuries and are in any case of pre-Roman date. The roads facilitated the movement not only of rural produce into the city, but also of objects of long-distance trade on which Veii's prosperity must have been largely based. An important recent study, which has provided much of the information for the above summary, has concluded that 'both roads and drainage schemes quite clearly reflect the control and organisation of a major city, setting its *territorium* in order'.[43]

The wars between Rome and Veii in the fifth century were organised conflicts between developed states, and had complex economic and political causes; and the two sides had long-term objectives that went beyond the mere acquistion of booty – although raiding naturally went on during the course of the fighting (e.g. Livy 2.48.5–6). The economic prosperity of both Rome and Veii depended to a large extent on their control of major natural lines of communication. As we saw in Chapter 2, traffic passing along the western side of Italy from north to south could go either through Rome or through the territory of Veii, crossing the Tiber at Fidenae or Lucus Feroniae. But the rivalry between the two cities arose from their attempts to control the routes along the Tiber valley from the coast to the interior. It seems that the Veientines could threaten Rome's control of the left bank by holding a bridgehead at Fidenae; while Rome, by occupying the right bank, could cut off the Veientines' access to the coast and the salt beds at the mouth of the river. It is not therefore surprising that in the wars between them the principal objective of the Romans should have been to gain permanent control of Fidenae, which changed hands frequently in the course of the fifth century, while the Veientines concentrated their efforts against the Roman possessions on the right bank.[44]

The most we can say about the First Veientine War (483–474 BC) is that Veii had the best of it. The sources record a Roman victory at a pitched battle in 480, the details of which are plausible but possibly imaginary.[45] In any event it did not stop the Veientines from advancing into Roman territory and occupying a fortified post on the Janiculum. It was in an attempt to counter this move that the Fabian clan, accompanied only by their own clients and 'companions', marched out in 479 BC to occupy a small frontier post on the river Cremera. Two years later they suffered a catastrophic defeat in which the entire clan, 306 persons in all, was wiped out, with the exception of a single youth who escaped to keep alive the name of the Fabii.[46]

Although later tradition embellished this tale with details taken from the nearly contemporary episode of the 300 Spartans at Thermopylae, its basic historicity should not be questioned. The story is obviously connected with the fact that the Fabia tribe was situated on the border of the *ager Veientanus*, which was marked by the river Cremera. The war of the Fabii was therefore fought in defence of their own private interests. The incident represents one of the last vestiges of an archaic form of social organisation which was probably already in an advanced state of obsolescence. Finally, we should note that in the years from 485 to 479 BC one of the annual consuls was invariably a Fabius; but after 479 the Fabii disappear from the *Fasti* until 467, when the supreme office was held by Q. Fabius Vibulanus, the survivor of the Cremera.

The truce that was made in 474 left the Veientines firmly in possession of Fidenae, which they must already have controlled before the Cremera disaster.[47] Thus Fidenae became the focus of the Second Veientine War, which broke out in 437 BC when four Roman ambassadors were murdered on the orders of Lars Tolumnius, the tyrant of Veii. Another memorable and certainly authentic event of this conflict was the battle in which Aulus Cornelius Cossus killed Lars Tolumnius in single combat. For this he was awarded the *spolia opima*, a distinction which had previously been achieved only by Romulus. The inscribed linen corslet which Cossus dedicated in the temple of Jupiter Feretrius was – notoriously – alleged to be still there in the time of Augustus, when it became the object of a political controversy (Livy 4.20.5–11). Shortly afterwards (435) Fidenae was besieged, and captured when Roman soldiers entered the citadel by means of a tunnel.

In the Third Veientine War (406–396 BC) the Romans took the initiative and launched a full-scale attack on the city of Veii itself. The siege that ensued is said to have lasted for ten years; it ended with the capture of the city by the dictator M. Furius Camillus. The bare facts – the fall of Veii in 396 BC and the subsequent incorporation of its territory in the *ager Romanus* – are historically certain and mark the end of an epoch in Italian history. But the traditional details of the war, as recorded by Livy and others, are mostly legendary.

The story of the fall of Veii was elaborated in two distinct ways. First, the idea of a ten-year siege was obviously modelled on the Greek legend of the Trojan War, and traces of a superficial attempt to assimilate the two events are clearly visible in the surviving narratives. Second, the whole account is pervaded by an atmosphere of mysticism and religiosity.[48] The story consists of a succession of supernatural happenings. The end of Veii, predicted in its 'Books of Fate' (Livy 5.14.4; 5.15.11), was the consequence of a religious offence committed by its king (Livy 5.1.4–5). The fall of the city was portended by a rise in the level of the Alban Lake, a prodigy which the Romans expiated by constructing a drainage tunnel on the orders of the Delphic oracle. This bizarre story must be connected in some way with the tradition that the Romans entered Veii by means of a tunnel, a motif which itself has a bewildering variety of associations (the earlier siege of Fidenae, the *cuniculi* in the countryside around Veii, etc.).[49]

Camillus, the Roman commander, is portrayed as an instrument of Fate (*dux fatalis*) carrying out a religious mission. The story ends with the 'evocation' of Juno Regina, the goddess of Veii, who was persuaded to abandon the city and go over to Rome. Her cult statue was transported – with miraculous ease – to Rome, where it was installed in a temple on the Aventine dedicated by Camillus (Livy 5.22.3–6).

The wars between Rome and Veii illustrate an important fact about Etruscan political history, namely the particularism of the individual cities. The fact that Veii received no significant support from the other Etruscan cities evidently ran counter to the expectations of the Roman annalists. In Livy's account there is an underlying assumption that the other cities ought to have assisted Veii and would have done so had it not been for special circumstances, such as the impious behaviour of the Veientine king at the national games (Livy 5.1.3–5). We hear repeatedly of meetings of the 'Etruscan League' at the Fanum Voltumnae (near Volsinii) at which the representatives of the Etruscan cities refused, for one reason or another, to give aid to Veii (e.g. Livy 4.24.2; 4.61.2; 5.1.7; 5.17.6–7).

In fact it is highly questionable whether the assembly that met at the shrine of Voltumna ever functioned as a political or military league. There is no historically verified instance in the sources of an action involving an Etruscan federal army, and many scholars have supposed that the league of Voltumna was a purely religious association.[50] On the other hand, there is abundant evidence of antagonism and warfare between the Etruscan cities. This state of affairs is now documented by the *elogia Tarquiniensia*, Latin inscriptions of the first century AD which refer to events of the history of Tarquinii in the fifth (and perhaps also the fourth) century BC.[51] The inscriptions refer to hostile interventions by magistrates of Tarquinii in the affairs of Caere and

Arretium, as well as a war against the Latins.

During the wars between Rome and Veii Tarquinii seems, if anything, to have supported Veii (Livy 5.16.4). Clusium on the other hand remained neutral (Livy 5.35.4), while Caere favoured the Romans. Any suggestion that the wars were part of a continuing racial conflict between Latins and Etruscans (cf. above, pp. 224 ff.) can therefore be ruled out.

This conclusion is confirmed by the fact that the most consistent and loyal supporters of Veii were the Capenates and Faliscans. These peoples, who lived in the region to the north of Veii between the Tiber and the Lakes of Vico and Bracciano, spoke a dialect of Latin and were ethnically distinct from the Etruscans. But both politically and geographically Capena and Falerii belonged to the catchment area of Veii, and they never failed to give her active support in the struggle against Rome. After the fall of Veii, the Romans quickly reduced them to submission (in 395 and 394 respectively).

These events all form part of a new phase in the history of Rome's external relations. In the last years of the fifth century there are clear signs of a more aggressive policy, not only against Veii and its satellites, but also in southern Latium. In a series of sparse notices, Livy records the capture of Bola (415 BC), Ferentinum (413), Carventum (410) and Artena (404). These successes were matched by occasional setbacks, but there can be little doubt about the overall success of the thrust, which had the effect of driving the Aequi out of the Algidus region and extending Roman control in the direction of the Sacco valley. In the coastal region Rome defeated the Volscians at Antium in 408, captured Anxur (Terracina) in 406 and colonised Circeii in 393. The details are confused, but the basic trend is unmistakable.

This change of stance coincides with a reform of the Roman army (the precise details of which remain obscure) and the introduction of pay (*stipendium*) for the troops (Livy 4.59–60; Diod. 14.16.5). At the same time the sources first begin to refer to the *tributum*, a property tax that was levied in order to meet the cost of military expenditure, and to the imposition of indemnities on defeated communities, starting with Falerii in 394 (Livy 5.27.15). These innovations are probably connected with the reform of the centuriate system, and the introduction of graded property classes in place of the old 'Servian' *classis* (see above, p. 187).[52]

Our knowledge of this period is still pitifully inadequate. But through the gloom we can dimly discern the outlines of a decaying archaic society in a state of radical and dynamic transition. This process was only momentarily affected by the Gallic disaster, which forms the subject of the next section.

6 THE GALLIC CATASTROPHE

In the summer of 390 BC (Varronian) a horde of Celts from the Po valley crossed the Apennines into northern Etruria. Advancing southwards down the Tiber valley they reached the outskirts of Rome, and defeated a hastily assembled Roman army at the river Allia. A few days later they entered the defenceless city and sacked it. A small garrison on the Capitol held out for a time, but was eventually forced to surrender and to hand over a large payment of gold. The Gauls then departed, leaving the Romans to pick up the pieces.

These basic elements make up one of the most dramatic episodes in Roman history. That it happened is certain. The sack was referred to by Greek writers of the fourth century BC,[53] and there is almost certainly a sound historical basis for the statement of Polybius (1.6.1) that it occurred in the same year as the Peace of Antalcidas and the siege of Rhegium by Dionysius I of Syracuse – that is, in 387 or 386 BC. It follows that the traditional, 'Varronian', chronology was three or four years adrift at this point.[54]

From a Roman point of view the event was straightforward: a humiliating disaster. But viewed from the other side it is extremely puzzling. Gallic raids into northern Etruria were probably common enough, but an attack on Rome is another matter. What was a band of Gauls doing so far south? Before tackling this question we need to examine the general background of the movement of Celtic peoples into northern Italy during the sixth and fifth centuries BC. The most useful source for this is Livy, himself a native of Cisalpina, who devoted two chapters to the subject (5.34–5). Livy describes a succession of migrations by different tribes, beginning with the Insubres, who moved into the region around Milan under the leadership of the legendary Bellovesus in around 600 BC. They were followed, in the course of the next two centuries, by the Cenomani, Libui, Salui, Boii and Lingones. The last group to arrive were the Senones, who by the start of the fourth century BC had occupied the strip of land along the Adriatic later known as the *ager Gallicus* (see Map 6).

It was these same Senones who crossed the Apennines and invaded the peninsula in 390. Their aim, according to Livy, was to find land for settlement. This view is corroborated by other sources which, although less informative, tell much the same story (e.g. Polyb. 2.17; Dion. Hal. 13.10–11; Plut., *Camill.* 15). All of them are agreed that it was the produce of its land, and especially of its vineyards, that tempted the Gauls to invade Italy. In the traditional story they were enticed by a certain Arruns of Clusium in Etruria, who wanted their assistance in his efforts to take revenge on his wife's lover. In any event Clusium was the Gauls' first destination.[55] Rome became involved when three Roman ambassadors fought alongside the men of Clusium in a battle against the Gauls and thus provoked their anger.

This account is not very satisfactory as it stands. Livy's description of the Celtic occupation of the Po valley may well be correct in general terms; critics who have argued that his 'long' chronology is incompatible with the versions of other sources are mistaken.[56] The other sources are much less precise than Livy, and do not offer anything that can be called an alternative chronology. The archaeological evidence is equivocal, and serves neither to support nor to undermine Livy's account. This is because it is not clear how Celts are to

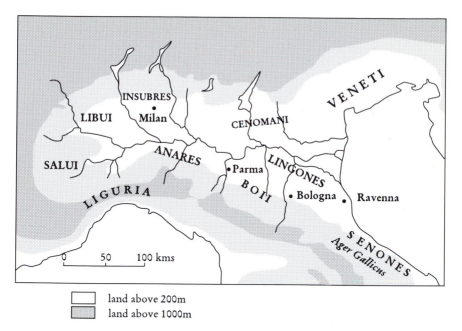

land above 200m
land above 1000m

Map 6 The Celtic peoples of northern Italy

be recognised archaeologically. For example, there are close resemblances between some burials of the Golasecca culture in Lombardy and those of the Hallstatt culture beyond the Alps. These same Golasecca sites during the fifth and fourth centuries contain increasing amounts of La Tène material (the characteristic culture of the Celts of Gaul), but at no stage is there any recognisable break in continuity. All one can say is that there is nothing in the archaeological evidence to contradict Livy's version.[57]

More explicit evidence is provided by the famous grave stelae of Bologna, showing combats between Etruscan horsemen and naked Celtic warriors, which confirm Livy's account of the insecure position of the Etruscan cities of the Po valley in the years after 400.[58] A much more questionable element of the traditional account is the notion that the Gauls were tempted into peninsular Italy by the hope of finding more productive land. The tale of Arruns of Clusium was certainly an old tradition (it was known both to Polybius and to Cato[59]), but its connection with the Gallic invasion of 390 BC is nonsensical.

Tradition is itself guilty of inconsistency when it presents the invading force as a warrior band – the followers of Brennus – rather than as a mass folk migration in search of land for settlement.[60] A migrating tribe would not have advanced as far as Rome, at least not in the first instance: on the other hand, the story makes more sense if Brennus and his men were warriors who

315

moved into the Italian peninsula in search of plunder and adventure. Stripped of its romantic details, the story of Arruns of Clusium would imply that the Gauls intervened in an internal political struggle in Clusium at the bidding of one of the warring factions;[61] in other words, they were a mercenary band, not a migrating tribe.

As it happens, this interpretation is confirmed by a report that, a few months after the sack of Rome, some Gauls enlisted as mercenaries in the service of Dionysius of Syracuse, and helped him in his wars against the Italiot Greeks (Justin 20.5.1–6). That the Syracusan tyrant should have employed Gauls as mercenaries is likely enough on general grounds; but the strongest argument for accepting this information as genuine is that it solves the puzzle of what the Gauls were doing in central Italy. Their route, via Clusium and Rome, becomes comprehensible if we assume that their ultimate destination was the Mezzogiorno, since the natural route to Campania and Magna Graecia was across the Apennines and down the valleys of the Chiana and Tiber. This reconstruction can also make sense of an otherwise mysterious notice in Diodorus, that on their way back *from the south* the Gauls were caught and defeated in the 'Trausian Plain' (wherever that was) by an Etruscan army from Caere (Diod. 14.117.7). Strabo confirms this story, and adds that it was the Caeretans who recovered the gold which the Romans had paid over to the Gauls (Strabo 5.2.3, p. 220 C).

It has been suggested that subsequent Gallic attacks were orchestrated by Dionysius of Syracuse, whose principal aim was to undermine the power of Rome's ally Caere.[62] In 384 the Caeretan port of Pyrgi, with its rich sanctuaries, was sacked by a Syracusan fleet (Diod. 15.14.3); the battle of the Trausian Plain can be explained on the assumption that Dionysius had organised a simultaneous attack on Caere from the interior by his Gallic mercenaries. This hypothetical reconstruction, though unprovable, is most attractive.

In any case close friendship between Rome and Caere is presupposed in the traditional story, which records that the Vestal Virgins and the sacred objects in their care were given refuge in Caere. They were escorted there by a plebeian named Lucius Albinius, who is probably a historical figure and certainly belongs to the very earliest level of the tradition. Aristotle is quoted (by Plutarch, *Camill.* 22.3) as saying that the city was saved by 'a certain Lucius', who is presumably to be identified with Albinius. Aristotle's statement is one of the reasons why scholars tend to reject the idea, much trumpeted in late annalistic sources but not mentioned in e.g. Polybius, that Camillus played a part in the story, and was indeed responsible for driving the Gauls away.

In the developed legend Camillus was in exile at Ardea when the Gauls descended (he had been wrongfully accused of mishandling the spoils of Veii), and was appointed dictator only after the fall of the city. He then proceeded to form a new army from the survivors of the Allia disaster, marched on Rome and defeated the Gauls in the Forum at the very moment when the gold was being paid out. It is obvious that this legend was fashioned in an attempt to compensate for the most humiliating fact of all: the payment of the ransom. It is said that when the gold was being weighed out the Romans complained about the weights; whereupon Brennus threw his sword into the scales with the words *'vae victis'* ('woe to the vanquished!') – an incident which has immortalised the Gallic chief in contrast to the lifeless figure of Camillus, the most artificially contrived of all Rome's heroes.

The part played by Camillus in the Gallic saga is demonstrably a late and artificial accretion. Even the story of his exile may be no more than a device to dissociate him from the disaster of the Allia. It is not simply that Aristotle and Polybius seemingly knew nothing of him. It is equally significant that other traditions existed concerning the recovery of the gold. For instance, the family of the Livii Drusi claimed that the gold was paid, but then recovered at a later date by their ancestor, who defeated a Gallic chief in single combat during a campaign in northern Italy (Sueton., *Tib.* 3.2). Another version, as we have seen, gave the credit to Caere. These alternative traditions would not have grown up if the Camillus story had been either true or part of the earliest tradition.

In general, it can be said that the Camillus legend serves to replace the historical role of Caere, and that he himself is a substitute for the person of L. Albinius, who is an integral part of an original tradition in which Caere held the centre of the stage. An older story, but one that is not for that reason necessarily more true, is that of M. Manlius Capitolinus, who supposedly saved the Capitol from capture during a night attack; it was he who was aroused by the cackling of the sacred geese of Juno, just as the Gauls were about to scale the citadel. Some experts believe that an alternative tradition existed, according to which the Gauls actually succeeded in storming the Capitol.[63] But this supposed alternative version is based on a misunderstanding of certain texts (such as Silius Italicus, *Punica* 1.625; 4.150; 6.555) which actually refer to the surrender of the Capitol and the payment of the ransom (which is in Livy!).

In conclusion we may ask how serious were the effects of the Gallic raid. The sources certainly do not attempt to minimise the extent of the disaster. They report widespread loss of life, total moral collapse and the physical destruction of the city. But there are good grounds for thinking that these reports are exaggerated. The Allia was certainly a rout, but casualties may have been light since we are given to understand that the Romans ran away at the first encounter. It has been reasonably suggested that the flight of the soldiers to Veii was not a spontaneous act arising in the panic of the moment, but part of a prearranged plan;[64] in other words the Romans, realising that their cause was hopeless and that they would be unable to save the city, evacuated it in advance. This would be consistent with the story of Albinius and the Vestals.

Moreover, the physical damage to the city does not seem to have been nearly as extensive as tradition would have us believe. The notion that the haphazard and unplanned character of the city resulted from the haste with which it was rebuilt after the sack (Livy 5.55) is naive and almost certainly mistaken. So too is the belief that the scarcity of documentary sources for early Roman history was due to their destruction at the hands of the Gauls. This is a false solution to a non-existent problem. The important point to make about records in relation to the sack is not that so many ancient documents, buildings, monuments and relics were destroyed, but rather that so many of them survived. The best explanation of all the evidence is that the Gauls were interested in movable booty, and that they left most of the monuments and buildings alone. They ransacked the place, and made off with whatever they could carry. The story that they had to be bought off with gold is consistent with this interpretation – and is most probably true.

This conclusion is in line with common sense and is moreover consistent with the fact that no archaeological trace of the Gallic disaster has yet been positively identified. The 'burnt layer' beneath the second paving of the Comitium is clear evidence of a destructive fire which was once thought to have been the work of Brennus, but it is now clear that it dates from the sixth century BC and is if anything to be connected with the upheavals of the late monarchic period.[65] But the strongest argument for a 'minimalist' interpretation of the Gallic disaster is the speed and vigour of the Roman recovery in the following years. This recovery will be dealt with next.

7 THE ROMAN RECOVERY

The effects of the Gallic raid have been much exaggerated in the ancient tradition and in some modern accounts. The sack was a severe psychological blow, but was only a momentary setback and did not radically affect the pattern of Roman military success and territorial expansion which became evident at the end of the fifth century. The successful Roman campaigns that are recorded in the years immediately following the sack can only be understood in this light. The alternative is to dismiss the entire annalistic record of the period down to the middle of the fourth century as a fabrication. This sceptical view was most forcefully argued by Beloch, and has subsequently been widely accepted.[66] The arguments offered in its support are quite baseless, however, and it depends more on a general feeling that the annalistic sources 'must be' unreliable than on any serious reasoning.

The principal argument is that Camillus' victories are not mentioned by Polybius or Diodorus, who are usually considered much more reliable than the annalistic tradition followed by Livy, Dionysius, Plutarch and Cassius Dio. But this is a false dichotomy. The two groups of sources do not, in fact, represent two parallel but conflicting traditions. Polybius does not give a systematic account of the events of the period, but merely alludes to them in passing in the course of an interesting digression on Rome's Gallic Wars (Poly. 2.18–35). As for Diodorus, his references to events of early Roman history are so scarce, and his selection is so idiosyncratic, that nothing can legitimately be inferred from his silence on any particular topic. Livy remains the only full-length narrative source for the fourth century, and it is foolish to reject information in Livy simply on the grounds that it is not corroborated by other sources.[67]

We need not spend time on the other arguments against Livy's account, which mostly beg the question by setting out to explain why the Roman victories of the 380s were invented, a conclusion that is assumed in advance. There is a perceptible anti-Roman strain in much modern writing on this subject;[68] some people seem to derive pleasure from being able to point out not only that the hated Romans were liars but also that many of their vaunted military victories did not take place. This anti-Roman position tells us more about the liberal attitudes and post-colonial guilt of its advocates than about the history of the fourth century BC.

Of course, if the events reported in the traditional account cannot be proved false, it does not follow that they are genuine. It is likely enough that the details have been elaborated, that the role of Camillus has been over-played, that some of the events have been mechanically duplicated, and that the scale of Roman successes has been exaggerated.[69] Nevertheless, there are sound reasons for accepting that Rome's aggressive and expansionist policy, which became evident in the 420s and was most clearly seen in the annexation of Veii, continued after the departure of the Gauls. Camillus, whose importance in Roman public life at this time is proved by the *Fasti*, probably had much to do with the planning and execution of this drive.

The events in question include campaigns in Etruria, principally directed against Tarquinii, a savage attack on the Aequi, who were decisively beaten in 388, and victories over the Volsci in 389 and 386. The Romans then consolidated these victories by founding Latin colonies at Sutrium and Nepet in south Etruria, probably in 383,[70] and at Satricum and Setia (385 and 383 respectively) on sites taken from the Volscians. Colonial foundations are among the most reliable items recorded in the annalistic sources, and there is no reason to doubt the accuracy of these reports. But the strongest argument for accepting the broad pattern of events as presented in Livy is that it accords more closely with what we know of Rome's circumstances in 390 than any of the modern alternatives.

This last point is paradoxical and needs some further explanation. The disastrous humiliation of the Gallic raid might seem at first sight to have weakened Rome's position and left her vulnerable to hostile attack; that indeed is how the sources visualise the situation, and what enabled them to present the subsequent recovery as little short of miraculous. The perception is false, however, and not only because it exaggerates the damage done by the Gauls to the fabric of the city. It is important not to forget that in the 390s

Rome was expanding rapidly, and had already achieved a level of power and dynamism that made it radically different from what it had been for most of the fifth century. The momentary setback of the Gallic raid did not seriously affect this new situation, the main features of which may be briefly outlined.

The most important factor contributing to the strength of Rome at this time was the annexation of Veii and its territory in 396 BC, which had increased the size of Rome's territory by some 562 km². If account is taken of other territorial gains made during the later fifth century (Fidenae, Labici), it is possible to calculate that the *ager Romanus* had increased by over 75 per cent since the beginning of the fifth century, from around 900 km² in 495 BC to *c.* 1582 km² in 396.[71] It is reasonable to assume a corresponding increase in manpower resources.

After the capture of Veii, and before the Gallic sack, the Romans had distributed some of the territory of Veii in small allotments to Roman citizens (Livy 5.30.8; Diod. 14.102.4). After the sack they hastened to confer Roman citizenship on the surviving native population, as well as on the inhabitants of the territory that had been seized from the Capenates and Faliscans in 395 and 394. Livy regards this grant of citizenship as a reward for a handful of pro-Roman quislings (6.4.4), and suggests that the bulk of the population had been sold into slavery (5.22.1). Although some historians accept Livy's version,[72] it seems in fact to reflect the attitudes and practices of a later age, when Roman citizenship was highly prized, and mass enslavements were a regular feature of Roman policy. It is much more likely, given the absence at this period of a market for such a vast number of slaves, that only a minority of the defeated Veientines were sold, and that the enfranchisement of the rest in 389 was a concession designed to prevent them from rebelling in the aftermath of the sack. If so, it worked. The resettlement of the *ager Veientanus* was probably complete by 387 BC, when four new local tribes were created: the Stellatina, Tromentina, Sabatina and Arniensis (Livy 6.5.8).

The Romans' control of the region was symbolised by the fact that a few years later they began to construct a new city wall of ashlar masonry: the stone came from the Grotta Oscura quarries in the newly won territory of Veii. Two further points can be made about the wall in the present context. First, it was probably built in recognition of the inadequacy of the earlier defences, which the Gauls had so fatally exposed (cf. above, p. 200). Second it is worth reflecting on the immense scale of the undertaking, which only a powerful and well-organised city-state could have contemplated. When finished, the wall extended for over 11 kilometres and enclosed an area of *c.* 426 hectares. In the years after the Gallic raid Rome was without a doubt the largest urban settlement in central Italy.[73]

Another circumstance that worked to the Romans' advantage was their alliance with Caere. Caere had supported Rome against Veii and had provided a refuge for the Vestal Virgins at the time of the Gallic attack. This was the product of a long-standing entente that continued after the sack. But the precise juridical terms of the relationship are uncertain and have been the object of a long and rather arid debate, which need not detain us long.

Some sources suggest, and some modern historians accept, that the people of Caere were incorporated in the Roman state at this time with a restricted form of citizenship known as *civitas sine suffragio* ('citizenship without suffrage'), and that Caere was the first Italian city to be so incorporated.[74] The case rests on antiquarian and legalistic arguments that make sense only in abstract terms; a moment's reflection is enough to show that it is historically impossible. It is unthinkable that Caere, a powerful independent city, would have allowed itself to be annexed, or that the Romans, who owed a debt of gratitude to the city that helped them against the Gauls, would or could have responded by politically annihilating it.

What in fact happened was that the two cities agreed to extend some of the rights of citizenship to each other's citizens by a reciprocal treaty. The result was that when in Rome a citizen of Caere could enjoy all the private rights and privileges of Roman citizenship but would be free from its burdens and obligations. The same would apply to Romans at Caere. This is no doubt what Livy means when he defines the relationship between Rome and Caere as 'public hospitality' (*hospitium publicum*: Livy 5.50.3). It is sometimes said that in this passage Livy misconstrued the institution of citizenship without suffrage.[75] But the truth is evidently the other way round: Livy's version is the correct one, and it is the alternative tradition, and its modern supporters, that are guilty of misunderstanding by assuming that the arrangement implied the incorporation of Caere in the Roman state. Here, as so often, the ingenuous Livy turns out to have a better grasp of the truth than the sophisticated modern experts who affect to know better.

This interpretation of the evidence is borne out by the treaty Rome made with another city to which she was indebted, namely Massilia, which is said to have helped pay the ransom to the Gauls. Justin tells us that in 389 BC Rome made a formal alliance with Massilia, and adds the specific information that Massiliot visitors to Rome were to enjoy certain privileges (Justin 43.5.10). This clause appears to recall the institution of *hospitium publicum*, which was probably a common feature of international treaties at this period, and not a native Roman institution at all.[76]

To return to our main theme, we may conclude that after the Gallic attack Caere cemented its alliance with Rome. Its incorporation in the Roman state occurred much later, probably in 273 BC.[77] In 389 the continuing support of Caere was a major factor in Rome's rapid recovery, and her capacity to carry on an expansionist policy. The entente with Caere can probably also help to explain some scattered allusions in the sources to Roman activity overseas, in particular the foundation of a colony on Sardinia in 386 BC (Diod. 15.27.4). The foundation of a fortified settlement at Ostia is now placed by archaeologists in the period between 380 and 350 BC; and a Roman expedition to Corsica, mentioned in a passage of the Greek philosopher Theophrastus (*c.*

370–288 BC), should perhaps also be dated to this period.[78]

Taken together, the evidence clearly shows that Rome was able to shake off the effects of the sack with comparative ease and to continue with an aggressive and expansionist policy. The results confirm the general reliability of the record. At the end of the 360s Rome was in a position of strength from which she was able to begin the drive leading to the conquest of Italy. The period from *c.* 376 to 363 was one of comparative peace; it follows, therefore, that the position of strength was the result of a successful policy of conquest and consolidation that was enacted between 389 and 377. Livy's account of the triumph of Roman arms during this period must therefore be historical, at least in its main outlines.

8 THE BEGINNINGS OF ROMAN EXPANSION

One of the most puzzling questions about this period concerns the state of Rome's relations with the Latins and Hernici. The orthodox modern view is that the allies rebelled after the Gallic raid, and that it took the Romans thirty years to regain their former hegemony. The authority usually cited in support of this assertion is Polybius, but he plainly says nothing of the kind.[79] It is nevertheless true that the treaties with the Latins and the Hernici were not functioning properly at this time. Although Livy speaks of secession (*defectio*), there was no armed uprising by the Latins and Hernici; rather, the arrangements of the *foedus Cassianum* simply lapsed, and the military partnership ceased to function. The probable reason was that it no longer suited the Romans to enforce the treaty, most obviously because it limited their freedom of action, and above all inhibited their chances of territorial expansion to the south.

Many of the Latin communities seem to have remained loyal to Rome. This is attested in the case of Tusculum and Lanuvium, and is probably true of other cities as well, such as Aricia, Lavinium and Ardea,[80] but others were overtly hostile, and joined the Volscians in armed resistance to Rome. The result was a reversal of what had happened in the fifth century, when the Latins had joined forces with Rome in response to Volscian attacks; now they were uniting with the Volscians against the threat of Roman encroachment.

The rebels included the Latin colonists of Velitrae and Circeii, whose action can be explained partly on the assumption that many of them were the original Volscian inhabitants, and partly by the fact that they were especially threatened by the Romans' plan to overrun the Pomptine Plain. It is not at all surprising that the nearest of the old Latin communities, Lanuvium, is also recorded as joining the Volscians in 383 BC, although it had hitherto been loyal (Livy 6.21.2).

The most important of the Latin cities that fought against Rome at this time were Tibur and Praeneste. These cities had not belonged to the Latin League in the fifth century (see above, p. 306), and only began to play a part in the affairs of the region after the withdrawal of the Aequi. Hostilities between Rome and Tibur did not begin until 361 BC, but already in 382 the Praenestines are recorded as attacking Rome's allies and joining the Volscians. The Roman success against Praeneste in 380 BC is of particular interest because it was commemorated by a triumphal monument and an inscription that survived to the late Republic. Livy's account is as follows:

> Titus Quinctius then returned in triumph to Rome. He had won one victory in pitched battle, taken nine towns by assault and accepted the surrender of Praeneste, and brought with him a statue of Jupiter Imperator which he had carried off from Praeneste. This he dedicated on the Capitol between the shrines of Jupiter and Minerva, with a plaque fixed below it to commemorate his exploits bearing an inscription to this effect: 'Jupiter and all the gods granted that the dictator Titus Quinctius should capture nine towns.'[81]

To the south there was fierce fighting in the Pomptine district, with Satricum and Velitrae at the centre of the action. Satricum was repeatedly taken and retaken in the period between 386 and 346 BC (Livy 6.8; 6.16.5; 6.22; 6.32; 7.27); Velitrae was the object of frequent Roman assaults, and its capture is reported in 380 (Livy 6.29.6) and again in 367 after a long siege (Livy 6.36.1–6; 6.42.4; Plutarch, *Camill.* 42.1).

The expansionist nature of Roman intentions at this time is most clearly revealed by their seizure of Tusculum in 381. In a sense this was a logical step, since Tusculum by this date was almost completely surrounded by Roman territory. The sources suggest that the Tusculans had become disaffected, and had actually joined the Volscians (Livy 6.25.1); given the menacing character of Rome's recent actions, that would not be altogether surprising. Camillus was dispatched with an army against Tusculum, which surrendered without a blow. The free inhabitants were forthwith admitted to Roman citizenship. They nevertheless kept their corporate identity and a degree of internal autonomy, but were subject to all the duties and obligations of Roman citizens (above all the payment of *tributum* and service in the legions). Tusculum thus became the first Roman *municipium* (Cic., *Planc.* 19), a word whose original significance is uncertain, but which in later times was the standard term for any community incorporated into the Roman state as a self-governing body of Roman citizens.[82]

The later Roman tradition was pleased to regard this act as one of great generosity (Livy 6.25.6; Dion. Hal. 14.6), but this view is anachronistic and reflects the conditions of later times, when municipal status was highly prized by cities within the Roman Empire. The fact that the Romans occupied Tusculum and made its inhabitants into Romans should not necessarily be seen as a sign of Roman benevolence. Read, say, 'Germans' for 'Romans', and 'France' for 'Tusculum', and it at once becomes clear what this action really meant. We need not be surprised that Tusculum joined the insurgents at the time of the great Latin revolt (340 BC), nor should we cast doubt on reported attempts by the other Latins to detach Tusculum from Rome (e.g. Livy 6.36.1–6: 370 BC).

As has been noted, the period from 376 to 363 BC is presented as one of comparative peace, interrupted only by the siege of Velitrae (370–367 BC) and a Gallic raid in 367 which may be apocryphal.[83] But the resumption of warfare in 362 BC opened a new phase in the history of Rome's external relations. A decade of vigorous and successful campaigning brought an unprecedented series of victories (eight triumphs and one ovation are recorded in the period from 361 to 354) and placed Roman power on a new footing.

The new offensive began with a war against the Hernici (362), which ended with the renewal, in 358, of the alliance which had been in abeyance since the Gallic sack. The treaty with the Latins was also revived in 358 (Livy 7.12.7). The new agreements were probably made on terms more favourable to the Romans than in the original treaties; in any case the Latins had to accept the Roman occupation of the *ager Pomptinus*, and the Hernici were forced to cede part of their territory in the Trerus valley for occupation by Roman settlers. These annexations were formally carried out in 358 BC, when the two districts were formed into new Roman tribes, respectively the Pomptina and the Publilia (Livy 7.5.11).

The Romans renewed their alliances with the Latins and Hernici at a time when Latium was once again being threatened by Gallic invasions – a fact that is unlikely to be a coincidence. Indeed this very point is made explicitly by Livy (7.12.7–8) and implicitly by Polybius (2.18.5), both of whom refer to the renewal of the Latin treaty in the context of an attack by the Gauls, one of several that Livy records during these years.[84]

At the same time the Romans became involved in a war against Tibur (361–354 BC), in which the Tiburtines joined the Gauls in their attacks on Rome. Evidently Tibur was excluded from the new agreement Rome had made with the Latin League in 358 BC. There is nothing particularly surprising about this, since as far as we can see Tibur had not been a member of the Latin League since the sixth century. The same goes for Praeneste, which was also hostile to Rome in the 350s. In 354 both Tibur and Praeneste were compelled to surrender and to make separate agreements with Rome (Livy 7.19.1; Diod. 16.45.8).

In 358 BC the Romans also found themselves at war with the Etruscans of Tarquinii, who were joined in 357 by Falerii and by Caere in 353. In 356 Livy records a victory by the dictator C. Marcius Rutilus over the entire Etruscan nation (7.17.6–9), but this is probably an annalist's misunderstanding of a notice in which the Tarquinienses and their allies were referred to by the general name of Etruscans. The outcome of the war was a truce of 100 years with Caere (353 BC) and truces of forty years each with Tarquinii and Falerii (351).[85]

In 350 and 349 the Gauls once again attacked Latium. In 349 the Latin

League refused to send troops to the army, and a Greek fleet ravaged the coast. But in spite of these difficulties the Romans managed to defeat the Gauls (in a battle in which M. Valerius Corvus fought a celebrated duel with a Gallic champion – Livy 7.26), and the Greek fleet eventually withdrew. No further Gallic attacks are recorded for several decades, and according to Polybius (2.18.9) in 331 the Romans made peace with the Gauls, who did not return for another thirty years.

The significance of the Gallic Wars of the fourth century BC is difficult to assess. It is not clear whether we should visualise the periodic attacks as large-scale invasions from beyond the Apennines, which is how they are presented by Polybius, or as petty raids by marauding bands operating from within the peninsula (which is the model that some historians have drawn from Livy).[86] On this view they represented little more than a minor irritation to Rome, once she had learned how to deal with them. Either way the attacks – even the great invasion of 390 BC – had little long-term effect on wider developments and did not upset the general pattern of inter-state relationships in central Italy.

That is not to say, however, that the inhabitants of peninsular Italy were able to view the Gauls with equanimity. The raids were terrifying and unpredictable, and aroused deep and irrational fears. In later times the mere threat of a '*tumultus Gallicus*' called for emergency troop levies and induced a state of extreme panic. On at least three later occasions, in 228, 216 and 114 BC, the threat of Celtic invasions of Italy caused the Romans to carry out human sacrifices by burying alive in the Forum Boarium a pair of Gauls and a pair of Greeks. It has been suggested that this barbaric ritual was a magical performance designed to avert a danger that threatened to destroy the city. If so it probably dates from the first half of the fourth century, when the main threat to Rome came from the Gauls and the Sicilian Greeks.[87]

There can be no doubt, however, about the main direction of events at this time. The Romans' military power was growing inexorably, their foreign policy was becoming more ambitious, and the scope and scale of their warlike operations were continually increasing. There is no good reason to deny the historicity of the Roman raid against Privernum in 357 (Livy 7.16.3-6), the attack on the Aurunci in 345 (Livy 7.28.1-3) or the capture of Sora in the same year (Livy 7.28.6). These ventures make sense in relation to the events that were to follow; and the widening horizons of Rome are confirmed by two cardinal pieces of evidence – the treaty between Rome and the Samnites in 354 BC and that between Rome and Carthage in 348.

About the former we have no detailed information,[88] but the latter is almost certainly to be identified with the second of the three Carthaginian treaties listed by Polybius (3.24). The text given by Polybius is vague about the precise extent of Roman power, but it recognises Roman overlordship of Latium and the fact that there were other peoples outside Latium with whom Rome had formal relations. It also envisages, as we have seen (above, p. 212), the possibility of Roman colonisation overseas, which is consistent with the evidence for Roman activity in Corsica and Sardinia in the first half of the fourth century, and confirms that Roman power was already beginning to be felt beyond the confines of Italy.

13

THE EMANCIPATION OF
THE *PLEBS*

1 ECONOMIC AND SOCIAL PROBLEMS: PUBLIC LAND

The years of recovery and gradual expansion after the Gallic sack also witnessed far reaching social and political changes. Although the Gallic raid was only a temporary setback in the growth of Roman power in central Italy, it must nevertheless have aggravated the difficulties of the poor and widened social divisions. The period is represented as one of political tension and strife, leading to an attempted *coup d'état* in 384 and culminating in a period of anarchy in the years around 370. These events are not well documented, however, and the details are uncertain; but the sources are agreed that the main underlying issues were land, debt and the political rights of the plebeians. Although the Roman historians and antiquarians have much to say on these matters, it is clear that they did not understand them very well. In a way this is not surprising, since many of the institutions of the archaic period had become obsolete by the beginning of the third century BC, and its true character had long been forgotten by the time Fabius Pictor began to write.

Nevertheless, some of the major events and issues of the struggle were recorded in documentary sources and preserved in oral memory down to the time of the first Roman historians. These historians did their best to make sense of the traditional facts, and to construct a coherent narrative that would explain the motives and aspirations of those who took part in the events. In doing so they distorted the historical reality; in particular, they un-consciously modernised the story by making anachronistic assumptions about the economic and social organisation of Rome in the fifth and fourth centuries BC. They modelled their accounts of political struggles on the experience of more recent times, adopting the political vocabulary of the late Republic and assimilating the early leaders of the *plebs* to the Gracchi and Saturninus.[1]

This process of assimilation was not completely arbitrary. The issues that dominated the crisis of the early fourth century were not dissimilar to those of the second and first centuries BC. This point deserves emphasis. It is sometimes assumed that the traditional stories of agitation about *ager publicus* and debt-bondage were fabrications modelled on the events of the age of the Gracchi and later. But such scepticism is unwarranted. Land and debt were constant issues in political struggles in the Graeco-Roman world. Moreover, the conflicts of the fourth century BC as recorded in our sources have certain distinctive features which clearly puzzled later historians – which suggests that the record was not the product of wholesale fabrication.

Everything suggests that the sources were right to stress the issues of land and debt in their accounts of the social conflicts of the fourth century. However obscure the details, it seems certain that the plebeians' efforts were essentially a struggle against oppression by a large class of poor peasants who were in subjection to the rich. The domination of the rich rested on their control of large landed estates; while the small size of the majority of peasant holdings was the cause of the indebtedness of the poor and of the state of bondage to which they were reduced.[2]

It is important to stress that the power of the ruling class and the oppression of the *plebs* derived from the peculiar system of tenure that characterised the *ager publicus*. It is this that gives Roman agrarian history its distinctive character. Niebuhr's epoch-making work at the beginning of the nineteenth century established once and for all that movements for agrarian reform during the Roman Republic were not aimed at redistribution of land in private ownership, but were concerned solely with the manner of disposal and use of the *ager publicus*. This fundamental thesis, which is now universally accepted, is as valid for the period of the early Republic as it is for the age of the Gracchi.[3] The discontent of the plebeians was caused by the fact that the public land, on which they depended for survival, was controlled and permanently occupied by the wealthiest families and their clients.

In their struggle for reform the *plebs* adopted a two-pronged approach. First, they pressed for newly conquered land to be distributed in allotments which would become the private property of the individual recipients (*assignatio viritana*), rather than remaining the property of the state and thus a target for encroachment by wealthy possessors. Second, they demanded a statutory limit on the amount of *ager publicus* that any one *paterfamilias* could occupy, and on the numbers of animals he could graze on it. This was one of the principal ingredients of the Licinio-Sextian legislation, which, in spite of fierce opposition, became law in 367 BC. The aim of the law was to allow poor plebeians some access to the *ager publicus*. There is no evidence that before 367 plebeians had been legally denied the right to occupy *ager publicus*, as is sometimes asserted, but it is likely enough that that is what happened in practice.[4]

It is important to note that the Lex Licinia merely imposed fines on those who held public land in excess of the prescribed limit. It did not set up any machinery for reclaiming the excess in the name of the state, nor did it contain any provision for the assignation of public land to the *plebs*. It was concerned solely with rights of *possessio*, and in this respect it differed from the agrarian law of Tiberius Gracchus, for which it provided only a partial model. This crucial distinction is a strong argument in favour of the authenticity of the Lex Licinia, and clearly undermines the view that it was a fictitious anticipation of the legislation of the Gracchi.[5]

It is generally agreed that the Lex Licinia was a genuine early example, if not in fact the earliest example, of a law to limit holdings of public land (*lex de modo agrorum*). The details of the prescribed limits, however, are a matter of controversy. Livy and other sources maintain that a maximum of 500 *iugera* was laid down for individual holdings; but in the course of a precise digression on the subject Appian adds two further clauses – that the number of animals that could be put to pasture on public land should not exceed 100 cattle or 500 smaller animals (i.e. sheep or pigs),[6] and second that a certain number of the workers should be free men (Appian, *B.C.* 1.8.33). These details are said by some historians to be anachronistic, more appropriate to the age of the great slave-run estates of the second century BC than to the simple peasant society of the fourth century. That may be so; in any event it is probable that the two additional clauses mentioned by Appian were later modifications of the original Lex Licinia. That does not mean, however, that we should reject the statement of other sources, including authoritative writers like Varro (*RR* 1.2.9), that the Lex Licinia imposed a limit of 500 *iugera*.

The territory of Rome must have embraced large areas of *ager publicus* already at the beginning of the fourth century. We cannot know how much of the territory of Veii was assigned to freeholders, how much was left in the possession of the original inhabitants, and how much was left as *ager publicus*, but on any reasonable estimate the latter category must have been a substantial proportion of the total; modern scholars have suggested as much as half or two-thirds – that is, *c.* 112,000 or *c.* 150,000 *iugera*.[7] If we remember that this amount would have been an addition to the *ager publicus* that already existed in the original Roman territory, then it becomes evident that some individual holdings might well have exceeded 500 *iugera*, or at least threatened to do so. It is probable that the 500 *iugera* limit, so far from being a second-century figure applied anachronistically to the early fourth century, was on the contrary a fourth-century figure that had become little more than an archaic survival by the second, when some landowners possessed estates embracing thousands of *iugera* of *ager publicus*. That would explain the hysterical reaction of the Roman ruling class when Ti. Gracchus proposed to enforce the ancient limit. A moment's reflection is sufficient to show that, unless some holdings of *ager publicus* in 133 BC were vastly in excess of the ancient limit, Gracchus' land commission would not have been able to obtain much land for distribution to the poor.

2 ECONOMIC AND SOCIAL PROBLEMS: THE DEBT CRISIS

We may now turn to the problem of debt, which was one of the main issues in the conflict over the Licinio-Sextian Laws and had always been a major grievance of the *plebs*. Debt was a direct consequence of poverty and land hunger, and itself gave rise to the condition of servitude to which many of the plebeians were reduced. As we have seen (pp. 266ff., 282ff.) the most important function of debt-bondage (*nexum*) was to provide dependent labour for exploitation by large landowners. This conclusion becomes inescapable if we accept the standard view that there was no alternative source of available labour.

Although chattel slavery existed in early Rome (see above, p. 280), and probably some form of hired wage labour as well, these categories cannot have accounted for more than a small part of the total labour force. For the most part wealthy landowners must have relied upon the labour of their dependants. Some of these may have been clients who were granted privileged tenancies on lands controlled by their patrons; but many of them will have been debt bondsmen. If we accept this, together with the tradition that much of the power of the wealthy came from their occupation of the *ager publicus*, we can see that the issues of *ager publicus* and *nexum* are directly related. As the control of the public land became concentrated in the hands of a small class of wealthy aristocrats, more and more peasants were reduced to servitude. They were denied the possibility of working the *ager publicus* for their own benefit, and instead worked it for their rich patrons under constraint. In this way the majority of the peasants were prevented from rising above the level of subsistence, and from obtaining a share of the surplus, which was entirely expropriated by the wealthy and their clients.

This state of affairs forms the background to the crisis of the early fourth century. Livy refers frequently to the problem of debt at this period, and affirms that it was greatly aggravated by the Gallic sack. There may be some justification for this opinion. Although the economic effects of the sack were negligible in the long term, the presence of a hostile barbarian army living off the land for several months would have been catastrophic for those living on the margins of subsistence. The poorest peasants would have lost everything and been faced with starvation. In such circumstances a growing incidence of debt and debt-bondage was inevitable.

The sources indicate that the problem was widespread and affected large numbers of citizens. According to Livy the tribunes of 380 BC complained that one class of citizens had been ruined by the other (*demersam partem a parte civitatis*: Livy 6.27.6). Shortly before this the debt crisis had given rise to the celebrated affair of M. Manlius Capitolinus, who was condemned and executed in 384 for allegedly aiming at tyranny. The surviving accounts of this obscure event are rhetorical and untrustworthy. They make much of the fact that Manlius, who had saved the Republic when he prevented the Gauls from storming the Capitol, was later condemned for attempting to subvert it. There was further irony in the manner of his death: he was hurled from the Tarpeian rock (an outcrop of the Capitol), the very precipice from which he had once thrown the Gallic intruders. This romance was spun out of a very few authentic facts. But we can be sure that some kind of upheaval did take place, and that Manlius was a historical person.[8] This is borne out by certain incidental details, for example the story that after his death the Manlii decreed that in future no member of the clan should ever again be called Marcus (a rule that was rigidly observed, so far as we know). But in the present context the important fact about the event is that it arose out of the debt crisis. Manlius obtained the mass support of the *plebs* by taking up their cause (he was the first patrician to do so, according to Livy, 6.11.7) and paying their debts out of his personal fortune.

The suppression of Manlius did nothing to relieve the crisis.[9] Unrest over debt is recorded in 380 and again in 378, when Livy reports the construction of the new city wall (Figure 25), and adds that taxes levied to pay for it caused an increase of indebtedness among the *plebs*. It is difficult to know how much truth there might be in this statement. The wall was certainly an immense undertaking, and must have imposed heavy demands on the available workforce. It was over 11 kilometres long, over 10 metres high and 4 metres thick at the base. The huge blocks of tuff with which it was built (measuring on average *c.* 1.5 m x 0.5 m x 0.6 m) came from the Grotta Oscura quarries near Veii, which was 15 kilometres from Rome (see above, p. 320). As far as I know, the economics of the wall's construction have never been seriously studied.[10] But even on the roughest estimate it can be conjectured that the labour expended on the tasks of quarrying, transporting and laying the hundreds of thousands of blocks must have amounted to at least 5 million man-hours.[11]

The problem is that we do not know who supplied the labour or how it was organised. Livy speaks of taxes and censorial contracts, but in this he may have been guilty of anachronism. It is perhaps more probable that the government distrained directly on the labour services of Roman citizens as a form of tax or an extension of military service, and only contracted with specialised craftsmen and engineers, some of whom perhaps came from abroad.[12] On the other hand, if Livy is correct, and the whole of the work was farmed out to contractors (the fact that the wall was built in distinct and clearly identifiable sections may give some support to this idea), we still do not know how the contractors obtained the necessary labour. If slaves and debt bondsmen were used, the wealthy contractors would themselves have been the sole beneficiaries of a major public investment of funds raised from taxes, booty and indemnities. The plebeians cannot have gained anything from the work unless there was some redistribution of resources through the

Figure 25 Rome: the 'Servian' Wall.

payment of wages. If this did not happen, Livy must be right that the building of the wall increased the burdens of the poor.

The debt issue featured prominently in the struggle over the Licinio-Sextian Laws of 367 BC. The legislation apparently laid down that on all outstanding debts the interest paid should be deducted from the capital sum and the remainder paid off in three annual instalments (Livy 6.35.4). This measure, if authentic, is important as the first ever enactment to take positive steps to relieve debt. The following decades saw further measures restricting interest rates and easing the terms of repayment (e.g. in 357 and 347). In 344 Livy records that severe penalties were inflicted on usurers (7.28.9); two years later a Lex Genucia prohibited interest charges altogether, a law that remained in being for centuries, but was only rarely enforced (cf. Appian, *B.C.* 1.54). Like all laws regulating loans and restricting usury, it was no doubt easy to circumvent by 'under-the-counter' deals which the desperate would have had no alternative but to accept. Under 352 Livy records a law which apparently introduced a system of state mortgages and bankruptcy proceedings under the supervision of a commission of five men, two patricians and three plebeians.

Some of the details of these various reports may seem anachronistic or improbable, but there is no reason in general to doubt that debt relief was the object of much legislation in this period. There may also have been laws to alleviate the conditions and terms of debt-bondage, but if so they too would have been difficult to enforce. *Nexum* certainly continued to exist as an institution (see e.g. Livy 7.19.5 – 354 BC) but in 326 BC it was formally abolished by a Lex Poetelia.[13]

The Lex Poetelia marks the end of a long process of social change. By that time the land hunger of the *plebs* had been largely satisfied by the conquest and settlement of new territories. The improved economic conditions that resulted from successful warfare, land assignation and colonisation would have meant that the plebeians were gradually freed from the necessity of entering into bondage. It is probable that by the start of the Second Samnite War (327–304 BC) the institution of *nexum* had already become a relic of a bygone age. Its disappearance did not, however, put an end to indebtedness, which persisted as a major social evil to the end of the Republic. The Lex Poetelia merely abolished the *nexum* as an institutionalised form of labour contract; from now on only defaulting debtors were placed in bondage, following a judgement in court.[14]

The decline and eventual abolition of debt-bondage at the end of the fourth century presupposes the development of an alternative supply of labour to work the large estates of the rich. This need was met by slaves. The growing importance of slavery in fourth-century Rome is indicated by a tax on manumissions which was introduced in 357 BC (Livy 7.16.7). The tax implies that manumissions were frequent, which in turn presupposes a large number of slaves. By the end of the century freedmen were so numerous and so influential that their status became a major political issue (see below, p. 374). From the beginning of the Samnite Wars our sources regularly record mass enslavements of prisoners of war, which must imply that the Roman economy was by that time heavily dependent on slave labour.

The idea that Rome did not become a slave society until after the Hannibalic War is unacceptable;[15] in fact the process was already well advanced by the end of the fourth century, together with the closely related phenomenon of imperialism. War and conquest both created and satisfied the demand for slaves. Finally, we should note that the emancipation of the citizen peasantry and the increasing use of slave labour on the land made it possible for the Roman state to commit a large proportion of the adult male population to prolonged military service, and thus to pursue a course of imperialism and conquest.

3 THE LICINIO-SEXTIAN ROGATIONS

The transformation of the social and economic structures of the Roman Republic in the fourth century coincided with a reform of the constitution and the emergence of a new governing class. These changes resulted from the power struggle that accompanied the legislation of 367 BC, and it is to this struggle that we must now turn.

In general we are better informed about the history of Roman political institutions than about other matters. There are two reasons for this. First, politics was a matter of direct concern to the ruling class, to which the Roman historians and antiquarians themselves belonged, and upon which they concentrated their attention. Second, the results of political reforms can be monitored through the evidence of the *Fasti* and other reliable indicators. Even so, the background remains obscure, and although we can document the changes we are not always able to explain them satisfactorily. Once again the literary sources do not seem to have been able to account adequately for the facts at their disposal, and we cannot trust their interpretations of them. This is particularly true of Livy's narrative of the Licinio-Sextian 'Rogations'.[16]

Livy tells us that in 376 BC two tribunes, C. Licinius Stolo and L. Sextius Lateranus, brought three proposals (*rogationes*) before the *plebs*. Two of them, concerning land and debt, have already been mentioned; the third dealt with the admission of plebeians to the consulship. The proposals aroused opposition, and a stalemate resulted; Licinius and Sextius persisted with their demands in spite of patrician intransigence and the obstruction of some of their own colleagues. The conflict lasted for ten years (376–367 BC), during which the two reformers were continually re-elected. They countered the veto of their colleagues by themselves blocking the election of magistrates; for a period of five years (375–371 BC) the state was without magistrates and no public business could take place (Diodorus (15.75) shortens the anarchy to one year). The crisis ended in 367, when the rogations were finally enacted by the *plebs* and accepted by the patricians; the compromise was overseen by the aged Camillus, who emerged once again as the saviour of the state (Livy 6.35–42).

Very little of this narrative can be accepted as it stands. As far as political institutions are concerned, however, the results of the episode are reasonably certain. The consulship was restored as the chief annual magistracy and made accessible to plebeians. A new magistracy, the praetorship, was created; its principal functions were judicial, although the praetor held *imperium* and could be appointed to military commands if necessary. At first the praetorship was held only by patricians, but in 337 BC a plebeian was elected. Another innovation was the appointment of two 'curule' aediles on the model of the existing plebeian aediles. Though confined to patricians at first, the curule aedileship was soon made accessible to plebeians, who held it in alternate years. Finally the Board of Two in charge of sacred performances (*duumviri sacris faciundis*) was enlarged to a Board of Ten (*decemviri sacris faciundis*), comprising five patricians and five plebeians.

The most important of these measures was undoubtedly that concerning the consulship. Its precise significance is unclear, however, and the background is extremely puzzling. This is largely because of the obscurity that surrounds the institution of 'military tribunes with consular power' (*tribuni militum consulari potestate*), which had replaced the consulship in the late fifth century.[17] These officials were traditionally instituted in 445 BC, when it was decided that in certain years the consulship should be suspended and that 'consular tribunes' (as we may call them for convenience) should hold office instead. The difference between the two magistracies was that the consular tribunes numbered three or more, to a normal maximum of six,[18] in one year, and that the consular tribunate, unlike the consulship, was open to plebeians. That at least is what Livy and Dionysius tell us (Livy 4.6.8; Dion. Hal. 11.56.3). But their statements are contradicted by their own evidence.

The most notable discrepancy is the fact that, among the consular tribunes who held office in the period down to 400 BC, plebeians are conspicuous by their absence. The *Fasti*, of which Livy himself provides the most reliable version, indicate that the patricians did not have a monopoly of the consulship in the first half of the fifth century (see above, p. 252ff.); but from 444 to 401, that is, from the moment the consular tribunate was introduced, all senior magistrates, whether consuls or consular tribunes, were patricians![19]

Even more peculiar is the narrative Livy offers in 4.6–7. He tells us that the decision to have consular tribunes was taken in 445 as a concession to the *plebs*, who had been agitating for admission to the consulate. But when elections were held, the people rejected all the plebeian candidates, and elected three patricians. Livy comments on the moderation of the people, who were content with the principle that plebeians could stand, but were not biased in their favour when casting their votes (4.6.11–12). That is not as silly as it sounds, if we exclude Livy's high-minded explanation of the motive; we should remember that the *comitia centuriata* was heavily weighted in favour of the well-to-do, and that in the absence of secret ballot citizens were not free to vote as they might wish. Livy may be right to suggest that it was one thing for plebeians to be allowed to stand, and quite another for them to secure election.[20]

But that is not the end of the puzzle. Although Livy says that the three consular tribunes elected in 445 were patricians, one of them, L. Atilius, has a plebeian name. More curious still, he tells us that after three months in office (in 444) they were forced to resign because of a technical flaw in the election process, and were replaced by suffect consuls. His account makes clear, however, that his sources disagreed about the magistrates for this year (4.7.10–12). In the following years consuls held office, until 438 when there were three consular tribunes. An irregular pattern of alternation between consuls and consular tribunes then continued until the Licinio-Sextian Law. This pattern is best illustrated by a table.

The table reveals some interesting patterns. First, it shows that the alternation of consuls and consular tribunes was not random, but ran in blocks. Second, it indicates that consular tribunates were originally less common than consulships, but became more frequent in the 420s; after 420, apart from a run of five years from 413 to 409 and a two-year interlude in 393–392, consular tribunes replaced consuls altogether. Third, the number of consular tribunes in each annual college gradually increased from three to

Table 8 Consular tribunes, 444–367 BC

Date[a]	No.	Pl.	Date	No.	Pl.	Date	No.	Pl.
444[b]	3	1	418	3		392	cos.	
443	cos.		417	4		391	6	
442	cos.		416	4		390	6	
441	cos.		415	4		389	6	
440	cos.		414	4		388	6	1
439	cos.		413	cos.		387	6	
438	3		412	cos.		386	6	
437	cos.		411	cos.		385	6	
436	cos.		410	cos.		384	6	
435	cos.		409	cos.		383	6	1
434[c]	3		408	3		382	6	
433	3		407	4		381	6	
432	3		406	4		380	9	
431	cos.		405	6		379[d]	6	3
430	cos.		404	6		378	6	
429	cos.		403	8		377	6	
428	cos.		402	6		376[e]	4	
427	cos.		401	6		375	anarchy	
426	4		400	6	4	374	anarchy	
425	4		399	6	5	373	anarchy	
424	4		398	6		372	anarchy	
423	cos.		397	6		371	anarchy	
422	3	1	396	6	5	370	6	
421	cos.		395	6		369	6	
420	4		394	6		368	6	
419	4		393	cos.		367	6	

Notes: [a] The first column gives the (Varronian) date BC, the second the number of consular tribunes, and the third the number of plebeians, if any.
[b] According to some of Livy's sources, the three consular tribunes of 444 resigned after three months in office and were replaced by consuls.
[c] There was much dispute in the sources about the magistrates of 434.
[d] Livy lists 6, including 3 plebeians; Diodorus gives 8 (5 plebeians).
[e] Livy leaves this year out. The 4 consular tribunes are listed by Diodorus, who does not normally give a full list.
Source: For the names, and full references to all the sources, see Broughton, *MRR* I.

four to six, until by the end of the fifth century six had become the regular number. Fourth, it can be said that as time went on the consular tribunes began to include increasing numbers of plebeians, although this is far from being a clear statistical trend. In 400, 399 and 396 the colleges were predominantly plebeian, but these years were quite exceptional. In only one other year did the consular tribunes include more than one plebeian (379); otherwise there were only four occasions when a single plebeian was elected, and these are widely scattered (444, 422, 388, 383).

These facts have never been satisfactorily explained; indeed, many commentators, ancient and modern, do not seem even to be aware of them.[21] In all humility we have to admit that we do not know why the new magistracy was instituted, nor what determined the decision to have tribunes rather than consuls in any given year or series of years. That the aim was to give plebeians a chance to share in the government is difficult to accept, as we have seen. On the other hand, the alternative offered by the sources, and accepted by many modern authorities, that consular tribunes could provide more army commanders in times of military difficulty, is open to the objection that consular tribunes were often elected in years of peace, or when there was no obvious need for several commanders; usually one or two of the consular tribunes commanded the army while the rest stayed at home. In times of extreme emergency the Romans continued to appoint dictators. An interesting fact noted by our sources is that no consular tribune ever celebrated a triumph.[22]

The patricians had a virtual monopoly of the consular tribunate down to 400, but the subsequent presence of plebeians, although unevenly distributed, shows that their eligibility was not in question. This fact inevitably raises the question of why there should have been such resistance to the measure proposed by Licinius and Sextius, and why, if plebeians were already eligible for the chief magistracy, the enactment of the Licinio-Sextian Laws in 367 BC should have been regarded as such a landmark in the struggle for plebeian rights.

The answer given by the sources is that the law was a breakthrough, not because it made plebeians eligible for the consulship, but because it required that one of the two annual consulships be reserved for a plebeian. The problem with this interpretation is that the alleged rule was not adhered to, and in several years between 355 and 343 both consuls were patricians. The system whereby the two orders shared the consulship between them began only in 342; from that year onwards, down to the time of Caesar, the consuls of every year always included at least one plebeian. The introduction of this regular system must be connected with a plebiscite which some of Livy's sources recorded under the year 342 BC and attributed to the tribune L. Genucius (Livy 7.42).

Strangely enough, however, Livy's sources claimed that the Lex Genucia allowed plebeians to hold both consulships, a possibility that was not in fact realised until 172 BC. Thus we find an apparent discrepancy between the annalists and the *Fasti* concerning the laws of 367 and 342. According to the annalists the first law stated that one of the consuls must be plebeian, the second that both might be. The *Fasti*, on the other hand, suggest that the law of 367 made it possible for a plebeian to hold one of the annual consulships, and that the law of 342 made it obligatory.

The second of these two alternatives is clearly preferable, and not only because, in a straight fight between the *Fasti* and the annalists, the smart money will always be on the *Fasti*.[23] If a law of 342 BC had allowed the voters to elect two plebeian consuls they would certainly have done so long before 173 BC. The annalists' mistake can be explained, however, if we assume that the Lex Genucia gave plebeians a guaranteed right to one of the consulships but did not specify any similar guarantee for patricians. At the time it was not necessary; the patricians' right to hold one of the consulships would have been taken for granted, and was in practice guaranteed by traditional custom.

When two plebeians were first elected in 173 BC it was no doubt argued that the change did not contravene the provisions of the Lex Genucia, since that law had only specified that plebeians should have a reserved right to one of the consulships. In 342 BC it had not been necessary to go further than that in order to ensure power-sharing. Once it was accepted that an all-plebeian college was in accordance with the Lex Genucia, historians could easily have made the mistake of supposing that it was what Genucius had originally intended.

If it was the Lex Genucia that introduced the system of power-sharing, it would seem to follow that the law of 367 BC had done no more than restore the consulship in place of the consular tribunate. It has in fact been argued that the purpose of the Licinio-Sextian Laws was administrative reform.[24] On this view the undifferentiated college of six consular tribunes was replaced by a more sophisticated system of five magistrates with specialised functions: two consuls, one praetor and two curule aediles. In this respect the reform continued a trend that had been initiated in 443 BC when the censorship was created. The difficulty with this interpretation is that it does not explain why the law should have been regarded as a victory for the *plebs*.

Tradition clearly implies that before 367 plebeians had been systematically excluded from the consulship.[25] The famous achievement of L. Sextius Lateranus, the first plebeian consul in 366 BC, becomes rather less impressive if he simply happened to be the first to hold an office after an administrative adjustment. The point is surely that he was the first plebeian to hold any kind of supreme office, just as L. Genucius (cos. 362) was the first plebeian to conduct a military campaign under his own auspices (Livy 7.6.8). Unless we dismiss the whole tradition as worthless, we must accept that the Licinio-Sextian Laws radically changed the plebeians' rights in relation to the magistracies.

In one significant way L. Sextius did set a precedent. As far as we know, he was the first Roman to hold both plebeian and curule offices in the course of his career. Admittedly our knowledge of the tribunician *Fasti* at this early period is extremely limited; but the tribunes we do hear about were the leaders of the plebeian movement, and it is surprising not to find any of them among the plebeian consular tribunes. Is it possible that before 367 BC former tribunes (and aediles) of the *plebs* were excluded from the curule magistracies?

The suggestion is admittedly hypothetical, but it has several points in its favour.[26] In the first place it is compatible with the theory, outlined above (p. 258), that the so-called plebeian consuls of the early fifth century were clients of the patricians, and were 'plebeian' only in the negative sense that they did not belong to the patriciate. They had nothing in common with the plebeians who took part in secessions, met in the *concilium plebis*, attended to the cult of Ceres, and held office as tribunes or aediles. In terms of this model the problem of eligibility is easily resolved. If it is accepted that there were Roman citizens who were neither patricians nor plebeians, it is a simple step to conclude that the consular tribunate (like the consulship in the early fifth century) was not exclusively reserved for patricians, but was nevertheless closed to plebeians, and *a fortiori* to men who had held plebeian office.

The most compelling argument in support of this reconstruction is that it makes sense of the story of the Licinio-Sextian Rogations. The aim of Licinius and Sextius was to abolish all forms of discrimination against plebeians as such. The enactment of the law was a victory for the leading plebeians, many of whom were wealthy, socially aspiring and politically ambitious. Such men had been attracted into the vigorous and well-organised plebeian movement in preference to the alternative of attaching themselves to a patrician patron. The latter course offered nominal prestige, but no opportunity to exercise independent power. On this view the non-patricians who held the consular tribunate in the years before 367 were mere ciphers; not surprisingly they played no part in the leadership of the reformed state.

However that may be, it is certain that only a small group of rich and aspiring plebeians derived any advantage from the constitutional reforms of 367 BC. In the struggle against patrician exclusiveness this group had made common cause with the poor and had used the institutions of the plebeian movement to gain entry into the ranks of the ruling class. Whether the mass of the *plebs* benefited from their success is more doubtful. The poor gained some temporary economic relief, but lost control of their own organisation. Once the plebeian leaders were admitted into the ruling class on an equal footing with the patricians they immediately acquired all the characteristics of the incumbent group and ceased to represent the interests of the *plebs*. The plebeian leaders were themselves wealthy landowners, and shared the same economic interests as the patricians. The point is well illustrated by the story that C. Licinius Stolo, one of the legislators of 367, was later fined for occupying more *ager publicus* than had been permitted by his own law (Livy 7.16.9). There is no way of knowing whether this story is historical. But if it is not true, it is *ben trovato*.

It seems clear that the plebeian leaders, having scaled the patrician citadel, pulled the ladder up after them. The process is a familiar one in all societies. That the outcome of the Licinio-Sextian Laws should have been the emergence of a joint patrician–plebeian aristocracy (the so-called *nobilitas*) is not in the least surprising, and could perhaps have been foreseen at the time. In Livy's account of the struggle over the Rogations the opposition is said to have come not only from the patricians, but also from within the plebeian movement itself. The two reformers were resisted both by their fellow tribunes and by a body of radical plebeians, who favoured the proposed laws on land and debt but opposed the admission of plebeians to the consulship. We are told that at one stage the plebeian assembly was on the point of enacting the first two proposals and rejecting the third, but that Licinius and Sextius were somehow able to insist that all three measures were voted on together (Livy 6.39.2).

Livy's account naturally raises procedural questions that we are not equipped to answer. Our ignorance in this matter does not, however, give us the right to reject the whole narrative out of hand, as some historians have done.[27] The basic point of Livy's story, that the rogations contained two very different kinds of reform, is clearly true, and there is every reason to suppose that Licinius and Sextius found some way of ensuring that the *plebs* would not be able to enact the laws on land and debt unless they also passed the measure on the consulship. Livy's version merely confirms what many historians have rightly supposed, namely that the plebeian leaders gained what they wanted 'because they linked the interests of the masses with those of their own small class'.[28] His suggestion that the plebeian movement was divided over the issues is also perfectly credible. The radical opposition had good reason to be suspicious of the proposed admission of plebeians to the consulship. Such a measure, they knew, would destroy the plebeian movement.

4 THE RISE OF THE NOBILITY

The Licinio-Sextian Laws transformed the political structure of the Roman state. By ending all forms of discrimination against plebeians the reform had the effect of assimilating all non-patrician Roman citizens under the general designation of *plebs*. In other words the division of the citizen body into two antithetical groups – patricians and plebeians – was the consequence, not the cause, of the struggle over the Licinio-Sextian Laws. Another paradoxical consequence was that the plebeian movement lost its revolutionary identity and ceased to exist as a state within the state. Its institutions were incorporated into the normal machinery of government. The tribunate and aedileship became the equivalent of junior magistracies, open to all except patricians, and were increasingly occupied by young nobles who treated them as rungs on the ladder to the consulship.

Since these plebeian offices no longer entailed disqualification from curule magistracies, they ceased to be an institutionalised form of opposition, and the men who held them no longer felt bound to challenge the ruling class in the interests of the poor. The plebeian assembly (*concilium plebis*) was assimilated to an assembly of the people (*comitia populi*) and its resolutions (*plebiscita*) eventually became equivalent to laws (*leges*). The two terms are used interchangeably, not only in the ancient literary sources, but also in official documents from the late Republic.[29] But once again the result was not that the *plebs* became free to legislate in their own interest, but rather that the plebeian institutions became a convenient mechanism for legislation promoted by the nobility.

It is important to recognise that the aim of the reform of 367 BC was to remove the civil disabilities suffered by plebeians, rather than to abolish the privileges enjoyed by patricians. In fact, the patricians retained their prestige and many of their political prerogatives; although these were gradually eroded in the course of the next two centuries they were never entirely eliminated. The fact that a tiny number of patrician clans were able to claim the right to one of the consulships each year until the second century BC should not be forgotten. But their monopoly of important magistracies was rapidly ended in the years after 367. The first plebeian dictator was appointed in 356, and a plebeian censor soon followed (in 351).

An important stage in the process is represented by the Leges Publiliae of 339, proposed by the dictator Q. Publilius Philo (who was subsequently to become the first plebeian praetor in 336). Three Publilian Laws are recorded. The first, modelled on the Genucian plebiscite of three years earlier, laid down that one of the censors must be a plebeian. The second, which stated 'that a decision of the *plebs* should be binding on the people' (Livy 8.12.14), has been discussed in an earlier chapter (above, pp. 277f.). The third was a closely related measure which laid down that the 'authorisation of the Fathers' (*auctoritas patrum*) should be given before a law was voted on by the assembly rather than afterwards.[30] The right of the patricians to sanction the people's decisions before they could become law was apparently a powerful weapon in their arsenal.

It is very uncertain precisely what the *auctoritas patrum* (cf. above, p. 249) amounted to, and what effect the Lex Publilia had on the people's freedom to make laws. It does not seem likely that the *auctoritas patrum* had given the patrician senators a general right of veto over measures of which they did not approve. If it had been a general power of assent the Lex Publilia would have increased rather than diminished the power of the patricians; obviously the capacity to kill off a proposal before it could be put to the vote would have been more effective than the right to sanction a decision that had already received the support of a majority of the people. But Publilius' law was certainly a progressive measure which reduced the patricians' capacity to obstruct legislation. It follows that the *auctoritas patrum* must have been some kind of confirmation that the law in question was technically acceptable, and in particular that it did not contain any religious flaws (the word *auctoritas* is etymologically related to augury, and implies religious 'authority'). The Lex Publilia therefore reduced the *auctoritas patrum* to a formality by laying down that any proposed measure had to be checked for religious defects in advance of the people's vote. It took away the patricians' power to overturn a popular enactment on a technicality.[31]

The *auctoritas patrum* was one aspect of a more general religious aura that surrounded the patriciate. It was believed that the gods were especially intimate with the patricians, who consequently had exclusive control of many religious institutions and monopolised the chief priesthoods. The change in the composition of the committee in charge of sacred performances (*decemviri sacris faciundis*, see above, p. 334) in 367 was the first attempt to break the patricians' hold on the priesthoods. The second and decisive stage occurred in 300 BC when a plebiscite (the Lex Ogulnia) admitted plebeians to the two major colleges of priests on a power-sharing basis (Livy 10.6–9). Four plebeians were added to the four existing pontifices, and five plebeians were added to the four existing augurs. These priests held office for life; but whenever death created a vacancy in one of the colleges a successor was chosen from the same order as the deceased (see e.g. Livy 23.21.7). Thus the ratio of plebeians to patricians in the colleges of pontiffs and augurs remained constant (at 4:4 and 5:4 respectively) until the end of the Republic. In the late Republic only minor priesthoods, such as the corporation of the Salii, and obsolete relics, like the posts of *flamen dialis* and *rex sacrorum*, were exclusively filled by patricians.

Reforms like the reduction of the *auctoritas patrum* to a formality, and the extension of power-sharing to the priestly colleges, form part of a political shift from an exclusive aristocracy of birth (the patriciate) to a competitive oligarchy whose prestige depended on a mixture of personal distinction (through office-holding) and birth (i.e. descent from former office-holders). This new aristocracy, the so-called *nobilitas*, comprised both patricians and plebeians, and emerged as a natural consequence of the formal division of all major political and religious offices between the two orders – the system I have described, in modern constitutional parlance, as 'power-sharing'.

The character of this nobility, which arose from the reforms of 367 BC, can be illustrated by an analysis of the consular *Fasti* for the succeeding years. They make it clear that the beneficiaries of the reform were a restricted group of aspiring plebeian leaders together with a relatively small caucus of patricians who supported them. The principal figures of this liberal or progressive wing of the patriciate were C. Sulpicius Peticus, L. Aemilius Mamercinus and Q. Servilius Ahala (who between them shared all the patrician consulships in the years 366–361), and M. Fabius Ambustus (censor in 363 and father-in-law of Licinius Stolo), who is said by Livy to have given active support to the reformers.[32]

The victory of this 'centre party' (as it has been called) was won at the expense of the rest of the patricians, who found themselves excluded from office in the years after 367. It is striking, for instance, that not one of the eighteen patricians who held office as consular tribunes in the years 370–367 went on to hold a consulship after the reform;[33] moreover, several old-established patrician clans faded away altogether and do not reappear in the *Fasti* after 367 BC. 'Disappearing' patrician *gentes* include the Horatii, Lucretii, Menenii, Verginii, Cloelii and Geganii – to mention only some of those that are well represented among the consular tribunes in the early fourth century. One could add the Sergii and the Julii, who came in from the cold only at the end of the Republic.[34]

An important result of the new situation was that the two groups forming the patricio-plebeian nobility were not locked in conflict, but on the contrary were bound together by the peculiar rules of the power-sharing system. In this connection it is worth noting a curious feature of the group-voting procedure in consular elections. On these occasions the constituent voting units, the centuries, announced their results in succession, each one returning two names. As soon as one candidate achieved a majority of the centuries – i.e. 97 out of 193 – he was declared elected; the process then went on until a second candidate had gained 97 votes, whereupon the election was brought to a close and the citizens went home.[35] The problem is that since each century had two votes the total number of votes cast was not 193 but 386. It follows that, if the people had had a free choice among all the candidates, the first two to obtain 97 votes would not necessarily be the winners, since a third-place candidate with sufficient support among the centuries not yet called could overtake one or indeed both of them.

How are we to explain this peculiarity? In the late Republic it had the effect of giving the power of decision to the wealthier centuries which voted first.[36] But it cannot have been instituted for such a purpose. It is much more probable – indeed virtually certain – that the explanation lies in the system of power-sharing that began in 342 BC. Under this arrangement a consular election was not an open competition for two places within an undifferentiated group of candidates; rather, patrician candidates competed for one of the annual places, and plebeian candidates competed for the other. Each century thus returned the name of a patrician and the name of a plebeian, which meant that the first of each category to achieve 97 votes would naturally be the winner.

An inevitable result was that patricians and plebeians were able to form alliances for their mutual benefit, and to pool their resources in electoral campaigns. One fact that can be deduced from the *Fasti* is that the two consuls of a given year were often political allies who had stood as joint candidates on an electoral 'ticket'. The point is well illustrated by the example of the patrician Q. Fabius Maximus Rullianus and the plebeian P. Decius Mus, who were consuls together three times (in 308, 297 and 295). This case is far from exceptional. The close association between Q. Aemilius Papus and C. Fabricius Luscinus (cos. 282, 278 BC) was legendary (Cic., *de amic.* 39), as was that between L. Valerius Flaccus and the elder Cato (consuls in 195, censors in 184).

These patrician–plebeian combinations were a natural consequence of the reforms of the fourth century. They also serve to explain how so many important measures during this period came to be passed by means of plebiscites. As we have seen, before the Lex Hortensia (287 BC) plebiscites were passed subject to some form of patrician or senatorial approval; it follows that in order to be binding plebiscites required the support of both patricians and plebeians. The sequence of measures passed by plebiscite can be explained if they were proposed in the interests, and with the support, of the emerging patricio-plebeian nobility.

It is not an accident that many of the plebiscites in question favoured the oligarchic nobility and were often concerned to extend the principle of power-sharing. The most important of these measures were the Lex Ogulnia (300 BC), the Lex Ovinia (before 318), the Leges Genuciae (342) and the Leges Liciniae-Sextiae themselves. The opposition from exclusive and hard-line patricians was gradually marginalised, while the tribunate, which fast became a stepping-stone for aspiring young nobles, was used as an instrument of policy by the nobility (cf. Livy 10.37.11, where some tribunes are described as 'slaves of the nobles' – *mancipia nobilium*). Plebiscites became the normal method of legislation, proposed by the tribunes on behalf of the Senate. On this view the Lex Hortensia removed the last vestiges of patrician obstruction, but kept the legislative process firmly in the hands of the nobles. So far from opening the floodgates of radical popular legislation, the Lex Hortensia marks the triumph of the patricio-plebeian oligarchy.[37]

14

THE ROMAN CONQUEST
OF ITALY

1 THE OUTBREAK OF THE SAMNITE WARS

In Chapter 12 we saw that Roman expansion in Italy began, after a long period of stagnation in the fifth century, with the capture of Veii in 396 BC. Although the Gallic raid held things up for a time, the next fifty years witnessed the gradual spread of Roman power in central Italy, the growth of Rome's territory and an increase in the size of her population. The wars of 343–338 caused this process to accelerate dramatically, and made possible the phenomenal expansion of the succeeding half century, in which the Romans extended their sway over the whole peninsula. The period was dominated by the struggle between Rome and the Samnites, which began in 343 BC.

The Samnites were a federation of tribes who inhabited a large inland area of the southern central Apennines. The region consists of a mountainous plateau intersected by fertile upland valleys, which were densely settled even in the pre-Roman period. Recent archaeological research has confirmed this pattern of dense rural settlement in Samnium, supported by the production of arable crops, vines and olives, as well as by stock-raising.[1] But if recent research has shown that the Samnite economy was more complex and diversified than is suggested by the traditional picture of a predominantly pastoral society, it remains true that in pre-Roman times the region was relatively poor and backward, with few urban centres, no coinage and little trade. The inhabitants supplemented their livelihood by warfare and raiding, and in times of extreme hardship their only remedy was forced emigration in the form of a *ver sacrum* (see above, p. 305).

The political organisation of the Samnites was based on local units called (in Latin) *pagi*. The *pagus* was a canton comprising one or more villages (*vici*) and governed by an elected magistrate called a *meddíss* (Latin *meddix* – Festus p. 110 L). A group of such *pagi* would together form a larger tribal unit, for which the Oscan term was *touto* (Latin *populus*). The chief magistrate of the *touto* had the title *meddíss tovtiks* (*meddix tuticus*).[2] The Samnite federation comprised four tribal groups, each forming a separate *touto*. They were the Hirpini, who occupied southern Samnium, the Caudini, whose territory in

345

the west bordered Campania, the Carricini, the smallest of the four, who lived in the extreme north east, and the Pentri, the largest group, who inhabited central and eastern Samnium.

The general pattern of settlement in the pre-Roman period seems to have been one of scattered villages with associated hill-forts and rural sanctuaries, which, however, remained separate from the villages. For instance, the elaborate sanctuary at Pietrabbondante, which goes back to the pre-Roman period although the impressive standing remains date only from the second century BC, seems to have been a religious meeting place for the people of the surrounding districts, but it did not form part of a large nucleated settlement.[3]

The hill-forts are the most significant physical relics of pre-Roman Samnium. Standing ruins, in the form of rough polygonal walls, can still be seen on remote hilltops in many parts of the central Apennines. A few were substantial permanent settlements; but the majority of Samnite hill-forts are small and inaccessible, and cannot have been places of permanent habitation. No doubt they were used as temporary refuges, although some of them may have had a more positive strategic purpose as military strongholds.[4]

In time of war the several tribes formed a single federation under a commander in chief (Livy 9.1.2; 9.3.9; 10.12.1, etc.) and maintained a remarkable unity in the face of common enemies. This sense of ethnic solidarity distinguishes the four tribes of the Samnite League from their neighbours. But we should not forget that in cultural terms the Samnites belonged to a much wider community of Oscan-speaking peoples who had spread throughout the Mezzogiorno during the fifth century (see above, p. 305). Bruttium, Lucania, northern Apulia, Samnium and Campania were all inhabited by peoples who spoke the same language and shared common religious beliefs, social customs and political institutions. This Oscan *koinē* also included the peoples of the Abruzzi region which, then as now, belonged economically, socially and culturally to the south, although it is geographically on a parallel with Rome. The region was a patchwork of fragmented tribal groups: the Marsi, Paeligni, Vestini, Marrucini and Frentani.

In Campania the Oscan-speaking invaders had occupied a wealthy and highly developed region which had been colonised by both Greeks and Etruscans and in which urbanised city-states were well established. Although the immediate effects of the Oscan invasion at the end of the fifth century were dramatic, the city-states soon began to flourish once again under their new overlords. A remarkable mixture of influences led to the formation, in the fourth century, of a distinctive Campanian culture, in which many of the old Greek and Etruscan traditions were adapted to the social needs and values of the Oscan conquerors. A case in point is their addiction to horse breeding and cavalry prowess, which, as Frederiksen showed, was a legacy from the classical Greek past of the city.[5] A similar development can be seen at Paestum in Lucania, where the remarkable painted tombs, recently published by

Angela Pontrandolfo and Agnès Rouveret, bear witness to the hellenising lifestyle and artistic taste of its Oscan ruling class.[6]

An intense rivalry characterised the relations between the city states in these coastal regions. In the fourth century the cities of northern Campania formed a league, centred on Capua and led by a *meddix tuticus*. Among the member states of this confederation were Casilinum, Atella and Calatia. Other Campanian towns such as Nola and Abella remained separate, while the Alfaterni in the south formed their own league under the hegemony of Nuceria. Naples, the only surviving Greek city in Campania, was strongly affected by Oscan influences, but retained its political independence. An equally strong antagonism existed between them and their Samnite kinsmen in the interior. This tangled web of internecine rivalry and conflict was further complicated, in 343 BC, by the intervention of Rome.

This decisive intervention, which led to the so-called First Samnite War, came about when the Samnites attacked the Sidicini, an Oscan-speaking people who lived in the region between the rivers Liris and Volturnus, and subsequently the Campanians, who had gone to their assistance. When the Samnites began to besiege Capua, the Campanians appealed to Rome. In spite of their alliance with the Samnites (above, p. 325), the Romans responded positively to the appeal and declared war on their erstwhile allies. This strange turn of events, which causes Livy no little embarrassment, is presented as the result of an act of submission by the Campanians, who surrendered themselves into the power of Rome. Scholars have expressed disbelief, but it has been shown that such 'voluntary submissions' were a regular feature of inter-state diplomacy at this period.[7]

A year of successful campaigns, which earned triumphs for both consuls and the congratulations of a Carthaginian embassy (Livy 7.38.2), was followed in 342 by an army revolt and a political crisis, of which the Genucian Laws were among the results (see below, p. 371); when the Romans resumed hostilities in 341 the Samnites immediately sued for peace. The Romano-Samnite alliance was then renewed, whereupon the Sidicini and the Campanians at once joined up with the Latins and Volscians, who were already in revolt against Rome. There was, therefore, a complete reversal of the situation of two years earlier, when the Romans had aided the Campanians and Sidicini against the Samnites. This volte-face is puzzling, and may well be connected with internal political upheavals in Rome. At all events, there is no justification for the old-fashioned view that the First Samnite War was an annalistic fabrication.[8]

2 THE LATIN REVOLT AND ITS CONSEQUENCES

The Romano-Latin War, which began in 341, was a major turning-point in Italian history. Its cause, according to Livy, was the Latins' resentment at being treated as subjects rather than allies. It is also likely that the events of the preceding years had made them justifiably afraid of Roman territorial encroachment. The events of the war are described in some detail by Livy, but the reliability of his account is open to question. The substantial accuracy of the main outline is widely recognised, however, and there can be no doubt about the results.[9]

After several years of fierce campaigning, the revolt was crushed. The Volscians of Privernum were defeated in 341; in the following year the Latins and Campanians suffered at least two major defeats, one of them at a celebrated battle which Livy locates at Veseris near Mount Vesuvius, although modern experts place it further north, near Roccamonfina.[10] The battle was remembered in the Roman tradition for two incidents. First, T. Manlius Torquatus, the son of one of the consuls, slew an enemy champion in single combat, but was executed by his father for disobeying a command not to engage the enemy. The second incident involved the other consul, P. Decius Mus, who 'devoted' himself and the enemy to the gods of the underworld, and by riding headlong into the opposing ranks brought about their destruction along with his own. Whether these episodes are in any sense historical naturally cannot be known, but neither should be ruled out a priori. The first possibly, and the second probably, has some basis in fact.

The campaign of 340 brought a temporary end to the fighting. Rome punished her enemies by confiscating some of their territory, and rewarded those who had remained loyal. The latter included Lavinium, which was given a privileged status that is now obscure to us, and 1,600 of the *equites campani*, the aristocracy of Capua, who received economic privileges and honorary Roman citizenship.[11] Some of the Latin peoples took up arms again in 339, but were defeated after two or more years of warfare. In 338 the Romans captured the stronghold of Pedum, and then proceeded to reduce the other rebel communities one by one (Livy 8.13.8). In the following years mopping-up operations were carried out in Campania, and against the Sidicini, Aurunci and Volsci.

The settlement which the Romans imposed after 338 established a pattern for the future development of Roman expansion in Italy.[12] It combined a number of constitutional innovations and created a unique structure which made possible the rise of the Roman Empire. In the opinion of De Sanctis this was the turning-point of Roman history.[13] The settlement was based on two broad principles. First, the Romans dealt with the various defeated communities individually rather than in groups. Leagues and confederations were dissolved, and their constituent units bound to Rome by separate ties. Second, a set of distinct types of relationship was established, so that Rome's subjects were divided into formal juridical categories defined by the specific rights and obligations of each community in relation to the Roman state. In this way a 'Roman commonwealth' was created, based on a hierarchy of statuses among its various members.[14]

The details of the settlement are systematically outlined by Livy (8.14), who lists them under three headings (see Map 7).

(1) In Latium many of the defeated Latin communities were incorporated into the Roman state and their inhabitants made Roman citizens. Livy specifies Lanuvium, Aricia, Nomentum and Pedum. Each of these places became a self-governing *municipium* on the model of Tusculum (see above, p. 323). Tusculum itself had taken part in the revolt, but its citizenship was restored in 338 after the ringleaders had been executed.

Harsh treatment was reserved for Velitrae and Antium. Velitrae's walls were razed and its ruling class was banished. The land of the dispossessed aristocrats was distributed to Roman settlers, and the remaining Veliterni were given Roman citizenship.[15] The inhabitants of Antium also became Roman citizens, but were forced to surrender their fleet. Some of the ships were immediately destroyed; their prows or beaks were displayed as trophies in the Roman Forum on the front of the speakers' platform, which was afterwards known as the *rostra* ('the Beaks').

Livy makes it clear that these incorporated communities acquired full Roman citizenship, and distinguishes them from the states that received half citizenship (*civitas sine suffragio*). There is no warrant for the widely held view that full citizenship (*civitas optimo iure*) was reserved exclusively for Latins, and that the Volscians of Antium and Velitrae had to be content with *civitas sine suffragio*.[16] It is only modern scholarship, not Roman policy, that has discriminated between communities on the grounds of race and language.

The practical business of registering the new citizens was carried out by the censors of 332 BC. Most of the communities in question were registered in existing tribes, but Lanuvium and Velitrae were incorporated in two new tribes, respectively the Maecia and the Scaptia (Livy 8.17.11). The new tribes also included Roman citizens who had been settled on land confiscated from the two cities. The inclusion of both old and new citizens in newly created tribes had occurred earlier in the settlement of the *ager Veientanus* in 387 BC, and had become the normal practice.

(2) Of the Latin cities that were not incorporated, Tibur and Praeneste retained their status as independent allies, but were forced to cede some of their territory. The Latin League was broken up, and many of its constituent members became Roman *municipia*. The rest continued to exist as sovereign communities and to possess the rights of *conubium* and *commercium* with Roman citizens (see above, p. 295). But they were no longer permitted to exercise such rights, or to have political relations, with one another. Paradoxically, their geographical isolation minimised the effects of these prohibitions, since their immediate neighbours were now mostly Roman citizens, with whom they *were* permitted to have dealings; but at the same time their chances of adopting an independent foreign policy were reduced practically to nil.

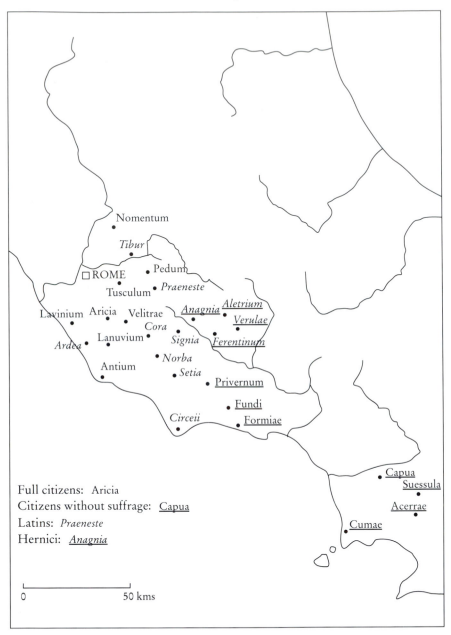

Nomentum

Tibur

Pedum

□ROME
Tusculum *Praeneste*

Lavinium Aricia Velitrae *Anagnia* *Aletrium*
             Cora   *Verulae*
        Lanuvium *Signia* *Ferentinum*
Ardea
           Norba
Antium   *Setia*
              Privernum

            Fundi
Circeii   Formiae

                          Capua
                          Suessula

                          Acerrae

                    Cumae

Full citizens: Aricia
Citizens without suffrage: Capua
Latins: *Praeneste*
Hernici: *Anagnia*

0   50 kms

Map 7 The settlement of 338 BC (*source*: Livy 8.14)

(3) In the part of the Roman commonwealth that lay outside the boundaries of Latium Vetus – the region later known as Latium Adiectum (Pliny, *n.h.* 3.56–9) – the Romans imposed partial citizenship (*civitas sine suffragio*) on the peoples whom they had defeated. Livy specifies the Campanian cities of Capua, Suessula and Cumae, to which Acerrae was added in 332 (8.17.12), and the Volscian towns of Fundi and Formiae, with the addition of Privernum in 329 (8.21.10). This partial citizenship was the most important innovation of the whole settlement. The citizens without suffrage were liable to all the burdens and obligations of full citizens – especially military service – but possessed no political rights. They could not vote in Roman assemblies nor hold office at Rome. As communities they retained their native institutions, and became self-governing *municipia*. Since they possessed the rights of *conubium* and *commercium* their status was in practice similar to that of the Latins, although the two categories were juridically quite distinct, since the Latins were technically foreigners (*peregrini*), whereas the Oscan-speaking Campanians and Volscians were technically citizens (*cives*).

The size and population of the Roman commonwealth after the Latin War have been analysed in detail by A. Afzelius, who estimated the size of the *ager Romanus* (i.e. the territory occupied by Roman citizens of all kinds) at 5,525 km², and of the commonwealth as a whole at 8,505 km². The corresponding population figures, according to Afzelius, were 347,300 free persons for the *ager Romanus*, and 484,000 for the commonwealth as a whole.[17] Although considerably smaller than the territory of the Samnite League, the Roman commonwealth included the best agricultural land in peninsular Italy, and in terms of manpower Rome commanded resources that were at least equal to, and perhaps greater than, those of the Samnites.[18] The foundation for this was the Roman annexation of Campania, a vital step in their drive towards expansion, and the key to their success in the struggle against the Samnites.

In the longer term, however, the most important feature of the Roman commonwealth was its potential for further growth. This manifested itself in three ways. First, the institution of the self-governing *municipium* enabled the Roman state to go on extending its territory and incorporating new communities without having to make any radical changes to its rudimentary system of centralised administration. Second, by the invention of the *civitas sine suffragio* the Romans could increase their citizen manpower but still maintain the essential character of Rome as a city-state and the integrity of its traditional political institutions. The third vital innovation of this period was the resurrection, in changed circumstances but essentially the same form, of the institution of the Latin colony. After the settlement of 338 BC, Latin status ceased to have a distinct ethnic or linguistic significance, and came instead to depend on possession of legally defined rights and privileges that could be exercised in dealings with Roman citizens. A Latin state could therefore be created simply by an enactment of the Roman people conferring Latin rights on it. By the same token, a new Latin community could be founded *ex novo*. The fact that the Latin League no longer existed did not matter; the city became 'Latin' because it possessed certain rights in relation to Rome. This juridical shift was important because it meant that Latin communities no longer had to be located in Latium, but could be placed anywhere.

The new programme of Latin colonisation, which began in 334 BC, gave the Romans and their allies the chance to acquire conquered land even in distant regions, and thus to benefit directly from the commonwealth's territorial expansion; while the state was able to consolidate its conquests by planting strategic garrisons in troublesome areas. Since the colonies were self-sufficient autonomous communities, their distance from Rome did not place any strain on its traditional city-state structure. As Arnold Toynbee noted in his masterly account of this period, the main constitutional innovations of the settlement 'gave the Roman commonwealth the maximum capacity for expansion, combined with the maximum solidity of structure'.[19]

The first colony to be established under these conditions was at Cales (Calvi), a crucial strategic site on the main route from Rome to Capua; it protected the vulnerable stretch of this route at the point where it swerved inland in order to cross the river Volturnus, and shielded Capua from the Sidicini.[20] The 2,500 families who occupied Cales in 334 BC were drawn largely from the Roman proletariat, but also included Latins and other allies. They received allotments of land and were constituted as an autonomous community. The government of the colony was placed in the hands of a small group of well-to-do colonists (*equites*) who formed its ruling class and received large plots of land.[21] Cales became a model for later colonies which were established at strategic points throughout the Italian peninsula during the course of the next two generations. As well as being military strongholds, these colonies were romanised enclaves in which Latin was spoken and the Roman way of life was practised; as such they contributed more than any other single factor to the consolidation of the conquest and the eventual unification of Italy under Rome.

3 THE SECOND SAMNITE WAR

In 328 BC the Romans founded a colony at Fregellae (Ceprano) on the eastern bank of the Liris, at the junction with the Trerus (Sacco). The colonisation of Fregellae provoked the hostility of the Samnites, who saw it as an act of aggression against themselves, since they had overrun the region a few years previously (Livy 8.23.6). Relations between Rome and the Samnites deteriorated rapidly, and within two years they were formally at war. The sources, describing events from a Roman point of view, naturally see things differently. In particular, they allege that the Samnites had incited the Greek city of Neapolis (Naples) to attack Rome's possessions in Campania, and that they were encouraging Privernum, Fundi and Formiae to revolt.

The Naples affair, the object of much confusion in the sources, was evidently crucial. When the Romans declared war on Naples, the Samnites went to its assistance and installed a garrison (327 BC). The city was internally divided, however, with the mass of the people (the 'demos') favouring the Samnites, and the propertied class supporting Rome (Dion. Hal. 15.6.5). In 326 the pro-Roman group succeeded in getting rid of the Samnites and handing over the city to the Roman commander Q. Publilius Philo. This was the first action of the Second Samnite War, which lasted, on and off, for twenty years.

In the early years the Romans seem to have adopted a broadly offensive strategy. At no point in the period down to 320 BC did the Samnites attack the territory of Rome or its allies;[22] on the contrary, the Romans invaded western Samnium in 326 (Livy 8.25.4) and attacked the Vestini, who were allies of the Samnites, in the following year (8.29.1, 6, 11–14). Large-scale victories are recorded in 325 and 322, the former apparently somewhere 'in Samnium', although the exact site of the battle (Imbrinium) is not identifiable. Finally, in 321 a full-scale Roman invasion of Samnite territory ended in disaster at the Caudine Forks, where the army was ambushed in a remote mountain glen and forced to surrender. The Romans were set free under an agreement, after being compelled to march, unarmed and half-naked, under a 'yoke' of spears.[23]

The fact of a Roman surrender is undeniable. Although the sources maintain that the Romans subsequently repudiated the truce and avenged the humiliation by a series of victories, there can be little doubt that the overall result was a major reverse. They were forced to give up Fregellae and Cales (Livy 9.4.4; Appian, *Samn.* 4.5), and this may have formed the basis of a peace that lasted until 316 BC.[24]

The Romans used the lull to strengthen their position in Campania, and in 318 they created two new tribes, the Oufentina and the Falerna, on territory that had been settled twenty years previously. At the same time they campaigned in Apulia and Lucania, and forced a number of communities there to make treaties of alliance (including Arpi, Teanum Apulum, Canusium, Forentum and Nerulum – Livy 9.20). These regions had for some time been the object of Roman attention, and earlier alliances are recorded by Livy in 326 BC (8.25.3). Rome's efforts on this front form part of a broad strategic policy aimed at isolating and encircling the Samnites. The pattern is one of consistent aggression, a conclusion that is not necessarily incompatible with the modern view that the Romans' principal intention was to preserve their own security.[25]

On the other hand, there is little sign of any corresponding aggression or urge to expand on the part of the Samnites, although both ancient and modern writers frequently assert the contrary.[26] The only occasion when the Samnites invaded the territory of the Romans or their allies in force was in 315 BC, an attack that was itself a response to Roman aggression, as Livy admits

(9.21.2: a Roman assault on Saticula). In 315 the Samnites advanced across the Liris and defeated the Romans in a pitched battle at Lautulae near Terracina; it must have been on this occasion that they entered Latium and devastated the coastal region as far as Ardea (Strabo 5.3.5 p. 232 C; 5.4.11 p. 249 C). But in the following year they were themselves defeated by the Romans, possibly again at Terracina.[27] The Romans then proceeded to reassert their control of Campania, where some cities had become disaffected, and dealt severely with a revolt of the Aurunci, who were massacred (9.25.9).

The Romans recovered Sora in 314 and Fregellae in 313. Colonies were established at Luceria in 314, at Suessa Aurunca and Saticula in 313, and at Interamna on the Liris and on the island of Pontia in 312. The result was that by 312 Samnium was encircled by military allies of Rome, and confronted in the sensitive Liris-Volturnus region by a string of Latin colonies on strategic sites stretching from Fregellae to Saticula. At the same time the Romans strengthened their grip on the lowlands by the Tyrrhenian coastline. A potent symbol of their permanent control of this area was the construction of the Appian Way, the great highway from Rome to Capua, which was started in 312 BC. These events marked the turning-point of the war. In the years that followed the Romans were able to extend the scope of their military activities to other parts of central Italy, and to embark on a series of vigorous offensives which in little more than a decade transformed the political map of Italy.[28]

The increased scale of Roman operations during this period is indicated by a law of 311 BC which laid down that the military tribunes of the four legions should be elected by the people rather than appointed by their commanders (Livy 9.30.3). This innovation presupposes an increase in the normal size of the army from two to four legions, and probably coincides with it. It was perhaps also at this time that the tactical organisation of the Roman army was reformed; under the new system the legion ceased to fight as a single compact phalanx, and was subdivided into smaller units called 'maniples' which could operate independently.[29]

Our sources do not give a very clear picture of the last years of the Second Samnite War; instead they provide a shapeless catalogue of annual campaigns, the details of which are often uncertain. But the general trend of events is clear enough, and shows the Romans pressing ahead with an aggressive strategy. It is evident, moreover, that they were no longer in any serious danger of defeat. Roman campaigns in Samnium were conducted every year down to 304 BC with varying success. The outcome of the campaign of 311 under C. Junius Bubulcus Brutus is uncertain and the cause of serious disagreement between our sources.[30] A major victory is attributed to L. Papirius Cursor in 310, but in 307 the Samnites staged a late rally and seized Sora and Caiatia; although apparently defeated in a battle (Livy 9.43.8–21), they returned to the attack in 306 and invaded northern Campania (Livy 9.44.5; Diod. 20.90.3). The Romans retaliated with a full-scale invasion of Samnium and captured the stronghold of Bovianum; the Samnites were then destroyed in a pitched battle in which their leader Statius Gellius was killed. The Romans proceeded to recapture Sora and to take Arpinum and Cesennia (Livy 9.44.16). In 304 the Samnites sued for peace; the 'old treaty' (presumably that of 354 and 341) was renewed, and the twenty years war was at an end.

The conclusion of the Samnite War did not, however, result in an immediate or drastic reduction in the level of Rome's military commitments. The reason is that, from around 312 BC onwards, the Samnite War as such had ceased to be the Romans' principal concern. Other theatres of war now predominated, as the Romans concentrated their efforts in other directions, first in Etruria and Umbria, and then in the mountainous region of central Italy.

4 THE ROMAN CONQUEST OF CENTRAL ITALY

In 311 BC the Etruscans attacked Sutrium (we are not told why) and prompted Roman intervention in a region that had been quiet since the 350s. It is not clear precisely who these 'Etruscans' were, but the more or less vague indications in the sources suggest that they were from the inland cities of Volsinii, Perusia, Cortona, Arretium and, probably, Clusium. The coastal cities, such as Caere, Tarquinii and Vulci, seem not to have been involved.

The Romans responded with a vigorous advance up the Tiber valley which resulted in the submission of Perusia, Cortona and Arretium in 311, and of Volsinii in 308. A celebrated episode of this war was the expedition to Umbria led by the consul Q. Fabius Maximus Rullianus in 310, and particularly the reconnaissance mission, by the consul's brother or half-brother, through the trackless Ciminian forest (Livy 9.36.1–8). Disguised as a peasant and accompanied only by a slave, the scout, who had been educated at Caere and therefore spoke fluent Etruscan, made his way through the forest and continued as far as Camerinum in Umbria, which he persuaded to become an ally of Rome.[31]

The historical reliability of this and similar stories has been much discussed by scholars, some of whom remain deeply sceptical. But there are good reasons for thinking that the sources for this period are much more reliable than anything relating to earlier times. We should note, first, that Livy's account of this period is much more detailed than his earlier narrative. It is important to be aware of this fact and to understand its implications. An improvement in both the quantity and the quality of information becomes clearly evident in Livy's account of the last years of the Second Samnite War. The later part of book 9 and book 10 contain far more substantive data of a routine kind than previous books, and the account begins to resemble the narrative format of the later sections of his work.

There are two reasons for this. First, the increasingly detailed record of routine annual events must imply that better and more abundant documentary evidence was available for this period. Second, the elaborate circumstantial detail that accompanies the main narrative of military events is best explained by the increasing availablity to historians of oral memory and even of eyewitness reports. The earliest Roman historians, who were writing before 200 BC, could easily have had access to such information. For instance Fabius Pictor, who was born probably in the second quarter of the third century, would have met people who had lived through the Samnite Wars. The romantic story about the brother of Fabius Rullianus who reconnoitred the Ciminian forest might well have reached him at first hand. It is quite possible, not to say probable, that the intrepid explorer entertained his relatives and friends with reminiscences for years afterwards, and that the young Fabius Pictor was among them. The same goes for Fabius Rullianus himself, who might well have lived long enough to dandle the young Fabius Pictor on his knee.[32]

A further point about the sources for this period is that they themselves reveal more discrepancies and disagreements about what exactly happened. This is not necessarily a bad sign. Rather, it suggests that Roman historians and antiquarians had access to a wider diversity of materials, and that as events came increasingly within the range of living memory, they provided more scope, and more pressing reasons, for debate and disagreement. The age of the Samnite Wars was a living past which Romans of Fabius Pictor's time were still arguing about. It is not an accident that Livy's exasperated comment (8.40.4–5) about aristocratic families falsifying the record relates to an event of 322 BC.

From 318 BC onwards Livy can be supplemented by the regular annual notices of Roman events in Diodorus (down to 302), and by the entries in the triumphal *Fasti*.[33] Discrepancies between these sources occur frequently; but we should not necessarily infer that when two different sets of events are reported one or both sources must be wrong. Sometimes both could be right; in other words, they may complement, rather than contradict, one another. It is also worth noticing that in this section of his work Livy refers frequently to discrepancies between his sources. A remarkable instance occurs at 10.17.11–12, where he reveals his acquaintance with four distinct versions of a campaign in 296 BC. As far as Livy is concerned, these instances bear witness to his conscientiousness, and increase the value of his account.

While the details of particular campaigns may be suspect, there is every reason to accept the basic structure of the narrative, as many historians are now inclined to do. This 'conservative' position has been defended in detail in William Harris' study of Roman policy in Etruria and Umbria.[34] Harris argues convincingly that the extreme scepticism of earlier scholars such as Pais and Beloch is unjustified, and that the main outline of the traditional account is probably reliable and based on authentic records. Although he confines his discussion to events in Etruria and Umbria, Harris' conclusions have a general validity, and can be applied to the period of the Samnite Wars as a whole.

The broad outline of the war in Etruria and Umbria in the years 311–308 may be taken as historical; the same goes for the Roman campaigns in Samnium down to 304. But the main thrust of Rome's efforts at this time, according to an equally believable part of Livy's account, was directed towards the conquest of the centre of the Italian peninsula. An annalistic notice, which almost certainly comes from a documentary source, records the Roman decision, in 307, to construct the Via Valeria, the military road which extended beyond Tibur into the central Apennines and eventually reached the Adriatic (Livy 9.43.25).

The conquest of this region began with the reduction of the Hernici, who were accused of rebellion, in 306, and a brutal campaign against the Aequi in 304. In a mere fifty days the Aequi were overwhelmed; their hill towns were systematically destroyed, and the population was massacred. If the object of the exercise was to encourage the others, it was highly effective. The neighbouring peoples of the Abruzzi region lost no time in concluding permanent treaties of alliance with Rome: the Marsi, Paeligni, Marrucini and Frentani in 304 (Livy 9.45.18; Diod. 20.101.5), the Vestini in 302 (Livy 10.3.1).

These military and diplomatic successes were consolidated by the foundation of colonies at Sora (303 BC), Alba Fucens (303) (Figure 26) and Carseoli (298). In 299 the Umbrian stronghold of Nequinum was captured, and the colony of Narnia (modern Narni) founded on its site. In 303 the towns of Trebula Suffenas (Ciciliano), Arpinum (Arpino) and Frusino (Frosinone) were annexed with *civitas sine suffragio* (Livy 10.1.3). In 299 the tribes

Figure 26 Alba Fucens.

357

Aniensis and Teretina were created; the former was situated on land taken from the Aequi in the upper Anio valley, and the latter in the Liris valley on land that had been annexed from the Aurunci in 314 BC.

These acts of enfranchisement and annexation mark the end of a further stage in Rome's conquest of Italy (Map 8). The process of expansion had by now developed its own momentum; the logical result was Roman domination of the entire Italian peninsula. This outcome could only have been averted by positive and concerted action by the peoples who still retained their independence. It was perhaps around the turn of the century that the free peoples of Italy first perceived what might be in store for them; at any rate it was then for the first time that they began to make serious efforts to organise a united front against Rome.

Map 8 The Roman conquest of Italy, fourth–third centuries BC

5 THE BATTLE OF SENTINUM AND ITS CONSEQUENCES

By 298 BC the Romans were once again fighting on several fronts. Annual Roman campaigns in Etruria and Umbria are recorded from 302 onwards, and in 298 hostilities between Rome and the Samnites were resumed. This 'Third Samnite War' (298–290 BC) began when the Romans made an alliance with the Lucanians, who had been attacked by the Samnites. An early Roman success is recorded in the epitaph of L. Cornelius Scipio Barbatus, the consul of 298. The inscription, which was composed some time after Scipio's death and probably dates from the early second century BC, claims that he 'captured Taurasia and Cisauna in Samnium, subdued all Lucania and brought back hostages' (Figure 27).[35]

Figure 27 Sarcophagus of Scipio Barbatus.

In itself this information does not present any great problem. We could reasonably infer that it was Scipio who negotiated the Lucanian alliance and received the hostages whom, as our literary sources tell us, the Lucanians gave as a pledge of their good faith (Livy 10.11.13; Dion. Hal. 17/18.1.2). The intimation that the Lucanians' submission was the result of military action is a good example of how events could be improved in the telling. The reported achievements in Samnium are credible enough, although the location of Taurasia and Cisauna is uncertain. The problem is that Livy has none of this. Instead he places Scipio's activities in Etruria, and gives the Samnite province to his plebeian colleague Cn. Fulvius Maximus Centumalus (who is credited with several successes and a triumph). To make matters worse, the *Fasti Capitolini* state that Fulvius triumphed over both the Samnites and the Etruscans.

On present evidence no satisfactory resolution of this puzzle is possible. The sources could be reconciled by supposing that both consuls operated in both theatres; but if so neither Livy nor the inscription would emerge with much credit. Once again the evidence seems to show that there was a great deal of confusion in the tradition about the distribution of consular commands in the Samnite Wars, and that many different versions proliferated in the late Republic.[36]

As consuls for 297 the Romans chose two of their most experienced military leaders, Q. Fabius Maximus Rullianus and P. Decius Mus. Both men had their commands extended in 296 and were again elected consuls for 295. In 295 at least five men held *imperium* as 'pro-magistrates'. They included one of the consuls of the previous year, L. Volumnius Flamma, who was retained *pro consule* (his colleague in the consulship of 296, Ap. Claudius Caecus, was praetor in 295). The other four, who held commands *pro praetore*, were the two consuls of 298, L. Cornelius Scipio Barbatus and Cn. Fulvius Maximus Centumalus, and two other ex-consuls, M. Livius Denter (cos. 302) and L. Postumius Megellus (cos. 305).

The pattern is extraordinary and unprecedented. In the later Republic it was normal practice for magistrates to have their commands extended if their term of office ended before their tasks were complete.[37] At this period, however, it was a rare novelty. If we ignore some doubtful fifth-century cases, there had only been two previous instances of commands being prorogued – those of Q. Publilius Philo in 326 (below, p. 370) and of Q. Fabius Maximus Rullianus in 307 (Livy 9.42.2). But now in 296–295 several simultaneous instances are recorded. Even more remarkable is the fact that four of the promagistrates of 295 did not have regular commands prorogued, but had *imperium* conferred upon them at a time when their legal status was that of private citizens (*privati*). Appointments of this kind were always regarded as anomalous – and, in conservative eyes, undesirable.

How then are we to account for the multiple prorogations and extra-ordinary commands in 296–295 BC? The sources offer no explanation, but their accounts of the events themselves suggest an answer: at this time the state faced a grave military threat. Our sources give no hint of an impending military crisis until the end of 296. In 297 the consuls Fabius and Decius had both commanded in Samnium, and ravaged it continuously for four months (Livy 10.15.3–6); in the following year they continued their operations. At the same time the consul L. Volumnius Flamma put down a revolt in Lucania and defeated the Samnites at the river Volturnus. But in spite of these successes the Romans were not able (or did not choose) to prevent the Samnite general Gellius Egnatius from leading an army northwards into Etruria and joining forces with the leaders of the Etruscan states.

At the end of the year the Roman commander in Etruria, the consul Ap. Claudius, reported to the Senate that a grand coalition had been formed in northern Italy, comprising Samnites, Etruscans, Umbrians and Gauls (Livy 10.21.11–15). This unlikely alliance must have been several years in the making, as Livy himself implies (10.16.3); and the extraordinary pattern of military appointments in 296 and 295 shows that the Romans had been conscious of a growing threat since the end of 297 at the latest.

Matters came to a head in 295 when a combined army of Samnites and Gauls met the Romans at Sentinum in Umbria. At this celebrated battle the Romans fielded four legions together with contingents of allied soldiers who, according to Livy, outnumbered the citizen troops. If we estimate the size of a legion at around 4,500 men, the total number of troops on the Roman side will have been over 36,000, a huge army by the standards of the time, and probably the largest that the Roman state had ever put into the field. The size of the opposing force is completely unknown. The sources naturally maintain that the Romans were heavily outnumbered, and fantastic figures such as 650,000 were given in some accounts known to Livy (10.30.5). The Greek historian Duris of Samos, who was a contemporary of the event, apparently reported that 100,000 men were killed (*FGrHist* 76 F. 56). Livy's more modest account gives a figure of 8,700 killed on the Roman side, and 25,000 of the enemy (10.29.17–18). Such figures are more realistic, and may be based on more than guesswork.[38]

However that may be, there can be little doubt that, in terms of the size of the forces engaged, the ferocity of the fighting and the decisiveness of the result, Sentinum was the greatest military engagement that had ever taken place in Italy. Livy's detailed account of the battle may well contain authentic elements, probably for the first time. The reference to it in the work of a contemporary Greek historian has already been noted; moreover, Romans of the generation of Fabius Pictor would have been able to speak to survivors of the battle, and it would be extraordinary if Pictor himself had not in fact done so.

The Roman victory was total, but apparently far from easy. In Livy's opinion, the result might have been different if the Etruscan and Umbrian contingents had been present (Livy 10.27.11); as it was they were drawn away from Sentinum when the Roman reserve armies moved up from Rome and attacked Clusium. The battle itself was closely fought, but at the critical moment the consul P. Decius Mus followed the example of his father and devoted himself (cf. above, p. 348). This undoubtedly historical incident turned the tide of the battle in favour of the Romans. After the victory Fabius returned to Rome in triumph, with an assured place in the Roman tradition as the hero of the Samnite Wars.

Sentinum sealed the fate of Italy. After the battle the Romans lost no time in settling accounts with the Etruscans and Umbrians, and pressed home their advantage in Samnium, where fierce fighting is reported in 295 and 294. In 293 they inflicted a crushing defeat on the Samnites at the battle of Aquilonia.[39]

At this point events become hard to follow because Livy's text breaks off in 293 at the end of book 10, and we are compelled to rely on later epitomes and secondary accounts that preserve only the bare bones of Livy's narrative. The complete text of Diodorus ceased with the events of 302, and to round off the dismal picture of our sources for this period the section of the *Fasti Capitolini* containing triumphs from 290 to 283 is missing.[40] A proper narrative of the final stages of the Roman conquest of peninsular Italy is not really possible from the few surviving scraps of evidence, from which we can reconstruct only the barest outline of events.

It seems certain, however, that from 292 to 290 the Romans overran Samnium, and annexed a large area of territory in the south east where they founded the colony of Venusia in 291. A year later the Samnites surrendered and were forced to become allies of Rome, no doubt on unequal terms. In 290 the consul M' Curius Dentatus conquered the Sabines and Praetuttii, who were made Roman citizens *sine suffragio*; some of their land was seized and distributed to Roman settlers. As a result of this poorly documented episode Roman territory was extended right across the peninsula to the Adriatic coast, where a colony was founded at Hadria (Atri) probably between 290 and 286. Some years later the territory of Picenum was added, following a revolt in 269 BC. The Picentes were made *cives sine suffragio* (with the exception of Asculum, which remained an ally), and a colony was established at Firmum in 264.

After their defeat at Sentinum the Gauls seem to have remained quiet for a time; ten years later, however, they once again penetrated into Etruria. The Gallic War that followed appears to have been a major conflict.[41] The Romans were heavily defeated at Arretium in 284, but in the following year they won a decisive victory at Lake Vadimon (in the Tiber valley, about 80 km north of Rome). They then annexed the territory along the northern Adriatic that was occupied by the Senones, and secured their control of this district (the so-called *ager Gallicus*) by founding a Latin colony at Ariminum (Rimini) in 268 BC.

Warfare in Etruria and Umbria continued, although very few details are preserved. Vulci and Volsinii were defeated in 280, and Caere in 273. The process of conquest was certainly complete by 264, when Volsinii was destroyed in the aftermath of a revolution in the city. The Etruscan and Umbrian communities remained nominally independent but were bound to Rome by treaties of alliance. The exception was Caere, which was incorporated with citizenship *sine suffragio* following its defeat in 273; in the same year a colony was founded on the Tuscan coast at Cosa.

6 THE INVASION OF PYRRHUS AND THE UNIFICATION OF ITALY

At the beginning of the third century BC the Greek cities of southern Italy were in a state of advanced decline, resulting from the continuous pressure of hostile natives and centuries of internecine strife. The Romans became directly involved in the affairs of Magna Graecia in 285 BC when the city of Thurii appealed to them for aid against the Lucanians; within a few years Locri, Rhegium and Croton had also placed themselves under Rome's protection. These developments were viewed with alarm in Tarentum, the most powerful of the Greek cities, which had for some time been suspicious of the growing power of Rome. A generation earlier, around 303, Rome and Tarentum had made a treaty in which the Romans agreed not to sail beyond the Lacinian promontory (near Croton); and when in 282 a squadron of Roman ships appeared off Tarentum, in direct contravention of the treaty, the Tarentines responded with force and sank several of them. They then marched on Thurii, expelled the Roman garrison, and replaced the ruling oligarchy with a democratic government.[42]

The episode illustrates a consistent feature of Rome's foreign policy, namely her support for the upper classes in the communities of Italy, who regarded Rome as their natural ally, whereas the masses were normally hostile. This is an underlying theme of the Tarentum episode. It was the *demos* (people's assembly) that ordered the attack on the Roman ships and the subsequent march on Thurii; and when the Romans protested, their envoy had to face the people in the theatre at Tarentum, and to bear their insults.[43] Finally, it was the people's assembly that decided, after the Romans had declared war and driven the Tarentines behind their walls, to appeal to King Pyrrhus of Epirus.

This was not the first time that the Greeks of Italy had looked overseas for help. Archidamus of Sparta in 343 BC, Alexander the Molossian in 334 and Cleonymus of Sparta in 302 had all tried their hand, ostensibly assisting the Greek cities against hostile 'barbarians', but also furthering their own ambitions, which did not always coincide with what the cities wanted. The same applies to the frequent interventions of Agathocles, the tyrant of Syracuse, between 298 and 295. So when they approached Pyrrhus in 281 the Tarentines knew, or should have known, that the king, if he answered the appeal, would be likely to have more far-reaching ambitions than saving Tarentum from the Romans. When Pyrrhus decided to abandon a risky attempt to conquer Macedonia and to accept the Tarentine offer instead, he is said to have been aiming not only at an empire in Italy, but also at the conquest of Sicily and Carthage (Plut., *Pyrrh.* 14.3–5).

Pyrrhus set out for Italy in 280 BC with an army of 25,000 men and 20 elephants. This was the first time that the Romans had had to face a fully equipped and professionally trained Hellenistic army, and in the first engagement at Heraclea they were defeated, but not before they had inflicted heavy losses on their opponents.[44] Pyrrhus then offered peace, but the Senate rejected his terms, evidently persuaded by the aged Appius Claudius not to treat with the enemy as long as he remained on Italian soil. This detail, if authentic, gives an interesting glimpse of how the Romans now saw themselves in relation to Italy.[45] Pyrrhus then attempted to march on Rome, and advanced as far as Anagnia before turning back; Capua and Naples had closed their gates, and none of Rome's allies joined him. He must have begun to realise the size of the task he had set himself; Rome was a well-organised state whose resources he could not hope to match.[46]

In 279 he won a second battle at Ausculum, but his losses were even greater than at Heraclea. His response to a soldier who congratulated him has become proverbial: 'One more victory over the Romans and we are completely done for' (Plut., *Pyrrh.* 21.9). A year later he decided to cut his losses and to try his hand in Sicily, where the Greek cities had requested his help against the Carthaginians. The result was a renewed alliance between Rome and Carthage (Polyb. 3.25.1–5). In Sicily Pyrrhus promised much but again achieved little, and when he returned to Italy in 275 he was met and defeated by a Roman army at Beneventum. Pyrrhus then sailed back to Greece where he continued to waste his talents and the lives of his followers in fruitless enterprises. His brilliant but ultimately worthless career came to an end a few years later when he was struck on the head and killed by a roof-tile during a street battle in Argos.

After Pyrrhus' departure the Romans overran Magna Graecia, and captured Tarentum in 272. But Pyrrhus' invasion had prompted a revolt of the Samnites, Lucanians and Bruttians which lasted for over a decade. Although our meagre sources provide few details about this war, it was evidently serious since the Capitoline *Fasti* list no fewer than ten triumphs over these peoples (in varying combinations) between 282 and 272 BC. The final defeat of Samnium and Lucania was marked by the foundation of colonies at Paestum in 273 BC, Beneventum in 268, and Aesernia in 263. By then the Roman conquest of peninsular Italy was complete.

7 THE NATURE OF ROMAN CONTROL IN ITALY AND THE DYNAMICS OF IMPERIALISM

The Roman conquest of Italy was a remarkable achievement, if only because it happened so quickly. A little over seventy years before the capture of

Volsinii in 264 Rome's power was confined to the relatively minute region of Latium Vetus. On the other hand, the Romans established their control so thoroughly that, if we exclude the special circumstances of the Hannibalic War, they faced no serious revolts in Italy for nearly 200 years. The only exceptions were the isolated and short-lived rebellions of Falerii (241 BC) and Fregellae (125 BC), which attracted no support from the other allies and were both easily crushed. The speed and thoroughness of the Roman conquest are astounding, and demand some kind of explanation.

Recent studies of Roman imperialism have tended to stress the belligerence of Roman society, and the frequency and intensity of its military activity.[47] For most of its history the Roman Republic was constantly at war, and a very high proportion of its citizen manpower was committed to military service. Its institutions were military in character and function, and its culture was pervaded by a warlike ethos. These facts are important, but they do not explain Roman imperialism; rather, they are themselves symptoms of the phenomenon that needs to be explained. Why were the Romans so belligerent? How did they manage to conquer Italy so quickly, and why was their control of the conquered peoples so thorough and long-lasting? In the last analysis, the answer to all these questions is the same, and is to be found in the nature of Rome's relations with her neighbours from the earliest times.

The foundations of Roman military power were firmly laid in the settlement that followed the Latin revolt in 338 BC. This settlement, it can be argued, only modified the institutions and structures that had been established in dealings with the Latin League, the Hernici, Veii, Caere and Tusculum. But the systematic application of these institutions to the relationships that were set up in 338 marked a new departure, and propelled the Romans along the road to empire. As we have seen, the settlement of 338 established a hierarchy of relationships in which the subject peoples were categorised as full citizens, citizens *sine suffragio*, Latins and allies. These various groups had one thing in common: the obligation to provide troops for the Roman army in time of war. The result was that the Roman commonwealth possessed enormous reserves of military manpower, and in 338 was already the strongest military power in Italy.

As it proceeded on its triumphant course, the Roman state expanded by adding an ever widening circle of dependent communities to the commonwealth. Defeated peoples were annexed with either full or partial citizenship, Latin colonies were founded, and an increasing number of states became allies. By 264 BC Rome had concluded permanent treaties with over 150 nominally independent Italian communities, which had either been defeated in war or had voluntarily agreed to become allies.[48] The treaties (*foedera*) probably differed from one another in detail, but the basic provision common to all of them was the allies' obligation to supply military aid to Rome. In military enterprises.

From 338 BC onwards, every Roman army that took the field comprised both citizen troops (in the legions) and contingents of allies. This fact is often overlooked by our Rome-centred sources, but it should not be overlooked by us. The presence of the allies was essential to Rome's military success. We have already noted that at the battle of Sentinum the Latins and other allies outnumbered the Roman legionaries (above, p. 361). We know from Polybius (2.24) that in the third century the Italian allies could have mobilised some 360,000 men of military age on Rome's behalf; and that, of the troops actually under arms, the allies outnumbered the Romans by three to two.

It is not difficult to see how these facts bear on the question of Roman imperialism. The availability of Italian manpower gave the Roman state vast military potential and the capacity to absorb heavy losses, as the events of the Pyrrhic War demonstrated. It meant that Rome could use war as an instrument of policy with a minimum of risk to herself. But the system also had a more dynamic effect. Since the alliances had a purely military function, they were of use to the Romans only in time of war. The Romans therefore had to engage in warfare if they were to avail themselves of the services of the allies and to keep the system in being. This functional interpretation of the Roman alliance was first outlined by Momigliano, who observed that the Romans

> passed from war to war without giving thought to the very meta-physical question of whether the wars were meant to gain power for Rome or to keep the allies busy. Wars were the very essence of the Roman organisation. The battle of Sentinum was the natural prelude to the battle of Pydna – or even to the destruction of Corinth and the Social War.[49]

It follows that the Roman conquest was the result of efficient exploitation of the resources of the allies. Certainly the allies had to bear the burden of the wars of conquest, and a substantial share of the risks. In particular, they incurred a proportion of the cost, since they were obliged to pay for their contingents out of their own resources.[50] In this way the Romans were able to tax the allies without imposing a direct tribute, and to fight wars at a relatively low cost to themselves. For their part the allies were evidently prepared to accept this state of things, and remained consistently loyal to Rome. This compliant attitude, although at first sight surprising, can be accounted for in two ways.

In the first place the Romans could count on the support of the propertied classes in the allied states, who turned naturally to Rome whenever their local interests were threatened. During the wars of conquest the Romans were often helped by pro-Roman elements within the Italian communities; the events at Naples in 326 BC (above, p. 353) provide a good example. On several occasions the Romans intervened with military force to defend local aristocracies against popular insurrections, for example at Arretium in 302 BC (Livy 10.3–5), in Lucania in 296 (Livy 10.18.8) and at Volsinii in 264 (Zonaras 8.7.4–8). In return they received the active co-operation of the ruling classes of the allied states, an arrangement that ensured their continuing loyalty even in times of crisis. It was especially effective in regions where deep social divisions existed, as in northern Etruria, where archaic forms of dependence and clientage appear to have survived well into the Roman period.[51]

The second reason for the co-operation of the Italian allies is that as military partners of Rome they obtained a share of the profits of successful warfare. This was a standard clause in all treaties and went back to the original *foedus Cassianum* of 493 BC (see above, p. 299). It applied not just to movable booty, which was shared equally between Romans and allies alike, but also to land, which was confiscated as a matter of course from defeated enemies. This land was used for colonisation and distribution to individuals. Although the sources do not say so explicitly, it is virtually certain that the recipients of land allotments included non-Roman Italians (Latins and allies) as well as Roman citizens.

This inference is based not only on what we know of colonisation at later periods (e.g. Livy 34.42.5–6; 42.4.3–4; etc.), but also on the simple demographic argument that the Roman population on its own could not have sustained such a high rate of emigration as the record implies.[52] According to the sources Latin colonies comprised between 2,500 and 6,000 adult males. This means that in the period from 334 to 263 BC, when nineteen such colonies were established (see below, Table 9, p. 381), as many as 70,000 adult males and their dependants were resettled. It is unlikely that the Roman population on its own could have withstood such a drain on its citizen manpower. The only reasonable explanation of the facts is that a substantial proportion of these settlers were drawn from the allied communities.

We should not forget that many of the allies had themselves been defeated in war and compelled to join the Roman alliance. Allied participation in the settlement of conquered territories is directly connected with the Roman practice of confiscating large areas of land from conquered states. The Roman system has been compared to a criminal operation which compensates its victims by enrolling them in the gang and inviting them to share the proceeds of future robberies.[53] This brutal analogy brings us back to the point about the Roman state's need to make war. Any self-respecting criminal gang would soon break up if its boss decided to abandon crime and 'go legitimate'.

By joining a large and efficient operation and sacrificing their political independence, Rome's Italian allies obtained security, protection and profit for a relatively modest premium. Although the allied soldiers serving in the Roman army might often (if not always) outnumber their Roman counterparts, the burden placed on the manpower of Roman citizens was proportionately much heavier. In 225 BC the Roman citizen troops accounted for about 40 per cent of the combined Roman and Italian army, but at that time Roman citizens represented only about 27 per cent of the total population of peninsular Italy.[54] By drawing up this kind of balance sheet it becomes possible to understand the loyalty of the allies to Rome, and to explain both the dynamics and the cohesiveness of the system.

ROME IN THE AGE OF
THE ITALIAN WARS

1 THE TRANSFORMATION OF THE STATE

During the period of the wars of conquest the Roman state was internally transformed. It was at this time that the characteristic political, social and economic structures of the classical Republic began to take shape. As far as political institutions are concerned, the most striking development was the emergence of the Senate as the principal organ of government, and of the nobility as the controlling element within the Senate. When and how this came about is not easy to say, but there is no doubt that it happened. In the second century BC the Senate dominated all aspects of public life. According to Polybius it had complete control of state finances, military policy, foreign affairs, and law and order.[1] We may add that it also had full charge of all matters relating to the state religion. That, one is tempted to say, covers just about everything.

In the early Republic, however, the Senate had not possessed these all-embracing powers. Indeed, as we have seen (above, pp. 247f.), the Senate of the archaic age is an elusive entity, with no formal authority and an ill-defined membership. As far as we can judge, it was purely an advisory council whose members were chosen at the whim of the magistrates in office. It may well be (although no source says this) that the magistrates fell into the habit of including among their advisers all surviving ex-magistrates; and it is also likely enough that it became their normal practice to continue with the council they inherited from their predecessors, so that in practice membership of the Senate became a lifelong position. If so, the Senate, like many other Roman institutions, would have acquired a tralaticious character.

Even so, the Senate did not become a permanent independent body until the Lex Ovinia handed over to the censors the task of enrolling senators according to set criteria (cf. above, p. 248). The date of the Lex Ovinia is unknown, but it was certainly earlier than 318 BC, when we know the Senate was selected by the censors, and probably later than 339, when the Lex Publilia enacted that one of the censors must be a plebeian.[2] Indeed the most likely date would be some time between 339 and 332 BC, when Publilius Philo himself was censor.

However that may be, the important consequence of the Lex Ovinia was that those who were chosen became senators for life; their position was no longer dependent on the favour of the magistrates in office. It is not clear from the evidence (Festus p. 290 L) precisely how the censors were to carry out their task. The text merely says that they were 'sworn to enrol the best men of all ranks' without further explanation;[3] this is no doubt a résumé of regulations that were set out in detail in the law. We might imagine that the persons in question included all former curule magistrates, both patrician and plebeian, but more than that we cannot say. In any event we can be sure that the law specified the criteria of selection, and in doing so it necessarily restricted the discretionary powers of the censors. Although it gave them the right to omit names from the roll of the Senate, it appears to have allowed them only to pass over those who had shown themselves to be morally unfit for membership. The Lex Ovinia therefore marks an important stage in what Mommsen called 'the emancipation of the Senate from the power of the magistrates'.[4]

Everything suggests that the Senate gradually acquired its control of the government in the generations following the passage of the Lex Ovinia. This reconstruction is consistent with other political trends that can be observed at this time, and can be explained in the same way. First we may note that before the late fourth century government appears to have been conducted by the magistrates acting in concert with the popular assemblies. At this period all major decisions concerning the mobilisation of armies, the declaration of war, the conclusion of treaties, the foundation of colonies, the creation of new tribes, the extension of citizenship, as well as all kinds of reforming legislation, were decided on by popular assemblies summoned by the magistrates.[5]

Although the magistrates would have consulted their advisers, it does not follow that at this date popular enactments were merely formal ratifications of decisions that had been initiated by the Senate. That is not to say that the advisory role of the Senate was unimportant; but when the Roman state was a relatively compact territorial unit with only simple administrative needs, the popular assemblies probably took a more central part in determining policy than they did later. Again, the Senate's control of finance would have been less important and perhaps less absolute in the pre-coinage economy of the fourth century than in the relatively complex world of the second.

A simple example will suffice to illustrate the difference between the political system of the fourth century and that of the 'classical' period. In the third and second centuries the Senate's right to terminate or extend the *imperium* of a serving commander (*prorogatio*) was an important weapon in its arsenal, as Polybius himself points out (6.15.6). But in the fourth century the practice of *prorogatio* hardly existed. Moreover, the earliest known instance, the appointment of Q. Publilius Philo *pro consule* against Naples in 326 BC, was the result of a popular vote (Livy 8.23.11–12).

We must surely reckon with the possibility that in the mid-fourth century political power rested not with a collective oligarchy but with a handful of talented and charismatic individuals who shared the senior magistracies among themselves and largely directed the policy of the state by acting with the people. Their own position depended on tenure of the magistracies and consequently on popular support. The clearest sign of this is the frequency of 'iteration' – that is, the repeated tenure of the same office by the same man.

Iteration was extremely common in the fourth century, when the majority of consuls held the office more than once, and a number of leading figures had careers including four or more consulships, as well as holding office frequently as praetor, censor, dictator and Master of the Horse.[6] In the seventy-two years between 366 and 291 BC 54 consulships were held by only fourteen individuals, 38 of them by just eight, each of whom was consul four or more times. They include the patricians C. Sulpicius Peticus, L. Papirius Cursor, M. Valerius Corvus and Q. Fabius Maximus Rullianus, and the plebeians M. Popillius Laenas, C. Marcius Rutilus, Q. Publilius Philo and P. Decius Mus.

It is important to stress what an unusual pattern this is. The *Fasti* allow us to trace the history of the consulship right down to the time of its demise in AD 542; but in the whole of this immense period the careers of fourth-century BC politicians are quite exceptional. The only parallels, and this must be significant, are the careers of late republican dynasts such as Marius and Caesar, and of the emperors themselves. It is legitimate to conclude that the political leaders of the fourth century BC ruled by virtue of the offices they held, and that their tenure of office was dependent on popular appeal and electoral success. This point highlights the fact that the system involved a substantial democratic element that was largely absent in the later period when the Senate controlled the government and the outcome of the annual elections had little effect on the general direction of policy.

This 'plebiscitary system' (as it may be called)[7] was gradually undermined in the period of the Samnite Wars. The first signs of an oligarchic reaction appeared in 342 BC, when L. Genucius attempted to curtail the practice of iteration. Two of Genucius' laws, concerning usury and the sharing of the consulship between patricians and plebeians, have already been discussed (above, pp. 332 and 337). But he is also credited with a third law, that no one be permitted to hold more than one magistracy at a time, or to hold the same office twice within ten years. The latter clause seems to be reflected in the *Fasti*, which not only register the presence of several 'new men' in the years after 342, but also reveal that in the next twenty years no one held two consulships within ten years of each other, with one doubtful exception. The contrast with the preceding period is so striking that we must conclude that the Lex Genucia was not only enacted but, for a time, enforced.[8]

The election in 321 of two able and experienced men (L. Papirius Cursor II, Q. Publilius Philo III), in both cases in breach of the ten-year rule, was clearly a response to exceptional circumstances; 321 BC was after all the year of the Roman defeat at the Caudine Forks. The general crisis of the Second Samnite War caused a revival of frequent iterations. Not for the last time the Romans sacrificed constitutional principle on the altar of military expediency. In the space of just thirteen years (326–313) L. Papirius Cursor managed to hold five consulships, two of them in succession (in 320 and 319).

But Cursor's remarkable record was an exception and stands out against a more general trend away from multiple iterations and towards a wider distribution of consular honours among the elite. In the critical year 295 the two consuls were men who between them could boast nine consulships (Q. Fabius Maximus Rullianus V, P. Decius Mus IV), but nothing like this was to occur again until the Second Punic War, when the military emergency caused another temporary reversion to multiple iterations. In the period from 295 to 215 only three men held as many as three consulships each, of whom M' Curius Dentatus (cos. III, 274) was the last. The most telling statistic is that in the thirty-five years from 289 to 255 the seventy consulships were shared among sixty-five different individuals; in other words there was virtually no iteration at all.

We may conclude by saying that from the end of the Third Samnite War (290 BC) Roman nobles could normally expect, at best, to be consul just once in their careers. After the multiple iterations of the fourth century this represents a remarkable transformation. Its political effects can be listed under three headings. First, a system was now in place which ensured that honours would be more equally destributed among a wider elite. Second, it served to curtail the rise of ambitious and charismatic individuals. Third, the fact that individual nobles held high office only occasionally and for short periods meant that the exercise of real power was bound to shift to the Senate, of which they were all permanent members. These three features are classic symptoms of oligarchy, a system of government which depends on rotation of office within a competitive elite, and the suppression of charismatic individuals by peer-group pressure, usually exercised by a council of elders.[9] In these respects Rome in the second and third centuries comes very close to an oligarchic ideal type.

Two further developments at the beginning of the third century point in the same direction. First, this period witnessed the demise of the dictatorship as a regular office. During the fourth century dictators were appointed almost as a matter of course. In the period from 367 to 300 BC dictators held office in two out of every three years, but hardly ever thereafter.[10] This pattern is especially evident in the case of dictators appointed to military commands in times of emergency (as opposed to those chosen for other reasons, for example to hold elections, or to 'hammer the nail'). Military dictators are recorded frequently down to 310, but are then attested only in 302, in 249 at a critical moment of the First Punic War, and finally in the emergency that followed the battle of Trasimene in 217. After that, we wait for Sulla. The second of the two developments referred to is the mechanism that came to replace the dictatorship as the standard response to an emergency, namely prorogation. As we have seen, the first extensive use of this device occurred in 296–295, during the sort of crisis that would earlier have called for a dictator. The difference is that, from the 290s onwards, prorogations were handled by the Senate, not by the magistrates or the people. The significance of this development is unmistakable.

There can be no doubt that the rise of the senatorial oligarchy occurred in the years on either side of 300 BC. Apart from anything else, it fulfilled some obvious practical needs The growth of the Roman state and the increasing complexity of its affairs were bound to enhance the power and standing of its only permanent council. The popular assemblies, cumbersome in their procedures and only able to accept or reject specific proposals, were quite unsuitable for the administration of matters such as finance. In the military field the days were long gone when the consuls could simply ask the assembly whether or not war should be declared on some threatening neighbour. Now that campaigns were taking place in far-flung regions of Italy, strategic decisions had to be made about the tasks that needed to be undertaken and the logistic resources required to carry them out. This function – the allocation to the executive magistrates of specific tasks (the original meaning of the term 'provinces')[11] – could only be handled by a permanent body with sufficient skill and experience to make informed decisions. That body, needless to say, was the Senate.

The changes we have been discussing were not brought about solely by administrative pressures. Political and ideological forces were also at work. The political tensions of the late fourth century, which are vaguely outlined but not satisfactorily explained in the literary sources, can be interpreted in terms of a struggle between two conflicting tendencies: an oligarchic tendency, reflecting the interests of the rising patricio-plebeian nobility, and a plebiscitary tendency, represented by charismatic and populist individuals.

2 THE CAREER OF APPIUS CLAUDIUS CAECUS

The existence of such a conflict can help to explain the extraordinary career of Appius Claudius Caecus, the dominant figure in Roman public life in the years on either side of 300 BC. Of Appius' early life nothing is known. An account of his career on an inscription from the Forum of Augustus records a number of junior magistracies, but he first appears in the literary sources as censor in 312 BC, when he created a sensation by his bold and controversial actions.[12]

The main events of Appius Claudius' censorship can be briefly summar-ised. He first ordered the construction of the great public works that bore his name: the Via Appia, the road from Rome to Capua, and the Aqua Appia, Rome's first aqueduct, which brought fresh water into the city from the Sabine hills. Both projects entailed considerable expenditure of public funds, but, according to Diodorus (20.36), Appius acted without the Senate's authority and emptied the treasury. In drawing up his list of the Senate he outraged the establishment by choosing men considered unworthy and passing over some of their betters (Livy 9.30.1–2). His selection of new senators was regarded as wilful and partisan; and great offence was caused by the fact that many of them were the sons of freedmen.

Appius Claudius' most important measure as censor was a reorganisation of the tribes, which had the effect of increasing the voting power of the city proletariat in the tribal assemblies. The precise nature of the change is unclear; Livy merely says that Appius corrupted the Forum and the Campus (that is, probably, the electoral and legislative assemblies) by distributing the lower classes (*humiles*) throughout all the tribes. The *humiles* were presumably the propertyless inhabitants of the city (artisans, traders and so forth), who had hitherto been confined to only four of the thirty-one tribes, and were therefore under-represented in the assemblies in proportion to their numbers. A large number of them, probably the great majority, appear to have been freedmen or the descendants of freedmen.[13] Appius' reform distributed them among all the tribes, including the so-called rustic tribes, which had formerly been the exclusive preserve of country dwellers and landowners. The measure had far-reaching implications; in Livy's words it transferred the control of the assembly from the 'honest citizens' (*integer populus*) to the faction of the Forum, the 'lowest of the low' (*forensis factio . . . humillimi*: Livy 9.46.13–14).

Appius also interfered with the organisation of the state religion; our sources have some entertaining ancedotes about his activities in this sphere, but we are not in a position to understand their political significance (if any).[14] What is clear is that his radical reforms aroused a storm of protest from conservative nobles. Even his own colleague in the censorship, C. Plautius, was so scandalised by the new senatorial roll that he resigned his office, leaving Appius to carry on alone (and with a free hand). It is further alleged that Appius failed to lay down his office when the full eighteen-month term had elapsed. Indeed, according to some sources he was still in office as censor in 308 BC, when he stood (successfully) for the consulship (Livy 9.42.3).

However that may be, there is no doubt that Appius' measures aroused intense opposition. His new list of senators was not recognised by the consuls of 311 BC, who continued to summon the Senate using the old list that had been drawn up by the previous censors. Conceivably the consuls' justification was that by enrolling his own clients and passing over more 'worthy' choices Appius had contravened the Lex Ovinia.[15] In any event, Appius' designs in regard to the Senate were thwarted. His reform of the tribes, however, remained in force for a time, and was directly responsible, according to Livy, for the election of Cn Flavius as curule aedile for 304 BC (Livy 9.46.10).

Cn Flavius, a secretary (*scriba*) of Appius Claudius, was the son of a freedman and the first of his class to hold a curule magistracy. The conservative establishment was appalled, and many nobles refused to treat Flavius with the customary respect due to a curule magistrate (Piso fr. 27 P); some even removed their gold rings and military decorations in protest. As aedile Cn Flavius published an account of the legal procedures known as *legis actiones*, which had not hitherto been accessible to the people, and published a calendar indicating the *dies fasti* – the days on which legal business was permitted. There is no reason to question the view of all the sources that the publication of the *ius Flavianum* (as it was later called) and the calendar was a politically motivated act, nor the clear implication of most of them that Flavius was acting as Appius Claudius' agent.[16]

A reaction soon followed. In the year of Flavius' aedileship, the censors, those old cronies Q. Fabius Rullianus and P. Decius Mus, reversed Appius' tribal reorganisation, and confined the *humiles* once again to the four 'urban' tribes. Then, when Cn Flavius dedicated a shrine of Concord in the Comitium, much to the annoyance of the leading nobles, a law was immediately enacted that no one should dedicate a temple or an altar without the approval of the Senate or of a majority of the tribunes of the *plebs*.[17]

How are we to interpret this confusing jumble of data? The actions attributed to Appius and his agents mark him out as a radical populist who aimed to build a personal following among the mass of the people. This general assessment of Appius Claudius as a revolutionary democrat is clearly set out in the surviving sources, especially in Diodorus, who gives the most coherent account of his censorship (20.36). It was accepted by Mommsen (who likened Appius to Cleisthenes and Pericles) and remains the standard view, in spite of some recent hypercritical and revisionist challenges.[18]

It is true that the later annalistic tradition was hostile to the whole clan of the patrician Claudii,[19] and that Livy's stereotyped picture of Appius Claudius Caecus as a tyrannical patrician cannot be accepted as it stands (it is contradicted by Livy's own narrative!); on the other hand, there is no reason to doubt the basic outline of Appius' actions, as they are reported in the sources, nor to modify the record so as to reduce him to the level of a run-of-the-mill politician who did nothing out of the ordinary.[20] Some of the traditional hostility to Appius may even reflect contemporary rhetoric; as we have seen, Fabius Pictor could have had access to traditions going back to the time of Fabius Rullianus, who was a personal enemy of Appius Claudius.

The chief difficulty in seeing Appius as a populist is the fact that on a number of occasions he appears as the upholder of patrician privileges and an opponent of the *plebs*. In 300 BC he vigorously opposed the Ogulnian plebiscite, which admitted plebeians to the two senior priestly colleges, and on two separate occasions he attempted to exclude plebeians from the consulship and to bring about the election of an all-patrician college.

But aristocratic pride is perfectly compatible with demagogic methods, as Mommsen noted (citing the examples of Pericles and Caesar). Appius' opposition to the Lex Ogulnia is not really a major difficulty because that law was in no sense a democratic measure. Like other political reforms in the

Conflict of the Orders, it benefited only a narrow group of well-to-do plebeians and did nothing for the rights of the lower classes. Under the Lex Ogulnia the major priestly colleges became self-perpetuating oligarchic cliques, divided equally between the patrician and plebeian members of the new nobility and recruiting new members by co-optation. The choice of pontiffs and augurs was not in any way subjected to popular will (the colleges were not opened to election until much later), and anyone not acceptable to the conservative establishment could be excluded. Appius himself was not a member of either college.[21]

As for his attempts to contrive the election of an all-patrician college of consuls, the most probable explanation is that Appius was challenging the system of power sharing between the two Orders, rather than the right of plebeians as such to hold the consulship (which is how Livy and his sources interpreted it – 10.15.8–9). The target was not the political rights of plebeians in general, but rather the privileged position of the plebeian nobility, which had acquired a guaranteed share of the senior magistracies, irrespective of the wishes of the electorate, whose power of decision was restricted by the power-sharing rule.

The point can be illustrated by the consular elections of 297 BC, in which Appius himself was a candidate (Livy 10.15.7–12). When it became clear that the people's first choice was Q. Fabius Rullianus, who was not even a candidate (as consul in office Fabius was presiding over the elections; his candidature would have been technically illegal), Appius proposed that the rules should be waived and that both he and Fabius should be consuls. This was evidently what the result of a free election would have been.

In the event Fabius withdrew, allowing Appius Claudius to take the patrician place in the consular college, and thus resolving the immediate issue. But the point of principle was whether or not the *comitia* should be entitled to elect whomsoever they wished, regardless of the rules. Appius evidently contended that they should, on the basis of the clause of the Twelve Tables (XII.5) which stated that 'the people's last decree is the effective law' (Livy 7.17.12; Cic., *pro Balbo* 33). The argument, in other words, was that an electoral vote constituted a decree of the *populus*, and as such automatically overruled any previous enactment that might conflict with it.

Livy explicitly attributes this line of reasoning to Appius at the time when his prolonged tenure of the censorship came under attack (9.33.9); and the case is outlined in full in a speech ascribed to Appius Claudius Crassus, Caecus' grandfather, at the time of the Licinio-Sextian Rogations (Livy 6.40.15–20; cf. 10.7.2). The argument which Livy or his source(s) thus foisted on the Claudian house is so distinctive, and so obviously accords with Appius Claudius Caecus' actual view of popular rights, that we might reasonably conjecture that the tradition has preserved a genuine example of the political thought of Appius Claudius Caecus.

This speculation is not necessarily improbable, given that much reliable information about the political debates of this period would have been available to Fabius Pictor; moreover, we happen to know that some of Appius' own words survived in written form. Appius Claudius has a place in the history of literature as the Father of Latin prose.[22] Works attributed to him include political speeches, most famously the one in which he opposed peace with Pyrrhus in 279 BC (Cic., *Cat. maior* 16; *Brutus* 61), and a work of jurisprudence (Pomponius in Dig. 1.2.2.36). A collection of his sayings (*carmina*) circulated in the late Republic, and was already known to the Greek philosopher Panaetius in the second century BC. The most famous of the sayings to survive is the adage *faber est suae quisque fortunae* ('each man is the architect of his own fortune'). The various works attributed to Appius Claudius are sometimes dismissed as late forgeries, but without any good reason.[23] The fact is that the traditional picture of Appius does have some authentic touches. That is what makes him so different from Furius Camillus, Manlius Torquatus, Valerius Corvus and the other lifeless heroes of the early Republic. As De Sanctis observed, he stands out as the first living personality in Roman history.[24]

3 THE LEX HORTENSIA AND ITS EFFECTS

It is clear that in his political actions Appius Claudius was swimming against the tide. His efforts to democratise the assembly and to assert its sovereignty were ultimately abortive; popular government was never established in Rome. On the contrary, the outcome of the political struggles of the fourth century was the formation of a self-serving and self-perpetuating oligarchy which restricted the magistrates' scope for independent political action and at the same time emasculated the theoretical sovereignty of the people's assemblies.

This may seem at first sight a somewhat paradoxical result, given that the Roman tradition regarded the political history of this period as a long but ultimately successful struggle for liberty and the assertion of the rights of Roman citizens. Moreover, some modern scholars have argued that at this time Rome was progressing towards democracy.[25] But we must recognise that there is a great difference between what the Romans regarded as liberty and the modern (or for that matter the ancient) concept of democracy. For the ordinary citizen *libertas* signified equality before the law, and the right of appeal (*ius provocationis*) against the arbitrary decisions of a magistrate. Both principles were enshrined in the Twelve Tables, and reinforced by subsequent legislation, for example the Lex Valeria of 300 BC (see above, p. 277). But the Roman ideal of juristic liberty and equality for all citizens was never matched by true political liberty or equality of political rights. In political terms *libertas* was an aristocratic concept, which signified the unhindered operation of a system of hierarchical institutions, and the freedom of members of a noble elite to compete equally and openly for political honours.[26]

The theory that in the fourth and early third centuries Rome was gradually advancing towards democracy is based on the fact that at this time the people's assemblies gradually acquired the right to pass legally binding enactments. The final stage in the process was the Lex Hortensia, a measure passed in circumstances that are entirely obscure to us.[27] Even the date is uncertain, but it was between 289 and 286 BC. We are told that Q. Hortensius, a plebeian who is otherwise unknown, was appointed dictator to deal with a plebeian secession caused by debt. How the emergency arose, and how it was resolved, we cannot say (but it is interesting to observe that the Lex Poetelia of 326 BC had not, in fact, abolished the problem of indebtedness). The memorable result of the crisis of *c.* 287 BC, however, was a law that appeared to endorse the principle of popular sovereignty.

But this impression is illusory. The problem is that the apparent success of the *plebs* did not in the event result in democratic government. This has led historians to speak about the 'frustration of democracy by the Roman establishment', and to argue that the embryonic growth was somehow aborted almost at the moment of its birth.[28] Alternatively it has been suggested that the Roman state became so prosperous through war and imperialism that the masses were content to leave the conduct of affairs to the Senate and did not bother to exercise the democratic rights which they had managed to acquire.[29]

There is certainly some truth in these propositions. The alleviation of economic discontent by successful conquest undoubtedly caused the people to acquiesce in the rule of the oligarchy, and created a consensus that was to last until the time of the Gracchi. But that is not to say that Rome was a latent democracy, or that the people possessed the constitutional means to withdraw their consent at any time. In fact the political reforms of the fourth century had had the effect of reducing the powers of the plebeian assembly. As we have seen (above, pp. 339–44), the leading plebeians fulfilled their aspirations and obtained admittance to the nobility, but by doing so they ceased to represent the political interests of the rest of the *plebs*.

The Lex Hortensia was certainly an important concession (the legislation of the Gracchi would have been impossible without it), but it did not radically affect the structure of Roman political institutions. Democracy never materialised at Rome because the popular assemblies could not function as autonomous institutions. They did not meet as a matter of course, as the Athenian *ecclesia* did, but only when summoned by a magistrate – a consul or praetor in the case of the *comitia*, a tribune in that of the *concilium plebis*. Moreover, they could not initiate anything; they merely answered 'yes' or 'no' to questions (*rogationes*) that were put to them by the magistrates, or chose between candidates who were presented to them.

The assembly's role in politics was therefore passive rather than active, and depended absolutely on the magistrates who had the right to 'deal with the people' (*agere cum populo*). In this sense every election, enactment or judicial verdict was a bilateral act, as Mommsen saw.[30] The problem was that the two parties to this form of contract were potentially, and often actually, antagonistic. The magistrate did not necessarily share the people's interests, and was under no obligation to represent them; although elected by the people, he was not in any way accountable to them either during or after his term of office. The fact that consuls could not be re-elected for consecutive terms, and that iteration was eventually eliminated altogether, meant that they had no cause to heed the wishes, or the wrath, of the electorate.

Ordinary citizens had little freedom of speech, in the basic sense that they were denied access to all formal means of making their views known and of taking political initiatives. Only magistrates had an automatic right to address the people and only they could propose laws. The citizens had no right either to debate or to amend the proposals put to them. It follows that the Roman people could advance their own interests only in collusion with a magistrate; and for them to do so against the wishes of the ruling class required a kind of conspiracy between magistrate and people. Not surprisingly, this did not occur very often, and when it did the oligarchy was still able to use a variety of devices to thwart a proposal, for instance by using the tribunician veto or by the announcement of unfavourable omens before or during an assembly. When in 133 BC the tribune Tiberius Gracchus allied himself with the assembly in a systematic attempt to promote the interests of the poor against those of the possessing classes, the result was an explosion of violence and the start of the Roman Revolution.[31]

Two further points need to be made in connection with the subject of democracy (or its absence) at Rome. First, the voting in the assemblies was organised by groups, rather than on the basis of a simple majority of all those present and voting. In the *comitia tributa* and the *concilium plebis* the voting units were the local tribes, which numbered thirty-three after 299 BC (the definitive figure of thirty-five was reached in 241 BC, when the last two tribes were added). Four of them were the so-called 'urban' tribes, the rest were 'rustic' tribes. The significance of this distinction is that (after the failure of Appius Claudius' reform) only landowners and country dwellers were registered in the rustic tribes, while the landless inhabitants of the city were confined to the four urban tribes, and consequently had very limited voting power in proportion to their numbers. Since the assemblies were held only in Rome, the system artificially favoured the wealthy landowners who lived in the city but owned country estates, and discriminated against both the urban proletariat and the far-flung peasant smallholders who for practical reasons were unable to attend the *comitia* in person.

The voting units of the *comitia centuriata* were the 193 centuries, which were distributed among five economically defined classes (see above, pp. 179ff.). But the distribution of the centuries among the classes went in inverse proportion to the actual numbers of citizens, so that the wealthiest class, which was numerically relatively small, contained by far the largest number of centuries; together with eighteen centuries of *equites*, the eighty centuries of the first class could command an absolute majority of the total. At the other extreme, proletarians who fell below the minimum property qualification for membership of the fifth class were enrolled in a single century, and were often not called upon to vote at all.[32]

The assemblies were thus organised to give the greatest influence to the propertied classes. Another factor that gave the *comitia centuriata* in particular an inherently conservative character was the division of the centuries between *iuniores* (men aged between 17 and 45) and *seniores* (men aged 46 and over). Since both had an equal number of centuries within each class, it follows that the seniors, who represented fewer than 30 per cent of the total electorate, carried more than twice as much political weight as the juniors.

The second point is that only members of the elite could stand for magisterial office. Whether or not there was a formal property qualification, it is obvious that only the wealthy could put themselves forward for positions that were unpaid and might entail considerable expense. Moreover, given the restrictions on canvassing and the absence of any means of making oneself known to the electorate, an outsider without powerful connections and backing would have had no chance at all.[33] It is significant that the term *nobilis* means literally 'well-known'.

4 ECONOMIC DEVELOPMENTS

The period of the Samnite Wars saw an unparalleled increase in the public and private wealth of the Romans. Their most obvious gain was in land. The *ager Romanus*, which after the conclusion of the Latin War in 338 BC had comprised *c.* 5,525 km^2 and supported a population of around 347,300 persons (see above, p. 351), had expanded by 264 to 26,805 km^2 with a population in the region of 900,000. On these figures the Romans possessed more than 20 per cent of the total land surface of peninsular Italy (reckoned at 125,455 km^2) and nearly 30 per cent of its population (estimated in total at something over 3 millions).[34]

This expansion was accompanied by a considerable redistribution of landed property within the annexed territories, where impoverished Roman citizens and others (p. 367, above) were resettled on small allotments. The principal stages in this process were marked by the formation of new rustic tribes, the Scaptia and the Maecia in 332 BC, the Oufentina and Falerna in 318, and the Aniensis and Teretina in 299. A further large-scale resettlement of Roman citizens took place on land annexed from the Sabines and Praetuttii after the campaigns of M' Curius Dentatus in 290 BC. The original proprietors were wholly or partly dispossessed, and many of them were killed, enslaved or deported *en masse* to other areas.

We have no means of knowing how many people were involved in these schemes, but a reasonable guess would be that between 20,000 and 30,000 adult male Romans were resettled, together with their dependants. In addition, Romans and their allies benefited from the foundation of Latin colonies, which in the period 334–264 BC took up a further 7,000 km² of conquered land and involved the resettlement of over 70,000 men and their families (see below, Table 9; Map 9).

Rome's increasing prosperity is reflected in the development of the city and the growth of its population. The profits of conquest, in the form of booty and indemnities, were used to finance a programme of public building on a scale that had not been seen since the great age of the Tarquins. The literary sources record the construction of fourteen temples in the years from 302 to 264 BC (see below, Table 10), but this is certainly not a complete list of those actually built; eight of the fourteen are known from Livy, and belong to the period before 293 BC, for which his text is fully preserved. Moreover, archaeology provides evidence of other temple constructions, either not mentioned in literary sources, or not securely identified with otherwise known buildings. These include the temples of Portunus and Hercules Invictus (see below), and two of the temples of the Largo Argentina (temple C and temple A (Figure 28)) which probably date from the late fourth and early third centuries BC (respectively).[35]

These public undertakings are a symptom of the rapid development of the city of Rome in the early third century. Its precise rate of growth and the size of its population at any particular stage cannot be accurately measured, but

Table 9 Latin colonies, 334–263 BC

Date BC	Colony	Region	Adult male settlers	Cum. total	Area (km²)	Cum. total
334	Cales	Campania	2,500*	2,500	100	100
328	Fregellae	Latium	4,000	6,500	305	405
314	Luceria	Apulia	2,500*	9,000	790	1,195
313	Saticula	Samnium	2,500	11,500	195	1,390
313	Suessa Aurunca	Latium	2,500	14,000	180	1,570
313	Pontiae Islands	(Latium)	300	14,300	10	1,580
312	Interamna Lirenas	Latium	4,000*	18,300	265	1,845
303	Sora	Latium	4,000*	22,300	230	2,075
303	Alba Fucens	Central Apennines	6,000*	28,300	420	2,495
299	Narnia	Umbria	2,500	30,800	185	2,680
298	Carseoli	Central Apennines	4,000*	34,800	285	2,965
291	Venusia	Apulia	6,000	40,800	800	3,765
289	Hadria	Central Apennines	4,000	44,800	380	4,145
273	Paestum	Lucania	4,000	48,800	540	4,685
273	Cosa	Etruria	2,500	51,300	340	5,025
268	Ariminum	Umbria	6,000	57,300	650	5,675
268	Beneventum	Samnium	6,000	63,300	575	6,250
264	Firmum	Picenum	4,000	67,300	400	6,650
263	Aesernia	Samnium	4,000	71,300	385	7,035

Note: All figures are estimates, except for those marked *, which are recorded by Livy.
Source: A. Afzelius, *Die römische Eroberung Italiens* (Copenhagen 1942), with modifications.

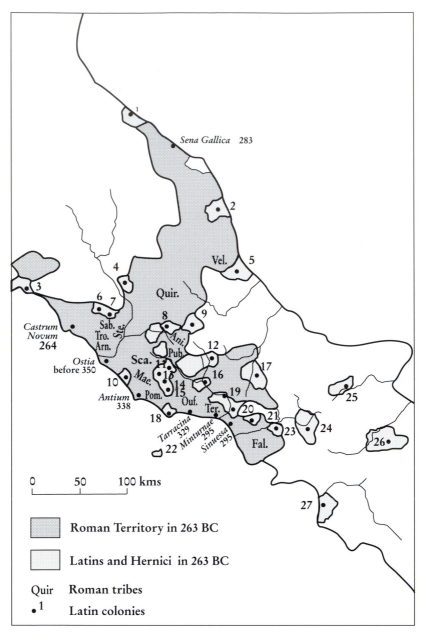

Map 9 Roman settlement and colonisation in Italy to 241 BC

KEY TO MAP 9

Latin Colonies, with dates (BC)

1. Ariminum, 268
2. Firmum, 264
3. Cosa, 273
4. Narnia, 299
5. Hadria, 290–86
6. Sutrium, 383
7. Nepet, 383
8. Carseoli, 298
9. Alba Fucens, 303
10. Ardea, 442
11. Signia, 495
12. Sora, 303
13. Cora, before 500
14. Norba, 492
15. Setia, 383
16. Fregellae, 328
17. Aesernia, 263
18. Circeii, 393
19. Interamna, 312
20. Suessa Aurunca, 313
21. Cales, 334
22. Pontia, 313
23. Saticula 313
24. Beneventum, 268
25. Luceria, 314
26. Venusia, 291
27. Paestum, 273

Roman tribes, with dates (BC)

Arn.	Arniensis,	387
Sab.	Sabatina,	387
Ste.	Stellatina,	387
Tro.	Tromentina,	387
Pom.	Pomptina,	358
Pub.	Publilia,	358
Mae.	Maecia,	332
Sca.	Scaptia,	332
Fal.	Falerna,	318
Ouf.	Oufentina,	318
Ani.	Aniensis,	299
Ter.	Teretina,	299
Qui.	Quirina,	241
Vel.	Velina,	241

Table 10 Roman temple construction, 302–264 BC

Date BC	Temple	Location
302	Salus	Quirinal
296	Bellona Victrix	Circus Flaminius (Campus Martius, SE)
295	Jupiter Victor	Quirinal?
295	Venus Obsequens	Circus Maximus
294	Victoria	Palatine
294	Jupiter Stator	Palatine
293	Quirinus	Quirinal
293	Fors Fortuna	Right bank of Tiber, at 6th milestone
291	Aesculapius	Tiber Island
278	Summanus	Circus Maximus
272	Consus	Aventine
268	Tellus	Carinae (Esquiline)
267	Pales	Unknown
264	Vertumnus	Aventine

Source: G. Wissowa, *Religion und Kultus der Römer*² (1912), 594–5; Wissowa lists a further 18 temples which certainly or probably belong to the period 293–218, for which Livy's full text is missing.

Figure 28 Largo Argentina: temple A.

we can make informed guesses. According to one recent estimate the city of Rome had a population of around 30,000 in the middle of the fourth century, rising to 60,000 by 300 and exceeding 90,000 at the time of the war against Pyrrhus.[36] If anything these figures err on the side of caution, but they are certainly of the right general order of magnitude; on any reasonable estimate, Rome was one of the largest cities in the Mediterranean world in the early third century. A significant indication of its growth was the need to construct aqueducts, of which the Aqua Appia of 312 BC was the first; it ws followed by the Anio Vetus, begun by the censor M' Curius Dentatus in 272 BC.[37]

As for its food supply, a city with a population of 90,000 could not possibly have been maintained from the agricultural surplus of its own hinterland, and must have imported a substantial proportion of its requirements, which would have amounted in total to more than 11,000 tonnes of wheat (or calorific equivalent) per year.[38] The only realistic assumption is that the necessary imports were transported by water. As there was as yet no harbour in use at Ostia (the small Roman settlement founded early in the fourth century was no more than a fort to guard the estuary), we must suppose that the traffic made its way along the Tiber to the Portus Tiberinus, the river landing situated opposite the eastern tip of the Tiber island.

The use of the Tiber for grain transport naturally raises the question of the scale and nature of Rome's maritime trade in general. Recent archaeological work has shown that the area of the Portus had been frequented from a very remote epoch (see above, p. 69); more important for the purposes of the present discussion is the fact that a substantial redevelopment seems to have taken place there at the end of the fourth century BC (Map 10). The earliest phase of the temple of Portunus, the god of the harbour, belongs to this period, as does the temple of Hercules Invictus, which stood beside the Ara Maxima. The Ara Maxima was itself the site of a cult of Hercules and had long-standing associations with foreign trade. It is tempting to speculate that the late fourth-century buildings reflect the growing importance of Rome's maritime trade at that period; and the attractive suggestion has been made that the redevelopment of this part of the city should be dated to the censorship of Appius Claudius, since it was he who transformed the worship of Hercules at the Ara Maxima from a private concern of the Potitian clan into a publicly administered cult.[39]

At this point it may be noticed that the picture of Rome as a major importing centre conflicts with the conventional view of the Roman economy at the start of the third century. This view maintains that Rome was a simple agrarian community with a near-subsistence economy and little trade.[40] Local craft production was at a rudimentary level and of poor quality; such luxuries as were to be found at Rome must have been imported from more advanced centres of production in Etruria, Campania or Magna Graecia. The Roman ruling class was culturally unsophisticated and not particularly rich by comparison with other contemporary elites or in relation to the mass of the

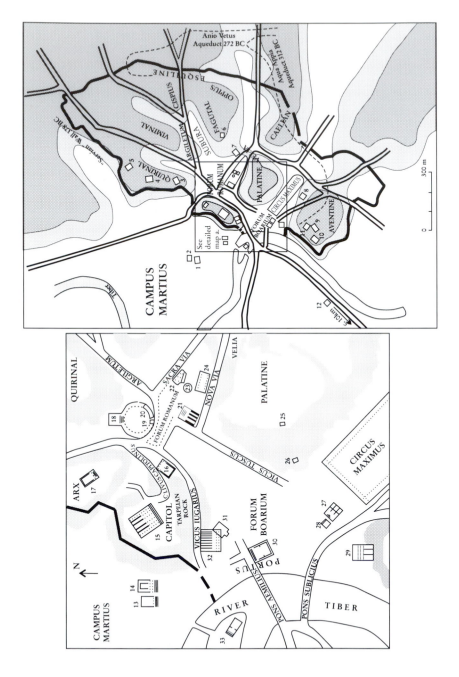

Map 10 The city of Rome: major public buildings

KEY TO MAP 10

1. Largo Argentina, Temple C, late 4th century BC
2. Largo Argentina, Temple A, early 3rd century BC
3. Temple of Semo Sancus, 466 BC
4. Temple of Salus, 302 BC
5. Temple of Quirinus, 293 BC
6. Temple of Tellus, 268 BC
7. Temple of Jupiter Stator (pre-Republican?)
8. Temple of Mercury, 495 BC
9. Temple of Diana (pre-Republican)
10. Temple of Juno Regina, 392 BC
11. Temple of Minerva, 3rd century BC?
12. Temple of Fors Fortuna, 293 BC
13. Temple of Apollo, 431 BC
14. Temple of Bellona, 296 BC
15. Temple of Jupiter Optimus Maximus, 509 BC
16. Temple of Saturn, 497 BC
17. Temple of Juno Moneta, 344 BC
18. Curia Hostilia (pre-Republican)
19. Volcanal – Niger Lapis (pre-Republican)
20. Rostra, 338 BC
21. Temple of Castor, 484 BC
22. Regia (pre-Republican)
23. Temple of Vesta (pre-Republican)
24. Atrium Vestae (pre-Republican)
25. 'Hut of Romulus'
26. Lupercal
27. Temple of Hercules Invictus, late 4th century BC
28. Ara Maxima Herculis (pre-Republican)
29. Temple of Ceres, 493 BC
30. Temple of Portunus, late 4th century BC
31. Archaic Temple at Sant'Omobono (pre-Republican)
32. Temples of Fortuna and Mater Matuta, 396 BC
33. Temple of Aesculapius, 291 BC

peasantry. Tradition itself told stories of horny-handed senators who worked their own fields, lived in unplastered hovels and cooked their own turnips (see especially the account of M' Curius Dentatus in Plutarch, *Cato maior* 2.1). Above all the Romans were indifferent to maritime activity. According to Seneca (*de brev. vit.* 13.4) the man who first persuaded the Romans to take to the sea was Appius Claudius Caudex, consul in 264 BC. Polybius tells us that in 260 the Romans possessed no naval resources at all, because 'they had never given a thought to the sea' (1.20.12).

This traditional view has recently been challenged, however, and in the extreme form outlined above it is certainly unacceptable.[41] We cannot take Polybius literally, nor Seneca seriously. The foundation of coastal garrison colonies, the Latin settlement on the Pontine islands (313 BC), and the Decian plebiscite of 311 BC, which established a small fleet under two naval commanders (*duumviri navales*: Livy 9.30.4), show that the Romans had not been entirely unconcerned about naval defence in the late fourth century. Nevertheless, it remains true that the object of these measures was primarily to guard the coast of Latium against pirates or enemy attacks, and possibly to provide naval assistance for land forces where appropriate (as in 310 BC – Livy 9.38.2); they do not necessarily have any bearing on the question of Rome's status as a commercial centre. The negative point made by the traditionalists, that the Roman government cannot be shown to have had any 'commercial policy', remains valid. The second treaty between Rome and Carthage of 348 BC (it was renewed in 305 according to Livy 9.43.26) contains clauses dealing with trade; but while they envisage the possibility that Roman traders might visit Sicily or Africa, the primary object of these clauses was clearly to protect the commercial interests of Carthage, not those of Rome.[42]

On the other hand, it cannot be seriously maintained that the Romans were not engaged in trade at all. Recent studies of the archaeological evidence have shown beyond doubt that Rome was an important manufacturing and trading centre in the years before and after 300 BC. As usual, pottery is the most plentiful category of material, and the evidence it provides is decisive in this case. It is now virtually certain that several different kinds of pottery, including wares of high quality, were manufactured in Rome in the early third century. The material includes not only decorated plates of the so-called 'Genucilia' type, but also black-glaze ware – of which the *pocula* (cups bearing dedications to divinities) form a particularly interesting group (Figure 29).[43] The most characteristic body of material, however, is a group of black-glaze pots decorated with small embossed stamps which come from a Roman workshop known as the 'Atelier des petites estampilles'. The significant point about this high-quality ware, which was produced in large quantities in the early years of the third century, is that it was widely exported; examples have been found not only in many parts of central Italy, but also along the coasts of southern France and north-east Spain, in Corsica and the Punic part of Sicily, and in the Carthaginian territory in North Africa.[44]

Figure 29 Roman black-glazed cup of the *poculum* type.

It is important that we should be clear about the limitations of this evidence. We might reasonably argue that the distribution of finds of Roman fine pottery represents the tip of an iceberg, and implies a geographically extensive trade, not only in ceramics but in other items as well. But we have no means of reconstructing the content, volume or mechanism of this trade, nor of assessing its general economic importance. We cannot say, for instance, what percentage of Rome's gross product (itself unknowable) was represented by manufacture and trade.

The evidence that is currently available nevertheless supports a position that is qualitatively different from the traditional idea of third-century Rome as a simple rustic community. It should be emphasised that the original proponents of the traditional view were not attempting to set up a 'primitivist' model of the early third-century economy in the manner of the Cambridge school.[45] On the contrary, they were (if anything) 'modernists', whose purpose in stressing the supposedly primitive character of Rome was precisely

389

to isolate it from the more advanced economic and cultural conditions that prevailed elsewhere in the Mediterranean (and even in Italy) at the beginning of the third century BC.[46]

5 EPILOGUE: ROMAN SOCIETY AND CULTURE ON THE EVE OF THE PUNIC WARS

An unprejudiced assessment of the archaeological facts clearly shows that on the eve of the Punic Wars Rome was neither isolated nor culturally backward. A high level of material culture is attested not only by the products of fine-pottery workshops, but by a whole range of artefacts: terracotta sculptures and miniature funerary altars ('arule'), carved stone monuments (among which the sarcophagus of L. Cornelius Scipio Barbatus, cos. 298, holds pride of place: see above, p. 359), bronzes, and even a fragment of an extremely fine fresco painting. The latter item, from a tomb on the Esquiline, depicts a historical scene involving a certain Q. Fabius. According to the most probable interpretation, the tomb was that of Q. Fabius Rullianus, and the painting part of an illustrated account of episodes from the Samnite Wars.[47] The finest example of Roman craftsmanship to survive from this period is the Ficoroni cista, an engraved bronze casket that was found in a tomb at Palestrina (Praeneste) (Figure 30); a recent study has dated it to around 315 BC.[48] An inscription on the handle tells us that the cista was made in Rome by a craftsman named Novius Plautius. Although it is sometimes dismissed as a unique exception, there is in fact no reason to suspect that the Ficoroni cista is not a representative example of the bronzework that was being produced in Roman workshops in the years around 300 BC. It is exceptional only in the sense that no other surviving cista is demonstrably of Roman origin.

Literary evidence moreover indicates that at this time bronze statues began to be erected in Rome. They include the equestrian statue of Q. Marcius Tremulus, consul in 306 BC (Pliny, *n.h.* 34.23; Livy. 9.43.22; Cic., *Phil.* 6.13), and the bronze group of the twins Romulus and Remus with the she-wolf, which was set up by the curule aediles Cn and Q. Ogulnius in 296 BC. These two also placed a bronze statue of Jupiter in a four-horse chariot on the roof of the Capitoline temple, in place of the terracotta one that had been there since the end of the sixth century.[49] Three years later colossal bronze statues of Jupiter and Hercules were set up on the Capitol; and in the Comitium, according to a strange story in Pliny, the Romans put up statues of Pythagoras and Alcibiades, 'the wisest and bravest of the Greeks' (historians have not failed to point out the 'western' bias apparent in this strange choice). The only surviving remnant of republican bronze sculpture is the head of the so-called 'Capitoline Brutus' (Figure 31). Although it is usually ascribed to this period, the date – and even the authenticity – of the 'Brutus' remain controversial.[50]

The only testimony that conflicts with this picture of Rome as a prosperous and culturally sophisticated place is the fact that later tradition portrayed its

Figure 30 The Ficoroni cista.

Figure 31 The 'Capitoline Brutus'.

aristocratic leaders as models of frugality and simplicity. But in reality the supposed poverty of men like M' Curius Dentatus and C. Fabricius Luscinus is a myth. The stories that were told about them are more revealing of later Roman ideology than of the economic conditions of the early third century; in any case the later tradition was less concerned with the economic status of these men than with the moral example they set. It is relevant to note that these improving tales were propagated by the elder Cato, who fashioned Dentatus and his like in his own self-made image; and it would be unwise to base a historical account of the lifestyle of Roman aristocrats in the third century on the ideological constructs of the elder Cato.[51]

The nature of the economic and cultural changes we have been discussing can be further illustrated by an examination of three specific developments that occurred during the age of the conquest. The first is the growth of slavery. We have already seen that Rome was well on the way to becoming a slave society before the end of the fourth century BC (above, p. 333); the mass enslavements that are recorded in the early years of the third century must have advanced the process still further. We have little specific information about the social and economic effects of the process, but it is possible to construct a plausible account of the changes that occurred.

It is reasonable to suppose, first, that many slaves were employed in the houses of the rich and in trading and manufacturing enterprises in the city; they added to the size of the urban population and in the course of time changed its composition. Throughout the history of the Republic the most important single cause of the growth of the urban *plebs* was the importation, and subsequent manumission, of slaves.[52] The social effects of the process were already beginning to be felt at the time of Appius Claudius' censorship, as we have seen.

It is also extremely probable that slave labour was being used on a large scale in agriculture. This contention is not seriously weakened even if we choose to accept the moralising tales about third-century senators working their own land. It is sufficient merely to notice a revealing story about Cato the Elder (born in 234 BC), who took pride in the fact that as a young man he had worked with his own hands *together with his slaves* (Plut., *Cato maior* 3.2).

The development of large slave-run estates in Italy is normally dated to the period after the Hannibalic War (218–202 BC), but there is no warrant for this assumption. On the contrary, there is good reason to believe that slaves were employed on the land from the late fourth century onwards. The case rests on three connected arguments. First, as we have seen, the ending of debt-bondage (formally abolished by the Lex Poetelia of 326 BC) must have created a demand for an alternative supply of agricultural labour to work the estates of the rich, a demand that can only have been met by slaves. Second, the impoverished peasants who were freed from dependence on the rich were left with no means of livelihood other than their own inadequate landholdings. Their plight was remedied by successful war and the colonisation of conquered territories. Third, the mass emigration of tens of thousands of poor peasant families must have led to a gradual depopulation of the old *ager Romanus* – a phenomenon that is in fact referred to in the sources of the classical period[53] – and implies a radical change in the organisation of landholdings and the manner of their exploitation. What must have happened is that the land was concentrated into larger holdings, which were worked by slaves who were brought in to replace the former peasant smallholders.

The model therefore implies a continuous exchange of populations; poor Roman citizens were sent away to colonise lands whose original inhabitants were brought back to Roman territory as slaves. The process was complicated by a change in the relative distribution of the inhabitants in the old *ager Romanus*, with a greater proportion than before living in the city, and a corresponding reduction in the population of the countryside. The same land was worked by a smaller number of people; since they were slaves they could be worked harder and organised more effectively so as to produce a greater surplus. Increased productivity was stimulated by the development of an urban market in the growing and prosperous city of Rome.

In the absence of any specific testimony this reconstruction must remain hypothetical; but it has the virtue of being able to account for the mass enslavement of war captives, who must have been employed somehow, and the economic growth that is presupposed by the increase in the non-agricultural population of the city.

The second exemplary development is the appearance of Rome's first coinage. Precisely when, where and why the Roman state first issued coined money are much debated questions, involving complex technical issues. The following is a brief summary of what seems the most convincing modern reconstruction, presented in the knowledge that many areas of doubt remain.[54]

The use of coined money was a Greek practice and was introduced into Italy by the cities of Magna Graecia at an early date. Coins produced by the Italiot Greeks mostly had a local circulation, but by the end of the fourth century had begun to penetrate into some of the native regions of the Mezzogiorno. Indeed by this time some non-Greek communities (especially in Campania, but also in Apulia and Lucania) were producing their own coins on the Greek model. Moreover, some formerly Greek communities such as Cumae, which had been overrun by Oscan-speaking natives at the end of the fifth century, had continued to mint coins after the Oscan takeover without any noticeable break in the regularity of issues.

Early Roman coinage forms part of the monetary history of Campania, which is where the first coins to be issued in the name of the Republic were minted. Coinage was therefore a consequence of Rome's political involvement in Campania. The earliest 'Romano-Campanian' coins can be dated to the fourth century, and belong to isolated and sporadic issues. A small group of bronze coins, with a head of Apollo on the obverse, and the forepart of a man-headed bull with the Greek legend PΩMAIΩN on the reverse (Crawford no. 1), was probably the first. The types are purely Neapolitan, and it is reasonable to infer that they were minted at Naples shortly after the treaty with Rome in 326 BC, and perhaps in commemoration of it. These coins probably circulated only in Campania, and belong more properly to the monetary history of Naples than to that of Rome.

Figure 32 Early Roman coins. (a) Helmeted head of bearded Mars/Horse's head on base; behind, corn-ear; on base ROMANO. Crawford no. 13. (b) Laureate head of Apollo; before, ROMANO/Galloping horse; above, star. Crawford no. 15. (c) Head of Hercules/She-wolf suckling twins; in exergue, ROMANO. Crawford no. 20. (d) Helmeted head of Roma; behind, club/Winged Victory attaching wreath to palm branch; behind, ROMANO; before, control letters HH. Crawford no. 22.

Much more important is the first issue of Roman silver coins (Figure 32a), the didrachms with a picture of the head of Mars on one side, and a horse's head and the word ROMANO on the other (Crawford no. 13). This now appears to have been an isolated coinage datable to the years around 310 BC. It was a substantial issue, to judge from the number of dies, and it circulated widely in the south (though not, apparently, in Rome). The mint is uncertain, but probably Campanian; the weight standard is that of Naples. An isolated issue of this kind was almost certainly minted for a specific purpose, presumably on the occasion of some project involving large state expenditure. The most likely candidate is the construction of the Via Appia in the years 312–308 BC. Once again a major innovation appears to be associated with Appius Claudius Caecus.[55]

These sporadic and isolated coinages did not give way to a regular sequence of Roman coins until the time of the Pyrrhic War, which seems to have been a crucial event for the monetary history of Italy. The demands of the war led many Greek cities to reduce the weight of their coins; some ceased to strike coins altogether. On the other hand, coined money began to circulate much more widely in non-Greek Italy than it had done previously; and for the first time coins penetrated into Samnium and the region of the central Apennines. This development was a consequence of Roman activity, and almost certainly reflects the fact that men from these regions were now serving in the allied contingents of the Roman army.

The Pyrrhic War witnessed a second issue of Roman silver didrachms (Apollo/Galloping Horse ROMANO – Crawford no. 15: Figure 32b) and the beginning of a remarkable series of bronze issues. The bronze coins were cast rather than struck, in units weighing a Roman pound (324 g) and fractions of a pound. The basic unit was the *as*, and the fractions the *semis* ('half'), *triens* ('third'), *quadrans* ('quarter'), etc. Associated with the cast bronze coins were large bronze ingots ('currency bars') weighing about 5 Roman pounds each (Crawford nos. 3–12). The cast bronze coinage is a very characteristic form, unparalleled outside Italy. Within central Italy, however, it was widespread, and was produced at a number of different centres, mostly, if not entirely, in imitation of Rome.

The date at which silver coins were first minted at Rome (as opposed to Campania) is uncertain, but the most probable answer is 269 BC, which the literary sources regard as a crucial date in the history of Rome's silver coinage. The coinage that can be ascribed to this year is the very large issue of silver didrachms with Hercules/Wolf and Twins ROMANO (Crawford no. 20: Figure 32c). The types are interesting, and serve to remind us that coined money was a medium through which a state could advertise itself to the world at large. The Hercules/Wolf and Twins coinage was followed, on the eve of the First Punic War, by an issue of didrachms with a helmeted head of Roma/Victory ROMANO (Crawford no. 22: Figure 32d). Such types are an indication of Rome's growing self-confidence, and awareness of her immense power.

In economic terms the introduction of coinage is not of great significance in itself; the important stage in the early history of money is the official designation of a specific quantity of metal as a monetary unit, irrespective of whether the fixed unit is issued in the form of a coin. In Rome the fixed metallic unit was the *as*, a pound of bronze, which had existed as an official measure of value long before the introduction of coins (see above, p. 288).

It follows that we need not search for elaborate explanations of the introduction of coinage by Rome. In general ancient states issued coins for financial, rather than for economic, reasons. That is to say, coinage was a convenient means of distributing the proceeds of booty, or of making payments to large numbers of people such as soldiers or workmen. It was not produced in order to facilitate exchange, or in furtherance of any kind of monetary policy. For the Romans of the fourth century BC, the decision to issue money in the form of coin must have been taken principally for reasons of prestige. Its economic importance may have been minimal, but the appearance of Roman coins was an event of great cultural significance. Coinage was a Greek device, and the Romans' adoption of it marks a conscious effort on their part to enter the cultural milieu of the Hellenistic world. This brings us to the last of the three developments referred to earlier, namely the increasing influence of Hellenism on Roman life.

The influence of Greek culture on Rome can be traced back to the beginning of Roman history. The archaeological record shows that Greek artefacts and techniques were being imported as early as the eighth century BC, and we have seen that in the archaic age the influence of Greek ideas on Roman political, legal and religious institutions was pervasive. But during the course of the fifth century Rome's contacts with the Greek world diminished, as the city entered a long period of relative isolation.

When Rome emerged in the second half of the fourth century as a powerful military state, relations with the Greek world were re-established on a new footing. The renewed influence of Greek culture manifested itself not only in monuments and artefacts, as Rome, along with the rest of Italy, adopted Hellenistic styles and techniques, but also in the fields of politics and religion.[56] That leaders such as Q. Publilius Philo and Appius Claudius Caecus were infected by democratic political ideas and practices seems certain. A point of particular interest is that the former was, as far as we know, the first Roman noble to adopt a Greek surname. He was followed by P. Sempronius Sophus (cos. 304 BC) and Q. Marcius Philippus (cos. 281).

A number of Greek cults were established in Rome at this time. The most spectacular example is that of the healing god Aesculapius, to whom a temple was dedicated on the Tiber island in 291 BC. A series of appropriately militaristic cults were set up in the period of the Samnite Wars; they include those of Victoria, Jupiter Victor, Bellona Victrix and Hercules Invictus. These 'victory cults' were evidently based on contemporary Hellenistic models.[57]

In contrast to the one-sided relationship of the archaic age, the long and not always easy love affair that began in the fourth century was reciprocated. The Romans' enthusiasm for Greek culture was matched by the close attention which the Greeks began to pay to Rome. A list of the Greek intellectuals who were attracted to the subject of Rome and the Romans at this time reads like a *Who's Who* of contemporary Greek learning: the philosophers Aristotle, Theophrastus and Heraclides Ponticus, the historians Duris, Hieronymus and Timaeus, the poets Callimachus and Lycophron, and the scientist Eratosthenes. The detailed evidence is well known and has been assembled many times; there is no need to reproduce it here.[58]

The Greeks were attempting to understand the little-known Italian Republic which had grown from nothing into a world power, and which in 275 BC had won a sensational victory in the war against Pyrrhus. But one senses that at the same time the Romans were also trying to come to terms with the position in which they found themselves. The enthusiastic adoption of Hellenism was itself a part of this search for an identity. This became apparent at the end of the third century when Fabius Pictor presented to the public a definitive account of the Roman tradition. His History of Rome, the first ever by a Roman, was written in Greek.

APPENDIX: A NOTE ON
EARLY ROMAN
CHRONOLOGY

The Romans dated events by the names of the annual consuls. For us to give a 'Christian' date (BC or AD) to any given consular year is relatively straightforward for the period after 300 BC, for which we possess a full and accurate list of consuls (the *Fasti*); it is simply a matter of counting the number of consular years before and after the consulship of Gaius Caesar and L. Aemilius Paulus, who held office in the year we call AD 1. Whether or not Jesus was really born in that year is irrelevant to the question of dating. What matters is that the universally recognised system of dating starts from that point, 1995 years ago. The list of consuls is complete from 300 BC onwards, but before then matters are more complicated because the *Fasti* are reconstructed differently by different sources, and because there are discrepancies between the several versions of the *Fasti* and chronological data provided by independent evidence.

In ths book I have followed the standard convention in using the so-called 'Varronian' system, established by scholars (including Varro) at the end of the Republic, and used in the list of consuls set up on a stone inscription in the Forum in the time of Augustus. The surviving portions of this list are in the Capitoline Museum, whence the title *Fasti Capitolini*. The Varronian chronology places the first consuls in 509, the Decemvirs in 451–450, the Gallic sack in 390 and the first plebeian consul in 366.

The problem is that the Varronian chronology is a secondary reconstruction based on an artificially revised version of the *Fasti*. In particular there are clear signs of an attempt to lengthen the chronology by means of bogus insertions into the list. The most notorious are the four so-called 'dictator-years' – i.e. (Varronian) 333, 324, 309 and 301 BC. In each of these years, according to the *Fasti Capitolini*, a dictator and *magister equitum* held office instead of consuls, and gave their names to the year. It is obvious, however, that the dictator-years were a relatively late fabrication. They do not appear in any sources other than the *Fasti Capitolini*, and it is impossible to believe that such an extraordinary constitutional anomaly as a dictator-year should have gone unnoticed by historians if it had had any foundation either in fact or in tradition. The conclusion is that the Varronian years 333, 324, 309 and

301 did not exist; in other words the year we are conventionally obliged to call '310 BC' was immediately followed by '308 BC'.[1]

The *Fasti Capitolini* also include five years of 'anarchy' (Varronian 375–371 BC) during the turmoil of the Licinio-Sextian Rogations, in which no curule magistrates were elected. Livy's version is similar (6.35.10, and cf. above, p. 334), but Diodorus, more plausibly, has only one year without magistrates. The five-year anarchy is obviously unlikely to be historical, and is best seen as a device, similar to the dictator-years, for extending the chronology of the fourth century. The need for such lengthening was already implicit in the Roman historical tradition at an early stage. For example, Fabius Pictor wrote that the election of the first plebeian consul (Varronian 367 BC) occurred in the 22nd year after the Gallic sack (Gellius, *N.A.* 5.4.3), although the known versions of the Fasti record only nineteen colleges of consular tribunes for the period in question. It follows, if Fabius Pictor's arithmetic was correct, either that his version of the *Fasti* included some annual colleges that were not present in later versions of the list (which seems extremely unlikely), or that his version included a period of anarchy lasting several years. Again, Polybius maintains (2.18.6) that the Gauls returned to Latium (Varronian 361 BC) in the 30th year after the sack, a period covered in the surviving *Fasti* by only twenty-five colleges of consuls (and consular tribunes). This can be explained in a number of ways, the most probable being that by Polybius' time a five-year anarchy was already accepted in authoritative versions of the *Fasti*.

The most important piece of independent evidence was the synchronism of the Gallic sack with the Peace of Antalcidas (the 'King's Peace') and the siege of Rhegium by Dionysius of Syracuse. The synchronism, which was recorded by Polybius (1.6.2), but was probably worked out by an earlier historian such as Philistus or Timaeus, would place the sack in the summer of the Julian year 386 BC. The Romans knew that the sack had occurred under the consular tribunes Q., K. and N. Fabius Ambustus, Q. Sulpicius Longus, Q. Servilius Fidenas and P. Cornelius Maluginensis; but in the *Fasti* only eighty-one colleges of consular tribunes and consuls were listed between that year and the consulship of M. Valerius Corvus V and Q. Appuleius Pansa (i.e. 300 BC).

Those who attempted to establish a general chronology in the late Republic would have been able to infer from such evidence that the available versions of the *Fasti* were deficient in the period after the sack. In particular, the synchronism of the sack with the Peace of Antalcidas would have indicated that the list of magistrates was four years short. It is probable that the four dictator-years and the extension of the 'anarchy' from one to five years were alternative ways of lengthening the *Fasti* by the appropriate amount. But by adopting both devices, the Varronian chronology placed the sack in 390, four years earlier than the Polybian date.

The precise mechanics of the Varronian chronology need not concern us.

The several versions of the *Fasti* in our sources differ from each other, and from the Varronian system, by only a few years at most. Whether the Gallic sack actually happened in 386 BC or 390 BC is of little consequence in itself; the problem is that discrepancies, however small, can lead to confusion, particularly in the minds of modern readers, who are used to a simple and universal numerical system of dating and have no familiarity with the sort of difficulties the ancients had to face as an everyday fact of life. Ancient scholars, such as Dionysius of Halicarnassus, who was an expert on chronology, understood the problems very well.[2] These scholars made great efforts to synchronise rival dating systems, such as the Attic archons and the Roman consuls, and to create a universal scheme using Olympiads, the quadrennial cycles associated with the Olympic Games which were first held in the summer of 776 BC.[3]

Throughout his work on early Rome Dionysius carefully correlated the Roman *Fasti* with the Attic archon list and the succession of Olympic cycles. His normal practice is to mark the first year of each Olympiad with the number of the Olympiad, the name of the winner in the foot race at the Games, the Athenian archon, and finally the consuls. For example, 8.77.1: 'The following year, at the beginning of the seventy-fourth Olympiad (the one at which Astylus of Syracuse won the foot race), when Leostratus was archon at Athens, and Quintus Fabius and Servius Cornelius had succeeded to the consulship. . .' The year is 484 BC, although on the Varronian system (which Dionysius of course does not follow) Fabius and Cornelius were consuls in 485. Dionysius' chronology is consistent and is applied, with extreme skill, to the whole of the period covered in his work, going back to the Trojan War, which he places 432 years before the founding of Rome in Olympiad 7.1 (752/1 BC).

Dionysius had a grasp of the issues and an understanding of the complexities of ancient chronology that few if any of today's scholars can rival. Those who criticise his efforts usually do no more than reveal their own ignorance. The technicalities of early Roman chronology are too difficult to go into here, even if I understood them properly, which I don't. The standard modern works were produced in the nineteenth century by Mommsen (naturally), W. Soltau, and O. Leuze; present-day scholars are not competent to match their efforts.[4]

For practical purposes the important thing to remember about Roman dates is that events were associated in the first instance with the names of the consuls of the year in which they took place. Locating that year in any general scheme of chronology, whether Olympiads, or years after the founding of the city, or years before or after Christ, is a secondary and necessarily somewhat artificial process. If this is not kept firmly in mind, confusion can result. For instance, one historian has recently written that the capture of Veii occurred 'in (Varronian) 396 according to Livy, in 388 according to Diodorus'.[5] This implies that Livy and Diodorus reported the fall of Veii under different years, but actually they place the event in the same 'Roman' year – the consular tribunate of L. Titinius, P. Licinius, P. Maelius, Q. Manlius, Cn. Genucius and L. Atilius; and as it happens their accounts also coincide in absolute terms, since both record the same number of years between the fall of Veii and 300 BC. Although they get there by different methods, both contrive to place the capture of Veii in 392 BC.[6] Diodorus also synchronises the year in question with Olympiad 96.4, the archonship of Demostratus (393–392 BC). It is hardly necessary to point out that neither Livy nor Diodorus (nor any other literary source) follows the Varronian chronology.

Many readers of Livy are quite unaware that his chronological scheme is different from the Varronian one. The reader is not affected by this because Livy records events under the heading of the annual magistrates, who by a simple process of conversion can be given their appropriate Varronian dates (which are inserted in the margins of many modern editions). No doubt ancient readers were equally unconcerned about the absolute chronology of the annalistic histories they consulted. It has become conventional to use the Varronian chronology, but it is important to remember that Varronian dates are no more that numerical symbols for specific consular years.

NOTES

1 INTRODUCTION: THE EVIDENCE

1 A. Momigliano, *The Classical Foundations of Modern Historiography* (Berkeley 1990), 54.

2 Good general books on Livy include P.G. Walsh, *Livy: his historical aims and methods* (Cambridge 1961); T.A. Dorey (ed.), *Livy* (London 1971); T.J. Luce, *Livy: the composition of his history* (Princeton 1977). R.M. Ogilvie's *Commentary on Livy Books 1–5* (Oxford 1965), a towering scholarly achievement, is an indispensable aid to study. A commentary on books 6–10 by Stephen Oakley is currently in preparation.

3 E. Gabba has recently published an important study, *Dionysius and the History of Archaic Rome* (Berkeley 1991). See also two recent collections of essays: 'Autour de Denys d'Halicarnasse', in *MEFRA* 101 (1989), 9–242, and 'Denys d'Halicarnasse, historien des origines de Rome', ed. P.M. Martin, in *Pallas (Revue d'études antiques)* vol. 39 (Toulouse 1993). A French translation of books 1 and 2 has recently appeared, with introduction and notes by V. Fromentin and J. Schnäbele (Paris: Les Belles Lettres, 1990).

4 On Cicero's historical interests and approach see E. Rawson, *JRS* 62 (1972), 33–45 = Rawson, *Roman Culture and Society* (Oxford 1991), 58–80 (pp. 75ff. on the historical work Cicero planned but never got around to writing). See also P.A. Brunt, in *Miscellanea in onore di E. Manni* (Rome 1979) I, 311–40.

5 K. Sacks, *Diodorus Siculus and the First Century* (Princeton 1990). On Diodorus' History in general see also E. Rawson, *Intellectual Life in the Late Roman Republic* (London 1985), 223–7. Much has been written on Diodorus' 'Roman annals'. Among older work notice especially Ed. Meyer, *Rh. Mus.* 37 (1882), 610–27. Recent surveys, with full discussion and bibliography, include G. Perl, *Kritische Untersuchungen zur Diodors römischer Jahrzählung* (Berlin 1957); F. Càssola, *ANRW* II.30.1 (1982), 724–73, and, on the legends of early Rome, F. Càssola in E. Galvagno and C. Molè Ventura (eds), *Mito, storia, tradizione: Diodoro Siculo e la storiografia classica* (Catania 1991), 273–324.

6 The standard general account of Dio is F.G.B. Millar, *A Study of Cassius Dio* (Oxford 1964), but it deliberately omits consideration of the early books. Millar's observation (p. 3) that a special study of the early books would be worth the effort still holds true.

7 On Strabo's account of Italy see the papers collected in G. Maddoli (ed.), *Strabone: contributi allo studio della personalità e dell'opera* (Perugia 1986), and D. Musti, *Strabone e la Magna Grecia* (Padua 1988).

8   On Plutarch's Roman Lives see especially C.P. Jones, *Plutarch and Rome* (Oxford 1971).

9   F.W. Walbank's *Historical Commentary on Polybius* I–III (Oxford 1957–87) is indispensable, as is his book *Polybius* (Berkeley 1972). On the lost *archaeologia*, see F. Taeger, *Die Archäologie des Polybios* (Stuttgart 1922) and, briefly, Walbank, *Comm.* I, 663ff. See also the excellent Budé edition of book VI, by R. Weil, with text, notes and French translation (Paris 1977).

10 For discussion of Tacitus' antiquarian digressions, R. Syme, *Tacitus* (Oxford 1958), 311–12, 397–8, 514–5, 703–8.

11 I have discussed this further in I.S. Moxon *et al.* (eds), *Past Perspectives* (Cambridge 1986), 67–86. The best discussion of Livy's working methods is by Luce, *Livy* (1977), esp. 185–229, a work that has the unusual merit of treating Livy as (in the author's words) 'a thinking adult'.

12 For this view, T.P. Wiseman, *Clio's Cosmetics* (Leicester 1979), 12–20.

13 Momigliano, *Classical Foundations* (1990), 92ff. (and cf. his earlier study in *Terzo contributo*, 55–68). On Fabius Pictor see further Frier, *Libri annales* (1979), 210ff. Important new information about Pictor is contained in a text painted on the wall of a building at Taormina in Sicily. This 'dipinto' is quoted and discussed by Frier, 230f.

14 On Ennius see the definitive text and commentary by O. Skutsch, *The Annals of Quintus Ennius* (Oxford 1985). English translation of the fragments by E.H. Warmington, *Remains of Old Latin* I (Loeb). In general A.S. Grattwick, in *The Cambridge History of Classical Literature* II.1 (1982) 60–76; T.J. Cornell, *JRS* 76 (1986), 244–50; A. von Albrecht, *Geschichte der römischen Literatur*, 2 vols (Berne 1992), 106–19.

15 The explanation is that Cato was the inspiration for both Polybius and Cicero. See D. Timpe, *ANRW* I.2 (1972), 928ff.; T.J. Cornell, in H. McK. Blake *et al.* (eds) *Papers in Italian Archaeology* I (Oxford 1978), 135–6.

16 Fragments of the *Origines* are now collected in the Budé edition, with French translation and commentary, by M. Chassignet: Caton, *Les origines* (Paris 1986). On Cato's *Origines* see further A.E. Astin, *Cato the Censor* (Oxford 1978), 211–39; W. Kierdorf, *Chiron* 10 (1980), 205–24; C. Letta, *Athenaeum* 42 (1984), 3–30, 416–39; Albrecht, *Gesch. röm. Lit.* (1992), 314–26.

17 On these historians see E. Badian, in T.A. Dorey (ed.), *Latin Historians* (London 1966), 11ff.; E. Rawson, *Latomus* 34–5 (1976), 689–717 = *Roman Culture* (1991), 245–71; G. Forsythe, *Phoenix* 44 (1990), 326–44; Albrecht, *Gesch. röm. Lit.* (1992), 298–313.

18 Badian, *in Latin Historians* (1966), 11ff.; Ogilvie, *Comm.* (1965), 7–17; Walsh, *Livy* (1961), 110ff.

19 Cicero, *de orat.* 2.54: 'Cato, Pictor and Piso . . . do not understand the adornment of composition . . . and, so long as their narrative is understood, regard conciseness as the historian's single merit . . . they did not embellish their facts, but were chroniclers and nothing more' (*non exornatores rerum, sed tantummodo narratores*) (Loeb translation).

20 R.M. Ogilvie, *JRS* 48 (1958), 40–6; *Comm.* (1965), 544f.

21 Cf. my remarks in I. Moxon *et al.* (eds), *Past Perspectives* (1986), 67–86. On Livy's citations see M.L.W. Laistner, *The Greater Roman Historians* (Berkeley 1947), 83–8; Luce, *Livy* (1977), 139–84.

22 Dion. Hal. 1.6.1. The fragments of Hieronymus are assembled by F. Jacoby, *FGrHist* IIB, no. 154. On Hieronymus see J. Hornblower, *Hieronymus of Cardia* (Oxford 1981).

23 For fragments of Timaeus, Jacoby, *FGrHist* IIIB, no. 566. On Timaeus see A. Momigliano, *Essays in Ancient and Modern Historiography* (Oxford 1977), 37–66;

cf. P.M. Fraser, *Ptolemaic Alexandria* (Oxford 1972) I, 765. L. Pearson, *The Greek Historians of the West: Timaeus and his predecessors* (Atlanta 1987), argues that Timaeus invented most of the information about Italy in his first five books. Recent archaeological discoveries suggest otherwise, and in general Pearson's case is unconvincing.

24 E. Gabba in *Entretiens* 13 (1967), 135ff.

25 E. Rawson, *Intellectual Life* (1985), 231.

26 This was undoubtedly the thrust of the observations of a certain Clodius, cited by Plutarch, *Numa* 1.1, a frequently misunderstood passage. On the fictitious genealogies see T.P. Wiseman, *Greece and Rome* 21 (1974), 153–64.

27 Oral tradition has been little studied in the Roman context, as W.V. Harris has rightly observed, in Eder (ed.), *Staat und Staatlichkeit* (1990), 496; cf. Poucet, *Les Origines* (1985), 65–70. But see now J. von Ungern-Sternberg in *Vergangenheit in mündlicher Überlieferung*, ed. J. von Ungern-Sternberg and H. Reinau (Stuttgart 1988), 237–65; T.P. Wiseman, *JRS* 79 (1989), 129–37.

28 O. Szemerényi, *Hermes* 103 (1975), 307–19.

29 T.P. Wiseman, *JRS* 79 (1989), 136–7; *Historiography and Imagination* (Exeter 1994), ch. 1.

30 The theory goes back to the seventeenth-century Dutch scholar Jacob Perizonius. A full account of the theory, with a judicious assessment of its worth, is given by A. Momigliano, *JRS* 47 (1957), 104–14 (= *Secondo contributo* 69–87).

31 Cicero, *Brutus* 75, is usually taken to imply that the songs went out of use many centuries before Cato's time (Momigliano, *Secondo contributo* 81; Harris, in Eder (ed.), *Staat und Staatlichkeit* (1990), 497 n. 12). I am not sure that that is what Cicero really means; all we can deduce for certain is that the songs were no longer extant in his (Cicero's) time.

32 Thus, rightly, Frier, *Libri annales* (1979), 79–81, against M. Gelzer, *Kleine Schriften* (Wiesbaden 1964) III, 93–103. Gelzer's argument that Cicero referred only to style amounts to special pleading.

33 Frier, *Libri annales* (1979), 27–67, argues convincingly that all the later sources are dependent on Verrius Flaccus.

34 This is the view of C. Cichorius, *RE* 1 (1894), 2248–55, s.v. 'annales'; J.E.A. Crake, *CPh* 35 (1940), 375–86; Ogilvie, *Comm.* (1965), 6 n.1. M.I. Henderson, *JRS* 52 (1962), 277, rightly considers the idea of *tabulae* stacked inside the Regia absurd.

35 Frier, *Libri annales* (1979), 116, correctly points out that Ennius, whom Cicero quotes at this point (*Rep.* 1.25, cf. Ennius, *Ann.* 153 Sk.), cannot himself have dated the eclipse by the founding of the city; that must have been the result of Cicero's own calculation (cf. Skutsch, *Annals of Ennius* (1985), 312). It is also possible that in the late Republic someone added a.u.c. dates to the year-entries in the *Annales maximi*. This would explain Dionysius' reference to the 'tablet preserved by the high priests' (1.74.3) as evidence for the foundation date.

36 This position is not undermined, indeed it is positively strengthened, by the arguments of R. Drews, *CPh* 83 (1988), 189–99, who makes a good case for saying that the *Annales maximi* were no longer extant in the second half of the first century BC. I agree that they were never 'published' in multiple copies, but I still find it hard to believe that Verrius Flaccus could not and did not consult them directly.

37 On Roman archives see E. Rawson, *Intellectual Life* (1985), 238–9; *ANRW* I.4 (1973), 334f. = *Roman Culture* (1991), 145f.; Mommsen, *Staatsr.* II³ (1887), 546 n. 1, and *Ges. Schr.* III (Berlin 1907), 290–313.

38 The starting-point of the *Annales maximi* is a problem. Cicero says that they went back to 'the beginning of Roman history', and the *Origo gentis Romanae* (see p. 85) purports to cite the fourth book of the chronicle as evidence for the Alban

kings (*OGR* 17.1–3, 4–6; 18.2–3). This must mean that someone edited the chronicle (cf. n. 35) and added a section on the legendary prehistory of the city. This was clearly seen to be a secondary conflation, and no source refers to it as possessing any authority. The main question, which I have been concerned with in the text, is: when did genuine records begin? To which the only certain answer is: before 400 BC.

39 See my paper in M. Beard *et al.*, *Literacy in the Roman World* (Ann Arbor 1991), 7–33, esp. 24ff.

40 Hayden White, *Metahistory* (Baltimore 1973).

41 On the distinction between structural facts and narrative superstructure see Momigliano, *Sesto contributo*, 484.

42 Momigliano, *Classical Foundations* (1990), 67ff.

43 Momigliano, *Classical Foundations* (1990), 77ff.

44 N. Horsfall, in *The Cambridge History of Classical Literature* II.2 (1982), 112.

45 Livy's failure to make use of Varro has often been noticed, e.g. by Ogilvie, *Comm.* (1965), 6, and his extremely rare digressions on antiquarian themes (e.g. 7.2.3ff. on the origins of the Roman theatre, 5.33.4ff. on the Gallic migrations, and 8.8.3ff. on the Roman army) stand out very obviously from the rest. On Dionysius' use of Varro, see Gabba, *Dionysius* (1991), 99ff.; but NB J. Poucet, *Pallas* 39 (1993), 41–70, with some important reservations.

46 There is a desperate need for a serious study of the life and work of Varro, which will explain, in language that can be understood by the ordinary reader, exactly what is known of Varro's antiquarian works, and what these remnants amount to. The standard account is that of H. Dahlmann, *RE* suppl. VI (1935), 1172–1277, s.v. Terentius (84) Varro. For a brief orientation, N. Horsfall, *Cambr. Hist. Class. Lit.* II.2 (1982), 110–16; E. Rawson, *Intellectual Life* (1985), 235–47 and *passim*; Albrecht, *Gesch. röm. Lit.* (1992), 472–90. Rawson notes (p. 236) that the *Res humanae* have not been comprehensively studied for over a century. The only usable edition of the surviving fragments is that of P. Mirsch, *Leipzig Studien* 5 (1882) 1ff. For the *Res divinae*, see B. Cardauns (ed.), *M. Terentius Varro. Antiquitates rerum divinarum*, 2 vols (Mainz 1976).

47 B. Riposati, *M. Terenti Varronis de vita populi Romani* (2nd edn, Milan 1972); P. Fraccaro, *Studi Varroniani. De gente populi Romani* (Padua 1907), for the fragments of the *de vita* and the *de gente*. See also H. Peter, *Historicorum Romanorum reliquiae* II (Leipzig 1906), 9–25.

48 On Varro's *Annales*, and other late republican works on chronology, see Rawson, *Intellectual Life* (1985), 245–6.

49 Rawson, *Intellectual Life* (1985), 246–7; *JRS* 62 (1972) 33–45 = *Roman Culture* (1991), 58–79.

50 The editing of the text, first by K.O. Müller and later by W.M. Lindsay, is one of the great achievements of classical scholarship; nevertheless, in spite of its importance, it has never been translated, and there is no convenient monograph or general article that gives the basic information in easily digestible form. The principal scholarly studies are R. Reitzenstein, *Verrianische Forschungen* (Breslau 1887); W. Strzelecki, *Quaestiones Verrianae* (Warsaw 1932: in Latin); A. Dihle, *RE* VIII A, 2 (1958), 1636–45, s.v. 'Verrius Flaccus'.

51 The Loeb edition of Ovid's *Fasti*, by Sir James Frazer, is reproduced from his monumental edition and commentary, *The Fasti of Ovid* (London 1929). For a more recent scholarly commentary and German translation, F. Bömer, *P. Ovidius Naso, Die Fasten*, 2 vols (Heidelberg 1957–8). For discussion of the work and its sources, Bömer I, 22–8; W. Fauth, *ANRW* II.16.1 (1978), 104–86; R. Schilling, *Rites, cultes, dieux de Rome* (Paris 1979), 1ff. See also the papers in 'Reconsidering Ovid's *Fasti*', *Arethusa* 25.1 (1992).

52 On Pliny's *Natural History* see now M. Beagon, *Roman Nature: the thought of Pliny the Elder* (Oxford 1992).

53 The parallel passages are listed by W.M. Lindsay in *Glossaria Latina* IV (Hildesheim 1965), 85. H.J. Rose, *The Roman Questions of Plutarch* (Oxford 1924) is still important.

54 For a general account of Gellius' life and work, L. Holford-Strevens, *Aulus Gellius* (London 1988).

55 On Macrobius see H. Bloch in A. Momigliano (ed.), *The Conflict between Paganism and Christianity in the Fourth Century* (Oxford 1963), 204ff.; A. Cameron, *JRS* 56 (1966), 25–38; Albrecht, *Gesch. röm. Lit.* (1992), 1179–83.

56 The text of Servius is edited by G. Thilo and H. Hagen, 3 vols (Leipzig 1881–7); and by E.K. Rand, A.F. Stocker *et al.*, 2 vols (Lancaster, Pa. 1946–65: the 'Harvard edition', so far covering Aeneid 1–5). There are no translations. The Servian commentaries and their citations of earlier authors are discussed in an important and informative article by R.B. Lloyd, *HSCPh* 65 (1961) 291–341.

57 See Lloyd, *HSCPh* 65 (1961), 294f. on Ennius, and 299ff. on Cato, with comparative statistics for other authors cited. For relative frequency of quotations in Servius and other direct sources, see, for Ennius, Skutsch, *Annals of Ennius* (1985), 8–46, and, for Cato, Chassignet, *Caton* (1986), 111–15.

58 See my comments in *PCPhS* 21 (1975), 16–27. The principal sources, all dependent on antiquarians, are Dion. Hal. 1.72; Plutarch, *Romulus* 2; Festus, pp. 326–8 L, s.v. 'Romam'; Servius (*auctus*), *Aen.* 1.273.

59 Cicero, *de legibus* 2.55ff., and see Rawson, *Roman Culture* (1991), 67–8.

60 See F. Coarelli, *Annales ESC* 37 (1982), 742–40.

61 The basis of all modern studies is Mommsen, *Staatsr.* I³ (1887), 22ff., 61ff., 116ff. On the *lex curiata* see, e.g., E.S. Staveley, *Historia* 5 (1956), 84–90; J. Nicholls, *AJPh* 88 (1967) 257–78; A. Magdelain, *Recherches sur l'imperium* (Paris 1968); R. Develin, *Mnemosyne* 30 (1977), 49–65. For sixteenth-century studies, W. McCuaig, *Athenaeum* 74 (1986), 147–83.

62 J.A. North, *CAH²* VII.2 (1989), 573ff.

63 A. Momigliano, *JRS* 53 (1963), 99–101 = *Terzo contributo*, 553–8.

64 E. Gjerstad, *Early Rome*, 6 vols (Lund 1953–73).

65 Sequence dating was first pioneered by the Egyptologist Flinders Petrie at University College London in 1897. See M.S. Drower, *Flinders Petrie: a life in archaeology* (London 1985), 251–2 (with a brief account of the method and relevant bibliography). For its application to Italian cemeteries see T.W. Potter, *The Changing Landscape of South Etruria* (London 1979), 67–8. Notice also Potter's account (ibid.) of 'horizontal stratigraphy' – the idea that as a cemetery takes over more and more land for burials, it will 'move' in a certain direction, with the result that the location of a tomb will provide prima-facie evidence of its relative date.

66 Excellent examples (from Lanuvium) can be seen in the British Museum (currently in room 71). A. Andrén, *Architectural Terracottas from Etrusco-Italic Temples* (Lund 1940), is still the basic work of reference. Among recent studies see M. Cristofani, in *Etruria e Lazio arcaico* (1987), 95–120.

67 Cf. M. Torelli, *CAH²* VII.2 (1989), 40.

68 Not everyone is convinced by this kind of argument, however, and there is still much scepticism, particularly (for some reason) in America. See e.g. K. Raaflaub's remarks in Raaflaub (ed.), *Social Struggles* (1986), 15f.; W.V. Harris in Eder (ed.), *Staat und Staatlichkeit* (1990), 497 n. 11; Ross Holloway, *Archaeology* (1994), 10–11, and *passim*.

69 Thus N. Spivey and S. Stoddart, in their book *Etruscan Italy: an archaeological history* (London 1990), attempt to write the history of the Etruscans without the

aid of written sources. The result is a useful corrective to some modern fantasies, and is an excellent *jeu d'esprit*. But history by definition cannot exist without written documents, and it will not do to relegate the historical Etruscans to prehistory. In fact the task Spivey and Stoddart set themselves is impossible; the underlying framework of the book, and its key concepts – including 'Etruria' and 'the Etruscans' – are historical categories, known only from written sources.

70 The idea that the Latins were cremators, and the Sabines inhumers, was made famous (or notorious) by F. von Duhn, *Italische Gräberkunde* I (Heidelberg 1924); but it had been current since the first excavations in the Forum. See e.g. R. Lanciani, *The Athenaeum* (London 1902), 632–3. For criticism see Poucet, *Origines* (1985), 140; A. Momigliano, *CAH²* VII.2 (1989), 65.

71 A. Carandini, *Archeo* 48 (Feb. 1989), 57–9; *Boll. Arch.* 1–2 (1990), 159–65; in *GRT* (1990), 97; and see the report in *Current Archaeology* 139 (1994), 261–5; for comment on the finds: A. Grandazzi, *La fondation de Rome* (Paris 1991), 203–7; A. Mastrocinque, *Romolo* (Este 1993), 94–5; Ross Holloway, *Archaeology* (1994), 101–2. For a sceptical judgement, see J. Poucet, *Latomus* 53 (1994), 99.

72 Poucet, *Les origines* (1985), 125.

2 THE PRE-ROMAN BACKGROUND

1 For an account of the peoples of Italy in *c.* 350 BC, see Salmon, *Making of Roman Italy* (1982), ch. 1. See also his chapter in *CAH²* IV (1988), 676–719; Potter, *Roman Italy* (1987), 28ff.

2 See R. Peroni in *Italy before the Romans* (1979), 7–30.

3 S.M. Puglisi, *La civiltà appenninica* (Florence 1959); M.A. Fugazzola Delpino, *Testimonianze di cultura appenninica nel Lazio* (Florence 1976).

4 Puglisi, *Civiltà appenninica* (1959); G.W. Barker in E.J. Higgs (ed.), *Palaeo-economy* (Cambridge 1975), 111–75; *Landscape and Society: prehistoric central Italy* (London 1981).

5 C.E. Oestenberg, *Luni sul Mignone e problemi della preistoria d'Italia* (Lund 1967); on Narce: T.W. Potter, *A Faliscan Town in South Etruria* (London 1976); N. Negroni Catacchio, *Sorgenti della Nova: una comunità protostorica e il suo territorio nell'Etruria meridionale* (Rome 1981).

6 Bronze-age finds in Rome and Latium: M.A. Fugazzola Delpino, *Testimonianze* (1976), updated by a contribution to a symposium on the Bronze Age in Latium in *Arch. Laz.* 2 (1979), 129–92. A brief account in A.P. Anzidei *et al.*, *Roma e il Lazio dall'età della pietra alla formazione della città* (Rome 1985), 124–5.

7 R. Peroni in *Italy before the Romans* (1979), 24–5. On the late Bronze Age in general see M.A. Fugazzola Delpino, *Testimonianze* (1976), 31–51; R. Peroni (ed.), *Il Bronzo Finale in Italia* (Atti XXI riunione scientifica dell'IIPP, Florence 1977); a brief account in English in Bietti Sestieri, *Iron Age Community* (1992), 29ff.

8 A.-M. Bietti Sestieri, *PPS* 39 (1973), 383–424.

9 The culture is named after the mounds of fertile black earth ('terra mara' in the local dialect), which marked the remnants of the bronze-age settlements. They were made famous by L. Pigorini, *BPI* 29 (1903), 189–211, who saw the 'Terramaricoli' as Indo-European invaders from the Danube region who brought a new type of civilisation to Italy and were the ancestors of the Romans. See L. Barfield, *Northern Italy before Rome* (London 1971), 90–5; M.A. Fugazzola Delpino, in *Italy before the Romans* (1979), 32–4. Rightly or wrongly, Pigorini's theories have recently been revived in the wake of new excavations. See L. Bernabò Brea, *La terramara di Poviglio. Le campagne di scavo 1985–1989* (Reggio Emilia 1989).

10 M.A. Fugazzola Delpino, in *Italy before the Romans* (1979), 31–51.

11 See above, p. 30 and n. 70. The idea continues to appear in general books on early Rome, e.g. Ogilvie, *Early Rome* (1976), 11.

12 F.R. Ridgway, in *Italy before the Romans* (1979), 419–87.

13 Ridgway, in *Italy before the Romans* (1979), 419–87; L. Bonfante, *Out of Etruria* (Oxford 1983).

14 On the origin and use of the term 'Villanovan', M. Pallottino, *Miscellanea . . . T. Dohrn dedicata* (Rome 1982), 67ff.; D. Ridgway, *CAH*² IV (1988), 640ff. For an excellent and fully documented account of the Villanovan culture see G. Bartoloni, *La cultura villanoviana* (Rome 1989).

15 See the important contributions of R. Peroni, *Arch. Laz.* 2 (1979), 171–6, and in Momigliano and Schiavone (eds), *StdR* I (1988), 10–11.

16 In general see D.H. Trump, *Central and Southern Italy before Rome* (London 1960); J. de la Genière, in *Italy before the Romans* (1979), 59–93; B. D'Agostino, in *Popoli e civiltà dell'Italia antica* II (Rome 1974), 11–91; V. Cianfarani *et al.*, *Culture adriatiche antiche di Abruzzo e Molise* (Rome 1978); M. Mazzei (ed.), *La Daunia antica* (Milan 1984); E. De Juliis, *Storia e civiltà della Puglia preromana* (Milan 1988).

17 V. Cianfarani, *Culture adriatiche d'Italia* (Rome 1970).

18 I have discussed this possibility in *ASNP* ser. III, VI.2 (1976), 411–39.

19 On Dionysius' account of pre-Roman Italy see Pallottino, *Earliest Italy* (1991), 41ff.; Gabba, *Dionysius* (1991), 11ff., 107ff.

20 On the Pelasgians in Italy see the exhaustive study of D. Briquel, *Les Pelasges en Italie: recherches sur l'histoire de la légende* (Rome 1984). On Dionysius and the Etruscans, see H.H. Scullard, in *Ancient Society and Institutions: Studies . . . V. Ehrenberg* (Oxford 1966), 225–31; E. Gabba, *RAL* ser. 8, vol. 30 (1975), 35–49; D. Briquel, *REL* 61 (1983), 65–86.

21 On Hercules see J. Bayet, *Les origines de l'Hercule romain* (Paris 1926); A. Mastrocinque (ed.), *Ercole in occidente* (Trento 1993).

22 Cf. P.M. Martin, *Athenaeum* 50 (1972), 252–75.

23 On the festival of the Argei, Scullard, *Festivals and Ceremonies* (1981), 120–1; B. Nagy, *AJAH* 10 (1985), 1–27.

24 See e.g. J. de la Genière, in *Italy before the Romans* (1979), 89–91; Pallottino, *Earliest Italy* (1991), 40–5 (both are cautiously optimistic). The improbable theories of E. Peruzzi, *Mycenaeans in Early Latium* (Rome 1980), have no secure foundations.

25 Lord William Taylour, *Mycenaean Pottery in South Italy* (Cambridge 1958); L. Vagnetti (ed.), *Magna Graecia e mondo miceneo – nuovi documenti* (Taranto 1982). For a recent discovery in southern Latium, M. Angle, A. Zarattini, *Arch. Laz.* 8 (1987), 250–2; *PdP* 48 (1993), 190–217.

26 E.J. Bickermann, *CPh* 47 (1952), 65–81 = *Religion and Politics in the Hellenistic and Roman Periods* (Como 1985), 399–417.

27 On the languages of ancient Italy see E. Pulgram, *The Tongues of Italy* (Cambridge, Mass. 1958); G. Devoto, *Gli antichi italici* (3rd edn, Florence 1967); *Popoli e civiltà dell'Italia antica* VI (Rome 1977?), with contributions by various linguistic experts; J.H.W. Penney, in *CAH*² IV (1988), 720–38; and the extremely useful survey by R.G.G. Coleman, *Trans. Phil. Soc.* (1986), 100–31.

28 R.G.G. Coleman, *Trans. Phil. Soc.* (1986), 120–2, thinks the inscription, the so-called Lapis Satricanus (see below, p. 144), is Volscian.

29 C. Renfrew, *Archaeology and Language* (London 1987), 123ff., for a discussion of 'models for linguistic replacement'.

30 These developments are discussed in a series of studies by M. Torelli: *DdA* 8 (1975), 3–78; *Storia degli Etruschi* (2nd edn, Bari 1984), 47ff.; in Momigliano and Schiavone (eds), *StdR* I (1988), 53–74; in P. Gros and M. Torelli, *Storia*

dell'urbanistica: il mondo romano (Bari 1988), 5–45. A brief statement in English: *CAH²* VII.2 (1989), 31–9.

31 D. Ridgway, *CAH²* IV (1988), 655; cf. Pallottino, *Earliest Italy* (1991), 52.

32 *TLE²* 559 (B.M. Bronzes 678). The translation is adapted from L. Bonfante, in J.T. Hooker (ed.), *Reading the Past* (London 1990), 365.

33 On the Etruscan language see Bonfante, in Hooker, *Reading the Past*; Pallottino, *Etruscans* (1975), 189ff.; M. Cristofani in *Italy before the Romans* (1979), 373–412. Understandable irritation at popular misconceptions has caused some experts to exaggerate the level of scholarly knowledge of Etruscan. Thus, I believe, Ridgway in *CAH²* IV (1988), 638–9.

34 A clear statement of the issues can be found in Scullard, *Etruscan Cities and Rome* (1967), 34ff.

35 The Lemnos stele, an Etruscan inscription of (probably) sixth-century date, discovered in 1885, indicates that there were Etruscans on the island of Lemnos at that time. But there is no warrant for the modern notion that they were the descendants of migrating Lydians who, like Philoctetes, had been left behind on Lemnos at the time of the original migration. See now, for a wholly different interpretation, M. Gras, in *Mélanges J. Heurgon* (1976), 355–63; *Trafics tyrrhéniens archaiques* (Rome 1985), 625–32.

36 M. Pallottino, *L'origine degli Etruschi* (Florence 1947); *Etruscans* (1975), 64ff.

3 THE ORIGINS OF ROME

1 Old Latium is the region bounded to the north west by the rivers Tiber and Anio, and to the east and south by a line running from the mouth of the Astura to Palestrina and Tivoli. The term 'Old Latium' (Latium Vetus) is used to distinguish it from the later Roman district, sometimes known as Latium Adiectum, which extended south to the borders of Campania, and the modern region of Lazio, which includes much of southern Etruria and the Sabine country.

2 R. Peroni, *BCom* 77 (1959–60), 7–32.

3 M.A. Fugazzola Delpino, *Testimonianze* (1976); *CLP* (1976), 65–7; the various papers in *Arch. Laz.* 2 (1979), 129–90; G. Bergonzi, A.-M. Bietti Sestieri, *DdA* NS 1 (1980), 47–8 (with full references); *Iron Age Community* (1992), 45–62.

4 Some Italian archaeologists are more optimistic, and hold that 'continuous occupation of the hills and lower ground of Rome goes back, in all probability, at least to the Recent Bronze Age and possibly to the Middle Bronze Age' (M. Pallottino in *Italy before the Romans* (1979), 200). Ross Holloway also states (*Archaeology* (1994), 14) that 'there was a settlement at Rome in the second millennium BC'. The transition from the 'Recent Bronze Age' to the 'Final Bronze Age' in central Italy is very problematic (in general see R. Peroni in *Italy before the Romans* (1979), 7–30). Peroni has also suggested that material from beneath the Arch of Augustus in the Roman Forum should be attributed to a settlement of the Recent Bronze Age – that is the thirteenth or twelfth century BC: *Arch. Laz.* 2 (1979), 171–6.

5 The material in question, a group of ten cremation tombs, has only been briefly published by M. Cataldi Dini in *Arch. Laz.* 6 (1984), 91–7; cf. T.J. Cornell, *Arch. Reports* 32 (1985–6), 129. If these tombs are correctly assigned to phase I, this is the largest group so far discovered.

6 Palombara Sabina: *NSc* (1902), 20ff.; Campo Reatino: *BPI* 65 (1956), 449ff.

7 This widely accepted chronological scheme is based on the classification of material from Rome and the Alban Hills by H. Müller-Karpe, *Vom Anfang Roms* (Heidelberg 1959); *Zur Stadtwerdung Roms* (Heidelberg 1963), as refined and

applied to all of Latium Vetus by G. Colonna, in *Popoli e civiltà dell'Italia antica* II (Rome 1974), 275–347. The method is essentially that of sequence dating (above, p. 27 and n. 65). The alternative scheme proposed by E. Gjerstad, *Early Rome* I–IV (Lund 1953–66), and P.G. Gierow, The Iron-Age Culture of Latium I (Lund 1966); II.1 (Lund 1964), is based on dubious premises and is now generally rejected, although it is taken seriously by Ross Holloway, *Archaeology* (1994), 37–50 (with some important reservations about the Müller-Karpe scheme). On this see D. Ridgway, *JRS* 58 (1968), 235–40, and in *Italy before the Romans* (1979), 187–93. Most recently see the detailed discussion of Meyer, *Pre-Republican Rome* (1983), with a detailed refutation of Gjerstad and further refinements of Müller-Karpe.

8 C. Ampolo, V. Giovannini, *CLP* (1976), 347f.; L. Crescenzi, *Arch. Laz.* 1 (1978), 51f.

9 The complete report of the excavations has now been published: A.-M. Bietti Sestieri, *La necropoli laziale di Osteria dell'Osa*, 3 vols (Rome 1992). The main results are conveniently summarised in Bietti Sestieri, *Iron Age Community* (1992). See also Ross Holloway, *Archaeology* (1994), 103–13; C. Smith, *Early Rome and Latium* (forthcoming), *passim*.

10 On all this see A.-M. Bietti Sestieri, *Ricerca su una comunità* (1979), 99–114.

11 A.-M. Bietti Sestieri, *La necropoli laziale* (1992), 130, 564–5 (tomb 126); 130, 563 (tomb 128).

12 See Bietti Sestieri, *Iron Age Community* (1992), 141ff.

13 This point is made briefly by A.-M. Bietti Sestieri in A.P. Anzidei *et al.*, *Roma e il Lazio dall'età della pietra alla formazione della città* (Rome 1985), 171.

14 There are some minor differences; for instance at Rome there seem to be some examples of female cremations. But the basic cultural features are remarkably uniform in all early iron-age sites so far discovered in Old Latium. See Bietti Sestieri, *Iron Age Community* (1992), 221ff.

15 H. Haelbeck in E. Gjerstad, *Early Rome* (1953–73) I, 155; II, 289; III, 464. Cf. C. Ampolo, *DdA* NS 1 (1980), 16.

16 C. Ampolo, *DdA* NS 1 (1980), 34–6, 44.

17 On the possibilities, as well as the difficulties, of such types of analysis see G. Barker, *Prehistoric Farming in Europe* (Cambridge 1985), 19–23.

18 Bietti Sestieri, *Iron Age Community* (1992), 102.

19 This speculation is based on two pieces of evidence. The discovery of a cremation grave under the so-called House of Livia (G. Carrettoni, *BPI* 64 (1954–5), 299; Gjerstad, *Early Rome* III (1960), 72), between the Palatium and the Cermalus, suggests that there were originally two villages (one on each summit), separated by a cemetery. The same idea is implied in the annual Roman festival of the Septimontium (11 December) in which the inhabitants of seven hills celebrated a joint festival. According to Varro, *LL* 6.24, the seven hills in question included the Palatium and the Cermalus. Cf. Scullard, *Festivals and Ceremonies* (1981), 203.

20 On the process of nucleation in Old Latium see M. Guaitoli, *Arch. Laz.* 6 (1984), 364–81; A.-M. Bietti Sestieri, in A.P. Anzidei *et al.*, *Roma e il Lazio* (1985), 151–5. For Rome note especially A. Guidi, *Opus* 1 (1982), 279–89.

21 On these sites see the brief summaries in the exhibition catalogue *Enea nel Lazio* (1981), 48–9 (Antemnae), 49–50 (Crustumerium), 38–42 (Tibur); on Corniculum see Z. Mari, M. Sperandio, *Arch. Laz.* 6 (1984), 35–46; in more detail see the volumes by L. Quilici and S. Quilici Gigli in the series 'Latium Vetus': *Antemnae* (Rome 1978); *Crustumerium* (Rome 1980); *Fidenae* (Rome 1986); *Ficulea* (Rome 1993).

22 On the problem in general see A. Guidi, *Rivista di Archeologia* 6 (1982), 31–4.

23 A.-M. Bietti Sestieri, in A.P. Anzidei *et al.*, *Roma e il Lazio* (1985), 156–9; *Iron Age Community* (1992), 70–5.

24 On the hut settlements of central Italy see G. Bartoloni, A. Beijer and A. De Santis in C. Malone and S. Stoddart (eds), *Papers in Italian Archaeology* IV, iii (Oxford 1985), 175–202; G. Bartoloni, F. Buranelli, V. D'Atri, A. De Santis, *Le urne a capanna rinvenute in Italia* (Rome 1987); and now the first report on the excavations at Satricum, M. Maaskant-Kleibrink and R. Olde-Dubbelink, *Borgo Le Ferriere (Satricum)*, (Groningen 1987), 47–89. On present-day shepherd huts see J. Close-Brooks and S. Gibson, *PPS* 32 (1966), 349–52; for the comparison with the Apennine culture, G. Barker, *Landscape and Society: prehistoric central Italy* (London 1981), 192–3.

25 The most exhaustive treatment of the legends, with full references to the sources, remains that of A. Schwegler, *Römische Geschichte* I-III (1853–5). Among recent accounts notice M. Grant, *Roman Myths* (London 1971), and N.M. Horsfall, J. Bremmer, *Studies in Roman Myth and Mythography* (London 1987). Poucet, *Les Origines* (1985), deals at length with questions of veracity. A. Grandazzi, *La fondation de Rome* (Paris 1991), asks fundamental questions and deals with methodological issues in a subtle and original manner. Cf. also the interesting study by A. Mastrocinque, *Romolo* (Este 1993).

26 I have discussed these variants at length in *PCPhS* 21 (1975), 1–32, where I estimated that between 25 and 30 distinct versions of the foundation story could be isolated in the sources. These are conveniently assembled in *FGrHist* 840 (and cf. above, p. 23, n. 58).

27 The *Origo gentis Romanae* was long thought to be a document of little value. Indeed B.G. Niebuhr dismissed it as a Renaissance forgery (*History of Rome*[3] (1837) I, 68 n. 274). Its true character was firmly established by A. Momigliano in *JRS* 48 (1958), 56–73 (= *Secondo contributo* 145–76). The most recent edition is the Budé text by J.-C. Richard (Paris 1983) with French translation and full notes.

28 This is the version of Promathion, cited by Plutarch, *Romulus* 2; see further *PCPhS* 21 (1975), 21 n. 4; 25 n. 4; 26 and n. 2, and cf. above, p. 132.

29 *Origo gentis Romanae* 23.6, with Richard's notes ad loc. Cf. the comment of A. Momigliano, *JRS* 53 (1963), 97 (= *Terzo contributo* 549).

30 On the disappearance of Romulus see D. Briquel, *Latomus* 36 (1977), 253–82; Coarelli, *Il foro romano* I, 189–99; Poucet, *Les origines*, 289f.

31 Dionysius' account of the 'constitution of Romulus' in 2.7–29 is unlike anything in any other historical source. It probably derives not from an annalist but from a political pamphlet, possibly of the age of Sulla. Thus, E. Gabba, *Athenaeum* 38 (1960), 175–225. J.P.V.D. Balsdon, *JRS* 61 (1971), 18–27 argues, in my view unconvincingly, that the passage was an original composition by Dionysius himself.

32 Beginning probably with the annalist L. Calpurnius Piso Frugi (cos. 133), on whom see E. Rawson, *Latomus* 35 (1976), 368–717 = *Roman Culture* (1991), 245–71.

33 Dion. Hal. I.79.11. The site has now been tentatively identified near the temple of Magna Mater on the Palatine. See P. Pensabene, in *GRT* (1990), 87–90, and cf. Mastrocinque, *Romolo* (1993), 93–4.

34 This point is well made by A. Momigliano in *Mededelingen der koninklijke Nederlandse Akademie van Wetenschappen* NS 45, 9 (1982), 231–54 (= *Settimo contributo* 437–62). As a refugee himself, Momigliano was well qualified to speak on the matter. He drew attention to the popularity of the *Aeneid* in the USA, a society which is rightly conscious of having much in common with ancient Rome.

35 According to P.A. Brunt, *Italian Manpower* (Oxford 1971), 387, 'slaves and

freedmen accounted for well over two-thirds of the urban population in 70 [BC], perhaps three-quarters.'

36 H. Strasburger, *Zur Sage von der Gründung Roms* (Heidelberg 1968); cf. H.D. Jocelyn, *PCPhS* 17 (1971), 51ff.

37 It is true that we do not know the provenance of the statue, but there is no reason to suppose that it is 'Etruscan' (cf. Grandazzi, *La fondation de Rome*, 308 n. 63), and it is perverse to suggest that it originally had no connection with the story of Romulus and Remus. On any reasonable view it must have had. The arguments of E.J. Bickerman, *RFIC* 97 (1967), 394–5 = *Religions and Politics in the Hellenistic and Roman Periods* (Como 1985), 526–7 and M.H. Crawford, *Roman Republican Coinage* (Cambridge 1974) I, 403–4, are unconvincing. My comments in *PCPhS* 21 (1975), 7 n. 4 are too cautious. In general see O.W. von Vacano, *ANRW* I. 4 (1973), 523–83; C. Dulière, *Lupa Romana* (Brussels 1979).

38 In 296 BC, according to Livy X.23.12, the aediles Cn. and Q. Ogulnius set up a statue group of the wolf and twins at the Ficus Ruminalis, the sacred fig tree at the foot of the Palatine beneath which the twins were said to have been washed ashore. This statue (not to be confused with the Capitoline Wolf) was reproduced on the reverse of the silver didrachms issued between 269 and 266 BC (Crawford no. 20).

39 I argued the case against Strasburger in more detail in *PCPhS* 21 (1975), 1–32.

40 G. Binder, *Die Aussetzung des Königskindes* (Meisenheim 1964), for a list of 'exposure' myths. See also S. Thompson, *Motif-Index of Folk-Literature* (rev. edn, Copenhagen 1955–7) V, 279ff.

41 Alföldi, *Struktur*, 69–73; M. Eliade *From Zalmoxis to Gengis Khan*, 10–25; J.-P. Roux in *La naissance du monde (Sources Orientales* 1) (Paris 1959), 287. S. Mazzarino, *Il pensiero storico classico* II.1 (Bari 1966), 310 and n. 555, cites a native Australian example.

42 Silvius: Cato, *Orig.* I.11; Dion. Hal. 1.70.2; *Origo gentis Romanae* 16; Alföldi, *Early Rome*, 238–9. Caeculus: Cato, *Orig.* II.29; Serv., *Aen.* 7.678; Bremmer and Horsfall, *Roman Myth*, 49–62; L. Deschamps, in *Hommages H. Le Bonniec* (Brussels 1988), 144–57.

43 The Bologna stele: P. Ducati, *Monumenti Antichi* 20 (1910), 531, fig. 24, no. 195. It is normally said to represent a wolf, but see T.P. Wiseman, *LCM* 16.8 (1991), 117. The Bolsena mirror: R. Adam, D. Briquel, *MEFRA* 94 (1982), 33–65. The Praenestine cista: F. Jurgeit, in *Tainia R. Hampe . . . dargebracht* (Mainz 1980), 272–5, and see Wiseman, *LCM* 16.8 (1991), 117, and *PBSR* 61 (1993), 1–6.

44 On the Aeneas legend see the controversial book by J. Perret, *Les origines de la légende troyenne de Rome* (Paris 1942). Recent accounts include Galinsky, *Aeneas* (1969); Dury-Moyaers, *Enée et Lavinium* (1981); the exhibition catalogue *Enea nel Lazio* (1981); A. Momigliano, *Settimo contributo* 437–62; N.M. Horsfall in Horsfall and Bremmer, *Roman Myth* (1987), 12–24; Dubourdieu, *Culte des Pénates* (1989); Gruen, *Culture and National Identity* (1992), 6–51.

45 *Iliad* 20.307f. A similar point is made in the Homeric Hymn to Aphrodite (*Hom. Hymns* 5. 195–7).

46 Some historians, such as Strabo (13.1.53, p. 608 C), believed that in Homer's time a dynasty claiming descent from Aeneas had ruled over a refounded city at or near the site of Troy, and many modern scholars have followed them. But the inference is open to question: see P.M. Smith, *HSCPh* 85 (1981), 17–58.

47 B.V. Head, *Historia Numorum*[2] (Oxford 1911), 214; F. Canciani, *LIMC* I (Munich 1981), s.v. 'Aeneias', no. 92.

48 N.M. Horsfall, *JHS* 99 (1979), 35–43.

49 Thuc. 6.2.3; cf. Antiochus of Syracuse *FGrHist* 555 F.6; Plutarch, *Nicias* 1.3; and

many others. Further references and discussion in Galinsky, *Aeneas* (1969), 76–8; J. Perret, *Mélanges J. Heurgon* (Rome 1976), 791–805.

50 Dion. Hal. I.72.2 = Hellanicus, *FGrHist* 4 F.84 and Damastes, *FGrHist* 241 F.45. N.M. Horsfall has challenged the authenticity of these quotations in *CQ* 29 (1979), 372–390, but see A. Momigliano, *ASNP* IX.9.3 (1979), 1223–4 (= *Settimo contributo* 108–9).

51 N.M. Horsfall, *CQ* 29 (1979), 384f., decisively refuting the view that the piety of Aeneas is a late and distinctively Roman contribution to the story, as maintained by Galinsky, *Aeneas* (1969), 41ff. and by me in *PCPhS* 21 (1975), 13.

52 Zonaras 8.9.12; cf. Cicero, *Verr.* 4.72. Galinsky, *Aeneas* (1969), 173; Gruen, *Culture and National Identity* (1992), 44–5.

53 Livy 38.9.7; 37.2; 38.39.10; Dittenberger, *Syll.*³ 591; Ennius, *Annals* 344–5 Sk., with Skutsch's commentary pp. 514f. See further Gruen, *Culture and National Identity* (1992), 48–50.

54 For example Demetrius of Skepsis, writing in the second century BC, asserted that Aeneas and his descendants had ruled in the Troad, and that there had never been a Trojan migration to Italy (Strabo 13.1.53 p. 608 C) This can be seen as a piece of anti-Roman polemic: E. Gabba, *RSI* 86 (1974), 630–2; in M. Sordi (ed.), *I canali della propaganda nel mondo antico* (Milan 1976), 84–91; Smith, *HSCPh* 85 (1981), 42–3; J.-L. Ferrary, *Philhellénisme et impérialisme* (Paris 1988), 223–9; *contra*: Gruen, *Culture and National Identity* (1992), 40–2.

55 A. Momigliano, *Settimo contributo* 456–9.

56 Perret, *Origines* (1942); cf. the review by A. Momigliano, *JRS* 35 (1945), 99–104 (= *Terzo contributo* 677–87).

57 Amphora: Canciani, *LIMC* I, s.v. 'Aeneias', no. 94; Horsfall, *JHS* 99 (1979), 40–1 and plate IIIa; F. Castagnoli, *SR* 30 (1982), 5. Scarab: P. Zazoff, *Etruskische Skarabäer* (Mainz 1968), no. 44; Horsfall, *JHS* 99 (1979), 40–1 and plate IIIb.

58 L. Vagnetti, *Il deposito votivo di Campetti a Veio* (Rome 1971), 88; M. Torelli, *DdA* 7 (1973), 399–400; Canciani, *LIMC* I, s.v. 'Aeneias', no. 96.

59 The Trojan Penates of Lavinium were described by Timaeus, drawing upon local sources (Dion. Hal. I.67.4 = *FGrHist* 566 F.36). On the supposed relics at Lavinium M.H. Crawford, *JRS* 61 (1971), 153f.; Dubourdieu, *Culte des Pénates* (1989), 264–85.

60 The definitive publication of the excavations at the sanctuary of the thirteen altars is in L. Cozza and F. Castagnoli (eds), *Lavinium* II (Rome 1975). On Lavinium in general see Dury-Moyaers, *Enée et Lavinium* (1981); *Enea nel Lazio* (1981), esp. 156ff.; J. Poucet, *RBPhH* 61 (1983), 144–59; M. Torelli, *Lavinio e Roma* (Rome 1984); Ross Holloway, *Archaeology* (1994), 128–41.

61 Ross Holloway, *Archaeology* (1994), 7–8; and see further below, p. 109, and n. 4.

62 S. Weinstock, *JRS* 50 (1960), 112ff.; *contra*: F. Castagnoli, *PdP* 32 (1977), 351ff.; Dury-Moyaers, *Enée et Lavinium* (1981), 221–6; Dubourdieu, *Culte des Pénates* (1989), 430–9.

63 On the 'heroon of Aeneas' see P. Sommella, *RPAA* 44 (1972), 47–74; *Gymnasium* 81 (1974), 273–97. The objections to the identification were pointed out by me, *LCM* 2 (1977), 77–83; *Arch. Reports* 27 (1979–80), 86, and independently by J. Poucet, *AC* 48 (1979), 181–3; *Mélanges R. Schilling* (Paris 1983), 187–201, and now *LEC* 57 (1989), 231–8. These objections have not been answered; they are either ignored, e.g. by F. Zevi, in *Gli Etruschi e Roma* (1981), 145–58, or brushed aside, e.g. by F. Castagnoli, *SR* 30 (1982), 13; Ross Holloway, *Archaeology* (1994), 135–8.

64 See Gruen, *Culture and National Identity* (1992), 24–5, with further refs.

65 Dion. Hal. I.79.8, citing Fabius Pictor, Cincius Alimentus and Cato. See also Fabius fr. 1 P; Cincius fr. 1–2 P; Cato, *Orig.* I.19; II.26.

66 Hesiod fr. 168 M.-W. (= Serv. Auct., *Aen.* 8.130); J. Bayet, *MEFR* 38 (1920), 63–144; *Hercule romain* (1926).

67 Plut., *Romulus* 1.1 (*FGrHist* 840 F.40e). The play on words ('Ρώμη = 'strength') is found also in Promathion (*ap.* Plut., *Romulus* 2), Lycophron (*Alex.* 1233) and Hyperochus (Festus p. 328 L = *FGrHist* 576 F.4), the author of a Cumaean history. Hyperochus wrote that the original settlement was called Valentia (Latin for 'strength'), which was changed to 'Ρώμη by Greek-speaking followers of Evander and Aeneas.

68 J. Bayet, *MEFR* 38 (1920), 63–144.

69 E. La Rocca, *DdA* 8 (1974–5), 86–103; *CLP* 367–71; *PdP* 32 (1977), 375–97; Ross Holloway, *Archaeology* (1994), 166–7.

70 *Hercule romain* (1926).

71 On Hercules-Melqart see A. Piganiol, *Hommages A. Grenier* (Brussels 1962), 1261–4; D. van Berchem, *RPAA* 32 (1959–60), 61–8; *Syria* 44 (1967), 73–109, 307–38; Phoenician merchants at Rome: R. Rebuffat, *MEFR* 78 (1966), 7–48.

72 e.g. E. Peruzzi, *Aspetti culturali del Lazio primitivo* (Florence 1978); *Mycenaeans in Early Latium* (Rome 1980), on which see above, p. 409, n. 24.

73 The metaphors, when not audio-visual ('echoes', 'reflects') are usually either fruity ('a historical core') or nutty ('a kernel of fact', 'un noyau historique', etc.).

74 E. Pais was the leading figure of the so-called 'hypercritical' school. See especially his *Storia di Roma* I (1898). On Pais notice especially the critique of C. Barbagallo, *Il problema delle origini di Roma* (Milan 1926).

75 Poucet, *Les origines* (1985). Cf. my review in *TLS*, 1 August 1986, 848.

76 E. Peruzzi, *Mycenaeans in Early Latium* (Rome 1980).

77 Thus, rightly, Heurgon, *Rise of Rome* (1973), 24.

78 The canonical date of 1184 BC was established by the Alexandrian scholar Eratosthenes in the early third century BC. How this date was calculated we do not know, and it may not be as well founded as modern scholars seem to think.

79 These versions include that of Eratosthenes himself: *FGrHist* 241 F.45. Also Lycophron, *Alex.* 1232f.; Hegesianax, *FGrHist* 45 F.9; Dionysius of Chalcis, *FGrHist* 840 F.10; Apollodorus (Festus s.v. 'Romam', p. 326 L); and the anonymous authors cited by Dion. Hal. I.72.1. We may take it that these writers either did not know of the Roman foundation date, or chose to ignore it. More surprisingly, the Roman poets Naevius and Ennius also made Romulus the grandson of Aeneas (Serv. Dan., *Aen.* 1.273; cf. Ennius, *Ann.* 58–60 with Skutsch's commentary ad loc.). Naevius may not have been aware of the chronological difficulties this created, but Ennius represents a more serious problem, on which see my comments in *JRS* 76 (1986), 247 (where the question is raised but not answered).

80 Cincius *ap.* Festus, s.v. 'praetor', p. 276 L: *Albanos rerum potitos usque ad Tullum regem* ('the Albans were in charge of affairs down to the time of King Tullus').

81 Poucet, *Les origines* (1985), 146–9; cf. Heurgon, *Rise of Rome* (1973), 136. Heurgon was taken to task for this and described as 'hypercritical' by M. Pallottino, whose own view is that 'the period traditionally assigned to Tullus Hostilius coincides precisely [*sic*] with the decline of the protohistoric centres in the Alban Hills' (*Italy before the Romans* (1979), 218).

82 Varro, *de re rust.* 2.4.17f. On the myth of the sow see Alföldi, *Early Rome* (1965), 271ff.

83 C. Ampolo, *CLP* (1976), 144–5. The cremation grave under the house of Livia is reported in G. Carrettoni, *BPI* 64 (1954), 299; E. Gjerstad, *Early Rome* III (1960), 72. I can find no evidence to support M. Pallottino's statement that 'the summit of the Palatine was already occupied by *vast concentrations* of huts in the Early Iron Age' (my italics): *Italy before the Romans* (1979), 202.

84 If we are to believe R. Peroni, *Arch. Laz.* 2 (1979), 171–6, the earliest traces of habitation in Rome belong to the Recent Bronze Age (thirteenth–twelfth centuries BC), and are to be located at the feet of the hills rather than on the hills themselves. Cf. the remarks of M. Pallottino and G. Colonna in the discussion following Peroni's paper, on p. 185.

85 See above, p. 408, n. 71.

86 Some speculations can be found in Gjerstad, *Early Rome* VI (1973), 86.

87 M. Pallottino, in *Italy before the Romans* (1979), 201.

88 Momigliano, *Terzo contributo*, 553.

89 Pliny, *n.h.* III.69. There is argument about the reading of several of the names, but this problem need not concern us here. For historical discussion see A. Rosenberg, *Hermes* 54 (1919), 113–73, esp. 121ff.; M. Pallottino, *Arch. Class.* 12 (1960), 27–30; A. Bernardi, *Athenaeum* 42 (1964), 223–60; Alföldi, *Early Rome* (1965), 13–15; Richard, *Origines* (1978), 136–8; Pallottino, *Origini* (1993), 120–32.

90 A. Rosenberg, *Hermes* 54 (1919), 133 and 137.

91 Pallottino, *Origini* (1993), 126–32.

92 We know that Cato copied documents of precisely this kind in his *Origins* (II.28), and in my view he is the most likely source for this text.

93 Festus pp. 474–6 L; p. 458 L. Antistius Labeo, cited by Festus, included the Subura in his list, which creates a problem because the Subura is a valley not a mount, and would increase the number of participating groups to eight. The problem still remains if we accept L.A. Holland's interpretation that the groups were not *septem montes* ('seven mounts') but *septi* (or *saepti*) *montes* (i.e. 'fortified mounts') – *TAPhA* 84 (1953), 16–34, and J. Poucet, *BIBR* 32 (1960), 25–73. Cf. R. Gelsomino, *Varrone e i sette colli di Roma* (Rome 1975). Most scholars tend to ignore the reference to the Subura. The theory of De Sanctis, *StdR* I² (1960), 182, that the Subura was incorporated into the group of the Septimontium at a secondary stage, remains attractive.

94 Cf. A. Momigliano, *Terzo contributo*, 555. The cremation grave beneath the House of Livia (above, n.81) supports the idea that there was a stage when the Palatine was occupied by two separate villages.

95 Varro tells us that the festival of the Septimontium was not included in the calendar because it involved only the *montani*, not the whole people (*LL* 6.24).

96 Wissowa, *RuK²* (1912), 555f.

97 As has long been recognised: Momigliano, *Terzo contributo* 554; Grandazzi, *Fondation* (1991), 260ff.; Pallottino, *Origini* (1993), 155–60.

98 Ovid, *Fasti* 5.143; cf. the denarius of L. Caesius, of 112 or 111 BC (Crawford no. 298).

99 See my comments in *PCPhS* 21 (1975), 30–1.

100 Mommsen, *Ges. Schr.* IV.1 (1906), 22–35; E. Pais, *Ricerche sulla storia e sul diritto pubblico di Roma* I (Rome 1915), 347–64; G. Dumézil, *La naissance de Rome* (Paris 1944), 128–93; *L'héritage indo-européenne à Rome* (Paris 1948), 125–42; *Mythe et épopée* I (Paris 1968), 290–302; *Archaic Roman Religion* (Chicago 1970), 60–78; J. Poucet, *Recherches sur la légende sabine des origines de Rome* (Kinshasa 1967); *ANRW* I.1 (1972), 48–135; *Les origines* (1985), 213ff. and *passim*. Poucet's view is that the Sabine invasions of Roman territory from the end of the sixth century to the middle of the fifth, together with some events of the early third century, provided the historical model for the fabrication of the pseudo-history of the age of Romulus.

101 Recent work in Sabina: *Civiltà arcaica dei Sabini*, 3 vols (Rome 1973–7). The principal sites are Palombara Sabina, Camporeatino, Colle del Forno, Magliano Sabina, and Poggio Sommavilla. P. Santoro, *NSc* 31 (1977), 211–98 (Colle del Forno); *Arch. Class.* 43 (1991), 349–62 (Poggio Sommavilla); M.P. Muzzioli,

Cures Sabini (Florence 1980); and see the regular annual reports on archaeology in Sabina in *Archeologia Laziale*.

102 Momigliano, *Terzo contributo*, 562 n. 40.

103 Thus, rightly, Poucet, *Les origines* (1985), 79–81.

104 L. de Beaufort, *Dissertation sur l'incertitude des cinq premiers siècles de l'histoire romaine* (Utrecht 1738; rev. edn, Paris 1866), 26.

105 Dumézil, *Archaic Roman Religion* (1970), 4.

106 Dumézil, *Archaic Roman Religion* (1970), 66ff.; *Jupiter, Mars, Quirinus* (Paris 1941), 155–98; *L'héritage indo-européen à Rome* (Paris 1948), 125–42; *Mythe et épopée* I (Paris 1968), 285–302.

107 Dumézil, *Archaic Roman Religion* (1970), 163

108 Dumézil, *L'héritage indo-européen à Rome* (1948), 143–59; *Mythe et épopée* I (1968), 274–84.

109 Dumézil, *Tarpeia* (Paris 1947), 176–93.

110 Momigliano, *Terzo contributo*, 581–3; *Ottavo contributo*, 135–59; *Studies on Modern Scholarship* (Berkeley 1994), 286–301.

111 Momigliano, *Terzo contributo*, 583.

112 Cf. Heurgon, *Rise of Rome* (1973), 133–4.

113 Dumézil, *Archaic Roman Religion* (Chicago 1970), 73.

114 Dumézil, *Jupiter, Mars, Quirinus* (1941), *passim*, esp. 69ff.; *L'héritage indo-européen à Rome* (1948), esp., 72ff.; *L'idéologie tripartite des indo-européens* (Brussels 1958), esp. 48–53; id., *Archaic Roman Religion* (1970), 141ff.

4 THE RISE OF THE CITY-STATE

1 On the use of the potter's wheel and the development of specialisation in ceramic production see e.g. A.-M. Bietti Sestieri in A.P. Anzidei *et al.*, *Roma e il Lazio* (1985), 190–1, 213–16. On craft production in general G. Colonna in Momigliano and Schiavone (eds), *StdR* I (1988), 291–316.

2 Castel di Decima. Only a handful of tombs have so far been published in detail. See T.J. Cornell, *Arch. Reports* 26 (1979–80), 77, for a concordance of all the available publications and full references. For discussion and analysis see F. Zevi, *PdP* 32 (1977), 241–73; A. Bedini and F. Cordano, ibid., 274–311; G. Bartoloni, M. Cataldi Dini, F. Zevi, in G. Gnoli and J.-P. Vernant (eds), *La mort, les morts dans les sociétés anciennes* (Cambridge, Paris 1982), 257–73. For a brief synthesis, Ross Holloway, *Archaeology* (1994), 114–20.

3 *CLP* (1976), 213–49; F. Canciani, F.W. von Hase, *La tomba Bernardini di Palestrina* (Rome 1979); Ross Holloway, *Archaeology* (1994), 156–60.

4 Tomb XV: *NSc* 29 (1975), 251–94; *CLP* (1976), 260–7. Tomb CLIII: *CLP* (1976), 287.

5 Tomb CI: *CLP* (1976), 287–8; cf. L. Quilici, *Roma primitiva e le origini della civiltà laziale* (Rome 1979), 303–4. On the Vestal Virgins as the king's daughters see Mommsen, *Röm. Forsch.* I (1864), 80; *Staatsr.* II³ (1887), 54.

6 Ross Holloway, *Archaeology* (1994), 120–2, drawing on A. Bedini in M.R. Di Mino, M. Bertinetti (eds), *Archeologia a Roma* (Rome 1990), 48–64, and in *Roma, 1000 anni di civiltà* (Rome 1992), 83–96.

7 Chamber tombs at Laurentina and Torrino: T.J. Cornell, *Arch. Reports* 32 (1985–6), 132; at Osteria dell'Osa: M. Cataldi Dini in A.-M. Bietti Sestieri (ed.), *Ricerca su una comunità* (1979), 187–94.

8 G. Colonna, *CLP* (1976), 337–9.

9 Formal definitions: Cicero, *Top.*, 6.29; Paul.- Fest. p. 83 L, s.v. 'Gentilis'. For a minimalist interpretation, based largely on these texts, P.A. Brunt, *JRS* 72 (1982),

2–4; there is an abundance of more elaborate theories, attributing a high degree of organisation and solidarity to the *gens*, especially in early times. See e.g. Fustel de Coulanges, *Ancient City* (Baltimore 1980), 32ff., esp. 92ff.; P. Bonfante, *Scritti giuridici* I (Turin 1926), 18–63; De Martino, *Storia* I² (1972), 4–19; *Diritto e società nell'antica Roma* (Rome 1979), 51–74; G. Franciosi (ed.), *Ricerche sulla organizzazione gentilizia romana* 1–2 (Naples 1984–8); a balanced account in Richard, *Origines* (1978), 181ff. Among earlier studies in English, note especially G.W. Botsford, *Political Science Quarterly* 21 (1906), 498–526; 22 (1907), 663–92.

10 Examples include V. Giuffrè, *Labeo* 16 (1970), 329–34; De Martino, *Storia* I² (1972), 77–9; A. Guarino, *La rivoluzione della plebe* (Naples 1975), 158–60. These scholars tend to cite 10.8.9, which actually says someting quite different. Cf. Richard, *Origines* (1978), 182 n.172; A. Momigliano, *CAH²* VII.2 (1989), 99.

11 The theories of Fustel de Coulanges, Bonfante, and the rest (see above, n.9), were attacked by Eduard Meyer, *Sitzber. Preuss. Ak.* (1907), 508 (cf. *Gesch. des Altertums* I² 1 (1907), 1ff.; *Klio* 2 (1899), 514), who argued that the formation of the *gens* occurred after the foundation of the state.

12 J. Bremmer in Horsfall and Bremmer, *Roman Myth* (1987), 47–8.

13 Frederiksen, in *Italy before the Romans* (1979), 291ff.; *Campania* (1984), 71ff.

14 J. Heurgon, *Capoue préromaine* (1942), 74; I. Strom, *Problems concerning the . . . Etruscan Orientalizing Style* (Odense 1971), 47.

15 Ross Holloway, *Archaeology* (1994), 160, 168–9.

16 H. Payne, *Necrocorinthia* (Oxford 1931); R.M. Cook, *Greek Painted Pottery* (2nd edn, London 1972), 43–62.

17 G. Colonna, *Arch. Class.* 13 (1961), 9–25; D. Williams, in J. Swaddling (ed.), *Italian Iron Age Artefacts in the British Museum* (London 1986), 295–304; for the general context, Ridgway, *First Western Greeks* (1992), 139–44.

18 See now the readable account of Ridgway, *First Western Greeks* (1992), with further references and bibliography.

19 Ridgway, *First Western Greeks* (1992), 91f., 99f.

20 Ridgway, *First Western Greeks* (1992), 108.

21 On the nature and purpose of Greek colonization see O. Murray, *Early Greece* (London 1980), 100ff.; J. Boardman, *The Greeks Overseas* (2nd edn, London 1980); A.J. Graham, *CAH²* III.3 (1982), 83–162.

22 Ridgway, *First Western Greeks* (1992), 129ff.

23 O. Murray, *Early Greece* (1980), esp. 38ff.; in *Tria Corda* (1983), 257–72; and the contributions in O. Murray (ed.), *Sympotica* (Oxford 1989).

24 M.I. Finley, *The World of Odysseus* (2nd edn, London 1978).

25 The classic study is that of M. Mauss, *The Gift* (1925; English edn, London 1970); in the Homeric context, Finley, *World of Odysseus²* (1978), 64ff., 95ff., 120ff. On the institution of guest-friendship see the excellent account of G. Herman, *Ritualised Friendship and the Greek City* (Cambridge 1987).

26 Frederiksen, *Italy before the Romans* (1979), 292–3.

27 The uncivilised nature of the Cyclopes is underlined in *Odyssey* 9, 108ff. Their attitude to guest-friendship: Finley, *World of Odysseus²* (1978), 101–2.

28 M. Cristofani, *PdP* 30 (1975), 132–52. On gift-giving in archaic Italy see also A. Rathje, *Opus* 3 (1984), 341–7.

29 A. Rathje, *ARID* 12 (1983), 7–29; in O. Murray (ed.), *Sympotica* (Oxford 1989), 279–93. Ross Holloway's scepticism (*Archaeology* (1994), 191 n.3) does not persuade me.

30 G. Colonna, *Arch. Class.* 25–6 (1973–4), 132ff.

31 Fondo Artiaco: G. Buchner, in *Italy before the Romans* (1979), 129–44; Frederiksen, *Campania* (1984), 72. Eretria: C. Bérard, *Eretria* III: *l'heroon à la porte de*

l'ouest (Berne 1970), 13–32; in G. Gnoli and J.-P. Vernant (eds), *La mort, les morts, dans les sociétés anciennes* (Cambridge 1982), 89–105.

32 M. Torelli, in P. Gros and M. Torelli, *Storia dell'urbanistica: il mondo romano* (Bari 1988), 5–36.

33 M. Guaitoli, *PdP* 36 (1981), 152–73; *Arch. Laz.* 6 (1984), 364–81.

34 M. Torelli in Gros and Torelli, *Storia dell'urbanistica* (1988), 31–2.

35 E. Nielsen, K. Phillips, *NSc* 30 (1976), 113–47 (Murlo); C.E. Oestenberg, *Case etrusche di Acquarossa* (Rome 1975); M. Torelli, *CAH*² VII.2, 39–48; in Momigliano and Schiavone (eds), *StdR* I (1988), 249ff.; S. Stopponi (ed.), *Case e palazzi d'Etruria* (Milan 1985), 41ff., 64ff.

36 G. Colonna in *Naissance de Rome* (1977), intro. to items 706–10; G. Bartoloni, M. Cataldi Dini, *DdA* NS 2 (1980), 126; the existence of huts in the preceding stage (Gjerstad, *Early Rome* I.75) has been questioned by A. Ammermann, *AJA* 94 (1990), 627–46, who believes that the material beneath the first paving was a fill brought in to raise the level of the Forum valley.

37 C. Ampolo, *DdA* NS 2 (1980), 166–7; Gjerstad, *Early Rome* III (1960), 79–83, 132–8.

38 Gjerstad, *Early Rome* III (1960), 217–59. For the date, Coarelli, *Foro romano* I (1983), 122, 127–30.

39 Cf. Momigliano, *Quinto contributo*, 294–5. For contemporary reactions to the find see R. Lanciani, *New Tales of Old Rome* (London 1901), 1–30; but notice the vigorous response of E. Pais, *Ancient Legends of Roman History* (London 1906), 15–42.

40 For the text, R. Wachter, *Altlateinischer Inschriften* (Berne 1987), 66–9. Discussion in R.E.A. Palmer, *The King and the Comitium* (Wiesbaden 1969); G. Dumézil, *Mariages indo-européens à Rome* (Paris 1979), 259–93; Coarelli, *Foro romano* I (1983), 178–88, and see 138–78 for the monumental context.

41 Tomb of Romulus: Horace, *Ep.* 16.13f., and scholia *ad loc.* (quoted by Coarelli, *Foro romano* I, 167 n. 9). On the 'disappearance' of Romulus, see above, p. 59 and n. 30. On founders' tombs, see my remarks in 'Gründer', *Reallexikon für Antike u. Christentum* 12 (1983), 1139ff.

42 Festus says that the black stone *locum funestum significat … Romuli morti destinatum*, which is difficult to interpret, and is taken by some to be corrupt (e.g. De Sanctis, *RFIC* 28 (1899), 4). The best I can do is 'indicates a deathly place, intended for the death of Romulus' (not 'for the dead body of Romulus' as some scholars seem to understand it. In Latin that would be *Romulo mortuo*, not *Romuli morti*).

43 Coarelli, *Foro romano* I (1983), 177.

44 Gjerstad, *Early Rome* III (1960), 310–20, 359–74; C. Ampolo, *DdA* NS 2 (1980), 166; L. Vendittelli, in *GRT* (1990), 62.

45 Gjerstad, *Early Rome* III (1960), 190–201; 145–65; A. Sommella Mura, in *CLP* (1976), 145–6; C. Ampolo, *DdA* NS 2 (1980), 167; M. Albertoni, in *GRT* (1990), 73–4. On votive deposits in general see C.J. Lowe, in H.McK. Blake *et al.* (eds), *Papers in Italian Archaeology* I (Oxford 1978), 141–52; G. Bartoloni, *Scienze dell'antichità* 3–4 (1989–90), 747–59; Ross Holloway, *Archaeology* (1994), 88–90.

46 P. Virgili, in *Il viver quotidiano in Roma arcaica* (Exhibition catalogue, Rome 1989), 45–61; *GRT* (1990), 129–30; Ross Holloway, *Archaeology* (1994), 70–5. On the inscriptions, G. Colonna, in *Etruria e Lazio arcaico* (1987), 58–9.

47 On the terracottas, A. Sommella Mura, *Bollettino Musei Comunali di Roma* 23 (1977), 3–15; *PdP* 32 (1977), 68–128; 36 (1981), 59–64; M. Cristofani, *Arch. Laz.* 10 (1990), 31–7; Ross Holloway, *Archaeology* (1994), 75–80.

48 Gjerstad, *Early Rome* III (1960), 168–89. The dimensions of the foundations fit the description given by Dionysius of Halicarnassus, 4.61. Dionysius clearly

describes the temple, not the platform on which it was built, which effectively demolishes the sceptical arguments of F. Castagnoli, *Studi Romani* 22 (1974), 433–4; PBSR 52 (1984), 7–9; see Colonna, in *Etruria e Lazio arcaico* (1987), 64, n. 65; Ross Holloway, *Archaeology* (1994), 8. But Ross Holloway's view that the temple was dedicated in 378 BC (cf. Alföldi, *Early Rome* (1965), 323–9) is an arbitrary speculation.

49 Even the most sceptical are prepared to concede this; e.g. A. Drummond, *CAH²* VII.2 (1989), 22.

50 Cf. J.B. Ward Perkins, *PBSR* 29 (1961), 27–8, noting the continuation of wattle-and-daub huts at Veii down to 396 BC.

51 A. Carandini in *GRT* (1990), 97–9; *Boll. Arch.* 2 (1990), 159–65.

52 M. Grant, *Cities of Vesuvius* (London 1974), 111.

53 The theory was first outlined in *BCom* 73 (1947–50), 15ff., and subsequently in many other publications, e.g. *Legends and Facts of Early Roman History* (Lund 1962), 24ff.; *Historia* 16 (1967), 257–78; *ANRW* I.1 (1972), 136–88; *Early Rome* V (1973), 365ff.; VI (1973), 136ff.

54 M. Pallottino in *Italy before the Romans* (1979), 208–11.

55 H. Müller-Karpe, *Zur Stadtwerdung Roms* (Heidelberg 1962).

56 The idea of unification goes back long before Gjerstad, and is to be found e.g. in G. Pinza, *Monumenti primitivi di Roma e del Lazio* (Monumenti Antichi XV, Rome 1905). Pallottino (*Italy before the Romans* (1979), 210) points out that the two theories are not mutually exclusive, since the expansion of the 'Palatine-Forum nucleus' could have entailed the absorption of minor settlements on other hills.

57 *AJAH* 6 (1981), 133–65.

58 See above, p. 96 and n. 50.

59 Müller-Karpe, *Zur Stadtwerdung Roms* (1962), 61ff.

60 V. Gordon Childe, *Town Planning Review* 21 (1950), 7–16. The ten criteria are: (1) the concentration of a large number of people in a restricted area, (2) craft specialisation, (3) the appropriation by a central authority of an economic surplus, (4) monumental public architecture, (5) developed social stratification, (6) the use of writing, (7) the emergence of exact and predictve sciences, (8) naturalistic art, (9) foreign trade, and (10) group membership based on residence rather than kinship.

61 A. Guidi, *Opus* 1 (1982), 279–89.

62 For example, Rome in the eighth century had no monumental public architecture (no. 4) and did not yet use writing (no. 6); and at no time did a single central authority appropriate the society's economic surplus (no. 3). For criticisms see the discussions in *Opus* 2 (1983), 425–46, with Guidi's reply, 447–8.

63 See the instructive comments of P. Wheatley in P.J. Ucko, R. Tringham, G.W. Dimbleby (eds), *Man, Settlement and Urbanism* (London 1972), 608–13. Wheatley's whole article (601–37) is an important general discussion of theoretical issues.

64 This is made clear in Childe's more detailed account of the origins of urbanism in *New Light on the Most Ancient East* (London 1952), ch. 7, and *The Prehistory of European Society* (London 1958), ch. 6 ('The urban revolution in the orient').

65 The point is made by C. Ampolo in *MEFRA* 92 (1980), 567–76; and in D. Papenfuss, V.M. Strocka (eds), *Palast und Hütte* (Mainz 1982), 319–24; cf. also *Opus* 2 (1983), 425–30. The present discussion owes much to Ampolo's work.

66 See e.g. *Legends and Facts* (1962), 33; further references in n. 53, above.

67 The establishment of a 'poliadic' sanctuary – that is, one dedicated to a recognised patron deity – is rightly held to be crucial by A.M. Snodgrass, *Archaeology and*

the Rise of the Greek State (Cambridge 1977), 24; and see F. de Polignac, *Les origines de la polis grecque* (Paris 1984), 86–9.

68 On the votive deposit – the so-called *favissa capitolina* – see the references cited in n. 45 above. A precursor to the temple of Jupiter: J. Martinez-Pinna, *Arch. Laz.* 4 (1981), 249–52.

69 Gjerstad, *Legends and Facts* (1962): 'the *political* synoikismos of the villages into a single community' (my emphasis).

70 Cf. the remarks of M. Moggi, *ASNP* ser. III, 5.3 (1975), 915ff.

71 There is much dispute about the significance of the Greek innovation, which consisted in using some of the Phoenician signs as vowels. The standard view is that this created a true alphabet, which can therefore be seen as a Greek invention. Others argue that the addition of vowels was only a minor modification, and that the alphabet had a long history in the Near East going back to the second millennium BC. This intrinsically meaningless debate has become more than an academic quibble, for reasons that will be clear to anyone who has read M. Bernal, *Black Athena* (London 1987). Basic studies of the origins of the (Greek) alphabet include L.H. Jeffery, *The Local Scripts of Archaic Greece* (2nd edn, Oxford 1990), 1–42 and suppl. 425–8; O. Murray, *Early Greece* (1980), 91–9; B.S.J. Isserlin, *CAH²* III.1 (1982), 794–818; L.H. Jeffery, ibid., 819–33; J.F. Healey, in J.T. Hooker (ed.), *Reading the Past* (London 1990), 197–257; R. Thomas, *Literacy and Orality in Ancient Greece* (Cambridge 1992), 53.

72 I have discussed this whole issue in more detail in M. Beard *et al.*, *Literacy in the Roman World* (1991), 7–33.

73 On the famous 'Nestor cup' see Jeffery, *Local Scripts* (1990), 235–6; Ridgway, *First Western Greeks* (1992), 55–7.

74 A. La Regina, *Scienze dell'antichità* 3–4 (1989–90), 83–8; Bietti Sestieri, *Iron Age Community* (1992), 184–5; Ross Holloway, *Archaeology* (1994), 112–13.

75 I have argued the point in *Literacy* (1991), 16–21.

76 My view of this matter – in *Literacy* (1991), 24ff. – differs from that of W.V. Harris, *Ancient Literacy* (Cambridge, Mass. 1989), 149–53, and S. Stoddart and J. Whitley, *Antiquity* 62 (1988), 761–72, who argue that writing was barely known and little used in archaic Italy.

77 J. Goody and I. Watt, *CSSH* 5 (1962–3), 304–45 = Goody (ed.), *Literacy in Traditional Societies* (Cambridge 1968), 27–68; see also Goody, *The Domestication of the Savage Mind* (Cambridge 1977); *The Logic of Writing and the Organization of Society* (Cambridge 1986); *The Interface Between the Written and the Oral* (Cambridge 1987). For some criticisms: P. Cartledge, *JHS* 98 (1978), 37; B.V. Street, *Literacy in Theory and Practice* (Cambridge 1984), 44–65; Harris, *Ancient Literacy* (1989), 40–2; an important and wide-ranging discussion of the issues, with a critical account of recent work, in Thomas, *Literacy and Orality* (1992), 15–28.

78 Mommsen's view was set out in the first edition of CIL I (1863), 361ff. For an important contribution in English, accepting Mommsen's basic principles, see W. Warde Fowler, *The Roman Festivals* (London 1899) and *The Religious Experience of the Roman People* (London 1911), 94ff. A critical account of scholarship since Mommsen is given by A.K. Michels, *The Calendar of the Roman Republic* (Princeton 1967), 207–20, who is herself one of the few to disagree with Mommsen and to date the calendar after the fall of the monarchy. For a recent general account: Scullard, *Festivals and Ceremonies* (1981), esp. 41ff.

79 For the calendar as the product of a literate mentality see R.L. Gordon, in M. Beard and J. North (eds), *Pagan Priests* (London 1990), 184–91.

80 This change in funerary practice is discussed by G. Colonna, *PdP* 32 (1977), 131–65; *Arch. Laz.* 4 (1981), 229–32; C. Ampolo, *AION* 6 (1984), 71–102; A. Naso, in *GRT* (1990), 249–51; Ross Holloway, *Archaeology* (1994), 168–70.

81 For a sobering example of this see K. Hopkins, *Death and Renewal* (Cambridge 1983), 209–10, and esp. n. 10.

82 Colonna, *PdP* 32 (1977), 158ff.

83 Ross Holloway, *Archaeology* (1994), 168–71.

84 See the important discussion of M. Toher, in Raaflaub (ed.), *Social Struggles* (1986), 301–26, esp. 322ff.

85 M.I. Finley, *Aspects of Antiquity* (London 1968), 111.

86 Thus, rightly, Ross Holloway, *Archaeology* (1994), 171.

87 Coarelli, *Foro romano* I (1983), 199–210.

88 On the sanctuary of Minerva see my comments in *Arch. Reports* 26 (1979–80), 86; 32 (1985–6), 129; F. Castagnoli, *Il culto di Minerva a Lavinium* (Quaderno Lincei no. 246, Rome 1979); *BCom* 90 (1985), 7–12; M. Fenelli *et al.*, in *Enea nel Lazio* (1981), 187–271; M. Torelli, *Lavinio e Roma* (Rome 1984); Ross Holloway, *Archaeology* (1994), 138–41.

89 F. Castagnoli *et al.*, *Lavinium* II: *Le tredici are* (Rome 1974); Ross Holloway, *Archaeology* (1994), 129–35.

90 On Gravisca see M. Torelli, *PdP* 32 (1977), 398–458; G. Colonna (ed.), *Santuari d'Etruria* (Milan 1985), 141–4; on the 'Sostratos amphorae' A.W. Johnston, *PdP* 27 (1972), 416–23; M. Torelli, *PdP* 37 (1982), 304–25. Briefly, Spivey and Stoddart, *Etruscan Italy* (1990), 94.

91 On Pyrgi, see the reports in *NSc* 13 (1959), 143–263; 24 (1970), Suppl. II; M. Pallottino *et al.*, *Arch. Class.* 16 (1964), 49–117; G. Colonna (ed.), *Santuari d'Etruria* (Milan 1985), 127–41; Coarelli, *Foro Boario* (1988), 328–63. Brothels: Coarelli, *Foro Boario* (1988), 351; Spivey and Stoddart, *Etruscan Italy* (1990), 123–5.

92 Coarelli, *Foro Boario* (1988), 113–27 and *passim*; in Momigliano and Schiavone (eds), *StdR* I (1988), 127–51; briefly, Torelli, *CAH*² VII.2 (1989), 48–51.

93 Exhaustive discussion, with full references to the sources, in Poucet, *Légende sabine* (1967), 333–410; Palmer, *Archaic Community* (1970), 5–25; Richard, *Origines* (1978), 195–222.

94 Thus Cicero, *Rep.* 2.14; Varro, *LL* 5.55, citing Junius Congus Gracchanus (on whom see above, p. 19). Other sources derived Luceres from Lucerus, king of Ardea (Paul.-Fest. p. 106 L), or from the grove (Latin *lucus*) where Romulus established his asylum (Plut., *Rom.* 20). Livy (1.13.8) reserved judgement.

95 P. Willems, *Le sénat de la république romaine* I (Louvain 1885), 22; G. Devoto, *Athenaeum* 31 (1953), 335–43; U. von Lübtow, *Das römische Volk* (Frankfurt 1955), 39–40; A. Bernardi, *Nomen Latinum* (Pavia 1973), 17–18.

96 Niebuhr, *Hist. Rom.*³ (1837), I, 289ff.; A. Piganiol, *Essai sur les origines de Rome* (Paris 1917), 244–6.

97 D. Roussel, *Tribu et cité* (Besanon 1976); F. Bourriot, *Recherches sur la nature du genos* (Paris 1976). In brief: M.I. Finley, *Ancient History: evidence and models* (London 1985), 90–2; O. Murray in O. Murray and S. Price (eds), *The Greek City* (Oxford 1990), 12–16; C. Ampolo, in Momigliano and Schiavone (eds), *StdR* I (1988), 169f.

98 Discussions of the curiae include Botsford, *Roman Assemblies* (1909), 152–200; Momigliano, *JRS* 53 (1963), 108–17 = *Terzo contributo*, 571–90; Palmer, *Archaic Community* (1970); Richard, *Origines* (1978), 197–222.

99 Niebuhr, *Hist. Rom.*³ (1837), I, 306ff.; Mommsen *Staatsr.* III.1 (1887), 9 n., 90 n.

100 O. Murray, in *The Greek City* (1990), 14–16.

101 P. Kretschmer, *Glotta* 10 (1920), 145–57; Palmer, *Archaic Community* (1970), 67.

102 On the names of the curiae, Palmer, *Archaic Community* (1970), 75–9; Richard, *Origines* (1978), 207–8, with full references to sources and bibliography.

103 J.W. Poultney, *The Bronze Tables of Iguvium* (Philadelphia 1959); for discussion

of their relevance to the Roman curiae, see above all Momigliano, *JRS* 53 (1963), 115–17 = *Terzo contributo*, 585–90.

104 The uniqueness of the Roman tribal system is rightly stressed by C. Ampolo, in Momigliano and Schiavone (eds), *StdR* I (1988), 169–72.

105 On 'archaic rationality', O. Murray, in *The Greek City* (1990), 1–25, and *PBSR* 46 (1991), 1–13.

5 TRADITIONAL HISTORY: KINGS, QUEENS, EVENTS AND DATES

1 See e.g. Poucet, *Origines* (1985), 99.

2 None of the kings has been formally authenticated by contemporary evidence. The earliest literary reference is a fragment of Timaeus (third century BC) which may refer to Servius Tullius (*FGrHist* 566 F.59); the François Tomb (*c.* 320 BC) refers to a Gnaeus Tarquinius. See below.

3 Unlike 'Romulus', they do have authentic-sounding names; what is more, the forenames Numa and Tullus are unusual – indeed unique – and their gentile names are relatively obscure, which at least proves that they are not crude inventions of family history. See Heurgon, *Rise of Rome* (1973), 135; on the other hand, the conclusion that the names are historical does not take us very far. Cf. M.I. Finley, *Ancient History: evidence and models* (London 1985), 10.

4 The story was celebrated in Roman tradition (it may have been the subject of one or more ballads: Heurgon, *Rise of Rome* (1973), 136, but cf. Momigliano, *Secondo contributo*, 84–5), and was associated with local relics and monuments in and around the city. These included the *pila Horatia*, the *tigillum sororium*, the Fossae Cluiliae, and the tombs of the Horatii and Curiatii, no doubt ancient tumuli of the orientalising period.

5 *bonus Ancus*: Ennius, *Ann.* 137 Sk.; Lucretius III.1025.

6 Even the most stable monarchies rarely attain an average length of reign of more than twenty years. The average for the British monarchy since the start of the seventeenth century is just over 21 years. This compares with the more established ancient dynasties: Attalids 22 years, Antigonids 20 years, Achaemenids 19 years, Ptolemies 15 years. Data in E.J. Bickermann, *Chronology of the Ancient World* (rev. edn, London 1980), 126ff. The absurdity of the Roman king list was first pointed out by Lorenzo Valla in the fifteenth century, and systematically exposed by Sir Isaac Newton, *The Chronology of Ancient Kingdoms Amended* (London 1728). Note the comments of C. Ampolo, in Momigliano and Schiavone, *StdR* I (1988), 216–17.

7 Poucet, *Origines* (1985); Heurgon, *Rise of Rome* (1973), 137; id., *BAGB* (1971), 219–30.

8 On this phrase, see p. 208 and n. 34.

9 A. Bernardi, *RSI* 66 (1954), 5–20; in Momigliano and Schiavone (eds), *StdR* I (1988), 194f.; Richard, *Origines* (1978), 287ff.; Pallottino, *Origini* (1993), 205.

10 See the works cited in n. 9, and many others, e.g. Alföldi, *Early Rome* (1965); Scullard, *Etruscan Cities and Rome* (1967); Ogilvie, *Early Rome* (1976).

11 F. Schachermeyr, *RE* IV A, 2 (1932), s.v. 'Tarquinius', 2351–2; T.N. Gantz, *Historia* 24 (1975), 539–54; L. Bessone, *RFIC* 110 (1982), 394–415.

12 These difficulties are discussed in an excellent article by O. Cazenove, *MEFRA* 100 (1988), 615–48, esp. 619–22.

13 For comparison see L. Heusch, *Essais sur le symbolisme de l'inceste royale en Afrique* (Brussels 1958). Note that even if Tarquinius Superbus was the grandson

of Tarquinius Priscus, the marriages would still be incestuous, since the marriage of first cousins was equally forbidden in Roman law.

14 J. Beloch, *Griechische Geschichte* II² 2 (1913), 274–82; E. Will, *Korinthiaka* (Paris 1955), 363–440; R. Sealey, *REG* 70 (1957), 318–25.

15 A. Blakeway, *JRS* 25 (1935), 129–49.

16 C. Ampolo, *DdA* 9–10 (1976–7), 333–45; some reservations on this by D. Musti in *Etruria e Lazio arcaico* (1987), 139–53. On p. 139 Musti points out in passing that Dionysius' account of Demaratus' commercial activities (3.46) is virtually a textbook definition of the mechanisms of archaic trade.

17 E. Gabba in *Entretiens* 13 (1967), 135–69; in *Bilancio critico* (1993), 13–24.

18 Cic. *Rep.* 2.28; *Tusc.* 4.3; Livy 1.18; Dion. Hal. 2.59; Plut., *Numa* 18. Ovid still has Numa as a pupil of Pythagoras: *Met.* 15.4.481; *Fasti* 3.153.

19 J. Ducat, *BCH* 85 (1961), 418–25; J. Servais, *Ant. Class.* 38 (1969), 28–81.

20 The revised chronology being offered here is compatible with that proposed for Servius Tullius by Thomsen, *King Servius* (1980), 31f. M. Pallottino defends the traditional account in *Italy before the Romans* (1979), 218–19.

21 F.E. Brown, *RPAA* 47 (1974–5), 15–36; Coarelli, *Foro romano* I (1983), 59f.; F.E. Brown, R.T. Scott in S. Stopponi (ed.), *Case e palazzi d'Etruria* (Milan 1985), 186–7 (in the first line on p. 187 the phrase 'alla fine del VIII a.C.' is evidently a misprint for 'alla fine del VII a.C.').

22 C. Ampolo, *DdA* NS 2 (1980), 166. The earliest construction of the Comitium also belongs to this time. It too is attributed to Tullus Hostilius by Cicero, *Rep.* 2.31.

23 De Sanctis, *StdR* I² (1960), 360–1. E.S. Staveley, *Historia* 32 (1983), 38, evidently misreads the sources when he argues that 'the use of the *interregnum* was apparently abandoned with the coming of the elder Tarquin'.

24 Cicero (*Rep.* 2.35) and Dionysius (3.46.1) are careful to report these details. Livy, who is generally uninterested in constitutional niceties (cf. Momigliano *Nono contributo*, 511–14), mentions only the popular vote.

25 Cic., *Rep.* 2.37: *Servius Tullius primus iniussu populi regnavisse traditur*. Livy 1.41.6: *Servius . . . primus iniussu populi voluntate patrum regnavit*. Cf. Dion. Hal. 4.8–12.

26 Livy 1.47.10. I have italicised the words that translate the phrase *ut antea*.

27 Dion. Hal. 5.35.3 must mean that Horatius' name was inscribed on the temple. The objections of K. Hanell, *Entretiens* 13 (1967), 40, are not decisive, in view of Dion. Hal. 9.60.8, where the same terminology is used. See M.J. Pena, *Faventia* 3.2 (1981), 149–70.

28 Apiolae: Pliny, *n.h.* 3.70 (= Valerius Antias fr. 11 P); Livy 1.35.7; Dion. Hal. 3.49.1–4; Strabo 5.3.4 p. 231. C. Suessa Pometia: Cic., *Rep.* 2.44; Livy 1.53.3; Dion. Hal. 4.50.2–5; 59.1; Tac., *Hist.* 3.72. The identity of the two sites was first suggested by E. Pais, *Storia di Roma* I.1 (1898), 347 n. 2.

29 Tacitus, whose account is the most coherent we have, clearly states that the building work continued under Servius Tullius (*Hist.* 3.72). Gjerstad arbitrarily dismisses this as 'a late and worthless notice': *Legends and Facts* (1962), 50.

30 Gjerstad, *Legends and Facts* (1962), 50; *Early Rome* V (1973), 366ff. Critical discussion in Thomsen, *King Servius* (1980), 49–54.

31 G. Colonna has recently tried to uphold both the traditional date and the story that Vulca was commissioned by Tarquinius Priscus (*PdP* 36 (1981), 41–59, esp. 56ff.) by arguing that Vulca made only the cult statue, which was set up on the Capitol before the temple proper was built, and that the rest of the terracotta sculptures, including that of Jupiter in a quadriga, were ordered at the end of the sixth century from different craftsmen. But this unlikely theory does violence to the text of Pliny 35.157, where Vulca is clearly connected with the quadriga as well as the cult statue.

32 The data from the ancient sources are listed in a table by C. Ampolo, *DdA* NS 2 (1980), 170. The column under Tarquinius Priscus is conspicuously blank.

33 Livy 1.35.10; Dion. Hal. 3.67.4. Some scholars have made an epic out of this, speaking of the pavement of the Forum, the new 'axiality' of the city, the construction of up-market shopping precincts, and so on (e.g. Musti, *GRT* (1990), 11).

34 The problems are set out with admirable clarity in Thomsen, *King Servius* (1980), with full references to sources and bibliography. The question of origins is dealt with in ch. III (57–104); see also Valditara, *Studi sul magister populi* (1989), 41–136.

35 Thomsen, *King Servius* (1980), 64, with earlier bibliography in n. 27.

36 There are many examples among the Sulpicii of the Republic. Servius is also occasionally found in other *gentes* – e.g. Ser. Cornelius Lentulus, cos. 303 BC; Ser. Fulvius Paetinus Nobilior, cos. 255 BC; Ser. Cornelius Cethegus, cos. AD 24, etc.

37 Justin 38.6.7. *Servus* is a general word for slave; *verna* denotes a person born in slavery – a 'house-born slave'. It does not matter whether the passage in question goes back to a genuine speech of Mithridates. Even if it was the free composition of a Roman historian (in this case Trogus Pompeius, whom Justin epitomised), it clearly indicates that the Romans were acutely conscious of the shameful nature of the tradition about Servius.

38 Thus Livy 4.3.12 (the speech of Canuleius): *captiva Corniculana natus patre nullo, matre serva* – 'son of a war-captive from Corniculum, a man with nobody for his father and a slave for his mother'.

39 Versions of the 'phallus in the hearth' story. Servius Tullius: Dion. Hal. 4.2.1ff.; Ovid, *Fasti* 6.627–36; Pliny, *n.h.* 36.204; Plut., *de fort. Rom.* 10. Romulus: Plut., *Romulus* 2.3–6. Caeculus: Paul.-Fest. p. 38 L, s.v. 'Caeculus'; Virg., *Aeneid.* 7.678–81 and Servius, ad loc.; Solinus 2.9; Cato, *Origines* II.29. Cf. the story of Mutinus Titinus, founder of Cures, in Dion. Hal. 2.48, and the remarks of F. Altheim, *Griechische Götter im alten Rom* (Giessen 1930), 53f. On Caeculus see above, p. 63 and n. 42.

40 Binder, *Aussetzung des Königskindes* (1964). Cf. T.J. Cornell, in *Reallexikon f. Antike u. Christentum*, s.v. 'Gründer', 1107–45, esp. 1125.

41 Claudius' main point, that outsiders had been accepted as kings, would be made more than adequately by reference to the Latin tradition of Servius as the son of the captive Ocresia of Corniculum. The whole digression is in any case overblown. In Tacitus' version of the speech (*Annals* 11.24) the argument is much more economical and elegant. On Tacitus' improvements see e.g. M.T. Griffin, *CQ* 32 (1982), 404–18.

42 In the earlier parenthesis (*nam et hoc inter auctores discrepat*: 'for this too is disputed among writers') the words 'this too' (*et hoc*) refer forward to the more important discrepancy between writers – i.e. between the Roman and Etruscan writers on the origin of Servius Tullius. I failed to see this in my earlier study in *ASNP* ser. III, 6.2 (1976), 418. My suggestion that the Etruscan version might derive from oral tradition can be ruled out.

43 This was established in an important paper by J. Heurgon, *CRAI* (1953), 92–7. Cf. my remarks in *ASNP* ser. III, 6.2 (1976), 417–18.

44 This point was made by Momigliano, *Quarto contributo*, 489, and is decisive against those who claim that the Etruscan tradition was known to earlier historians – e.g. Alföldi, *Early Rome* (1965), 134; Harris, *Rome in Etruria and Umbria* (1971), 26; F. Coarelli, *DdA* ser. 3, 3 (1983), 50, 65.

45 Varro, *LL* 5.46; Festus p. 486 L, s.v. 'Tuscum vicum'; Dion. Hal. 2.36.2.

46 The preserved portions can best be set out as follows:

Tuscum vicum con
tores dictum aiunt ab

decedente ab obsi
Romae locoque [h]is dato
entes fratres Caeles et Vibenn
Tarquinium Romam se cum max
rint.

The following restoration and translation may be proposed:

Tuscum vicum con<plures scrip>
tores dictum aiunt ab <is qui Porsena rege>
decedente ab obsi<dione e Tuscis remanserint>
Romae locoque [h]is dato <habitaverint; aut quod Volci>
entes fratres Caeles et Vibenn<a quos dicunt ad regem>
Tarquinium Romam se cum Max<tarna contulisse, eum incoluer>
rint.

'Many writers say that the Tuscus Vicus was named after those Etruscans who remained in Rome after King Porsena had abandoned his siege; and they [who remained] lived in the district which had been granted to them. Or [it is so called] because it was occupied by the Volcentane brothers Caeles and Vibenna, who, they say, came to Rome with Maxtarna (?) to help King Tarquinius' (or 'against King Tarquinius').

47 *Res Etruscae*: H. Peter, *Historicorum Romanorum reliquiae* II (2nd edn, Leipzig 1906), 78–9; M. Schanz, C. Hosius, *Gesch. d. röm. Literatur* II (Munich 1935), 366–7.

48 The evidence is discussed by Thomsen, *King Servius* (1980), 85–7, and by me in *ASNP* ser. III, 6.2 (1976), 418–19; see also Valditara, *Studi sul magister populi* (1989), 88ff.; Pallottino, *Origini* (1993), 237–50 (to be used with caution).

49 *TLE*² 942. The provenance of the cup, now in the Musée Rodin, is unknown. A hero cult (Ampolo in Momigliano and Schiavone (eds), *StdR* I (1988), 207–8) is more probable than J. Heurgon's suggestion of a fraud by a potter wishing to pass off his product as the possession of Aulus Vibenna – *Mélanges Carcopino* (Paris 1966), 515–28.

50 M. Pallottino, *SE* 13 (1939), 455–7 (= *TLE*² 35). For the date, F. Boitani, in Buranelli (ed.), *Tomba François* (1987), 234 n.95; cf. M. Cristofani, in *GRT* (1990), 19–20; and see Ampolo's discussion in Momigliano and Schiavone (eds), *StdR* I (1988), 206–8.

51 The pictures were removed from the tomb shortly after its discovery in 1857 and are now in the Villa Torlonia, where they are inaccessible to the public and to professional scholars. This disgraceful state of affairs is aggravated by the fact that the paintings have deteriorated badly, and much of what was once visible has now vanished. This means that drawings and reproductions made in the nineteenth century have become sources in their own right, and the paintings have to be studied in several different versions, using the methods of source criticism. The starting-point for any study must now be the exhibition catalogue *La Tomba François* (ed. F. Buranelli, Rome 1987); but the publication of F. Messerschmidt and A. von Gerkan, *Nekropolen von Vulci*, *JdI* Suppl. 12 (1930), 62–163, remains indispensable. The date was firmly established by M. Cristofani, *DdA* 1 (1967), 86–129.

52 F. Coarelli, *DdA* ser. 3, 3 (1983), 56.

53 Alföldi, *Early Rome* (1965), 223–4.

54 However, I do not accept Alföldi's view that the victorious warriors are themselves to be seen as Trojans. His theory that Vulci claimed a Trojan origin is mistaken. Equally unacceptable is Coarelli's view that the victims are in some sense Roman, so that 'Trojans' are being killed in both pictures: *DdA* ser. 3, 3 (1983), 56–7, 68.

Only Cneve Tarchunies is described as Roman, and it is far from clear that the episode has anything to do with Rome as such.

55 On the names see e.g. Alföldi, *Early Rome* (1965), 221–2; Thomsen, *King Servius* (1980), 74–6.

56 As Coarelli rightly points out, however, this need not exclude the possibility that some of them originally hailed from elsewhere, just as Cneve Tarchunies is described as Roman, although his family originated from Etruria: *DdA* ser. 3, 3 (1983), 63. This leaves open the possibility of Mastarna being a Latin; and Coarelli makes an interesting case for the Tiburtine origin of Marce Camitlnas (pp. 64–5).

57 Thomsen, *King Servius* (1980), 90 (with earlier bibliography); Coarelli, *DdA* ser. 3, 3 (1983), 49. A more prudent approach is adopted by C. Ampolo in Momigliano and Schiavone (eds), *StdR* I (1988), 217 and M. Pallottino in Buranelli (ed.), *Tomba François* (1987), 232; *Origini* (1993), 203–4.

58 This is one of the instances where different versions of the painting offer different information. The originals seem to show that *Tarchunies'* companions are beardless, but in some drawings, including that reproduced in *CAH²* VII.2 (1989), 95, they are shown with beards.

59 Pallottino's suggestion (*CRAI* (1977), 231) that Rasce is connected with *Rasenna* (Dion. Hal. 1.30.3), and means 'the Etruscan', is rightly dismissed by Thomsen, *King Servius* (1980), 98 n. 191, and Coarelli, *DdA* ser. 3, 3 (1983), 63 n. 86. See the interesting discussion of Valditara, *Studi sul magister populi* (1989), 87 n. 184.

60 First suggested by J.G. Cuno, *Neue Jahrbücher Phil. u. Pedagogik* (1873), 669 n. 7. Further bibliography in Thomsen, *King Servius* (1980), 97 n. 183.

61 Mazzarino, *Dalla monarchia* (1945), 175ff.; Valditara, *Studi sul magister populi* (1989), 116–22 (with bibliography), and cf. below, p. 226.

62 It sounds more plausible, and more sinister, in other languages: *Der Führer, Il Duce, El Caudillo.*

63 Pallottino has argued (in Buranelli (ed.), *Tomba François* (1987), 228–9; cf. *Origini* (1993), 245–6) that the suffix signifies the possessive case, and that the man was not himself the *magister*, but one who 'belonged to' the *magister* as a dependant or client, the *magister* in this instance being Caeles Vibenna. This strikes me as improbable. Why should an Etruscan leader (Caeles Vibenna), in an Etruscan town (Vulci), be known by the Latin title *magister*?

64 Pallottino goes too far when he says (In *Tomba François* (1987) and *Origini* (1993)) that *Macstrna* derives 'with absolute certainty' (*con assoluta certezza*) from the Latin word *magister*.

65 Nevertheless, I cannot resist pointing to the fact that in Varro (*LL* 5.46; 5.55) and Dionysius (2.36.2; 2.37.2) Caeles Vibenna and Lucumo are doublets of one another (cf. Paul.-Fest. p. 38 L; Serv., *Aen.* 5.560). See also Poucet, *Recherches* (1967), 356 n. 85.

66 This is essentially the view of A. Momigliano, *Claudius* (2nd edn, Cambridge 1960), 14; *CAH²* VII.2 (1989), 96. This still seems to me to be the most acceptable way to resolve the puzzle.

67 Numa too had sons, who became the ancestors of famous noble families, according to a tradition that is at least as old as the historian L. Calpurnius Piso (second century BC), who himself belonged to a clan that traced its descent back to Calpus, one of the sons of Numa. This claim was, however, contested by other historians (Wiseman, *Clio's Cosmetics* (1979), 11). The important point here is that the sons of Numa did not succeed him.

68 A rather more complex relationship existed in the case of Ancus Marcius, who was the son of Numa's daughter. Similarly the foundation story revolves around the fact that the sons of Rhea Silvia, the daughter of Numitor, are regarded as a potential threat by Amulius.

69 Thus Martin, *Royauté* (1982), 19ff., for an extended discussion.

70 This is explicitly recognised by Livy 4.3.10–17 (speech of Canuleius). Note also that the clans that traced their descent back to the sons of Numa (cf. above, n. 67) were plebeian.

71 J. Goody in Goody (ed.), *Succession to High Office* (Cambridge 1966), 10ff.

72 A. Magdelain, *Hommages J. Bayet* (Paris 1964), 427–73; J. Linderski, *ANRW* II.16.3 (1986), 2146–312.

73 This useful Italian word has no easy English equivalent. Momigliano called them 'band leaders' (*Settimo contributo*, 417 etc.), which has misleading resonances. The editor of *CAH²* VII.2 (1989) changed this to 'band chiefs'. I have stayed with *condottieri*, or 'warlords'.

74 On Appius Claudius see below, p. 157. On Coriolanus' following, Dion. Hal. 7.21.3 (the wording is highly significant). Clients and companions of the Fabii: Dion. Hal. 9.15.3. Clients of the Fabii are mentioned by Paul.-Fest. p. 451 L and Serv., *Aen.* 8.337. Livy calls them *cognati* and *sodales* (2.49.5). On the Fabii at the Cremera, see p. 311 and n. 46.

75 The text reads:

> *. . . iei steterai popliosio valesiosio*
> *suodales mamartei*

i.e. (probably) '. . . the companions of Poplios Valesios (= Publius Valerius) set this up to Mamars (= Mars).'

76 Arnobius, *Adv. nat.* 6.7 (= Fabius Pictor fr. 12 P); Chron. AD 354 (*Chronica minora*, ed. Mommsen, I.144; Frick I.114). See further Alföldi, *Early Rome* (1965), 216ff.; Thomsen, *King Servius* (1980), 93ff.; Coarelli, *DdA* ser. 3, 3 (1983), 50–2. The chronicle is the only source to say that Olus was a king (Momigliano, *Quarto contributo*, 494).

77 Livy 3.15–18; Dion. Hal. 10.14–17. The story was already in Cato, *Origines* I.26. On the episode in general, M. Capozza, *Movimenti servili nel mondo romano nel periodo repubblicano* I (Rome 1966), 37ff.; Cornell, *CAH²* VII.2, 286.

78 On this linkage see Coarelli, *Foro romano* I (1983), 161–78; Mastrocique, *Romolo* (1993), 60–2.

79 Ovid, *Fasti* 6.569–80; Plut., *Fort. Rom.* 10 (*Moralia* p. 322 C). *Fenestella* is a diminutive of *fenestra* ('window').

80 S.N. Kramer, *The Sacred Marriage Rite* (Bloomington 1969); see also the French edition, *Le mariage sacré*, adapted by J. Bottéro (Paris 1983).

81 Plutarch, *Qu. Rom.* 36 (*Moralia* 273 B-C). On this subject see the important discussions of M. Verzar, *MEFRA* 92 (1980), 35–84; F. Coarelli, *Foro Boario* (1988), 301–28; C. Grottanelli, *DdA* ser. 3, 5 (1987), 71–110. The study of J.J. Bachofen, *Die Sage von Tanaquil* (1870), should not be forgotten.

82 A. Sommella Mura, *BMCR* 23 (1977), 3–15; *PdP* 32 (1977), 62–128; *PdP* 36 (1981), 59–64; *GRT* (1990), 15–20. See also Coarelli, *Foro Boario* (1988), 301–28 (not accepting the identification of the armed goddess with Athene-Minerva).

83 J. Boardman, *Rev. Arch.* (1972), 57–72; (1978), 227–34.

84 C. Ampolo, *PdP* 36 (1981), 32–3. A similar statue-group showing the apotheosis of Heracles has recently been identified among the sculptured fragments from the Portonaccio sanctuary at Veii, and can be interpreted in the same way. G. Colonna, *Op. Rom.* 16 (1987), 7–41; A. Sommella Mura, *GRT* (1990), 119–20.

85 On the Greek tyrants in general, see O. Murray, *Early Greece* (London 1980), 132–52; N.G.L. Hammond, in *CAH²* III.3 (1982), 341–51; A. Andrewes, ibid., 392–416.

6 THE MYTH OF 'ETRUSCAN ROME'

1 See B. Croce, *Storia della storiografia italiana nel secolo decimonono* (3rd edn, Bari 1947), I. 52; P. Treves, *L'idea di Roma e la cultura italiana nel sec. xix* (Milan 1962), 19ff.; A. Momigliano, *Studies in Historiography* (London 1966), 18–20.

2 K.O. Müller, W. Deecke, *Die Etrusker*, 2 vols (Stuttgart 1877). On Müller see A. Momigliano, *Studies on Modern Scholarship* (Berkeley 1994), 302–14.

3 L. Lanza, *De'vasi antichi dipinti volgarmente chiamati etruschi* (1806). Cf. M. Cristofani, *Prospettiva* 4 (1976), 16–21.

4 Niebuhr, *Hist. Rome*³ (1837) I, 385. Note that although the second German edition of Niebuhr's History was published in 1827, he was still able to take account of Müller's *Etrusker* (1828), because in 1826 it had been submitted to the Berlin Academy for a prize, for which Niebuhr was one of the judges. Müller won the prize, but his work still infuriated Niebuhr.

5 Mommsen, *History of Rome*² (1864) I, 132–3.

6 For the debate about Etruscan art, see e.g. G. Cultrera, *SE* 1 (1927), 71ff.; C. Anti, *SE* 4 (1930), 151ff.; and note the useful study of M. Harari, *Accordia Research Papers* 3 (1992), 101–6.

7 A.C. Vaughan, *Those Mysterious Etruscans* (New York 1964), a typical example of the genre. On the revival of *etruscheria*, M.I. Finley, *Aspects of Antiquity* (London 1968), 102–12.

8 De Sanctis, *StdR* I² (1960), 360–2; Beloch, *Röm. Gesch.* (1926), 227–30.

9 The Etruscans in Campania: the main sources include Polyb. 2.17.1; Strabo 5.4.3, p. 242 C; Pliny, *n.h.* 3.60. Capua and Nola: Velleius 1.7; Livy 4.37.1; Dion. Hal. 15.13; Serv., *Aen.* 10.145. Pompeii and Herculaneum: Strabo 5.4.8, p.247 C; Theophrastus, *H.P.* 9.16.6. Etruscan inscriptions: below, n. 12.

10 Frederiksen, *Campania* (1984), 174ff. (on terracottas). Frederiksen's discussion of the Etruscans in Campania (pp. 117–33) is fundamental; cf. his detailed treatment in *Italy before the Romans* (1979), 277–311. J. Heurgon, *Capoue préromaine* (1942) is still the main work of reference.

11 Frederiksen, in *Italy before the Romans* (1979), 299. Influence of Clusium and Vulci: Heurgon, *Capoue préromaine* (1942), 70ff.

12 Frederiksen, *Campania*, 124. The number of Etruscan texts now exceeds 100. For a selection see *TLE*², 23–7.

13 Cato, *Origines* III.1 (= Velleius 1.7). For a lucid discussion of this text, see Heurgon, *Capoue préromaine* (1942), 63.

14 J. Beloch, *Campanien* (Berlin 1879), 8f.

15 Thus Beloch (who was never afraid to change his mind), *Griech. Gesch.* I², 1 (Berlin 1924), 245 n. 1. Followed by L. Pareti, *La tomba Regolini-Galassi* (Vatican City 1949), 498ff.

16 J. Heurgon, *Capoue préromaine* (1942), 63. More recently, cf. G. Colonna in *Gli etruschi e Roma* (1980), 165; *Annali Fond. Museo Faina* 1 (1980), 50ff.; M. Cristofani, *Saggi di storia etrusca arcaica* (Rome 1987), 77–88.

17 Colonna in *Gli etruschi e Roma* (1980), 159. The same considerations apply to Cato, *Origines* I.12, on which see Momigliano, *Quarto contributo*, 492–3.

18 Alföldi, *Early Rome* (1965), 206ff.

19 E.g. P.G. Walsh, *Livy* (1961), 276–7: 'patriotic distortion has concealed the fact of Etruscan dominance.' Cf. Scullard, *History of the Roman World*⁴ (1980), 53, in almost exactly the same words.

20 E. Meyer, *Röm. Staat u. Staatsgedanke*² (1961), 19: 'Dieser etruskische Einfluss ist so stark und so durchdringend, dass er ohne die Annahme einer auch politisch etrusckischen Herrschaft nicht erklärlich ist.' The idea that cultural imperialism

and political domination go together is one of the themes of E. Said, *Culture and Imperialism* (London 1993).

21 The Romans themselves were fully conscious of this. See Livy 4.3–4, and the speech of Claudius of AD 48 (*ILS* 212; Tac., *Ann.* 11.24; see above, p. 133). Its historical importance has been highlighted by C. Ampolo, *DdA* 4–5 (1970–1), 37–68.

22 C. Ampolo, in *Gli etruschi e Roma* (1980), 57ff., with further bibliography.

23 G. Colonna in *Etruria e Lazio arcaico* (1987), 55–66, esp. p. 58. Scholars disagree about the number of Etruscan inscriptions found in Rome. This is because it is difficult to tell, with some very fragmentary texts, which language they are written in. A later Etruscan text, dating from the third century BC, has recently been unearthed on the Palatine: see M. Cristofani, *Arch Laz.* 11 (1993), 37–8.

24 For example, the inscribed bucchero *kylix* from the temple of Mater Matuta at Satricum was dedicated by Lars Velchaina, who also made a similar dedication at Caere, probably his native city. See M. Cristofani, *CLP* 374–5, no. 128. Another example is the dedication at Veii made by Aulus Vibenna of Vulci (see above, p. 135, and n. 50).

25 G. Colonna, in *Etruria e Lazio arcaico* (1987), 58–9.

26 M. Guarducci, *RPAA* 49 (1976–7), 92; G. Colonna, in *Etruria e Lazio arcaico* (1987), 58.

27 The idea is already embodied in the Aeneas story; see above, p. 60 and n. 34. Rossellini's film, *Roma, città aperta* (1946), takes its title from the decision of the Allied Command to make Rome an 'open city' in 1944. For the use of the phrase *città aperta* to define archaic Rome, see Ampolo's study, *DdA* 9–10 (1976–7), 333–45.

28 *TLE²*, 155 (*rutile hipukrate*), 865 (*ate peticina*), 65 (*kalatur phapena*); G. Colonna, *CLP* 376, no. 131 (*tite latine*).

29 C. Ampolo, *DdA* 9–10 (1976–7), 333–45.

30 G. Colonna, in *Etruria e Lazio arcaico* (1987), 55–66, has argued the case convincingly. Naturally the conclusion applies *a fortiori* if we assume, as I believe we should, that the Tarquins came to power in the second quarter of the sixth century, rather than in the last quarter of the seventh.

31 It hardly needs to be said that the relationship can easily be expressed in terms of sexual imagery. This point is frequently made in feminist literature and in modern accounts of cultural imperialism. See E. Hall, *Inventing the Barbarian* (Oxford 1989), esp. 201ff.; E. Said, *Orientalism* (London 1978), *passim*.

32 Cf. J.A. North, *CAH²* VII.2 (1989), 578–9, from whom I have borrowed the idea and much of the wording for this paragraph. North is dealing specifically with religion, but his remarks can be extended to cover all aspects of archaic Roman culture.

33 Gjerstad, *Early Rome* IV (1966), 516ff. Cf. R. Bloch, *The Origins of Rome* (London 1960), 96; 107ff.; *Tite-Live et les premiers siècles de Rome* (Paris 1965), 68ff.; Toynbee, *Hannibal's Legacy* I (1965), 369; Ogilvie, *Early Rome* (1976), 137, etc.

34 Ogilvie, *Early Rome* (1976), 30.

35 Thus, e.g., Ogilvie, *Early Rome* (1976), 40–2; cf. F. Altheim, *History of Roman Religion* (London 1938), 106f.; H.J. Rose, *CJ* 40 (1943–4), 65–76; K. Latte, *Römische Religionsgeschichte* (Munich 1960), 36; Heurgon, *Rise of Rome* (1973), 117, 140; Scullard, *Festivals and Ceremonies* (1981), 41.

36 Latte, *Römische Religionsgeschichte* (1960), 36.

37 G. Wissowa, *RuK²* (1912), 224–5, citing Mommsen's opinion (CIL I², 327) that the name derives from the (IE) Latin verb *volvere* (= 'to roll'). On the complexities

surrounding Volturnus see Momigliano, *Terzo contributo*, 631–3. The difficulties are not fully resolved by C. de Simone, *SE* 43 (1975), 145ff.

38 W. Warde Fowler took the absence of Etruscan elements to be evidence that the calendar was of 'pre-Etruscan' origin: *Roman Festivals* (1899), 338; *Religious Experience of the Roman People* (1911), 94f.

39 E.g. Ogilvie, *Early Rome* (1976), 37; Scullard, *Festivals and Ceremonies* (1981), 19; etc.

40 On religious evolutionism the classic text is E.B. Tylor, *Primitive Culture* (London 1871). For Rome the most important expression of evolutionism can be found in the works of Warde Fowler (see n. 38), and *Roman Ideas of Deity* (London 1914), and of his pupil H.J. Rose, *Primitive Culture in Italy* (London 1926) and *Ancient Roman Religion* (London 1948); cf. Rose's article '*Mana* in Greece and Rome', *HTR* 42 (1949), 155–74. Notice also the aptly titled *Phases in the Religion of Ancient Rome* by C. Bailey (Oxford 1932). Chapter 4 'The gods: anthropomorphism and foreign cults' follows three previous chapters on magic, charms, taboos, spirits, etc.

41 Varro, quoted by Augustine, *C.D.* 4.31, and Tertullian, *Apol.* 25.12 (= frs 18 and 38 Cardauns). Probably what Varro had in mind was the cult statue of Jupiter, which on his view was ordered by Tarquinius Priscus (see above, p. 129).

42 Pallottino, *Etruscans* (1975), 140. It should be said that in the following sentence Pallottino qualifies this statement somewhat (though not enough, in my view).

43 Pallottino, *Etruscans* (1975). Cf. A.J. Pfiffig, *Religio Etrusca* (Graz 1975), 231ff.

44 See above, p. 148 (Chapter 5) and n. 83.

45 E. La Rocca, *DdA* 8 (1974–5), 86–103; *CLP* (1976), 367–71; *PdP* 32 (1977), 375–97.

46 Against evolutionism in general: J.A. North, *CAH*[2] VII.2 (1989), 581. That the Roman gods were always personalised, even before they were identified with Greek equivalents: G. Dumézil, *Les dieux des Indo-Européens* (Paris 1952), ch. 4; *Archaic Roman Religion* (Chicago 1970), 18ff.; J. Scheid, *Religion et piété à Rome* (Paris 1985), 59–94.

47 Coarelli, *Foro romano* I (1983), 161–78.

48 The pioneer in this field was S. Mazzarino, *Dalla monarchia* (1945). A good example of the use of an 'interaction' model is the volume on 'la formazione della città nel Lazio', *DdA* NS 2 (1980).

49 C. Renfrew, J. Cherry (eds), *Peer Polity Interaction and Socio-Political Change* (Cambridge 1986).

50 C. Renfrew in Renfrew and Cherry, ibid., 7–8.

51 Note that the exhibition catalogue, *Case e palazzi d'Etruria*, ed. S. Stopponi (Milan 1985), includes material from Rome and Latium but does not attempt to justify its inclusion in a work supposedly devoted to Etruria.

52 S. Etruria and N. Latium: S. Judson and A. Kahane, *PBSR* 31 (1963), 74–99; Potter, *Changing Landscape* (1979), 84–7. Southern Latium: M.R. de la Blanchère, *MEFR* 2 (1882), 94–106, 207–11; 'cuniculus' in Daremberg-Saglio, *Dict. des antiquités* I.2, 1591–4; S. Quilici Gigli, *Arch. Laz.* 5 (1983) 112–23; F. Coarelli in *Crise et transformation* (1990), 143–6.

53 Potter, *Roman Italy* (1987), 142.

54 J.-C. Meyer, *Pre-Republican Rome* (1983), 142.

55 Cf. Coarelli, in *Crise et transformation* (1990), 146–8, making the excellent point that this archaic corvée system is unlikely to have been invented by annalists living at a time when the system of labour was wholly different.

56 Livy 1.8.3; 1.44.4; Dion. Hal. 3.61; Florus 1.5.5–6; Silius Italicus, *Punica* 8.483–7; 10.41; Diod. 5.40; Strabo 5.2.2 p. 220 C.

57 Cic., *Rep.* 2.31; Macrob., *Sat.* 1.6.7; Pliny, *n.h.* 9.136. For the versions of Strabo

Livy and Dionysius see previous note. For discussion, P. De Francisci, *SE* 24 (1955–6), 33–4.

58 L. Bonfante Warren, *JRS* 61 (1971), 49.

59 De Martino argues that *imperium* was an Etruscan concept: *Costituzione romana* I² (1972), 118ff. (with further bibliography). *Contra*: U. Coli, *Regnum* (1951), 25ff.; P. De Francisci, *SE* 24 (1955–6), 19–43.

60 Cic., *de nat. deorum* 2.11; *de div.* 1.3; 2.70; 2.75ff. Cf. De Francisci, *SE* 24 (1955–6), 27–8.

61 Wissowa, *RuK²* (1912), 547; De Sanctis, *StdR* IV.2.1 (1953), 361ff.; Beloch, *Röm. Gesch.* (1926), 103; P. Fraccaro, *JRS* 47 (1957), 61.

62 Plut., *Rom.*, 11.1. Recent attempts to identify archaeological traces of Romulus' sacred *pomerium* (see above, p. 30 and n. 71) seem misguided. J. Le Gall in G.A. Mansuelli, R. Zangheri (eds), *La città etrusca e italica preromana* (Bologna 1970), 59–65, questions the Etruscan origin of the ritual.

63 Ogilvie, *Early Rome* (1976), 30; A. Boethius, *Etruscan and Early Roman Architecture* (Harmondsworth 1970), 64ff. J. Rykwert's remarkable book, *The Idea of a Town* (London 1976), mystical in conception but nonetheless extremely stimulating, is not really concerned with the historical issues being discussed here.

64 G. Colonna, in *Etruria e Lazio arcaico* (1987), 62–4 (an important discussion). On the development of Tuscanic temples see also G. Colonna (ed.), *Santuari d'Etruria* (Milan 1985), 60ff.

65 M. Pallottino, *La scuola di Vulca* (2nd edn, Rome 1948).

66 L. Banti, *SE* 17 (1943), 187–224. Note that Serv., *Aen.* 1.422, cited ever since Müller as evidence for the Etruscan origin of the Capitoline triad, refers to later Roman practices and has no bearing on Etruscan religion. Thus, rightly, De Sanctis, *StdR* I² (1960), 267; A.J. Pfiffig, *Religio etrusca* (Graz 1975), 33–4.

67 A. Ernout, *Bull. Soc. Ling.* 30 (1930), 82–124 (= Ernout, *Philologica* I (1946), 21–51); more recently, L.R. Palmer, *The Latin Language* (London 1954), 46–8.

68 G. Devoto, *SE* 6 (1932), 243–60; C. De Simone in *Gli Etruschi e Roma* (1981), 99–101. The derivation from Etruscan *puple strikes me as anything but certain.

69 L. Polacco, *Tuscanicae dispositiones* (Padua 1952), 137–9, speaks of the 'etruscheria' of the Augustan age, and of a 'tendenza snobistica'; cf. Harris, *Rome in Etruria and Umbria* (1971), 30: 'Etruscan ancestry had a well-attested snob value in the early empire.'

70 Harris, *Rome in Etruria and Umbria* (1971), 114ff., 202ff.; E. Gabba, *CAH²* VIII (1989), 236–7.

71 Cicero, *de nat. deor.* 2.11 (citing Ti. Gracchus the Elder). Passages such as Livy 7.17.3 are instructive as evidence for Roman attitudes.

72 *Ineditum Vaticanum*, ed. H. von Arnim, *Hermes* 27 (1892), 118–30 (F. Jacoby, *FGrHist* 839 F.1), 3. Cf. the very similar passages, clearly drawn from the same source, in Diod. 23.2.1; Athenaeus 6.273f. The *topos* recurs in Sallust, *Cat.* 51,37f.

73 E.S. McCartney, *MAAR* 1 (1915–16), 121–67, esp. 156; Thomsen, *King Servius* (1980), 158; C. Saulnier, *L'armée et la guerre dans le monde étrusco-romain, VIII–VI s.* (Paris 1980); P.F. Stary, *Zur eisenzeitliche Bewaffnung und Kampfesweise in Mittelitalien* (Mainz 1981); P. Fraccaro, *Della guerra presso i Romani* (Opuscula IV, Pavia 1975). H. Last, *CAH* VII (1928), 385, is rightly sceptical.

74 Cf. my comments in E. Campanile (ed.), *Alle origini di Roma* (Pisa 1989), 91ff.

75 A. Snodgrass, in Renfrew and Cherry, *Peer Polity Interaction* (1986), 52.

76 L. Bonfante, *Etruscan Dress* (Baltimore 1975), 93.

77 J.B. Ward Perkins, *PBSR* 29 (1961), 39ff.; M. Torelli, *DdA* 8 (1974–5), 57ff.; and my observations in M. Beard *et al.*, *Literacy in the Roman World* (Ann Arbor 1991), 14–15.

7 THE REFORMS OF SERVIUS TULLIUS

1 Essential bibliography on the tribes includes Mommsen's youthful work *Die römische Tribus in administrativer Beziehung* (Altona 1844), largely superseded by his discussion in *Staatsr.* III.1 (1887), 161ff., but still worth consulting in parts. See also W. Kubitschek, *De Romanorum tribuum origine ac propagatione* (Vienna 1882); *RE* VI A (1917), 2492–2518, s.v. 'tribus'. The standard modern treatment is Taylor, *Voting Districts* (1960).

2 The reading of most MSS is *una et triginta* (= 31), but the alternative *una et viginti* (= 21) appears in two of the best codices and is undoubtedly the correct reading, since it is found also in the *Periochae* and is consistent with Livy's own statement (6.5.8) that the addition of four tribes in 387 BC brought the total to 25.

3 The principal exception is Gjerstad, *Legends and Facts* (1962), 57; *Early Rome* V (1973), 120, who uses the former interpretation in support of his contention that Servius Tullius was ruling in 495 BC. This theory has won little support.

4 Some scholars, notably Beloch (*Röm. Gesch.* (1926), 175ff.), have questioned the date, on the grounds that Crustumerium cannot have been in Roman hands until after the capture of Fidenae in 426 BC. But this argument has no weight, since Fidenae was only an enclave guarding the river crossing, just as the land controlled by Rome on the right bank was a bridgehead in Veientine territory. Thus Ogilvie, *Comm.* (1965), 292.

5 Botsford, *Roman Assemblies* (1909), 48–65; Taylor, *Voting Districts* (1960), 3–7.

6 Dion. Hal. 4.15. This chapter apparently contradicts what Dionysius himself had said previously in 4.14, where Servius is credited with only the four urban tribes.

7 Vennonius is otherwise mentioned in a list of annalists in Cicero, *Leg.* 1.2.6 (cf. *Att.* 12.3.1), and is quoted, along with Fabius Pictor, as a source for a detail in the Romulus legend in the *Origo gentis Romanae*, 20.1 (see J.-C. Richard's note.).

8 Nonius, p. 62 Lindsay = B. Riposati, *M. Terenti Varronis de vita populi Romani* (1939), p. 104.

9 Niebuhr, *Hist. Rome* I[3] (1837), 418–19; F. Cornelius, *Untersuchungen* (1940), 106f.

10 The basic objections are stated by Taylor, *Voting Districts* (1960), 5 n. 9. For a detailed refutation see Thomsen, *King Servius* (1980), 119–21.

11 A connection between *pagi* and tribes is also implied in a fragmentary Latin papyrus, POxy 2088 – quoted, with discussion and bibliography, in Thomsen, *King Servius* (1980), 14ff. But the text is too fragmentary for its sense to be recovered, and in its present state it does not throw any further light on the problem.

12 De Sanctis, *StdR* II[2] (1960), 19 n. 58, Botsford, *Roman Assemblies* (1909), 53, and Thomsen, *King Servius* (1980), 122–3, are overconfident in asserting that Varro took his information solely from Pictor. How can we possibly be certain about a matter such as this?

13 I leave aside those sceptical historians who deny any connection whatever between Servius Tullius and the local tribes, and who in some cases treat Servius himself as a wholly legendary figure: Pais, *Storia di Roma* I (1898), 320; Beloch, *Röm. Gesch.* (1926), 270f.; U. Coli, *Scritti di diritto romano* (Milan 1973), 586; G.V. Sumner, *JRS* 60 (1970), 76f.

14 This was Mommsen's view in *Die römische Tribus* (1844), 17, 215, although he later repudiated it (*Röm. Forsch.* I (1864), 151; *Staatsr.* III.1 (1887), 163 n. 3), arguing that the four urban tribes were always confined to the city; the rustic tribes had not yet been formed, because at the time of Servius land outside the city was not yet held in private ownership, but was the common property of the patrician clans. This view is untenable, if only because the tribes were divisions of the Roman

people based on domicile, not divisions of the territory conferring citizenship exclusively on its owners. See the refutations of P. Fraccaro, *Athenaeum* 21 (1933), 150–72 (= *Opuscula* II, 149–70); H. Last, *JRS* 35 (1945), 40–2.

15 A. Magdelain, *REL* 49 (1972), 103ff.; Thomsen, *King Servius* (1980), 142–3.

16 Servius Tullius is said to have conducted four censuses in all (Val. Max. 3.4.3), whereas Tarquinius Superbus did not conduct any (Dion. Hal. 5.20). The implication is that the rustic tribes were created either under Servius Tullius or after the fall of the monarchy. See Taylor, *Voting Districts* (1960), 6; L. Capogrossi Colognesi, *Dalla tribù allo stato* (Rome 1990), 169.

17 Cf. Taylor, *Voting Districts* (1960), 6–7, with n. 13.

18 Beloch, *Röm. Gesch.* (1926), 270–3; Alföldi, *Early Rome* (1965), 310–18.

19 Botsford, *Roman Assemblies* (1909), 55 n. 1.

20 Mommsen, *Die römische Tribus* (1844), 7; Beloch, *Röm. Gesch.* (1926), 334; Taylor, *Voting Districts* (1960), 7 n. 6; Ogilvie, *Comm.* (1965), 292.

21 Camilius: W. Schulze, *Zur Geschichte lateinische Eigennamen* (Berlin 1904), 140; Pollius: Martial, *Ep.* 1.113.5; Pupinius: CIL V, 7055; Voltinius: CIL XI, 3208, and Schulze, 259.

22 Taylor, *Voting Districts* (1960), 39.

23 Thus, Alföldi, *Early Rome* (1965), 316–17; Thomsen, *King Servius* (1980), 130.

24 H. Last, *JRS* 35 (1945), 30–48.

25 Spivey and Stoddart, *Etruscan Italy* (1990), 127, are mistaken in suggesting that the Servian reforms entailed the issue of citizen armour.

26 Livy says that the engineers and musicians were attached to the first and fifth classes respectively, Dionysius to the second and fourth. The census rating of the lowest class changed during the course of the Republic (Gabba, *Republican Rome* (1976), 1–19), and it may be that the different figures given by Livy (11,000 *asses*) and Dionysius (12,500) refer to different periods.

27 Mommsen, *Staatsr.* III.1 (1887), 245 n. 1; see Thomsen, *King Servius* (1980), 153, for further references.

28 Thomsen, *King Servius* (1980), 151–2.

29 Thus e.g. J. Heurgon, *Tite-Live* book I (Paris 1963: Collection 'Erasme'), note on 1.43.

30 If heavy 'libral' *asses* (i.e. *asses* weighing a pound) are meant, the property qualifications would seem to be set rather high: thus Gabba, *Republican Rome* (1976), 3. This impressionistic argument tells in favour of sextantal *asses*.

31 P. Fraccaro, in *Atti II congresso naz. studi romani* (1931), 91–7 (= *Opuscula* II, 287–92). Fraccaro was challenged by De Sanctis, *RFIC* 61 (1933), 289–98 (= *Scritti minori*, 5, 239–47), but responded in *Athenaeum* 12 (1934), 57–71 (= *Opuscula* II, 293–306).

32 This important distinction between the weaponry of classes I–III and that of IV–V was first emphasised by Mommsen, *Die röm. Tribus* (1844), 138.

33 See below, p. 354; see further Polyb. 6.19.7; Meyer; Fraccaro *della guerra presso i romani* (*Opuscula* IV (1975), 73).

34 H. Delbrück, *History of the Art of War* I (Engl. trans., Westport, Conn. 1975), 263; G. Veith in Kromayer and Veith, *Heerwesen und Kriegsführung* (1928), 261.

35 It is hard to know why Gellius gives a higher figure (sc. 125,000) for the rating of the first class than Livy or Dionysius (100,000). Festus (p. 100 L) gives 120,000, while Gaius (2.274) agrees with Livy and Dionysius. Possibly they refer to different periods (cf. n. 26 above). Notice incidentally that the use of *classicus* to mean 'belonging to the first rank' is the origin of the modern term 'classical' (cf. Gellius 19.8.5, for the earliest example of this transference).

36 Thomsen, *King Servius* (1980), 176–7.

37 Botsford, *Roman Assemblies* (1909), 76ff., Beloch, *Röm. Gesch.* (1926), 291, and

Momigliano, *SDHI* 4 (1938), 511 (= *Quarto contributo*, 365), also argue strongly in favour of this twofold distinction between *classis* and *infra classem*.

38 The intimate connection between hoplite weaponry and the phalanx is stressed by V.D. Hanson, in Hanson (ed.), *Hoplites: the classical Greek battle experience* (London 1991), 63–84, rightly arguing that the former presupposes the latter.

39 On the adoption of hoplite equipment and tactics in Italy see A.M. Snodgrass, *JHS* 85, 116ff.; M. Torelli, *DdA* 8 (1974–5), 13–17; C. Saulnier, *L'armée et la guerre dans le monde étrusco-romain (VIIIe–IVe s.)* (Paris 1980), 115–20; P.F. Stary, *Zur eisenzeitlichen Bewaffnung und Kampfesweise in Mittelitalien* I–II (Mainz 1981) 307–12; Spivey and Stoddart, *Etruscan Italy* (1990), 127–39; B. D'Agostino, in Murray and Price (eds), *The Greek City* (1990), 59–82.

40 De Sanctis, *StdR* II² (1960), 181ff.; *RFIC* 61 (1933), 189ff.; Beloch, *Röm. Gesch.* (1926), 283ff.; Cornelius, *Untersuchungen* (1940), 80; Meyer, *Röm. Staat²* (1961), 52ff.; G.V. Sumner, *JRS* 60 (1970), 67ff. The rather feeble paper of M.P. Nilsson, *JRS* 19 (1929), 1–11, has, for some unaccountable reason, been very influential.

41 Hanson, *Hoplites* (1991), 70–1.

42 Botsford, *Roman Assemblies* (1909), 76ff.

43 D. Kienast, *Bonner Jahrbücher* 175 (1975), 93ff.

44 Momigliano, *Terzo contributo*, 596.

45 Cf. Kienast, *Bonner Jahrbücher* 175 (1975), 94. Rawson, *JRS* 72 (1982), 180, points out that some figured monuments from northern Italy appear to show soldiers in the same army carrying both round and oblong shields.

46 Thus, e.g., W. Kunkel, *Introduction to Roman Legal and Constitutional History* (Oxford 1966), 11.

47 De Sanctis, *StdR* II² (1960), 198; Nicolet, *Tributum* (1976), 27ff.

48 Crawford, *Coinage and Money* (1985), 22–3.

49 Polyb. 6.19.5 with Walbank's note. Gabba, *Republican Rome* (1976), 53–6, argues that tribal recruitment dates from the early third century, but his arguments are not conclusive.

50 Crawford, *Coinage and Money* (1985), 23.

51 Fraccaro, *Opuscula* II, 292.

52 Pre-hoplite warfare in Italy see Stary, *Zur eisenzeitliche Bewaffnung* (1981) 1, 128ff.

53 Beloch, *Röm. Gesch.* (1926), 270f., 290ff.; A. Bernardi, *Athenaeum* 30 (1952), 22; U. Coli, *Scritti di diritto romano* II (1973), 583, 588; E. Meyer, *Röm. Staat²* (1961), 57ff.

54 Taylor, *AJPh* 78 (1957), 339.

55 Mommsen, *Staatsr.* II³ (1887), 232 n. 1.

56 Taylor, *AJPh* 78 (1957), 340.

57 Gabba, *Republican Rome* (1976), 53f.

58 Gabba, *Republican Rome* (1976), 54; but note the different view adopted in *Athenaeum* 39 (1961), 107f.

59 E.g. Gabba, *Republican Rome* (1976), 210 n. 21, with further refs; Ogilvie, *Comm.* (1965), 604, with an explanation that is as unlikely as it is ingenious.

60 Taylor, *AJPh* 78 (1957), 341–2; Thomsen, *King Servius* (1980), 189 n. 175.

61 Cf. Momigliano, *Quinto contributo*, 317.

62 H. van Effenterre, *REG* 89 (1976), 1–17; P. Siewart, *Die Trittyen Attikas und die Heeresreform des Kleisthenes* (Munich 1982); G.R. Stanton, *Chiron* 14 (1984), 1–41; F.J. Frost, *Historia* 33 (1984), 283–94.

63 Dion. Hal. 4.20.2. Although Livy does not record any act by the *comitia centuriata* before the election of the first consuls (1.60.4), it is not correct to say, as Botsford does (*Roman Assemblies* (1909), 201), that for Roman historians the centuriate assembly came into existence at the beginning of the Republic.

64 Mommsen, *Staatsr.* III.1 (1887), 246; Botsford, *Roman Assemblies* (1909), 201; H. Last, *JRS* 35 (1945), 35; Ogilvie, *Comm.* (1965), 172.

65 Last, *JRS* 35 (1945), 35; Thomsen, *King Servius* (1980), 156–7.

66 Thus, rightly, W. Kunkel, *Introduction to Roman Legal and Constitutional History* (Oxford 1966), 10–11. Others who accept that the centuriate organisation functioned as an assembly from the start include De Martino, *Storia* I² (1972), 153ff.; Heurgon, *Rise of Rome* (1973), 149; Ogilvie, *Early Rome* (1976), 64–5.

67 Momigliano, *Quarto contributo*, 377–94; *Quinto contributo*, 635–9.

68 Some scholars have questioned the historical existence of P. Valerius Publicola (Pais, *Storia di Roma* I (1898), 489); others doubt the authenticity of all events involving Valerii, which they consider inventions by the annalist Valerius Antias. I have criticised this approach in I.S. Moxon *et al.* (eds), *Past Perspectives* (1986), 77–8.

69 Table X.1. Cf. Cic., *Rep.* 2.54. The phrase *maximo comitiatu* is usually taken to mean 'in the most important of the assemblies', i.e. the *comitia centuriata*, and to imply the existence of lesser assemblies (thus, e.g., Taylor, *Voting Districts* (1960), 9); but see E. Gabba, *Athenaeum* 75 (1987), 203–5, arguing persuasively that it means 'in a well-attended assembly'.

70 A. Drummond, *CAH²* VII.2 (1989), 220.

71 The general point is made by Cicero, *Rep.* 2.54, who cites documentary evidence in his support (the *libri pontificii* and *libri augurales*). Cf. Livy 1.26.5; 8.33.8; Cic., *Mil.* 37; Festus p. 297 L (all referring to the supposed appeal of Horatius, in the reign of Tullus Hostilius).

72 Curt. 6.8.25; Arrian 3.26.2. See F. Granier, *Die makedonische Heeresversammlung* (Munich 1931).

73 Mommsen, *Staatsr.* II³ (1887), 11; *Strafr.* (1899), 474.

8 THE POWER OF ROME IN THE SIXTH CENTURY

1 The information is conveniently tabulated by Ampolo in *DdA* NS 2 (1980), 170–1.

2 The standard work on the Servian wall is G. Säflund, *Le mura di Roma repubblicana* (Lund 1930). See also *Roma medio-repubblicana* (Exhibition catalogue, Rome 1973), 7–31; for a brief account, M. Todd, *The Walls of Rome* (London 1978), 13–20. On the size of the enclosed area see Beloch, *Röm. Gesch.* (1926), 208.

3 Säflund, *Le mura di Roma* (1930), 231ff. The wall was built of stone from the Grotta Oscura quarries at Veii, which did not come under Roman control until 396 BC. For a full discussion see Thomsen, *King Servius* (1980), 219ff.

4 P. Quoniam, *MEFR* 59 (1947), 41ff.; F. Coarelli, *Guida archeologica di Roma* (Milan 1974), 297–8.

5 E. Gjerstad, *Studies Robinson* 1 (1951), 412–22; *Op. Rom.* 1 (1954), 50–65; 3 (1960), 69–78; *Early Rome* III (1960), 27ff.

6 R.E.A. Palmer, *AJA* 79 (1975), 389–90.

7 A. Boethius, *Op. Rom.* 4 (1962), 29–43; L. Quilici, *Arch. Class.* 20 (1968), 137–40; C. Morselli, E. Tortorici, *Ardea*, Forma Italiae I.16 (Rome 1982); S. Quilici Gigli, *GRT* (1990), 192–3.

8 F. Coarelli, *Il foro romano* I (1983), 111–17.

9 A. von Gerkan, *Rh. Mus.* 100 (1957), 95ff.; 104 (1961), 138; Alföldi, *Early Rome* (1965), 322.

10 Full discussion of literary sources in Thomsen, *King Servius* (1980), 218ff.

11 F. Castagnoli, *PdP* 32 (1977), 346.

12 Tarquinii: P. Romanelli, *NSc* 73 (1948), 206–7; Caere: M. Pallottino, *EAA* 2 (1959), 519.

13 Veii. J.B. Ward Perkins, *PBSR* 27 (1959) 66–71; 29 (1961), 32–9.

14 Old Smyrna and Asia Minor: J.M. Cook *et al.*, *BSA* 53–4 (1958–9), 1–137; A.W. Lawrence, *Greek Aims in Fortification* (Oxford 1979), 30ff.

15 Cumae: W. Johannowsky in *EAA* 2 (1959), 970–2 (s.v. 'Cuma').

16 On the phrase *lustrum condere*, R.M. Ogilvie, *JRS* 51 (1961), 31–9. New foundation of the city: Mommsen, *Staatsr.* II³ (1887), 232 and n. 1.

17 Coarelli, *Foro romano* I (1983), 196–9.

18 On the pomerium, Varro, *LL* 5.143; Gell. 13.14.1; Plut., *Rom.* 11; Livy 1.44.3ff., with Ogilvie's note. See Mommsen, *Röm. Forsch.* II (1879), 23–41; A. Magdelain, *REL* 54 (1976), 71–109; P. Catalano, *ANRW* II (1978), 479–91; F. Coarelli, *Foro Boario* (1988), 386ff.

19 J. Poucet, *Recherches sur la légende sabine* (Kinshasa 1967), 102ff.

20 Seneca, *de brev. vit.* 13.8; NB especially Sallust, *Hist.* 1.55.5M (*Oratio Lepidi*), where Sulla is described as *scaevus iste Romulus* ('that twisted Romulus').

21 Cf. Ampolo, *DdA* NS 2, (1980), 168f.

22 From Ampolo, ibid.; cf. in Momigliano and Schiavone (eds), *StdR* I (1988), 232, 583; M. Guaitoli, *Röm. Mitt.* 84 (1977), 7–25.

23 Beloch, *Röm. Gesch.* (1926), 169ff.; Alföldi, *Early Rome* (1965), 304ff.; S. Quilici Gigli, *MEFRA* 90 (1978), 567–75; Humbert, *Municipium* (1978), 49–84.

24 Beloch, *Röm. Gesch.* (1926), 178; the figure of 822 km² needs to be increased by the addition of the territories of Ficulea (37), Crustumerium (39.5) and Nomentum (72) to give a figure for 495 BC. Cf. Gjerstad, *Early Rome* 193 n. 3.

25 This was the fundamental basis of Beloch's pioneering study, *Die Bevölkerung der griechisch-römischen Welt* (Leipzig 1886). On Beloch's population studies see A. Momigliano, *Studies on Modern Scholarship* (Berkeley 1994), 100ff.

26 Beloch, *Röm. Gesch.* (1926), 209; F. De Martino, *Diritto e società nell'antica Roma* (Rome 1979), 162–82.

27 Ampolo, *DdA* NS 2 (1980), 15–31; cf. Cornell, *CAH²* VII.2 (1989), 247.

28 J. Heurgon, *Daily Life of the Etruscans* (London 1964), 145–8 (a brilliant piece of analysis).

29 The figure implies a total population of more than 266,000, a physical impossibility. It also conflicts with all ancient accounts of the *comitia centuriata*. Other versions of the same figure occur in Dionysius 4.22.2 (84,700) and Eutropius 1.7 (83,000). The fact that in the accounts we have the Servian system included 85 centuries of *iuniores* makes one wonder if someone (Fabius or his source) did not confuse centuries with thousands.

30 This was Beloch's view, decisively confirmed by P.A. Brunt, *Italian Manpower* (1971), 15–25.

31 F. Coarelli, in Momigliano and Schiavone (eds), *StdR* I (1988), 317ff.

32 B.G. Niebuhr, *History of Rome* I³ (1837), 552; II³ (1838), 68ff.

33 Brunt's rejection of the figures: *Italian Manpower* (1971), 27, but see Coarelli, in Momigliano and Schiavone (eds), *StdR* I (1988), 319.

34 *La Nuova Antologia* (16 August 1936), 405–16 = G. Pasquali, *Terze pagine stravaganti* (Florence 1942), 1–24. On this see C. Ampolo, in E. Campanile (ed.), *Alle origini di Roma* (Pisa 1988), 77–87.

35 T. Frank, *Economic Survey of Ancient Rome* I (Baltimore 1927); I.G. Scott, *Mem. Am. Acad. Rome* 7 (1929), 63ff.; see also I.G. [Scott] Ryberg, *An Archaeological Record of Rome from the Seventh to the Second Century* BC (London 1940).

36 Alföldi, *Early Rome* (1965), 318–35.

37 See especially the criticisms of A. Momigliano, *JRS* 57 (1967), 211–16 (= *Quarto*

contributo, 487–99); *Essays in Ancient and Modern Historiography* (Oxford 1977), 99–105 (= *Sesto contributo* 69–75); *Quinto contributo*, 293–331.

38 *GRT*, ed. M. Cristofani (Rome 1990). On the exhibition see e.g. A.J. Ammerman, *JRA* 4 (1991), 200f.

39 R. Righi in *Enea nel Lazio* (1981), 72, on item A.121.

40 Momigliano, *Quarto contributo*, 490–1; *Quinto contributo*, 308. For the date, M.L. West, *Hesiod: Theogony*, (Oxford 1966), 435–6.

41 For full discussion of all the problems, see Walbank's *Commentary on Polybius* I (1957), ad loc.; B. Scardigli, *I trattati romano-cartaginesi* (Pisa 1991), 47–87. The presence of Lavinium in the list of Latin towns is based on an emendation (challenged by Rosenberg, who would delete it altogether – *Hermes* 54 (1919), 164). See Walbank on 3.22.11.

42 T. Mommsen, *Die römische Chronologie*[2] (Berlin 1859; 1st edn 1858), 320ff. Subsequent bibliography to *c.* 1963 is given by Alföldi, *Early Rome* (1965), 350 n. 2; see also H. Bengtson, *Die Staatsverträge des Altertums* II[2] (Munich 1975), 16–20, 306–9, 339–40, 345. Important recent discussions include Werner, *Beginn röm. Rep.* (1963), 299–368; Toynbee, *Hannibal's Legacy* I (1965), 519–55; K.-E. Petzold, *ANRW* I.1 (1972), 364–411; Heurgon, *The Rise of Rome* (1973), 250–7; H.H. Scullard, *CAH*[2] VII.2 (1989), 520–30; C. Ampolo, in Momigliano and Schiavone (eds), *StdR* I (1988), 231 n. 82; *Alle origini* (1988), 82–4. Most recently see the fully documented study of B. Scardigli, *I trattati romano-cartaginesi* (Pisa 1991), 24–33.

43 See Walbank's note on 3.21.9–10.

44 Especially A. Aymard, *REA* 59 (1957), 277–93 (= Aymard, *Etudes d'histoire ancienne* (Paris 1967), 373 ff.), and Alföldi, *Early Rome* (1965), 354.

45 This point is well made by Ampolo, *Alle origini* (1988), 83. On the oaths in general see Walbank on Polyb. 3.25.6–9.

46 Founding cities: Ampolo, *Alle origini* (1988); archaic language: Polyb. 3.22.3, and see e.g. Heurgon, *Rise of Rome* (1973), 253.

47 A strong argument, frequently advanced. See e.g. Toynbee, *Hannibal's Legacy* I (1965), 522f. (also advocating a *terminus post quem* of 351 BC for the second treaty).

9 THE BEGINNINGS OF THE ROMAN REPUBLIC

1 Shakespeare's *Lucrece* (1594), a poem of 1,855 lines, enjoyed immense acclaim when it was first published (it was reissued five times between 1598 and 1624), but is little read nowadays and has been reviled by critics for centuries. It tells the story of Lucretia in melodramatic rather than narrative fashion, and is preceded by an 'argument', a prose account of the fall of the Tarquins based on Livy. Shakespeare's main source for the poem, however, seems to have been Ovid (*Fasti* 2. 721–852). He also drew upon Chaucer, who included the rape of Lucretia in *The Legende of Good Women* (*c.* 1382), lines 1,680–1,885, with explicit acknowledgement of 'Ovyde and Titus Lyvius' (l.1683). On Shakespeare's sources for *Lucrece* see G. Bullough, *Narrative and Dramatic Sources of Shakespeare* (London 1957) I, 179–83. On the history of the legend in general see I. Donaldson, *The Rapes of Lucretia* (Oxford 1978).

T.B. Macaulay's *Lays of Ancient Rome* (1842), once extremely well known, are today not even in print. In my experience few English students have even heard of them.

2 Tarquin had three sons, Titus, Sextus and Arruns. Arruns was killed at the battle of Silva Arsia, and Titus at Lake Regillus. Sextus (the rapist) was lynched by the inhabitants of Gabii. See further below.

3 He and Arruns Tarquinius (see previous note) had killed each other in single combat during the battle. Brutus was replaced as consul by Sp. Lucretius, the father of Lucretia. Lucretius died after a few days in office, and was replaced in his turn by M. Horatius. Thus there were five consuls in all in the first year of the Republic, an unparalleled state of affairs which many critics regard as inherently improbable, although the traditional narrative makes reasonable sense as it stands. Livy tells us (2.8.5) that some sources omitted Lucretius, and made Horatius the immediate successor of Brutus. Polybius evidently followed a different version, when he refers to 'the consulship of L. Junius Brutus and M. Horatius' (3.22.1, cited below, pp. 218–19).

4 They include the deeds of C. Mucius Scaevola, who stole into Porsenna's camp and tried to assassinate him; on being discovered he showed his indifference to the prospect of torture by thrusting his right hand into a fire – whence his surname, Scaevola (= 'left-handed'); and of Cloelia, the girl who was given as hostage to Porsenna but who persuaded her fellow prisoners to escape and led them to safety by swimming across the Tiber. These episodes are narrated in Livy 2.12–13.

5 The sources call him Octavius (sic) Mamilius, but such a combination of two gentile names is most odd. It is better to presume a praenomen Octavus (cf. Quintus, Sextus, Septimus, Decimus). See Beloch, Röm. Gesch. (1926), 189 n. 1.

6 An extreme statement to this effect in Alföldi, Early Rome (1965), 84, although even Alföldi does not question the historicity of Porsenna. That is left to Werner, Beginn röm. Rep. (1963), 377–86.

7 Macaulay's preface to the Lays of Ancient Rome is extremely important; the poems are an imaginative attempt to reconstruct the lost ballads which, he believed, lay behind the ancient tradition. In other words he accepted the famous 'ballad theory' of Niebuhr and Perizonius, on which see above, p. 12.

8 J. Heurgon, L'information littéraire 7 (1955), 56–64.

9 Ed. Meyer, Geschichte des Altertums III², 752 n. 1; Alföldi, Early Rome (1965), 77. Notice also the interesting suggestion of Momigliano (Terzo contributo, 601–2) that it was Claudius who unearthed the unpalatable fact of Porsenna's capture of Rome.

10 They would include his relatives Brutus and Collatinus, but perhaps also Valerius Publicola, who held the consulship for three years in succession, and in the traditional story was suspected of aiming at kingship. He is said to have ruled as sole consul for a period after the death of Brutus, and had built his house on the Velia where former kings had lived (on the significance of this see below, p. 240, and cf. Coarelli, Foro romano I (1983), 79ff.). The recently discovered Satricum inscription recording a dedication by 'the companions of Poplios Valesios' (see above, p. 144) can be used to fuel such speculation. If Publicola is to be identified with this Poplios Valesios (admittedly a big if) then it is possible to see him as an independent warlord whose activities extended as far as southern Latium.

11 It is clear that our principal sources, Livy, Dionysius, Diodorus, and the Fasti Capitolini, themselves depended on different sources, because of innumerable minor discrepancies in matters such as praenomina, cognomina, the order of consuls' names, etc. The several versions are tabulated in A. Degrassi (ed.), Inscriptiones Italiae, XIII.1: Fasti consulares et triumphales (Rome 1947). This publication gave rise to an important series of papers on the Fasti by L.R. Taylor: CP 41 (1946), 1–11; 45 (1950), 84–95; PAPS 94 (1950) 511–16; and (with T.R.S. Broughton) MAAR 19 (1949), 3–14. For a useful survey of scholarship on the Fasti see R.T. Ridley, Athenaeum 58 (1980), 264–98.

12 On the Varronian chronology, see pp. 589ff. Livy, whose version of the Fasti is generally regarded as the most reliable of those we have, leaves out Varronian 490 and 489 as well as the four dictator-years. He also omits Varronian 507 (P. Valerius

Publicola III, M. Horatius Pulvillus II), but this may be his mistake, since he refers to Publicola in his next consulship (504 Varr.) as 'consul for the *fourth* time' (2.16.2). Livy thus lists 202 colleges (but perhaps it should have been 203) before 300 BC.

13 Polyb. 3.22.1–2. In referring to the 'crossing of Xerxes to Greece' Polybius probably meant the year of Salamis (i.e. 480/479 BC). This would date the first consuls to 508/507 BC. See Walbank's note ad loc. (Walbank's whole discussion of the beginning of the Republic, pp. 339–40, is indispensable).

14 Thus, e.g. Werner, *Beginn röm. Rep.* (1963), 12 n. 1, harking back to the old idea of Mommsen, *Röm. Forsch.* I (1864), 57–68, and Cichorius, *De fastis consularibus antiquissimis* (Diss. Leipzig, 1886) that *cognomina* were not used in early documents; but this view is untenable, as Beloch demonstrated: *Röm. Gesch.* (1926), 46–52.

15 As maintained by E. Gabba in *Synteleia V. Arangio-Ruiz* (Naples 1964) I, 486–93.

16 A. Drummond, *CAH²* VII.2 (1989), 178.

17 R. Werner, *Beginn röm. Rep.* (1963), on which see Momigliano, *Terzo contributo*, 669–72.

18 Livy's text makes it clear that the purpose of the nails was to mark the passing of years (but see below, n. 22), and that a similar practice was observed at the temple of Nortia in the Etruscan city of Volsinii. Livy took his information from L. Cincius, an antiquarian of the first century BC, on whom see J. Heurgon, *Athenaeum* 42 (1964), 432–41.

19 Werner, *Beginn röm. Rep.* (1963), 482: '. . . die römische Republik ihre Entstehung einem griechischen Sieg über die Etrusker verdankte.'

20 For example T. Geganius (cos. 492) is rejected because of his *praenomen* Titus, which Werner believes would not have been borne by a Geganius in the early fifth century (p. 271). We know that certain *praenomina* were shunned by certain clans (for example Marcus by the Manlii), but we are told nothing about the naming habits of the Geganii. No one can possibly know what the parents of a fifth-century Geganius might have been moved to call their son.

21 Momigliano, *Quinto contributo*, 303.

22 Livy confuses the issue, however, by associating his account of the annual nail ceremony with the occasional practice of appointing a special dictator to hammer a nail in order to ward off a plague. The appointment of such a *dictator clavi figendi causa* is attested for 363 BC (the present instance), 331, 313, and 263 BC (Livy 7.3.3; 8.18.12; 9.28.6; and *Fasti Capitolini* under 363 and 263 BC). The two types of ceremony – the annual performance on the 13 September and the occasional apotropaic ritual – are clearly incompatible; and one is bound to assume either that both forms of ritual were practised (in which case we can only speculate whether there were two distinct sets of nails in the wall, or whether the two types of nail were mixed together indiscriminately); or that the annual nail ceremony lapsed, and was replaced by a ritual that occurred only intermittently, in time of plague or other sign of divine anger. Livy seems clearly to favour the second of these alternatives, if that is the correct interpretation of the sentence *intermisso deinde more digna etiam per se visa res propter quam dictator crearetur*: 'then the custom (sc. the annual ceremony) lapsed, but the thing itself (sc. the hammering of a nail) seemed important enough in itself to warrant the appointment of a dictator'.

23 It is possible that a formal record was kept of the magistrates who fixed the annual nails, or even that the nails themselves were inscribed with the names of the magistrates who fixed them. Near-eastern parallels for this apparently exist: see *Entretiens* 13 (1967), 192.

24 T. Mommsen, *Die römische Chronologie²* (Berlin 1859; 1st edn, 1858), 199.

25 K. Hanell, *Das altrömische eponyme Amt* (Lund 1946). Hanell's ideas were first formulated in Δραγμα *M.P. Nilsson dedicatum* (Lund 1939), 156ff. A later summary in *Entretiens* 13 (1967), 177–91.

26 Hanell, *Das altrömische Eponyme Amt* (1946), 95–117. The arguments are complex and technical. The details need not concern us here, but note that Hanell's interpretation has been strongly criticised, e.g. by E. Meyer, *Mus. Helv.* 9 (1952), 176–81; A.K. Michels, *Calendar of the Roman Republic* (1967), 215–17.

27 Gjerstad's views were published in the same form in a number of different works, among which notice *Op. Rom.* 3 (1961), 69–102; *Legends and Facts of Early Roman History* (Lund 1962), esp. pp. 44ff.; *Early Rome* IV (Lund 1965), 517ff.; *Entretiens* 13 (1967), 3–30.

28 The monuments in question are the archaic temple at Sant'Omobono, and the earth rampart on the Viminal (the *agger*). On these monuments see above, pp. 147, 199. The point made in the text is well illustrated by the latter case. What tradition attributed to Servius Tullius was the massive stone wall surrounding the city, of which substantial portions are still standing. This wall dates from 378 BC, and was clearly misattributed to Servius Tullius. It is only a secondary (modern) interpretation that associates the *agger* with Servius.

29 Cf. Momigliano, *Terzo contributo*, 552, 570–1, 607–8. On the Etruscan names in the early *Fasti* see M. Pallottino, *SE* 31 (1963), 31–7; Ranouil, *Recherches sur le patriciat* (1975), 188–9.

30 When the final volumes of *Early Rome* appeared in the 1970s they were simply dismissed, or even ridiculed, e.g. by R.E.A. Palmer, *AJA* 79 (1975), 386–90.

31 This description of the fall of the Roman Empire comes from A. Cameron, *The Mediterranean World in Late Antiquity* (London 1993), 33.

32 Thus, rightly, C. Ampolo, *PdP* 30 (1975), 410–16; in *Gli etruschi e Roma* (1981), 45–67. Cf. Scullard, *Etruscan Cities and Rome* (1967), 263.

33 Momigliano, *Terzo contributo*, 667; and cf. the works cited in the previous note.

34 On this question I find myself in agreement with J.C. Meyer, *Pre-Republican Rome* (Odense 1983), 163–5; cf. his remarks in *ARID* 9 (1980), 62–6.

35 On the 'age of crisis', see generally M. Pallottino, *Earliest Italy* (1991), 97ff., and the contributions to the volume *Crise et transformation* (1990), especially that of G. Colonna, 7–21.

36 Thus, rightly, M. Pallottino, *SE* 31 (1963), 31; J. Heurgon, *Rise of Rome* (1973), 158–9.

37 That the consuls were originally called praetors is confirmed by Livy 3.55.12 and Festus p. 249 L. The word *praetor* is derived from *prae-ire* (Varro, *LL* 5.80, 87; Cicero, *Leg.* 3.8), meaning 'to go in front'; but whether this means 'to lead' in the sense of military command (as *TLL*, s.v. 'praeeo') is open to dispute. See G. Luzzatto, *Eos* 48 (1956), 439ff.; A. Giovannini, *Mus. Helv.* 41 (1984), 15–30; in *Bilancio critico* (1993), 75–96. The traditional view is upheld by C.J. van Leijenhorst, *Mus. Helv.* 43 (1986), 177–9, and G. Valditara, *Studi sul magister populi* (1989), 336–8 n. 149.

38 Important remarks on *provocatio* in Giovannini, *Bilancio critico* (1993), 93–6.

39 Whether or not there was any legal prohibition on successive consulships, the rule was stringently observed in practice, as the *Fasti* confirm. The only exception in the early Republic is, significantly, P. Valerius Publicola, cos. 509, 508, 507, 504, on whom see above, n. 10.

40 Valditara, *Studi sul magister populi* (1989), 202ff; G. Labruna, *Index* 15 (1987), 291ff. argues convincingly, however, that some dictators were appointed for political reasons, in opposition to the *plebs*.

41 Hanell, *Das altrömische Eponyme Amt* (1946), 165ff.

42 Beloch, *Röm. Gesch.* (1926), 231–6; De Martino, *Storia* I² (1972), 191ff.; *ANRW*

I.1 (1972), 234ff., with further bibliography in n. 60; in Momigliano and Schiavone (eds), *StdR* I (1988), 356f.; Valditara, *Studi sul magister populi* (1989), 182ff.

43 *Storia* I² (1972), 191ff.

44 A. Bernardi, *Athenaeum* 30 (1952), 12.

45 College of three praetors: De Sanctis, *StdR* I² (1960), 391ff.; C. Gioffredi, *BCom.* 71 (1943–5), 129ff.; A. Heuss, *ZSS* 64 (1944), 69; criticised by J. Heurgon, in *Entretiens* 13 (1967) 108–9.

46 J. Heurgon, in *Entretiens* XIII (1967), 119ff.

47 Momigliano, *Quarto contributo*, 411ff.; note also the interpretation of Mommsen, *Röm. Chronol.*² (1859), 178, who argued that *praetor maximus* meant, in a generic sense, the chief magistrate, whoever that might be (that is, consul, dictator, or *interrex*). The phrase *qui praetor maximus sit idibus Septembribus* should then be translated 'whoever may be head of state on the 13th September'.

48 Mazzarino, *Dalla monarchia* (1946), 67–80.

49 Momigliano, *Terzo contributo*, 674; J. Heurgon, in *Entretiens* 113 (1967), 114.

50 The principal studies of Etruscan magistrates include Rosenberg, *Staat der alten Italiker* (1913); S.P. Cortsen, *Die etruskischen Standes- und Beamtentitel* (Copenhagen 1925); M. Pallottino, *SE* 24 (1955–6), 45–72; J. Heurgon, *Historia* 6 (1957), 63–97; Lambrechts, *Essai sur les magistratures* (1959); J. Heurgon, in *Entretiens* 13 (1967), 99–127.

51 Heurgon, *Historia* 6 (1957), 83–4; Lambrechts, *Essai sur les magistratures* (1959), 202–3.

52 Salmon, *Samnium and the Samnites* (1967), 85–7, and see Ennius, *Ann.* 289, with Skutsch's note.

53 Rosenberg, *Staat der alten Italiker* (1913), 72.

54 Ibid., 46–7.

55 E.g. the two *meddices* of the Marrucini: Vetter, *Handbuch* (1953), no. 219.

56 This view was applied axiomatically to all the evidence by H. Rudolph, *Stadt und Staat im römischen Italien* (Leipzig 1935), a procedure that is generally regarded as unjustified.

57 Salmon, *Making of Roman Italy* (1982), 5, 27; Pallottino, *Earliest Italy* (1991), 85ff.

58 On Lars Porsenna, see now J.-R. Jannot, *MEFRA* 100 (1988), 601–11.

59 Ogilvie, *Comm.* (1965), 632, on Livy 5.1.3.

60 Torelli, *Elogia Tarquiniensia* (1975), 45ff.; my own view is presented in detail in *JRS* 68 (1978), 170–2. See further below, p. 459 n. 51.

61 Lambrechts, *Essai* (1959), 89ff.

62 Pallottino, *Earliest Italy* (1991), 92; Torelli, *Storia degli Etruschi* (1981), 81–2.

63 Rosenberg, *Staat der alten Italiker* (1913), 79–84.

64 E. Campanile, C. Letta, *Studi sulle magistrature indigene e municipali nell'area italica* (Pisa 1979), 34f.

65 Cf. Crawford, *Roman Republic*² (1992), 31 and *passim*.

66 Momigliano, *Quinto contributo*, 316.

67 Mommsen, *Hist. Rome*² (1864), 253ff.; Rosenberg, *Staat der alten Italiker* (1913), 81.

68 E.g. Ovid, *Fasti* 2,685ff.; Paul.-Fest. p. 346 L, s.v. 'regifugium'; Warde Fowler, *Roman Festivals* (1899) 327–30; Scullard, *Festivals and Ceremonies* (1981), 81–2.

69 CIL I², 4, 2830; M. Guarducci, *Vestigia* 17 (1972), 381–4; M. Cristofani, in *GRT* (1990), 22–3.

70 Cf. J.A. North, *CAH*² VII.2 (1989), 611–12.

71 K. Latte, *Röm. Religionsgesch.* (1960), 195ff. Contra: Dumézil, *Archaic Roman Religion* (1970), 102ff.

72 Suggested e.g. by P. De Francisci, *Primordia civitatis* (1959), 727–32.

73 E. Gabba, *Athenaeum* 39 (1961), 98–121.

74 Mazzarino, *Dalla monarchia* (1945), 177ff.

75 J.W. Hall, in *The Cambridge History of Japan* III (1990), 189–93; J.P. Mass, *Warrior Government in Early Medieval Japan* (New Haven, Conn. 1974); H. Bolitho in I.W. Mabbett (ed.), *Patterns of Kingship and Authority in Traditional Asia* (London 1975), 24–43, on Japanese kingship. Briefly, G. Cameron Hurst in *Kodansha Encyclopedia of Japan* 8 (Tokyo 1983), 228–30, s.v. 'warrior government'.

76 S. Weinstock, *Divus Julius* (Oxford 1971), 29.

77 Dio. 7.8 (Euseb., *Chron.* p. 138 Karst): 'Julios aber, verlustig gegangen des Fürstentums, wurde in das Hohepriestertum eingesetzt, und war wie ein zweiter König.'

78 Dictator: Plut., *Rom.* 27; Dion. Hal. 5.74; *ILS* 4955. *Rex sacrorum*: *ILS* 4942, with G. Wissowa, *RuK²* (1912), 520 n.6; and see Momigliano, *Quarto contributo*, 397.

79 Dictator: *ILS* 6194 (= CIL XIV, 2097); CIL XIV, 2112, 2121, etc.: see further Rosenberg, *Staat der alten Italiker* (1913), 73. *Rex sacrorum*: CIL XIV, 2089; *Eph. Ep.* IX, 608.

80 Alföldi, *Early Rome* (1965), 63ff.; T.J. Cornell, *Mus. Helv.* 31 (1974), 206–7; Frederiksen, *Campania* (1984), 96–9.

81 Momigliano, *Quinto contributo*, 303: 'This synchronism with the history of Cumae is the strongest single argument for the correctness of Roman republican chronology.'

82 Cf. J.A. North, *CAH²* VII.2 (1989), 614.

83 Coarelli, *Foro romano* I (1983), 137–8.

84 Coarelli, *Foro Boario* (1988), 209ff.

85 A. Bernardi, *Athenaeum* 30 (1952), 24ff.

86 For an account of these excavations see C. Huelsen, *Jahrb. d. Inst.* 4 (1889), 228–53; G. Boni, 'Regia', *Atti congr. int. scienze storiche* 5 (1904), 518–26. A brief summary in T. Frank, *Roman Buildings of the Republic* (Rome 1924), 81–5; I.S. Ryberg, *An Archaeological Record of Rome* (1940), index s.v. 'Regia'.

87 F.E. Brown, *Entretiens* 13 (1967), 47–60; *RPAA* 47 (1974–5), 15–36. Cf. Brown, in *In Memoriam O.J. Brendel* (Mainz 1976), 5–12.

88 The importance of Brown's conclusions is stressed by Momigliano, *Quinto contributo*, 303, 312; cf. Ogilvie, *Early Rome* (1976), 85.

89 Thus for example several contributors to *CAH²* VII.2 (1989): Torelli, p. 48; Momigliano, p. 76; Drummond, p. 177. A more detailed exposition in Coarelli, *Foro romano* I (1983), 56ff.; on p. 64 he speaks of 'sclerotizzazione'.

90 Coarelli, *Foro romano* I (1983), 21–3, argues that the two were identical. The issue is not touched on by L. Richardson Jr, *A New Topographical Dictionary of Ancient Rome* (Baltimore 1992) s.vv. 'Regia', 'domus publica', 'domus regis sacrorum', etc.

91 Plut., *Numa* 14.1; Dio, fr. 6.2. On the kings' houses see further below, n. 95.

92 Brown, *RPAA* 47 (1974–5), 36; De Francisci, *Primordia civitatis* (1959), 727–32.

93 Coarelli, *Foro romano* I (1983), ch. 1, esp. pp. 56–78.

94 The palace complexes at Murlo (Poggio Civitate) and Acquarossa are described by E. Nielsen and K.M. Phillips, *NSc* 30 (1976), 113–47 (Murlo), and C.E. Östenberg, *Case etrusche di Acquarossa* (Rome 1975). Discussion of the historical implications in Torelli, *Storia degli Etruschi* (1981), 174–81; *CAH²* VII.2 (1989), 40–8. See also S. Stopponi (ed.), *Case e palazzi degli Etruschi* (1985), 1ff., 64ff.

95 The key text on the kings' houses is Solinus I, 21–6, which probably draws upon Varro. See Coarelli, *Foro romano* I (1983), 56f.

96 That the Vestal Virgins were originally the daughters of the royal household is an old theory going back to the nineteenth century at least. Mommsen believed that when the *pontifex maximus* punished unchaste Vestals he was exercising a form

of *patria potestas*, which he had taken over from the former king (*Röm. Strafr.* 1899). In general see my remarks in J. Scheid (ed.), *Le délit religieux dans la cité antique* (Rome 1981), 30 (with bibliography). For a dissenting view, J.A. North, *CAH²* VII.2 (1989), 608, 613.

97 Coarelli's radical revision of the topography of the Sacra Via has been criticised, e.g. by F.E. Brown, *Gnomon* 56 (1984), 381–3; F. Castagnoli, *Quad. Top.* 10 (1984), 99–114; F. Buranelli La Pera, L. D'Elia, *BCom* 91 (1986), 241–62.

98 The importance of these epithets is rightly stressed by Coarelli, *Foro romano* I (1983), 77.

10 PATRICIANS AND PLEBEIANS

1 I have dealt with these issues in more detail in Raaflaub (ed.), *Social Struggles* (1986), 73–6; and in I.S. Moxon *et al.* (eds), *Past Perspectives* (1986), 67–86.

2 Mommsen, *Hist. Rome²* (1864) I, 59ff. (ch. 6); Niebuhr, *Hist. Rome³* (1837) I, 306ff., 309ff. N.D. Fustel de Coulanges, *The Ancient City* (Baltimore 1980), passim, esp. 221ff., 257ff.

3 For an excellent survey of relevant publications down to 1910 see G. Bloch, *Rev. Hist.* 106 (1911), 241–75; 107 (1912), 1–42. Recent surveys include De Martino, *Storia* I² (1972), 73ff.; Richard, *Origines* (1978), 27ff.; and see the important discussions of Momigliano, *Sesto contributo*, 482f., and Ampolo, in *Gli etruschi e Roma* (1981), 48ff.

4 Most notoriously, G. Sergi, *Origine e diffusione della stirpe mediterranea* (Rome 1895), and above all *Arii e Italici: attorno all'Italia preistorica* (Turin 1898). See also G. Boni, *Atti del congresso internaz. di scienze storiche* 5 (Rome 1904) and F. Bernhöft, *Staat und Recht in der römischen Königszeit* (Stuttgart 1882). Among English-language publications, W. Ridgeway, *PBA* (1907–8), 3–60, and R.W. Husband, *TAPhA* 40 (1909), 63–81, make grim reading.

5 Boni, *Atti del congresso internaz. di scienze storiche* 5 (1904), 493–584.

6 For a critical review of these theories, which still recur in modern publications (e.g. N. Rouland, *Rome, democratie impossible?* (Paris 1981), 20), see C. Ampolo, in C.R. Whittaker (ed.), *Pastoral Economies in Classical Antiquity* (Cambridge 1988), 120–33.

7 Matriarchal natives and patriarchal Aryan invaders: F. Bernhöft, *Staat und Recht*, following the ideas of J.J. Bachofen, *Das Mutterrecht* (Stuttgart 1861), 166. Cf. J. Binder, *Die Plebs* (Leipzig 1909), 403. Critical discussion in De Martino, *Storia* I² (1972), 81–4.

8 For instance A. Alföldi's ideas on the origins of the Roman population are based on the supposed link between the early Latins and the nomadic tribes of eastern Europe; see in particular his *Die Struktur des voretruskischen Römerstaates* (Heidelberg 1974), which adopts methods and assumptions that would not have been out of place in the 1880s.

9 De Sanctis, *StdR* I² (1960), 219ff.

10 H. Last, *JRS* 35 (1945), 30–48; A. Magdelain, in *Hommages J. Bayet* (Brussels 1964), 427–73; Ranouil, *Recherches sur le patriciat* (1977); Palmer, *Archaic Community* (1970), 197ff., 243ff., 290ff.

11 A. Momigliano, *RSI* 79 (1967), 297–312 (= *Quarto contributo*, 437–54; English translation in Raaflaub (ed.), *Social Struggles* (1986), 175–97); in *Entretiens* 13 (1967), 199–221 (= *Quarto contributo*, 419–36); *Labeo* 23 (1977), 7–15 (= *Sesto contributo*, 477–86); J.C. Richard, *Origines* (1978); in Raaflaub (ed.), *Social Struggles* (1986), 105–29; in *Bilancio critico* (1993), 27–41.

12 K. Raaflaub in Raaflaub (ed.), *Social Struggles* (1986), 198–243; in *Bilancio critico* (1993), 129–57.

13 Ateius Capito, ap. Gellius 10.20.5, and cf. 17.21.27. Notice also Livy's habit of describing an individual patrician as 'a man of patrician lineage' (*vir patriciae gentis*) 3.27.1; 3.33.9; 7.39.12. It is of course illegitimate to deduce from these texts, as many Romanists do, that plebeians did not have *gentes*.

14 Notice, however, that the sources do not use *pater* in the singular in this context. As a collective term meaning 'senators' or 'patricians', *patres* is always plural. In the singular it has the sense of 'father' (with all the complications involved in that term).

15 Niebuhr, *Hist. Rome*³ (1837) I, 338ff. The Senate of the middle Republic was indeed a body of 300 men, but it is uncertain how far back this goes (Romulus' senate supposedly contained only 100 men) or what connection there was, if any, between the 300 senators and the 30 curiae.

16 P. Bonfante, *Scritti* I (1926), 1–17; *Storia*⁴ (1957) I, 67ff.; P. De Francisci, *Primordia civitatis* (1959), 175ff. The alternative phrase *princeps gentis* (e.g. De Martino, *Storia* I² (1972), 15) is based on a complete misunderstanding of the texts in which it occurs (viz. Cic., *Fam.* 9.21.2; Suet., *Tib.* 1; cf. Dion. Hal. 6.69.1 – ὁ ἡγεμὼν τοῦ γένους), where it clearly means either 'the ancestor of the *gens*' (Suet., Dion. Hal.), or 'the first of the *gens* to achieve curule office' (Cic.).

17 Willems, *Sénat* (1878), I. 38; Cornelius, *Untersuchungen* (1940), 93; De Martino, *Storia* I² (1972), 265–6; Ogilvie, *Comm.* (1965), 236; E.S. Staveley, *Historia* 32 (1983), 29–30; A. Drummond, in *CAH*² VII.2 (1989), 181. The only text to support this intepretation is Isidorus, *Orig.* 9.4.11, a secondary source with no independent authority. Cicero's reference to a *pater conscriptus* (*Phil.* 13.28) is ironical. This text 'ist natürlich ein Scherz', said Mommsen (*Staatsr.* III. 863 n.), who knew a joke when he saw one.

18 For the formula *qui patres quique conscripti* see Livy 2.1.11; Festus. p. 304 L. For the view stated in the text cf. Mommsen, *Staatsr.* III (1887), 836ff.; A. O'Brien Moore, *RE* Suppl. 6, 674; A. Magdelain, in *Hommages J. Bayet* (1964), 453; Momigliano, *Quarto contributo*, 423ff.; Richard, *Origines* (1978), 479ff.; D. Musti, *MEFRA* 101 (1989), 207–27.

19 The enrolment of *conscripti* is traced back to the regal period by several sources, in one case to Romulus. The evidence is set out by Ogilvie, *Comm.* (1965), 236.

20 Momigliano, *Terzo contributo*, 591 n. 93, citing Mommsen, *Röm. Forsch.* I (1864), 228 n.; Richard, *Origines* (1978), 233f.

21 Willems, *Sénat* II (1878), 121ff.; U. Coli, *Regnum* (1950) = *Scritti* I (1973), 387.

22 These distinctive features of the domestic *consilium* are stressed by Mommsen, *Staatsr.* III.2 (1888), 1028f., in contrast to the Senate of the late Republic. The distinction makes it clear that the early Roman Senate was different from its late republican counterpart precisely because it was more like a *consilium*.

23 Festus. p. 290 L. On the Lex Ovinia in general, see p. 369. The interpretation of the penultimate sentence is problematic, but does not affect the present discussion. I prefer the reading *iurati* to the corrupt *curiati* (below, p. 370 n. 3) and the widely accepted emendation *curiatim*. If this is right, it removes one of the main supports for the theory that the Senate was connected with the curiae.

24 Cf. Momigliano, *Quarto contributo*, 439: 'Le scoperte degli antiquari lasciarono di solito indifferenti gli storici; né mai gli antiquari, come Varrone, riconobbero loro compito di far saltare in aria i racconti degli storici come avrebbero potuto.'

25 This was the 'patrician senate', whose separate existence was divined by Mommsen, *Röm. Forsch.* I (1864), 218–49 ('Der Patriciersenat der Republik').

26 Palmer, *Archaic Community* (1970), 197–9, makes much of a supposed distinction between *patres* and *patricii*.

27 Livy 3.11.6–14.5. On the episode, see A.W. Lintott, *Violence in Republican Rome* (Oxford 1968), 56–60. Ogilvie, *Comm.* (1965), ad loc., dismisses it as an invention, which cannot be right. For the present discussion what matters is the use of the word *patres*. Note incidentally that Kaeso's patrician followers are described as his *sodales* (3.14.3, with Ogilvie's note), and in Dion. Hal. 10.5.1 as ἑταῖροι.

28 The Loeb translation (B.O. Foster) translates *patres* variously as 'senators' and 'patricians'. The *iuniores, seniores patrum* (3.14.2–3) are wrongly taken to be younger and older senators! In 3.11.7 *in medio patrum agmine* cannot mean 'in the midst of a band of senators' (Foster). In this scene the (young) patricians were literally lined up for battle.

29 Cic., *Rep.* 2.63: *conubia . . . ut ne plebi cum patribus essent.* Liv. 4.4.5: *ne conubium patribus cum plebe esset.* On this clause, see pp. 255, 291–2.

30 Quite apart from its use as an honorific title for gods, e.g. Mars and Jupiter, the Latin word *pater* has five distinct meanings: (1) father in a biological sense: a begetter of children; (2) 'father' in a legal sense: a legally independent male citizen (technically defined as an adult male citizen with no surviving male ascendants); (3), usually in the plural, *patres*: patricians, members of the patrician order; (4) also plural: senators (short for *patres conscripti*, or *patres et conscripti*); (5) also plural: patrician senators (*patres* as opposed to *conscripti*).

31 The explanation is obvious enough to anyone who has read Thorstein Veblen. Horses are expensive to maintain and of little practical value (we are not dealing with carthorses here). They are therefore natural objects of conspicuous consumption. Momigliano is misleading when he suggests that mounted aristocracies are a peculiarity of the European Middle Ages (*Quarto contributo*, 377–402, esp. 397).

32 Mommsen, *Staatsr.* III.1 (1887), 245; E. Meyer, *Kl. Schriften* 2 (1924), 279 n. 3; De Sanctis, *StdR* I (1907), 247–8; H. Hill, *The Roman Middle Class* (Oxford 1952), 208–11; F. De Martino, *PdP* 35 (1980), 143–60. There is a big difference between saying, as these scholars do, that the cavalry centuries were reserved for patricians, and saying that the patriciate was an aristocracy of knights, which is Alföldi's view. He argues in particular that the 300 *celeres* (mounted guards) organised the coup to overthrow the kings, and set themselves up as an exclusive aristocracy: see A. Alföldi, *Der frührömische Reiteradel* (Baden-Baden 1952); in *Festschr. K. Schefold* (Berne 1967), 13–45; *Historia* 17 (1968), 444–60.

33 Festus p. 290 L, where we have to understand *centuriae* before *procum patricium*, which is only partially justified by Cicero, *Orator* 156. For reasons explained above, I take *patricium* to be an adjective qualifying *procum*. For full discussion of these difficult texts, see Momigliano, *Quarto contributo*, 377–402.

34 H. Last, *JRS* 35 (1945), 30–3; P. De Francisci, *Primordia civitatis* 776–85; E.S. Staveley, *Historia* 32 (1983), 24–57.

35 De Sanctis, *StdR* I (1907), 224 55, esp. 234.

36 De Martino, *Storia* I² (1972), 75–7, on the economic basis of class divisions in early Rome, a view that was first advanced by G.W. Botsford, *Political Science Quarterly* 21 (1906), 489–526; 22 (1907), 663–92. On the archaeological evidence, C. Ampolo, *DdA* 4–5 (1970–1), 46–9. See further J. C. Richard, in Raaflaub (ed.), *Social Struggles* (1986), 110ff., with further bibliography.

37 H. Jordan, *Die Könige im alten Italien* (Berlin 1887), 15ff., taken up by H. Last, *JRS* 35 (1945), 30f. Some scholars are impressed by the fact that certain toponyms within the city of Rome, for instance the hills named Oppius, Cispius and Caelius, are also personal names belonging to plebeian gentes (C. Huelsen, *RPAA* 2 (1923–4), 83ff.; cf. Last). To this one can only say: so what?

38 Momigliano, *Terzo contributo*, 590–1; *Quarto contributo*, 427; Richard, *Origines* (1978), 235–8. Contra: A. Magdelain, *REL* 40 (1962), 220; Ogilvie, *Comm.* (1965),

87–8; Staveley, *Historia* 32 (1983), 38; see further my comments in *Tria Corda* (1983), 105 and n. 10.

39 The exception is the Vestal Virgins, who included plebeians from at least as early as 483 BC (Livy 2.42.11, with Ogilvie's note). The priestly character of the patriciate is stressed in the interesting book by R.E. Mitchell, *Patricians and Plebeians* (Ithaca, N.Y. 1992).

40 Attus Navius: Livy 1.36.2–5; Dion. Hal. 3.71.1–5. See J. Linderski, *ANRW* II.16.3 (1986), 2207–8; M. Beard in *Images of Authority, Festschr. J. Reynolds*, ed. M.M. McKenzie and C.M. Roueché (Cambridge 1989), 50ff.

41 Enemies of Brutus the conspirator challenged this claim, on the grounds that the original Brutus had put his sons to death (see above, p. 216), and cannot therefore have had any descendants. But this argument, which is not conclusive, as Posidonius pointed out (Plut., *Brut.* 1.5), went against the generally accepted tradition and was a late (and maliciously inspired) variant. See Plutarch, *Brut.*, and Rawson, *Roman Culture* (1991), 490–1.

42 Interpolations in the *fasti*: Beloch, *Röm. Gesch.* (1926), 9–22; Werner, *Beginn röm. Rep.* (1963), 275ff. For a thorough refutation, A. Bernardi, *Athenaeum* 30 (1952), 12. Cf. Heurgon, *Rise of Rome* (1973), 165–6.

43 *Transitio ad plebem*: see Mommsen, *Röm. Forsch.* I (1864), 123ff.; B. Kübler, *RE* VIA (1936), 2154 s.v. 'transitio ad plebem'; Ranouil, *Recherches sur le patriciat* (1977), 160–6.

44 It is widely assumed that clients also took the names of their patrons, but there are no good grounds for this assumption, which does not accord with the meagre evidence we have (e.g. Plutarch, *Marius* 5.4).

45 De Sanctis, *StdR* II² (1960), 200 n. 71. A clear restatement of this view by A. Drummond, *CAH²* VII.2 (1989), 175f.

46 A. Sempronius Atratinus (cos. 497, 491) was certainly a patrician, since he is recorded as *interrex* in 482 (Dion. Hal. 8.90.4–5). His descendants served as consuls and consular tribunes down to the end of the fifth century, whereupon the family disappears from the *Fasti* until the end of the Republic, when C. Sempronius Atratinus (cos. suff. 34 BC) achieved prominence as a supporter of Mark Antony. Meanwhile, the plebeian Sempronii, starting with P. Sempronius Sophus (cos. 304), enjoyed enormous success in the last three centuries of the Republic. Ranouil, *Recherches sur le patriciat* (1977), 172–5, 218–20, gives full details.

47 As far as the Veturii are concerned, only one plebeian Veturius is certainly known, namely T. Veturius Calvinus (cos. 334, 321 BC), who was probably born a patrician but transferred to the *plebs* in order to give himself a chance of the consulship, as Münzer surmised: *Röm. Adelsparteien* (1921), 123; Ranouil, *Recherches sur le patriciat* (1977), 145–7. *Contra*: Beloch, *Röm. Gesch.* (1926), 344–5, who believed that all Veturii were patrician, and that in 334 and 321 both consuls were patricians, and Palmer, *Archaic Community* (1970), 294–6, who wrongly supposes that all Veturii were plebeian. See further I. Shatzman, *CQ* 23 (1972), 65–77. So too the plebeian Servilii were the consequence of a transition to the *plebs* by the sons of C. Servilius Geminus (IIIvir a.d.a. 218 BC): Ranouil, 226. It follows that the Claudii and Sempronii are the only known examples of plebeian consular families that had no known connection with their patrician namesakes.

48 Of the clans listed in Table 5, the following produced plebeian consuls in the later Republic: Aquilii, Cassii, Genucii, Junii, Minucii, Tullii, Volumnii.

49 Q. Antonius Merenda. See Ranouil, *Recherches sur le patriciat* (1977), 106, 111; Drummond, *CAH²* VII.2 (1989), 193f.

50 The greatest concentration of 'plebeian' consuls is to be found in the years 509–486 (probably twelve of them). But from 485 to 470 all consuls were patricians. During

this same period a new patrician clan, the Fabii, dominate the *Fasti*. These facts must be linked in some way; and it is not fanciful to connect them with the fall of Sp. Cassius. Cf. Heurgon, *Rise of Rome* (1973), 164.

51 P.E. Corbett, *The Roman Law of Marriage* (Oxford 1930), 50; Drummond, *CAH²* VII.2 (1989), 180, 184.

52 There is a major difficulty in the fact that Coriolanus, traditionally presented as an arrogant patrician, belonged to the ostensibly plebeian *gens Marcia*. There is no need to enter into a discussion of this complex issue, since the point about mixed marriages is established either way. Plutarch (*Coriolanus* 33.2-3) names Coriolanus' wife Virgilia, his mother Volumnia. This (certainly incorrect) version was followed by Shakespeare.

53 In essence this view goes back to Mommsen, *Staatsr.* III.1 (1887), 33-6, 78-80, who believed that originally *confarreatio* was the only legitimate form of marriage among Roman citizens (who were, on Mommsen's view, *ipso facto* patricians). A full discussion, with bibliography, by J. Linderski, in Raaflaub (ed.), *Social Struggles* (1986), 244-61 (though I do not share Linderski's view that *confarreatio* was limited to patricians).

54 K. Raaflaub in Raaflaub (ed.), *Social Struggles* (1986), 198, 243.

55 Cic., *Rep.* 2.58: *contra consulare imperium tribuni plebis ... constituti*. Incidentally this interpretation presupposes the existence of a dual collegiate consulship before 494 BC. Cicero and Livy (2.58.1) give the original number of tribunes as two, though other sources suggest that there were four or five: Ascon., *in Cornel.* p. 76 C; Diod. 11.68.8.

56 A comparable instance is the English word 'tory', originally a term of abuse meaning 'bandit'.

57 K. Raaflaub, in *Bilancio critico* (1993), 148, misrepresents my view of this matter. I did not say (in *Tria Corda* (1983), 106, 118) that the plebeians were either wholly or mainly an urban group, but on the contrary that they were 'undifferentiated', by which I meant that they included all sorts, including poor peasants, as is clear from the sentence which Raaflaub quotes from my article.

58 Thus Momigliano, *Quarto contributo*, 434. The reconstruction offered in the text owes much to Momigliano's work, and to the development of it given in Richard's monumental study (*Origines*, 1978).

59 K. Raaflaub, in *Bilancio critico* (1993), 150.

60 Momigliano, *Quarto contributo* 430, 444f. *Populus* in the sense of 'heavy infantry' is found in the title *magister populi* (Cic., *Rep.* 1.63; Varro, *LL* 5.82; 6.61; Festus. p. 216 L), in the verb *populari* ('to devastate'), and the formula in the *carmen saliare* (Festus p. 224 L): *pilumnoe poploe* ('pilum-bearing people').

61 Dion. Hal. 6.63.3; cf. 5.67.5; 5.68.5. These references are to fictional speeches, but they indicate that Dionysius, or his source, envisaged the army as consisting largely of clients of the patricians who were separate from the *plebs*.

62 Cf. Momigliano, *Quarto contributo*, 446.

63 See my comments in *Tria Corda* (1983), 105.

64 'A state within a state' was Mommsen's description of the plebeian organisation: *Staatsr.* III (1887), 145. The notion goes back ultimately to the sources themselves – e.g. Livy 2.44.9: *duas civitates ex una factas, suos cuique parti magistratus, suas leges esse* ('Two states had been created out of one; each faction had its own magistrates, its own laws'). Cf. 3.19.9.

65 The parable is not as inept as it sounds (and perhaps Menenius was not as foolish as Shakespeare presents him). He compared the patriciate to the belly, and argued that although it might appear a completely parasitic consumer of food acquired by the labour of the limbs, the limbs are in fact dependent on sustenance supplied by the belly through the bloodstream. The story, which presupposes quite

sophisticated medical knowledge, may be of Greek origin, as argued by W. Nestle, *Klio* 21 (1927), 350–60.

66 Diod. 11.68.8. The word order makes it clear that what happened for the first time was not the election of tribunes, but the election of four of them. Thus Ogilvie, *Comm.* (1965), 382.

67 Livy 3.30.7, stating that two tribunes were elected from each of the five 'Servian' classes. This looks like an inept attempt to explain the number of tribunes; it seems unlikely that the different property classes would need to be represented among the *plebs*; in any case, there are good reasons for thinking (cf. above, p. 187) that the division of the people into five property classes dates only from the end of the fifth century.

68 Festus p. 422 L: *sacratae leges sunt, quibus sanctum est, qui[c]quid adversus eas fecerit sacer alicui deorum sicut familia pecuniaque* ('Sacred laws are laws which have the sanction that anyone who breaks them becomes 'accursed' to one of the gods, together with his family and property'). The formula occurs in the Twelve Tables (VIII.21) and in the Forum Cippus, where it is probably directed against anyone who defiles the sanctuary. Thus Coarelli, *Foro romano* I (1983), 178.

69 For an excellent discussion see Ogilvie, *Comm.* (1965), 500–2, with earlier bibliography.

70 Livy 4.26.3; 7.41.4; 9.39.5; 10.38.2–12; 36.38.1. For discussion see F. Altheim, *Lex sacrata* (Amsterdam 1940); T.J. Cornell, *Mus. Helv.* 31 (1974), 199–202.

71 Cic., *Sest.* 79; Dion. Hal. 7.15.5; Dio 53.17.9.

72 Sulla's restriction of the veto: Cic., *Leg.* 3.22; Caes., *BC* 1.5; 1.7. On Sulla's attempt to restore the 'original form' of the tribunate, see my remarks in *Tria Corda* (1983), 116–17.

73 Cicero, *pro Cornelio ap.* Ascanius p. 67; Dion. Hal, 6.89.1; 9.41.2. See further Mommsen, *Straatsr.* III. 1 (1887), 151–2; Richard, *Origines* (1978), 559ff.

74 Stressed by Momigliano, *Quarto contributo*, 451f.; *Quinto contributo*, 328f. O. Cazenove in *Crise et transformation* (1990), 373–99.

75 Others include the Lex Icilia of 492 on the power of the tribunes (Dion. Hal. 7.17.5; Cic., *Sest.* 79), and the Lex Verginia of 457 increasing the number of tribunes to ten (Livy 3.30.5–7; Dion. Hal. 10.30.2–6).

76 Livy 3.31.1 speaks simply of a law *de Aventino publicando*; later he speaks of a *lex Icilia de Aventino* (3.32.7), evidently referring to the same law, in view of Dion. Hal. 10.31–2. On this law see De Sanctis, *StdR* II² (1960), 23–5; Beloch, *Röm. Gesch.* (1926), 205–7; Ogilvie, *Comm.* (1965), 446–7; F. Serrao, *Legge e società* I (1981), 121–73; Flach, *Die Gesetze* (1994), 95–8.

77 This point is most clearly set out by Binder, *Die Plebs* (1909), 473f.

78 F. Serrao, however, accepts the account of Dionysius as fully historical: *Legge e società* I (1981), 129f.

79 Dion. Hal. 10.32.4. On the importance of this kind of documentary evidence see C. Ampolo, in *Tria Corda* (1983), 9–26.

80 Livy 3.32.7: *postremo concessum patribus, modo ne lex Icilia de Aventino aliaeque sacratae leges abrogarentur.*

81 De Sanctis, *StdR* II² (1960), 23–5.

82 Cicero (II *Verr.* 5.36) calls the Plebeian Games the earliest of all, and it is possible that games as such were a novelty first introduced into Rome by the *plebs*. Traditionally the *ludi Romani* were instituted by Tarquinius Priscus (Livy 1.35.9) or by Superbus (Dion. Hal. 6.29); these intermittent performances were distinguished by Dionysius from the regular annual games first set up after Lake Regillus together with the temple of Ceres, Liber and Libera (6.10.1; 6.17.2). This fact led A. Piganiol to connect the origin of the *ludi Romani* with the *plebs*: A. Piganiol, *Recherches sur les jeux romains* (Strasburg 1923), 75ff.

83 Cf. A. Drummond, *CAH*² VII.2 (1989), 226.

84 H. Le Bonniec, *Le culte de Cérès à Rome* (Paris 1958), 279ff. for an exhaustive discussion.

85 O. de Cazenove, in *Crise et transformation* (1990), 384, suggests Cumae (the whole article, pp.373–99, is important on the early history of the cult).

86 Le Bonniec, *Culte de Cérès*, 381ff., argues for a third-century date on the basis of a passage of the highly unreliable Arnobius, *Adv. nat.* 2.73, who appears to state that the *sacra* of Ceres were introduced 'shortly before' the cult of the Magna Mater (209 BC).

87 On the original meaning of *thesmophoros* see W. Burkert, *Greek Religion* (Oxford 1985), 243f. Demeter as lawgiver: Callimachus, *Hymn.* 6.18; Diod. 1.14.4; 25.1; Cic., II *Verr.* 5.187; Ov., *Met.* 5.343.

88 Alföldi, *Early Rome* (1965), 94: 'an obvious forgery'; Drummond, *CAH*² VII.2 (1989), 225: 'difficult to accept'.

89 Zonaras 7.15. The same tradition in Pomponius (*Dig.* I.2.2.21): *ut essent qui aedibus praeessent, in quibus omnia scita sua plebs deferebat, duos ex plebe constituerunt, qui etiam aediles appellati sunt.* 'They chose two men from the *plebs* to be in charge of the temple, in which all resolutions of the *plebs* were kept, and they were even called *aediles.*'

90 Drummond, *CAH*² VII.2 (1989), 241–2. For the 'state within the state', see above, n. 64.

91 Tacitus, our source for this innovation (*Annals* 11.22), says that quaestors had formerly been chosen by the consuls, and that the institution went back to the time of the kings. This may be a reference to judicial officers called *quaestores parricidii*, who prosecuted cases of homicide and are referred to in the Twelve Tables (IX.4). Whether these *quaestores parricidii* were the forerunners of the regularly elected quaestors, or remained a separate institution, is unknown. For discussion see Drummond, *CAH*² VII.2 (1989), 195ff.

92 Essential data can be found in E. Pais, *Fasti triumphales populi Romani* (2nd edn, Turin 1930), 489ff., showing that 70 out of 86 recorded temples down to the age of Augustus were founded in consequence of military victories. This important point has recently been restated by C. Ampolo, in Eder (ed.), *Staat und Staatlichkeit* (1990), 482–9, whom I have followed in the text.

93 The general point is made by Cicero, *Rep.* 2.58. Livy (2.23) and Dionysius (6.26) both give the story of 'the distinguished veteran'; their versions agree very closely.

94 On the institution of *tributum* see p. 187. The detail about taxation also means that the story cannot be a fabrication of the Gracchan age, because at that period the *tributum* was no longer being levied on Roman citizens in Italy.

95 Specifically, an episode in 385 BC, Livy 6.14.3–6. Cf. L. Peppe, *Esecuzione* (1981), 40ff., 99ff. The motif of the long-serving veteran also appears in other contexts, e.g. Livy 3.58.8 and, especially, 42.34.

96 Dion. Hal. 6.83.4f.; 6.88.3; Dio fr. 17 vol. I, p. 47 Boiss.; Zonar. 7.14; *Inscriptiones Italiae* XIII.3, nos. 60, 78, all suggest that debtors were released from servitude as part of the compromise offered by Agrippa Menenius; but this looks like a secondary addition introduced to make sense of the story (Drummond, *CAH*² VII.2 (1989), 214), though there may be something in it.

97 Garnsey, *Famine and Food Supply* (1988).

98 Listed by Garnsey, *Famine and Food Supply* (1988), 168–72, with full discussion. See also Momigliano, *Quarto contributo*, 331–49; Ogilvie, *Comm.* (1965), 256–7; Frederiksen, *Campania* (1984), 164–6; C. Virlouvet, *Famines et émeutes à Rome* (1985), 11ff.

99 E.g. Livy 3.31.1. Cato, *Origines* IV.1, makes it clear that the *Annales maximi* recorded shortages and eclipses as a matter of routine (that is the sense of *quotiens*

annona cara, etc.). Drummond's scepticism (*CAH²* VII.2 (1989), 133–4) is perverse.

100 The possibility of a connection is widely accepted, e.g. by Le Bonniec, *Culte de Cérès* (1958), 243ff., and has been explored in detail by D. van Berchem, *BCAR* 63 (1935), 91–5, and A. Momigliano, *Quarto contributo*, 344ff. The need for caution is stressed by O. de Cazenove, in *Crise et transformation* (1990), 378 and nn. (with further bibliography).

101 Garnsey, *Famine and Food Supply* (1988), 170–1, with bibliography in n. 10, to which add Cornell in Raaflaub (ed.), *Social Struggles* (1986), 58–61. The main sources for the episode are Livy 4.13–16; Dion. Hal. 12.1–4. Livy calls Maelius an equestrian, meaning that he was not a senator or a patrician. A Sp. Maelius is recorded as tribune in 436 (Livy 4.21.3–4); Momigliano speculates that he may be the same man, and that the story of his assassination should be redated (*Quarto contributo*, 338f.).

102 The best account in English is in Momigliano, *Studies on Modern Scholarship* (1994), 225–36. For a fully documented study see L. Capogrossi Colognesi, *La terra in Roma antica* (Rome 1981).

103 E.g. Terracina, in 329 BC (Livy 8.21.11). The practice is also reflected in the use of the word *centuria* for an area of land measuring 200 *iugera* (i.e. 100 minimum plots). On Romulus' distribution see Varro, *RR* 1.10.2; Pliny, *n.h.* 18.7. Modern discussions include: L. Capogrossi Colognesi, *La terra in Roma antica* (1981); E. Gabba, *RIL* 112 (1978), 250–8; M. Crawford, *Coinage and Money* (1985), 24.

104 Mommsen, *Staatsr.* III.1 (1887), 22–7. An important element of this re-construction was the statement of Pliny (*n.h.* 19.50) that in the Twelve Tables (VII.3) the term *heredium* (i.e. the traditional 2-*iugera* plot?) stood for the *hortus* (= 'garden'). Fundamental criticisms of Mommsen's theory were made by R. von Pöhlmann, *Gesch. der sozialen Frage und des Sozialismus in der antiken Welt* (3rd edn, Munich 1925) II, 328–40.

105 The main accounts of this process occur in sources dealing with the background to the Gracchan crisis, in particular Appian, *B.C.* I.7; Plutarch, *Ti.Gracch.* 8; both must be referring to *ager publicus*, since they refer to the *lex de modo agrorum* (i.e. the Lex Licinia of 367 BC?) as an attempt to halt the trends they were describing.

106 Cassius Hemina fr. 17 P: *quicumque propter plebitatem agro publico eiecti sunt* ('All those who, because they were plebeians, were evicted from public land'). Drummond's statement, *CAH²* VII.2 (1989), 238, that this is 'clearly [*sic*] retrojected from later abuses' is unjustified, especially as Hemina was writing before Ti. Gracchus' tribunate. G. Forsythe, *Phoenix* 44 (1990), 334, argues unconvincingly against this dating.

107 B. Niese, *Hermes* 23 (1888), 410–23; Beloch, *Röm. Gesch.* (1926), 344; Ogilvie, *Comm.* (1965), 340; Flach, *Die Gesetze* (1994), nos. 16, 20, 36, 48, 49, 50, 52, 62c.

108 Examples of unembellished notices: Livy 4.12.4; 4.43.6; 4.52.2; 5.53.2; etc. A list (not fully complete) of recorded agrarian proposals to 367 BC can be found in Flach, *Die Gesetze* (1994); refs in previous note.

109 De Martino, *Storia economica* I (1979), 15.

110 E. Badian, *ANRW* I.1 (1972), 699.

111 See A. Santilli in F. Serrao (ed.), *Legge e società nella repubblica romana* I (Naples 1981), 281–306.

112 That Italians from the allied communities were to be included among recipients of Gracchus' allotments is the only possible interpretation of Appian's account, and I agree with Gabba that Dionysius' version of the Sp. Cassius affair is an indirect confirmation of this: *Athenaeum* 42 (1964), 29–41. Incidentally the formula 'the allies and the Latin name' (*socii et nomen Latinum*) (Livy 2.41.6)

was current usage in the Gracchan period, but is anachronistic for 486 BC, when Rome had no allies other than the Latins.

113 De Sanctis, *StdR* II² (1960), 8–9.

114 De Sanctis based his argument partly on the notice of Diodorus (11.37.7) that Cassius was executed after being convicted of aiming at tyranny; but Diodorus is not necessarily the pure gold that he was once thought to be (see above, p. 3). One might equally rely on the bare statement of Cicero, *Phil.* 2.114: *Sp. Cassius auctor legis agrariae propter suspicionem regni* (sc. *interfectus est*). Cf. De Martino, *Storia economica* I (1980), 14–15.

11 THE TWELVE TABLES

1 Cic., *Rep.* 2.1.3. I have discussed this passage in H. McK. Blake *et al.* (eds), *Papers in Italian Archaeology* I (1978), 135–6; and briefly in *JRS* 66 (1976), 261.

2 Dionysius says (10.58.4) that three – Q. Poetelius, K. Duilius and Sp. Oppius – were plebeian. Moderns would add L. Minucius, T. Antonius and M' Rabuleius to the list. Livy (4.3.17) seems to have thought that all were patricians.

3 Beloch, *Röm. Gesch.* (1926), 236ff.; Ogilvie, *Comm.* (1965), 451, 461–2 (with earlier bibliog.); A. Drummond, *CAH²* VII.2 (1989), 114.

4 Livy 3.37.4; Dion. Hal. 10.60.5–6 and esp. 11.6.5. On this see J. von Ungern Sternberg in Raaflaub (ed.), *Social Struggles* (1986), 95ff.

5 The theory goes back to Niebuhr, *Hist. Rome³* (1837), II. 334; cf. Schwegler, *Röm. Gesch.* III (1858), 10; recently revived by De Martino, *Storia* I² (1972), 308. Mommsen (whom I have followed) attacked it on the grounds that it has no support in the sources; he argued, moreover, that the Decemvirate must have been open to plebeians from the start: *Röm. Forsch.* I (1864), 296.

6 The clause about intercalation is normally entered as Table XI.2, with Table XII containing a ragbag of odds and ends. But the traditional order is partly conventional, and there is no clear evidence about what Table XII contained (except for the rules concerning 'noxal surrender', a means of making slaves and persons *in potestate* liable for damages – XII.2). What we do know is that intercalation was dealt with in one of the last two tables – Sempronius Tuditanus *ap.* Macrobius, *Sat.* 1.13.21.

7 Livy 3.57.10; Dion. Hal. 10.57.7. Diodorus 12.26.1 seems to say that Valerius and Horatius were themselves the authors of Tables XI and XII.

8 This seems to me the only way to make sense of Polybius' comment that the cycle of constitutions (by which kingship degenerated into tyranny, aristocracy into oligarchy, etc.) applies especially to Rome (6.9.12–14). On this see Poma, *Tra legislatori e tiranni* (1984), 79ff.

9 J. von Ungern Sternberg, in Raaflaub (ed.), *Social Struggles* (1986), 95ff. argues that the 'common source of Livy and Dionysius' must have been writing after 37 BC, because their reference to the Decemvirs refusing to give up power reflects the action of the Triumvirs in that year. But many regimes have refused to give up power after the expiry of their mandate. Ungern Sternberg himself cites the example of Hitler in 1943 (p. 97), and thus effectively destroys his own argument.

10 Traces of an anti-Claudian tradition are evident enough in the surviving accounts, as Mommsen showed: *Röm. Forsch.* I (1864), 285–318. But Mommsen did not on that account reject the second Decemvirate, or the story of Verginia, or any other substantive element of the narrative. See further T.P. Wiseman, *Clio's Cosmetics* (1979), 57–139; and my review in *JRS* 72 (1982), 203–6.

11 The anti-Claudian tradition need not be the work of a late republican annalist; it could equally be the product of family rivalry going back to the fourth and third

centuries. As for the names, it is possible that in the earliest versions of the story the dramatis personae were not named, but referred to simply as 'a maiden' and 'one of the Decemvirs', as in Diodorus (12.24.2–4); cf. Ogilvie, *Comm.* (1965), 477. The widespread notion that in the original version Verginia was a patrician is based on a mistranslation of a phrase in Diodorus (12.24.2). See e.g. E. Täubler, *Untersuchungen z. Gesch. des Decemvirats* (1922), 21–2; Beloch, *Röm. Gesch.* (1926), 244; Gundel, *RE* VIIIA.2 (1958), s.v. Verginius, 1351–2; Ogilvie, *Comm.* (1965); Ungern Sternberg in Raaflaub (ed.), *Social Struggles* (1986), 91. For the correct interpretation, E. Pais, *Storia critica* II (1913), 205 n. 1; J. Bayet, *Tite-Live, Hist. romaine* III (Paris 1942), 134.

12 Momigliano, in *Entretiens* 13 (1967), 357; in general see G. Crifò, *ANRW* I.2 (1972), 124–7.

13 Table VIII.3,4. The word is a direct borrowing from the Greek ποινή (= 'recompense', 'requital'), and has given us the words 'penal', 'punish', etc.

14 Pliny, *n.h.* 34.21; Strabo 14.1.25, p. 642 C; Pomponius, *Dig.* 1.2.2.4. Strabo's statement that Hermodorus was known to Heraclitus (early fifth century) makes the chronology strained, but not impossible.

15 See above all E. Pais, *Ricerche storiche* I (Rome 1915), 147–79. His conclusion, that the Twelve Tables date from the second century BC, seems quite absurd today. More recently see De Martino, *Storia* I² (1972), 304 (with extensive bibliog. in n. 28); F. Wieäcker, *Studi Volterra* III (Milan 1971), 757–84; P. Siewert, *Chiron* 8 (1978), 331–44; M. Ducos, *L'influence grec sur la loi des douze tables* (Paris 1978) (generally dismissive).

16 Livy 3.35.7. The existence of another college of plebeian officers suggests that the plebeian organisation was even more complex than is usually recognised. The *iudices decemviri* are sometimes seen as forerunners of the later board for judging lawsuits (*decemviri stlitibus iudicandis*): thus Mommsen, *Staatsr.* II³ (1887), 605, but see Ogilvie, *Comm.* (1965), 501, for a different view.

17 Livy 3.55.8–11. For a good discussion see Ogilvie, *Comm.* (1965), 502–3.

18 E. Pais, *Storia critica* I.2 (1913), 465; De Sanctis, *StdR* II² (1960), 49; E.S. Staveley, *Historia* 3 (1955), 412–15; J. Bleicken, *ZSS* 76 (1959), 356ff.; Ogilvie, *Comm.* (1965), 252; Drummond, *CAH²*, VII.2 (1989), 312ff.; Flach, *Die Gesetze* (1994), 59–62, 216–18. *Contra*: De Martino, *Storia* I² (1972), 312ff.; B. Santalucia, in Momigliano and Schiavone (eds), *Storia di Roma* I (1988), 437f.

19 De Sanctis, *StdR* II² (1960), 50 and 208f.; J. Bleicken, *Das Volkstribunat* (1968), 13ff.; *Lex publica* (1975), 217–25; De Martino, *Storia* I² (1972), 373–7; M. Elster, *Studien zur Gesetzgebung* (1976), 75–119; A. Drummond, *CAH²* VII.2 (1989), 223; Flach, *Die Gesetze* (1994), 213–15.

20 This calculation is based on the laws listed in Rotondi, *Leges publicae populi Romani* (1912), a work that is not to be relied upon in detail.

21 Cf. E.S. Staveley, *Athenaeum* 33 (1955), 3–31; Ogilvie, *Comm.* (1965), 498–9; Scullard, *History of the Roman World*⁴ (1980), 469–71.

22 A. Drummond, *CAH²* VII.2 (1989), 223.

23 A Lex Trebonia apparently laid down that tribunician elections should not be brought to an end until ten tribunes had been elected: Livy 3.65.4; Diod. 12.25.3; and a Lex Duilia laid down the death penalty for anyone 'who left the plebs without tribunes or declared the election of magistrates not subject to appeal' (Livy 3.59.2; Dion. Hal. 11.46.5). See Flach, *Die Gesetze* (1994), 221–2.

24 Dion. Hal. 10.57.7; Diod. 12.26.1; Livy 3.57.10. Pomponius (*Dig.* 1.2.2.4) says they were inscribed on tablets of ivory: *in tabulas eboreas*, which editors have emended to *in tabulas roboreas* ('on tablets of oak'), which sounds more plausible, although whether it comes closer to what Pomponius actually wrote may be questioned.

25 H.E. Dirksen, *Übersicht der bisherigen Versuche zur Kritik u. Herstellung d.*

Textes d. Zwölf-Tafel Fragmente (Leipzig 1824). Dirksen was largely followed by R. Schoell, *Legis duodecim tabularum reliquiae* (Leipzig 1866), C.G. Bruns, *Fontes iuris Romani antiqui* (7th edn, Tübingen 1909), S. Riccobono, *Fontes iuris Romani antejustiniani*[2] (Florence 1941). English translation (with Latin text) by E.H. Warmington in *Remains of Old Latin* III (Loeb Classical Library, 1938), 424ff. A new edition, with English translation and commentary, will shortly be published in M.H. Crawford (ed.), *Roman Statutes* (London 1995?). I am grateful to Michael Crawford for allowing me to consult his edition in typescript.

26   The earliest commentary was by Sex. Aelius Paetus Catus (cos. 198 BC), on whom see F. D'Ippolito, *I giuristi e la città* (Naples 1978), 53–70; R.A. Bauman, *Lawgivers in Roman Republican Politics* (Munich 1983), 139–48; Rawson, *Intellectual Life* (1985), 202f.

27   Watson, *Rome of the Twelve Tables* (1975), 92–3.

28   According to Livy (2.5) the practice was instituted as a reward for the slave who revealed the conspiracy of the sons of Brutus (see above, p. 216). Scholars are divided on the question of whether *manumissio vindicta* existed before the Twelve Tables. In general see W.W. Buckland, *The Roman Law of Slavery* (Cambridge 1908), 441–2; H. Lévy-Bruhl, *Quelques problèmes du très ancien droit romain* (Paris 1934), 56–76; M. Kaser, *Das römische Privatrecht*[2] (1971), 115–19; ZSS 61 (1941), 153–86. On different forms of manumission see D. Daube, *JRS* 36 (1946), 57–75.

29   H. Lévy-Bruhl, *Quelques problèmes* (1934), 16. The whole article, 'Théorie de l'esclavage', 16–33, is fundamental.

30   Alföldi, *Early Rome* (1965), 295.

31   This conclusion supports, and is itself supported by, the tradition that the seventeen rural tribes had been established by the early fifth century, since the territory of at least two, the Romilia and the Galeria, were on the right bank.

32   Gellius (20.1.48ff.) adds that the law indemnified the creditors in the event of their not cutting the man into pieces of exactly the right size (the Shylock problem: Shakespeare, *Merchant of Venice*, Act IV, scene 1, lines 325ff.).

33   Most obviously, that the creditors were entitled to divide, not the person of the insolvent debtor, but his property (Radin, *AJPh* 43 (1922), 40ff.; E. Gjerstad, *Early Rome* V (1973), 327). For a magico-religious interpretation, H. Lévy-Bruhl, *Quelques problèmes* (1934), 154–67. See also G. MacCormack, *TvR* 36 (1968), 509ff., arguing, most implausibly, that the debtor's body was cut up if he died within the period of sixty days.

34   Watson, *Twelve Tables* (1975), 123–4.

35   W. Eder, in Raaflaub (ed.), *Social Struggles* (1986), 262–300, accepted by W.V. Harris, *Ancient Literacy* (1989), 153.

36   E.g. Livy 7.19.5. See G. MacCormack, ZSS 84 (1967), 350–5.

37   There is an immense literature on *nexum* in works on Roman law, much of it incomprehensible and little of it useful to the social historian. I have found the following most valuable: L. Mitteis, 'Ueber das *Nexum*', ZSS 22 (1901), 96–125; F. De Zulueta, *Law Quarterly Review* 29 (1913), 137–53 (a masterpiece of lucidity); Watson, *Twelve Tables*, 111–24. Cf. my account in *CAH*[2], VII.2 (1989), 329–34. On debt-bondage as a social institution see above all M.I. Finley, *Economy and Society in Ancient Greece* (London 1981), 150–66; and the excellent pamphlet by J. Ennew, *Debt Bondage: a survey* (London 1981), published by the still active (and much-needed) Anti-Slavery Society, and available from Third World Publications, 151 Stratford Road, Birmingham B11 1RD, England.

38   Later this law was used as a dodge for releasing sons from paternal authority in a 'collusive' action – that is, one in which threefold sale and manumission were ceremoniously acted out among consenting parties by prior agreement. But this

is unlikely to have been the original purpose of the law, *pace* H. Lévy-Bruhl, *Nouvelles études sur le très ancien droit romain* (Paris 1947), 80ff.

39 R. Yaron, *TvR* 36 (1968), 57ff.; J.M. Kelly in *Daube Noster* (Edinburgh 1974), 183–6; H. Kaufman, *Die altrömische Miete* (Cologne 1964), 243f.

40 Watson, *Twelve Tables* (1975), 119–20.

41 On *patria potestas* see Mommsen, *Hist. Rome²* (1864) I, 59ff.; J.A. Crook, *CQ* 17 (1967), 113–22.

42 On the practice of infanticide see Brunt, *Italian Manpower* (1971), 148–54.

43 E. Gabba, *Athenaeum* 38 (1960), 175–225, and see above, p. 59 and n. 31.

44 J. Gardner, *Women in Roman Law and Society* (London 1986), 11.

45 Watson, *Twelve Tables* (1975), 9f.

46 Assuming, that is, that her husband had been *sui iuris*. If he had still been *in potestate*, she would have had to wait until the death of her husband's last surviving male ascendant before she achieved independence. In that case her tutor would be chosen from among her late husband's agnates. If her husband had been *sui iuris* (i.e. a *paterfamilias*), he could have given her in his will the right to choose her own tutor. A woman married without *manus* would be likely to achieve independence earlier, since fathers of married women were normally older than their husbands; but in that event her tutor would be chosen from her father's agnates, and might insist that she leave her property to her family of origin rather than to her own children.

47 Cf. M. Kaser, *Eigentum und Besitz im älterem römischen Recht* (2nd edn, Cologne 1956), 169–99; *Das altrömische Ius* (Göttingen 1949), 149ff., 160ff.

48 As I stated in Cornell and Matthews, *Atlas of the Roman World* (1982), 19.

49 For this and what follows, see C. Ampolo in C.R. Whittaker (ed.), *Pastoral Economies in Classical Antiquity* (Cambridge 1988), 120–33.

50 J.A. North, *CAH²* VII.2 (1989), 601.

51 R. Besnier, *RHDFE* 13 (1934), 405–63; L. Clerici, *Economia e finanza dei Romani* (Bologna 1943) 55–8; L.R. Ménager, *RIDA* ser. 3, 19 (1972), 367–97.

52 A. Piganiol, *Essai sur les origines de Rome* (Paris 1917); De Martino, *Storia* I² (1972), 39–43. For a recent restatement of Piganiol's view see N. Rouland, *Rome: démocratie impossible?* (1981), 20.

53 Dion. Hal. 10.50.2; Gellius, 11.1.2; Cic., *Rep.* 2.60; Festus, pp. 129 L, 220 L, 268–70 L; and see Crawford, *Coinage and Money* (1985), 19–20.

54 Crawford, *Coinage and Money* (1985), 19–20: 'I regard the whole apparatus of fines in kind recorded by the sources as so much learned speculation starting from the etymology of *pecunia* and cognate words.' Note that the derivation of *pecunia* from *pecus* is rejected by E. Benveniste, *Le vocabulaire des institutions indo-européennes* I (Paris 1969), 47ff.

55 Pliny, *n.h.* 33.43 (= Timaeus, *FGrHist* 566 F.61); Cassiodorus, *Variae* 7.32.4; Charis., *Inst. Gramm.* p. 105 Keil; *de vir. ill.* 7.8. See Momigliano, *Terzo contributo*, 649–56. For the interpretation offered in the text see Crawford, *Roman Republican Coinage* (1974) I, 35ff.; *Coinage and Money* (1985), 19; Thomsen, *King Servius* (1980), 202ff.

56 On 'ramo secco' bars: Crawford, *Coinage and Money* (1985), 3–6, with a map showing find spots (to which Satricum should now be added). The sixth-century date is assured by the archaeological context of a hoard found at Bitalemi in Sicily in the 1960s. For the link with Servius Tullius, C. Ampolo, *PdP* 29 (1974), 382–8, and in Momigliano and Schiavone (eds), *StdR* I (1988), 227–8.

57 This would hardly need saying were it not for the fact that some scholars persist in dating the centuriate reform to the late fifth century. See above, p. 184 n. 40.

58 E.g. A. Drummond, in A. Wallace-Hadrill (ed.), *Patronage in Ancient Society* (London 1989), 90.

59 General works on patronage (on which the literature is enormous) include E. Gellner and J. Waterbury (eds), *Patrons and Clients* (London 1977); J. Boissevain, *Friends of Friends* (Oxford 1974). The best accounts of patron-client relations in Roman society are those of E. Badian, *Foreign Clientelae* (Oxford 1958), and R. Saller, *Personal Patronage under the Early Empire* (Cambridge 1982). The modern fashion is to minimise (I think wrongly) the importance of patronage in Roman political life. See e.g. P.A. Brunt, in *The Fall of the Roman Republic and Other Essays* (Oxford 1988), 382–442. Drummond's useful survey of early Roman *clientela* (see previous note) is heavily dependent on Brunt.

60 Mommsen, *Hist. Rome*[2] (1864) I, 90ff.; *Staatsr.* III.1 (1887), 61f.; Fustel de Coulanges, *The Ancient City* (1980), 221f.; Gjerstad, *Early Rome* 5 (1973), 188ff.

61 See especially Plautus, *Menaechmi* 574–9:

> To have a large following of clients is everyone's ambition. Whether the clients are honest men or worthless is immaterial; nobody bothers about that; a client's wealth is what matters, not his reputation for honesty. A decent poor man is of no account at all, but a rich rogue is considered a most desirable client.

(trans. E.F. Watling, Penguin Classics)

61 Cf. my comments in *Tria Corda* (1983), 110.

12 WARS AND EXTERNAL RELATIONS, 509–345 BC

1 M. Torelli, *Storia degli Etruschi* (Bari 1981), 186–8; G. Colonna, in *Crise et transformation* (1990), 10–14 (with detailed bibliography).

2 The miraculous appearances of the Dioscuri at Lake Regillus and later in the Forum are mentioned by Cicero, *de nat. deor.* 2.6; Dion. Hal. 6.13; Plut., *Coriolanus* 3.4. Livy makes no reference to them, but instead mentions the vow of a temple to the Dioscuri by the dictator A. Postumius in the heat of the battle (2.20.12).

3 On the Lavinium inscription (CIL I[2] 4, 2833) see further F. Castagnoli, *Lavinium II: Le tredici are* (Rome 1975), 441–3; Dury-Moyaers, *Enée et Lavinium* (1981), 198–205; Dubourdieu, *Culte des Pénates* (1989), 285–972; Ross Holloway, *Archaeology* (1994), 130–4.

4 I. Nielsen, J. Zahle, *Acta Arch.* 56 (1985), 1–29; I. Nielsen, *Acta Arch.* 59 (1988), 1–14; *ARID* 19 (1990), 89–104; C. Grønne, *ARID* 19 (1990), 105–17; A. Naso, C. Grønne, in *GRT* (1990), 62–3. The temple was subsequently rebuilt under the emperor Tiberius; three standing columns from the later structure now constitute the most famous landmark in the Roman Forum.

5 A full account of epiphanies in Greek sources (with some later parallels) is given in W.K. Pritchett, *The Greek State at War* III (Berkeley 1979), 11–46. On supposed cases in the First World War, such as the 'Angel of Mons', note the cautionary remarks of P. Fussell, *The Great War and Modern Memory* (New York 1975), 115–16.

6 Cf. J.A.O. Larsen, *Representative Government in Greek and Roman History* (Berkeley 1966), 24–5.

7 On the Feriae Latinae and the early organisation of the Latins see above all Alföldi, *Early Rome* (1965), 1–46 (to be used with caution).

8 Dion. Hal. 4.26.5. The inscription should probably be identified with the *lex arae Dianae in Aventino* ('law of the altar of Diana on the Aventine'), which served as the model for all later sanctuaries of the same kind: CIL XII. 4333, etc. Mommsen, *Staatsr.* III.1 (1887), 614ff.; Thomsen, *King Servius* (1980), 303–4.

9 The cult statue: Strabo 4.1.5, p. 180 C. The coins: Crawford, *RRC* no. 448.3; cf. C. Ampolo, *PdP* 25 (1970), 200–10.

10 Alföldi, *Early Rome* (1965), 49–52 (with earlier bibliography); V. Ciccala, *RSA* 6–7 (1976–7), 301–5; Humbert, *Municipium* (1978), 66–7n.; Thomsen, *King Servius* (1980), 297–314; C. Ampolo, *PdP* 38 (1983), 321–6; in *Crise et transformation* (1990), 125–6.

11 L. Morpurgo, *Monumenti Antichi* 13 (1903), 297–368; *NSc* (1931), 237–305; E. Gjerstad, *Acta Arch.* 41 (1970), 99–107; G. De Palma, P. Pensabene, in *Enea nel Lazio* (1981), 19–27.

12 C. Ampolo, *PdP* 36 (1981), 219–33.

13 J.G. Frazer, *The Golden Bough*, 3rd edn, 12 vols (London 1911–15), esp. I, ch. 1.

14 I have explained my reasons for this opinion in *CAH*² VII.2 (1989), 273. For detailed arguments, see Thomsen, *King Servius* (1980), 313–14; C. Ampolo, *PdP* 38 (1983), 321–6.

15 See further *CAH*² VII.2 (1989), 274; C. Ampolo, in *Crise et transformation* (1990), 126–7.

16 Thus, rightly, Humbert, *Municipium* (1978), 68–9 (with bibliography).

17 It is clear that Dionysius gives only a brief summary of what must have been a longer document. Elsewhere he states that the treaty established a relationship of 'isopolity' between Romans and Latins (6.63.4; 7.53.5, etc.), no doubt a reference to the 'Latin rights' discussed earlier (p. 295). On 'isopolity' see the extensive discussion of Humbert, *Municipium* (1978), 85ff.

18 Thus e.g. Schwegler, *Röm. Gesch.* II (1855), 346ff., and many others. The view of Rosenberg, *Hermes* 54 (1919), 147ff. and Alföldi, *Early Rome* (1965), 119, that there was a system of rotation by which all Latin cities, including Rome, took turns to hold the command, can be ruled out as incompatible with the text of the *foedus Cassianum*.

19 Thus Mommsen, *Staatsr.* III.1 (1887), 619 n. 2.

20 De Sanctis, *StdR* II² (1960), 98.

21 Roman antiquarians derived their name from the Sabine or Marsic word *herna* = 'rock' (Schol. Veron. and Serv., *Aen.* 7.684; Paul.-Fest. p. 89 L). Cf. E.T. Salmon, *The Making of Roman Italy* (London 1982), 7–8.

22 On booty in ancient warfare see now the exhaustive study of W.K. Pritchett, *The Greek State at War* V (Berkeley 1991), 68–541 (see 363ff. on clauses about the division of booty in treaties). For general discussion of this topic, A. Aymard, *Rev. Hist.* 217 (1957), 233–49 (= *Etudes d'histoire ancienne* (Paris 1967), 499–512), and M.I. Finley, *Ancient History: evidence and models* (London 1985), 77.

23 J. Beloch, *Der italische Bund unter Roms Hegemonie* (Leipzig 1880), 134, 152.

24 Originally suggested by A. Rosenberg, *Hermes* 54 (1919), 161ff.; and established as the standard view by E.T. Salmon, *Phoenix* 7 (1953), 93–104, 123–35; *Roman Colonization* (1969), 40ff.; Toynbee, *Hannibal's Legacy* I (1965), 391–7. The opposite opinion was voiced, in my view correctly, by M. Gelzer, 'Latium', *RE* 12 (1924), 958–9. Sherwin-White, *Roman Citizenship*² (1973), 36–7, is elliptical and obscure.

25 See the discussion in Toynbee, *Hannibal's Legacy* I (1965), 391–7.

26 According to the traditional chronology the colonies at Signia (495) and Velitrae (494) were founded before the *foedus Cassianum* (493), but the dating of events at this period is so unsure that it would be unwise to press the point.

27 On the Volscian advance see E. Manni, *Athenaeum* 17 (1939), 233–79; F. Coarelli, in *Crise et transformation* (1990), 135–54; M. Cristofani in S. Quilici Gigli (ed.), *I Volsci* (Rome 1992), 13–24; R. van Royen, ibid., 33–6.

28 E. Vetter, *Handbuch der italischen Dialekte* I (Heidelberg 1953), no. 222; cf. J.W. Poultney, *AJPh* 72 (1951), 113–27. M. Crawford has suggested that the *tabula*

Veliterna need not have been inscribed at Velitrae in the local language, but may have been brought there as booty from somewhere else (Umbria?) at a later date: *Athenaeum* 59 (1981), 542. If so, all bets are off. The recent discovery at Satricum of a Volscian text, inscribed on a lead axe-head from a fifth-century tomb, proves that the Volsci had their own language and their own distinctive script; but the text is too short and too obscure to resolve the problem of the *tabula Veliterna*. On the Satricum find, see G. Colonna, *Arch. Laz.* 7 (1984), 104–6; T.J. Cornell, *Arch. Reports* 32 (1985–6), 127–8; on the Volscian language in general, H. Rix, in *I Volsci* (1992), 37–49.

29 G. Devoto, *Gli antichi Italici* (3rd edn, Florence 1968), 113–14. On the Volsci in general, apart from the items cited in n. 27, see G. Radke, 'Volsci', *RE* IX A, 1 (1961), 773–827; Salmon, *Making of Roman Italy* (1982), 9–10; and the papers collected in *I Volsci*, ed. S. Quilici Gigli (*Quaderni di Archeologia etrusco-italica* 20, Rome 1992).

30 On the *ver sacrum* see J. Heurgon, *Trois études sur le 'ver sacrum'* (Brussels 1957); Salmon, *Samnites* (1967), 35–6.

31 On the Oscan expansion in southern Italy see Heurgon, *Capoue préromaine* (1942), 82ff.; Toynbee, *Hannibal's Legacy* I (1965), 21f., 93f.; B. D'Agostino, in *Popoli e civiltà* II (1974), 179–271; Frederiksen, *Campania* (1984), 134–57; Lomas, *Rome and the Western Greeks* (1993), 33–4.

32 On the Samnite seizure of Capua (Livy 4.37.1; cf. Diod. 12.31.1), apart from the items cited in n. 31, see T.J. Cornell, *Mus. Helv.* 31 (1974), 193–208.

33 On the Aequi, see M.A. Tomei, in *Enea nel Lazio* (1981), 58–9; Salmon, *Making of Roman Italy* (1982), 8–9. Vetter, *Handbuch* I (1953), no. 226 is a possible Aequian text, on which see C. Letta, *I Marsi e il Fucino nell'antichità* (Milan 1972), 34.

34 The connection is established by the inscription 'Vetusia' (i.e. Veturia) on a silver cup found in the Tomba Bernardini (7th century BC); see M. Torelli, *DdA* 1 (1967), 38–45; F. Canciani, F.W. von Hase, *La Tomba Bernardini di Palestrina* (Rome 1979), 39–40; T.J. Cornell, in M. Beard *et al.*, *Literacy in the Roman World* (Ann Arbor 1992), 18.

35 The Coriolanus legend was subjected to systematic negative criticism by Mommsen, *Röm. Forsch.* II (1879), 113–42, but is to some extent rehabilitated by De Sanctis, *StdR* II² (1960), 103–7. See also E.T. Salmon, *CQ* 24 (1930), 96–101, and my comments in *CAH²* VII.2 (1989), 288.

36 Ogilvie, *Comm.* (1965), 285f., 577.

37 The information is tabulated in *CAH²* VII.2 (1989), 290. For full discussion of the evidence, see A. Degrassi, *Inscriptiones Italiae* XIII.1, *Fasti consulares et triumphales* (Rome 1947), 535ff. E. Pais, *Fasti triumphales populi Romani* (2nd edn, Turin 1930), is still worth consulting.

38 Harris, *War and Imperialism* (1979), 26.

39 For example against the Volsci in 484 (Dion. Hal. 8.84–6) and 478 (Livy 2.58–60). These were fairly 'routine' campaigns, and as such to be distinguished from major disasters like the Cremera, the Allia, or Verrugo (423 BC, Liv. 4.38), which were too well known to be concealed.

40 A clear summary in Potter, *Changing Landscape* (1979), 1–18.

41 It is not fanciful to attribute the Portonaccio terracottas to the school of Vulca, the Veientine sculptor who was summoned to Rome by the Tarquins to make the statues for the Capitoline temple. See M. Pallottino, *La scuola di Vulca* (Rome 1945).

42 Beloch, *Röm. Gesch.* (1926), 620.

43 Potter, *Changing Landscape* (1979), 87.

44 Thus Ogilvie, *Comm.* (1965), 627.

45 A sceptical verdict in De Sanctis, *StdR* II² (1960), 120.

46 On the story of the Fabii at the Cremera see the series of studies by J.-C. Richard, *Latomus* 47 (1988), 526–53; *RPh* 63 (1989), 75–84; *MEFRA* 101 (1989), 159–73; *Gerión* 7 (1989), 65–73; *Latomus* 48 (1989), 312–25; in Eder (ed.), *Staat und Staatlichkeit* (1990), 174–99; in *Crise et transformation* (1990), 245–62.

47 De Sanctis, *StdR* II² (1960), 122.

48 J. Hubaux, *Rome et Véies* (Liège 1958); Sordi, *I rapporti romano-ceriti* (1960), 177ff.; Ogilvie, *Comm.* (1965), 626–30.

49 Another legend connected with the tunnel is the story (Livy 5.21.8–9; Plut., *Camillus* 5.4) of the sacrificial entrails. When the king of Veii was offering a sacrifice, a priest foretold that whoever removed the entrails would win the war. His words were overheard by some Roman soldiers in the tunnel, who thereupon burst out, snatched the entrails, and took them back to Camillus. For an interesting discussion see Ogilvie's note ad loc.

50 E.g. L. Pareti, *RPAA* 7 (1931), 89–100; G. Camporeale, *PdP* 13 (1958), 5–25; Scullard, *Etruscan Cities* (1967), 231–5; Banti, *Etruscan Cities* (1973), 206–8; M. Grant, *The Etruscans* (London 1980), 119–22.

51 Torelli, *Elogia Tarquiniensia* (1975); T.J. Cornell, *JRS* 68 (1978), 167–73; E. Gabba, *NAC* 8 (1979), 143–7; G. Colonna, *MEFRA* 96 (1984), 557–78.

52 Crawford, *Coinage and Money* (1985), 22–3. A reference in Livy to the '*classis*' operating at Fidenae in 426 BC (4.34.6) suggests that the Servian system was still in being at that date.

53 See Plutarch, *Camillus* 22.2–3, citing Heraclides Ponticus and Aristotle. The event was also mentioned by the historian Theopompus (*FGrHist* 115 F.317 = Pliny, *n.h.* 3.57).

54 On the synchronism (which also occurs in Justin 6.6.5, and probably goes back to Timaeus: Beloch, *Röm. Gesch.* (1926), 140), see F.W. Walbank, *Hist. Comm. Polyb.* I (Oxford 1957), 46–7; 185–6. On the Varronian chronology, see below, pp. 399ff.

55 Doubted by J. Wolski, *Historia* 5 (1956), 37–9; Ogilvie, *Comm. (1965)*, 699–700; but see below, n. 61.

56 The literary accounts are discussed by G.A. Mansuelli in *I Galli e l'Italia* (1978), 71–5. On Livy's sources, H. Homeyer, *Historia* 9 (1960), 345–61; Ogilvie, *Comm.* (1965), 700–2.

57 For discussion see R. Chevallier, *Latomus* 21 (1962), 366–70; G.A. Mansuelli, *Hommages A. Grenier* (Brussels 1962), 1067–93; *Studi Etruschi* 33 (1965), 3–47; L. Barfield, *Northern Italy before Rome* (London 1970), 127ff.; P. Santoro (ed.), *I Galli e l'Italia* (1978); V. Kruta, *Studi Etruschi* 46 (1978), 151–74; E. Campanile (ed.), *I Celti d'Italia* (Pisa 1981); D. Vitali (ed.), *Celti ed etruschi nell'Italia centro-settentrionale dal V secolo a.C. alla romanizzazione* (Imola 1987); G. Bandelli, in Momigliano and Schiavone (eds), *Storia di Roma* I (1988), 509–10; M.T. Grassi, *I Celti in Italia* (Milan 1991); A. Calvetti, *I Celti in Romagna* (Ravenna 1991); *I Celti* (Exhibition catalogue, Milan 1991); D. Foraboschi, *Lineamenti di storia della Cisalpina romana* (Rome 1992), 63ff.

58 For a succinct account of the Bologna stelae see Scullard, *Etruscan Cities* (1967), 201–4, with plate 93.

59 Polyb. 2.17.3 with Walbank's note ad loc.; Cato, *Origines* II.5 Chassignet.

60 Celtic war-bands are described by Polybius 2.17.11; Caesar, *BG* 6.15.2; and in many other texts. Cf. esp. Diod. 5.29.2; Tac., *Germ.* 13–14. Basic modern discussions include C. Jullian, *Histoire de la Gaule* II (Paris 1909), 76ff.; E. Norden, *Die germanische Urgeschichte in Tacitus* (Leipzig 1920), 124–7; J. de Vries, *Kelten und Germanen* (Berne–Munich 1960), 108ff.

61 Thus, e.g. G. Mansuelli, *Hommages A. Grenier* (Brussels 1962), 1085; Heurgon, *Rise of Rome* (1973), 182; R. Jannot, *MEFRA* 100 (1988), 611–14. An interesting detail in the Arruns story is that his cuckolding rival is called Lucumo, elsewhere attested as the Etruscan word for king (Serv., *Aen.* 2.278; 8.65 and 8.475; cf. above, pp. 139ff.). It is possible, therefore, that the story is a garbled reference to an attempted coup against the ruler of Clusium.

62 Sordi, *I rapporti romano-ceriti* (1960), 62–72.

63 O. Skutsch, *Annals of Ennius* (1985), 405–8; N.M. Horsfall in Horsfall and Bremmer, *Roman Myth* (1987), 63–75; but see my comments in *JRS* 76 (1986), 247–8.

64 Alföldi, *Early Rome* (1965), 356–7.

65 Coarelli, *Foro romano* I (1983), 130; see further above, pp. 237–8.

66 Beloch, *Röm. Gesch.* (1926), 314–20.

67 See further *CAH²* VII.2 (1989), 310f.

68 Nobody likes the Romans, and political correctness requires that imperialists be damned. An interesting and consciously anti-Roman discussion of the aftermath of the Gallic sack can be found in Toynbee, *Hannibal's Legacy* I (1965), 372–7, where Beloch's scepticism is used as a stick to beat the Romans. An anti-Roman, anti-imperialist stance is also clearly evident in recent work such as Harris' *War and Imperialism* (1979).

69 See Beloch, *Röm. Gesch.* (1926), 314–20, for details. On Camillus notice especially A. Momigliano, *CQ* 36 (1942), 111–20 (= *Secondo contributo*, 89–104).

70 The dates of these foundations are problematic. Livy (6.21.4) dates Nepet to 383, but does not mention Sutrium. Velleius Paterculus (1.14.2) places Sutrium seven years after the sack (i.e. 383), and Nepet ten years later. See the discussion of Harris, *Rome in Etruria and Umbria* (1971), 43–4.

71 Beloch, *Röm. Gesch.* (1926), 620.

72 Harris, *Rome in Etruria and Umbria* (1971), 41 and n. 6.

73 Cf. Crawford, *Roman Republic²* (1992), 33. F. Coarelli, in Momigliano and Schiavone (eds), *Storia di Roma* I (1988), 328, argues that Grotta Oscura stone was chosen deliberately in order to advertise the fact of Veii's subjection. This is not as unlikely as it sounds; Coarelli is right to observe that better-quality stone was available nearer to Rome, which makes his 'ideological' interpretation more than persuasive.

74 Gellius 16.13.7; Strabo 5.2.3, p. 220 C. Among modern scholars see Sordi, *I rapporti romano-ceriti* (1960), 36–49; Harris, *Rome in Etruria and Umbria* (1971), 45–7.

75 Harris, *Rome in Etruria and Umbria* (1971), 45–7. But see Brunt, *Italian Manpower* (1971), 515–18; M. Humbert, *MEFRA* 84 (1972), 247ff.; *Municipium* (1978), 29–32.

76 Sordi, *I rapporti romano-ceriti* (1960), 111ff.; Brunt, *Italian Manpower* (1971), 516.

77 Dio fr. 33 (and see below, p. 363); Beloch, *Röm. Gesch.* (1926), 363; Brunt, *Italian Manpower* (1971), 517.

78 See further *CAH²* VII.2 (1989), 315, and add A. Fraschetti, *Quaderni Urbinati* 24 (1977), 157–62.

79 Polybius says (2.18.4–6) that after the sack of Rome the Gauls of Cisalpina were occupied with domestic conflicts and wars against neighbouring Alpine peoples. 'During this time the Romans regained their own power and once again achieved mastery over the Latins. In the thirtieth year after the sack the Gauls once again invaded . . .', etc. The statement 'Polybius says that, after the Gallic disaster, it took the Romans thirty years to re-establish their position *vis-à-vis* the Latins' (Toynbee, *Hannibal's Legacy* I (1965), 372, 277) is a gross distortion of the text.

Sordi's view, *I rapporti romano-ceriti* (1960), 59–60, that the figure of thirty years had a mystical significance, is far-fetched.

80   De Sanctis, *StdR* II² (1960), 232–3.

81   Livy 6.29.9; cf. Diod. 15.47.7. Festus p. 498 L gives a different version of the text. Cicero, II *Verr.* 4.129 wrongly connects the dedication with T. Quinctius Flamininus, cos. 198 BC. On this see De Sanctis, *StdR* II² (1960), 237 n. 31; J. Heurgon, *Athenaeum* 42 (1964), 435f.

82   Humbert, *Municipium* (1978), 283–4. *Contra*: e.g. Sherwin-White, *Roman Citizenship²* (1973), 40ff.

83   The episode is suspicious not only because it serves to crown Camillus' career with one final Gallic triumph; Livy himself indicates a difficulty when he notes that some of his sources made this event the setting for a single combat between T. Manlius Torquatus and a Gallic champion (6.42.5; cf. Claudius Quadrigarius fr. 10 P), an episode which he himself narrates under 361 BC (7.10). This looks horribly like a doublet.

84   Livy records Gallic incursions in 367 (see previous note), 361, 360, 358 and 357 BC, whereas Polybius refers to just one, in the thirtieth year after the sack (see n. 79). Livy's account also includes a number of Roman victories, whereas Polybius says that the Romans avoided meeting the Gauls in the field (2.18.6). See further below, n. 86.

85   This war is treated cursorily by De Sanctis, *StdR* II² (1960), 241–3, and Harris, *Rome in Etruria and Umbria* (1971), 47–8; but it has recently received more attention, especially from Torelli, *Elogia Tarquiniensia* (1975), 82ff. There has been some discussion of the interesting detail that an Etruscan victory in 358 BC was followed by the ritual killing of 307 Roman prisoners of war in the Forum of Tarquinii (Livy 7.15.10), to which the Romans responded, three years later, by killing 358 Tarquinian aristocrats in the Forum Romanum (7.19.2–3). On these episodes see M. Torelli, in *Le délit religieux dans la cité antique* (Rome 1981), 1–7; D. Briquel, in *La Rome des premiers siècles* (1992), 37–46.

86   Sordi, *I rapporti romano-ceriti* (1960), 164–5. Her argument is that the attacks recorded by Livy (above, n. 84) were carried out by war bands operating from southern Italy (NB esp. 7.1.3, Apulia; 7.11.1, Campania), whereas Polybius took note only of invasions from the north.

87   A. Fraschetti, in *Le délit religieux dans la cité antique* (1981), 51–115, esp. 90ff.; A.M. Eckstein, *AJAH* 7 (1982), 69ff.

88   See the discussion in Salmon, *Samnites* (1967), 192–3, with a speculative reconstruction of its terms.

13   THE EMANCIPATION OF THE *PLEBS*

1   I have discussed the approach of our sources in more detail in Raaflaub (ed.), *Social Struggles* (1986), 52–76; cf. A. Momigliano, ibid., 177–8.

2   By this statement I do not mean to rule out the possibility that the plebs included landless artisans and traders, but I doubt if such persons were more than a minority. See further above, p. 257 with n. 57.

3   Niebuhr, *History of Rome* II (1838), 129ff. On Niebuhr and *ager publicus* see A. Momigliano, *Studies on Modern Scholarship* (Berkeley 1994), 225ff.

4   Cassius Hemina fr. 17 P.; G. Tibiletti, *Athenaeum* 26 (1948), 216.

5   The Lex Licinia is rejected as complete fiction by B. Niese, *Hermes* 23 (1888), 410–29; Pais, *Storia di Roma* II (1899), 141–3; De Sanctis, *StdR* II² (1960), 204–5; E. Meyer, *Römische Staat²* (1961), 286–7; D. Flach, *Römische Agrargeschichte* (Munich 1990), 32; *Die Gesetze* (1994), 285–94. The question is critically reviewed

by Toynbee, *Hannibal's Legacy* II (1965), 559–64; Forsén, *Lex Licinia Sextia* (1991), 15ff.

6 G. Tibiletti, *Athenaeum* 28 (1950), 248f., and E. Gabba (*Comm.* on Appian, ad loc.) argue that these figures are cumulative, not alternatives.

7 De Martino, *Diritto e società* (1979), 183–93; *Storia economica* (1979) I, 26. The general point was made already by H. Last, in *CAH* VII (1928), 539–40. *Contra*: Forsén, *Lex Licinia Sextia* (1991), 42–4.

8 Cf. Momigliano, *Secondo contributo*, 92. Manlius is listed in the *Fasti* as consul in 392 BC, and was *interrex* in 388 (Livy 6.5.6). For a recent discussion of the episode, I. Valvo, *La sedizione di Manlio Capitolino in Tito Livio* (Milan 1983).

9 Livy records attempts to resolve the crisis by the foundation of colonies, making the connection explicit in the case of Satricum (6.16.6–7 – 385 BC).

10 Detailed accounts of the wall can be found in G. Säflund, *Le mura di Roma repubblicana* (Lund 1932); M.G. Picozzi and P. Santoro, in *Roma medio-repubblicana* (1973), 7–31; but these experts deal with technical matters, and do not touch upon social and economic issues.

11 Calculated on the assumption that a force of 100 men could quarry, cut, transport and lay no more than two or three blocks in the course of a ten-hour day. At this rate of progress the wall would have taken twenty years to build – a fact that is borne out by Livy's statement (7.20.9) that work was still going on in 353 BC (note that the five-year 'anarchy' from Varronian 375–371 should probably be reduced to one year – see below, pp. 399–402).

12 Picozzi and Santoro in *Roma medio-repubblicana* (1973), 7ff.

13 Livy 8.28; Dion. Hal. 16.5; Cic., *Rep.* 2.34. Varro, *LL* 7.105 places the law in 313 BC, when a C. Poetelius was dictator. See Rotondi, *Leges publicae* (1912), 230–1. For discussion see De Martino, *Diritto e società* (1983), 193–203; Hölke-skamp, *Entstehung* (1987), 159–60, with further bibliography.

14 P.A. Brunt, *JRS* 48 (1958), 168; *Social Conflicts* (1971), 56–7; Hölkeskamp, *Entstehung* (1987), 159ff.

15 M.I. Finley, *Ancient Slavery and Modern Ideology* (London 1980), 83; and see further below, pp. 393–4.

16 The Latin word *rogatio* means 'a question' or 'an enquiry'. The magistrate or tribune proposing a law asked the people if they wished to enact such-and-such, to which the individual voters replied *uti rogas* ('as you ask' – i.e. yes), or *antiquo* ('I make old' = leave things as they are – i.e. no). A rogation is therefore a legislative proposal, a bill.

17 There is a large literature on the consular tribunate. Curiously (and inexplicably) this is the one topic in archaic Roman history where English-speaking scholars predominate (although the results of their efforts are not much of an advertise-ment). The main discussions include: Mommsen, *Staatsr.* II³ (1887), 182–93; Beloch, *Röm. Gesch.* (1926), 247–64; E.S. Staveley, *JRS* 43 (1953), 30–6; F.E. Adcock, *JRS* 47 (1957), 9–14; A. Boddington, *Historia* 8 (1959), 356–64; R. Sealey, *Latomus* 18 (1959), 521–30; Palmer, *Archaic Community* (1970), 222ff.; J. Pinsent, *Military Tribunes and Plebeian Consuls* (Wiesbaden 1975); V. Kirby, *Mundus Antiquus* 1 (1976), 24–9; A. Drummond, *Athenaeum* 58 (1980), 57–72; T.J. Cornell, in *Tria Corda* (1983), 101–20, esp. 111f.; R.T. Ridley, *Klio* 68 (1986), 444–65; F. Càssola, in Momigliano and Schiavone (eds), *Storia di Roma* I (1988), 453ff.; J.-C. Richard, *MEFRA* 102 (1990), 767–99; in *La Rome des premiers siècles* (1992), 235–46.

18 Eight or nine member colleges are extremely rare (see Table 8), and may not be historical. But Claudius, in his speech to the Senate (see above, pp. 133–4), says that colleges of eight were 'frequent' (*ILS* 212, 33–6). For discussion, A. Drummond, *Athenaeum* 58 (1980), 57–72, esp. 67ff.

19 The only exceptions are L. Atilius (444) and Q. Antonius Merenda (422); but even if these are admitted, the period from 444 to 401 is still that in which the patricians came closest to a monopoly. See above, pp. 254ff., and Table 6.

20 Livy's account, and the various modern alternatives, are examined by R.T. Ridley, *Klio* 68 (1986), 444–65, esp. 452–5.

21 Livy is certainly unaware of patterns that are present in his own data; and the problem with many modern accounts is that they concentrate on one or more selected aspects of the problem (e.g. the number of consular tribunes, or the eligibility of plebeians), but overlook others. The starting-point should be an accurate table of data (useful examples in Beloch, *Röm. Gesch.* (1926), 254–5 and Ridley, *Klio* 68 (1986), 462–5) and a clear grasp of what our sources, particularly Livy, actually say (again, Ridley has the right approach).

22 Zonaras 7.19.5, confirmed by the rest of the evidence we have, which records no triumph by a consular tribune. It is true that the section of the Capitoline *Acta triumphalia* from 437 to 367 is missing, but the Zonaras passage shows that no record of a triumph by a consular tribune was known to Dio or (presumably) his annalistic sources. But it does not follow that the consular tribunes lacked the right to triumph (*pace* Richard, in *Rome des premiers siècles* (1992) 239ff.), still less that they lacked *imperium* (Sealey, *Latomus* 18 [1959], 529; cf. E. Badian, in Eder (ed.), *Staat und Staatlichkeit* (1990), 469), or were in some other way inferior to consuls (J. Linderski, in Eder (ed.), *Staat und Staatlichkeit* (1990), 45).

23 This point is well made by R. Billows, *Phoenix* 43 (1989), 112–33; note, however, that his explanation of the annalists' error is radically different from the one presented here.

24 K. von Fritz, *Historia* 1 (1950), 3–44. Sordi, *I rapporti romano-ceriti* (1960), 73–9, argues that the reforms were the work of an 'Etruscan' group, and were inspired by the institutions of Caere.

25 Most clearly stated by Fabius Pictor, ap. Gellius 5.4.3 (Fabius 'Latinus' fr. 6 P.): *tum primum ex plebe alter consul factus est, duovicesimo anno postquam Romam Galli ceperunt* ('then for the first time one of the consuls was elected from the *plebs*, in the twenty-second year after the Gauls captured Rome').

26 I have argued the case more fully in *Tria Corda* (1983), 101–20.

27 E.g. von Fritz, *Historia* 1 (1950), 11 and n. 17; Elster, *Gesetzgebung* (1976), 13; Flach, *Die Gesetze* (1994), 281–2.

28 Brunt, *Social Conflicts* (1971), 55.

29 E.g. the *lex agraria* of 111 BC (*FIRA* I, n.8), lines 77–82.

30 At an unknown date, but later than *c.* 298 BC, a Lex Maenia extended the provisions of the Lex Publilia to elections (Cic., *Brut.* 55). The standard view (following Mommsen, *Röm. Forsch.* I (1864), 242) is that it must have been enacted between 292 and 219 BC, when Livy's full text is missing, but this cannot be certain. Cicero tells us that it was later than the occasion when Appius Claudius, as *interrex*, refused to admit a plebeian candidate for the consulship; this was perhaps in 298 BC (see Broughton, *ad ann.*).

31 On the *auctoritas patrum* and the Lex Publilia see E. Siena, *Studi Romani* 4 (1956), 509–22; Hölkeskamp, *Entstehung* (1987), 110–13 (with full bibliography).

32 Livy 6.34. Beloch (*Röm. Gesch.* (1926), 352–3) rejects this passage as legendary, and substitutes an arbitrary reconstruction of his own, whereby Fabius is presented as an upholder of patrician privilege and an opponent of the plebs! This has unfortunately had wide influence (e.g. *OCD*², s.v. Fabius Ambustus, 2).

33 Data in Broughton, *MRR* I, 110ff. The point was already made by F. Münzer, *Römische Adelsparteien und Adelsfamilien* (Stuttgart 1920), 10–11.

34 Data in Ranouil, *Recherches sur le patriciat* (1975), 205ff.

35 On Roman voting procedures see the standard accounts of L.R. Taylor, *Roman*

Voting Assemblies (Ann Arbor 1966); E.S. Staveley, *Greek and Roman Voting and Elections* (London 1972), 133–216; C. Nicolet, *The World of the Citizen in Republican Rome* (London 1980), 207–315.

36 Staveley, *Greek and Roman Voting* (1972), 186.

37 This is also one of the conclusions of Hölkeskamp's excellent book (*Entstehung*, 1987), now reinforced by two further studies: *Arch. f. Kulturgesch.* 70 (1988), 271–312; and in Eder (ed.), *Staat und Staatlichkeit* (1990), 437–57.

14 THE ROMAN CONQUEST OF ITALY

1 Note especially the field survey, by a British team, of the Biferno (Tifernus) valley: G. Barker *et al.*, *PBSR* 46 (1978), 135–51; some good general comments in A. La Regina, *Poszbna Isdanja* 24 (1975), 273; for a concise statement of the traditional view, see G. Tibiletti, *Popoli e civiltà dell'Italia antica* VII (Rome 1978), 15–49.

2 A full account of the meagre evidence in Salmon, *Samnites* (1967), 77–101.

3 Salmon, *Samnites* (1967), 137–40; A. La Regina *et al.*, *Sannio: Pentri e Frentani dal VI al I sec. a.C.* (Rome 1980), 131ff.; M.J. Strazzulla, B. di Marco, *Il santuario sannitico di Pietrabbondante* (Rome 1972).

4 I am indebted to Stephen Oakley for much helpful information on this topic. Published information is still confined to the brief general account of A. La Regina, *Poszbna Isdanja* 24 (1975), 271ff., and G. Conta Haller, *Ricerche su alcuni centri fortificati in opera poligonale nell'area campano-sannitica* (Naples 1978), which is unfortunately restricted to the lower Volturnus valley.

5 M.W. Frederiksen, *DdA* 2 (1968), 3–31.

6 A. Pontrandolfo, A. Rouveret, *Le tombe dipinte di Paestum* (Modena 1993).

7 Frederiksen, *Campania* (1984), 188f.

8 F.E. Adcock, *CAH* VII (1928), 588; Walsh, *Livy* (1961), 280; but see De Sanctis, *StdR* II² (1960), 256ff.; Frederiksen, *Campania* (1984), 185ff.

9 Frederiksen, *Campania* (1984), 185ff.; and see my comments in *CAH²* VII.2 (1989), 360–4.

10 Frederiksen, *Campania* (1984), 185ff.

11 Livy 8.11.16; defended by Humbert, *Municipium* (1978), 172–6; full discussion in Frederiksen, *Campania* (1984), 191ff.

12 On the settlement of 338 BC, see De Sanctis, *StdR* II² (1960), 265ff.; Beloch, *Röm. Gesch.* (1926), 375ff.; Toynbee, *Hannibal's Legacy* I (1965), 129–41; Sherwin-White, *Roman Citizenship²* (1973), 38ff., 202ff.; Humbert, *Municipium* (1978), 176ff.; Salmon, *Making of Roman Italy* (1982), 40–56; Frederiksen, *Campania* (1984), 194ff.; Crawford, *Roman Republic²* (1992), 34ff..

13 De Sanctis, *StdR* II² (1960), 267: 'Fu questo il momento critico della storia di Roma.'

14 The 'Roman Commonwealth' is an expression coined by Arnold Toynbee, *Hannibal's Legacy* (1965), *passim*.

15 Livy's statement (8.14.5) that they were already citizens must be a mistake, probably arising from the fact that Velitrae was a colony; in Livy's time colonies were communities of Roman citizens, not of Latins.

16 Most clearly Salmon, *Roman Colonization* (1969), 46–7 and *passim*, followed by Sherwin-White, *Roman Citizenship²* (1973), 205, 212. The old idea of Mommsen (*Staatsr.* III.1 (1887), 571ff.), that all incorporated communities, including Latins, received *civitas sine suffragio*, is no longer widely accepted; it seems to be contradicted by Dio VII.35.10. In general cf. Humbert, *Municipium* (1978), 177 n. 78.

17 Afzelius, *Die römische Eroberung* (1942), 153.

18 By adjusting the figures presented by Afzelius, *Die römische Eroberung* (1942), 138, we may reckon the land area of Samnium to have measured some 12,500 km², and its population to have been of the order of 450,000. For details see *CAH²* VII.2 (1989), 352–3, and n. 2.

19 Toynbee, *Hannibal's Legacy* I (1965), 140.

20 On the strategic importance of Cales see Toynbee, *Hannibal's Legacy* I (1965), 136–7; Frederiksen, *Campania* (1984), 207ff.

21 This is not specifically attested for the early colonies but can safely be assumed. Strangely enough the text that refers most clearly to the practice (Plut., *C. Gracch.* 9.1) is usually misunderstood, e.g. by Salmon, *Roman Colonization* (1969), 120.

22 Thus, rightly, Harris, *War and Imperialism* (1979), 177; cf. Salmon, *Samnites* (1967), 217–18. For the traditional view of 'Samnite aggressiveness', De Sanctis, *StdR* II² (1960), 281; Frederiksen, *Campania* (1984), 207–8, with nn. 7 and 17.

23 The affair and its sequel form one of the most celebrated, and one of the most questionable, episodes in Roman history. Further details in *CAH²* VII.2 (1989), 370–71; NB also N.M. Horsfall, *PBSR* 50 (1983), 45–52.

24 It is much disputed whether this peace was the result of the agreement made at the Caudine Forks (thus Salmon, *Samnites* (1967), 226ff.), or whether it was concluded in 318 BC after a series of Roman successes in 320–319, which is Livy's version. On this debate note especially Frederiksen's remarks in *JRS* 58 (1968), 226. No significance should be attached to the fact that Diodorus' first reference to the Second Samnite War occurs under Varronian 318 BC (Salmon, *Samnites*, 228 n. 3). The reason is that his books 17 and 18 (dealing with Alexander the Great and the Successors, from 336 to 319 BC) exclude Roman events altogether.

25 This is an aspect of the more general theory of 'defensive imperialism', which goes back to Mommsen. See Harris, *War and Imperialism* (1989), 163ff., for full discussion and bibliography. In my opinion Harris' seminal work is an important and much needed corrective, but does not make sufficient allowance for the possibility that what the Romans thought they were doing may have been different from what they actually did.

26 See the references cited by Harris, *War and Imperialism* (1979), 176 nn. 1–2.

27 Diod. 19.76.2, assuming that the MS reading περὶ κίνναν τὸλιν should be corrected to περὶ Ταρακίναν πόλιν.

28 On the importance of the events of 313–312 BC, see Toynbee, *Hannibal's Legacy* I (1965), 147.

29 The sources that date this reform to the period of the Samnite Wars (Sallust, *Cat.* 51.37–8; *Ineditum Vaticanum* – see above, p. 170) are to be preferred to an alternative tradition in Livy, who assumes that a manipular army existed long before 340 BC (8.18.3–4). In general see the standard works on the Roman army, esp. J. Kromayer, G. Veith, *Heerwesen und Kriegsführung der Griechen und Römer* (Munich 1928), 288ff.; P. Fraccaro, *Della guerra presso i Romani* (Opuscula V, Pavia 1975), 41ff.; for a brief account, L. Keppie, *The Making of the Roman Army* (London 1984), 19ff. Eduard Meyer's essay 'Das römische Manipularheer', *Kleine Schriften* II (Halle 1924), 193–329, remains fundamental. On the sources see E. Rawson, *PBSR* 39 (1971), 13–31 = *Roman Culture and Society* (Oxford 1991), 34–57.

30 Livy credits Brutus with a decisive victory over the Samnites (9.31), and the *Fasti Capitolini* record his triumph. This account is flatly contradicted by Zonaras (8.1), who says the Romans were defeated. On the other hand, Diodorus' narrative (20.26.3–4) bears no relation at all to the other extant versions. One reasonably certain fact is that Brutus vowed a temple to Salus, which he subsequently dedicated in 302 (Livy 9.43.25; 10.1.9). His campaign cannot therefore have ended

in total disaster, but a vow to 'Safety' may imply something less than a complete victory.

31 Camerinum seems rather out of the way; but it may be a mistaken reference to Clusium, which Livy says was originally called 'Camars' (10.25.11). This would make better sense of the story.

32 According to the reconstruction of Frier, *Libri annales* (1979), 225, the historian Fabius Pictor was a great-nephew of Rullianus.

33 The so-called *Fasti triumphales* (or *Acta triumphalia*) were set up on an inscription in the Forum under Augustus, and together with the consular lists form part of the *Fasti Capitolini*. An antiquarian compilation, they represent a tradition independent of the extant literary sources (but are not to be regarded as more reliable; the first recorded triumph is that of Romulus). The standard edition is that of A. Degrassi, *Inscriptiones Italiae* XIII.1 (Rome 1947). See also the important study of E. Pais, *Fasti triumphales populi Romani*[2] (1930).

34 *Rome in Etruria and Umbria* (1971), esp. 49–84.

35 *ILLRP* 309. It is important to note that the original inscription on the third-century sarcophagus was erased, probably around 200 BC, and replaced by the one we can now read. This was the period when the first histories of Rome were being written, which is not a coincidence. See above, pp. 355–6, and cf. the remarks of F.G.B. Millar, *JRS* 79 (1989), 138–9.

36 On the Scipio Barbatus problem see B. Bruno, *La terza guerra sannitica* (Rome 1906), 21–5; Beloch, *Röm. Gesch.* (1926), 437–8; Salmon, *Samnites* (1967), 260.

37 On prorogation in general see W.F. Jashemski, *The Origins and History of the Proconsular and Propraetorian Imperium* (Chicago 1950); H. Kloft, *Prorogation und ausserordentliche Imperien, 326–81 v. Chr.* (Meisenheim 1977). On the early period in particular R. Develin, *Latomus* 34 (1975), 716–22. The interpretation offered here and in *CAH*[2] VII.2 (1989), 377ff. (written in 1983), is very similar to that arrived at independently by Hölkeskamp, *Entstehung* (1987), 138ff.

38 On the battle of Sentinum see De Sanctis, *StdR* II[2] (1960), 337–41; P. Sommella, *Antichi campi di battaglia in Italia* (Rome 1967), 35–47; Salmon, *Samnites* (1967), 265–8; Harris, *Rome in Eturia and Umbria* (1971), 69–74. The frieze of a temple at Civitalba, near Sentinum, depicts armed Gauls being pursued by goddesses and heroes, and has been interpreted as a representation of the rescue of the sanctuary at Delphi from a Gallic attack in 278 BC (Pausanias 10.23). It dates from the early second century BC, and was perhaps set up to commemorate the defeat of the Gauls at Sentinum a century earlier. See A. Andrén, *Architectural Terracottas from Etrusco-Italic Temples* (Lund 1940), 297–308; M. Verzar, F.-H. Pairault-Massa, in *I Galli e l'Italia* (1978), 196–203.

39 Aquilonia is only one of a number of Roman military successes recorded for 293, including the capture of Duronia, Cominium, Aquilonia, Saepinum, Velia Palumbinum and Herculanum. The location of these places is a longstanding puzzle, on which see A. La Regina, *Poszbna Isdanja* 24 (1975), 271–82, and my brief discussion in *CAH*[2] VII.2 (1989), 358.

40 The scrappy material for the period 292–265 BC is conveniently assembled by M.R. Torelli, *Rerum Romanarum fontes ab anno ccxcii ad annum cclxv a.Ch.n.* (Pisa 1978), with helpful commentary.

41 The Gallic War of 284–282 BC is a major puzzle. The best account is in Polybius, 2.19.7–20, on which see Mommsen, *Röm. Forsch.* II (1879), 365–75, and Walbank's notes ad loc. Other sources, with commentary, in Torelli, *Rerum Romanarum fontes* (1978), 80–92. See further De Sanctis, *StdR* II[2] (1960), 357–9; E.T. Salmon, *CPh* 30 (1935), 25–31; Harris, *Rome in Etruria and Umbria* (1971), 79–81; J.H. Corbett, *Historia* 20 (1971), 656–64; M.G. Morgan, *CQ* 22 (1972), 309–25.

42 Sources and discussion in Torelli, *Rerum Romanarum fontes* (1978), 78–9, 93ff.

On Rome's relations with Tarentum, W. Hoffmann, *Hermes* 71 (1936) 11–24; J.H. Thiel, *A History of Roman Sea-Power before the Second Punic War* (Amsterdam 1954), 23–6; H.H. Schmitt, *Die Staatsverträge des Altertums* III (Munich 1969), 60, no. 444; P.R. Franke, *CAH*[2] VII.2 (1989), 456ff.; Lomas, *Rome and the Italian Greeks* (1993), 50f.

43 The appearance of the Roman envoy, L. Postumius Megellus, in the theatre at Tarentum is a famous scene, described by Dion. Hal. 19.5.1–5; Appian, *Samn.* 7.2; Dio, fr. 39, 6–9 (quoted, with other sources, in Torelli, *Rerum Romanarum fontes* [1978], 100–3). An interesting and certainly authentic detail is that Postumius spoke in Greek, and was jeered for his mistakes and funny accent.

44 On the size of Pyrrhus' forces, and the losses at Heraclea, see De Sanctis, *StdR* II[2], 272–5 nn. 22–3, 27. On Pyrrhus in general, apart from the works cited in n. 42, P. Lévêque, *Pyrrhos* (Paris 1957); D. Kienast, *RE* XXIV (1963), 135–45, s.v. 'Pyrrhos'; E. Garoufalias, *Pyrrhus* (London 1979).

45 A published version of Ap. Claudius' speech was still extant in the time of Cicero (*de Sen.* 16; *Brut.* 61; cf. De Sanctis, *StdR* II[2] (1960), 485); but the sources do not make it clear whether or not the demand that Pyrrhus should leave Italy occurred in the speech. On the peace negotiations in general see M.R. Lefkowitz, *HSCPh* 64 (1959) 147–77.

46 Notice especially the anecdote reported by Dio 9, fr. 40.27 (quoted in *CAH*[2] VII.2 (1989), 391).

47 Hopkins, *Conquerors and Slaves* (1978), 25ff.; Harris, *War and Imperialism* (1979), 9ff. and *passim*. For the fifth and fourth centuries, see now S. Oakley, in J. Rich and G. Shipley (eds), *War and Society in the Roman World* (London 1993), 13–16.

48 V. Ilari, *Gli italici nelle strutture militari romane* (Milan 1974); for a list of allies see Afzelius, *Die römische Eroberung* (1942), 134–5.

49 A. Momigliano, *Alien Wisdom* (Oxford 1975), 45–6; cf. Crawford, *Roman Republic*[2] (1992), 47–8; J. North, *JRS* 71 (1981), 6–7. Harris' criticisms of this thesis in *The Imperialism of Mid-Republican Rome* (ed. W.V. Harris, Rome 1984), 89–109, are curiously ill-directed. See now the useful remarks of Oakley, in *War and Society* (1993), 17–18.

50 Polyb. 6.21.5, on which see C. Nicolet, *PBSR* 46 (1978), 1–11; E. Gabba in *Armées et fiscalité dans le monde antique* (Paris 1977), 22–3; *CAH*[2] VIII (1989), 223–4.

51 Harris, *Rome in Etruria and Umbria* (1971), 114–44.

52 Hopkins, *Conquerors and Slaves* (1978), 21 and n. 17, questions the authenticity of the records; but his figures are in need of modification (see Badian, *JRS* 72 (1982), 165), and he overlooks the possibility of allied participation.

53 E.J. Bickerman and M. Smith, *The Ancient History of Western Civilization* (New York 1976), 149.

54 Afzelius, *Die römische Eroberung* (1942), 133–5.

15 ROME IN THE AGE OF THE ITALIAN WARS

1 Polybius 6.13, with Walbank's notes ad loc. Modern accounts of the Senate in the classical Republic include P. Willems, *Le sénat de la république romaine*, I-II (Louvain 1878–83); Mommsen, *Staatsr.* III.2 (1888), 835ff.; De Sanctis, *StdR* IV.1[2] (1969), 499–515; A. O'Brien-Moore, *RE*, Suppl. B. VI (1935), 660ff.; E. Meyer, *Römische Staat*[2] (1961), 202–15; M. Bonnefond-Coudry, *Le sénat de la république romaine* (Rome 1989). F.G.B. Millar's important paper in *JRS* 79 (1989), 138–50, a refreshing corrective to many current misconceptions, is nevertheless wrong in my opinion to minimise the importance of the Senate in the middle Republic.

2 The Lex Ovinia is one of the most important but least noticed of early tribunician laws. It is normally dated after 318 BC, which cannot be right, in view of Diod. 20.36.5; see *CAH²* VII.2 (1989), 393 n. 54. The same point was made by L. Lange, *De plebiscitis Ovinio et Atinio disputatio* (Leipzig 1878), one of the few modern discussions of the law. The most recent account is that of Hölkeskamp, *Entstehung* (1987), 142ff., with bibliography.

3 The text is unfortunately corrupt at the crucial point. The manuscript reading is *curiati*, which most commentators, following Ursinus, emend to *curiatim* ('by curiae'). This strikes me as meaningless, and I prefer to accept Meier's suggestion of *iurati* (i.e. the censors were 'sworn', 'bound by oath', etc.). I regard this as virtually certain, in view of the parallel case in Cicero, *pro Cluentio* 121: ... *praetores urbani, qui iurati debent optimum quemque in lectos iudices referre* ...

4 Mommsen, *Staatsr.* III.2 (1888), 880.

5 The importance of popular laws in the regulation of the state is stressed by Millar, *JRS* 79 (1989), 145. The collection of material in Rotondi, *Leges publicae* (1912), is still useful, but is incomplete and full of mistakes. A new edition is in preparation by a research team of the CNRS (Paris).

6 Our knowledge of magistrates other than consuls is very patchy for this period. Accounts of individual careers in the *elogia* set up in the Forum of Augustus in 2 BC record several otherwise unknown dictatorships, praetorships, etc. See Broughton, *MRR* I, 187, with references. These are just the tip of an iceberg.

7 I use the term 'plebiscitary' in its modern sense (for want of anything better), as in M. Weber, *Wirtschaft und Gesellschaft* (5th edn, Tübingen 1976), 156 = *Economy and Society* (ed. G. Roth and C. Wittich, Berkeley 1978), 268–9, and index, s.v. 'democracy, plebiscitary'.

8 This has frequently been denied, (e.g. R. Billows, *Phoenix* 43 (1989), 116 and notes.) It is true that one of the consuls of 341 and one of those of 340 had held the consulship a few years previously; but we need not suppose that the law was made retrospective. The apparent exception of the consuls of 336 and 330 (L. Papirius Crassus) is explained by the fact that they were probably two men of the same name: F. Münzer, *RE* 18 (1949), 1035–6, s.v. 'Papirius' nos. 46, 47. In any case, a real change in patterns of office-holding is evident in the *Fasti* from 342 onwards. See R. Rilinger, *Chiron* 8 (1978), 247–312; R. Develin, *Patterns in Office-Holding, 366–49* BC (Brussels 1979), 13ff.; Hölkeskamp, *Entstehung* (1987), 94–5, 126–9.

9 Cf. S.C. Humphreys, in Eder (ed.), *Staat und Staatlichkeit* (1990), 293–302, esp. 299f.

10 Cf. K.-J. Hölkeskamp, in Eder (ed.), *Staat und Staatlichkeit* (1990), 442–3.

11 On the meaning of '*provincia*', see J.S. Richardson, *Hispaniae* (Cambridge 1986), 5–10; A.W. Lintott, *Imperium Romanum* (London 1993), 22ff.

12 Discussions of the career of Appius Claudius include Niebuhr, *Hist. Rome³* III (1842), 294–313; Mommsen, *Röm. Forsch.* I (1864), 301–13; A.G. Amatucci, *RFIC* 22 (1894), 227–58; F. Münzer, *RE* III (1899), 2681–5, s.v. 'Claudius'; De Sanctis, *StdR* II² (1960), 213–18; P. Lejay, *RPh* 44 (1920), 91–141; A. Garzetti, *Athenaeum* 25 (1947), 175–224; E.S. Staveley, *Historia* 8 (1959), 410–33; C. Nicolet, *Latomus* 20 (1961), 683–720; F. Càssola, *I gruppi politici romani nel III sec. a.C.* (Trieste 1962), 128–37; E. Ferenczy, *From the Patrician State to the Patricio-Plebeian State* (Budapest 1976) 120–217; B. MacBain, *CQ* 30 (1980), 356–72; M. Crawford, *The Roman Republic* (2nd edn, London 1992), 43–5.

13 As implied by Plutarch, *Publ.* 7. The matter is highly controversial. See S. Treggiari, *Roman Freedmen during the Late Republic* (Oxford 1969), 39–42, whom I have followed.

14 R.E.A. Palmer, *Historia* 14 (1965), 293–324; Wiseman, *Clio's Cosmetics* (1979), 87–8 (both excessively sceptical); Coarelli, *Foro Boario* (1988), 81–2, 111.

15 Thus Staveley, *Historia* 8 (1959), 413. Staveley's alternative suggestion, that the purpose of the Lex Ovinia was not to give the censors the job of enrolling the Senate, but to regulate their procedures (cf. *OCD*², s.v. 'Ovinius'), is flatly contradicted by Festus p. 290 L, the only evidence.

16 Pomponius in *Digest* I.2.2.7 claims that Flavius stole the *formulae* from Appius, who had been planning to publish them himself.

17 Livy 9.46.7. The reference to the college of tribunes is very strange in this context, and is unlikely to be an invention. Cicero (*Dom.* 127) mentions a tribunician Lex Papiria which laid down that dedications could not take place without the command of the *plebs* (i.e. except by plebiscite). This may be the same law, in which case one could suppose that any such plebiscite would have to be proposed by at least five (or six?) of the tribunes.

18 Recent 'hypercritics' include Palmer, *Archaic Community* (1970), 269–79, and most recently Wiseman, *Clio's Cosmetics* (1979), 85–9; revisionists include Garzetti, Staveley, Càssola and MacBain (see n. 12).

19 Mommsen, *Röm. Forsch.* I (1864), 287ff.; Wiseman, *Clio's Cosmetics* (1979), 85–9 and *passim*.

20 This is the approach adopted by Garzetti, *Athenaeum* 25 (1947), 175–224.

21 We can be sure of this because no priesthood is mentioned in his *elogium* – A. Degrassi, *Inscriptiones Italiae* XIII.3, 79 and 12.

22 See the standard histories of Latin literature, e.g. M. Schanz, C. Hosius, *Gesch. d. röm. Lit.* I (Munich 1927), 41f.; see also Ferenczy, *From the Patrician State* (1976), 212–17.

23 E.g. A.S. Gratwick, in the *Cambridge History of Latin Literature* II.1 (Cambridge 1982), 138–9.

24 De Sanctis, *StdR* II² (1960), 216.

25 E.g. F. Càssola, *I gruppi politici romani* (1962), 241–2.

26 The difference between ancient and modern ideas of liberty was first noted by Benjamin Constant, *De la liberté des anciens comparée à celle des modernes* (1819); English translation in B. Constant, *Political Writings*, ed. B. Fontana (Cambridge 1988), 309–28. Important recent discussions include C. Wirzubski, *Libertas as a Political Idea at Rome* (Cambridge 1950); A. Momigliano, *Quinto contributo*, 949–75; P.A. Brunt, *The Fall of the Roman Republic and Other Essays* (Oxford 1988), 281–350.

27 Sources and commentary in Torelli, *Rerum Romanarum fontes* (1978), 69–73. See further K.-J. Hölkeskamp, *Arch. f. Kulturgesch.* 70 (1988), 271–312.

28 Toynbee, *Hannibal's Legacy* I (1965), 315ff.

29 E.g. Scullard, *Hist. Roman World*⁴ (1980), 129–30.

30 Mommsen, *Staatsr.* III.1 (1887), 303–4.

31 It has become traditional to reject the view of the sources that Ti. Gracchus' aim was to promote the interests of the poor. See, most clearly, E. Badian, *ANRW* I.1 (1972), 707, 716–20. A different, and to my mind more convincing, view can be found in Brunt, *Social Conflicts* (1971), 74–81; and cf. M.I. Finley, *Politics in the Ancient World* (Cambridge 1983), 4–6 and *passim*.

32 On the operation of the Roman assemblies see above, p. 343 and n. 35; on the political implications of group voting see e.g. Brunt, *Social Conflicts* (1971), 8ff., 61ff.

33 The chances of a parvenu ('new man') gaining entry to the elite were further curtailed by restrictions on canvassing, particularly the Lex Poetelia of 358 BC (Livy 7.15.12). This was a tribunician law, carried with the backing of the patricians (*patribus auctoribus*), on the proposal of the tribune C. Poetelius, possibly the same Poetelius (Libo Visolus) who had held the consulship two years earlier. The law is probably authentic (Hölkeskamp, *Entstehung* (1987), 28 with n. 133; and see pp. 83ff. for valuable discussion).

34 Afzelius, *Die römische Eroberung* (1942), 192; cf. Brunt, *Italian Manpower* (1971), 59.

35 F. Coarelli, in *Roma medio-repubblicana* (1973), 117–20.

36 C.G. Starr, *The Beginnings of Imperial Rome* (Ann Arbor 1980), 15–26.

37 On Roman aqueducts the standard work (with full descriptions of existing remains) is T. Ashby, *The Aqueducts of Ancient Rome* (Oxford 1935). See pp. 49ff. for the Aqua Appia, 54ff. for the Anio Vetus. More recently see A.T. Hodge, *Roman Aqueducts and Water Supply* (London 1992).

38 This figure is based on an annual consumption rate of 120 kg of wheat (or calorific equivalent) per person, for which see Ampolo, *DdA* NS 2 (1980), 15–31, esp. 25. The figure of 18,000 tonnes given in *CAH²* VII.2 (1989), 408, was based on a consumption rate of 200 kg per person year, which is probably too high (cf. Hopkins, *Conquerors and Slaves* (1978), 98). A hinterland of 1,000 km² would probably be able to support about half the population (at most), if we assume, following Ampolo, that around 15 per cent of the land was under cultivation at any one time, and that the annual yield was *c.* 350 kg per hectare. It follows that a minimum of 5,500 tonnes would have had to be imported each year around 280 BC.

39 Livy 9.29.9–11; cf. Coarelli, *Foro Boario* (1988), 80–2.

40 E.g. T. Frank, *Economic Survey of Ancient Rome* I (Baltimore 1933), 6; M. Rostovtzeff, *Social and Economic History of the Roman Empire* (2nd edn, Oxford 1957), 13. For a recent statement of this traditional view, R.W. Wallace in Eder (ed.), *Staat und Staatlichkeit* (1990), 278–92.

41 For a reasoned critique of the traditional view, see Starr, *Beginnings of Imperial Rome* (1980), based on the archaeological evidence presented in the 1973 exhibition catalogue *Roma medio-repubblicana*. Wallace's attempt to dismiss this evidence (see previous note) is misconceived. See the fiercely critical remarks of M. Torelli in the discussion following Wallace's paper (ibid. 303–5).

42 H.H. Scullard, *CAH²* VII.2 (1989), 526–30; Scardigli, *Trattati romano-cartaginesi* (1991), 115ff.

43 J.-P. Morel, in *Roma medio-repubblicana* (1973), 43–6.

44 J.-P. Morel, *MEFRA* 81 (1969), 59–117.

45 For a lucid summary of the views of the 'Cambridge primitivists' (principally A.H.M. Jones and M.I. Finley), see K. Hopkins in P. Garnsey *et al.*, *Trade in the Ancient Economy* (London 1983), x–xiv.

46 This is clear at least as far as T. Frank is concerned. His explicit rejection of all theory (*Economic Survey* I (1927), viii) makes him an unconscious modernist. Wallace too is inclined to argue that the Rome was different from its neighbours, in Eder (ed.), *Staat und Staatlichkeit* (1990), 291, prompting the obvious question from Sally Humphreys – why? (ibid., 293).

47 F. Coarelli, in *Affreschi romani dalle raccolte dell'Antiquarium comunale* (Exhibition catalogue, Rome 1976), 3–11.

48 T. Dohrn, *Die ficoronische Cista* (Berlin 1972).

49 Livy 10.23.11–12. This information comes from archival sources (probably the *Annales maximi*) and should not be doubted. A full account of all the construction, monumentalization and decoration recorded by Livy for this period is given by S.P. Oakley, in J. Rich and G. Shipley (eds), *War and Society in the Roman World* (London 1993), 33–5.

50 For the standard date (early third century BC), see R. Bianchi Bandinelli, *Rome the Centre of Power* (London 1972), 29.

51 On Cato's ideological fabrications see Toynbee, *Hannibal's Legacy* II (1965), 501–21. The standard work on Cato is A.E. Astin, *Cato the Censor* (Oxford 1978).

52 Brunt, *Italian Manpower* (1971), 377, 386: 'it can hardly be doubted that slaves

and freedmen formed the larger part of the urban population.'

53 Brunt, *Italian Manpower* (1971), 345ff., with refs. Brunt notes that ancient writers who complained about depopulation had in mind only the free population, and ignored the slaves.

54 I have followed the version of Crawford, *Roman Republican Coinage* (1974), 35–46; *Coinage and Money*, 25ff.; A Burnett, *SNR* 56 (1977), 92–121; *NAC 7* (1978), 121–42.

55 Crawford, *Coinage and Money* (1985), 28ff., revising the opinion given in *Roman Republican Coinage* (1974), 37–8, 133.

56 The archaeological evidence is summarised in the contributions to P. Zander (ed.), *Hellenismus in Mittelitalien* (Göttingen 1976).

57 S. Weinstock, *HTR* 50 (1957), 211–47.

58 P.M. Fraser, *Ptolemaic Alexandria* (Oxford 1972); N. Petrochilos, *Roman Attitudes to the Greeks* (Athens 1974); A. Momigliano, *Alien Wisdom* (Oxford 1975), 12–21; E.S. Gruen, *Studies in Greek Culture and Roman Policy* (Leiden 1990), 158–62; *Culture and Identity* (1992), 227ff.

APPENDIX: A NOTE ON EARLY ROMAN CHRONOLOGY

1 On the dictator-years see A. Drummond, *Historia* 27 (1978), 550–72.

2 Dionysius wrote a specialised work on chronology entitled *Chronoi* or *Chronica*; he refers to it in *Rom. ant.* 1.74.2. The few surviving fragments are collected by F. Jacoby, *FGrHist* 251. On this topic I am indebted to Clemence Schulze, who kindly allowed me to read her important paper on 'Dionysius of Halicarnassus and Roman Chronology', which will be published shortly in *PCPhs*.

3 As with the birth of Jesus, it does not matter for dating purposes whether the first Olympic Games really did take place in 776 BC. The important point was that the series of Olympiads was counted from that year.

4 Mommsen, *Die römische Chronologie²* (Berlin 1859); W. Soltau, *Römische Chronologie* (Freiburg i. B. 1889); O. Leuze, *Die römische Jahreserzählung* (Tübingen 1909). Recent accounts include Werner, *Beginn röm.Rep.* (1963); E.J. Bickermann, *Chronology of the Ancient World* (2nd edn, London 1980).

5 Harris, *Rome in Etruria and Umbria* (1971), 41.

6 In *CAH*² VII.2 (1989), 349 and n. 56 I wrongly stated that Livy's chronology placed the fall of Veii 391 BC, on the grounds that his version missed out the Varronian year 376 BC. But although Livy strangely fails to name the consular tribunes of 376, he does record their election and his narrative implies the existence of this year, in which Licinius and Sextius were tribunes for the first time, and in which they votoed the election of consular tribunes for the following year, i.e. Varronian 375, the first year of the anarchy. Thus rightly, F. Càssola, *ANRW* II.30.1 (1982), 731 n.16.

BIBLIOGRAPHY

This list does not include all the items cited in the notes, but only those that make an important contribution to subjects discussed in the text. It also includes some titles that are important for the same reason, but are not mentioned in the notes. The works of an individual author are listed in chronological order of publication.

Affreschi romani delle raccolte dell'Antiquarium comunale (Exhibition catalogue), Rome 1976.

Afzelius, A., *Die römische Eroberung Italiens (340–264 v. Chr.)*, Copenhagen 1942.

von Albrecht, A., *Geschichte der römischen Literatur*, 2 vols, Berne 1992.

Alföldi, A., *Der frührömische Reiteradel und seine Ehrenabzeichen*, Baden-Baden 1952.

—— *Early Rome and the Latins*, Ann Arbor n.d. (1965).

—— 'Die Herrschaft der Reiterei in Griechenland und Rom nach dem Sturz der Könige', in *Gestalt und Geschichte, Festschrift K. Schefold*, Berne 1967, 13–45.

—— *Die Struktur des voretruskischen Römerstaates*, Heidelberg 1974.

Altheim, F., *Griechische Götter im alten Rom*, Giessen 1930.

—— *History of Roman Religion*, London 1938.

—— *Lex sacrata: die Anfänge der plebeischen Organisation*, Amsterdam 1940.

Ampolo, C., 'L'Artemide di Marsiglia e la Diana dell'Aventino' *PdP* 25, 1970, 200–210.

—— 'Su alcuni mutamenti sociali nel Lazio tra l'VIIIe il V secolo', *DdA* 4–5, 1970–1, 37–68.

—— 'Servius rex primus signavit aes', *PdP* 29, 1974 382–8.

—— 'Gli Aquilii del V secolo a.C. e il problema dei Fasti consolari più antichi', *PdP* 30, 1975, 410–16.

—— 'Demarato, osservazioni sulla mobilità sociale arcaica', *DdA* 9–10, 1976–7, 333–45.

—— 'Le origini di Roma et la 'cité antique', *MEFRA* 92, 1980, 567–76.

—— 'I gruppi etnici in Roma arcaica: posizione del problema e fonti', in *Gli Etruschi e Roma*, Rome 1981, 45–70.

—— 'Il gruppo acroteriale di S. Omobono', *PdP* 36, 1981, 32–5.

—— 'Ricerche sulla lega latina I: caput aquae Ferentinae e lacus Turni', *PdP* 36, 1981, 219–33.

—— 'Ricerche sulla lega latina II: la dedica di Egerius Baebius (Cato fr. 58 Peter)', *PdP* 38, 1983, 321–6.

—— 'Sulla formazione della città di Roma', *Opus* 2, 1983, 425–30.

—— 'Il lusso funerario e la città antica', *AION* 6, 1984, 71–102.

—— 'Il lusso nelle società arcaiche', *Opus* 3, 1984, 469–76.

—— 'Roma arcaica fra Latini ed Etruschi: aspetti politici e sociali', in *Etruria e Lazio arcaico*, 1987, 75–88.

—— 'La 'grande Roma dei Tarquini' revisitata', in E. Campanile (ed.), *Alle origini di Roma*, Pisa 1988, 77–87.

—— 'La nascità della città' and 'La città riformata', in A. Momigliano, A. Schiavone (eds), *Storia di Roma* I, 1988, 153–80; 203–39.

—— 'Rome archaïque: une société pastorale?', in C.R. Whittaker (ed.), *Pastoral Economies in Classical Antiquity*, Cambridge 1988, 120–33.

—— 'Roma arcaica ed i Latini nel V secolo', in *Crise et transformation*, 1990, 117–33.

—— 'Aspetti dello sviluppo economico agl'inizi della repubblica romana', in W. Eder (ed.), *Staat und Staatlichkeit*, 1990, 482–93.

Ampolo, C. et al., *La formazione della città nel Lazio, DdA* NS 2, 1980.

Andrén, A., *Architectural Terracottas from Etrusco-Italic Temples*, Lund 1940.

Anzidei, A.P. et al., *Roma e il Lazio dall'età della pietra alla formazione della città*, Rome 1985.

von Arnim, H., 'Ineditum Vaticanum', *Hermes* 27 1892, 118–30.

Astin, A.E., *Cato the Censor*, Oxford 1978.

Aymard, A., 'Les deux premiers traités entre Rome et Carthage', *REA* 59, 1957, 277–93 (=*Etudes d'histoire ancienne*, Paris 1967, 373–86).

Badian, E., *Foreign Clientelae, 264–70 BC*, Oxford 1958.

—— 'The Early Historians', in T.A. Dorey (ed.), *Latin Historians*, London 1966, 1–38.

Balsdon, J.P.V.D., 'Dionysius on Romulus, a Political Pamphlet?', *JRS* 61, 1971, 18–27.

Banti, L., 'Il culto del cosidetto tempio di Apollo a Veio e il problema delle triadi etrusco-italiche', *SE* 17, 1943, 187–224.

—— *The Etruscan Cities and their Culture*, London 1973.

Barbagallo, C., *Il problema delle origini di Roma, da Vico a noi*, Milan 1926.

Barfield, L., *Northern Italy before Rome*, London 1971.

Barker, G., *Landscape and Society: prehistoric central Italy*, London 1981.

Bartoloni, G., 'I depositi votivi di Roma arcaica', *Scienze dell'antichità* 3–4, 1989–90, 747–59.

—— *La civiltà villanoviana*, Rome 1989.

Bartoloni, G., Beijer, A., De Santis, A., 'Huts in the Central Tyrrhenian Area of Italy during the Protohistoric Age', in C. Malone, S. Stoddart (eds), *Patterns in Protohistory*, Oxford 1985, 175–202.

Bartoloni, G., Buranelli, F., D'Atri, V., De Santis, A., *Le urne a capanna rinvenute in Italia*, Rome 1987.

Bartoloni, G., Cataldi Dini, M., Zevi, F., 'Aspetti dell'ideologia funeraria nella necropoli di Castel di Decima', in G. Gnoli and J.-P. Vernant (eds), *La mort*, Cambridge–Paris 1982, 257–73.

Bartoloni, G. and Grottanelli, C., 'I carri a due ruote nelle tombe femminili del Lazio e dell'Etruria', *Opus* 3, 1984, 383–410.

Bayet, J., 'Les origines de l'arcadisme romain', *MEFR* 38, 1920, 63–143.

—— *Les origines de l'Hercule romain*, Paris 1926.

—— 'Tite-Live et la précolonisation romaine', *RPh* 12, 1938, 97–119.

Beard, M. and North, J.A. (eds), *Pagan Priests*, London 1990.

Beard, M., et al., *Literacy in the Roman World*, Ann Arbor 1991 (*JRA* suppl. 3).

de Beaufort, L., *Dissertation sur l'incertitude des cinq premiers siècles de l'histoire romaine*, Utrecht 1738 (rev. edn, Paris 1866).

Bedini, A. and Cordano, F., 'L'ottavo secolo nel Lazio e l'inizio dell'orientalizzante antico alla luce di recenti scoperte nella necropoli di Castel di Decima', *PdP* 32, 1977, 274–311.

Beloch, J., *Campanien*, Berlin 1879.

—— *Die Bevölkerung der griechisch-römischen Welt*, Leipzig 1886.

—— *Römische Geschichte bis zum Beginn der punischen Kriege*, Berlin 1926.

Bernardi, A., 'Dagli ausiliari del *rex* ai magistrati della *respublica*', *Athenaeum* 30, 1952, 3–58.

—— 'Periodo sabino e periodo etrusco nella monarchia romana', *RSI* 66, 1954, 5–20.

—— 'Dai *populi Albenses* ai *Prisci Latini* nel Lazio arcaico', *Athenaeum* 42, 1964, 223–60.

—— *Nomen Latinum*, Pavia 1973.

Bessone, L., 'La gente Tarquinia', *RFIC* 110, 1982, 394–415.

Bickermann, E.J., 'Origines gentium', *CPh* 47, 1952, 65–81 (= *Religions and Politics*, 1985, 399–417).

—— 'Some Reflections on Early Roman History', *RFIC* 97, 1969, 393–408 (= *Religions and Politics*, 1985, 525–40).

—— *Chronology of the Ancient World*, rev. edn, London 1980.

—— *Religions and Politics in the Hellenistic and Roman Periods*, Como 1985.

Bietti Sestieri, A.-M., *Ricerca su una comunità del Lazio protostorico*, Rome 1979.

—— 'Evidence of Social Change in Lazio in the 8th Century BC: the case of the iron-age cemetery of Osteria dell'Osa', in C. Malone, S. Stoddart (eds), *Patterns in Protohistory*, Oxford 1985, 111–44.

—— *The Iron-Age Community of Osteria dell'Osa*, Cambridge 1992.

—— *La necropoli laziale di Osteria dell'Osa*, 3 vols, Rome 1992.

Bilancio critico su Roma arcaica fra monarchia e repubblica (Convegno in memoria di F. Castagnoli: Atti dei Convegni Lincei 100), Rome 1993.

Binder, G., *Die Aussetzung des Königskindes Kyros und Romulus*, Meisenheim am Glan 1964.

Binder, J., *Die Plebs, Studien zur römischen Rechtsgeschichte*, Leipzig 1909.

Blakeway, A., 'Demaratus', *JRS* 25, 1935, 129–49.

Bleicken, J., 'Ursprung und Bedeutung der Provocation', *ZSS* 76, 1959, 324–77.

—— *Das Volkstribunat der klassischen Republik*, Munich 1960.

—— *Lex publica: Gesetz und Recht in der römischen Republik*, Berlin 1975.

Bloch, G., *Les origines du Sénat romain*, Paris 1883.

—— 'La plèbe romaine, Essai sur quelques théories récentes', *Rev. Hist*, 106, 1911, 241–75; 107, 1912, 1–42.

Bloch, R., *The Origins of Rome*, London 1960.

—— *Tite-Live et les premiers siècles de Rome*, Paris 1965.

Boethius, A., *Etruscan and Early Roman Architecture*, Harmondsworth 1970.

Bonfante, L., 'Roman Triumphs and Etruscan Kings: the changing face of the triumph', *JRS* 60, 1970, 49–66.

—— *Etruscan Dress*, Baltimore 1975.

—— 'Etruscan', in J.T. Hooker (ed.), *Reading the Past*, London 1990.

Bonfante, P., 'La gens e la famiglia', in *Scritti giuridici varii* 1, Turin 1926, 1–17.

—— 'Teorie vecchie e nuove sulle formazioni sociali primitive', ibid., 18–63.

—— *Storia del diritto romano*, 2nd edn, 2 vols, Turin 1957.

le Bonniec, H., *Le culte de Cérès à Rome*, Paris 1958.

Botsford, G.W., 'The Social Composition of the Primitive *populus*', *Political Science Quarterly* 21, 1906, 498–526.

—— 'Some Problems Connected with the Roman *gens*', *Political Science Quarterly* 22, 1907, 663–92.

—— *The Roman Assemblies from their Origin to the End of the Republic*, New York 1909.

Bremmer, J.N., 'The *suodales* of Poplios Valesios', *Zeitschrift für Papyrologie und Epigraphik* 47, 1982, 133–47.

Bremmer, J.N. and Horsfall, N.M., *Roman Myth and Mythography*, London 1987.

Briquel, D., 'Perspectives comparatives sur la tradition relative à la disparition de Romulus', *Latomus* 36, 1977, 253–82.

—— *Les Pelasges en Italie: recherches sur l'histoire de la légende*, Rome 1984.

Brown, F.E., 'New Soundings in the Regia', in *Les origines de la république romaine*, Foundation Hardt *Entretiens* 13, Geneva 1967, 47–60.

—— 'La protostoria della regia', *RPAA* 47, 1974–5, 15–36.

—— 'Of Huts and Houses', in *In Memoriam O.J. Brendel*, Mainz 1976, 5–12.

Bruno, B., *La terza guerra sannitica*, Rome 1906.

Brunt, P.A., *Italian Manpower, 225 BC – AD 14*, Oxford 1971.

—— *Social Conflicts in the Roman Republic*, London 1971.

—— 'Cicero and Historiography', in *Miscellanea di studi classici in onore di Eugenio Manni*, Rome 1979, I, 311–40.

—— 'Clientela', in *The Fall of the Roman Republic and Other Essays*, Oxford 1988, 382–442.

Buchner, G., 'Early Orientalizing: aspects of the Euboean connection', in *Italy before the Romans*, 1979, 129–44.

Buranelli, F., (ed.), *La Tomba François de Vulci* (Exhibition catalogue), Rome 1987.

Campanile, E., (ed.), *Alle origini di Roma*, Pisa 1988.

Campanile, E. and Letta, C., *Studi sulle magistrature indigene e municipali nell 'area italica*, Pisa 1979.

Canciani, F. and von Hase, F.W., *La Tomba Bernardini di Palestrina*, Rome 1979.

Capdeville, G., 'Le nom de Servius Tullius', in *La Rome des premiers siècles*, 1992, 47–68.

Capogrossi-Colognesi, L., *La terra in Roma antica*, Rome 1981.

—— *Dalla tribù allo stato*, Rome 1990.

Carandini, A., 'Campagne di scavo delle pendici settentrionali [sc. del Palatino]', *Boll. Arch*. 1–2, 1990, 159–65.

Càssola, F., *I gruppi politici romani nel III sec. A.C.*, Trieste 1962.

—— 'Diodoro e la storia romana', *ANRW* II.30, 1, 1982, 724–73.

Castagnoli, F., *Lavinium I: topografia generale, fonti e storia delle ricerche*, Rome 1972.

—— 'Roma arcaica e i recenti scavi di Lavinio', *PdP* 32, 1977, 340–55.

—— 'Les sanctuaires du Latium archaïque', *CRAI* 1977, 460–76.

—— *Il culto di Minerva a Lavinium* (Accademia Nazionale dei Lincei, Quaderno 246), Rome 1979.

—— 'La leggenda di Enea nel Lazio', *SR* 30, 1982, 1–15.

—— 'Ancora sul culto di Minerva a Lavinio', *BCom* 90, 1985, 7–12.

Catalano, P., 'Aspetti spaziali del sistema giuridico-religioso romano: mundus, templum, urbs, ager, Latium, Italia', in *ANRW* II.16, 1978, 440–553.

de Cazenove, O., 'La chronologie des Bacchiades et celle des rois étrusques de Rome', *MEFRA* 100, 1988, 615–48.

—— 'Le sanctuaire de Cérès jusqu' à la deuxième sécession de la plèbe', in *Crise et transformation*, 1980, 373–99.

—— 'La détermination chronographique de la durée de la période royale de Rome', in *La Rome des premiers siècles*, 1992, 69–98.

I Celti (Exhibition catalogue), Milan 1991.

Chevallier, R., 'La Celtique du Pô', *Latomus* 21, 1962, 356–70.

Cianfarani, V. *et al.*, *Culture adriatiche antiche di Abruzzo e Molise*, Rome 1978.

Cichorius, C., *De fastis consularibus antiquissimis*, Diss. Leipzig 1886.

—— 'Annales', *RE* 1, 1894, 2248–55.

Civiltà del Lazio primitivo (Exhibition catalogue), Rome 1976.

Coarelli, F., *Guida archeologica di Roma*, Milan 1974.

—— 'Topographie antique et idéologie moderne: le Forum romain revisité', *Annales (ESC)* 37, 1982, 724–40.

—— *Il foro romano* I: *Periodo arcaico*, Rome 1983.

—— 'Le pitture della tomba François di Vulci: una proposta di lettura', *DdA* ser. 3, 3, 1983, 43–69.

—— *Il foro Boario*, Rome 1988.

—— 'I santuari, il fiume, gli empori' and 'Demografia e territorio' in A. Momigliano and A. Schiavone (eds), *StdR* I, 1988, 127–51; 318–39.

—— 'Roma, i Volsci e il Lazio antico', in *Crise et transformation*, 1990, 135–54.

Coleman, R.G.G., 'The Central Italic Languages in the Period of Roman Expansion', *Trans. Philol. Soc.* 1986, 100–31.

Coli, U., 'Regnum', *SDHI* 17, 1951, 1–168 (= *Scritti di diritto romano*, Milan 1973, I, 323–483).

—— 'Tribù e centurie dell'antica repubblica romana', in *SDHI* 21, 1955, 181–222 (= *Scritti*, 1973, II, 571–611).

Colonna, G., 'La ceramica etrusco-corinzia e la problematica storica dell'orientalizzante recente in Etruria', *Arch. Class.* 13, 1961, 9–25.

—— 'Nomi etruschi di vasi', *Arch. Class.* 25–6, 1973–4, 132–50.

—— 'Preistoria e protostoria di Roma e del Lazio', in *PCIA* 2, 1974, 273–346.

—— 'Scriba cum rege sedens', in *Mélanges Jacques Heurgon*, Rome 1976, 187–207.

—— 'Un aspetto oscuro del Lazio antico. Le tombe del VI–V sec. A.C.', *PdP* 32, 1977, 131–65.

—— 'The Later Orientalizing Period in Rome', in *Italy before the Romans*, 1979, 223–35.

—— 'Tarquinio Prisco e il tempio di Giove Capitolino', *PdP* 36, 1981, 41–59.

—— 'Quali etruschi a Roma?' in *Gli Etruschi e Roma*, 1981, 159–68.

—— 'I templi del Lazio fino al V secolo compreso', *Arch. Laz.* 6, 1984, 396–411.

—— 'Apollon, les Etrusques et Lipara', *MEFRA* 96, 1984, 557–78.

—— 'Etruria e Lazio nell'età dei Tarquini', in *Etruria e Lazio arcaico*, 1987, 55–66.

—— 'Il maestro dell'Ercole e della Minerva', *Op. Rom.* 16, 1987, 7–41.

—— 'La produzione artigianale', in A. Momigliano, A. Schiavone (eds) *Storia di Roma* I, 1988, 292–316.

—— 'Città e territorio nell'Etruria meridionale del V secolo', in *Crise et transformation*, 1990, 7–21.

Conta Haller, G., *Ricerche su alcuni centri fortificati in opera poligonale nell'area campano-sannitica*, Naples 1978.

Cornelius, F., *Untersuchungen zur frühen römischen Geschichte*, Munich 1940.

Cornell, T.J., 'Notes on the Sources for Campanian History in the Fifth Century BC', *Mus. Helv.* 31, 1974, 193–208.

—— 'Aeneas and the Twins: the development of the Roman foundation legend', *PCPhS* NS 21, 1975, 1–32.

—— 'Etruscan Historiography', *ASNP* ser. 3, VI.2, 1976, 411–39.

—— 'Principes of Tarquinia', *JRS* 68, 1978, 167–173.

—— 'The Foundation of Rome in the Ancient Literary Tradition', in H. McK. Blake *et al.* (eds), *Papers in Italian Archaeology* I, Oxford 1978, 131–40.

—— 'Rome and Latium Vetus, 1974–79', *Arch. Reports* 26, 1980, 71–89.

—— 'Some Observations on the *crimen incesti*', in *Le délit religieux dans la cité antique*, 1981, 27–37.

—— 'Gründer', in *Reallexikon für Antike und Christentum* XII, 1983, 1107–45.

—— 'The Failure of the *plebs*', in *Tria Corda: scritti in onore di Arnaldo Momigliano* (ed. E. Gabba), Como 1983, 101–20.

—— 'The Annals of Quintus Ennius', *JRS* 76, 1986, 244–50.

—— 'The Formation of the Historical Tradition of Early Rome', in I.S. Moxon *et al.* (eds), *Past Perspectives*, Cambridge 1986, 67–86.

—— 'Rome and Latium Vetus 1980–85', *Arch. Reports* 32, 1986, 123–33.

—— 'The Value of the Literary Tradition concerning Early Rome', in K. Raaflaub (ed.), *Social Struggles in Archaic Rome*, Berkeley 1986, 52–76.

—— 'La guerra e lo stato in Roma arcaica (VII–V sec.)', in E. Campanile (ed.), *Alle origini di Roma*, Pisa 1988, 89–100.

—— 'Rome and Latium to 390 BC', 'The Recovery of Rome', 'The Conquest of Italy', in *CAH²* VII.2, 1989, 243–419.

—— 'The Tyranny of the Evidence: a discussion of the possible uses of literacy in Etruria and Latium in the archaic age', in M. Beard *et al.*, *Literacy in the Roman World*, 1991, 7–33.

Cozza, L. *et al.*, *Lavinium II; le tredici are*, Rome 1975.

Crake, J.E.A., 'The Annals of the *pontifex maximus*', *CPh* 35, 1940, 375–86.

Crawford, M.H., *Roman Republican Coinage*, 2 vols, Cambridge 1974.

—— *Coinage and Money under the Roman Republic*, London 1985.

—— *The Roman Republic*, 2nd edn, London 1992.

Crifò, G., 'La legge delle XII tavole: osservazioni e problemi', in *ANRW* I.1, 1972, 115–33.

Crise et transformation des sociétés archaïques de l'Italie antique au Ve siècle av. J.C. (Proceedings of a conference at the École Française de Rome), Rome 1990.

Cristofani, M., 'Ricerche sulle pitture della Tomba François di Vulci. I fregi decorativi', *DdA* 1, 1967, 186–219.

—— 'Il 'dono' nell'Etruria arcaica', *PdP* 30, 1975, 132–52.

—— 'Sugli inizi dell'etruscheria', *MEFRA* 90, 1978, 577–625.

—— 'Recent Advances in Etruscan Epigraphy and Language', in *Italy before the Romans*, 1979, 373–412.

—— (ed.), 'I santuari: tradizioni decorative', in *Etruria e Lazio arcaico*, Rome 1987, 95–120.

—— *Saggi di storia etrusca arcaica*, Rome 1987.

—— 'Osservazioni sulle decorazioni fittili arcaiche dal santuario di S. Omobono', *Arch. Laz.* 10, 1990, 31–7.

Crook, J.A., 'Patria potestas', *CQ* 17, 1967, 113–22.

Daube, D., 'Two Early Patterns of Manumission', *JRS* 36, 1946, 57–75.

D'Agostino, B., 'Il mondo periferico della Magna Grecia', in *PCIA* 2, 1974, 177–271.

—— 'Military Organization and Social Structure in Archaic Etruria', in O. Murray, S. Price (eds), *The Greek City*, Oxford 1990, 59–82.

De Francisci, P., 'Intorno all'origine etrusca del concetto d'*imperium*', *SE* 24, 1955–6, 19–43.

—— *Primordia civitatis*, Rome 1959.

De Martino, F., *Storia della costituzione romana*, 5 vols, 2nd edn, Naples 1972–5.

—— 'Intorno all'origine della repubblica romana e delle magistrature', in *ANRW* II.1, 1972, 217–49 (= *Diritto e società*, 1979, 88–129).

—— *Diritto e società nell'antica Roma*, Rome 1979.

—— *Storia economica di Roma antica*, 2 vols, Florence 1980.

—— 'Sulla storia dell'*equitatus* romano', *PdP* 35, 1980, 143–60.

De Sanctis, G., *Storia dei Romani* I–II: *La conquista del primato in Italia*, Turin 1907 (2nd edn, Florence 1960).

—— 'Le origini dell'ordinamento centuriato', *RFIC* 61, 1933, 289–98.

De Zulueta, 'The Recent Controversy about *nexum*', *Law Quarterly Review* 29, 1913, 137–53.

Degrassi, A., *Inscriptiones Italiae* XIII.1: *Fasti consulares et triumphales*, Rome 1947.

Le délit religieux dans la cité antique (Proceedings of a conference at the Ecole Française de Rome). Rome 1981.

Develin, R., 'Prorogation of *imperium* before the Hannibalic War', *Latomus* 34, 1975, 716–22.

—— *Patterns in Office-Holding, 366–49 BC*, Brussels 1979.

Devoto, G., *Gli antichi italici* 3rd edn, Florence 1967.

Dohrn, T., *Die ficoronische Cista*, Berlin 1972.

Dorey, T.A. (ed.), *Livy*, London 1971.

Drews, R., 'The Coming of the City to Central Italy', *AJAH* 6, 1981, 133–65.

—— 'Pontiffs, Prodigies and the Disappearance of the *Annales maximi*', *CPh* 83, 1988, 189–99.

Drummond, A., 'The Dictator Years', *Historia* 27, 1978, 550–72.

—— 'Consular Tribunes in Livy and Diodorus', *Athenaeum* 58, 1980, 57–72.

—— 'Rome in the Fifth Century. I, The Social and Economic Framework; II, The Citizen Community', in *CAH²* VII.2, 1989, 113–242.

—— 'Early Roman *clientes*', in A. Wallace-Hadrill (ed.), *Patronage in Ancient Society*, London 1989, 89–115.

Dubourdieu, A., *Les origines et le développement du culte des Pénates à Rome*, Rome 1989.

Ducos, M., *L'influence grec sur la loi des douze tables*, Paris 1978.

von Duhn, F., *Italische Gräberkunde* I, Heidelberg 1924.

Dulière, C., *Lupa Romana*, Brussels 1979.

Dumézil, G., *Jupiter, Mars, Quirinus*, Paris 1941.

—— *La naissance de Rome*, Paris 1944.

—— *Tarpeia*, Paris 1947.

—— *L'héritage indo-européene à Rome*, Paris 1948.

—— *L'ideologie tripartite des indo-européens*, Brussels 1958.

—— *Mythe et épopée*, 3 vols, Paris 1968.

—— *Archaic Roman Religion*, Chicago 1970.

—— *Marriages indo-européens à Rome*, Paris 1979.

Dury-Moyaers, G., *Enée et Lavinium*, Brussels 1981.

Eder, W., 'The Political Significance of the Codification of Law in Archaic Societies: an unconventional hypothesis', in K. Raaflaub (ed.), *Social Struggles*, 1986, 262–300.

—— (ed.), *Staat und Staatlichkeit in der frühen römischen Republik*, Stuttgart 1990.

Elster, M., *Studien zur Gesetzgebung der frühen römischen Republik*, Frankfurt 1976.

Enea nel Lazio, archeologia e mito (Exhibition catalogue), Rome 1980.

Ennew, J., *Debt Bondage: a survey*, London 1981.

Ernout, A., 'Les éléments étrusques du vocabulaire latin', *Bull. Soc. Ling.* 1930, 82–124 (= Ernout, *Philologica* I, Paris 1946, 21–51).

Fauth, W., 'Römische Religion im Spiegel der 'Fasti' des Ovid', *ANRW* II.16.1, 1978, 104–86.

Ferenczy, E., *From the Patrician State to the Patricio-Plebeian State*, Budapest 1976.

Finley, M.I., *Ancient Slavery and Modern Ideology*, London 1980.

—— 'Debt Bondage and the Problem of Slavery', in *Economy and Society in Ancient Greece*, London 1981, 150–66.

—— *Ancient History, Evidence and Models*, London 1985.

Flach, D., *Die Gesetze der frühen römischen Republik*, Darmstadt 1994.

Foraboschi, *Lineamenti di storia della Cisalpina romana*, Rome 1992.

Forsén, B., *Lex Licinia Sextia de modo agrorum – fiction or reality?*, Helsinki 1991.

Forsythe, G., 'Some notes on the History of Cassius Hemina', *Phoenix* 44, 1990, 326–44.

Fraccaro, P., *Studi Varroniani, De gente populi Romani*, Padua 1907.

—— 'La storia dell'antichissimo esercito romano e l'età dell'ordinamento centuriato', *Atti II Congresso nazionale di studi romani* 3, 1931, 91–7 (= *Opuscula* II, 287–92).

—— '*Tribules* ed *aerarii*: una ricerca di diritto pubblico romano', *Athenaeum* 11, 1933, 150–72 (= *Opuscula* II, 149–70).

—— 'Ancora sull'età dell'ordinamento centuriato', *Athenaeum* 12, 1934, 57–71 (= *Opuscula* II, 293–306).

—— 'La storia romana arcaica', *RIL* 85, 1952, 85–118 (= *Opuscula* I, 1–23).

—— *Opuscula*, 4 vols, Pavia 1956–75.

—— 'The History of Rome in the Regal Period', *JRS* 47, 1957, 59–65.

—— *Della guerra presso i Romani*, Pavia 1975 (= *Opuscula* IV).

Franciosi, G., (ed.), *Ricerche sull'organizzazione gentilizia romana*, 2 vols, Naples 1984–8.

Frank, T., *Roman Buildings of the Republic*, Rome 1924.

—— *Economic Survey of Ancient Rome*. I: *Rome and Italy of the Republic*, Baltimore 1927.

Fraschetti, A., 'A proposito dei 'clavtie' ceretani', *Quaderni Urbinati* 24, 1977, 157–62.

Fraser, P.M., *Ptolemaic Alexandria*, Oxford 1972.

Frazer, J.G., *The Golden Bough*, 3rd edn, 12 vols, London 1911–15.

Frederiksen, M.W. 'Campanian Cavalry: a question of origins', *DdA* 2, 1968, 3–31.

—— 'The Etruscans in Campania', in *Italy before the Romans*, 1979, 277–311.

—— *Campania*, London 1984.

Frier, B.W., *Libri annales pontificum maximorum: the origins of the annalistic tradition*, Rome 1979.

von Fritz, K., 'The Reorganisation of the Roman Government in 366 BC and the so-called Licinio-Sextian Laws', *Historia* 1, 1950, 3–44.

Fugazzola Delpino, M.A., *Testimonianze di cultura appenninica nel Lazio*, Florence 1976.

—— 'The Proto-Villanovan: a survey', in *Italy before the Romans*, 1979, 31–51.

Fustel de Coulanges, N.D., *The Ancient City* (with a foreword by A. Momigliano and S.C. Humphreys), Baltimore 1980.

Gabba, E., 'Studi su Dionigi da Alicarnasso. I. La costituzione di Romolo', *Athenaeum* 38, 1960, 175–225.

—— 'Studi su Dionigi da Alicarnasso. II. Il regno di Servio Tullio', *Athenaeum* 39, 1961, 98–121.

—— 'Studi su Dionigi da Alicarnasso. III. La proposta di legge agraria di Spurio Cassio', *Athenaeum* 42, 1964, 29–41.

—— 'Un documento censorio in Dionigi d'Alicarnasso 1.74.5', in *Synteleia V. Arangio-Ruiz*, Naples 1964, I, 486–93.

—— 'Considerazioni sulla tradizione letteraria sulle origini della repubblica', in *Les origines de la république romaine*, Fondation Hardt *Entretiens* 13, Vandœuvres–Geneva 1967, 133–69.

—— 'Storiografia greca e imperialismo romano (III–I sec. a.C.)', *RSI* 86, 1974, 625–42.

—— *Republican Rome: the army and the allies*, Oxford 1976.

—— 'Sulla valorizzazione politica della leggenda delle origini troiane di Roma fra III e II secolo a.C.', in M. Sordi (ed.) *I canali della propaganda nel mondo antico*, Milan 1976, 84–101.

—— 'Esercito e fiscalità a Roma nell'età repubblicana', in *Armées et fiscalité dans le monde antique*, Paris 1977, 13–33.

—— 'Per la tradizione dell'heredium romuleo', *RIL* 112, 1978, 250–8.

—— *Dionysius and the History of Archaic Rome*, Berkeley 1991.

—— 'Problemi di metodo per la storia di Roma arcaica', in *Bilancio critico*, 1993, 13–24.

Galinsky, G.K., *Aeneas, Sicily, and Rome*, Princeton 1969.
I Galli e l'Italia (Exhibition catalogue), Rome 1978.
Gantz, T.N.,'The Tarquin Dynasty', *Historia* 24, 1975, 539–54.
Gardner, J.F., *Women in Roman Law and Society*, London 1986.
Garnsey, P., *Famine and Food Supply in Graeco-Roman Antiquity*, Cambridge 1988.
Garoufalias, E., *Pyrrhus*, London 1979.
Garzetti, A., 'Appio Claudio Cieco nella storia politica del suo tempo', *Athenaeum* 25, 1947, 175–224.
de la Genière, J., 'The Iron Age in Southern Italy and Etruria', in *Italy before the Romans*, 1979, 59–93.
von Gerkan, A., 'Zur Frühgeschichte Roms', *Rh.Mus.* 100, 1957, 82–97.
—— 'Das frühe Rom nach E. Gjerstad', *Rh. Mus.* 104, 1961, 132–48.
Gierow, P.G., *The Iron Age Culture of Latium* I, Lund 1966; II.1, Lund 1964.
Giovannini, A., 'Les origines des magistratures romaines', *Mus. Helv.* 41, 1984, 15–30.
—— 'Il passaggio dalle istituzioni monarchiche alle istituzioni repubblicane', in *Bilancio critico*, 1993, 75–96.
Giuffrè, V., 'Plebeii gentes non habent',*Labeo* 16, 1970, 329–34.
Gjerstad, E., *Early Rome*, 6 vols, Lund 1953–63.
—— *Legends and Facts of Early Roman History*, Lund 1962.
—— 'Cultural History of Early Rome, Summary of archaeological evidence', *Act. Arch.* 36, 1965, 1–41.
—— 'Discussions concerning Early Rome: 3', *Historia* 16, 1967, 257–78.
—— 'The Origins of the Roman Republic', in *Les origines de la république romaine*, Fondation Hardt *Entretiens* 13, Vandœuvres–Geneva 1967, 3–30.
—— 'The Aventine Sanctuary of Diana', *Act. Arch.* 41, 1970, 99–107.
—— 'Innenpolitische und militärische Organisation in frührömischer Zeit', in *ANRW* I.1, 1972, 136–88.
Gnoli, G. and Vernant, J-P. (eds), *La mort, les morts dans les sociétés anciennes*, Cambridge–Paris 1982.
Goody, J. and Watt, I., 'The Consequences of Literacy', *CSSH* 5, 1962–3, 304–45 (= Goody (ed.), *Literacy in Traditional Societies*, Cambridge 1968, 27–68).
Grandazzi, A., *La fondation de Rome*, Paris 1991.
La grande Roma dei Tarquini (Exhibition catalogue), Rome 1990.
Grant, M., *Roman Myths*, London 1971.
—— *The Etruscans*, London 1980.
Gras, M., *Trafics tyrrhéniens archaïques*, Rome 1985.
Grassi, M.T., *I Celti in Italia*, Milan 1991.
Gros, P. and Torelli, M., *Storia dell'urbanistica: il mondo romano*, Bari 1988.
Grottanelli, C., 'Servio Tullio, Fortuna e l'oriente', *DdA* ser. 3, 5, 1987, 71–110.
Gruen, E.S., *Culture and National Identity in Republican Rome*, Ithaca, N.Y., 1992.
Guaitoli, M., 'Considerazioni su alcune città ed insediamenti del Lazio in età protostorica ed arcaica', *Röm. Mitt.* 84, 1977, 7–25.
Guarino, A., *La rivoluzione della plebe*, Naples 1975.
Guidi, A., 'Sulle prime fasi dell'urbanizzazione nel Lazio protostorico', *Opus* 1, 1982, 279–89.
Hanell, K., *Das altrömische eponyme Amt*, Lund 1946.
—— 'Probleme der römischen Fasti', in *Les origines de la république romaine*, Fondation Hardt *Entretiens* 13, Geneva 1967, 175–96.
Harris, W.V., *Rome in Etruria and Umbria*, Oxford 1971.
—— *War and Imperialism in Republican Rome, 327–70 BC*, Oxford 1979.
—— (ed.), *The Imperialism of Mid-Republican Rome*, Rome 1984.
—— *Ancient Literacy*, Cambridge, Mass., 1989.

—— 'Roman Warfare in the Economic and Social Context of the Fourth Century BC, in W. Eder (ed.), *Staat und Staatlichkeit in der frühen römischen Republik*, Stuttgart 1990, 494–510.

Harvey, F.D., 'Sostratos of Aegina', *PdP* 31, 1976, 206–14

Heurgon, J., *Recherches sur l'histoire, la religion et la civilisation de Capoue préromaine, des origines à 211 a.C.*, Paris 1942.

—— 'La vocation étruscologique de l'empereur Claude', *CRAI* 1953, 92–7.

—— 'Tite-Live et les Tarquins', *L'Information Littéraire* 7, 1955, 56–64.

—— 'L'état étrusque', *Historia* 6, 1957, 63–79.

—— *Trois études sur le 'ver sacrum'*, Brussels 1957.

—— *Daily Life of the Etruscans*, London 1964.

—— 'L. Cincius et la loi du *clavus annalis*', *Athenaeum* 42, 1964, 432–7.

—— 'La coupe d'Aulus Vibenna', *Mélanges J. Carcopino*, Paris 1966, 515–28.

—— 'The Inscriptions of Pyrgi', *JRS* 56, 1966, 1–15.

—— 'Magistratures romaines et magistratures étrusques', in *Les origines de la république romaine*, Fondation Hardt *Entretiens* 13, Geneva 1967, 99–127.

—— 'L'interprétation historique de l'historiographie latine de la République', *BAGB* 1971, 219–30.

—— *The Rise of Rome to 264 BC*, London 1973. (The original French version, *Rome et la Méditerranée occidentale*, Paris 1969, has been updated in a second edition, Paris 1980.)

Heuss, A., 'Zur Entwicklung des Imperiums des römischer Oberbeamter', *ZSS* 64, 1944, 57–133.

Hölkeskamp, K.-J., *Die Entstehung der Nobilität*, Stuttgart 1987.

—— 'Die Entstehung der Nobilität und der Funktionswandel des Volkstribunats: die historische Bedeutung der *Lex Hortensia de plebiscitis*', *Archiv für Kulturgeschichte* 70, 1988, 271–312.

—— 'Senat und Volkstribunat im frühen 3. Jh. v. Chr.', in W. Eder (ed.), *Staat und Staatlichkeit*, 1990, 437–57.

Holland, L.A., 'Septimontium or Saeptimontium?', *TAPhA* 84, 1953, 16–34.

Hopkins, K., *Conquerors and Slaves*, Cambridge 1978.

—— *Death and Renewal*, Cambridge 1983.

Horsfall, N.M., 'Some Problems in the Aeneas Legend', *CQ* 29, 1979, 372–90.

—— 'Stesichorus at Bovillae', *JHS* 99, 1979, 26–48.

—— 'Prose and Mime', in *The Cambridge History of Classical Literature* II.2, 1982, 112–20.

Hubaux, J., *Rome et Véies*, Liège 1958.

Huelsen, C., 'Die Regia', *JDAI* 4, 1889, 228–53.

Humbert, M., 'L'incorporation de Caere dans la civitas romana', *MEFR* 84, 1972, 231–68.

—— *Municipium et civitas sine suffragio: l'organisation de la conquête jusqu' à la guerre sociale*, Rome 1978.

Ilari, V., *Gli italici nelle strutture militari romane*, Milan 1974.

—— *Italy before the Romans: the iron age, orientalising and Etruscan periods*, ed. D. and F.R. Ridgway, Edinburgh 1979.

Jannot, J.-R., 'L'Etrurie intérieure de Lars Porsenna jusqu'à Arruns le jeune', *MEFRA* 100, 1989, 601–14.

Jashemski, W.F., *The Origins and History of the Proconsular and Propraetorian Imperium*, Chicago 1950.

Jocelyn, H.D., 'Urbs augurio augusto condita', *PCPhs* 17, 1971, 44–74.

Johnston, A.W., 'The Rehabilitation of Sostratos', *PdP* 27, 1972, 416–23.

Jordan, H., *Die Könige im alten Italien*, Berlin 1887.

Judson, S. and Kahane, A., 'Underground Drainageways in Southern Etruria and Northern Latium', *PBSR* 31, 1963, 75–99.

Kaser, M., 'Die Anfänge der Manumissio und das fiduziarisch gebundene Eigentum', *ZSS* 61, 1941, 153–86.

—— *Das altrömische Ius*, Göttingen 1949.

—— *Das römische Privatecht*, 2nd edn, Munich 1971.

Kienast, D., 'Die politische Emanzipation der Plebs und die Entwicklung des Heerwesens im frühen Rom', *Bonner Jahrbücher* 175, 1975, 83–112.

Kierdorf, W., 'Cato's 'Origines' und die Anfänge der römischen Geschichtsschreibung', *Chiron* 10, 1980, 205–24.

Kretschmer, P., 'Lat. *quirites* und *quiritare*', *Glotta* 10, 1920, 145–57.

Kromayer, J. and Veith, G., *Heerwesen und Kriegsführung der Griechen und Römer*, Munich 1928.

Kruta, V., 'Celtes de Cispadane et transalpines au IV et III siècles av. notre ère: données archéologiques', *SE* 46, 1978, 149–74.

Kubitschek, W., *De Romanorum tribuum origine ac propagatione*, Vienna 1882.

—— 'Tribus', *RE* VI A, 1917, 2492–2518.

Kunkel, W., *Introduction to Roman Legal and Constitutional History*, Oxford 1966.

La Regina, A., 'Centri fortificati preromani nei territori sabellici dell'Italia centrale adriatica', *Poszbna Isdanja* 46, 1975, 271–82.

La Regina, A., *et al.*, *Sannio: Pentri e Frentani dal VI al I sec. a.C.*, Rome 1980.

La Rocca, E., 'Due tombe dall'Esquilino. Alcune novità sul commercio euboico in Italia centrale nell'VIII sec. a.C.', *DdA* 8, 1974–5, 86–103.

—— 'Note sulle importazioni greche in territorio laziale nell'VIII secolo a.C.', *PdP* 32, 1977, 375–97.

Labruna, L., 'Adversus plebem dictator', *Index* 15, 1987, 289–314.

Laistner, M.L.W., *The Greater Roman Historians*, Berkeley 1947.

Lambrechts, R., *Essai sur les magistratures des républiques étrusques*, Brussels 1959.

Last, H., 'The Servian Reforms', *JRS* 35, 1945, 30–48.

Latte, K., *Römische Religionsgeschichte*, Munich 1960.

Letta, C., *I Marsi e il Fucino nell'antichità*, Milan 1972.

—— 'L'Italia dei mores Romani nelle *Origines* di Catone', *Athenaeum* 62, 1984, 3–30; 416–39.

Lévêque, P., *Pyrrhos*, Paris 1957.

Lévy-Bruhl, H., *Quelques problèmes du très ancien droit romain*, Paris 1934.

—— *Nouvelles études sur le très ancien droit romain*, Paris 1947.

Linderski, J., 'The Augural Law', in *ANRW* II.16.3, 1986, 2146–312.

—— 'Religious Aspects of the Conflict of the Orders: the case of *confarreatio*', in K. Raaflaub (ed.), *Social Struggles*, 1986, 244–61.

—— 'The Auspices and the Struggle of the Orders', in W. Eder (ed.), *Staat und Staatlichkeit*, 1990, 34–48.

Lintott, A.W., *Violence in Republican Rome*, Oxford 1968.

Lomas, K., *Rome and the Western Greeks, 350 BC – AD 200*, London 1993.

Lowe, C.J., 'The Historical Significance of Early Latin Votive Deposits', in H. McK. Blake *et al.* (ed.), *Papers in Italian Archaeology* (Oxford 1978), I, 141–52.

von Lübtow, U., *Das römische Volk*, Frankfurt 1955.

Luce, T.J., *Livy: the composition of his History*, Princeton 1977.

Maaskant-Kleibrink, M. and Olde-Dubbelink, R., *Borgo Le Ferriere (Satricum)*, Groningen 1987.

Macaulay, T.B., *Lays of Ancient Rome*, London 1842.

MacBain, B., 'Appius Claudius Caecus and the Via Appia', *CQ* 30, 1980, 356–72.

McCartney, E.S., 'The Military Indebtedness of Early Rome to Etruria', *MAAR* 1, 1915–16, 121–67.

MacCormack, G., 'Nexi, iudicati, and addicti in Livy', ZSS 84, 1967, 350–5.

Magdelain, A., 'Auspicia ad patres redeunt', Hommages J. Bayet, Paris 1964, 427–73.

—— Recherches sur l'imperium, Paris 1968.

—— 'Remarques sur la société romaine archaïque', REL 49, 1971, 103–27.

—— 'Le pomerium archaïque et le mundus', REL 54, 1976, 71–109.

Manni, E., 'Le tracce della conquista volsca nel Lazio', Athenaeum 17, 1939, 233–79.

Mansuelli, G.A., 'Problemi storici della civiltà gallica in Italia', in Hommages A. Grenier, Brussels 1962, 1067–93.

—— 'La formazione delle civiltà storiche nella valle padana orientale', SE 33, 1965, 13–47.

—— 'Etruschi e Celti nella valle del Po', in Hommages M. Renard, Brussels 1969, II, 485–504.

Martin, P.M., L'idée de la royauté à Rome, I: de la Rome royale au consensus républicain, Clermont-Ferrand 1982.

Martinez-Pinna, J., 'Evidenza di un tempio di Giove Capitolino a Roma all'inizio del VI sec. a.C.', Arch. Laz. 4, 1981, 249–52.

Mastrocinque, A., Romolo (la fondazione di Roma tra storia e leggenda), Este 1993.

Mazzarino, S., Dalla monarchia allo stato repubblicano; ricerche di storia romana arcaica, Catania 1945 (reprinted with an introduction by A. Fraschetti, Milan 1992).

—— Il pensiero storico classico, 3 vols, Bari 1966.

Ménager, L.R., 'Nature et mobiles de l'opposition entre la plèbe et le patriciat', RIDA ser. 3, 19, 1972, 367–97.

Messerschmidt, F. and von Gerkan, A., Nekropolen von Vulci (JDAI suppl. 12), Berlin 1930.

Meyer, Ed., 'Untersuchungen über Diodors römische Geschichte', Rh. Mus. 37, 1982, 610–27.

—— Geschichte des Altertums, 3 vols, 2nd edn, Stuttgart 1907–37 (vol. 1, 3rd edn, 1913).

—— 'Das römische Manipularheer', Kleine Schriften II, Halle 1924, 193–329.

Meyer, Ernst, Römische Staat und Staatsgedanke, 2nd edn, Zurich 1961.

Meyer, J.-C., 'Roman History in the Light of the Import of Attic Vases to Rome and South Etruria in the 6th and 5th Centuries BC', ARID 9, 1980, 47–68.

—— Pre-Republican Rome (ARID suppl. XI), Odense 1983.

Michels, A.K., The Calendar of the Roman Republic, Princeton 1967.

Millar, F.G.B., 'Political Power in Mid-Republican Rome: curia or comitium?', JRS 79, 1989, 138–50.

Mitchell, R.E., Patricians and Plebeians, Ithaca, N.Y. 1992.

Mitteis, L., 'Über das Nexum', ZSS 22, 1901, 96–125.

Momigliano, A., 'Due punti di storia romana arcaica', SDHI 2, 1936, 373–98 (= Quarto contributo, 329–61).

—— 'Studi sugli ordinamenti centuriati', SDHI 4, 1938, 509–20 (= Quarto contributo, 455–85).

—— Contributi alla storia degli studi classici (e del mondo antico), 14 vols, Rome 1955–95, in 10 parts, as follows: Contributo, 1955; Secondo contributo, 1960; Terzo, 1966; Quarto, 1969; Quinto, 1975; Sesto, 1980; Settimo, 1984; Ottavo, 1987; Nono, 1992; Decimo, forthcoming 1995.

—— 'Perizonius, Niebuhr and the Character of Early Roman Tradition', JRS 47, 1957, 104–14 (= Secondo contributo, 69–87; Essays, 231–51).

—— 'Some Observations on the 'Origo gentis Romanae'', JRS 48, 1958, 56–73 (= Secondo contributo 145–76).

—— 'Atene nel III secolo a.C. e la scoperta di Roma nelle storie di Timeo di Tauromenio', RSI 71, 1959, 529–56 (= Terzo contributo, 23–53; English translation in Essays, 1977, 37–66).

—— 'An Interim Report on the Origins of Rome', *JRS* 53, 1963, 95–121 (= *Terzo contributo*, 545–98).

—— 'Procum patricium', *JRS* 56, 1966, 16–24 (= *Quarto contributo*, 377–94).

—— *Studies in Historiography*, London 1966.

—— 'L'ascesa della plebe nella storia arcaica di Roma', *RSI* 79, 1967, 297–312 (= *Quarto contributo*, 437–54; English translation in Raaflaub (ed.)., *Social Struggles*, 1986, 175–94).

—— 'Osservazioni sulla distinzione fra patrizi e plebei', in *Les origines de la république romaine*, Fondation Hardt *Entretiens* 13, 1967, 199–221 (= *Quarto contributo*, 419–36).

—— Review of Alföldi, *Early Rome and the Latins*, in *JRS* 57, 1967, 211–16 (= *Quarto contributo*, 487–99).

—— 'Il *rex sacrorum* e l'origine della repubblica', in *Studi in onore di E. Volterra*, Milan 1969, I, 357–64 (=*Quarto contributo*, 395–402).

—— 'Praetor maximus* e questioni affini', *Studi in onore di G. Grosso*, Turin 1968 I, 161–75 (= *Quarto contributo*, 403–17).

—— 'The Origins of the Roman Republic', in C.S. Singleton (ed.), *Interpretation: theory and practice*, Baltimore 1969, 1–34 (= *Quinto contributo*, 293–332).

—— *Alien Wisdom, The limits of Hellenization*, Cambridge 1975.

—— *Essays in Ancient and Modern Historiography*, Oxford 1977.

—— 'Prolegomena a ogni futura metafisica sulla plebe romana', *Labeo* 23, 1977, 7–15 (= *Sesto contributo*, 477–86).

—— 'How to Reconcile Greeks and Trojans', *Mededelingen der Koninklijke Nederlandse Akademie van Wetenschappen* NS 45, 1982, 231–54 (= *Settimo contributo*, 437–62).

—— 'Georges Dumézil and the Trifunctional Approach to Roman Civilization', *History and Theory* 23, 1984, 312–30 (= *Ottavo contributo*, 135–59).

—— 'The Origins of Rome', in *CAH²* VII.2, 1989, 52–112 (= *Settimo contributo*, 379–436).

—— *The Classical Foundations of Modern Historiography*, Berkeley 1990.

—— *Studies on Modern Scholarship* (ed. G.W. Bowersock and T.J. Cornell), Berkeley 1994.

Momigliano, A. and Schiavone, A. (eds), *Storia di Roma* I: *Roma in Italia*, Turin, 1988.

Mommsen, T., *Die römische Tribus in administrativer Beziehung*, Altona 1844.

—— *Die römische Chronologie*, 2nd edn, Berlin 1859.

—— *The History of Rome*, (trans. W.P. Dickson), 4 vols, 2nd edn, London 1864.

—— *Römische Forschungen*, 2 vols, Berlin 1864–79.

—— *Römisches Staatsrecht*, 3 vols, 3rd edn, Leipzig 1887–8.

—— *Römisches Strafrecht*, Leipzig 1899.

Morel, J.-P., 'L'atelier des petites estampilles', *MEFR* 81, 1969, 1–59.

Morselli, C. and Tortorici, E., *Ardea*, Rome 1982 (Forma Italiae I.16).

Moxon, I.S., Smart, J.D. and Woodman A.J. (eds), *Past Perspectives: studies in Greek and Roman historical writing*, Cambridge 1986.

Müller, K.D. and Deecke, W., *Die Etrusker*, 2 vols, 2nd edn, Stuttgart 1877.

Müller-Karpe, H., *Vom Anfang Roms*, Heidelberg 1959.

—— *Zur Stadtwerdung Roms*, Heidelberg 1963.

Münzer, F., *Römische Adelsparteien und Adelsfamilien*, Stuttgart 1921.

Murray, O., 'The Greek Symposium in History', in *Tria Corda*, 1983, 257–72.

—— (ed.), *Sympotica*, Oxford 1989.

—— 'Cities of Reason', in Murray and Price (eds), *The Greek City*, 1990, 1–25.

—— *Early Greece*, 2nd edn, London 1993.

Murray, O. and Price S.R.F., *The Greek City from Homer to Alexander*, Oxford 1990.

Musti, D., *Tendenze nella storiografia romana e greca su Roma arcaica, Studi su Livio e Dionigi da Alicarnasso*, Urbino 1970.

—— 'Etruschi e greci nella rappresentazione dionisiana delle origini di Roma', in *Gli Etruschi e Roma*, 1981, 23–44.

—— 'Etruria e Lazio arcaico nella tradizione (Demarato, Tarquinio, Mezenzio)', in *Etruria e Lazio arcaico*, 1987, 139–53.

—— 'Patres conscripti (e minores gentes)', *MEFRA* 101, 1989, 207–27.

—— *La naissance de Rome* (Exhibition catalogue), Paris 1977.

Negroni Catacchio, N., *Sorgenti della Nova: una comunità protostorica e il suo territorio nell'Etruria meridionale*, Rome 1981.

Nestle, W., 'Die Fabel des Menenius Agrippa', *Klio* 21, 1927, 350–60.

Nicolet, C., *Tributum, Recherches sur la fiscalité directe à l'époque républicaine*, Bonn 1976.

—— 'Le *stipendium* des alliés italiens avant la guerre sociale', *PBSR* 46, 1978, 1–11.

—— *The World of the Citizen in Republican Rome*, London 1980.

Niebuhr, B.G., *The History of Rome* (trans. J.C. Hare and C. Thirlwall), 3 vols, 3rd edn, London 1837–42.

Niese, B., 'Das sogenannte Licinisch-Sextische Ackergesetz', *Hermes* 23, 1888, 410–29.

Nilsson, M.P., 'The Introduction of Hoplite Tactics at Rome', *JRS* 19, 1929, 1–11.

North, J.A., 'Religion in Republican Rome', in *CAH²* VII.2, 1989, 573–624.

Oakley, S., 'The Roman Conquest of Italy', in J. Rich and G. Shipley (eds), *War and Society in the Roman World*, London 1993, 9–37.

O'Brien Moore, A., 'Senatus', *RE* suppl. 6, 1935, 660–800.

Oestenberg, C.E., *Luni sul Mignone e problemi della preistoria in Italia*, Lund 1967.

—— *Case etrusche di Acquarossa*, Rome 1975.

Ogilvie, R.M., 'Livy, Licinius Macer, and the *libri lintei*', *JRS* 48, 1958, 40–6.

—— *A Commentary on Livy* 1–5, Oxford 1965.

—— *Early Rome and the Etruscans*, London 1976.

Les origines de la république romaine, Fondation Hardt *Entretiens* 13, Vandœuvres–Geneva 1967.

Pais, E., *Storia di Roma*, 2 vols, Turin 1898–9 (second, revised edn: *Storia critica di Roma durante i primi cinque secoli*, 4 vols, Rome 1913–20).

—— *Ancient Legends of Roman History*, London 1906.

—— *Ricerche sulla storia e sul diritto pubblico di Roma*, 4 vols, Rome 1915–21.

—— *Fasti triumphales populi Romani*, 2nd edn, Turin 1930.

Pallottino, M., *L'origine degli Etruschi*, Rome 1947.

—— *La scuola di Vulca*, 2nd edn, Rome 1948.

—— 'Nuovi spunti di ricerca sul tema delle magistrature etrusche', *SE* 24, 1955–6, 45–72.

—— 'Le origini di Roma', *Arch. Class.* 12, 1960, 1–36.

—— 'Fatti e leggende (moderne) sulla più antica storia di Roma', *SE* 31, 1963, 3–37.

—— 'Scavi nel santuario etrusco di Pyrgi', *Arch. Class.* 16, 1964, 49–117.

—— *The Etruscans*, London 1975.

—— 'Servius Tullius à la lumière des nouvelles découvertes archéologiques et épigraphiques', *CRAI* 1977, 216–35.

—— 'The Origins of Rome: a survey of recent discoveries and discussions', in *Italy before the Romans*, 1979, 197–222.

—— *A History of Earliest Italy*, London 1991.

—— *Origini e storia primitiva di Roma*, Milan 1993.

Palmer, L.R., *The Latin Language*, London 1954.

Palmer, R.E.A., *The King and the Comitium, A study of Rome's oldest public document* (*Historia* Einzelschriften 11), Wiesbaden 1969.

—— *The Archaic Community of the Romans*, Cambridge 1970.

—— Review of Gjerstad, *Early Rome* V–VI, *AJA* 79, 1975, 386–90.

Pareti, L., *La tomba Regolini-Galassi del Museo Gregoriano Etrusco e la civiltà dell'Italia centrale nel VII sec. a.C.*, Vatican City 1947.

Pasquali, G., 'La grande Roma dei Tarquini', *La Nuova Antologia*, 16 August 1936, 405–16 (= *Terze pagine stravaganti*, Florence 1942, 1–24).

Pearson, L., *The Greek Historians of the West: Timaeus and his predecessors*, Atlanta 1987.

Pena, M.J., 'La dedicación y el dedicante del templo de Júpiter Capitolino', *Faventia* 3.2, 1981, 149–70.

Penney, J.H.W., 'The Languages of Italy', in *CAH*[2] IV, 1988, 720–38.

Perl, G., *Kritische Untersuchungen zur Diodors römischer Jahrzählung*, Berlin 1957.

Peroni, R., 'S. Omobono: materiali dell'età del Bronzo e degli inizi dell'età del Ferro', *BCom* 77, 1959–60, 7–32.

—— 'From Bronze Age to Iron Age: economic, historical and social considerations', in *Italy before the Romans*, 1979, 7–30.

—— 'L'insediamento subappenninico della valle del foro e il problema della continuità di insediamento tra l'età del bronzo recente e quella finale nel Lazio', *Arch. Laz.* 2, 1979, 171–6.

—— (ed.), *Il Bronzo Finale in Italia*, Florence 1980.

Perret, J., *Les origines de la légende troyenne de Rome*, Paris 1942.

Peruzzi, E., *Aspetti culturali del Lazio primitivo*, Florence 1978.

—— *Mycenaeans in Early Latium*, Rome 1980.

Peter, H., *Historicorum Romanorum reliquiae*, 2nd edn, I–II, Leipzig 1906–14.

Petzold, K.-E., 'Die beiden ersten römisch-Karthagischen Verträge und das Foedus Cassianum', in *ANRW* I.1, 1972, 364–411.

Pfiffig, A.J., *Religio Etrusca*, Graz 1975.

Piganiol, A., *Essai sur les origines de Rome*, Paris 1916.

—— *Recherches sur les jeux romains*, Strasburg 1923.

Pinza, G., *Monumenti primitivi di Roma e del Lazio* (*Monumenti Antichi* XV), Rome 1905.

Poma, G., *Gli studi recenti sull'origine della repubblica romana. Tendenze e prospettive della ricerca 1963–73*, Bologna 1974.

—— *Tra legislatori e tiranni: problemi storici e storiografici sull'età delle XII Tavole*, Bologna 1984.

Potter, T.W., *A Faliscan Town in South Etruria*, London 1976.

—— *The Changing Landscape of South Etruria*, London 1979.

—— *Roman Italy*, London 1987.

Poucet, J., 'Le Septimontium et la Succusa chez Festus et Varron', *BIBR* 32, 1960, 25–73.

—— *Recherches sur la légende sabine des origines de Rome*, Louvain–Kinshasa 1967.

—— 'Les Sabins aux origines de Rome. Orientations et problèmes', in *ANRW* I.1, 1972, 48–135.

—— 'Le Latium protohistorique et archaïque à la lumière des découvertes archéologiques récentes', *AC* 47, 1978, 566–601; 48, 1979, 177–220.

—— 'Une culte d'Enée dans la région lavinate au IVe siècle a. C.n.?', in *Hommages R. Schilling*, Paris 1983, 187–201.

—— 'Enée et Lavinium', *RBPhH* 61, 1983, 144–59.

—— *Les origines de Rome: tradition et histoire*, Brussels 1985.

—— 'La diffusion de la légende d'Enée en Italie centrale et ses rapports avec celle de Romulus', *LEC* 57, 1989, 227–54.

—— 'Les grands travaux d'urbanisme dans la Rome 'étrusque': libres propos sur la notion de confirmation du récit annalistique par l'archéologie', in *La Rome des premiers siècles*, 1992, 215–34.

—— 'La fondation de Rome: croyants et antagonistes', *Latomus* 53, 1994, 95–104.

Poultney, J., *The Bronze Tables of Iguvium*, Philadelphia 1959.

Puglisi, S.M., *La civiltà appenninica: origine delle communità pastorali in Italia*, Florence 1959.

Pulgram, E., *The Tongues of Italy*, Cambridge, Mass., 1958.

Quilici, L., *Roma primitiva e le origini della civiltà laziale*, Rome 1979.

Quilici Gigli, S., 'Considerazioni sui confini del territorio di Roma primitiva', *MEFRA* 90, 1978, 567–75.

Quoniam, P., 'A propos du mur dit de Servius Tullius', *MEFR* 59, 1947, 41–64.

Raaflaub, K.A., (ed.), *Social Struggles in Archaic Rome: new perspectives on the Conflict of the Orders*, Berkeley 1986.

—— 'Politics and Society in Fifth-Century Rome', in *Bilancio critico*, 1993, 129–57.

Ranouil, P.C., *Recherches sur le patriciat, 509–366 av. J.-C.*, Paris 1975.

Rathje, A., 'A Banquet Service from the Latin City of Ficana', *ARID* 12, 1983, 7–29.

—— 'I *keimelia* orientali', *Opus* 3, 1984, 341–7.

—— 'The Adoption of the Homeric Banquet in Central Italy in the Orientalising Period', in O. Murray (ed.), *Sympotica*, Oxford 1989, 279–93.

Rawson, E., 'Prodigy Lists and the Use of the *Annales maximi*', *CQ* 21, 1971, 158–69 (= *Roman Culture and Society*, 1–15).

—— 'The Literary Sources for the Pre-Marian Army', *PBSR* 39, 1971, 13–31 (= *Roman Culture and Society*, 34–57)

—— 'Cicero the Historian and Cicero the Antiquarian', *JRS* 62, 1972, 33–45 (= *Roman Culture and Society*, 58–79).

—— 'The First Latin Annalists', *Latomus* 35, 1976, 689–717 (= *Roman Culture and Society*, 245–71).

—— *Intellectual Life in the Late Roman Republic*, London 1985.

—— *Roman Culture and Society*, Oxford 1991.

Rebuffat, R., 'Les Phéniciens à Rome', *MEFR* 78, 1966, 7–48.

Renfrew, C. and Cherry, J. (eds), *Peer Polity Interaction and Socio-Political Change*, Cambridge 1986.

Richard, J.-C., *Les origines de la plèbe romaine*, Paris 1978.

—— 'Sur le plébiscite *ut liceret consules ambos plebeios creari*', *Historia* 28, 1979, 65–75.

—— 'Patricians and Plebeians: the origin of a social dichotomy', in K. Raaflaub (ed.), *Social Struggles*, 1986, 105–29.

—— 'Recherches sur l'interprétation populaire de la figure du roi Servius Tullius', *RPh* 61, 1987, 205–25.

—— 'Historiographie et histoire: l'expédition des Fabii à la Crémère', *Latomus* 47, 1988, 526–53.

—— 'L'affaire du Crémère: recherches sur l'évolution et le sens de la tradition', *Latomus* 48, 1989, 312–25.

—— 'Les Fabii à la Crémère: grandeur et décadence de l'organisation gentilice', in *Crise et transformation*, 1990, 245–62.

—— 'Réflexions sur le tribunat consulaire', *MEFRA* 102, 1990, 767–99.

—— 'Tribuns militaires et triomphe', in *La Rome des premiers siècles*, 1992, 235–46.

—— 'Réflexions sur les 'origines' de la plèbe', in *Bilancio critico*, 1993, 27–41.

Ridgway, D., Review discussion of E. Gjerstad, *Early Rome* IV, and P.G. Gierow, *Iron-Age Culture of Latium*, *JRS* 58, 1968, 235–40.

—— 'The Etruscans', in *CAH*[2] IV, 1988, 634–75.

—— *The First Western Greeks*, Cambridge 1992.

Ridgway, D. and Ridgway, F.R. (eds), *Italy before the Romans*, Edinburgh 1979.

Ridgway, F.R., 'The Este and Golasecca Cultures: a chronological guide', in *Italy before the Romans*, 1979, 419–87.

Ridley, R.T., 'The Enigma of Servius Tullius', *Klio* 57, 1975, 147–77.

—— 'Fastenkritik, a Stocktaking', *Athenaeum* 58, 1980, 264–98.

—— 'The 'Consular Tribunate'. The testimony of Livy', *Klio* 68, 1986, 444–65.

—— 'Patavinitas among the Patricians? Livy and the Conflict of the Orders', in W. Eder (ed.), *Staat und Staatlichkeit*, 1990, 103–38.

Roma medio-repubblicana, Aspetti culturali di Roma e del Lazio nei secoli IV e III a.C. (Exhibition catalogue), Rome 1973.

La Rome des premiers siècles: légende et histoire (Actes de la table ronde en l'honneur de M. Pallottino), Florence 1992.

Rose, H.J., *The Roman Questions of Plutarch*, Oxford 1924.

—— *Primitive Culture in Italy*, London 1926.

—— 'The Pre-Caesarian Calendar', *CJ* 40, 1943–4, 65–76.

—— *Ancient Roman Religion*, London 1948.

—— 'Mana in Greece and Rome', *HTR* 42, 1949, 155–74.

Rosenberg, A., *Der Staat der alten Italiker*, Berlin 1913.

—— 'Zur Geschichte des Latinerbundes', *Hermes* 54, 1919, 113–73.

Ross Holloway, R., *The Archaeology of Early Rome and Latium*, London 1994.

Rotondi, G., *Leges publicae populi Romani*, Milan 1912.

Rudolph, H., *Stadt und Staat im römischen Italien*, Leipzig 1935.

Ryberg, I. Scott, *An Archaeological Record of Rome from the Seventh to the Second Century BC*, London 1940.

Sacks, K., *Diodorus Siculus and the First Century*, Princeton 1990.

Säflund, G., *Le mura di Roma repubblicana*, Lund 1930.

Salmon, E.T., 'Historical Elements in the Story of Coriolanus', *CQ* 24, 1930, 96–101.

—— 'Rome and the Latins', *Phoenix* 7, 1953, 93–104; 123–35.

—— *Samnium and the Samnites*, Cambridge 1967.

—— *Roman Colonization under the Republic*, London 1969.

—— *The Making of Roman Italy*, London 1982.

—— 'The Iron Age: the peoples of Italy', in *CAH²* IV, 1988, 676–719.

Saulnier, C., *L'armée et la guerre dans le monde étrusco-romain, VIIIe–VIe s.*, Paris 1980.

—— *L'armée et la guerre chez les peuples Samnites, VIIe–IVe s.*, Paris 1983.

Scardigli, B., *I trattati romano-cartaginesi*, Pisa 1991.

Schachermeyr, F., 'Tarquinius', *RE* IV A, 2, 1931, 2348–90.

Schanz, M. and Hosius, C., *Geschichte der römischen Literatur* I–II, Munich 1927–35.

Scheid, J., *Religion et piété à Rome*, Paris 1985.

Schilling, R., *Rites, cultes, dieux de Rome*, Paris 1979.

Schulze, W., *Zur Geschichte lateinische Eigennamen*, Berlin 1904.

Schwegler, A., *Römische Geschichte*, 3 vols, Tübingen 1853–5.

Scott, I.G.,'Early Roman Traditions in the Light of Archaeology', *MAAR* 7, 1929, 7–118. See also Ryberg.

Scullard, H.H., *The Etruscan Cities and Rome*, London 1967.

—— *A History of the Roman World, 753–146 BC*, 4th edn, London 1980.

—— *Festivals and Ceremonies of the Roman Republic*, London 1981.

—— 'Carthage and Rome', in *CAH²* VII.2, 1989, 486–569.

Serrao, F., (ed.), *Legge e società nella repubblica romana* I, Naples 1981.

Shatzman, I., 'Patricians and Plebeians: the case of the Veturii', *CQ* 23, 1973, 65–77.

Sherwin-White, A.N., *The Roman Citizenship*, 2nd edn, Oxford 1973.

Siena, E., 'La politica democratica di Quinto Publilio Filone', *SR* 4, 1956, 509–22.

Siewert, P., 'Die angebliche Übernahme solonischer Gesetze in die Zwolftafeln. Ursprung und Ausgestaltung einer Legende', *Chiron* 8, 1978, 331–44.

Skutsch, O., *The Annals of Quintus Ennius*, Oxford 1985.

Smith, C.J., *Early Rome and Latium: economy and society, c. 1000 to 500 BC*, Oxford 1995.

Smith, P.M., 'Aineiadai as Patrons of *Iliad* XX and the Homeric Hymn to Aphrodite', *HSCPh* 85, 1981, 17–58.

Snodgrass, A.M., 'The Hoplite Reform and History', *JHS* 85, 1965, 110–22.

Sommella, P., 'Heroon di Enea a Lavinium: recenti scavi a Pratica di Mare', *RPAA* 44, 1971–2, 47–74.

—— 'Das Heroon des Aeneas und die Topographie des antiken Lavinium', *Gymnasium* 81, 1974, 283–97.

Sommella Mura, A., '"La decorazione del tempio arcaico', *PdP* 32, 1977, 62–128.

—— 'L'introduzione di Ercole nell'Olimpo' in un gruppo arcaico in terracotta dall'area sacra di S. Omobono', *BCMR* 23, 1977, 3–15.

—— 'Il gruppo di Eracle ed Atena', *PdP* 36, 1981, 59–64.

Sordi, M., *I rapporti romano–ceriti e l'origine della 'civitas sine suffragio'*, Rome 1960.

Spivey, N. and Stoddart, S., *Etruscan Italy: an archaeological history*, London 1990.

Starr, C.G., *The Beginnings of Imperial Rome*, Ann Arbor 1983.

Stary, P.F., *Zur eisenzeitliche Bewaffnung und Kampfesweise in Mittelitalien*, Mainz 1981.

Staveley, E.S., 'The Significance of the Consular Tribunate', *JRS* 43, 1953, 30–6.

—— '*Provocatio* during the Fifth and Fourth Centuries BC', *Historia* 3, 1954–5, 412–28.

—— 'Tribal Legislation before the Lex Hortensia', *Athenaeum* 33, 1955, 3–31.

—— 'The Constitution of the Roman Republic, 1940–1954', *Historia* 5, 1956, 74–122.

—— 'The Political Aims of Appius Claudius Caecus', *Historia* 8, 1959, 410–33.

—— *Greek and Roman Voting and Elections*, London 1972.

—— 'The Nature and Aims of the Patriciate', *Historia* 32, 1983, 24–57.

Stibbe, C.M., *et al.*, *Lapis Satricanus: archaeological, epigraphical, linguistic and historical aspects of the new inscription from Satricum*, The Hague 1980.

Stopponi, S. (ed.), *Case e palazzi d'Etruria*, Milan 1985.

Strasburger, H., *Zur Sage von der Gründung Roms* (Sitzungsb. Heidelberg Akad., Phil.-hist. Kl., 1968 n. 5), Heidelberg 1968.

Strøm, I., *Problems concerning the Origin and Early Development of the Etruscan Orientalizing Style*, Odense 1971.

Sumner, G.V. 'The Legion and the Centuriate Organization', *JRS* 60, 1970, 61–79.

Swaddling, J. (ed.), *Italian Iron-Age Artefacts in the British Museum*, London 1986.

Taeger, F., *Die Archäologie des Polybios*, Stuttgart 1922.

Täubler, E., *Untersuchungen zur Geschichte des Decemvirats*, Berlin 1921.

Taylor, L.R., 'The Date of the Capitoline Fasti', *CPh* 41, 1946, 1–11.

—— 'Degrassi's Edition of the Consular and Triumphal Fasti', *CPh* 45, 1950, 84–95.

—— 'The Centuriate Assembly before and after the Reform', *AJPh* 78, 1957, 337–54.

—— *The Voting Districts of the Roman Republic*, Rome 1960.

—— *Roman Voting Assemblies*, Ann Arbor 1966.

Thomsen, R., *King Servius Tullius: a historical synthesis*, Copenhagen 1980.

Tibiletti, G., 'Il possesso dell'ager publicus e le norme de modo agrorum sino ai Gracchi', *Athenaeum* 26, 1948, 143–236; 27, 1949, 3–42.

—— 'Ricerche di storia agraria romana', *Athenaeum* 28, 1950, 183–266.

—— 'Considerazioni sulle popolazioni dell'Italia preromana', in *PCIA* VII, 1978, 15–49.

Timpe, D., 'Fabius Pictor und die Anfänge der römischen Historiographie', *ANRW* I.2, 1972, 928–69.

Toher, M., 'The Tenth Table and the Conflict of the Orders', in K. Raaflaub (ed.), *Social Struggles*, 1986, 301–26.

Torelli, M., 'L'iscrizione 'latina' sulla coppa argentea della tomba Bernardini', *DdA* 1, 1967, 38–45.

—— 'Tre studi di storia etrusca', *DdA* 8, 1974–5, 3–78.

—— *Elogia Tarquiniensia*, Florence 1975.

—— 'Il santuario greco di Gravisca', *PdP* 32, 1977, 398–458.

—— 'Delitto religioso, qualche indizio sulla situazione in Etruria', in *Le délit religieux dans la cité antique*, 1981, 1–7.

—— 'Per la definizione del commercio greco-orientale: il caso di Gravisca', *PdP* 37, 1982, 304–25.

—— *Lavinio e Roma*, Rome 1984.

—— *Storia degli Etruschi*, 2nd edn, Bari 1984.

—— 'Archaic Rome between Latium and Etruria', in *CAH*² VII.2, 1989, 30–51.

Torelli, M.R., *Rerum Romanarum fontes ab anno ccxcii ad annum cclxv a. Ch. n.*, Pisa 1978.

Toynbee, A.J., *Hannibal's Legacy*, 2 vols, London 1965.

Trump, D.H., *Central and Southern Italy before Rome*, London 1960.

von Ungern-Sternberg, J., 'The Formation of the Annalistic Tradition: the example of the Decemvirate', in K. Raaflaub (ed.), *Social Struggles*, 1986, 77–104.

von Ungern-Sternberg, J. and Reinau, H. (eds), *Vergangenheit in mündliche Überlieferung*, Stuttgart 1988.

Vagnetti, L., *Il deposito votivo di Campetti a Veio*, Rome 1971.

—— (ed.), *Magna Grecia e mondo miceneo – nuovi documenti*, Taranto 1982.

Valditara, G., *Studi sul magister populi: dagli ausiliari militari del rex ai primi magistrati repubblicani*, Milan 1989.

Valvo, I., *La sedizione di Manlio Capitolino in Tito Livio*, Milan 1983.

van Berchem, D., 'Il tempio di Cerere e l'ufficio dell'annona a Roma', *BCom* 63, 1935, 91–5.

—— 'Hercule-Melqart à l'Ara Maxima', *RPAA* 43, 1959–60, 61–8.

Versnel, H.S., *Triumphus. An inquiry into the origin, development and meaning of the Roman triumph*, Leiden 1970.

Verzar, M., 'Pyrgi e l'Aphrodite di Cipro. Considerazioni sul programma decorativo del Tempio B', *MEFRA*, 92, 1980, 35–86.

Il viver quotidiano in Roma arcaica (Exhibition catalogue), Rome 1989.

I Volsci, ed. S. Quilici Gigli (*Quaderni di Archeologia etrusco-italica* 20), Rome 1992.

Walbank, F.W., *A Historical Commentary on Polybius*, 3 vols, Oxford 1957–79.

Wallace, R.W., 'Hellenization and Roman Society in the Late Fourth Century BC', in W. Eder (ed.), *Staat und Staatlichkeit*, 1990, 278–92.

Walsh, P.G., *Livy: his historical aims and methods*, Cambridge 1961.

Ward Perkins, J.B., 'Veii: the historical topography of the ancient city', *PBSR* 29, 1961, 1–123.

Warde Fowler, W., *The Roman Festivals*, London 1899.

—— *The Religious Experience of the Roman People*, London 1911.

—— *Roman Ideas of Deity*, London 1914.

Watson, A., *Rome of the Twelve Tables*, Princeton 1975.

Weinstock, S., 'Victor and Invictus', *HTR* 50, 1957, 211–47.

—— 'Two Archaic Inscriptions from Latium', *JRS* 50, 1960, 114–18.

—— *Divus Julius*, Oxford 1971.

Werner, R., *Der Beginn der römischen Republik*, Munich 1963.

Wheatley, J., 'The Concept of Urbanism', in P.J. Ucko, R. Tringham, G.W. Dimbleby (eds), *Man, Settlement and Urbanism*, London 1972, 608–13.

Wieacker, F., 'Die XII Tafeln im ihrem Jahrhundert', in *Les origines de la république romaine*, Fondation Hardt *Entretiens* 13, Geneva 1967, 291–359.

—— 'Solon und die XII Tafeln', in *Studi in onore di E. Volterra*, Milan 1971, III, 757–84.

Willems, P., *Le sénat de la république romaine*, 2 vols, Louvain–Paris 1878–83.

Wirszubski, C., *Libertas as a Political Idea at Rome*, Cambridge 1950.

Wiseman, T.P., 'Legendary Genealogies in Late Republican Rome', *Greece and Rome* 21, 1974, 153–64.

—— *Clio's Cosmetics: three studies in Greco-Roman literature*, Leicester 1979.

—— 'Roman Legend and Oral Tradition', *JRS* 79, 1989, 129–37.

—— 'The She-Wolf Mirror', *PBSR* 61, 1993, 1–6.

—— *Historiography and Imagination*, Exeter 1994.

Wissowa, G., *Religion und Kultus der Römer*, 2nd edn, Munich 1912.

Wolski, J., 'La prise de Rome par les Celtes et la formation de l'annalistique romaine', *Historia* 5, 1956, 24–52.

Zevi, F., 'Alcuni aspetti della necropoli di Castel di Decima', *PdP* 32, 1977, 241–73.

—— 'Note sulla leggenda di Enea in Italia', in *Gli Etruschi e Roma*, 1981, 145–58.

INDEX